THE NEW LEGAL FRAMEWORK FOR E-COMMERCE IN EUROPE

This collection of essays by well known specialists in e-commerce and Internet law, drawn from both academe and practice, analyses recent crucial legislation which has created, for the first time, a legal regime governing European electronic commerce. The central focus is on the European Electronic Commerce Directive and its implementation in the UK since August 2002. The E-Commerce Directive develops a distinctive European strategy for regulating and promoting on-line business and the information society. Areas of the Directive analysed include contracting on-line, Internet service provider liability, consumer privacy including spam and 'cookies', country of origin regulation, and on-line alternative dispute resolution (ODR). Further chapters move beyond the Directive to discuss other important new laws in this domain, including the Privacy and Electronic Communications Directive, the Distance Selling Directives, the Electronic Money Directive, the Lawful Business regulations on employee surveillance, the disability discrimination rules affecting websites and the extension of VAT to on-line transactions. Both the European framework and the rules as implemented in the UK are examined and critiqued for how well they meet the needs of business and consumers.

30107

D0994640

The New Legal Framework for E-Commerce in Europe

Edited by
LILIAN EDWARDS

·HART·
PUBLISHING

OXFORD AND PORTLAND, OREGON
2005

Published in North America (US and Canada) by
Hart Publishing
c/o International Specialized Book Services
5804 NE Hassalo Street
Portland, Oregon
97213-3644
USA

Hart Publishing, Salters Boatyard, Folly Bridge,
Abingdon Rd, Oxford, OX1 4LB
Telephone: +44 (0)1865 245533 Fax: +44 (0) 1865 794882
email: mail@hartpub.co.uk
WEBSITE: http//:www.hartpub.co.uk

British Library Cataloguing in Publication Data
Data Available
ISBN 13: 978-1-84113-451-2 (paperback)
ISBN 10: 1-84113-451-1 (paperback)

Typeset by Hope Services, Abingdon Ltd.
Printed and bound in Great Britain by
Biddles Ltd, Kings Lynn

PREFACE

On 8 June 2000, the EC Electronic Commerce Directive[1] ('the ECD') was adopted. Throughout the extended and sometimes heated discussions surrounding its passage, it was plain that it would be a crucial piece of legislation paving the way for the entry of the European Single Market into the digital age. Its significance lay in two dimensions: first its sheer scope, and secondly, its underlying policy goals. Historically, it stands out as the first European Union omnibus legislative measure tailored to deal with the phenomenon of electronic commerce. Although a vast penumbra of EU legislation already existed in domains such as consumer protection, distance selling, digital signatures, taxation, competition law, privacy, telecommunications, and intellectual property which all affected e-commerce, the ECD was to be the key instrument which would define European e-regulatory policy and harmonise significant legal domains which represented major obstacles to the development of the electronic Single Market. The areas it covered, broadly, were

— founding a common jurisdictional basis for e-commercial actors ('country of origin' regulation) to reduce legal risk and doubt (see Chapter 1, Waelde);
— the provision of appropriate immunities for on-line intermediaries (including ISPs and hosts – see chapter 4, Edwards);
— clarification of how and when e-contracts were concluded on-line (see Chapter 3, Murray);
— regulation of commercial communications on-line, including 'spam' or junk email[2] (see Chapter 2, Edwards);
— encouragement of alternative dispute resolution ('ADR') and codes of conduct (see Chapter 5, Motion).

The *policy* goals meanwhile were, broadly and arguably,

(i) to promote the EC as a viable competitor in the ICT (information and communication technologies) market, especially as opposed to the US;
(ii) to protect the rights of EC citizens and consumers in the new on-line commercial, public and governmental information society; and

---

[1] 2000/31/EC.
[2] Although more significant legal developments in this area since followed in the Privacy and Electronic Communications Directive 2002.

(iii) to encourage trust in the on-line medium as a safe place for consumers, commerce and government to transact, deliver services and engage in social interaction.

The implementation of the ECD (as is often the case with European legislation) did not go entirely to plan. The transposition deadline, by which member states were to implement the Directive into their own domestic laws, was 22 December 2002 and 18 out of 25 EU/EEA states, including the UK, had met this deadline as of 2003.[3] However during and after the transposition period at least four significant changes overtook the ECD. First and most crucially, the so-called 'dot.com boom' the ECD was intended to regulate and exploit imploded (said 'implosion' is now semi-accurately dated as commencing around March 2000). The e-commerce market is now, after a period of slump in which many ill-conceived 'dot.coms' went to the wall, again regarded as healthy and 'maturing'[4].

Second, since 2000, ICT went from being the preserve of the software and telecoms sectors to an essential utility and part of the mainstream infrastructure, and strategic framework of most institutions, off-line or on-line, public, private or commercial—hence sparking a debate as to whether 'e-specific' legislation was the correct way to go, or whether it would make more sense simply to re-interpret existing commercial and other laws.

Thirdly, the ICT sector has moved from delivering electronic services almost exclusively via conventional personal computers or business mainframes, to a 'convergence' model where 'Internet' services are also delivered and accessed via TVs, digital radios and mobile devices, especially phones. Much legislation conceived to regulate a world of PCs and keyboards, struggles in its applicability to (inter alia) 3G phones, PDAs, RFID, and 'chips with everything'.

Finally, the EU itself has expanded significantly with the addition of 10 Accession states, for which e-commerce is a significant opportunity but which also have huge problems of 'digital inclusion' and law enforcement difficulties.[5] The Accession countries are relatively unsophisticated in the development of an information technology law sector and scholarly commentary is particularly needed to assist both European policy in this area and the Accession states themselves.

This book began with the objective of studying in depth the E-Commerce Directive, as a critical piece of legislation, and in particular, its implementation in

---

[3] A transposition table issued as part of the First Report on the ECD Brussels, 21.11.2003 COM(2003) 702 final in 2003 indicated 18 EU and EEA states had fully or partly transposed. See http://europa.eu.int/comm/internal_market/en/ecommerce/transposition_en.pdf. Information as to transposition status of Accession States does not seem to be publicly available.

[4] See Swire P 'Trustwrap: The Importance of Legal Rules to Electronic Commerce and Internet Privacy' (2003) 54 *Hastings Law Journal* 1.

[5] Kryczka K 'Ready to Join the EU Information Society? Implementation of the E-Commerce Directive 2000/31/EC in the EU Acceding Countries—the Example of Poland' (2004) 12 *IJLIT* 55.

the UK. We aimed not just to recount the laws that had been passed and how they fitted into existing UK law, but perhaps more importantly, to assess how far the European e-commerce policy cited above had been correctly formulated, and if the ECD itself successfully transposed those policy goals into legislation. Contributors were asked to consider if the Directive addressed 'the right' issues, if it focused on the real industry and consumer needs, not on 'paper tigers': the illustrative error that had preceded the ECD being the EC Digital Signatures Directive, which had effectively mandated a technology (PKI) for on-line security that has not in fact been readily embraced by either SMEs or consumers since.[6]

Other questions were also identified as worthy of attention. Were the provisions of the ECD really achieving harmonisation, or instead simply opening up new expanses for disagreement between member states' domestic laws? Was the ECD really creating greater certainty, and thus greater trust among consumers in the phenomenon of e-commerce? Were the rules of the ECD being implemented on paper, without sufficient practical ability or resources to enforce them? Did prospective e-consumers care or know about these legal developments at all? Would it have been better to put the effort and resources involved into public education, 'soft law' codes of conduct, alternative dispute resolution, or the building of technological aids (such as filters for censorship, or privacy-enhancing technologies (PETS))? These were all issues which this editor felt were not being fully answered or even addressed in most of the brief guides to the ECD appearing in the professional legal journals and conference circuit, or in standard commercial and IT textbooks.

Very swiftly it became apparent that the scope of the book could not, and should not, be restricted to the ECD. Many new pieces of legislation were emerging from Brussels and Westminster which were as apposite to the nascent European and UK regulatory framework for e-commerce as the ECD itself. For example, the Electronic Money Directive (EMI) was introduced in 2000 to regulate the novel area of digital or 'e-cash'. Guadamuz and Usher discuss this area in Chapter 6, expressing concern that, as with digital signatures, Brussels may have gone too far, too fast, in regulating around a technical paradigm—'stored value' cards—which has never in fact attained popularity in the commercial world, and perhaps thereby marginalising the newer 'account-based' payment methods, such as PayPal, which by comparison are a commercial success. It also seemed a rather obvious need in a book on European e-commerce to include a chapter on the distance-selling rules, and their recent update for financial services (see Chapter 8 by Nordhausen).

Meanwhile, some older areas of European law were being re-vamped to make them relevant to the challenges of digital trade. For example, taxation of electronic services, a vital issue for any merchant seeking to sell on-line either into, or out of,

---

[6] Ramberg C *Internet Marketplaces: The Law of Auctions and Exchanges Online* (Oxford, OUP, 2003).

the Single Market, had become an exasperatingly square peg in the round hole of existing laws on cross-border VAT. Amendments were consequently made to the existing EU tax law basic framework which Eden analyses in depth in Chapter 7. One area of the ECD itself was swiftly overtaken by newer laws. The original provisions of the ECD on control of junk email or 'spam', drafted when spam was more of a joke than the Internet-clogging pestilence it has subsequently become, were toothless and ineffective. The Privacy and Electronic Communications Directive,[7] discussed by Edwards in Chapter 2, attempts to take a sterner approach to stamping out spam by the adoption of an 'opt-in' regime, and, more widely, looks at the basic problem of how to balance the opportunities the Internet presents for marketing and collection of personal data, with the need to protect consumer privacy as a fundamental human right. These provisions and their UK implementation in the PECD regulations,[8] clearly had to find a home in this collection.

Once the decision had been made to expand the scope of the book, the choice of non-ECD topics was based on their relevance to the development of the European e-commerce market, their current topicality, and the degree to which commentary was already available elsewhere. There is, for example, no general chapter on data protection, relevant though it is, as several excellent texts already exist which spell out how it works and its application to European e-commerce markets. On the other hand, both surveillance of employees by electronic means (see Fraser, Chapter 9), and the application of disability discrimination law to web-based businesses (see Sloan, Chapter 10) appeared to be areas of compelling interest where academic guidance was lacking. In the end such selections must have an element of the arbitrary about them—but books (and editors) also have a need for finity.

We hope this will be a book which will meet the needs, as far as this is ever possible, of both legal practitioners and industry professionals, and academics and students. Five years on from the passing of the ECD, there is still an extensive need for in-depth analysis of it. Although much was written about the ECD *before* implementation, little has been added since domestic laws were put in place. Nor have gaps ben filled out by case law. Local research undertaken at Edinburgh found only a handful of reported cases in the EU on ISP liability, spam and privacy issues. In civilian countries, of course, the worth of judicial precedent as a gauge of certainty is limited. Even in the UK and Ireland, however, there have been no relevant cases to date. Commentaries on the implications of the ECD for member states have largely been provided (if at all) by large multinational law firms, whose product is often excellent but whose orientation, in the nature of things, will tend

---

[7] 2002/58/EC.
[8] SI 2003/2426.

to be towards the large business sector and who will not be too concerned with issues of human rights, privacy, freedom of expression etc. We hope this book, to some extent, fills that gap, at least for the UK.

The problem of simply finding out if and where the ECD has been implemented is hard enough. The Commission is, of course, itself tracking transposition status[9] and the First Report on the ECD has been issued.[10] However the Status page is unhelpful for a pan-European audience as it merely links without commentary to national legislation, usually only available in the local language, and is, at time of writing, out of date. One advance this editor would strenuously promote is the creation of an ECD website, updated by the Commission, which would provides links to primary legislation and case law implementing the ECD, not only in the local language, but translated into all the official working languages of the EC. One might hope that information of this kind would also appear as part of the currently in-preparation Second Report on the ECD.

I would like to thank a number of people who have been helpful in the production of this book. First, of course, the contributors, who have uniformly been both rigorous and imaginative in their treatment of their topics. Secondly, I would like to thank my research assistant, Ashley Theunissen, who was exceptionally helpful in locating commentaries on non-UK implementations of the ECD. Lastly, I would like to thank the motley crew of 'techies' (some of them lawyers as well!) whose aid I have drawn on during the various stages of my career as an Internet lawyer, and whose help this time round was again invaluable—including, but not limited to, Andrew Ducker, Simon Bisson, Mike Scott, Andres Guadamuz and Burkhard Schafer.

The law is stated as at February 2005. It has however sometimes been possible to include later developments.

Lilian Edwards
Edinburgh, August 2005

---

[9] Above n 3.
[10] 21 November 2003, COM (2303) 702 final.

CONTENTS

APPENDICES

KEY: European legislation
UK implementation

CONTRIBUTOR BIOGRAPHIES

Lilian Edwards
AHRC Research Centre for Studies in Intellectual Property and Technology Law
School of Law, University of Edinburgh

Lilian Edwards is Co-Director of the AHRC Research Centre for Studies in Intellectual Property and Technology Law and Senior Lecturer in the Law School at Edinburgh University. Her major research interest is the substantive law relating to computers and e-commerce, with a European and comparative focus, and she has recently focused on Internet content (pornography, libel, spam, etc); intermediary/ISP liability on the Internet; jurisdiction and other issues of international private law on the Internet; privacy on-line; cyber-crime and security; and consumer protection on-line. She has co-edited two prior collections on *Law and the Internet* (Hart Publishing, 1997 and 2000) (with Charlotte Waelde) and won the Barbara Wellbury Prize in 2004 for a major article on consumer privacy on-line. She also publishes extensively in family law.

Sandra Eden
School of Law, University of Edinburgh

Sandra Eden's main area of research interest is tax law and policy. She is also an expert in pension law, especially the taxation of pensions. She has published widely in these fields, and in particular on the taxation of e-commerce. She has also published articles on questions of legal process and access to justice.

Jane Fraser
Maclay Murray and Spens, Solicitors

Jane Fraser heads the Employment Pensions and Benefits team at MMS. Jane has extensive experience in representing clients in all areas of employment law. She makes regular appearances for clients at tribunals throughout the UK and before the Employment Appeal Tribunal. Her specialist areas of practice are business transfers and restructure, data protection and working time, and she has a particular interest in mediation and alternative dispute resolution. Jane is a regular speaker at conferences, has taught employment law topics at several Scottish universities and is a member of the Law Society of Scotland's Employment Law Specialisation Panel and Employment Law Group, as well as a member of the

Employment Lawyer's Association. Prior to joining MMS as a partner in 2001, Jane was a partner in the niche employment firm Mackay Simon.

Andres Guadamuz
AHRC Research Centre for Studies in Intellectual Property and Technology Law School of Law, University of Edinburgh

Andres Guadamuz is Co-Director of the AHRC Research Centre for Studies in Intellectual Property and Technology Law and lecturer in E-Commerce at the University of Edinburgh. Andres has both Bachelor and Licenciado degrees from the University of Costa Rica and obtained an LLM in International Business Law at the University of Hull. His research interests are centred on the interaction between technology and the law, the role of intellectual property on developing countries, open source and open access.

Andrew D Murray
London School of Economics

Andrew Murray is Lecturer in IT and Internet Law at the Department of Law, London School of Economics. He teaches courses in Information Technology & the Law, Internet & New Media Regulation and Media & Communications Regulation. Andrew is co-editor (with Mathias Klang) of *Human Rights in the Digital Age*, Glasshouse Press, 2005, and is the author of *Regulating Cyberspace: Regulatory Webs and Webs of Regulation*, Glasshouse Press, forthcoming 2006. He is a member of the Editorial Committee of the *Modern Law Review*, and currently serves as Production Editor for the *Review*. Andrew is an accredited 'Expert' for the Nominet .uk Domain Name Dispute Resolution Service.

Paul Motion
Ledingham Chalmers, Solicitors

Paul Motion is a Solicitor Advocate and partner at the firm of Ledingham Chalmers and was recommended in the Scottish Bar section of the 2004/5 'Legal 500' for information technology cases. He has extensive experience of general Commercial Court litigation. He is Chairman of the Scottish Society for Computers and Law and former Convener of the Law Society of Scotland's E-Commerce Committee. Paul sits on the Media Board for the UK Society for Computers and Law, a body that oversees the UK SCL website and content for 'Computers and Law' magazine. Paul has written many articles on IT law and has chaired and presented numerous seminars in the area.

Annette Nordhausen
University of Sheffield

Annette Nordhausen studied for her law degree (1st States Exam) at the University of Bremen, followed by a postgraduate program in European and International Law (LLMEur). She did her practical stage (Referendariat) and 2nd States Exam in Lower Saxony and worked at the University of Bremen as an assistant, before she joined the University of Sheffield in February 2002. Her doctoral thesis is on information duties in e-commerce contracts.

Martin Sloan
Brodies, Solicitors

Martin Sloan is a solicitor with the Technology & Information Group of the Edinburgh commercial law firm Brodies LLP and is one of the UK's leading authorities on Web accessibility and the law. Martin graduated from the University of Glasgow in July 2001, having researched the area of Web accessibility and the law for his honours dissertation. Martin has since published widely in this area and carried out research for the Digital Media Access Group at the University of Dundee (who supported the initial paper), the JISC-funded body TechDIS and JISC Legal Information Service on the accessibility of e-learning environments. Martin has also been invited to present seminars at a number of conferences and workshops, including the RNIB's Techshare conference, and co-authored a study of the accessibility problems encountered by people with disabilities when trying to access on-line manifestos of the main Scottish political parties prior to the last Scottish Parliament elections. In a professional context, Martin has advised a number of blue-chip clients and technology companies on their obligations under the Disability Discrimination Act 1995, particularly in relation to the accessibility of their websites and use of ICT. His website on disability issues is http://www.web-accessibility.org.uk.

John Usher
School of Law, University of Exeter

Professor Usher began his career as an Assistant Lecturer at Exeter in 1967. Together with Dominik Lasok he was part of the pioneering team that helped establish Exeter as a leading force in the field of European Law. He is a distinguished European lawyer and has held previous positions at the European Court of Justice, Luxembourg, and University College London. He held the Salvesen Chair of European Institutions and the Directorship of the Europa Institute at Edinburgh from 1995 to 2004, before returning to Exeter as Head of the Law School and Professor of European Law. He currently serves on the Executive Committee of the Committee of Heads of University Law Schools (CHULS). He is also a visiting Professor at the College of Europe in Bruges, and at the University of Amsterdam. Professor Usher was elected an Honorary Bencher of Lincoln's Inn in 1993, awarded an Honorary Jean Monnet Chair of European Law *(ad personam)* by the European Commission in 1997, and elected a Fellow of the Royal Society of Edinburgh in 1998.

Charlotte Waelde
AHRC Research Centre for Studies in Intellectual Property and Technology Law School of Law, University of Edinburgh

Dr Charlotte Waelde is Co-Director of the AHRB Research Centre for Studies in Intellectual Property and Technology Law. Charlotte was appointed to the Faculty of Law at the University of Edinburgh in 1996, having previously worked in private practice. Charlotte's main areas of interest lie in the field of intellectual property rights—particularly copyright and trade marks. Her main expertise lies in the area of intellectual property rights and the Internet. She has written and lectured extensively on this subject. She is co-editor (with Lilian Edwards) of *Law and the Internet: A Framework for Electronic Commerce*, Hart Publishing, 2000.

TABLE OF CASES

France

Germany

Netherlands

United Kingdom

United States of America

Part I
The Electronic Commerce Directive

1

Article 3, ECD: Internal Market Clause

International Private Law, Consumers and the Net: A Confusing Maze or a Smooth Path Towards a Single European Market?

CHARLOTTE WAELDE[1]

Trade across borders was once largely confined to business to business ('B2B') transactions. Where disputes in the international market place arose which involved parties from different legal systems, conflicts of applicable law could be settled by reference to established rules of international private law ('IPL'). Rooted in legal theory[2] these rules had long set guidelines for deciding which court or courts should have jurisdiction to hear the dispute (the 'forum'), which law should be applied (the 'applicable law', 'choice of law', or *lex causae*) and how resulting court judgments should be recognised and enforced.

Such commercial litigants would generally be well advised by lawyers and as such, could look after their own interests. Risk could be managed by dictating standard contractual terms which could stipulate what was to be borne by each party, and even in the event of dispute, could prescribe the forum where the dispute would be heard and the law that would be applied. Only the unwary or ill advised would need to fall upon the less predictable general rules of IPL. Case law precedents set by disputes also helped to predict outcomes and thus reduce risk and shape future commercial behaviour.

By contrast, seldom would a consumer step outside the confines of her home shores to make a purchase from another territory. If she did, it was generally small.

[1] Co-Director, AHRC Research Centre for Studies in Intellectual Property and Technology Law, University of Edinburgh. Thanks are due to Julia Pothmann, LLM Eur, PhD scholar at the Max-Planck-Institute for Intellectual Property Law, Munich for very helpful comments on an earlier draft.
[2] AE Anton and P Beaumont, *Private International Law,* 2nd edn, (W Green, 1990) ch 2.

Perhaps a trophy brought back from a holiday in the sun, or a memento for a partner when returning from a business trip. However with the Internet revolution, all this has changed. Now the international sourcing of goods and services is not confined to the larger commercial interests. Rather, the development of the Internet has meant that anyone can get involved in buying and selling across borders, including small businesses and consumers. Interestingly though, in Europe, statistics still suggest that the overwhelming majority of e-commerce transactions are still B2B.[3] However, most legislative initiatives have been designed to regulate the business to consumer ('B2C') marketplace.[4] It is in this sector that debate has been fierce over two regulatory paradigms: *country of origin* versus *country of destination.*

What is the difference? Roughly, the country of origin principle means that a business can carry with it and rely on, wherever it trades, its own home country regulations and laws. Conversely, the country of destination principle means that the laws and regulations of the country where goods or services are received, apply to a transaction.

Example 1

If a supplier of Sancerre based in France sells wine to a consumer based in Scotland, country of origin regulation would mean that it would be French law and rules that applied to the transaction: in other words, the rules of the place of the supplier. Conversely, country of destination regulation would mean that it would be the rules of Scotland and the UK (as appropriate) that applied: the rules of the place of the consumer.[5]

It is country of origin regulation that has, in principle, been chosen for incorporation into the Electronic Commerce Directive (ECD)[6] as transposed into the UK Regulations implementing that Directive.[7]

---

[3] See eg, http://www.oecd.org/dataoecd/34/61/2,077,266.pdf.

[4] A number of Directives have been passed in the EU in the field of consumer protection. For example Consumer Credit (90/88); Distance Selling (97/7 EC); Doorstep Selling (85/577 EEC); General Product Safety (92/59 EEC); Injunctions—Stop Now Orders (98/27 EC); Misleading and Comparative Advertising (84/450 EEC and 97/55 EC); Package Travel (90/314 EEC); Price Indications (98/6 EC); Product Liability (99/34 EEC); Sale of Goods and Associated Guarantees (99/44/EC); Timeshare (94/47 EC); and Unfair Contract Terms (93/13 EEC).

[5] For an article discussing the E-commerce directive and using *Yahoo! Inc v La Ligue Contre Le Racisme et L'Antisemitisme*, Final Order TGI, Paris, November 20, 2000 (English translation at http://www.lapres.net/yahweb-html) as a case study see MF Kightlinger, 'A Solution to the Yahoo! Problem? The EC E-Commerce Directive as a Model for International Cooperation on Internet Choice of Law' 24 *Michigan J Intl L* 719.

[6] Directive 2000/31/EC of the European Parliament and of the Council of 8 June 2000 on certain legal aspects of information society services, in particular electronic commerce, in the Internal Market (Directive on Electronic Commerce).

[7] The Electronic Commerce (EC Directive) Regulations 2002, SI 2002 No 2013.

Clearly such a rule is highly advantageous for businesses, as they need only be familiar with one set of rules, those of their home country. They can trade confident in the knowledge that so long as they comply with the regulations of their own domestic system, they will be legally compliant no matter the laws of the countries they trade with.

But matters are not quite this simple, particularly in the context of consumer contracts. There is a derogation from the country of origin principle in the ECD specifically for consumer contracts which may be seen as applying a country of destination approach through the application of the general rules of IPL, in particular the Brussels Regulation dealing with jurisdiction,[8] and the Rome Convention dealing with choice of law in contractual matters.[9] However, there is uncertainty as to which elements of the relationship between the supplier and consumer are subject to the country of destination principle, and which to the country of origin approach. As will be argued in this chapter, the result, in the context of consumer contracts, may be considered as having built a confusing maze rather than a smooth path to the Single European Market.

To explain the debate this article will first examine the genesis of the country of origin approach to regulation, and explain how it has operated in the broadcasting sector in Europe. The focus will then be on two arguments that have accompanied these instruments. The first is the debate as to the meaning of the country of origin principle, and the second is as to the scope of the derogation concerning consumers. Finally, we will move to the Rome Convention and the Brussels Regulation, analysing the rules on choice of law and jurisdiction in those instruments, and will ask whether all the complexities of this area really matter anyway, given that consumers are unlikely to go to court as most purchases are of low value or importance compared to litigation costs and difficulties. There are alternative mechanisms by which consumers may assert their rights in e-commerce disputes. It should be noted that the discussion in this chapter is limited to consumer contracts between a supplier and a consumer located within different countries in the EU[10] and so does not deal with, eg, transactions between a UK business and a US consumer.

---

[8] Council Regulation No 44/2001 of 22 December 2000 on jurisdiction and the recognition and enforcement of judgments in civil and commercial matters which came into force on 1 March 2002. The Regulation is applicable throughout the EU except for Denmark.

[9] EC Convention on the Law Applicable to Contractual Obligations (Rome 1980).

[10] Different rules apply where either the consumer or supplier are outwith the EU and also as between domiciliaries within the UK For the UK implementing provisions see Civil Jurisdiction and Judgments Act 1982 as amended eg, Sch 4 for intra UK disputes and Sch 8 for Scottish and non-EU disputes.

A. Meaning and Scope of 'Country of Origin' Regulation in the ECD

1. Terminology: Country of Origin and Country of Destination

Within the EU, the country of origin principle first appeared in the Television Without Frontiers Directive.[11] That Directive (as amended[12]) establishes a legal framework for the free movement of television broadcasting services in the EU to promote the development of a European market in broadcasting and related activities such as television advertising and the production of audiovisual programmes. It does this by seeking to ensure that only one Member State has competence to regulate activities within the fields co-ordinated by the Directive,[13] the intention being to ensure the freedom to provide services throughout the EU without being subject to possibly contradictory regulatory regimes. The Directives make it clear under which Member State's jurisdiction television broadcasters fall. This question is determined mainly by reference to where their central administration is located and where management decisions concerning programming are taken.[14]

However, the country of origin principle is not absolute and can give way to country of destination influence in certain circumstances. This can be seen in *Konsumentenombudsmannen v Agostini Förlag and TV-Shop i Sverige*[15] a case that concerned *inter alia* the re-transmission of broadcasts into Sweden, Norway and Denmark from the UK. These broadcasts contained advertisements that were lawful in the country of origin (the UK) but contrary to the Swedish law on Marketing Practices[16] (the country of destination). The question arose as to whether the Swedish authorities could exercise any control over the content of these advertisements. The ECJ held that the Directive does not in principle

---

[11] Council Directive 89/552/EEC of 3 October 1989 on the coordination of certain provisions laid down by Law, Regulation or Administrative Action in Member States concerning the pursuit of television broadcasting activities.

[12] Directive 97/36/EC of the European Parliament and of the Council of 30 June 1997 amending Council Directive 89/552/EEC on the coordination of certain provisions laid down by law, regulation or administrative action in Member States concerning the pursuit of television broadcasting activities. The Directives are currently under review with many broadcasters commenting favourably on the operation of the country of origin rule and expressing the view that the rule should not be changed. See generally http://europa.eu.int/comm/avpolicy/index_en.htm.

[13] Art 3 of Directive 89/552/EEC.

[14] The ECJ has made it clear that a Member State cannot object to the re-transmission on its territory of programmes broadcast by a television broadcaster body within the jurisdiction of another Member State where it considers that the programmes of the latter State do not meet requirements of Art 4 and 5 of the Directive, since this is a matter the assessment of which is within the field of control of the State of Origin, C–14/96 *Paul Denuit v Kingdom of Belgium* (29 May 1997, Preliminary Decision).

[15] C–34, C–35, C–36/95 (9 July 1997).

[16] Art 2 of the Swedish Marknadsföringslag (1975:1418).

preclude application of national rules with the general aim of consumer protection provided that does not involve secondary control of television broadcasts in addition to the control which the broadcasting Member State must carry out.[17] In other words, the Swedish authorities were able to exercise some control over the content of the advertisements in accordance with their domestic law, but that control only took effect after the re-broadcast had been transmitted and could not prevent transmission of the broadcast itself.[18]

So it seems that although the TV Without Frontiers Directive posits as a general rule country of origin regulation, it is not absolute. It does not preclude the authorities in the country of destination exercising regulatory oversight (and, as a result, no doubt influencing the behaviour of the advertisers). As will be seen in the discussion on the ECD, not only does the *meaning* of the country of origin paradigm seem to have troubled commentators more so than it did in the TV Without Frontiers Directive, but in addition, and in common with the broadcasting sector, the *scope* of the rule remains unclear.

B. The ECD and the 'Fudge' on Questions of Applicable Law

Arguments have raged as to the meaning of the country of origin rule to be found in the E-commerce Directive.[19] Three suggestions have been made as to the interpretation of the rule:

1. The rule amounts to an additional rule of IPL, which designates the applicable law (*lex causae*) in relevant e-commerce transactions;
2. the rule means that it is *the IPL rules of the country of establishment of the information society service provider*[20] (ISSP) which determine the applicable law in relevant e-commerce transactions;

---

[17] Above n 14, para 38.

[18] The ECJ noted in particular that that Council Directive 84/450/EEC of 10 September 1984 relating to the approximation of the laws, regulations and administrative provisions of the Member States concerning misleading advertising (OJ 1984 L 250, p 17), which provides in particular in Art 4(1) that Member States are to ensure that adequate and effective means exist for the control of misleading advertising in the interests of consumers as well as competitors and the general public, could be robbed of its substance in the field of television advertising if the receiving Member State were deprived of all possibility of adopting measures against an advertiser and that this would be in contradiction with the express intention of the Community legislature. Para 37.

[19] ECD, Art 3(1).

[20] '*Information society services*' are defined as services within the meaning of Art 1(2) of Directive 98/34/EC as amended by Directive 98/48/EC and a '*service provider*' as any natural or legal person providing an information society service. ECD, Art 2.

3. the rule only concerns *substantive law* (after the IPL rules of the forum have been applied normally) and prohibits the application of stricter rules than those of the country of origin (the 'restrictions' test).[21]

In laying out the country of origin principle, recital 22 of the ECD provides that: 'Information society services should be supervised at the source of the activity . . . such information society services should in principle be subject to the law of the member state in which the service provider is established', and Article 3, the Internal Market measure, provides: 'Each Member State shall ensure that the information society services provided by a service provider established on its territory comply with the national provisions applicable in the Member State in question which fall within the coordinated field.'

Suggestion 1: the rule amounts to an additional rule of IPL, which designates the applicable law (*lex causae*) in relevant e-commerce transactions.

   Under this suggestion, in order to determine whose law applies to an EC transnational e-commerce dispute, it is necessary to look at where the information society service provider (ISSP) is established[22] and apply that law as the applicable law (so long as the activity under question falls within the co-ordinated field[23]). So, in Example 1 above, since the supplier of Sancerre is based in France, the applicable law is French law. In other words, *the law of the country of origin is the applicable law.* This means Article 3 of the ECD is an IPL choice of law rule, and as such replaces prior common law or treaty IPL rules. This analysis is consistent with recital 55 and Article 3(3) of the ECD which refer to derogations from the internal market clause. Recital 55 provides that the Directive '*does not affect the law applicable to contractual obligations relating to consumer contracts*'; Article 3(3) specifically dis-applies the internal market Article in those fields specified in the Annex to the ECD. Included within those fields are '*contractual obligations*

---

[21] M Hellner, 'The Country of Origin Principle in the E-commerce Directive—A Conflict with Conflict of Laws?' (2004) 12(2) *European Rev Private L* 193, who argues that there are three ways in which the country of origin principle could be understood: (i) as a choice of law rule for the law applicable to e-commerce services; (ii) as only setting out certain limitations to the application of the designated law; (iii) as making the rules of the home country of the service provider internationally mandatory and thus applicable irrespective of what law is applicable to the contract or tort.

[22] An '*established service provider*' is defined as a service provider who effectively pursues an economic activity using a fixed establishment for an indefinite period. The presence and use of the technical means and technologies required do not, in themselves, constitute an establishment of the provider. ECD, Art 2.

[23] The coordinated field concerns requirements with which the service provider has to comply in respect of: (i) the taking up of the activity of an information society service, such as requirements concerning information society service; qualifications, authorisation or notification, the pursuit of the activity of an information society service, such as requirements concerning the behaviour of the service provider, including those applicable to advertising and contracts, or requirements concerning the liability of the service provider; (ii) The coordinated field does not cover requirements applicable to goods as such, requirements applicable to the delivery of goods, requirements applicable to services not provided by electronic means. See generally ECD, Art 2.

concerning consumer contracts'. It can be argued that these specific derogations are necessary because the country of origin rule is a choice of law rule. If it were not, what would be the point of including these derogations in the Directive? Thus one interpretation is that the country of origin rule is a choice of law rule which can be derogated from in the limited circumstances set out in the Annex to the ECD.

But this interpretation takes no account of the first sentence of recital 23[24] and Article 1(4) of the ECD, the latter of which states that '*This Directive does not establish additional rules on private international law nor does it deal with the jurisdiction of Courts'*. It is this measure that has caused much uncertainty as to the meaning of the country of origin rule. Suggestion 1 above, which is the most straightforward and therefore the most appealing interpretation of Article 3, appears to directly contradict Article 1(4). We turn therefore to Suggestion 2.

Suggestion 2: the rule means that it is *the IPL rules of the country of establishment of the information society service provider*[25] (ISSP) which determine the applicable law in relevant e-commerce transactions.

In this suggestion, the first step is to determine the establishment of the ISSP—that is, the country of origin. However, the second step is to apply not the substantive law but the *conflict laws of the country of origin* to determine the applicable law in a relevant dispute.

Example 2

A French based ISSP—a wine-selling website—supplies bottles of Sancerre to a Scottish retailer. The country of origin rule as interpreted according to Suggestion 2 means that the IPL rules of French law—*not* French substantive contract law—apply to solve any dispute. French IPL rules then may or may not designate French law as the applicable law of the dispute. If, for example, French IPL law says that in the case of a contractual dispute between two businesses the first law which should be applied should be that which the parties had chosen as the law of the contract, and a contractual term existed which named the law of England as the choice of law, then the French IPL rules would refer the dispute to the law of England. (Note this would *not* mean the dispute need be heard in the courts of England—that would be a matter of *forum* not choice of law.)

---

[24] Rec 23 states 'This Directive neither aims to establish additional rules on private international law relating to conflicts of law nor does it deal with the jurisdiction of Courts; provisions of the applicable law designated by rules of international law must not restrict the freedom to provide services established in this Directive.' ECD, Art 2.

[25] '*Information society services*' are defined as services within the meaning of Art 1(2) of Directive 98/34/EC as amended by Directive 98/48/EC and a '*service provider*' as any natural or legal person providing an information society service. ECD, Art 2.

Suggestion 3: the rule only concerns substantive law (after the IPL rules of the forum have been applied normally) and prohibits the application of stricter rules than those of the country of origin (the 'restrictions' test).

The third suggestion leads on from application of the second, but tries to take into account the wording of the second sentence in recital 23: 'provisions of the applicable law designated by rules of private international law must not restrict the freedom to provide information society services as established in this Directive', and of Article 3(2) 'Member States may not, for reasons falling within the coordinated field, restrict the freedom to provide information society services from another Member State.' This has been called by some the 'restrictions test'. Broadly it means that if after following suggestion 2's procedure, the applicable law turns out to be *more restrictive* than the country of origin law, ie, the home law of the ISSP, that would result in a restriction on the ability to provide information society services. Therefore the more restrictive law cannot be applied because it would 'restrict the freedom to provide information society services'.

Example 3

Leading on from Example 2, suppose that the law of England was more restrictive as to the activities of the French ISSP than the law of the country of origin—French law. In that case, English law could not be applied, and the law of the country of origin of the ISSP—French law—would prevail.

It is easy to see how complex these arguments can become.[26] Suffice it to say, academic argument in respect of these differing interpretations might have quietened, but it has not gone away. Attention has now shifted as to how Article 3 has been incorporated in the Member States. It is as to the decisions taken in the UK that we now turn.

C. The UK Regulations

In the first draft of the UK regulations which implement the ECD, ie, the Electronic Commerce (EC Directive) Regulations 2002, the UK Government included a slightly modified version of the internal market clause[27] and also

---

[26] For a proposal for a convention on country of origin regulation and the liability of online information publishers see C Reed, 'Liability of Online Information Providers—Towards a Global Solution' (2003) 17(3) *Intl Rev L Computers & Technology* 255.

[27] Cl 7, Draft Regulations at http://www.dti.gov.uk/industry_files/pdf/regulations.pdf.

sought to transpose Article 1(4) of the ECD almost verbatim.[28] Thus, the tension inherent in the ECD text, stating that no new rules on international private law were to be established, remained. The Government anticipated that that the effect of this was that: 'UK courts will continue to follow the requirements of the Private International Law (Miscellaneous Provisions) Act 1995 but that the application of the law dictated by them would be subject to a restrictions test in accordance with the internal market provisions of the Regulations.'[29]

Needless to say many commentators who responded to the consultation document rehearsed the points made in the last section of this paper and stressed the uncertainty that taking this course of action would result in for ISSPs who would be unsure of precisely which rules applied. The uncertainty would remain until such time (if ever) as the ECJ had the opportunity to resolve the conflict. Bowing to pressure, the Government removed the IPL clause (clause 5) from the final version of the Regulations saying not only that *'On balance, [the Government] agrees that the country of origin regulation should take precedence and has removed the provision on private international law accordingly',*[30] but also that:

> The Government has . . . looked to the purpose of the Directive in informing its approach. This is expressed in Article 1(1) as 'ensuring the free movement of information society services between the Member States' and qualified by the statement in recital 22 that 'such information society services should in principle be subject to the law of the Member State in which the service provider is established'. Taken together, Regulations 4(1) to 4(3) will, if replicated by other Member States, provide for what might be termed country-of-origin regulation.[31]

Whether the Government's optimism is overstated remains to be seen.

So in the final version of the UK Regulations, the internal market clause provides (with certain exclusions[32]) that:

- Any requirement that falls within the co-ordinated field will apply to the provision of an information society service by a service provider established in the UK irrespective of whether the information society service is provided in the UK or another Member State;[33]
- Enforcement authorities are required to ensure compliance with that requirement;[34]

[28] *Ibid*, Cl 5.
[29] Guide for Business to the Electronic Commerce (EC Directive) Regulations 2001. Interim Guidance, para 3.6. Available at http://www.dti.gov.uk/industry_files/pdf/guidance.pdf.
[30] Electronic Commerce (EC Directive) Regulations 2002, Public Consultation—Government Response, 2002.
[31] Guide for Business to the Electronic Commerce (EC Directive) Regulations 2003, para 4.8.
[32] Reg 4: Those activities excluded from this provision are set out in the Annex to the Directive and include contractual obligations concerning consumer contracts.
[33] Reg 4.1.
[34] Reg 4.2.

- Any requirement falling within the co-ordinated field is not to be applied to the provision of an information society service by a service provider established in a member State other than the UK.[35]

This is complex wording which would seem to fall short of what many may have wanted to see in the UK Regulations—a clear statement that ISSPs established in the UK must comply with UK law, and only UK law, if their activities fall within the co-ordinated field.[36] One assumes from the optimistic statements by the Government, noted above, that it is the Government's view that country of origin rule as it has been implemented in the Regulations means just that: that (subject to the discussion on consumer rights below) it will be the law of the place of establishment of the ISSP that is the applicable law where activities fall within the co-ordinated field. In essence, this corresponds to the *Suggestion 1* interpretation above.

D. The Derogation for Consumers

Although the UK Regulations may assert (arguably) that it is the 'home law' of the ISSP that takes precedence, it has to be appreciated that this is still not the whole story. Not only can UK based enforcement authorities take action against ISSPs where necessary for the protection of consumers[37] but in addition, contractual obligations concerning consumers[38] are exempt in both the Directive[39] and the UK implementing Regulations.[40] This exemption followed protracted argument about the protection of consumers who engage in e-commerce. This exemption implies that it is the law of the consumer's habitual residence that applies to contractual obligations concerning consumer contracts.[41] But that of course begs the question as to what a contractual obligation concerning a consumer contract is.

---

[35] Reg 4.3.

[36] As has been implemented in some other countries, eg, Luxembourg. Art 2(4) of their law states 'The legislation of the place of business of the information society service provider shall be applicable to providers and the services they provide, without prejudice to the freedom of the parties to choose the law applicable to their contract.' Law available at http://www.etat.lu/memorial/T01_a/tablealp.html.

    Austria Pt 6, § 20(1) 'In the co-ordinated field (§ 3(8)), the legal requirements for a service provider established in a Member State shall be determined in accordance with the law of such state'. Law available at http://www.bgbl.at/CIC/BASIS/bgblpdf/www/pdf/DDD/2001a15,201.

[37] ECD, Art 3(4)(1). UK Regulations, Reg 5(1)(d).

[38] ECD, Art 2(e). Reg 2 'consumer means any natural person who is acting for purposes other than those of his trade, business or profession'.

[39] Recs 55, 56. Art 3(3) and Annex.

[40] Reg 4(4) and Annex.

[41] Rec 55. For the reason why, see the section below on the EC Rome Convention.

1. The Suppliers and the Consumers: Poles Apart

There has been a bitterly contested war of words between suppliers and consumers as to whether the ECD should reflect the country of origin or the country of destination approach to regulation in the field of consumer contracts.[42] These opposing views can be simply stated. The suppliers argue that if they are to engage in B2C e-commerce, then they must be able to do so within an environment that not only promotes certainty in legal dealings, but does so in a manner in which legal and business risks are both known and capable of management. The application of the country of destination rule might result in a supplier being sued by a consumer in the courts of that consumer's domicile; logically therefore a supplier who traded across the EC might be exposed to the risk of suit in every one of the Member States of the EU. This risk was unacceptable. Equally, rules on choice of law that require a supplier to trade in accordance with the consumer protection laws in each of the Member States of the EU, and potentially liable if he does not, are unreasonable and unworkable both in terms of knowledge of the rules, and costs for compliance. As a result the supplier will not engage in e-commerce across borders, and the Single European Market will not become a reality.

Unsurprisingly, consumers (or, more usually, their representatives) take the opposite view. Consumers argue that they must both be able to sue in the courts of their home country, and that the consumer protection laws of their country should apply to a cross border transaction. Any other rule, and in particular a country of origin rule applying the laws of the supplier exclusively to any consumer transaction and requiring the consumer to sue in the courts of the supplier's domicile, would effectively deny the consumer access to justice. A consumer does not have the financial means to pursue an action in the trader's home courts, nor knowledge of the trader's laws. Any transaction in which the consumer engages is likely to be of (relatively) small value, and thus not worth pursuing across borders. If consumers cannot sue suppliers in their home courts and rely on their own familiar laws, then they will not engage in e-commerce across borders and the Single European Market will not become a reality.

2. Consumer Protection in the ECD and the UK Regulations

The Directive makes it clear that the scope of the co-ordinated field reaches into 'requirements relating to on-line activities such as on-line information, on-line advertising, on-line shopping, and on-line contracting' but that it does not cover

---

[42] This dichotomy was also one that bedevilled the negotiations surrounding the revision of the Brussels Convention. See generally *Hearing on Electronic Commerce Jurisdiction and Applicable Law 4–5 November 1999*. Position papers submitted to the European Commission at http://europa.eu.int/comm/scic/conferences/991,104/contributions.pdf.

'legal requirements relating to goods such as safety standards, labelling obligations or liability for goods'.[43] Further, consumer contracts 'should be interpreted as including information on the essential elements of the content of the contract, including consumer rights, which have a determining influence on the decision to contract'.[44] Does this include pre-contractual matters such as advertisements? Contractual matters as embodied in the agreement between the parties and relating to such measures as the quantity and description of the goods (ten bottles of Sancerre 1999)? Does it also encompass implied terms, such as the quality of the goods? Certainly it would appear that public law regulations relating to the process of manufacture are outwith the scope of the measures. But what lies within is far less certain.

When the UK Government was implementing these obligations the first approach was to transpose the text of the derogation in the ECD verbatim into the Schedule to the Regulations.[45] However, the advice given in the interim *Guide to Business*[46] went on to elaborate on what might be covered, and in doing so appears to have drawn on the Recitals laid out above. In this, the Government interpreted the derogation as applying to:

- the question of which law is applicable to the substance of a dispute, including contractual obligations/rights;
- essential information that has a determining influence on the decision to contract, which must be provided in accordance with the requirements of the consumer's Member State;
- requirements applicable to such contractual obligations, including requirements to do certain things before entering into a contract (eg, provide information about cancellation rights under the provisions of timeshare legislation).

Once again there was some disquiet from a number of commentators who considered that the extent of these derogations from the country of origin principle were excessive, in that they extended both to pre-contractual measures as well as to the terms of the contract. In particular it was argued that as most B2C commerce involves some sort of contract, if pre-contractual measures were included within the scope of the derogation, the derogation would swallow the rule. Having listened to the discussion, the Government clearly had sympathy for that argument. Whereas the wording of the final *Guide to Business* remains the same,[47] that wording differs from the Government response to the consultation which suggests that the derogation will apply to:

---

[43] Rec 21, Art 2(ii), UK Regulations, Reg 2.
[44] Rec 56.
[45] Schedule to the Draft Regulations at http://www2.dti.gov.uk/industry_files/pdf/regulations.pdf.
[46] Above n 27.
[47] Electronic Commerce (EC Directive) Regulations 2002, Public Consultation—Government Response 2002.

- the law applicable to the substance of a dispute, including contractual obligations/rights;
- information provided by traders about consumers' rights;
- other essential information that has a determining influence on the decision to contract;
- laws that bear on the terms of the contract (eg, rules on implied terms, certain cancellation rights and the circumstances in which an agreement is unenforceable).

It would appear that the scope of the advice is narrower than the wording in the Guide. For instance there is no reference to 'essential information having a determining influence on the decision to contract being supplied in accordance with the consumer's Member State'. Certainly the words 'other essential information' remain, but there is no reference to the consumer's Member State. In addition, the wording 'including the requirement to do certain things before entering into a contract' has been removed, even if the obligation to provide information in relation to cancellation rights remains albeit narrowed to '*certain* cancellation rights' [emphasis added]. Despite this, the *scope* of the derogation remains unclear.

3. The Rome Convention and the Applicable Law

This section will analyse the relevance of the Rome Convention on the Law Applicable to Contractual Obligations 1980 (the 'Rome Convention') which has been transposed into UK law by way of the Contracts (Applicable Law) Act 1990 (as amended). Both of these instruments deal with matters of applicable law.

The main principle in deciding the applicable law in the Rome Convention is that of freedom of choice.[48] In other words, the parties are free to choose which law should apply to their dealings. However, special provisions apply to consumer contracts.[49] These are set out in Article 5. These apply to a contract[50] the object of which is the supply of goods or services to a consumer for a purpose which can be regarded as being outside his trade or profession. In the absence of choice, the contract will be governed by the law of the country in which the consumer has his habitual residence. However, if the parties *have* expressly chosen the law that will govern the contract, that will not have the result of depriving the consumer of the protection afforded to him by the mandatory rules of the law of the country in

---

[48] Rome Convention, Art 3(1).

[49] See M Giuliano and P Lagarde, *Report on the Convention on the Law Applicable to Contractual Obligations* OJ No C 282, 31 October 1980, p 23. Available at http://www.rome-convention.org/instruments/i_rep_lagarde_en.htm.

[50] But not to a contract of carriage, except an inclusive tour contract providing for a combination of travel and accommodation, or a contract for the supply of services where the services are to be supplied to the consumer exclusively in a country other than that in which he has his habitual residence. Rome Convention, Arts 5(4) and (5).

which he has his habitual residence.[51] Thus if there is a choice of law clause which refers to some law other than the law of the consumers habitual residence, then the law referred to in the choice of law clause will apply except to matters falling within the mandatory rules of the consumers habitual residence. Thus different parts of a consumer contract may be governed by the laws of two (or more) countries.[52]

Example 4

A Scottish consumer purchases Sancerre from a French supplier under a contract that contains a choice of law clause making French law the applicable law of the contract. French law will govern except that UK mandatory rules protecting consumers will apply to protect the Scottish consumer.

Two key points. First, the derogation only applies if one of the tests in Article 5(2) of the Rome Convention is met:

- In that country the conclusion of the contract was preceded *by a specific invitation addressed to him or by advertising*, and he had taken in that country all the steps necessary on his part for the conclusion of the contract; or
- The other party or his agent received the consumer's order in that country; or
- The contract was for the sale of goods and the consumer travelled from that country to another country and there gave his order, provided that the consumer's journey was arranged by the seller for the purpose of inducing the consumer to buy.[53] [emphasis added]

Second, what is meant by the *mandatory rules* of the law of the country in which the consumer has her habitual residence?

(a) Specific Invitation and Advertising

If the protective provisions are to apply for the benefit of the consumer, the contract must meet one of the conditions set out in Article 5(2). Of particular note for e-commerce matters is the first indent. What is meant by the contract being preceded by *a specific invitation addressed to him* and by *advertising?* What amounts to a specific invitation? Would an email from an e-tailer advertising a sale and sent to a distribution list (to those who had opted in for such communications[54]) amount

---

[51] Rome Convention Art 5(2).
[52] *Green Paper on the Conversion of the Rome Convention of 1980 on the Law Applicable to Contractual Obligations into a Community Instrument and its Modernisation*, presented by the Commission, Brussels 14 January 2003, COM (2002) 654(01) final, p 28.
[53] Rome Convention, Art 5(1) and (2).
[54] See ch 2 by Edwards on unsolicited commercial communications.

to a specific invitation to each recipient? Would the techniques used by e-tailers such as amazon.com whereby a web site is 'personalised' each time you visit it with details of products that have been identified as potentially suitable amount to a specific invitation? Would (an intensely annoying) pop-up advertisement amount to a specific invitation? And what about *advertising*? A distinction is sometimes made between passive and active websites. A passive website is generally seen as one which supplies information but does little more. By contrast an active website is one with which the consumer can interact by, for example, ordering goods on line.[55] Does the mere provision of a passive website amount to advertising? In these circumstances a consumer has to take the initiative to seek out the website. Is this not more akin to a consumer reaching out to the e-tailer, rather than the e-tailer advertising his wares to the consumer? Is the test to be subjective; in other words, what appears to be the intention of the website owner assessed from the facts and circumstances? Or is the test objective; in other words what is to be inferred from an objective assessment of the website and the surrounding circumstances?

In the pre-Internet days, these questions may have had relatively clear answers. For instance, the French supplier of Sancerre might have decided to target consumers in the South of England by way of mail-shot, first checking out the law of England. Or he might have advertised in a newspaper with a circulation largely restricted to England. In these circumstances it would seem clear that the criteria in the Article would be met. The supplier would have taken active steps to enter the consumers' state (and taken risk management steps at the same time). It is a lot less clear that the mere provision of a passive website should fulfil the criteria necessary to bring it within Article 5(2). The analysis might tend to point to the opposite conclusion—that the consumer had entered the territory of the supplier. An analogy could perhaps be drawn with the UK cases of *800–Flowers Trade Mark*[56] and *Euromarket Designs Market v Peters Ltd*,[57] both cases concerning the

---

[55] This is a concept that has been used notably in the States when considering questions of jurisdiction. See *Zippo Manufacturing Company v Zippo Dot Com Inc*, 952 F Supp 1119 (1997):

> At one end of the spectrum are situations where a defendant clearly does business over the Internet. If the defendant enters into contracts with residents of a foreign jurisdiction that involve the knowing and repeated transmission of computer files over the Internet, personal jurisdiction is proper. Eg, *CompuServe, Inc v Patterson* 89 F3d 1257 (6th Cir, 1996). At the opposite end are situations where a defendant has simply posted information on an Internet Web site which is accessible to users in foreign jurisdictions. A passive Web site that does little more than make information available to those who are interested in it is not grounds for the exercise personal jurisdiction. Eg, *Bensusan Restaurant Corp v King*, 937 F Supp 295 (SDNY 1996). The middle ground is occupied by interactive Web sites where a user can exchange information with the host computer. In these cases, the exercise of jurisdiction is determined by examining the level of interactivity and commercial nature of the exchange of information that occurs on the Web site. Eg, *Maritz, Inc v Cybergold, Inc*, 940 F Supp 96 (EDMo 1996).

[56] [2000] FSR 697, 705, confirmed on appeal [2001] EWCA Civ 721.
[57] [2000] ETMR 1025, 1031.

question of whether a trade mark had been used in the UK. Jacob J said that the content providers could not be said to have intended to reach the UK market as: 'The mere fact that websites can be accessed anywhere in the world does not mean . . . that the law should regard them as being used everywhere in the world. It all depends on the circumstances, particularly the intention of the website owner and what the reader will understand if he accesses the site.'

Jacob J seems to be suggesting that the test is an objective one: what can be gleaned from an objective assessment of the intention of the website owner as evidenced by both the site and the surrounding circumstances.[58] An objective assessment of a website provided by an e-tailer might take into account such matters as the language of the site, the currency, and perhaps whether disclaimers are used stating which territories the trader is prepared to supply.

Suffice it to say that it is not yet clear as to what type of on-line e-tailing activity might satisfy these criteria. Some points may be clarified in due course as the European Commission is currently conducting a review of the Rome Convention suggesting *inter alia* that Convention should be converted into a Community Instrument and that the scope of the consumer protection measures might be revisited. Suggestions for reform include:

(a) broadening those circumstances in which the mandatory consumer protection rules of the consumer's habitual residence apply to a consumer contract provided the supplier is in a position to know where that is;[59]
(b) systematic application of the law of the consumer's place of residence;[60]
(c) bringing the test into line with that to be found in the Brussels Regulation which refers to 'directing activity to'[61] (see further the discussion below);
(d) making the main rule the law of the consumers habitual residence and allowing derogation for the application of a limited number of other laws only in narrowly defined circumstances.[62]

(b) Mandatory Rules

As discussed above, Article 5 of Rome provides that consumers are not to be deprived of the protection afforded by the *mandatory rules* of the law of the country in which they have their habitual residence. What are these mandatory rules? The definition of mandatory rules is not easy, and different Member States offer

[58] For a much fuller discussion in the context of jurisdiction see U Kohl, *An Analytical Framework on Regulatory Competence over Online Activity* (unpublished PhD dissertation, University of Canberra, 2003) 129.
[59] *Green Paper on the Conversion of the Rome Convention of 1980 on the Law Applicable to Contractual Obligations into a Community Instrument and its Modernisation,* presented by the Commission, Brussels, 14 January 2003, COM (2002) 654(01) final, p 28, para 3.2.7.3(iii).
[60] *Ibid,* para 3.2.7.3(v).
[61] *Ibid,* para 3.2.7.3(vi).
[62] *Ibid,* para 3.2.7.3(viii).

differing interpretations.[63] Very broadly, mandatory rules can be considered to be those rules from which the parties cannot derogate by contract.[64]

But that definition does not help deciding exactly which rules are mandatory in the context of consumer protection. There seems to be no European, or even UK list of exactly which consumer protection laws would fall under this head. In the Green Paper it is suggested that mandatory rules 'involve[s] in particular the right of the consumer to withdraw from the contract and to be protected against unfair terms, such as those releasing the professional from liability in the event of damage.'[65] But this of course raises further questions. Returning to the problem concerning the scope of the derogation from the country of origin rule for consumers outlined above,[66] the question that now arises is as to within the scope of that derogation, which elements of the contractual relationship between supplier and consumer might qualify as *mandatory rules*?

> ### Example 5
>
> A consumer in the UK contracts to purchase a case of Sancerre from a French supplier, but then wants to cancel the contract. UK law has implemented the minimum obligation in the EC Distancing Selling Directive to provide that the contract can be cancelled by the consumer within 7 working days.[67] But the French website states that the consumer has 10 working days during which the contract can be cancelled.[68] Is the UK cancellation period a mandatory rule of the consumer's habitual residence, designed to protect consumers? If it is, then Article 5 would appear to require that the UK 7-day

[63] For a discussion see M Hellner, 'The Country of Origin Principle in the E-Commerce Directive: A Conflict with Conflict of Laws', *Riga Graduate School of Law Working Paper* 2003, No 6, p 21 *et seq*.

[64] The mandatory provisions referred to in Art 7(1) of the Rome Convention are more deeply embedded than those relating to consumers in Art 5. Art 7 mandatory rules (also called overriding rules) 'are relevant only in an international context and involves provisions to which a state attaches such importance that it requires them to be applied whenever there is a connection between the legal situation and its territory, whatever law is otherwise applicable to the contract'. Green Paper, para 3.2.8.1. On mandatory rules see also eg, M Wojewoda, 'Mandatory Rules in Private International Law: With Special Reference to the Mandatory System under the Rome Convention on the Law Applicable to Contractual Obligations' (2000) 7(2) *Maastricht J European & Comparative L* 183. Cheshire and North, *Private International Law*, P North and J Fawcett, 13th edn, (Butterworths, 1999) 499. C Wadlow, *Enforcement of Intellectual Property in European and International Law* (Sweet and Maxwell, 1998) para 7–92.

[65] *Green Paper*, above n 59, p 28.

[66] See p 12 above.

[67] Consumer Protection (Distance Selling) Regulations 2000, SI 2000, No 2334. Working days means all days other than Saturdays, Sundays and Public Holidays. Reg 11 states that the period begins on the day on which the contract is concluded and ends on the expiry of 7 working days beginning with the day after the day on which the consumer received the goods.

[68] The French Code of Consumption requires 7 days from the day of the consumers order. The period can be extended by one day when the 7 days would end on a public holiday. Italian law provides for 10 working days. See http://www.retailing.org/ealaonline.pdf.

cancellation term be applied—even though the contractual provision given by the website is more favourable to the consumer. This seems an absurd result, especially if, perhaps, the extended cancellation period had a determining influence on the decision made by the consumer to buy from that particular supplier. An alternate interpretation might be to say that Article 5 demands the application of mandatory rules of the law of the consumer's habitual residence only when not to do so would indeed prejudice the consumer.

There appear to be no absolute answers to these difficult conundrums. This is acknowledged in the Green Paper on the revision of the Rome Convention although perhaps the most useful suggestion made in that Paper to try and untangle some of the confusion is that:

> For legal matters already harmonised at Community level . . . the consumer protection rules of the law chosen by the parties should apply. . . . Only in matters not harmonised at EC level, the consumer should not be deprived of the protection through the 'mandatory rules' of the law of the country of his habitual residence.

If the reader is looking for suggestions for a definitive list of what qualifies as a mandatory rule, she will be sorely disappointed.

4. The Brussels Regulation on Jurisdiction and Judgments[69]

So far the discussion has been on choice of law. In this section, questions of jurisdiction will be examined: that is, which courts have jurisdiction in the event of a dispute between a consumer and a supplier engaging in an e-commerce transaction. The country of origin rule does not touch on matters of jurisdiction. These matters are left within Europe to the Brussels Regulation on Jurisdiction and the Regulation and Enforcement of Judgments in Civil and Commercial Matters (the 'Brussels Regulation') to which we turn.[70]

The principal rule of the Brussels Regulation (implemented in the UK by way of the Civil Jurisdiction and Judgments Act 1990 as amended) is that the defendant should be sued in the State in which she is domiciled.[71] This is supplemented by

---

[69] Council Regulation No 44/2001 of 22 December 2000 on jurisdiction and the recognition and enforcement of judgments in civil and commercial matters.

[70] The Brussels Regulation replaced the Brussels Convention on 1 March 2002. For completeness it should be noted that negotiations are currently underway to draft a Rome II Convention which will deal with the law applicable to non-contractual obligations. As that Instrument goes beyond consumer contracts it will not be considered here. For further details see http://europa.eu.int/comm/justice_home/news/consulting_public/rome_ii/news_summary_rome2_en.htm.

[71] Brussels Regulation, Art 2.

special rules for contracts,[72] tort[73] and for the protection of consumers. The special rules determining jurisdiction in consumer contracts are to be found in Articles 13–15 of the Brussels Regulation.

These rules permit consumers to bring proceedings against another party to the contract in either courts of the Contracting State in which that other party is domiciled or in the courts of the state in which she (the consumer) is domiciled.[74] However, proceedings may only be brought *against* the consumer in the courts of the Contracting State in which the consumer is domiciled.[75] In addition, if the non-consumer party is not domiciled in a Contracting State but has a branch, agency or establishment in one state then as regards disputes arising out of the operation of that branch, agency or establishment that party shall be deemed to be domiciled in that state.[76] These rules may only be derogated from in limited circumstances which favour the consumer.[77]

The consumer rules only apply in three types of situation. The first two apply where goods have been purchased with the assistance of credit and cover (i) contracts for the sale of goods on instalment credit terms[78] and (ii) contracts for a loan repayable by instalments or any other form of credit made to finance the sale of goods.[79]

The third, and most troublesome provision for these purposes, covers contracts other than those for credit purchase where:

---

[72] Brussels Regulation, Art 5(1)(a). In relation to contractual jurisdiction the place of performance of the obligation in question is in relation to the sale of goods the place in a Member State where, under the contract, the goods were delivered or should have been delivered, and in the case of the provision of services, the place in a Member State where, under the contract, the services were provided or should have been provided.

[73] Brussels Regulation, Art 5(3). This has been interpreted by the ECJ to include both the place where the damage occurred and the place of the event giving rise to it: see Case 68/93 *Shevill v Presse Alliance* [1995] 2 AC 18. In Case 189/87 *Kalfelis v Schröder* [1988] ECR 5565, the ECJ ruled on the scope of 'matters relating to tort', and, in effect, excluded any case in which the parties are in a contractual relationship. This greatly reduces the relevance of this basis of jurisdiction in consumer cases.

[74] Brussels Regulation, Art 16(1).

[75] Brussels Regulation, Art 16(2).

[76] Brussels Regulation, Art 15(2).

[77] Brussels Regulation, Art 17 states:

The provisions of this Section may be departed from only by an agreement:

1. which is entered into after the dispute has arisen; or
2. which allows the consumer to bring proceedings in courts other than those indicated in this Section; or
3. which is entered into by the consumer and the other party to the contract, both of whom are at the time of conclusion of the contract domiciled or habitually resident in the same Member State, and which confers jurisdiction on the courts of that Member State, provided that such an agreement is not contrary to the law of that Member State.

[78] Brussels Regulation, Art 15(1)(a).

[79] Brussels Regulation, Art 15(1)(b).

The contract has been concluded with a person who pursues commercial or professional activities in the Member State of the consumer's domicile or, by any means, directs such activities to that Member State or to several States including that Member State, and the contract falls within the scope of such activities.[80]

The question is obviously raised of what '*directs such activities to*' means in the context of consumer e-commerce. Similar questions arise as those already explored under the test of 'advertising' in relation to the Rome Convention. Is the test subjective or is it objective? If objective would that indicate that by the mere placing of the website on the Internet the supplier was directing activities at any consumer who cared to respond? If the website is merely a passive one, giving information to the consumer but with little more can the supplier really be considered directing activity to the consumer? Or would the supplier merely be seen as inviting the consumer into his store, wherever that might be situated? What would be the position if only information about the products and services were made available on the site but that to enter into a contract a consumer was required to contact the trader by more conventional means, such as the telephone or by post? What if the supplier adds a facility to enable the consumer to make purchases using the website? Does it matter what currency is used on the site? Does it matter what language the site is in?

5. Disclaimers and Websites: Are They Effective?

One way for suppliers to minimise the risk of being sued in every member state of the EU might be to insert disclaimers specifying *where* they were prepared to do business, or perhaps more importantly, where they were *not*. Would such a disclaimer be effective, given it would act against the creation of a single European market? During the passage of the ECD, the European Parliament at one point proposed that one of the criteria determining whether activities were 'directed to [at][81]' one or more member states, should be whether an operator had attempted to confine its business to transactions with consumers domiciled in certain Member States,[82] eg, by the use of disclaimers. The amendment was not accepted by the Commission who opined: 'The existence of a consumer dispute requiring court action presupposes a consumer contract. Yet the very existence of such a contract would seem to be a clear indication that the supplier of the goods or services has directed his activities towards the state where the consumer is domiciled.'[83]

---

[80] Brussels Regulation, Art 15(1)(c).
[81] The words 'directed at' were used in the previous draft.
[82] See amended proposal for a Council Regulation on jurisdiction and the recognition and enforcement of judgements in civil and commercial matters COM (2000) 689 final, p 5.
[83] *Ibid*, p 6.

It would appear that the Commission considers the scope of the protection accorded to consumers to be broad.

Other changes to the wording of the Directive made during the legislative process also show how problematic defining the scope of this test has been.[84] A previous draft of the Regulation[85] had provided that:

> Account must be taken of the growing development of new communication technologies, particularly in relation to consumers; whereas, in particular, electronic commerce in goods or services by a means accessible in another Member Sates constitutes an activity directed to that State. Where that other State is the State of the consumer's domicile, the consumer must be able to enjoy the protection available to him when he enters into a contract by electronic means from his domicile.[86]

The explanatory memorandum to the draft noted that it was intended to include contracts concluded via interactive websites accessible in the consumer's state of domicile. However, passive websites that inform consumers about the possibility of goods and services would not be covered. In the latter instance, the consumer was to be treated as the active party who seeks out the site; just as she might travel to a foreign market or shopping mall. But the wording has been omitted from the final Instrument.

The Council and the Commission have issued a Joint Declaration on the interpretation of the phrase 'directs activities to'.[87] In this Declaration, it is suggested that it is not sufficient merely for activities to be targeted at a Member State of a consumer's residence but that in addition, any contract must be concluded within that framework. The mere fact that a site is accessible is not enough. However, a factor to be taken into account is that the Internet site solicits the conclusion of distance contracts and that a contract has actually been concluded by whatever means. The statement goes on to suggest that in this respect the language or currency does not constitute a relevant factor. The utility of this advice is questionable. Indeed, the UK's DTI, in their own guidance available on their website, have said that where a site is based in England, where prices are expressed in sterling and where orders are confined to UK customers, it might be hard to describe the site as directed at anywhere but the UK.[88] Admittedly the final decision will be for the ECJ when eventually called upon to adjudicate this matter, but the public disagreement between these regulatory bodies can do little to increase the levels of

---

[84] See generally *Hearing on Electronic Commerce Jurisdiction and Applicable Law 4–5 November 1999.* Position papers submitted to the European Commission at http://europa.eu.int/comm/scic/conferences/991,104/contributions.pdf.

[85] COM (1999) 348.

[86] Rec 13.

[87] The Brussels Regulation: The Council and Commission's Joint Statement on Arts 15 and 73, at http://www.dti.gov.uk/ccp/topics1/guide/jurisdiction_eustate.htm. Unfortunately the statement is undated.

[88] http://www.dti.gov.uk/ccp/topics1/guide/jurisdiction_brussels.htm.

confidence of either suppliers or consumers—something desperately needed if B2C e-commerce is to flourish.

Further comment has been made on the opaque nature of the test in the Green Paper proposing amendments to the Rome Convention where it is said that the opportunity might be taken during that review to reflect upon the meaning of the phrase 'directs activities to'. This would be particularly welcome if it is decided to amend the text of the Rome Convention to bring it into line with that chosen for the Brussels Regulation so that both instruments refer to the test of 'directs activities to'.[89]

6. Zoning

So what is the position in relation to applicable law and jurisdiction for consumer contracts on the Internet? The broad answer is that if a supplier sends a specific invitation or 'advertises' his wares on the Internet, and the activities of the supplier are directed to the consumer, then actions by the supplier must be raised in the consumer's domicile, and the mandatory consumer protection laws of the consumer's habitual residence will apply. The devil, however, is in the detail.

Although, as discussed above, the Commission appears to think that disclaimers will not be effective to ring-fence consumer contracts, if the test for interpreting both 'advertises' and 'directs activities to' is an objective one, then the inclusion of a disclaimer on a site must be a relevant factor in any analysis by a court. However, the use of such disclaimers will certainly encourage 'zoning' of the Internet. In other words, far from being a borderless world, application of the rules encourages suppliers to delimit those jurisdictions in which they are prepared to do business and thus contain the numbers of laws that may be applicable to their transactions.

The US case of *Euromarket Designs Inc v Crate & Barrel*[90] is one example of an attempt at zoning. A website run by Crate & Barrel from Ireland said 'Goods only sold in the Republic of Ireland', a clear attempt to limit the territorial applicability of the site. But unfortunately, at least for Crate & Barrel, the way the site was set up was not consistent with this statement as users were able: 'To select the United States as part of both their shipping and billing addresses, the fields in which users entered their . . . addresses were organised for a United States format address, ie, city, state, zip code, and there was evidence that the company sold to at least one

---

[89] Problems of determining jurisdiction have also arisen where a tort or delict is committed in one jurisdiction but its effects are felt in many others. In an attempt to limit the number of possible for a, commentators have suggested a variety of tests including that the website should 'target' a particular forum, that the 'effects' of the activity are felt in a particular forum, or that a 'single publication rule' should be introduced designating the (but only one) most appropriate forum in which a case should be heard. For further details see L Edwards, 'The Scotsman, the Greek, the Mauritian company and the Internet: Where on Earth do things Happen in Cyberspace?' (2004) 8 *Edinburgh L Rev* 99.

[90] 96 F Supp 2d 824 (ND 111, 2000).

person in the forum state through its website.'[91] An objective analysis indicated a 'mixed message'.

Zoning is also encouraged by some regulatory authorities. In Australia a policy statement by the Australian Securities and Investment Commission (ASIC) relating to online offers of securities states:

> [I]n order not to target persons in Australia . . . the offeror must . . . take a variety of precautions designed to exclude subscriptions being accepted from persons in Australia and to check that the precautions are effective . . . Examples of precautions are not sending notices to, or not accepting applications from, persons whose telephone numbers, postal or electronic addresses or other particulars indicate that they are applying from Australia . . . It is not acceptable to only use precautions that place the responsibility on the applicant. For example, it is not enough to simply ask an applicant whether they are applying from Australia.[92]

The purpose here is to advise offshore financial operators as to what they must do in order not to be subject to Australian jurisdiction and laws.

As consumer protection laws become harmonised throughout Europe, will this zoning activity remain necessary? It can be argued that as consumer protection laws converge, so the risk to the trader should lessen. Suppliers should be more easily aware of the laws that are relevant in a transaction with any consumer. Certainly suppliers could still face the risk of being hailed into court in the jurisdiction of the consumer, but the risk of unknown or unknowable laws should be significantly reduced.

Such an idea might sound good in theory, but in practice it is likely to be many years before the necessary level of harmonisation is attained.[93] Many of the consumer protection measures are minimum rather than absolute requirements. The period of notice for cancellation of a consumer contract is a case in point.[94] Further, different national courts will interpret requirements differently. The ECJ may be final arbiter in those areas in which it has competence, but it is unlikely that every potential conflict will be raised before that court for adjudication within the foreseeable future.

---

[91] G Smith, *Internet Law and Regulation*, 3rd edn, (Sweet & Maxwell, 2002).

[92] Australian Securities and Investment Commission (ASIC) Offers of Securities on the Internet. Policy Statement 141 (10 February 1999, reissued 2 March 2000) PS 141.14 at www.cpd.com.au/asic/ps.

[93] See the example given in *Green Paper on the Conversion of the Rome Convention of 1980 on the Law Applicable to Contractual Obligations into a Community Instrument and its Modernisation*, presented by the Commission, Brussels 14 January 2003, COM (2002) 654(01) final, p 29, n 58.

[94] Directive 97/7/EC Of The European Parliament And Of The Council of 20 May 1997 on the protection of consumers in respect of distance contracts Art 6(1): Right of Withdrawal: 'For any distance contract the consumer shall have a period of *at least* seven working days in which to withdraw from the contract without penalty and without giving any reason' [emphasis added].

E. The Smooth Path to the Single European Market:
Alternative Routes

Does it all matter anyway? The rules are complex and litigation is likely to be much too expensive for a consumer, particularly when compared to what maybe a transaction of (relatively) small value. Consumers might be much better served by looking at other means of self-protection.

One avenue might be through a careful choice of method of payment mechanism. When concluding a transaction on-line, consumers have a number of options, the most common being payment by way of credit or debit card.[95] If a consumer chooses to pay by credit card then some comfort may be found in the UK by virtue of Section 75 of the Consumer Credit Act 1974. Subject to a number of requirements,[96] Section 75 provides that the bank (or other credit grantor) is equally responsible with the supplier for any breach of contract or misrepresentation. This means that the consumer can choose to sue either the bank or the supplier. It had always been unclear as to whether Section 75 applied to purchases made abroad, for instance over the Internet. Anecdotal evidence from Trading Standards Officers would suggest that they have successfully assisted consumers in seeking redress from a bank where a purchase has been made from foreign parts. Further, three banks, HSBC, Bank of Scotland and Sainsbury's Bank, have in the past publicly confirmed that they would not differentiate between claims based on where a purchase was made.[97] In other words, they were willing to extend protection to purchases made overseas. However, this question on liability has now been referred to the High Court in a test case brought by the Office of Fair Trading (OFT) against a number of banks. The OFT lost, with the court ruling that purchases made overseas were not so protected.[98] Whether the banks mentioned above will now change their approach remains to be seen.

All of which begs the question as to how many people actually do shop on-line and make purchases from other European countries in any event? In November 2002, a Eurobarometer survey asked a number of questions of consumers about

---

[95] A variety of other options may also be available including PayPal. For information see http://www.paypal.com/ and A Guadamuz, ch 6 of this volume.

[96] 1. The cash price of the item being supplied is over £100 but not more than £30,000; 2. The credit agreement is regulated; 3. The credit grantor is in the business of granting credit and the credit agreement is made in the course of that business; 4. The credit is advanced under arrangements between the credit grantor and the supplier.

[97] http://www.oft.gov.uk/News/Press+releases/2002/PN+60–02+Protection+for+credit+card+holders+when+they+shop+abroad.htm.

[98] *The Office of Fair Trading v Lloyds TSB Bank plc, Tesco Personal Finance Ltd, American Express Services Europe Ltd* [2004] EWHC 260D (Comm).

their attitudes to cross border shopping.[99] Here are some of the questions and the responses:

One in eight Europeans had bought or ordered products or services for private use from shops or sellers located in another EU country during the last 12 months. Of those 57% did so when abroad on holiday, 34% when on a trip for shopping and only 18% on the Internet.

Reasons given for lack of confidence:

- It is harder to resolve after-sales problems such as complaints, returns and refunds and guarantees (59%).
- It is harder to ask public authorities or consumer associations to intervene on my behalf (47%).
- A greater risk of practical problems, eg, delivery hold-ups, errors etc (44%).
- I don't know the consumer protection laws in other EU countries (43%).
- I can't trust foreign shops or sellers—there is a greater risk of fraud or deception (36%).
- I can't trust the safety of goods and services purchased from foreign shops or sellers (34%).
- There are lower standards of consumer protection laws in other EU countries (32%).
- It is harder to take legal action through the courts (51%).

When asked about measures to increase confidence in cross border purchases consumer views were as follows:

- Strengthening consumer protection laws in all EU countries (80% fairly important).
- Harmonisation of consumer protection laws (79% fairly important).
- If national authorities could intervene on your behalf in other EU countries (43% fairly important).

However and notably, 57% would not buy more even if they were equally confident about making purchases from shops or sellers located in another EU country. Only 19% would buy a little more and only 4% would buy a lot more.[100]

---

[99] Standard Eurobarometer 57.2; Flash Eurobarometer 128; Press and Communication Directorate-General. Public Opinion Analysis Unit, 14 November 2002, Available at http://europa.eu.int/comm/consumers/cons_int/safe_shop/fair_bus_pract/green_pap_comm/studies/eb57–fb128_final_report_en.pdf.

[100] For an interesting survey carried out by the European Consumer Centres on *Realities of the European Marketplace: A cross-border e-commerce project by the European Consumer Centre's Network* see http://www.konsumenteuropa.se/Documents/Engelska/EEC_e-commerce_report.pdf. See also the speech made by David Byrne, (Speech/04/130) European Commissioner for Health and Consumer Protection, 'Consumer Confidence in the Online Marketplace Boosting Competitiveness' at the European Consumer Day Conference in Dublin, 15 March 2004, at http://europa.eu.int/rapid/pressReleasesAction.do?reference=SPEECH/04/130&format=HTML and aged=0&language=EN and guiLanguage=en.

It seems there is a room for a vigorous education campaign. It is also interesting to reflect on my own attitude to Internet shopping as a reasonably well-
travelled and frequent user of the Internet. I do purchase on-line from other
European countries (and further afield). Any decision I make on whether to
purchase from a particular supplier is based on my personal knowledge through
having shopped there before (brand value and reputation) or on personal recommendation. If I purchase from an unknown supplier (my Sancerre) I will always
make a small purchase first and see if it works. If all goes smoothly I might increase
the size of future purchases. I will always use my credit card sometimes suffering
the indignity of having to pay a premium for the privilege. Have I had any problems? No, never. One member of my family did have a problem with a computer—there was a failure to return the machine after a breakdown had been fixed
shortly after it had been purchased. It had been 'lost' somewhere in the warehouse.
Sadly he had not purchased the machine with his credit card. The supplier was
threatened with all sorts of doom laden scenarios including being set upon by
Trading Standards Officers as the website did not comply with the Distance Selling
Regulations. Eventually, but belatedly, the computer was returned. Will my nearest and dearest ever use that store again? No. Will I, or indeed anyone else to whom
I relate this story? No. If I compare this process with my 'real-time' shopping
habits there are differences. I do exercise a higher degree of caution when making
purchases on the Internet from abroad. I am more willing to take the risk of failure upon myself but take steps to manage the size of that risk. But the underlying
message from the consumer to the trader is the same. Be honest. Be upfront. You
will have nothing to worry about. Except, of course, the rogue consumer.

Finally, it should not be forgotten that there has been an active programme in
place in Europe for many years now, the purpose of which is to try and avoid disputes between suppliers and consumers, and if disputes do arise, then to provide
a mechanism for avoiding litigation and instead encouraging cheaper, faster and
easier resolution by out of court settlement and other means such as on-line
alternative dispute resolution ('ODR').[101] The EC is attempting to put in place a
network of ODR/ADR solutions for consumers across Europe, known as
EEJ-NET.[102] Furthermore, agreements between regulatory bodies in the EU (such
as trading standards officers) have been put into place to assist consumers and
maintain an oversight in relation to on-line B2C trading activity.[103] In reality, it is
this framework, if both sufficiently resourced and disseminated to consumer
knowledge, that is likely to provide the most realistic mechanism for redress in
the event that something goes wrong. If successful, such ADR and regulatory

---

[101] For full details, visit the European Commission Consumer Affairs website at
http://europa.eu.int/comm/consumers/index_en.htm.
[102] See further, P Motion, Chapter 5 of this volume.
[103] See EC Green Paper on Consumer Protection Memo 01/307 at http://europa.eu.int/comm/dgs/
health_consumer/library/press/press191_en.pdf.

assistance may far more successfully encourage consumers to engage in purchasing on-line throughout the Single Market than any amount of tinkering with the rules of IPL.

F. Conclusion

If there is a smooth path to the Single European Market through the creation of rules relating to choice of applicable law and jurisdiction for consumer purchases made on-line, it has yet to be completed. So many different interests, public and private, consumer and supplier, have to be accommodated, not to mention the historical traditions and theoretical underpinnings of each of the Member States of the EU in the areas of consumer protection and IPL, that there can be no easy solution to the risks posed by B2C e-commerce. There will always be a trade-off between certainty through the application of hard and fast rules, and the need for flexibility so that a court can do justice when faced with a particular dispute. Whether an equilibrium between these ideals has yet or can ever be attained remains open to debate.

2

Articles 6–7, ECD; Privacy and Electronic Communications Directive 2002

Canning the Spam and Cutting the Cookies: Consumer Privacy On-line and EU Regulation

LILIAN EDWARDS[1]

This chapter deals with the new European and UK laws relating to the control of 'spam' and 'cookies'. Spam is best defined as unsolicited junk email (though see below), while cookies (or 'web beacons') are small text files placed on the hard disc of a computer user, usually without the consent or knowledge of that user, and used extensively on e-commerce sites to store data records about that user's trans-actions for purposes of profiling and marketing.[2] To understand the current reg-ulation of spam and cookies and how European law has altered the shape of this area, we need now to extend our reach beyond the principal focus thus far in this volume on the Electronic Commerce Directive (ECD), to look at subsequent European laws. The provisions found in Articles 6 and 7 of the ECD relating to unsolicited (and solicited) commercial communications are only one piece, and at that now of somewhat limited significance, in a much larger jigsaw of regulation.

Spam and cookies, as we shall see below, raise important questions about pri-vacy invasion and consumer protection. Spam in particular however creates more purely economic problems in the domain of e-commerce and the global Internet,

[1] Co-Director, AHRB Centre for Intellectual Property and Technology Law, Edinburgh University. Parts of this chapter appeared in a much earlier form in L Edwards, 'Canning the Spam: Is there a Case for Legal Control of Junk Electronic Mail?' in L Edwards and C Waelde (eds), *Law and the Internet: A Framework for Electronic Commerce* (Hart Publishing, 2000). I am indebted to all at the Centre for Law and Technology at the University of California at Berkeley, where research for this chapter was carried out.

[2] See further http://www.allaboutcookies.org.

of significance to the public interest as a whole, not just to consumers. Thus global spam regulation, of late, has begun looking at ways to preserve the Internet as a whole from collapsing under the deluge of spam, rather than merely attempting to protect individual privacy and consumer rights.[3] In Europe however, regulation in this area has to date, and is indeed still, been embedded in the traditional sectors of data protection and consumer law. It has been a piecemeal affair, taking bites from the general law of privacy and data protection, moving through a guest appearance in the E-Commerce Directive and taking star billing in the controversial passage of the Privacy and Electronic Communications Directive 2002 (PECD),[4] which is the first EC Directive where the question of how to regulate cookies is directly addressed. We will deal below with spam and cookies in turn, considering also, given the global nature of these problems, what solutions to these problems have been found in the United States, from which most worldwide spam emanates.

A. Spam

Few Internet users will not at some point have received an email message of the following kind:

Subject: **you forgot the attachment**

From: 'ExtremePriceCuts.net' <extremepricecuts@extremepricecuts.net>

Reply-to: no-one@microsoft.com

From nothing to rich in 90 hours!! I cracked the Code! I made over $94,000!!!!!
You May Be Closer (Maybe Hours Away)
To Financial Freedom
If YOU Needed $24,000 In 24 Hours
And your life depended on it . . .
How Would YOU Do It?

http://www.esioffers.com/track_link.html?link=3664

Such unsolicited or 'junk' e-mails are colloquially known as spam.[5] They are usually sent out to thousands if not millions of electronic mailboxes simultaneously, most often for dubious commercial purposes, though some are also sent by

---

[3] A good example of this is the US Can-Spam Act, which combines traditional rules protecting the privacy of recipients of spam with rules aimed at merely reducing the amount of spam in the world, eg, forbidding the use of third party computers as 'zombie drones' to send out spam. See further below.

[4] Directive 2002/58/EC.

[5] The name 'spam' is, as a matter of Internet urban myth, supposed to derive from a well known Monty Python TV comedy sketch involving the chanting of 'spam, spam, spam' over and over again. Spam is of course, originally a trade marked term for a form of canned luncheon meat.

private individuals for non-commercial purposes, for example to spread racist or homophobic hate speech or for political or religious campaigning purposes. Spam can often be casually spotted by its use of multiple exclamation marks and capital letters (the Internet equivalent of shouting), or by enticing subject lines such as 'get rich quick' or 'hot sex here' (although recent iterations of spam tend most often to disguise its true nature in the subject line in a bid to up the 'click-through' rate, ie, to induce the reader to open it). Although most often found in the context of email, and Usenet newgroups, websites (such as the very popular web-log or 'blog' sites)[6] can also be spammed, and for this reason LINX, the London Internet Exchange, and may other leading spam-blocking sites,[7] have suggested the best description would be 'unsolicited bulk material' or UBM. This type of nomenclature also places the emphasis on the *bulk* in which the spam is sent, not its *contents*, fraudulent or otherwise, which as we shall see below, is a crucial point for would-be regulators of spam to note. Beyond the sheer question of bulk, it is not easy for an automated process to determine which are 'genuine' marketing messages and which are what is commonly regarded as 'spam'—for example, to distinguish between 10,000 emails promoting a Nigerian bank fraud scheme and 10,000 emails encouraging alumni of a major university to make tax-deductible gifts to that university. The presenting features of the *content* of spam are that they tend to advertise goods or services the recipient has not actively sought (typical examples being pornography, get rich quick schemes, pyramid selling schemes, 'phishing' emails,[8] dating agencies or software with which to become a spammer yourself); they are often misleading or outright fraudulent; and they are very often offensive, obscene, disgusting or illegal in content. Crucially, spam arrives without the consent of the recipient—hence 'unsolicited'. The leading spam country of origin is overwhelmingly the US currently, though it is hotly pursued by Far Eastern countries such as China and South Korea as spam havens.[9] Significantly, in late 2004

---

[6] The Mel Gibson directed film *The Passion* (released February, 2004) is noteworthy as the first Hollywood film to be promoted by an extensive spam campaign on weblog websites such as Live Journal. It is though the main aim of that campaign was not to spread the word (sic) but to up the Google page rankings of *The Passion* as viewings of blog pages contribute significantly to how these are worked out.

[7] Spamhaus, the UK based private spam filtering organization, which claims to serve up to 200 million Internet users, note that: 'The word Spam means "Unsolicited Bulk Mail". Unsolicited means that the recipient has not granted verifiable permission for the message to be sent. Bulk means that the message is sent as part of a larger collection of messages, all having substantively identical content. But ask a spammer and he'll claim it's something else. . . . The content of span is and always has been irrelevant. If it's sent unsolicited and in bulk, it is spam plain and simple.' See http://www.spamhaus.org.

[8] 'Phishing' entices the recipient to go to a fake site imitating a known banking or financial site and to there enter a password or other details. The aim of the scam is to give the fraudsters access to the recipient's details so that fraud can then be committed at the authentic site. Recent UK 'phishing' scams have afflicted customers *inter alia* of Lloyds Bank, the Royal Bank of Scotland and PayPal.

[9] The top ten spam origin countries as of February 2005 were USA, China, South Korea, Russia, Brazil, Canada, Taiwan, Japan, Argentina and Hong Kong. Earlier montbs have included EU countries such as UK and Italy at the lower end of this chart. See Spamhaus, above n 7.

only two EC countries were in the top 10 spamming countries (Italy and the UK at 9 and 10 respectively) and by February 2005 even they had fallen out of the ranks. It is a major problem for law enforcement, further discussed below, that the majority of spam that circulates in EC countries (estimated at 90% or more) comes from outside Europe.

Prior to 2000 or so, there was very little *legal* debate on how spam could, or should, be controlled in Europe. By contrast argument raged among 'techies' as to the best technological methods for controlling spam. When spam was still little more than a joke and a minor annoyance to consumers (and lawyers) in Europe, it was already becoming a major concern to network managers and system operators. In the US, always ahead in Internet litigation, running battles commenced in the courts between spammers and those who longed to stamp out the practice—notably Internet Service Providers (ISPs)—in the mid to late 1990s, and a flood of individual state statutes subsequently attempted to grapple with the problem in various ways.[10] More recently, a Federal statute has, after many prior attempts, finally passed which prescribes a uniform approach to spam regulation for the entirety of the USA—the CAN-SPAM Act of 2003.[11] UK and European interest, meanwhile, has increased in direct proportion to the increasing amount of email that is spam—spam in Europe has grown from only 7% of global email traffic in April 2001 to at least 50% of EU email traffic at January 2004,[12] while some extents put the proportion of spam in email as high as $\frac{3}{4}$ of the total in the run up to Christmas 2003. In the US, estimates vary but go as high as over 80% of all email traffic probably being designated as spam. At these levels, spam is not just an annoyance to users and service providers, but is on the way to making the entire Internet effectively unusable for those without highly effective filters in place. Since spam is also now frequently used as a delivery device for viruses, worms and distributed denial of service (DDOS) attacks it is not uncommon to view every spam email nowadays as a 'ticking bomb'.

More broadly, the European Union has clearly espoused the view that development of consumer confidence in the Internet as a commercial medium is dependent on consumer and retailer trust, and both spam and cookies are key problems which persistently remind users that the Internet has not yet attained the status of a safe and known environment. Accordingly, spam, once a matter of joke and urban legend, and cookies, of which most Internet users have still probably never

---

[10] See David Sorkin's useful inventory of spam laws at http://www.spamlaws.com/.

[11] This is the informal title of the Controlling the Assault of Non-Solicited Pornography and Marketing Act of 2003. The Act passed on 25 November 2003 and came into force on 1 January 2004.

[12] See EU press release, IP/o4/103, 27 January 2004. A variety of industry based pressure group in Europe are dedicated to the fight against spam, including E-CAUCE, the European Coalition against Unsolicited Commercial Email, web site at http://www.euro.cauce.org/en/index.html. A useful US and Europe based anti-spam site is Junkbusters at http://www.junkbusters.com. Spamhaus, see n 7 above, are a useful source of technical information and statistics: the European Commission also provides up to date information at its www.europa.eu.int pages under Information Society head.

heard, have become some of the most pressing issues for modern e-commerce legislation to grapple with all over the globe.[13]

Finally it is important to note that legislation in this area is an ongoing process as new types of privacy-invading technologies are invented. Cookies are by no means the end of the story: the PECD also attempts to grapple with the privacy implications of collection of traffic and locational data, which are increasingly likely to be used as means of targeting novel 'value added' commercial services at consumers. Most recently, the RFID—Radio Frequency Identity—chip, which reports back its whereabouts like a small microphone bug to nearby electronic readers, has made the leap from laboratory to shop floor and is currently stirring controversy as major High Street retailers and large distributors and manufacturers start to use it to improve efficiency and reduce costs, but at untried risks to privacy. Despite the often-made claims of the EC that it attempts to draft e-Directives in a technology-neutral fashion, it is quite probable that even fairly new legislation such as the PECD and the UK implementing Privacy and Electronic Communications (EC Directive) Regulations 2003 ('the UK PECD Regulations'),[14] are already out of date.[15] Do we need new legislation every time a new privacy invasive technology is invented and if so is there any hope that the law will not always lag futilely behind the potential harm created by the new privacy-invading technology (PIT)? One answer may be to use technology or 'code', not law, to effectively restrain technologies harmful effects; and in the final section of this chapter we will consider if legal regulation in this domain is not increasingly an irrelevance and even a distraction from the real solutions which may lie in the domains of technology and economics.

B. Why is Spam a Problem, and Whose Problem is it?

As noted above, the historic response to spam before the turn of the century was to regard it as a nuisance, and perhaps to take self help measures such as 'flaming' (sending abusive emails to the spammers)—but not to see it as a fit subject for legal or extra-legal regulation. However a number of factors have conspired to make spam, as noted above, a phenomenon to take very seriously indeed.

---

[13] See n 9 above and further below.

[14] SI 2003/ 2426. The Regulations finally came into force on 11 December 2003 following an extensive consultation exercise by the DTI.

[15] See for similar concerns in the field of e-money regulation, Guadamuz A and Usher J in Chapter 6 of this volume.

1. 'Living Persons' as Victims of Spam: Offence, Annoyance and Invasion of Privacy

Most obviously, much spam is annoying, objectionable, distasteful, and in some cases, deeply offensive, to its recipients. Furthermore, traditional direct marketing was usually only directed at solvent adults, while spammers will indiscriminately spam children and other vulnerable groups so long as the have an email address.[16] Spam also now appears in so many media that it is omnipresent both at home and at work. Spam that came as email was bad enough, but in the brave new world of the 21st century, unsolicited marketing also arrives as texts to mobile phones, spontaneous downloads to desktops, executable attachments alongside email spam which unknowingly plant viruses and spyware, and perhaps worst of all, 'pop-ups', windowed advertisement exploiting bugs in Windows soft ware, which obscure the user's desktop, arrive incessantly to some unlucky users, are difficult to close, endlessly repetitive, and sufficient to incite 'spam rage'[17] in the meekest of users.[18]

From a traditional European legal perspective, therefore, spam's worst offence is to be an invasion of the privacy of the individual whether the mail box is situated at home or work. Spam has been described as combining the worst aspects of junk mail, unwanted telephone solicitation ('cold calling') and junk faxes.[19] Looked at this way, spam is not a dissimilar problem to traditional, non electronic direct marketing, although it is important to note that the costs of marketing by spam are shifted almost wholly from the spammer, to the recipient who pays his ISP for Internet bandwidth and access. For the spammer, each spam costs less than 0.025 cents to send—for the recipient, the costs will generally be far higher, both in terms of time, money and personal irritation. Given the traditional European view that spam, like ordinary junk mail, was primarily an annoyance to living persons in their private sphere, it was natural that the main legal response in Europe

---

[16] Dallman and Dowling noted in 1998: 'The British Government is shortly due for a nasty shock due to their policy of connecting all schools to the Internet. Imagine the reaction when the tabloid press discovers that school children are being sent advertisements for pornography via the email accounts that the government has provided.' *Towards Useable Email*, p 2 at http://ww.davors.org/legal/dmaspam.html. Oddly there have been no such scandals, though most schools in the UK now have draconian filtering and firewall systems in place which may have forestalled such.

[17] 'Spam rage' was plead in defence in the case of a Silicon Valley computer programmer, who was arrested for threatening to torture and kill employees of the company he blamed for bombarding his computer with Web ads which offered to enlarge his penis: see report of 21 November 2003, at http://www.wired.com/news/culture/0,1284,61339,00.html.

[18] Or as the judge at first instance in the case of *U-Haul International v WhenU.com Inc*, 2003 WL 22071556 (F. Supp 2d), plaintively puts it: 'Computer users, like this trial judge, may wonder what we have done to warrant the punishment of seizure of our computer screens by pop-up advertisements that require us to click, click and click again in order to return to our Internet work.'

[19] See J Byrne, 'Squeezing Spam Off the Net: Federal Regulation of Unsolicited Commercial Email' (1998) 2 *W Va JL and Tech* 4.

was to cite the protection offered by data protection (DP) law, even though those rules not only pre-dated the deluge of spam, but also were largely formulated before the arrival of the modern Internet.[20] DP law does indeed in general forbid the processing, which includes collection and transmission, of 'personal data' which identifiably describes a 'living individual'[21] without the consent of that individual. It also bans in particular the use of personal data by direct marketers if the individual whom those details describe refuses to allow them use.[22] Such protection however is not available to corporations who are not living persons and thus incapable of being regarded as data subjects.[23] Since small to medium sized enterprises (SMEs) and sole traders suffer just as much or more economically from spam as individuals this is a major flaw in a DP-centric approach to spam regulation. The UK PECD regulations, as we shall see, do offer some limited extension of protection to juristic persons. In the US the situation is wholly different; not only is there of course no omnibus DP regime, but it has also long been accepted, albeit with some reluctance, that direct marketing is a form of speech and as such protected by First Amendments rights, although the protection given is much less than that which would be accorded non-commercial speech.[24]

And of course, for those few individual who do (mysteriously) take up the offers promoted by spammers, spam is not just a matter of disgust and invasion of privacy, but a serious cause of financial loss and personal dismay as a result of fraud. However such loss is usually covered by one or more existing laws relating to fraud in general, to mail fraud, credit card fraud or to abuse of phone lines or telecommunications.[25] Accordingly the EC approach has been that particular regulation of spam based on loss to living individuals should mainly be conceived as relating to dignitary (privacy) rather than economic loss.

---

[20] See EC Data Protection Directive (95/46/EC), implanted in the UK by the Data Protection Act 1998, and EC Telecoms Data Protection Directive, 97/66/EC, implemented in the UK by Telecommunications (Data Protection and Privacy) (Direct Marketing) Regulations SI 1998 No 3170 (relating to telephone solicitation).

[21] See Data Protection Act 1998, s 1(1) and discussion in Edwards, above n 1.

[22] See Data Protection Act 1998, s 11.

[23] This point is taken up interestingly by L Bygrave, *Data Protection Law: Approaching its Rationale, Logic and Limits* (Kluwer, 2002).

[24] *Virginia State Board of Pharmacy v Virginia Citizen's Consumer Council Inc* (1976) 425 US 748. See most recently the failure of telemarketers to have the 'Do Not Call' register set up by the Federal Trade Commission declared a breach of the First Amendment: see decision of the 10th US Circuit Court of Appeals in *Mainstream Marketing Service v FTC* (10th Cir) (2003) at http://www.ca10.uscourts.gov/opinions/03–1429.pdf.

[25] The Communications Act 2003, s 127(1) makes it an offence to send by means of a public telecommunications network a message that is 'grossly offensive or of an indecent, obscene or menacing character'. Section 127(2) further provides that a person is guilty of a crime if he persistently uses a public electronic communications network to send messages he 'knows to be false'—but, only if this is done 'for the purposes of causing annoyance, inconvenience or needless anxiety'. Arguably this will exempt most spammers, who just want to make a buck not cause alarm.

2. Economic Impacts of Spam: The Internet, the ISPs and Employers

If offence and annoyance to individuals, plus some significant economic loss to a few gullible souls[26] was all the damage spam caused, there would be good reason to leave it solely regulated by DP law, or indeed, to leave it unregulated by law but solely by technologies such as filtering. But spam can also be seen as a problem which is mainly economic, not emotional, in impact; which impacts disproportionately on certain industry groups; and affects the public interest in general, more than private individuals—and this analysis points towards why DP laws are perhaps not the best way to regulate spam after all. DP laws are mainly intended to encourage administrative compliance by responsible businesses, and are ill suited either to punishing in a way that hurts those who flagrantly disrespect the law, nor to compensating those who suffer financially as a result of spam. At the moment in the UK, the maximum fine for breaching an enforcement order served by the Information Commissioner is £5000 unless the trial goes before a jury, and in practice, prosecutions of any kind are rare to non-existent and fines low.[27] By comparison, ICSTIS, the regulator for breaches of the code of usage of premium rate phone lines, has recently imposed fines of up to £75,000 on spammers who came under its jurisdiction as they were fraudulently encouraging users to run up charges on premium rate lines.[28] There are no jail sentences available for even the most persistent spammers.[29] Individual compensation for victims of breaches of DP law is possible,[30] but there are no reported cases of an individual ever succeeding in gaining damages in the context of spam, and given the cost of legal

---

[26] It is often incredulously asked: 'But who actually responds to spam? How *do* spammers make money?' A number of explanations are put forward in the literature. One is that most spammers make money from selling other spammers software and mailing lists of spam-able addresses. A variation on this is that spammers are only trying to obtain personal details, not actual customers, so as to perpetrate further frauds and identity thefts. Another view is that the costs of spam are so low and billions of messages so easy to send, that a tiny return rate will still turn a profit. Victims are also often unlikely to complain and reveal their own gullibility so, as frauds go, it is a very safe one. See further, J Sauver, 'The Economics of Spam: The Spam Business Isn't Always What You'd Think' at http://cc.uoregon.edu/cnews/summer2003/spameconomics.html.

[27] See Annual Report of the UK INofrmation Commisioner 2002–03 at http://www.informationcommissioner.gov.uk/.

[28] See report on *ICSTIS v BW Telecom*, a New York company reported in *The Register*, 17 February 2004 at http://www.the register.co.uk/content/6/35,695.html; ICSTIS's website reports all such adjudications at http:www.icstis.org.uk/.

[29] Compare Italy, where jail sentences of up to three years are possible; and Virginia, where a spammer was recently jailed under the state spam statute for nine years (see http://news.bbc.co.uk/1/hi/technology/3981099.stm).

[30] 1998 Act, s 13.

proceedings, the lack of precedents and the likely nominal sum that might be awarded, it is unlikely any will arise.[31]

Upon whom does spam have the maximum detrimental impact? The European Commission has emphasised in the past, especially when introducing the ECD, that spam is one among several factors which fundamentally impedes the growth in public trust in the Internet as a serious commercial and social medium, by which governmental as well as private services can reliably be delivered. In this respect, the European debate around spam has begun to resemble the older debates around the regulation of encryption and pornography: in both cases, the private/moral interest in protection from offensive content, or protection of privacy rights, eventually carries less weight than the public/economic argument that unless the Internet is cleaned up and made secure for consumers and businesses, electronic commerce cannot thrive.[32] With spam however, the threat posed to the public interest has become somewhat more acute, as it has begun to threaten the potential destruction or at least retardation of the information society the EU has tried so strongly to promote. European Commissioner for the Information Society Erik Likannen put it thus in a speech in 2003: 'Combating spam has become a matter for us all and has become one of the most significant issues facing the Internet today. It is a fight over many fronts. . . . *We must act before users of e-mails or SMS stop using the Internet or mobile services,* or refrain from using it to the extent that they otherwise would.'[33] [emphasis added].

Certain actors suffer particularly direct economic losses as a result of spam. ISPs, especially the largest ones such as AOL, Comcast, BT Internet etc, suffer the brunt of the immediate damage. The sheer bulk of traffic sent out by spammers— who use special spamming software to sometimes send tens of millions of messages at one go—uses up bandwidth and slows Internet traffic down, not just email but also other services such as the Web. ISP servers from which spam is sent, or to which or through which it is transmitted, may crash, not just as a result of the initial volume of mail sent out but because of 'mail undeliverable' messages returned from inaccurate email addresses. Smaller ISPs tend to buy only as much bandwidth as they need to support the estimated traffic of their known subscribers

---

[31] Even Naomi Campbell, a global celebrity, was merely awarded nominal damages for the breach of her data privacy rights at the first stage of her recent battle with the press in the UK courts—see *Campbell v MGN* [2002] EWCA Civ 1373. (At the Court of Appeal, she then had her DP claim rejected on the grounds the breach of privacy was in the public interest—their 'right to know'—and although this was reversed in the House of Lords, the DP point was not pursued.) If even Ms Campbell only receives nominal damages for breach of DP rights, what would an ordinary mortal be granted?

[32] Dickie has described this as a 'market' rather than a 'welfarist' focus in regard to regulation of the Internet: see, J Dickie, *Internet and Electronic Commerce Law in the European Union* (Hart Publishing, 1999) p 101.

[33] Speech of 25 July 2003, quoted in DG Information Society Working Paper, *Issue Paper for EU Workshop on Unsolicited Commercial Communications or Spam,* 16 October 2003.

and massive surges of use caused by spammers, often sending vast amounts of spam from or to their server via multiple virus-enslaved computers known as 'zombie drones', will tend to crash the ISP's mail server or require the ISP to waste money buying excess bandwidth as preventative strategy. This represents a major problem to ISP and their system administrators who to retain customer confidence (and avoid potential suits for breach of contract) need to provide 24 hour access and keep networked workplaces going.[34] In *AOL v Prime Data Systems Inc*,[35] the court estimated that the real costs of AOL of dealing with each spam message were 0.078 cents per message. Since in that case 130 million junk emails were sent, the court awarded $4,000,000 against the spammer (including a punitive triple multiplier on the estimated damages). In another case it was estimated that handling spam had so degraded the performance of the server afflicted by spamming that emails that should have been delivered in minutes were taking three days to arrive.[36] Another major cost is filtering and its associated problems. Most major ISPs filter spam aggressively in an attempt to service their customer base. AOL estimated in 2003 that of the 2.5 billion email messages they delivered a day, nearly 80% were spam. AOL winnows these out, as the costs of filtering out spam are considerably less than the costs associated with storing and distributing it, plus efficient spam handling is a positive feature in attracting clientele. However the downside of such proactive filtering is dealing with complaints from customers whose emails are wrongly blocked as spam *and* from recipients who fail to receive email which was falsely identified as spam. Block of such 'false positives' may lead to valuable transactions falling through and important appointments being missed; although the issues of tort or delict law here are uncharted, it is clear that costs accrue to ISPs whichever way they decide to 'play safe'. MCI, a large Internet backbone carrier, now receive half a million complaints a month that its network is being used to transmit spam, and when it succeeds in evicting spammers from its network, finds that they rarely pay their accrued bills.[37] Less directly, large ISPs suffer brand tarnishing as they are associated with spam as their directories of customer addresses can be easily 'harvested' and thus tend to be heavily spammed. This damages customer loyalty and branch recognition and may have detrimental effects on their capital value or public stock price.

The other group who bear the cost of spam, it is often claimed, are employers. Spam wastes employee time, both when they examine and delete spam, or, worst still, become frustrated (or intrigued) and try to reply to it. Reports (usually commissioned by the writers of spam-blocking software, and so to be taken with a pinch of salt) repeatedly show that companies lose large amounts of money

---

[34] Compare the international furore caused, when Microsoft were forced in 2004 by hackers to shut down the free web based email system Hotmail for a few hours as a result of its compromise by hackers.

[35] ED Va No 97–1652–A, 12/10/98.

[36] *CompuServe Inc v Cyber Promotion Inc* No C2–96–1070 (SD Ohio 24/20/96).

[37] See generally, S Hansell, 'Diverging Estimates of the Cost of Spam', *New York Times*, 27 July 2003.

through spam, with some claiming that employees waste up 10% of their day opening and discarding spam email. Estimates of the annual cost of spam per US worker vary between $1400 and $49, depending on the analyst consulted.[38] The European Union, on whatever calculation, has based its legislative attack on spam on the claim that it is costing European businesses more than 2.25 billion Euros a year.[39]

C. Spam Law Prior to the E-Commerce Directive: The Data Protection Directive, the Distance Selling Directive and the Telecoms Data Protection Directive

The Data Protection Directive (DPD), and its UK implementation in the Data Protection Act 1998, imposes duties on 'data controllers' broadly to (i) to comply with the Data Protection Principles[40] and (ii) to notify with the Information Commissioner as persons who are processing personal data.[41] If these duties are breached, then the data controller may be liable to compensate any individual adversely affected, even if the Commissioner does not serve an enforcement notice,[42] and criminal liability may also be incurred.[43]

To determine if DP law regulated spam, then, it was first necessary to decide if spammers are 'data controllers'. A data controller is defined as '*a person who . . . determines the purposes for which and the manner in which personal data are, or are to be, processed.*'[44] This begs the question, do spammers process 'personal data'? Typically, spammers harvest from newsgroups, web sites or ISP mail programs, buy, or otherwise obtain, long lists of personal e-mail addresses, to which a spam e-mail is then sent by special software. Under section 1(1) of the 1998 Act, 'Processing' includes '. . . *carrying out any operation on the information or data*', which seems to fit these activities satisfactorily. 'Personal data' itself is defined in section 1(1) as '*data which relates to a living individual who can be identified (a) from those data, or (b) from those data and other information which is in the possession of, or likely to come into the possession of, the data controller.*' Does an e-mail address, without any other added information, identify an individual, in the same way that a name and physical address would? There has been doubt on

---

[38] *Ibid.*
[39] Cited by BBC News website, 15 July 2003.
[40] 1998 Act, s 4(4).
[41] *Ibid,* s 17(1).
[42] *Ibid,* s 13.
[43] *Ibid,* s 21.
[44] *Ibid,* s 1(1).

this matter in the past.[45] However, the PECD appears clearly to assume that email addresses if they do belong to a living person are to be regarded as 'personal data' and this is also the approach taken, with some caveats, in guidance supplied by the UK Information Commissioner.[46]

Assuming the 1998 Act does apply to spammers, it was clear that on most occasions, the act of spamming would be *prima facie* in breach of the 1998 Act in multiple ways. For example, spammers typically fail to register with the Data Commissioner as required, and also fail to respect requirements such as data security and use only for stated purposes. Most importantly however, spammers invariably failed to meet the most significant DP rule, deriving from the First Data Protection Principle, that the consent of data subjects to the processing of their data must be obtained. Admittedly, such consent is not required if one of the other exemptions in Schedule 2 is applicable, but the only one that seems relevant to spam is that the processing is 'necessary for the purposes of legitimate interests pursued by the data controller' which interests must be balanced against the data subject's rights, especially to privacy.[47] If the processing is detrimental to the interests of the data subject, as it arguably will always be in the case of spam, then the exemption is highly unlikely to exculpate the data controller.

The DPA 1998 furthermore gave the data subject the specific right under section 11 to demand to cease receiving—or to '*opt out*' from—the processing of his or her personal data for the purposes of direct marketing[48] by a data controller. This right was seen as important for consumer protection, even though anecdotal evidence showed that consumers rarely had either the knowledge or the impetus to seek out data controllers and express their desire to opt out. 'Opt-out' from traditional direct marketing was facilitated by the creation of the Mailing Preference Service, a voluntary 'opt out register' run by the Direct Marketing Association,[49] where consumers could register their preference not to receive direct marketing. Direct marketers then came by virtue of section 11 under an effective obligation to check the names on the register and remove 'opt-out' names before they sent out a mail-shot. Similar voluntary preference services were established for fax and telephone 'cold calling'. No such voluntary register however existed specifically for email spam, unsurprisingly as, as noted above, spam comes overwhelmingly from spammers who are outside the EU, anonymous and uninterested in complying with EC or UK law. Spammers, of course, nearly always failed to respect the

---

[45] See Edwards, above n 1.

[46] See Information Commissioner's Office DPA 1998: Legal Guidance at p 12, available at http://www.informationcommissioner.gov.uk/.

[47] 1998 Act, Sch 2, para 6(1).

[48] 'Direct marketing' is defined for these purposes as 'the communication (by whatever means) of any advertising or marketing material which is directed to particular individuals' (s 11(3)) and so includes spam as well as traditional junk mail.

[49] See further http://www.informationcommissioner.gov.uk/cms/DocumentUploads/The%20 Mailing%20Telephone%20and%20Fax%20Prerence%20Services.pdf.

opt-out right even where they ostensibly provided an opportunity to opt out within their own emails or websites (usually of the 'click here if you don't want to receive any more messages of this kind' type). Indeed, usually the spammer's reply-to email address proved either to be false or non-working or, as worst case scenario, to be a trap by means of which the spammers could verify the spam victim email address was indeed a valid one.

Other pieces of EC consumer legislation subsequent to the DPD also provided possible opportunities for enhancing protection from spam, but these were repeatedly not exploited, mainly due to the fervent opposition of the direct marketing industry. Consumers were, for example, guaranteed the right under the EC Distance Selling Directive 1997[50] not to receive unsolicited communications relating to distance selling from a business where they clearly objected.[51] This Directive, being of later vintage, was more clearly intended than the DPD to cover communications sent via the Internet as well as conventional mail and phone communications.[52] However since it again mandated only an 'opt-out' regime, effectively it required no more protection be given by the UK in relation to spam than section 11 of the DPA 1998 already gave.[53] An 'opt-in' minimum requirement, by contrast, would have meant that member states were required to legislate so that consumers would actually have to express a *prior preference* to receive unsolicited communications from the business in question before it would be legal for them to be sent such communications. Given consumer inertia, it was obvious (to everyone but the direct marketing industry) that such an approach would generally be more effective at controlling the increasing problem of spam, and protecting consumer privacy. It was not however at this time seen as the politically appropriate solution, at least in the UK, though several EC member states, notably Germany and Austria, did voluntary adopt an 'opt-in' regime (and thus ban spam) relatively early on.

Similarly, the Telecommunications Data Protection Directive 1997,[54] implemented in the UK by the Telecommunications (Data Protection and Privacy) (Direct Marketing) Regulations 1998,[55] was introduced to deal with the growing problem of unsolicited telephone calls and faxes and was aimed at cutting down on such 'cold calling' against the wishes of consumers. Article 12 of this Directive again gave states discretion to implement using either an 'opt-in' or 'opt-out' system, and again, the DTI chose after consultation to opt for the latter, so that those who wished *not* to receive unsolicited 'calls' still had to register their opt-out (with,

---

[50] Directive 97/7/EC, OJ No L 144/19. See further, A Nordhausen in ch 8 of this volume and Appendices.

[51] Art 10(1), Distance Selling Directive.

[52] See Art 2 of the DSD and Annex 1, which specifically refers to 'electronic mail'.

[53] The consultation paper issued by the DTI in November 1999 included draft regulations which contained alternate opt-out and opt-in schemes—however an opt-out scheme was in the end chosen.

[54] 97/66/EC. The Regulations came into force on 1 May 1999.

[55] SI 1998 No 3170.

this time, the Telephone Preference Service) to achieve this effect. The DTI also made it clear during the consultation period on implementing the Telecoms Directive, that the Regulations, and in particular, the word 'calls', were not to be interpreted to include e-mail solicitations,[56] and thus even the mild regime of opt-out was not extended to unsolicited email either (although mobile phone text messages *were* deemed to be included in the word 'calls' and thus, slightly oddly, did fall within the regime).

It became clear that there were two clear problems with both the Distance Selling Directive and the DPA 1998 in relation to spam. First, the jurisdictional and resources difficulties of enforcing EU and UK rules against predominantly American spammers were almost insuperable. But secondly, even leaving the enforcement difficulties aside, the 'opt-out' regime which both sets of rules imposed, was of very little practical help. Human nature is such that even faced with a constant source of annoyance, very few people are equipped to find out that a regulatory scheme exists which may help them, and even fewer will then make the effort to register their veto on spam. Most independent commentators agreed that an opt-in scheme for spam would be more appropriate, under which consumers would have to indicate (however bizarrely[57]) their actual *desire* to receive spam. Interestingly, the Distance Selling Directive of 1997 had already prescribed a very limited mandatory 'opt-in' regime for junk faxes and automated calling machines,[58] machines which repetitively call certain telephone numbers and then either hang up, play a pre-recorded message or connect the consumer to a human salesperson (if one is available)when the call is answered. The reason why these means of selling were distinguished from ordinary distance selling was, in the case of faxes, because the costs of marketing were transferred from seller to recipient, and in the case of automated calling machines, because of the extreme aggravation they caused. Both reasons applied just as strongly to spam, and therefore the case grew ever more compelling for the EC to unambiguously prescribe an opt-in regime for spam, especially as spam ceased to be a minor consumer problem, and became the scourge of the Internet around the turn of the millennium.

---

[56] See *Telecoms Data Protection Directive Implementation In the UK—Draft Regulations*, para 2.3.

[57] It has however been argued that 'opt-in' is rather easier for the seller to secure in relation to business-to-consumer (B2C) e-commerce than in the traditional postal or catalogue distance selling domain. Any consumer who buys something from a web site can be offered a box to click if they want to 'receive further information'. This will do as 'opt-in'; there is no need for it be done via a central register as with 'opt-out', so for small businesses, 'opt-in' may actually be a cheaper regime under which to operate than 'opt-out' where search fees of the opt-out register will be a significant overhead.

[58] See Art 12(1). It is noteworthy that even in the US, the home of free speech, automated calling machines are banned (although enforcement of this is patchy) and this ban has been upheld as constitutional (see *Moser v Federal Communications Commission* 46 F3d 970 (9th Cir, 1995)).

D. The Electronic Commerce Directive

At this point therefore, it was particularly puzzling and frustrating that the drafters of the ECD failed to grasp the nettle and impose a spam opt-in regime on reluctant member states such as the UK. Attempts were made in the European Parliament during the passage of the ECD both to ban both spam and cookies outright (see further below) but these were in the end repelled. Instead the EC Commission restricted the reforms introduced by the ECD in this connection to some rather redundant transparency provisions in Articles 6 and 7. First, Article 6 required that (all) 'commercial communications'[59] had to be 'transparent' in the sense that certain information had to be made available which identified the sender, adequately disclosed the nature and conditions of promotional offers made by the communication, etc.[60] In many respects, these requirements duplicated the work already done in the Distance Selling Directive. Secondly, only *unsolicited* commercial communications had to be 'identifiable clearly and unambiguously' as such to the recipient as soon as they arrive.[61] The obvious way to implement such labelling in the case of spam is by requiring a word such as 'advertising' to appear on the subject line of any spam e-mail. Spam filters can then in theory read the label and filter out the message. The UK Electronic Commerce (EC Directive) Regulations 2002 do not go into that degree of detail, however, merely demanding in addition to the general rule transposed from the Directive that any promotional offer or promotional competition or game be clearly identified (along with its qualifying or participation conditions).[62] Even if labelling is adopted by sellers, it is not much of a solution to spam. It may spare the sensibilities of recipients who are spared the experience of opening a message labelled (say) 'Advertising: red hot porn', but will do little for the more economic problems caused by spam discussed above, eg, the on-line time they waste being downloaded and deleted, and the clogging up of Internet bandwidth. Labelling *will* give email filtering systems a tag to act upon, but may also interfere with users forwarding spam to ISP postmasters and other spam 'vigilantes' so that they can be 'blacklisted' (see below) as they are currently encouraged to do. In any case, the

---

[59] Defined in the UK Regulations (see below n 62), Reg 2 as (with exceptions) 'a communication, in any form designed to promote, directly or indirectly, the goods, services or image of any person pursuing a commercial, industrial or craft activity, or exercisig a regulated profession'. The exceptions are a communication which contains merely an address, domain name or email address; and a communication promoting A but sent by an independent person B.

[60] The Commission has suggested that such information might satisfactorily be provided by a hyperlink in the case of a web page making a commercial communication; such a link could also be placed in an email.

[61] Art 7(1).

[62] SI 2002/1931, Regs 7 and 8.

practical evidence since the ECD was implemented in 2002 is that again, spam coming from outside the EC (and probably from within it as well) has resolutely ignored these injunctions. Enforcement certainly requires, even within the EC, a considerable budget for investigation, given the ease of falsifying one's origins on the Internet and the untraceability of most spammers operating from free ISP accounts and 'zombie drones'. Finally, on the great 'opt-in' debate, Article 7 finally provided merely that states must 'respect the opt-out registers'; a provision so redundant that the UK Regulations did not even transpose it.

E. The Privacy and Electronic Communications Directive 2002

It was thus left to the Privacy and Electronic Communications Directive 2002[63] to finally make some significant legal headway in Europe against the vice of spam. Article 13(1) of the PECD finally grasps the nettle and demands that all EU member states require prior consent—'opt in'—to the use of personal data to send junk electronic mail. 'Electronic mail' further more is widely defined to include 'any text, voice, sound or image message sent over a public communications network which can be stored in the network or in the recipient's terminal equipment until it is collected by the recipient'.[64] This is a clear attempt to make the Directive 'technology neutral' and less prone to immediate obsolescence as new forms of both communication and communications tools are invented and become popular. At present, this certainly covers not only email, but voicemail, video messaging to 3-G smartphones, text massages to phones, and more. It is interesting to ask why finally after so many lost opportunities the EC has caved in and demanded 'opt-in' to spam. One reason clearly is harmonisation—for many businesses, clarity on what they have to do throughout Europe is more important than the actual shape of the rule—but it is also down to the admission by the direct marketing industry itself that spam in its current form has rendered their industry untrustworthy and unprofitable; in short, most sentient human beings will delete unread any unsolicited mail message from unknown sender as fast as humanly possible, whether it comes from a respectable high street brand business, or from a Nigerian offering to deposit $8,000,000 in your account. Only by re-establishing a culture of trust via prior consent, the argument goes, can 'responsible' direct marketing businesses operate effectively on the Internet again.

---

[63] See above n 4.
[64] Art 2 (h), PECD.

So far, so good. There are, however, significant exceptions to the new 'opt-in to spam' rule. Prior consent is *not* required if the details of the recipient were previously obtained 'in the context of a sale of a product or service' so long as

- the recipient is given a clear, simple and free opportunity to opt-out of receiving spam each time a new communication is sent, and
- the goods or services were 'similar' to those now being marketed.[65]

Privacy advocates might suggest that the correct way to interpret this provision is to regard the exception as only operating where an *actual* prior sale had occurred—ie, *not* where the consumer had merely browsed the site to check out goods, decided not to buy, but perhaps inadvertently given away their details, eg, by having to register to gain access to the website; or by the collection of data via cookies (see below). The UK Regulations however take a different approach. So long as the business has legitimately obtained the contact details (in terms of the requirements of DP law concerning fair collection and processing), details can be used if they have been obtained in the course of the 'sale *or negotiations*' [italics added]. Is merely browsing a site, perhaps to gain information or for price comparison, 'negotiations'? Guidance from the Information Commissioner—who is of course perhaps more privacy-oriented than the DTI–suggests that 'negotiations' require some kind of active expression of interest by the data subject in the company's products and certainly do not include the case where all that has happened has been the browse of a site and deposit of a cookie.[66] It remains to be seen how courts or regulators will interpret this clause when or if a dispute arises.

And what are 'similar' goods or services? No elaboration is given in the Regulations but, again, according to the DTI during the consultation period, this should only be restricted by the reasonable expectations of the buyer at the time they gave their contact details. To give an illustrative example of the DTI approach, if a consumer buys baked beans on-line from Tesco's, it seems reasonable for Tesco's to then market TVs and DVDs (say) to that consumer without prior consent, because the consumer could reasonably have known that Tescos sold all these types of goods at the time she first gave away her personal information; however if Tesco's, *subsequent* to the baked bean purchase, acquired, say, a horse-riding stables business, it would *not* be reasonable for them to market horse-riding lessons to the consumer, as she could not have reasonably expected Tescos to offer that service.[67] The Information Commissioner guidance also focuses on the idea of

---

[65] Art 13(2), PECD.

[66] *Guidance to the Privacy and Electronic Communications (EC Directive) Regulations 2003, Pt 1: Marketing by Electronic Means* available at http://www.informationcommissioner.gov.uk/.

[67] Interestingly, the Art 29 Working Party Opinion on Art 13 of Directive 2002/58/EC also emphasises that 'only the same natural or legal person that collected the data may send marketing emails . . . subsidiaries or mother companies are not the ame company' (para 3.5, 11601/EN WP 90, 27 February 2004).

'reasonable expectation' and the availability of opt-out if the goods diverge from what the consumer expects to receive. Does the average consumer really view baked beans and TV sets, plain and simply, as 'similar goods'? This seems a technical and privacy-minimising interpretation, which is unlikely to be harmonious with several other member states which have already banned spam entirely and long ago—nor is it likely to instill the trust in consumers which is the whole object of the exercise.

What else does the PECD do to prevent spam? Article 12 (implemented in the UK Regulations, Regulation 18) strengthens the right of an on-line subscriber to withdraw their name from an on-line public directory of subscribers eg an AOL customer could ask for their email address not to be visible on a publicly accessible list of AOL subscribers. Since spam mailing lists were often culled in the past from easily harvestable open directories of ISP customers, this is a useful right for individuals.

Finally as noted above, the UK PECD regulations are significant in going some small way towards extending the protection of DP law to juristic persons as well as living individuals. Regulation 22, as discussed above, extends *only* to individual users, not to 'corporate subscribers' as defined in the Regulations. As Carey notes,[68] this is not that crucial an omission, as most spam emails sent to businesses will still go to a named individual's email inbox and fall within the rules; only spam emails addressed explicitly to the business name would remain legal. But Regulation 23,[69] which makes it unlawful to send a marketing email with no valid return address, or with the identity of the sender disguised or concealed, *does* apply to emails received by corporate subscribers, thus providing UK companies *as such* with their first real remedy in the fight against spam.

F. Assessment of Legal Solutions to Spam, and Alternative Solutions to Spam

The PECD brings one chapter in the battle to regulate spam by law to an end. The 'opt-in' wars are over. But it still has to be asked, as it has been repetitively in this chapter, if this time-consuming hard-fought legal effort has been worthwhile. What will happen to spammers who continue to operate without obtaining prior consent? Spammers mostly operate outside Europe and pay little attention to European law; they are generally very hard to trace; even if traced they can move swiftly from server to server in different countries; even if found, the work needed

---

[68] P Carey, *Data Protection*, 2nd edn, (Oxford, OUP, 2004) ch 12.
[69] Implementing Art 13(4) of the PECD.

to bring them within European enforcement jurisdiction will be enormous; the resources to fight spam in this way simply do not exist in most European countries where spam law enforcement is primarily the remit of the under-funded data protection authorities. There are very very many spammers and very very few data protection officials. To adopt Peter Swire's useful metaphor, spammers are 'mice' not 'elephants'.[70] To add insult to injury, as noted above, DP sanctions in most of Europe are hardly at the punitive level which would seriously cripple a determined spammer or put others off entering the trade, The obvious message is that there has to be a better way to fight spam than this.

The Americans, with more years of experience at fighting spam via the law than we Europeans, are faring no better. Impeded, as in Europe, by the lobbying forces of the direct marketing industry as well as by constitutional concerns about free commercial speech, the recent US Federal Can-Spam Act of 2003 is widely regarded as a damp squib and even by some more radical anti-spam campaigners as actively promoting spam. The main planks of the Can-Spam Act are (a) mandatory opt-*out (not* opt-in) and (b) prohibition of false or deceptive subject lines to spam email. 'Sexually oriented' spam must also be identifiable in advance by a warning label. So far, so very similar to European law at the stage of the ECD: and we have already seen how effective that was. The US's own relevant enforcement body, the Federal Trade Commission, is so unconvinced of the benefits of opt-out that it has indicated its unwillingness to set up a 'Do-Not-Spam' register to implement opt-out, on the perfectly sensible ground that such a public list will simply be used by spammers as a validated list of email addresses ripe to receive yet more spam.[71] To be fair, the US has the advantage over Europe of having a high proportion of spammers within its enforcement jurisdiction; and the Act also goes further in some ways than the ECD or even the PECD, particularly in prohibiting the use of third party computers ('open relays' or 'zombie drones') to send spam without the consent of that computer's owner. These provisions get nearer to the heart of what might actually make spam unworkable as opposed to traditional privacy and consumer law solutions. Most ISPs nowadays prevent any subscriber, guest or paying, named or anonymous, sending out mail-shots in the bulk which spammers need to use to have any hope of profit—that is, millions not thousands of messages. Spam is therefore now overwhelmingly sent either from ISPs or servers in developing countries which have no effective legal regulation in this area, from mail-server machines which have been, contrary to good security practice, left open so anyone can use them to send mail, not just registered users of that server ('open relays')—or far more commonly now, from networks of 'zombie

---

[70] See P Swire, 'Of Elephants, Mice and Privacy: International Choice of Law and the Internet' 32 *International Lawyer* 991—the metaphor of elephants and mice is then adapted to the landscape of on-line privacy in L Edwards, 'Reconstructing Consumer Privacy Protection On-Line: A Modest Proposal' (2004) 18 *Intl Rev L Computers & Technology* 313.

[71] See 'Do-Not-Email list is pointless, reasons FTC' at www.Out-Law.com, 17 June 2004.

drones'.[72] These are computers which, usually by means of a virus infection (or 'Trojan horse'), have been 'enslaved' by a remote user (the spammer, or zombie network owner) usually entirely without the knowledge of that computer's legitimate user or owner. If the enslaved computer has mail-server software on it, or (more commonly) if that software can be implanted by a virus attached to the spam email, then the 'zombie' can be used to send out spam without any of the usual problems of getting it past an ISP's safeguards. Legal provisions such as those in the Can-Spam Act making it plain that creating 'zombie drones' is itself a crime in spam law, are thus extremely useful, though again, hardly easy to enforce without detailed computer forensic help.

A second useful provision in the Can-Spam Act is a ban on falsifying the header information or origin of the email sent by spammers. Again, one of the key technical tricks spammers use is always to disguise the true origin of their messages, perhaps by using proxy servers, 'zombie drones' as discussed above, and anonymisers to modify originating IP address, as well as by more obvious tricks such as using dud return mail addresses. This prevents their being traced by law enforcement authorities or besieged by angry replies from disgruntled spam recipients. It also prevents the spam messages easily being caught by ISPs and system administrators who filter out email from known spamming domains and addresses. Thus again it is a sensible legal strategy to ban the falsification of email origin data. This prohibition arguably exists in UK law on the basis of common law fraud as well as regulation 23 of the PECD regulations, but it is not entirely clear how far modifying header information, say, as opposed to providing a false name or a non-existent email return address, would be a breach of regulation 23. The US clear statute law reference to 'origin of email' is to be preferred to the PECD emphasis on 'identity of sender'.

But although both these provisions are helpful to the cause of stamping out spam, again both fall foul to the problems of the resources needed for investigation, the number of spammers, the jurisdictional problems and the huge forensic difficulties of establishing that a particular Trojan horse virus (say) was released by a particular spammer. Just as in Europe, spam volume in the US has continued inexorably to rise, even since the Can-Spam Act came into force on 1 January 2004.[73] While it is of course essential to criminalise or otherwise sanction the activities that enable spamming, passing laws is really only a first and rather unsatisfactory step in the process of catching spammers or blocking spam activity.

---

[72] See for example, J Leydon, 'Zombie PCs Spew Out 80% of Spam' at *The Register*, 4 June 2004 (http://www.theregister.co.uk/2004/06/04/trojan_spam_study/) reporting that ⅘ of spam now emanates from computers contaminated with Trojan horse infections. Many well-known viruses are sent out, the report claims, purely to establish networks of compromised machines as future spam relays.

[73] However 'sexually explicit spam' *has* reportedly dropped by 78% since January 2004 reported the Internet company Postini, in October 2004. This bolsters the view taken in this article that spam regulation is mainly about economic loss and gain and not about 'privacy' primarily.

Would it not be better to concentrate the effort that has gone into legal solutions into technical solutions which might actually, conceivably succeed in reducing the actual volume of spam? Concentrating on technical standards rather than laws also has the key advantage that technology largely operates on a global basis. Difficult though the task still is, it is surely easier to get a few major IT players (all of whom hate spam) to agree on standards, than it is to globally harmonise *legal* regulation of spam via the slow and tortuous domain of international treaty making.[74] A third point is that although the EU has attempted to draft 'technology-neutral' laws to fight spam and more generally protect consumer privacy, it has inevitably and continually lagged behind in the spam 'arms race'. Technical standards in their nature would have at least a better chance of dictating to spammers, rather than, as is currently the case, spammers using technology to outwit and out-race the law.

1. Technical Solutions—the Answer?

Within the knowledgeable Internet community itself, there has been consensus for several years that the best results will come not from legal regulation, but from 'self regulation' by technical strategies.[75] There are a number of less or more successful approaches. The first line of defence has always been that ISPs, local network managers, and individual users can use filtering software to winnow out e-mails sent from the addresses (IP addresses and/or URLs) of known spammers. This however is only ever partially effective as the addresses of spammers change constantly and are in any case, as described above, usually disguised. There is some degree of co-operative 'blacklisting' of sites and ISPs known to harbour spammers: one such blacklist often consulted by system administrators is known as the Real Time Black Hole List and is available on the Web.[76] Traffic coming from a blacklisted site will not be transmitted on via other networks or ISPs where administrators have consulted the blacklist, with the effect that the black-listed site becomes isolated from the rest of the Internet, effectively 'sent to Coventry'. However no such system is foolproof, and a site which is being unknowingly made use of by spammers against its own policies (a 'zombie drone' perhaps), or one which is sending out multiple copies of an e-mail for a valid reason (eg an alumni e-mailing from a university)

---

[74] The EU have continually attempted for the last few years to broker international co-operation on spam, particularly between the EU and USA, as has the UN organization, the International Telecommunications Union (ITU), but the process remains slow despite mutual good intentions. Even intra-EU co-operation on spam law enforcement has been difficult to achieve. See latest communications from the EU Commission at http://europa.eu.int/rapid/pressReleasesAction.do?reference=IP/05/146&format=HTML and aged=0&language=en and guiLanguage=en on encouragement of cross-Europe spam hotlines accessible to all EU citizens for the reporting of spam, and EDRI comment at http://www.edri.org/edrigram/number3.3/spam.

[75] See Dallman and Dowling, above n 7 and Edwards (2000), above n 1.

[76] Run by the Mail Abuse Protection System (MAPS). See further http://maps.vix.com.

may find itself black-listed alongside the 'guilty' sites. It has also been suggested that mistaken placing of a site on the list might be seen as libelous, which provides a disincentive to co-operate in providing information to the organizers or re-publishing the list. Philosophically, Lawrence Lessig, the highly respected Internet law guru, has lead a movement against 'black hole lists' on the ground that they represent undemocratic unaccountable vigilante justice.[77] An extreme solution is to use a 'white-list', ie, to accept *only* email from a list of prior approved senders: this has obvious difficulties for agencies such as the government and universities, which constantly receive enquiries from strangers, as well as for most individuals.

The most currently promising technical solutions involve variations on configuring email servers, or more radically, redesigning the email standard format itself, to make it possible to spot any attempt to falsify or disguise the true origin of an e-mail message. Filtering out all mail with fake reply addresses or falsified header information will effectively filter out almost all spam. Promising attempts are being made, notably by the IETF (Internet Engineering Task Force) and a loose confederation of major industry players (the Anti-Spam Alliance[78]) to develop what are known as 'trusted email systems': systems where, by various different means, the standard format of email is altered so that the true domain origin of a message is always apparent and cannot be successfully disguised. Email can thus always be authenticated as coming from a verifiable, and traceable, source; if it does not, it is spam and can be filtered out or bounced back. There are many obstacles still in the way of developing a trusted email system acceptable to all players—technological interoperability, proprietary standards and patents, trade secrets, industry rivalry, and privacy concerns about the possible loss of anonymised email—but in the end this is likely to be the most promising route to stamping out spam. It is quite possible that in five years technology may have suc-ceeded where law has failed and succeeded in removing spam from the regulatory agenda.

2. Economic Solutions

While we wait for technology to do its stuff, another set of possible answers to the spam problem has emerged which might be termed economic solutions.[79] These

---

[77] See L Lessig, 'The Spam Wars', 31 December 1998 at http://www.lessig.org/content/standard/0,1902,3006,00.html. Lessigs' attitude may have been coloured by the fact that his former employer, Harvard University, was at one time black-listed on the Real Time Black Hole List.

[78] The group includes Yahoo!, Microsoft, EarthLink and America Online.

[79] It is interesting to note that spam as a problem has now engaged all four of the modalities of reg-ulation Lessig famously identified in his seminal text *Code and Other Laws of Cyberspace* (Basic Books, 1999). Spam was originally tackled by *norms* in the form of netiquette and flaming, as doled out by the early Internet community to the original Green Card spammers; then by *law*; then (or simultaneously) by '*code*'; and now finally solutions are emerging from looking at how *the market* propagates spam.

start from the not unobvious observation that spam is based on the fact that spamming costs spammers almost nothing regardless of how many emails are sent.[80] Both senders and receivers of email largely pay almost zero to send and receive spam, despite that fact that spam does have marginal costs, such as electricity, storage and network congestion. These costs are, however absorbed by persons other than the spammer. So for the spammer 'this represents a sure-win strategy: mail as much as you can, because even one hit out of a million is profitable'.[81] The obvious solution then is to charge (on top of dial-up or broadband costs) for sending each email. This will of course be unpopular with ordinary, non-spammer, users; but if the charge is kept very low, then arguably it will only really bite as an economic disincentive against those (like spammers) who send out millions, not tens or even hundreds of emails per day. With this in mind, Bill Gates, CEO of Microsoft, proposed in early 2004 that an email 'postage stamp' be purchased before email could be sent.[82] Set at a very low figure, of say, 0.01 cent per item, this would barely scrape the pockets of ordinary users but would be a real financial burden for spammers.

Although in some ways an attractive idea, charging for email has so far failed to gather overwhelming support. Many critics voice concerns in principle about abandoning the democratising and free speech advantages of 'free' email. What, for example, of non-commercial community information sites which send out notifications concerning, say, breast cancer news, or important public meetings to thousands of subscribers? Free 'weblog' sites also often regularly send out many hundreds of thousands of emails notifying participants of comments to their postings. Handling the many millions of micro-payments a 'postage stamp' system would demand is also problematic. Would such payments be made in only one currency or every local currency? Who would collect them—the ISP? Who would oversee their collection mechanisms and enforce the 'postage stamp' regime? What would be done with the money? The area is fraught with unanswered concerns. One possible retrenchment would be to make a would-be email sender do a short puzzle before they sent an email, with no monetary payment involved: plausible in time costs, it is argued, for a sender of a single email, but not for a spammer sending millions. However a quick and highly unscientific straw poll by this author found that ordinary users were even more unwilling to waste time doing puzzles to send their everyday email than they were to pay for 'postage stamps'. A final, slightly more promising wrinkle is to ask senders not to pay in advance, but to put a certain sum of money up front as a bond or guarantee:[83] if the email they send

---

[80] See J Leyden, 'The Economics of Spam', *The Register*, 4 March 2004 at http://www.theregister.co.uk.

[81] 'Make 'em pay', *The Economist*, 14 February 2002.

[82] See 'Fee-Based Email way to Can Spam?', 5 March 2004, at http:///www.CBSnews.com.

[83] *The Economist*, above n 81, cites IronPort Systems in Silicon valley as already offering such a bond system to 'legitimate bulk emailers' so they can differentiate themselves from spammers.

is then rejected by the intended recipient as spam, the bond comes into operation, and a cost per email would be deducted. However a solution like this virtually requires recipients involved in the scheme to maintain a 'white-list' of who they are willing to receive email from; which as noted above, is for many individuals and associations who anticipate email from strangers as well as friends, not a practical exercise.

Another quasi-economic approach focuses on *enforcement* of anti-spamming laws. As we have noted above, one of the obstacles to the success of all spam laws is the vast amount of spammers, the difficulties of bringing them to justice, and the limited amount of resources which can be devoted by law enforcement agencies, both criminal and civil, to the project. Lessig has suggested that one way round this would be for the law to offer a 'bounty' to private individuals who track down spammers. His proposal is for a law which would (a) require effective and mandatory labeling of all spam messages in their header so they could be filtered out—eg, by words such as 'SPAM' or 'ADVERT'; and (b) allot a 'bounty' of, say 10 cents per spam message to an individual who tracked down and produced evidence that a spammer had broken this law. The 'bounty' would be paid out of the fine imposed on the spammer once successfully prosecuted, and to reduce transaction costs, would be limited to cases involving the sending of at least 100 or more spam emails.[84] Superficially this seems a strange suggestion from a man who strenuously opposed in public the 'vigilante code justice' of 'black hole lists' (see above). However Lessig argues that while black-hole listers are using 'code' to make their own rules as to who should be punished for alleged spamming, without legal backing or evidential hearings, his bounty system merely employs effective incentives to enforce constitutional anti-spam laws made by normal democratic processes. *'[W]ith automated black holes, no judgment is required before harm is done, nor do the victims have any effective appeal.*[85]' Lessig's argument sufficiently convinced a US member of Congress to introduce a Bill based on these principles, though it has not come into force.

The argument, although neat, can again be criticised. The 'bounty' system is dependent financially on the successful prosecution of spammers once tracked down, which implies their being brought before the jurisdiction of the local courts with attachable assets. This may be a plausible assumption in the US, where the majority (though only just) of spammers are still based, but it is not a realistic expectation in Europe. (It also assumes successful prosecution, which surely cannot always be guaranteed.) From a constitutional perspective, would it not be better to use realistic and punitive fines paid by spammers (an excellent idea in

---

[84] See account in D McCullough, 'A Modest Proposal to End Spam', 28 April 2003, at http://news.com.com and also below.

[85] L Lessig, 'Code-Breaking: A Bounty on Spammers', 16 September 2002, at http://www.cioinsight.com/.

principle[86]) to provide adequate funding (possibly in arrears) to existing agencies,[87] already trained, accountable and responsible for tracking down spammers rather than pass it to 'trigger-happy' private bounty hunters with no knowledge of law, evidence, jurisdiction, human rights or due process?

3. Further Challenges to Consumer Privacy: Cookies, Traffic Data, Locational Data and the PECD

The PECD deals not only with spam, but with a variety of challenges to consumer and on-line privacy which the Data Protection Directive was perceived as not being able to manage satisfactorily. Indeed, the explicit intention of the PECD is to update the DPD for the Internet era. Recital 5 states that:

> New advanced digital technologies are currently being introduced in public communications network in the Community, which give rise to specific requirements concerning the protection of personal data and the privacy of the user. . . . The successful cross-border development of [digital network] services is partly dependent on the confidence of users that their privacy will not be at risk.

The PECD thus attempts to regulate not just spam but other threats to on line privacy such as, notably, cookies. Challengingly, the intention is also to be 'technology neutral', ie, to set up rules which may fairly and effectively regulate technologies not yet in existence as well as those already in the market. Whether the PECD actually achieves this goal is something we will briefly consider in this chapter's conclusion.

4. Cookies

Cookies are small text files (usually less than 1 Kbyte in size) which reside on the local hard disc of the computer, or terminal equipment of, a user, and contain a limited amount of profile information about that user.[88] Cookies are usually visible to users if you know where to look (the directories they are stored in depend on the configuration of the system, eg C:/Windows/Cookies) but frequently, the information in the cookie even if located will be apparently gibberish to the user,

---

[86] This is an area where UK DP law can certainly learn from US law. The Can-Spam Act provides for fixed damage levels of up to $100 per email sent to a cap of $2 million, or triple that amount if state attorneys prosecute in criminal courts. Compare the UK maximum penalty of £5000 in DP law (unless a jury trial is convened) and the actual highest fine in the last statistical year of around £3000.

[87] This writer has also proposed another model for the better funding of agencies such as the Information Commissioner's Office to meet under-resourced challenges such as the prevention of spam: see L Edwards, 'Reconstructing Consumer Privacy Protection On-Line: A Modest Proposal' (2004) 18 *Intl Rev L Computers & Technology* 313.

[88] See A Sharpe, 'The Way the Cookie Crumbles' (2002) 2 *Privacy & Data Protection* 6.

because it is merely acting as a unique identifier which connects the computer where it has been deposited, to information held server-side by the business which deposited the cookie. Typically, cookies are used on e-commerce sites such as Amazon, Ebay, etc. When a user browses such a site, or buys an item, then personal information is collected—what pages he views, what search terms he types in, what images he clicks on, what items he selects—and stored in the website's server-side database. That information is then connected to the user on subsequent repeat visits to that site via the cookie which acts to identify the user. (Sites cannot simply use IP address to recognize the user as many users access the Internet via ISPs such as AOL which dynamically assign different IP addresses to users each time they log in.)

Cookies of this kind are very useful to e-commerce businesses—and to on-line advertisers—as they enable a profile of the user's shopping habits and preferences to be built up. User X, for example, may be revealed by cookies to be repeatedly surfing various websites which sell Nike or other brand trainers. This is valuable information, which can be used by the business itself, sold to competing businesses or to advertisers or used in combination with other information for data mining purposes.[89] Cookies of this kind are also useful to users: they enable sites to know who you are, in essence, and are sometimes said to give the site a 'memory'; there is no need to log in every time, and data such as delivery addresses and credit card details can usefully be remembered and filled in automatically for the user. Cookies of this kind are called 'persistent' cookies, because they are not deleted but remain on the hard disc of the user more or less indefinitely. 'Session' cookies are a very different animal. These are used as a technical device to maintain continuity during one Internet website browsing session. Session cookies are deleted at the end of the visit to a particular website and do not normally involve the processing of personal data or any possible invasion of personal privacy.

Cookies became an object of contention during the debates over the 2002 Electronic Commerce Directive, when the European Parliament became aware that personal information about consumers browsing the Internet was being collected using cookies and processed in large amounts, usually without the consumers' consent, and almost invariably without even their knowledge. So horrified were the Parliament, that, at one point, the total banning of cookies without explicit prior consent appeared to be on the cards, to the utter consternation of European industry.[90] The matter was not resolved within the ECD and by the time of the PECD, as ever, a compromise had been reached. The final version enshrined in Article 5(3) of the PECD requires merely that cookies may only be set if the con-

---

[89] See further L Edwards and G Howells, 'Anonymity, Consumers and the Internet: Where Everyone Knows You're a Dog' in C Nicoll, JEJ Prins and MJM van Dellen (eds), *Digital Anonymity and the Law* (Asser Press, 2003).

[90] See G Mackay and M Lomas, 'The Cookie Monster' (2002) 12(6) *Computers and Law* 14.

sumer 'is supplied with *clear and comprehensive information . . .* about the purposes of the processing, and is offered the right to *refuse* such processing by the data controller' [italics added].

This is in many ways an extremely watered down version of the original intent which was to introduce a positive opt-in requirement in relation to cookies, just as was eventually the case with spam. Instead, the provision retains an opt-out system, albeit with added requirements of clear information. It seems that in Europe, cookies may no longer be simply invisibly set and collected. But how will this information and opt-out opportunity be supplied? Will a hyperlink to a privacy policy be sufficient? What if the privacy policy is unintelligible? In the UMIST/UK Information Commissioner study of compliance of websites with data protection law,[91] the study team found only 5% of privacy policies were intelligible to the average consumer, using recognised plain English indices. What if (as seems anecdotally to be the case) consumers never read privacy policies anyway? What if a tick box is supplied, already ticked, which gives permission to set cookies, unobtrusively tucked away at the bottom of the page? Or a box whose rubric reads 'Tick this box if you don't want us to set cookies', so putting the onus on the unsuspecting consumer? Neither of these would surely have been acceptable under a requirement of explicit prior consent, but may well be in an opt-out regime. The PECD recitals, from a consumer point of view, provide both bad and good news here. '*Information and the right to refuse,*' runs recital 25 of the PECD, '*may be offered once . . . also covering any further use.*' So it seems that if the consumer *once* has an 'opt-out' style tick box offered to her on her first visit to a particular web site, and fails to notice it and take the appropriate action (assuming she even knows what it means), she need never be offered it again; and meanwhile persistent cookies can be set which will continue to gather information every time she subsequently visits that site. On the other hand, the recital goes on to require that '*the method for giving information, offering a right to refuse or requesting consent should be made as user friendly as possible*'. One might hope that this might rule out the scenario described above.[92] However, leaving such important detail to the recital part of the Directive will do little for European uniformity, an obvious problem when websites largely operate without notice of or concern for national boundaries.

Another interesting point in Article 5(3) is that setting cookies is allowed without consent where '*strictly necessary* in order to provide an information

---

[91] This survey is unfortunately no longer available on the Web but can no doubt be obtained from the Information Commissioner's office.

[92] The NCC survey *Consumer Privacy in the Information Age* (December 1999, PD65/L/99) spoke to focus groups of consumers about privacy, and one of their strongest resulting findings was that consumers did not like the current variation in how consent is sought by tick boxes, and felt opt-in was much more in the best interests of consumers than opt-out. The report attaches a model standardised tick box format.

society service *explicitly requested* by the subscriber or user' [italics added]. Many web sites at present, whether by intent or laziness, are designed not to work without cookies. These are however often cookies of the non-privacy invasive, session cookie type. Some *will* work without cookies, but not as well; the Amazon site is a good example of this, as it (unusually) provides fairly good functionality without cookies, but popular features such as the 'shopping cart' and 'your preferences' do disappear. Many sites simply fall over if the user chooses to 'turn off' or delete the persistent cookies for that site cookies. So depending on the interpretation of 'strictly necessary', this provision may well be an open invitation to bypass the requirement of consent at all—in other words, to retain the *status quo*. What it should do, however, is clearly distinguish between the setting of site-specific cookies (eg when Amazon sets an Amazon cookie), and the setting of third party cookies by the likes of DoubleClick.[93] Since such ad-server cookies are invariably set invisibly, and not at the request of the consumer (for who would explicitly request ads?) it seems these cannot be covered. Hence it appears European consumers will in future have to be persuaded at least *not to opt out of* receiving cookie-enabled advertisements, at least once—an interesting opportunity if consumers are informed enough to grasp it.[94] In fact however, the majority of Internet ads are now served without the use of third party cookies at all, as popular browsers, such as later versions of Microsoft's Internet Explorer, are usually now set to block third party persistent cookies, using built in P3P[95] controls. The most pressing need to regulate cookies in the interests of consumer privacy may in fact thus have already come and gone. Again, as with the spam problem, the cookie problem seems to have been solved (or at least on the way to solution) more effectively and speedily by 'code' than by law.

The UK government has indicated in its consultation document and subsequent regulations for implementing the Privacy Directive[96] an approach which is, in this writer's opinion, disappointingly un-privacy friendly. On the question of *how* consumers should be offered the right to refuse cookies, the Regulations are entirely silent, except for asserting that the right to refuse cookies need not be offered more than once. The Information Commisioner's guidance suggests that the requirement to offer a way of refusing cookies can in fact be met if websites merely offer guidance on how consumers might use the facilities of their browser

---

[93] See further Edwards and Howells, above n 89.

[94] Of course most consumers ads are served to US web sites from US ad servers and hence at least in practical terms outside EC jurisdiction.

[95] P3P is the Platform for Privacy Preferences, a software means to (*inter alia*) control cookies. See discussion in L Edwards, 'Consumer Privacy, On-Line Business and the Internet: Looking for Privacy in All the Wrong Places' (2003) 3 *International Journal of Law and Information Technology* 226.

[96] Privacy and Electronic Communications (EC Directive) Regulations 2003, SI 2003/2426 and *Implementation of the Directive on Privacy and Electronic Communications*, DTI, March 2003, URN 03/762, at http://www.dti.gov.uk/industries/ecommunications/directive_on_privacy_electronic_communications_200258ec.html.

program (eg Internet Explorer, Netscape, Safari or Mozilla) to reject cookies.[97] This seems entirely inadequate to provide most consumers with a 'user friendly' way to vindicate their legal right to refuse. The position is muddied further in the UK regulations where the consumer is using a computer while at work; here it seems the person with the right to refuse cookies may well be the employer, as well as the employee/consumer—and whose wishes should prevail in the case of conflict is not entirely clear.[98] On the question of what is 'strictly necessary' in response to a request by the consumer, the Regulations again say nothing, although the guidance notes do specify that '*such storage of or access to information should be essential as opposed to reasonably necessary*' and most importantly, cookies must be set ' . . . for the provision of the service requested by the user, *rather than what might be essential for any other uses the service provider might wish to make of that data*' [italic added].[99] This looks a lot like like the cry of "essential!" cannot be co-opted for cookies which are there merely to enable third party advertising (or even advertising directly provided by the website owner?), as that is *not* usually the service the user was requesting.

G. What Next?

1. Locational and Traffic Data

Spam and cookies are no longer the only privacy invading technologies (PITs) in the e-commerce market. The most novel parts of the PECD relate to control of locational and traffic data, where their use by service providers might have negative impacts on consumer privacy. Locational data broadly refers to information that reveals the whereabouts of the user of a mobile phone or similar telecommunications device whose location can be traced and shared. It can also includes information as to *when* a particular user was using a mobile phone at a particular location. Traffic data is data processed by the provider of an electronic communications network (such as a telecommunications or cable company or ISP) which relates to routing, duration or time of a communication.[100] While traffic data has long been collected by telcos and ISPs for the purposes of billing, capacity management, and other internal procedures, locational data is a relatively new concept. It is hoped

---

[97] *Guidance to the Privacy and Electronic Communications (EC Directive) Regulations 2003*, Pt 2: Secuirity, Confidentiality, Traffic and Location Data, Itemised Billing, CLI and Directories, para 2.4.

[98] *Guidance*, para 2.6.

[99] *Guidance*, para 2.5.

[100] Full definitions of both terms for UK purposes can be found at Reg 2 of the UK PECD Regulations. Interestingly the UK definition of 'locational data' is wider than that stipulated by the PECD itself.

that exploitation of locational data to provide 'value added' services to mobile consumers will usher in a new profitable wave of mobile e-commerce ('m-commerce'). Locational data can be shared with or sold by the company originally collecting the data, to third parties who wish to provide services to users such as, eg, taxis, or fast food, or flowers. Typically, the third party service providers would use the locational data to provide the user with either information or the actual goods or services from the physically nearest relevant outlet. Locational data might also conceivably be used to serve relevant ads to mobile consumers direct to their phone, or even hypothetically to direct tailored ads at computer-equipped billboards the consumer is passing by—the 'intelligent billboard' concept.

In principle both traffic data and locational data have their quite proper, and potentially profitable, reasons to be collected. But they can also be privacy-threatening technologies. It hardly needs to be elaborated how useful it might be to a government, or an individual stalker, or a criminal, or a commercial competitor, to know exactly where a mobile phone user is; or who exactly a telephone subscriber has rung in the last month; or what websites they visited via their ISP and what individual pages they visited and what search terms they entered into a search engine. All this information can fall under locational and traffic data. When such data is stored and archived for long periods, rather than as is currently industry practice, deleted relatively fast when its billing or commercial purposes are done with, the potential privacy violation implications become even more severe. Yet in the post 9/11 world, enormous pressure is being put on telcos and ISPs, both by law and by extralegal means, to store and retain exactly such data for periods well beyond existing commercial good practice, in the interests of future hypothetical criminal or national security investigations. The balance between security and privacy is finely drawn in this area, and thus the regulation of traffic and locational data in particular is increasingly controversial. The data retention regime of the UK *for security and law enforcement purposes* is currently prescribed principally in the Regulation of Investigatory Powers Act 2000 and its subsidiary regulations, and is beyond the scope of this chapter; but it is worth noting that if the PECD restrictions on use of traffic and locational data noted below come into conflict with national security and law enforcement powers, then it is clearly the latter which win.[101]

The PECD and the UK implementing Regulations do explicitly attempt for the first time to place limits beyond those of general DP law on how traffic and locational data can be processed. Article 9 of the PECD provides that locational data can only be processed, which includes use, sale and sharing, with the consent of the user or subscriber, and only where it is necessary to provide 'value added' services. The key exception to this is if the data is anonymised. Furthermore, the service provider collecting and processing the locational data must inform the user or

---

[101] UK PECD Regulations, Regs 28 and 29.

subscriber *prior* to obtaining consent of what the locational data may be used for—eg, what third party it might be given to to provide 'value added' services, and for how long. Users must also have the option to 'opt out' of releasing locational data at any particular point, even if they have given this prior consent. The consent required thus resembles the positive opt-in required for spam more than the consent required to receive cookies, and thus reflects serious concerns about how locational data might be used.

Traffic data processing is also restricted. Traffic data, according to Regulation 8 of the UK PECD Regulations, can only be collected for limited purposes defined as:

- Management of traffic or billing;
- customer enquiries;
- prevention of detection of fraud;
- the marketing of electronic communications services;[102] or
- the provision of a value added service.

As discussed, a 'value added service' is an extra service provided to a user/subscriber by use of locational or traffic data—possibly by a third party other than the telco or ISP. It is technically defined as any service which requires the processing of traffic data or locational data beyond that which is necessary for the transmission of a communication or the billing in respect of that communication.[103]

Even when traffic data falls within one of these permissible categories, further restrictions apply.[104] If it is to be processed for the purpose of marketing electronic communications services, or to provide value-added services, the user or subscriber to whom the data relates must give their consent. This consent may be withdrawn at any time. Even then, the data must be processed and stored only for the duration necessary for the relevant purpose. Aside from these particular exceptions, the general principle is re-stated from general DP law that when traffic data has fulfilled its function—it aided the transmission of a communication—it should be either deleted or anonymised.[105]

2. The Future?

The outstanding question remaining is, is the PECD really 'technology neutral'? Does it update the DPD with sufficient generality to protect consumer privacy against all foreseeable threats arising from new technologies? Sadly, the answer already seems to be no. One type of technology currently under much scrutiny

---

[102] As defined by s 32 of the Communications Act 2003.
[103] UK Regulations, Reg 2(1).
[104] *Ibid*, Reg 7(2)(3)(4).
[105] *Ibid*, Reg 7(1).

from privacy activists worldwide is the RFID chip. RFID chips are tiny microchips attached to an antenna that receives and transmits location information by means of radio waves. RFID chips are small, very cheap (costing around 6p each), come in many varieties, and are currently used for a multiplicity of commercial purposes.[106] Most commonly, they are used for product tracking and inventory control, access control to sealed areas ('smart doors'), contact-less smart cards (eg the Oyster card used by London Transport commuters) and animal tagging. More novel applications include using it as a hands-free payment mechanism[107] and people-tagging.[108] Most consumer concern around RFID has centred on their use in high street stores, basically as a more advanced form of bar-code. If RFID tags, which are very small, are attached to, say, shirts, and not removed or de-activated at point of sale, whether deliberately or by accident, then the fear of privacy advocates and consumer groups is that they will operate as a sort of micro-bug, revealing the whereabouts of the buyer to unknown parties for an indefinite time after sale. In fact, RFID chips themselves usually carry no information except the inventory code and description for the particular item to which they were attached, and thus in themselves, do not identify the buyer, nor disclose personal data describing the buyer. However the identity of the buyer *could* conceivably be discovered if the RFID data was associated at point of sale with the personal identifying details of the buyer derived who bought the item using a means such as credit card, smart card or store card. Although this kind of scenario has caused a great deal of angst both in the US[109] and Europe,[110] the privacy concerns are actually rather limited. RFID chips are usually passive: that is, they do not broadcast their location as such, but need to be *detected* by readers at very short range, usually no more than six or seven metres away (many need even closer range).[111]

---

[106] See useful overview of RFID chip technology available at http://www.philips.com; also A Brown, 'RFID: An Unlawful or Just Unwanted Invasion of Privacy?' [2003–04] (December/January) *Computers & Law* 27.

[107] See S Morton, 'Barcelona Clubbers Get Chipped', 29 September 2004, at http://news.bbc.co.uk/1/hi/technology/3,697,940.stm.

[108] See description of tagging of school children in Tokyo to reassure parents, reported widely October 2004, eg http://www.cbsnews.com/stories/2004/10/11/tech/main648681.shtml. Anecdotal reports also exist of the RFID tagging of often absent academics in one US university so that they could be speedily located.

[109] See the site of CASPIAN, Consumers Against Supermarket Privacy Invasion and Numbering at http://www.nocards.org/, which asks, 'Is Big Brother in *your* grocery cart?'

[110] See 'Consumer Concern Over RFID Cards', at http://news.bbc.co.uk/1/hi/technology/4247275.stm, 9 February 2005, which claims that 50% of UK consumers polled were very concerned about the use of RFID in shops.

[111] RFID should not be confused, as it often is, with GPS, the Global Positioning System, which uses satellite technology to track locations or persons or objects from very great distances. RFID chip, by comparison to GPS systems, are extremely cheap and small and thus far more suitable to the inventory and stock control of many millions of manufactured items—however this cheapness comes at a price, in that the passive RFID chip can only be read at a very close distance by a specialised reader. Non-passive RFID chips, which have their own power supply and can broadcast over a wider range, do exist, but are currently too large and expensive to be used in most commercial applications.

RFID readers cost £250–£3000 each and therefore it is impractically expensive for RFID tags to be used as 'bugs' except within a relatively small and circumscribed area like a school, supermarket, library or campus.

The question of how far RFID chips are truly a significant threat to consumer privacy is not however the point here. What is germane is that it is not at all certain if RFID technology is controlled by data protection law, even as updated by the PECD, and if it is, *how* it is so controlled.[112] As noted, RFID chips themselves do not contain 'personal data', ie information identifying a living person. An RFID chip attached to a Gillette razor blade typically reveals nothing other than 'I am pack 23340000 [say] of this type of razor blades', sometimes with additional shelving, inventory, expiry date or supply chain history information. As such, *prima facie* RFID chips do not fall within the UK DP regime as it applies only to data which '*relates to a living individual who can be identified*' (DPA 1998, section 1). However as noted above in relation to spamming, conceivably RFID processing does fall within the data processing regime if the RFID chip data *taken with* credit card details (say), do, in the point-of-sale scenario described above, combine to identify a living individual. (The second part of the definition of 'personal data' in section 1 of the 1998 Act, it should be recalled, includes the case where a living individual can be identified from the data in question and any other information which is '*likely to come into the possession* of the data controller'.) If this were to be the case, the DPA 1998 duties of fairness in data processing, as laid down in the Eight Data Protection Principles,[113] might apply to some but not all data processors operating RFID chip systems in shops. So, for example, if Tesco's, the supermarket chain, attach RFID chips to the packets of razor blades they sell in order to monitor and prevent shoplifting, and legitimate buyers of razor blades pay by electronic means, then conceivably Tesco's will be able to tie the individual buyer to that packet of razor blades as it leaves the shop, and thus will be processing personal data during and after the purchase.[114] In that case, they might fall under duties including the need to give adequate notice of processing to consumers so as to obtain implied consent; they would have to notify the purposes for which they were collecting the data; and the security implications might have to be considered.[115] But if payment is made with cash, and Tesco's remove the tags at

---

[112] There is a small but growing legal literature on RFID. See Brown above n 106; E Ustaran, 'Data Protection and RFID Systems' (2003) *Privacy & Data Protection* 3.6(6); the Ontario Privacy Commissioner has published legal guidelines on using RFID tags in libraries at http://www.ipc.on.ca/docs/rfid-lib.pdf. In Europe, the EU Art 29 Working Party has published as Working Document on RFID, 10107/05/EN WP 105, 19 January 2005, at http://europa.eu.int/comm/internal_market/privacy/docs/wpdocs/2005/wp105_en.pdf.

[113] Data Protection Act 1998, Sch 1, Part II.

[114] See BBC website, 'Big Brother at the supermarket till?', 27 January 2005 at http://news.bbc.co.uk/1/hi/business/4211591.stm.

[115] Fuller consideration of how the DP Principles might apply to processors using RFID chips can be found in Art 29 Working Party Document on RFID, above n 112.

point-of-sale (as Marks and Spencers did, in their RFID test trials with clothing, to the approval of privacy activists) do any DP implications arise? Perhaps not. The area is grey in the extreme.

A further complicating factor is whether RFID tags fall under the new 'locational data' regime in the PECD described above. Locational data is technically defined solely as ' any data processed in an electronic communications network *indicating the geographic location of the terminal equipment of the user* of a public electronic communications service'. As Brown notes, it is hard to say that an RFID tag—or even the goods to which it is attached or embedded—are 'terminal equipment of the user'.[116] Undefined in the UK PECD Regulations, the obvious natural language interpretation would be that it refers to a mobile phone handset, a hand-held PC, a laptop, or the like. The PECD also fails to define 'terminal equipment' and interestingly, recital 35 of the PECD seems to imply that all locational data is also traffic data, ie data used to facilitate electronic communications—which makes it look even less like the kind of data stored in RFID chips or collected using them. RFID chips fundamentally track *objects* (including people); traffic data tracks electronic communications or *messages*. Yet if RFID chips are to fall within the DP regime, it would seem only sensible that they also fall within the locational data regime. What RFID does, then, is show that the supposedly 'technology neutral' regulation of the EC's latest Privacy Directive falls down badly as soon as applied to even the first major commercial privacy-invasive technology to be developed since cookies.

To add insult to injury, the scenario explored so far, of RFID in supermarkets, is one where it is relatively easy to minimise privacy violations by simple means such as removal of the tags before the purchaser leaves the store. What of the more novel applications of RFID mentioned above, such as tagging of children, and of hospital patients, and even the already common use of contact-less RFID-chipped smart cards in business HQs and on public transport?[117] In these scenarios, the RFID chip persists and stays active and associated with the card-holder, and the privacy risks seem much higher.

In conclusion then, the terrain we have surveyed above, of the legal regulation of privacy-invasive technologies such as spam, cookies, traffic data and RFID, is not an inspiring one for lawyers and legislators. Law faces many problems in this area; the problems of jurisdiction, of enforcement, of trans-nationality, of making the public aware of and comprehending of their rights; of financing and training

---

[116] Ustaran (above n 112) however seems to take the view that RFID tags do constitute 'locational data'. Interestingly though, the Art 29 Working party document, also above n 112, does not take a view on whether RFID tags collect or constitute locational data, though the document does assert that in many concrete cases, data processed via RFID tags *will* constitute 'personal data'.

[117] Out-Law.com reports at 14 October 2004 that the US Food and Drugs association has approved the implant sub-dermally of RFID chips into patients so that they can be used to access what drugs the particular patient needs, with less chance of human error. They could also recognise and record data about allergies.

of enforcement authorities, and of interpretation when new technologies or new tweaks on old technologies come along. Overwhelmingly, the conclusion cannot be resisted that law will always be running behind technology in this area and that solutions may perhaps best be found not in new legislation, but in international and business investment in technical standards and development. Spam has not been arrested in the slightest by international legal developments but may be decimated in a few years if changes are made to the basic Internet and email technical standards. Cookies were argued over sempeternally in the European Parliament, but now as of early 2005 are almost a forgotten problem for technologists, and third party advert serving is almost a thing of the past. RFID is the new privacy problem on the block and already has muddied the new legislation which might have been hoped to control it in advance. Real control of privacy invasion by RFID is more likely to come from good practice in the commercial sector or a supervening technology which (say) blocks or de-activates RFID chips, than DP law reform. As Lessig might have said, it is easier to fight code with code, than code with law. Indeed, code usually trumps law. It will be interesting to see if in five years time the legal framework for the protection of consumer and citizen privacy in Europe from technological threat has begun to recognize this hard truth. We need more, cheaper and easier to use privacy-enhancing technologies and less new law: discuss.

3

Articles 9–11, ECD

Contracting Electronically in the Shadow of the E-Commerce Directive

ANDREW D MURRAY*

The development of on-line retailing (or e-tailing) is an essential element of the commercial development of Cyberspace and has provided the foundation of a flourishing online business community.[1] The ability to enter into and perform contracts online is at the heart of this development. Without the certainty offered by a legal obligation to supply goods or services consumers may feel exposed. This can lead to faltering consumer confidence in electronic commerce with potentially harmful economic consequences. Such potential risks affect both consumers and the burgeoning e-tailing community and were sufficiently tangible to convince the United Nations to seek to provide a Model Law to provide certainty and protection for all parties involved in electronic data transactions. This programme, which began with a proposal for a model law on EDI transactions in 1984, led ultimately to the UNCITRAL Model Law on Electronic Commerce.[2] The Model

---

* Lecturer in Information Technology and Internet Law, Law Department, London School of Economics and Political Science.

[1] Evidence that e-tailing is growing strongly despite the global downturn can be found in recent data from the Pew Internet and American Life Project, which found that in 2004 $2/3$ of the US's adult Internet users are also online shoppers, corresponding to about 134 million purchasers, spending between $100 billion to $130 billion per annum. This is a considerable rise in dollar purchases from 2002 when Forrester Research put a figure of $78 billion on US consumer e-commerce for that year, see '2002 US eCommerce: The Year In Review' (http://www.forrester.com/ER/Research/Brief/Excerpt/0,1317,16086,FFhtml). There is evidence of similar trends elsewhere with the Interactive Media in Retail Group (IMRG) estimating that eCommerce revenues in the UK during 2004 totalled £17 billion. They reported that 'Internet shopping will become mass market in 2004, as millions of consumers routinely go online to research and buy every kind of product and service. Twenty million British shoppers will spend £17 billion online this year.' See: http://www.imrg.org/IMRG/press.nsf/(httpPressReleases)/BDCB1B7A0A17B30880256E5F0035C533.

[2] The UNCITRAL Model Law on Electronic Commerce (1996) with additional Art 5 bis as adopted in 1998 is available at: http://www.jus.uio.no/lm/un.electronic.commerce.model.law.1996/doc.html.

Law, through Article 5, provides formally for the legal recognition of electronic contracts. It requires States to ensure that: 'Information shall not be denied legal effect, validity or enforceability solely on the grounds that it is in the form of a data message.'[3] Building upon this principle, the Model Law then goes on to ensure that all supporting principles required to provide for recognition of electronic contracts are in place. Firstly, it endows equivalence for electronic documentation by requiring that, 'where the law requires information to be in writing, that requirement is met by a data message if the information contained therein is accessible so as to be usable for subsequent reference.'[4] Secondly, through Article 7, it requires that States give legal recognition to electronic signatures[5] and finally and perhaps most importantly, Article 11 formally provides for the legal recognition of electronic contracts.[6]

The Model Law has been adopted, and adapted, by leading digital economies such as the United States and the European Union. Both these major trading blocs have taken steps to legally recognize and enforce electronic contracts by providing for recognition of the principles contained therein, although not always by enacting all the provisions it contains. The United States has led the way through enactment of the Uniform Electronic Transactions Act (UETA)[7] and the Electronic Signatures in Global and National Commerce Act (E-Sign).[8] The primary implementation of the Model Law is by § 7 of UETA which provides for 'Legal Recognition of Electronic Records, Electronic Signatures and Electronic Contracts.' In a series of apparently innocuous provisions all the necessary principles for electronic contracting, as contained in the Model Law, are set out. Article

---

[3] The definition of 'data message' is given in Art 2 and is defined as 'information generated, sent, received or stored by electronic, optical or similar means including, but not limited to, electronic data interchange (EDI), electronic mail, telegram, telex or telecopy.'

[4] Art 6.

[5] Art 7 states:

Where the law requires a signature of a person, that requirement is met in relation to a data message if: (a) a method is used to identify that person and to indicate that person's approval of the information contained in the data message; and (b) that method is as reliable as was appropriate for the purpose for which the data message was generated or communicated, in the light of all the circumstances, including any relevant agreement.

[6] Art 11 states: 'In the context of contract formation, unless otherwise agreed by the parties, an offer and the acceptance of an offer may be expressed by means of data messages. Where a data message is used in the formation of a contract, that contract shall not be denied validity or enforceability on the sole ground that a data message was used for that purpose.'

[7] The model Uniform Electronic Transactions Act was approved and recommended for enactment in all States by the National Conference of Commissioners on Uniform State Laws (NCCUSL) at their 1999 Annual Conference in Denver, Colorado. It has since been adopted by 46 States and the District of Columbia. Only Georgia, Illinois, New York and Washington have failed to implement UETA In addition it has been federally recognized in § 102(a) of the Electronic Signatures in Global and National Commerce Act (2000) (see below) which specifies that State Law may modify, limit or supersede the electronic contracting provisions of E-Sign under limited conditions.

[8] 15 USC § 7001 (2000).

5 is enacted by § 7(a) which provides that, 'A record or signature may not be denied legal effect or enforceability solely because it in electronic form.' With the principle of equivalence for electronic documents established, the Act then quickly enacts the principles of Articles 6, 7 and 11 in the remainder of § 7.[9]

UETA does not have the force of law. It is merely a Uniform Act designed, like the Model Law, to act as a template for local lawmaker. To become effective the Uniform Act requires to be adopted by State Legislatures. UETA has, though, been extremely well received and by the end of 2004 the UETA model had been adopted in 46 States and the District of Columbia. Therefore despite its status as a Uniform Act it is reasonable to refer to UETA as the current law in regard of electronic contracting in the United States. The key provisions of UETA have further received Federal recognition through E-Sign which has federally enacted many of the key provisions of UETA, including the principles of equivalence for electronic documents and enforceability of electronic contracts, thus negating the need for state by state implementation.[10] E-sign is intended to clarify the legal status of electronic records and electronic signatures in the context of writing and signing requirements imposed by law. According to the Act, an electronic record is broadly defined as 'a contract or record created, generated, sent, communicated, received, or stored by electronic means'[11] and an electronic signature means 'an electronic sound, symbol, or process attached to or logically associated with a contract or record and executed or adopted by a person with the intent to sign the record'.[12] Between these two provisions therefore the State and Federal Governments of the United States have implemented the key provisions of the Model Law. Equivalence is given to electronic documents, electronic contracts are formally recognized and the mechanics of electronic signatures are provided for.

The European Union has set out to give recognition to the Model Law in two key Directives, one of which is only partially relevant to the discussion which follows, the other is at its heart. The first of these is the Directive on Electronic Signatures,[13] which although important to the formation of electronic contracts, is of restricted value. This is because it only comes to the fore when formality or

---

[9] § 7(b) enacts Art 11 by providing that 'a contract may not be denied legal effect or enforceability solely because an electronic record was used in its formation'; § 7(c) enacts Art 6 by requiring that 'if the law requires a record to be in writing, an electronic record satisfies the law', and Art 7 is enacted by § 7(d) which provides that, 'if the law requires a signature, an electronic signature satisfies the law.'

[10] E-sign § 101 provides that: '(1) a signature, contract or other record relating to such transaction may not be denied legal effect, validity or enforceability solely because it is in electronic form; and (2) a contract relating to such transaction may not be denied legal effect, validity or enforceability solely because an electronic signature or electronic record was used in its formation.'

[11] § 106(4).

[12] § 106(5).

[13] Directive 1999/93/EC of the European Parliament and of the Council of 13 December 1999 on a Community framework for electronic signatures.

proof is required. The second Directive is the E-Commerce Directive (ECD)[14] which lies at the heart of the discussion that follows.

A. Background—Why did We Need Articles 9–11 of the E-Commerce Directive?

This chapter focuses on electronic contracting. The provisions of the ECD relevant to this discussion may be found in Chapter II, Section 3: 'Contracts Concluded by Electronic Means'. This Section contains three Articles intended not only to fulfil the key principle of equivalence already seen in the UNCITRAL Model Law and in UETA and E-Sign within the United States, but to go further and determine some basic rules for the formation of electronic contracts. The key provision is Article 9, which, subject to some exclusions found in Article 9(2) (which shall be examined below) provides for equivalence for electronic documentation.[15] This mirrors both Article 6 of the Model Law and §§ 7(a) and (c) of UETA. The following provisions, Articles 10 and 11, are though quite unlike the provisions of the Model Law or UETA. Here the Directive attempts to harmonize some of the basic rules of contract formation as applied to electronic contracts. In Article 10 the Directive lays down minimum informational standards required for electronic B2C contracts. It should be said it quickly becomes clear that Article 10 is not a formation of contract provision at all, but rather a consumer protection provision embedded into the contract formation rules.[16] Finally, Article 11 attempts e-commerce alchemy. It is a brave attempt to define the moment at which an electronic contract is concluded. As we shall see, Article 11 went through many drafts before the text was settled. The final version is rather anodyne and may fairly be challenged as a missed opportunity. This line of argument, though, anticipates the discussion which follows. The logically prior question is what role do Articles 9–11 play in European Contract Law.

Given that most B2C and a significant amount of B2B contracts are of an informal nature is there need of the provisions of Articles 9–11 within the on-line community? Certainly e-businesses such as Amazon.com, Lastminute.com and Ticketmaster.co.uk flourished in the consumer environment in the period

---

[14] Directive 2000/31/EC of the European Parliament and of the Council of 8 June 2000 on certain legal aspects of information society services, in particular electronic commerce, in the Internal Market.

[15] Art 9(1) provides, 'Member States shall ensure that their legal system allows contracts to be concluded by electronic means. Member States shall in particular ensure that the legal requirements applicable to the contractual process neither create obstacles for the use of electronic contracts nor result in such contracts being deprived of legal effectiveness and validity on account of their having been made by electronic means.'

[16] Further, more detailed, discussion of Art 10 follows.

1996–2000 without the provisions of the Directive in place. Similar B2B success was achieved by Hewlett-Packard, Microsoft and Norton.[17] The reason for the Directive is that, as is so often the case within Europe, a lack of certainty and a lack of cross-border harmony was perceived to be hindering free movement of goods and services. The heart of this uncertainty, with regard to e-contracting, was not in the creation of informal contracts but in those contracts where a degree of permanence or durability was required by legislation. For example, the Consumer Credit Act 1974 required that consumer credit transactions be produced in compliance with published regulations[18] and that they be legible and are signed.[19] A Consumer Credit Agreement is consequently both a document of form and a formal document and could not therefore readily be concluded by electronic documentation. Similarly, a contract for the sale of heritable property must undergo several formal stages. The first stage is to agree a binding contract of sale between the seller and the buyer: the missives. In Scotland missives must comply with the Requirements of Writing (Scotland) Act 1995. Under the Act, the preparation of a formal contract for the 'transfer, variation or extinction of an interest in land' must be carried out in accordance with Ss 1(2) and 2.[20] Section 1(2) requires simply that the document in question must be 'written', while section 2(1) provides that, 'No document required by section 1(2) of this Act shall be valid in respect of the formalities of execution unless it is subscribed by the granter of it or, if there is more than one granter, by each granter.' Subscription is defined in section 7 and places an emphasis on physical recording of the signature on the document.[21] The

---

[17]   For example Lastminute.com increased its six month turnover from £300,000 (to 31 March 1999) to £11,417,000 (to 31 March 2000) with profitability in the same period increased from £25,000 to £1,112,000. In the same period it saw its subscriber base increase from 571,867 to 1,385,402 and its customer base increase from 28,687 to 65,387 (source: Lastminute.com interim results 4 May 2000). Meanwhile in January 2000, Microsoft invested $100M in VerticalNet Inc, an owner and operator of 55 industry-specific Web sites that function as online B2B vertical trade communities (source: P Greenberg, 'Microsoft To Invest $100M in B2B Venture', *E-Commerce Times*, 21 January 2000).

[18]   S 60(1) provides that, 'The Secretary of State shall make regulations as to the form and content of documents embodying regulated agreements.' Currently these regulations are to be found in the Consumer Credit (Agreement) Regulations 1983, SI 1983/1553.

[19]   S61(1) provides 'a regulated agreement is not properly executed unless a document in the prescribed form itself containing all the prescribed terms and conforming to regulations under section 60(1) is *signed in the prescribed manner* . . . by the debtor or hirer'. S 61(1)(c) provides that 'the document, when presented or sent to the debtor . . . [is] in such a state that all its terms are readily legible.'

[20]   S 1(2)(a)(i).

[21]   S 7:

> A document is subscribed by a granter of it if it is signed by him at the end of the last page. A document, or an alteration to a document, is signed by an individual natural person as a granter or on behalf of a granter of it if it is signed by him (a) with the full name by which he is identified in the document or in any testing clause or its equivalent; or (b) with his surname, preceded by at least one forename (or an initial or abbreviation or familiar form of a forename); or (c) with a name (not in accordance with paragraph (a) or (b) above) or description or an initial or mark if it is established that the name, description, initial or mark and (i) was his usual method of signing, or his usual method of signing documents or alterations of the type in question; or (ii) was intended by him as his signature of the document or alteration.

effect of these provisions is that every missive letter must be signed by the parties, or on their behalf by their agent. If the missives are physically signed (even if they are communicated to the other party by an electronic means such as facsimile transmission) the missives are formally valid:[22] without a signature they are not. Accordingly, a contract for the sale and purchase of land concluded by exchange of purely electronic transmissions was not possible in Scotland. As with Consumer Credit transactions, the requirements of formal validity prevented the effective use of electronic means for contracting.

These are two simple examples of everyday transactions where there was a lacuna in the prior law. Contracts of form ran into difficulties with the interpretation of generic terms such as 'in writing', 'readily legible' and 'in a durable medium'. Across Europe a divergent approach to this problem emerged. Some states such as Germany immediately moved to implement enabling legislation,[23] while others such as the UK took a more cautious approach. Within the UK a review undertaken by the DTI admitted that: 'the position on the requirement for information to be "written" or "in writing" . . . cannot at present be met using electronic means.'[24] The DTI recognized that 'these uncertainties and limitations . . . are important barriers to the development of electronic commerce',[25] and opened consultation on the best approach to removing these barriers.[26] Thus by the close of the last century, a clear divergence in Member States' approaches to e-commerce and e-contracting, was developing. Some countries such as Germany had already forged ahead with new, permissive, legislation. Others, such as the UK, were lagging behind mired in the process of consultation.[27]

---

[22] *McInto v Allan* [1998] SLT (Ct) 19. See also: R Rennie, 'Conclusion of Missives in the Modern Age' (2000) 5 *Scottish L & Practice Q* 346.

[23] See Federal Act Establishing the General Conditions for Information and Communication Services (Information and Communication Services Act) 1 August 1997. Available at: http://www.iid.de/rahmen/iukdgebt.html. See also: The Digital Signatures Ordinance 1997. (The original Digital signatures Ordinance of 1997 has now been superseded by the 2001 Ordinance passed to comply with the Directive on Electronic Signatures. The 2001 Ordinance is available at: http://www.iid.de/iukdg/gesetz/SigV161101-engl.pdf. Although the 1997 Ordinance may no longer be accessed it is referred to s 19 of the 2001 Ordinance).

[24] Building Confidence in E-Commerce: A Consultation Document, DTI, 5 March 1999, URN 99/642 at para 16.

[25] *Ibid*, para 17.

[26] In para 18 the DTI set out two broad approaches and asked for views to be expressed by members of the public. The approaches considered were (1) to allow for individual Acts and Statutory Instruments on a case-by-case basis or (2) allow, through enabling legislation, a power for Government Ministers to adopt changes through Statutory Instruments where necessary. This is the approach taken and may be found s 8 of the Electronic Communications Act. Note: the DTI did not seek responses on a third alternative already seen in the UNCITRAL Model Law and the German Information and Communication Services Act, that of blanket equivalence.

[27] The lack of progress by the UK government was noted mournfully by the Select Committee on Trade and Industry in their Seventh Annual Report of 1999, where they called for 'swift legislative action in this area' (*Building Confidence in Electronic Commerce: The Government's Proposals*, Seventh Annual Report of the Trade & Industry Committee, 12 May 1999, at para 58). They suggested the new Electronic Communications Bill (now Act) with its emphasis on the use of secondary legislation to

The need for some form of harmonisation was thus clear. A secondary benefit of legislation harmonising the European approach to electronic contracts, is that such a Directive would also allow the legislative draftsman to tackle the vexing issue of the point of creation of such contracts. To phrase it slightly differently, in tackling to issue of harmonisation of form, the Commission could also harmonize the rules of contract formation with regard to electronic contracts.[28] There is no doubt the opportunity to harmonize those actions which lead to conclusion of a contract is a powerful one. A major barrier to consumer confidence in e-commerce is simply consumers often don't know when they have entered into a legally binding contract with the supplier. A lack of harmony (and resultant lack of clarity) as to which acts lead to the creation of a legally binding contract has proven to be a barrier to development, both historically in traditional B2C commerce and in modern B2C e-commerce.[29] Thus in English Law (as in Scots Law) we can trace the development and deployment of a variety of tools to assist in the identification of the 'trigger' which creates an enforceable contractual relationship. These include the identification of contractual 'key stages' such as the concept of the 'invitation to treat', 'offer' and 'acceptance', and the use of rules of construction such as the delivery rule and the postal rule. In essence these tools are designed to provide us with the best possible identification of the moment '*consensus ad idem*' is (or was) achieved.[30]

The development and application of such tools were not though universal. Rules on offers and invitations to treat varied from Member State to Member State. For example, in Spain and Belgium the offering of goods or services by a retailer on a website constituted an offer to a buyer: the contract being deemed to be concluded when the buyer accepted the offer. This differed from leading economies such as Germany, France and the UK who all employed an invitation

---

create the new framework for e-documents and e-contracting would not make up for this shortcoming. It should be noted their views were not taken up by Government.

[28] For a discussion of the vexed issue of when an electronic contract is formed see: A Murray, 'Entering Into Contracts Electronically: The Real WWW' in L Edwards and C Waelde (eds), *Law and the Internet: A Framework for Electronic Commerce*, (Hart Publishing, 2000).

[29] This problem was noted by the DTI in ch 5 of the *DTI Consultation Document on Implementation of the E-Commerce Directive*, 10 August 2001 (available at: http://www2.dti.gov.uk/industry_files/pdf/ECD_consolidated_version.pdf) where it was noted:

> the act of clicking on an 'OK' icon may have different legal implications in different Member States. It might constitute either acceptance of an offer to provide a service or a customer's offer to contract. This, in turn, could give rise to uncertainty as to the time at which the contract was concluded. It might be the time of receipt or of sending the acceptance. In cross-border contractual relations, particularly for consumers, there is a risk to the development of the trust that is necessary for e-commerce (p 15).

[30] See E McKendrick, *Contract Law*, 5th edn, (Palgrave, 2003) ch 3 for a general discussion of these rules. See also R Zimmermann, *The Law of Obligations: Roman Foundations of the Civilian Traditions*, (OUP, 1996) 559–76 for a discussion of the roots of the Consensus Rule.

to treat principle when dealing with such advertisements.[31] Similarly rules on acceptances varied between Member States with Belgium only recognising an acceptance once the offeror has had the opportunity to review it, while under the Spanish Commercial Code a contract would be concluded when the buyer sent their acceptance to the vendor (offeror) whether or not such acceptance was received by the vendor.[32] This lack of harmony could, as with the rules on form, have been swept away by the ECD. Unfortunately in the drafting process this opportunity was lost: why?

B. Planning E-Contracts in Europe: Drafting the ECD

During the drafting process the Directive went through three clearly distinct incarnations, and in each the approach to electronic contracting was substantially different. The earliest incarnation was that of 18 November 1998.[33] This proposal, like the final text of the Directive, dealt with electronic contracting in Section III (Articles 9–11).

Article 9(1) was designed to deal with the problem of form. It provided that Member States should ensure that 'their legislation allows contracts to be concluded electronically.' In particular Member States were to ensure that 'the legal requirements applicable to the contractual process neither prevent the effective use of electronic contracts nor result in such contracts being deprived of electronic effect and validity on account of their having been made electronically.' Thus from its first draft Article 9(1) has provided that electronic documents should be deemed functionally equivalent to their paper counterparts fulfilling the equivalence principle found in Article 5 of the UNCITRAL Model Law. Further, when taken alongside the measures contained in the Directive on Electronic Signatures,[34] in particular Article 5,[35] the provisions of Article 9(1) would allow for electronic documentation to be used in the creation of both informal and formal contracts. Aware of the sensitivity attached to some formal documents such as documents relating to the transfer of an interest in land and testamentary and

---

[31] Source: Baker & McKenzie, *Doing E-commerce in Europe*, 2001. Available from: http://www.bmck.com/Doing%20E-Commerce%20in%20Europe/Doing%20E-Commerce%20In%20Europe.pdf.

[32] *Ibid.* In this case the UK, France and Germany would usually follow the Belgian approach rather than the Spanish approach, but see the effect of the Postal Rule in UK Contract Law as discussed in Murray, above n 28.

[33] A Proposal for a European Parliament and Council Directive on Certain Legal Aspects of Electronic Commerce in the Internal Market Com 1998 (586).

[34] Above n 13.

[35] Art 5 provides for the recognition of Digital Signatures and therefore fulfils the recognition requirement found in Art 7 of the UNCITRAL Model Law.

family documents, the Commission suggested national governments be allowed to exclude certain contracts from the equivalence principle. Documents which could be excluded were listed in Article 9(2):

(a) contracts requiring the involvement of a notary;
(b) contracts which in order to be valid require to be registered with a public authority;
(c) contracts governed by Family Law;
(d) contracts governed by the Law of Succession.

Any exceptions sought outwith this list would require to be individually agreed to by the Commission in a procedure set out Article 23.

With Article 9 giving equivalence to e-documents, Articles 10 and 11 could deal with the narrower issue of harmonisation of rules of contract formation. Article 10 was a general provision designed to provide consumer protection and to boost consumer confidence. As said above, Article 10 is not, and never was, a formation of contract provision, being instead in form a consumer protection provision.[36] As such it saw little amendment through the drafting process and so will be dealt with in full below when the final wording of the Directive is examined. Article 11, though, was the focus of intense scrutiny, debate and amendment throughout the drafting process and an examination of its various incarnations provides additional background to any analysis of the Directive. There is no doubt that the first draft of Article 11 was an ambitious piece of drafting. Grandly entitled 'Moment at which the Contract is Concluded', it was the aim of the Article to define, and thereby harmonize, the trigger event for B2C e-contracts throughout all Member States. If achieved, this would provide the degree of certainty required to boost consumer confidence, but at a cost to Member States, for the new regime would require some Member States to give up their current rules of contract formation.[37]

The draft Article 11 required Member States to:

(1) lay down in their legislation that, save where otherwise agreed by professional persons, in cases where a recipient, in accepting a service provider's offer, is required to give his consent through technological means, such as clicking on an icon, the following principles apply:

(a) The contract is concluded when the recipient of the service (i) has received from the service provider, electronically, an acknowledgement of receipt of the recipient's acceptance, and (ii) has confirmed receipt of the acknowledgement of receipt.
(b) Acknowledgement of receipt is deemed to be received and confirmation is deemed to have been given when the parties to whom they are addressed are able to access them

---

[36] Above, p 4.
[37] See above nn 31 and 32 and associated text.

(c) The acknowledgement of receipt by the service provider and confirmation of the service recipient shall be sent as quickly as possible.

If enacted this draft would have introduced a harmonized four stage contractual
structure. In effect a contract to buy a book from Amazon.co.uk would look like
this:

1 View details on web page	Offer (from Amazon)
2 Send 'order' to Amazon	Acceptance
3 Receive Confirmation from Amazon	Acknowledgement of receipt of the recipient's acceptance (Article 11(1)(a)(i))
4 Confirm Receipt to Amazon	**Confirmed receipt of the acknowledgement of receipt (Article 11(1)(a)(ii))**

According to this draft, the contract would be concluded only at stage four.
Unsurprisingly such a complex and unwieldy system was immediately attacked by
online retailers and service providers.[38] Then, when the provision came to be
reviewed by the European Parliament's Committee on Legal Affairs and Citizens'
Rights, as part of the co-decision procedure it was rejected.[39] The Committee
reported that:

On the surface, this procedure appears rather cumbersome. The Committee
considers that, while it is quite normal for the recipient to receive confirmation
from the service provider so as to be certain that his or her order has been
recorded, it is asking too much of recipients to require them to restate their desire
to conclude the contract.[40]

Obviously the Committee felt that stage four was an unnecessary and burdensome step. Why should e-businesses such as Amazon require to await confirmation from customers before processing an order? Further from the point of view
of the average UK consumer this is an unusual and onerous extra step: in UK Law
the contract would have been concluded at stage three.[41] The Report of the

---

[38] For example, the Library Association referred to Art 11 as 'very long-winded': Library Association
response to the UK consultation on the EC Proposal for a Directive on Certain Legal Aspects of
Electronic Commerce in the Internal Market, 23 March 1999.

[39] Report no.A4–0248/99 on the proposal for a European Parliament and Council Directive on certain legal aspects of electronic commerce in the internal market (COM(98)0586–C4–0020/99–98/
0325(COD)), Committee on Legal Affairs and Citizens' Rights, 23 April 1999.

[40] *Ibid*, p 39.

[41] Similarly consumers from Germany, France, Italy, Belgium and many other Member States
would equally be required to complete a further step above that usually required under existing law.
See Baker & McKenzie, above n 31.

Committee recommended several changes to the wording of Article 11, the key recommendation being the removal of stage four. The European Parliament, in plenary session on 6 May 1999, approved the Commission's proposal subject to the proposed amendments.[42] The draft Directive was thus remitted to the Commission for redrafting in light of these comments. This took place in Summer 1999 and on 17 August 1999 the Commission presented an 'Amended proposal for a European Parliament and Council Directive on certain legal aspects of electronic commerce in the Internal Market'.[43] The second draft made no revisions to Articles 9 and 10 but made substantial amendment to Article 11.

The newly proposed Article 11 still sought to harmonize the 'moment at which the contract is concluded', but now provided quite a different solution to that found in the first draft. It provided:

> Member States shall lay down in their legislation that, save where otherwise agreed by professional persons, in cases where a recipient, in accepting a service provider's offer, is required to give his consent through technological means, such as clicking on an icon, the contract is concluded when the recipient of the service has received from the service provider, electronically, an acknowledgement of receipt of the recipient's acceptance.[44]

Thus to return to our earlier example. A contract to buy a book from Amazon.co.uk would now look like this:

1 View details on web page	Offer (from Amazon)
2 Send 'order' to Amazon	Acceptance
3 **Receive Confirmation from Amazon**	**Acknowledgement of receipt of the recipient's acceptance (Article 11(1)(a)(i))**

The amended draft of Article 11, may therefore be characterized as following the three stage approach found in most leading European jurisdictions. This model would be familiar to UK consumers who could replace the terms 'Offer', 'Acceptance' and 'Acknowledgement' with the more familiar 'Invitation to treat', 'Offer' and 'Acceptance'. Similarly consumers in Germany, France and Belgium would be familiar with this model.[45] While no doubt some countries would be required to change their traditional approach to on-line contracting, Spain for example would traditionally have found the contract concluded at stage two,[46] this

---

[42] Amended proposal for a European Parliament and Council Directive on certain legal aspects of electronic commerce in the Internal Market COM (1999) 427 final, Explanatory Memorandum.

[43] COM (1999) 427 final.

[44] Art 11(1).

[45] See Baker & McKenzie, above n 31.

[46] *Ibid.*

settlement seemed straightforward and at this stage it was widely assumed it would be adopted. Unfortunately though the Directive had one last hurdle the clear, adoption by the Council.

For reasons which are not entirely clear the Council could not agree with the amended text of Article 11 found in COM (1999) 427. When the Common Position of the Council with regard to the draft Directive was published on 28 February 2000,[47] the wording of Article 11 had again been substantially redrafted. The newly proposed version of Article 11, now renamed 'placing of the order',[48] instead of seeking to harmonize the moment of contractual settlement, was now limited to listing requirements for the placing and receipt of orders on-line. The statement of the Council's reason for this extensive revision was somewhat enigmatic. It was simply recorded that, 'The Council considered that it was not appropriate to harmonize national law regarding the moment at which a contract is concluded.'[49] Then, on 12 April 2000, Rapporteur Ana Vallelersundi in her Recommendation for Second Reading,[50] proposed that the European Parliament approve the common position unamended on the basis that: 'this directive must be adopted as soon as possible to make sure that e-commerce can genuinely develop in the Community.'[51] On 4 May 2000 the Common Position was approved.[52] Thus the Directive, as finally enacted as Dir.2000/31/EC, carries though almost unchanged the terms of Articles 9 and 10 from the first draft, but Article 11 has been gutted of all meaning as we shall see in the following section.

C. Adopting E-Contracts in Europe: The ECD Dir.2000/31/EC

As we have seen, Articles 9–11 of the ECD were designed to fulfil three related, yet separable functions of equivalence, consumer protection and harmonisation of contract rules. The key function is the equivalence function. Without recognition of the equivalence of electronic documentation, electronic contracting is impossi-

---

[47] Common Position (EC) No 22/2000 adopted by the Council on 28 February 2000 with a view to adopting a Directive 2000/ 31/EC of the European Parliament and of the Council of . . . on certain legal aspects of information society services, in particular electronic commerce, in the internal market. OJ C 128, 8 May 2000, p 32.

[48] Up to the publication of the Common Position Art 11 had been consistently entitled 'moment at which the contract is concluded'.

[49] *Ibid*, p 49. The only clue to any dispute is that throughout the Council discussion of the draft Directive the Belgian Delegation abstained. As the wording of the second draft of Art 11 was compliant with current Belgian practice though this was unlikely to be the cause of this amendment.

[50] Report of the Committee on Legal Affairs and the Internal Market, Final A5–0106/2000.

[51] *Ibid*, p 12.

[52] OJ C 41, 7 February 2001, p 38.

ble except in relation to simple informal contracts. As it is Article 9 which provides equivalence it is to this critical provision that we shall first turn.

1. Article 9—Treatment of Contracts

Article 9(1) provides that

> Member States shall ensure that their legal system allows contracts to be concluded by electronic means. Member States shall in particular ensure that the legal requirements applicable to the contractual process neither create obstacles for the use of electronic contracts nor result in such contracts being deprived of legal effectiveness and validity on account of their having been made by electronic means.[53]

The final version of Article 9 varies little from the original version previously discussed. It retains the basic requirement that Member States ensure their legal system 'allows contracts to be concluded by electronic means'. The only substantive difference from the first and final drafts are that the final draft eliminates the reference to 'legislation' found in the first draft of Article 9(1). This is surely a sensible move as some member states may find that an expansive interpretation of their common law principles of contract may achieve such equivalence without the need to take recourse to enabling legislation. With such little change from inception to ratification, Article 9(1) adequately deals with the 'form' issue required by Article 5 of the UNCITRAL Model Law. As previously stated Article 9, alongside Article 5 of the Electronic Signatures Directive, creates a functional equivalence for e-documents in both informal and formal contracts.[54] It requires that anything which can be achieved through written documents must be in law achievable through e-documents.

The previously noted concerns regarding formality and sensitivity of some contractual relationships, and the use of paper documentation in such as a 'badge of formality' in such contractual relationships remains the focus of Article 9(2). The list of possible exceptions under Article 9(2) has in fact been expanded through the consultation process. As we saw, the original list of excludable documents consisted of:

---

[53] Art 9(2) lists 4 possible exemptions from the provisions of Art 9(1). It provides that

Member States may lay down that paragraph 1 shall not apply to all or certain contracts falling into one of the following categories (a) contracts that create or transfer rights in real estate, except for rental rights; (b) contracts requiring by law the involvement of courts, (c) contracts of suretyship granted and on collateral securities furnished by persons acting for purposes outside their trade, business or profession and (d) contracts governed by family law or by the law of succession.

[54] Above, p 9.

(a) contracts requiring the involvement of a notary;
(b) contracts which in order to be valid require to be registered with a public authority;
(c) contracts governed by Family Law;
(d) contracts governed by the Law of Succession.[55]

This list has altered considerably. The first two have been dropped in favour of a new wording 'Contracts that create or transfer rights in real estate.'[56] Although it is arguable that such contractual relations were always covered by either (a) or (b) previously, it may be argued that in both Scots and English Law it is possible to transfer an interest in real property without either the involvement of a notary or registration with a public authority. Although the interest transferred remains beneficial until registration, an interest in land can be transferred without either the involvement of a notary or registration by a public authority.[57] The new wording of Article 9(2)(a) makes it clear that interests in land were clearly the target of the wording found in draft Articles 9(2)(a) and (b) and as such are to be excludable from the effects of Article 9(1)(a).

Further, the original version of Article 9(2)(b)[58] has been replaced by a newly worded Article 9(2)(b), 'Contracts requiring by law the involvement of courts'. It is not clear why this has been done. One can think of many contracts which require to be registered, such as a Marriage Contract or a contract of security, such as a Floating Charge: few though, require the involvement of the Courts. The reason for the original wording of Article 9(2)(b) was the potentially prohibitive costs of computerising all public registries within the European Union. The reason for the alteration in the wording is therefore quite mystifying as with the removal of the public authority exemption governments will now be forced to computerize public records offices. Finally it should be noted that there is one new exception to be found in Article 9(2)(c): 'Contracts of suretyship granted and on collateral securities furnished by persons acting for purposes outside their trade, business or profession.' This was added following considerable lobbying from many in the consumer protection lobby as well as many in the financial services sector. There was concern that the digitisation of security agreements would remove from such agreements a degree of formality which is necessary to communicate to consumers the gravity of the agreement they are entering into. This was particularly sought by German and Scandinavian consumer protection groups and particularly opposed by UK financial services institutions.

---

[55] Above, p 10.
[56] Art 9(2)(a).
[57] See eg, *Sharp v Thomson* 1999 SC 66 (HL).
[58] 'Contracts which in order to be valid require to be registered with a public authority'.

2. Article 10—Information to be Provided

As previously stated, the focus of Article 10 is to provide transparency and consumer protection in on-line transactions. To achieve this Article 10 requires service providers to provide information regarding the technical steps which consumers are required to follow to conclude a contract, how to correct input errors, and to provide information about codes of conducts, contract terms and general conditions.[59] The aim of this Article is to provide the consumer with adequate protection measures required to stand in place of the 'badge of formality' previously associated with the written document. It reflects concerns that with digitisation:

(1) Formality in the contract-making process may be lost, meaning consumers may inadvertently enter into binding contacts without realising the gravity of the agreement into which they are entering;
(2) familiarity with counterparties can be lost when there is a lack of physical interaction;
(3) there is an increased risk of error in electronic documents due to the informal nature of the medium.

The method chosen to alleviate these concerns is though problematic. The majority of contracts can be formed without any particular exchange of information regarding how the contract is to be formed.[60] Such informal contracts rely upon default rules found in domestic rules of contract formation. Although it may be

---

[59] Art 10:

Information to be provided:

(1) In addition to other information requirements established by Community law, Member States shall ensure, except when otherwise agreed by parties who are not consumers, that at least the following information is given by the service provider clearly, comprehensibly and unambiguously and prior to the order being placed by the recipient of the service:

    (a) the different technical steps to follow to conclude the contract;
    (b) whether or not the concluded contract will be filed by the service provider and whether it will be accessible;
    (c) the technical means for identifying and correcting input errors prior to the placing of the order;
    (d) the languages offered for the conclusion of the contract.

[60] As has been noted, above, p 5, most B2C contracts are of an informal nature. Such contracts may be concluded on the basis of a set of previously agreed terms without the communication of 'the different technical steps to follow to conclude the contract'. Think for example of a simple sale of goods transaction. This can be concluded between the retailer and the consumer without a word being spoken, yet all terms are clear to all parties—transfer of title, payment, quality of goods. There is a concern that the provisions of Art 10 will make simple, informal contracts unnecessarily complex when pursued in an on-line environment. See C Hultmark Ramberg, 'The E-Commerce Directive and Formation of Contract in a Comparative Perspective' (2003) 1(2) *Global Jurist Advances*, Art 3. Available at: http://www.bepress.com/gj/advances/vol1/iss2/art3.

preferable that the parties to the contract have a common understanding rules of contract formation before they open negotiations, the provisions of Article 10 are not sufficiently flexible to meet the demands of the variety of contractual relationships and subject-matters encountered in e-commerce. As a result it will no doubt add a degree of resistance to the 'frictionless economy'. As noted by Professor Ramberg:

> Article 10 does not solve any practical problem. There are enough incentives in national general contract law for businesses to provide the information requested by the ECD. The implementation of Article 10 will only create confusion in the national laws of the Member States and contribute to a disharmony in law within EU.[61]

3. Article 11—Placing of the Order

As already discussed at some length Article 11 had the most turbulent path through the drafting process. In both a visionary first draft with a four-stage contract formation process, and a second draft containing a more recognisable three-stage process, the European Parliament and Commission sought to achieve harmonisation of the moment when e-contracts would be concluded. The advantages were clear: certainty would ensure that consumer confidence in cross-border trading would be greatly enhanced and harmonisation of the rules of contract formation would benefit e-businesses who could streamline their systems to a single European contract formation model. Unfortunately the title of the final version of Article 11 reveals all. While at first and second draft stage it was boldly declaiming '*Moment at which the Contract is Concluded*' by the final version it meekly states '*Placing of the Order*'. Any attempt to unite Europe to a single vision of e-contracting was abandoned. It was clear no compromise could be found after the Council of Europe agreed the Common Position on 28 February 2000.

The most valuable remaining provision of Article 11 is the second indent of Article 11(1).[62] A crucial question of contractual formation has been exactly how e-contracts fit the currently accepted models of contract formation. This issue is logically prior to that of actually going to the next step and harmonising rules of contract formation. Therefore although the Directive fails in that further step, it does finally answer the prior question. We now know that effective delivery (of an acceptance, and therefore *consensus ad idem* and conclusion of the contract) occurs when a party is able to access the communication. This means that the postal rule does not apply to e-mails but rather they are subject to the delivery

---

[61] *Ibid*, p 13.
[62] 'The order and the acknowledgement of receipt are to be received when the parties to whom they are able to access them.'

rule[63] it also confirms the delivery rule applies to on-line contracts as had been widely assumed.[64]

4. The Effect of Articles 9–11

Collectively the effect of Chapter II, Section 3 of the ECD is to require Member States to provide equivalence for e-documents in all contractual matters except those listed as exceptional by Article 9(2). Along with the provisions of the Electronic Signatures Directive, this should sweep away the final barriers to the use of e-documents in all formal contracts. It provides, in Article 10 (and Article 11(2)), measures designed to ensure consumer's are adequately compensated for the removal of the 'badge of formality' attached to written documentation and the framework to ensure consumer confidence is upheld. Finally, in Article 11 it prescribes the delivery rule for all methods of electronic communication, which will go some way towards providing a degree of harmonisation, but falls short of prescribing exactly when a contract will be concluded. How then has the UK Government implemented these provisions?

D. Implementing E-Contracts in the UK

The UK Government is not noted for its alacrity in implementing European Directives, and with its usual haste the DTI launched its initial public consultation on implementation of the Directive on 10 August 2001, some 13 months after the Directive was adopted.[65] This document set out the Government's initial position and sought response on a few narrow questions.

On the implementation of Article 9(1), the Government hinted that it did not intend to adopt the widespread equivalence provisions found therein. Instead they suggested that: '[t]he Government is still considering whether form requirements (eg, notices or copy documents) must be disapplied, such as those which have to be satisfied for a contract to be enforceable and where the context makes it clear that a physical instrument is required.'[66]

The reason for this becomes immediately and abundantly clear '[to do] so, could require considerable amendment of the legislation concerned.'[67] The UK

---

[63] This provision thereby deals a fatal blow to the five pages of analysis I carried out in my review of e-contracting in 'Entering Into Contracts Electronically: The Real WWW', above n 28, in only 22 words.

[64] *Ibid.*

[65] Consultation Document on Implementation of the E-Commerce Directive, DTI, above n 29.

[66] *Ibid*, p 16.

[67] *Ibid.*

Government had considered blanket equivalence previously in considering the drafting of the Electronic Communications Bill in 1999.[68] At this point they had rejected equivalence in favour of a 'case-by-case' approach.[69] It appeared they were about to do so again. Consultation was sought on more technical questions such as 'What are the consequences of failure to comply with the requirement of acknowledgement "without undue delay" and the other requirements in Articles 10 and 11?'[70] And 'Are there any likely circumstances in which it might not be straightforward to identify the point at which the parties to whom these messages are addressed are able to access them?'[71] It was clear the DTI had already made the major policy decisions relating to implementation over the previous months. Consultation was to be a mostly cosmetic exercise, where consultants where to be asked only to flesh out the detail.

When the responses were compiled following closure of the consultation period, it was clear consultees were at odds with the DTI's approach to the implementation of Article 9(1). There were renewed pleas for the Government to move faster on eliminating requirements for writing from existing statute and common law. It was suggested by several respondents, including the Alliance for Electronic Business, that the order-making power found in section 8 of the Electronic Communications Act 2000 did not implement Article 9 of the Directive and that a blanket equivalence for electronic writing (with a few specific exceptions) was required.[72]

Unsurprisingly though when the first draft of The Electronic Commerce (EC Directive) Regulations 2002, was published on 7 March 2002, there was a clear omission. The draft Regulations, by Regulation 11, would enact almost word for word Article 10 of the Directive. Further by Regulation 13, the provisions of Article 11 were to be fully enacted, including by Regulation 13(2), the first indent of Article 11(1) thus enshrining the delivery rule for e-contracts. The draft Regulations also gave the first insight into how the DTI intended to provide enforcement of the terms of Articles 10 and 11 of the Directive. By Regulation 16 individuals were to be given the right to cancel any contract entered into in breach of the provisions of Regulations 11(3) or 13(1) by giving 'notice of cancellation of the agreement'. By Regulation 16(2) the Service Provider would be required to

---

[68] See Building Confidence in E-Commerce: A Consultation Document, sup n 24 at paras 15–16.

[69] This was set out in House of Commons Research Paper 99/100, 8 December 1999, *The Electronic Communications Bill (revis edition) Bill 4 of 1999–2000*, where it was stated that 'obstacles in existing laws which insist on the use of paper will be swept away wherever it makes sense to give people the electronic option' (emphasis added) p 13. This then formed the basis s 8 of the Electronic Communications Act 2000.

[70] Consultation Document on Implementation of the E-Commerce Directive, DTI, above n 29, para 5.1.

[71] *Ibid*, para 5.3.

[72] See *DTI Consultation on Implementation of the Directive on Electronic Commerce (2000/31/ec) Summary of Responses*, 'Treatment of electronic contracts'. Available at: http://www.dti.gov.uk/ industries/content/dti_consultation_on_implementation_of_directive_on_electronic_ commerce_200031ec_summary_of_responses.html#contracts.

give restitution. There was though no attempt to provide implementation of Article 9. A glance through the Interim Guide for Business,[73] published contemporaneously gives the official answer for this omission. Firstly, the DTI, suggests that most contracts are already compliant with Article 9(1):

> The Government believes that the great majority of relevant statutory references (eg, to requirements for writing or signature) are already capable of being fulfilled by electronic communications where the context in which they appear does not indicate to the contrary.[74]

While this is certainly true, the overwhelming majority of contracts were capable of being fulfilled by electronic communications long before the process of drafting the ECD was begun: the 'stickiness' of the system was to be found in the minority of 'contracts of form' which, as was admitted by the DTI themselves, *did not* allow e-documents to be used. There is a clear contradiction here in the language used by the DTI in consultation on the Electronic Communications Bill and the language used in Consultation on the e-Commerce Regulations. Those contracts which were not compliant with Article 9(1), would, in the view of the DTI, be 'mopped up' by legislation passed under the Electronic Communications Act or the European Communities Act.

Where existing legal requirements applicable to the contractual process do create obstacles for the use of the electronic contracts or result in such contracts being deprived of legal effectiveness and validity on account of their having been made by electronic means, the Government will propose necessary amendments on a case-by-case basis. It will do so through appropriate proposals for primary legislation, Orders made under Section 8 of the Electronic Communications Act or Regulations made under Section 2(2) of the European Communities Act.[75]

Thus the DTI signalled its intent to take a robust view of 'contracts of form', showing no intention to depart from the approach first adopted in the Electronic Communications Act of recognition on a case-by-case basis, and an outright rejection of blanket equivalence, despite Article 9 being most clear on this matter.

The draft Regulations drew 77 published responses from industry, consumers and representative associations.[76] The majority of these responses focused on the Country of Origin principle (Regulation 7) and the 'Notice and Take Down' procedure introduced in Regulation 19. A sizable number of responses did though make comments in relation to electronic contracting. These comments were

---

[73] DTI, *A Guide for Business to the Electronic Commerce (EC Directive) Regulations 2002, Interim Guidance*, March 2002. Available at: http://www.dti.gov.uk/industry_files/pdf/guidance.pdf.

[74] *Ibid*, para 5.12.

[75] *Ibid*, para 5.13.

[76] The 77 responses may be accessed at: http://www.dti.gov.uk/industries/ecommunications/second_consult_responses.html There was a wide range of respondents from telecoms giants such as BT and AOL through retails groups such as the British Retail Consortium and the Alliance for Electronic Business to regulatory authorities such as the London Trading Standards Authorities.

overwhelmingly focused on two aspects of the proposed regulatory framework—
the enforcement provisions of Regulation 16, and the failure to directly implement
Article 9 of the ECD. The comments made with regard to Regulation 16 were uniformly critical of the scope of the Regulation as drafted. Typical of responses is that
of the Alliance for Electronic Business who pointed out that:

> The implementation of the prohibition on enforceability and the right to cancel under
> Regulation 16(1) goes beyond the scope of the Directive. It is open ended and the provi-
> sions are likely to breach the Human Rights Act 1998. The prohibition on enforceability
> is similar to that in the Consumer Credit Act 1974 that the Court of Appeal has already
> held to be incompatible with Convention Rights. The effect of this provision is that the
> Regulations would provide different sanctions for breach of statutory duty as would
> otherwise be provided for under the Directive. We believe that a consumer's right to can-
> cel should provide similar sanctions under these regulations as under the Distance
> Selling (Consumer Protection) Regulations 2000. Otherwise, disparity remains where a
> consumer could cancel on any minor issue, for example when a business fails to forward
> paperwork at the exact time that it said it would do so.[77]

The strong responses received in relation to the draft Regulation 16, caused the
DTI to reconsider their position. It was accepted that allowing customers to
rescind contractual obligations 'at any time' for minor technical breaches of the
Regulations 'would create disproportionate penalties for service providers.'[78] As a
result the Government redrafted Regulation 16 much more narrowly. Rescission
is now only allowed where 'the service provider has not made available means of
allowing [the individual] to identify and correct input errors in compliance with
Regulation 11(1)(b).'[79] Additionally, the requirement that the service provider
make restitution has been removed and there is a new defensive provision for
service providers who may under Regulation 15 seek a court order preventing
rescission taking place. Although this falls short of a three month time limit for
rescission as suggested by most respondents[80] it shows a degree of reflection and
flexibility on the part of the DTI.

The attack on the Government's decision not to directly implement Article 9
was equally forceful. Organisations as diverse as Abbey National plc,[81] the Digital

---

[77] Alliance for Electronic Business, *Response to the DTI Consultation on the Electronic Commerce (EC Directive) Regulations 2002*, 1 May 2002, p 6. Available at: http://www.dti.gov.uk/industry_files/pdf/ecommerce/AEBpdf.

[78] DTI, *Electronic Commerce (EC Directive) Regulations 2002: Public Consultation—Government Response*, 31 July 2002, p 4. Available at: http://www.dti.gov.uk/industry_files/pdf/govresponsetoconsultation.pdf.

[79] The Electronic Commerce (EC Directive) Regulations 2002, SI 2002/2013, Reg 15.

[80] This would have put Reg 15 on an equal footing with the rescission rights contained in Regs 11 and 12 of The Consumer Protection (Distance Selling) Regulations 2000 (SI 2000/2334).

[81] 'There is every chance that the approach being taken is resulting in a degree of uncertainty as to the precise legal position regarding electronic contracting. A primary aim of the E-Commerce Directive to enable the Community to benefit from consumer confidence and to give ISS providers legal certainty. It is possible that Government's approach maybe hampering this development.' *Abbey National Response*, p 1. Available at: http://www.dti.gov.uk/industry_files/pdf/ecommerce/AbbeyNational.pdf.

Content Forum,[82] Baker & McKenzie[83] and the Finance and Leasing Association[84] all stated with one voice that the Regulations as currently drafted *did not* meet the blanket equivalence requirement of Article 9 of the Directive. The DTI was urged in the strongest possible terms to reconsider on this point. The message was clear: the potential for consumer confusion and the resultant loss of consumer confidence (which had been a driving force behind the Directive in the first place) would remain high if the UK Government failed to implement Article 9 fully by giving immediate and blanket equivalence to all e-contracts.[85] The flexibility seen

[82] 'Section 8 of the Electronic Communications Act 2000 has allowed UK legislators to identify the legal barriers to allowing the conclusion of contracts by electronic means, and to amend them by Order. Until then the UK is in breach of its obligations to implement Art 9.' *DCF Second Response*, p 3. Available at: http://www.dti.gov.uk/industry_files/pdf/ecommerce/DigitalContentForum(2).pdf.

[83] To cite from Baker & McKenzie:

A key concern with the Regulations is that they do not implement Art 9. The Guidance provides that 'the Regulations do not transpose Art 9(1) . . . . The Government believes that the great majority of relevant statutory references (eg, to requirements for writing or signature) are already capable of being fulfilled by electronic communications where the context in which they appear does not indicate to the contrary.' There is clearly ambiguity as to whether or not existing requirements for writing can be satisfied by electronic means. We appreciate that there is a large volume of existing UK statutes with writing requirements which will require review and possible amendment to comply with Art 9 but this is a clear requirement of the E-Commerce Directive. The Government has had powers to remove obstacles to electronic contracting under Section 8 of the Electronic Communications Act 2000 since Section 8 of that Act came into force on 25 May 2000. Although there have been a number of consultations and regulations issued under Section 8, there has not been a comprehensive and systematic review of the obstacles to electronic contracting under existing UK laws. This is a key business concern as some of the existing UK statutory requirements *do* require hard copy (eg, the formal requirements for regulated agreements under the Consumer Credit Act 1974). Further delaying this process, as envisaged in paragraph 5.13 of the Guidance, is not permitted by the E-Commerce Directive and fails to remove existing obstacles which currently prevent the use of electronic contracts. To remove existing obstacles and lingering legal uncertainty, we urge the DTI to conduct an *immediate* review of all UK statutes with a view to removing any obstacles for the use of electronic contracts as soon as possible.

Baker & McKenzie Response, pp 1–2. Available at: http://www.dti.gov.uk/industry_files/pdf/ecommerce/Baker&McKenzie.pdf.

[84] *Finance & Leasing Association Response:*

In our view, Article 9 of the E Commerce Directive is clear. It requires all Member States to ensure that their legal system allows contracts to be concluded by electronic means. It also says that Member States shall, in particular, ensure that the legal requirements applicable to the contractual process neither create obstacles for the use of electronic contracts nor result in such contracts being deprived of legal effectiveness and validity on account of their having been made by electronic means. Accordingly, we cannot support the statement in 5.12 of the Interim Guidance that the Regulations should not seek to transpose Article 9(1) of the E Commerce Directive so as to ensure that UK law allows contracts to be concluded by electronic means.

Finance & Leasing Association Response, pp 3–4. Available at: http://www.dti.gov.uk/industry_files/pdf/ecommerce/Finance&LeasingAssociation.pdf.

[85] With the exception of 'contracts which create or transfer rights in real estate, except for rental rights' which by para 5.14 of *A Guide for Business to the Electronic Commerce (EC Directive) Regulations 2002, Interim Guidance, sup n* 73, were to be excepted.

in relation to rescission of contracts was not though extended to the implementation of Article 9. Although Articles 10 and 11 have been implemented almost perfectly by Regulations 9 and 11, which changed little from first to final draft, there remains no space in the final Regulations for the terms of Article 9. In the DTI publication, *A Guide for Business to the Electronic Commerce (EC Directive) Regulations 2002 (SI 2002/2013)*[86] the DTI blandly restates the text first seen in Paragraphs 5.12 and 5.13 of the Interim Guide for Business,[87] saying:

> The Government believes that the great majority of relevant statutory references (eg, to requirements for writing or signature) are already capable of being fulfilled by electronic communications where the context in which they appear does not indicate to the contrary.

Where existing legal requirements applicable to the contractual process do create obstacles for the use of the electronic contracts or result in such contracts being deprived of legal effectiveness and validity on account of their having been made by electronic means, the Government will propose necessary amendments on a case-by-case basis.[88]

It is almost as if the DTI never received the comments of those critical of this omission. No effort has been made to account for the difference between Article 9 of the Directive (blanket equivalence) and the wording of the Regulations which relies upon a piecemeal award of equivalence, first seen in the Electronic Communications Act. The Regulations came into force on 21 August 2002: the debate was closed.

E. Conclusion: What Does This Mean for E-Contracts in the UK?

The UK is left in a most unsatisfactory position by the failure of the UK Government to fully implement the ECD. Despite the assertions of the DTI that 'the great majority of relevant statutory references are already capable of being fulfilled by electronic communications' the failure to implement fully Article 9 left the UK in breach of the ECD. The actions of the DTI throughout the implementation process were driven by the advice they have received from the Law Commission. The Law Commission reported that: 'as English Law seldom imposes such form requirements in a contractual context, it is only in very rare

---

[86] DTI, 31 July 2002. Available at: http://www.dti.gov.uk/industry_files/pdf/businessguidance.pdf.
[87] Above n 73.
[88] A Guide for Business to the Electronic Commerce (EC Directive) Regulations 2002, sup n 86, at paras 5.15 and 5.16.

cases that the statute book will conflict with the obligation imposed by Article 9 of the ECD.'[89] That may be true, but Article 9 is seeking to harmonise *all* contracts of form throughout the EU (with the exception of those listed in Article 9(2) for which special exemptions are awarded). Thus these 'very rare cases' which remain cause unnecessary disharmony and may adversely effect consumer confidence. The Government has doggedly stuck to the position of the Law Commission that: General reform of the statute book is not required . . . Orders under section 8 (of the Electronic Communications Act) may be made where it is clear that an electronic communication can or cannot satisfy a form requirement, or where the position is uncertain. It will be possible to use an order under section 8 of the ECA to deal with form requirements which conflict (or which may conflict) with Article 9, to provide such clarification as may be required, and to impose such conditions as may be appropriate.[90]

This is clearly the wrong-headed approach. Although everything the Law Commission states is true, it does not comply with Article 9 which requires Member States to: '*ensure* that the legal requirements applicable to the contractual process neither create obstacles for the use of electronic contracts nor result in such contracts being deprived of legal effectiveness and validity on account of their having been made by electronic means' [emphasis added].

There is no doubt that a failure to fully implement Article 9 means that many contracts of form, not least contracts under the Consumer Credit Act 1974 remained deprived of legal effectiveness in the UK on account of their having been made by electronic means. Only in December 2002 did the DTI formally open consultation on enabling the conclusion of credit and hire agreements electronically. The Consultation process formally closed on 28 March 2003 with a view to publishing responses in June 2003,[91] but it was only in December 2003 that the results of the consultation were eventually published on the DTI website. By this time the On-line Agreements Consultation, as it had become known, had become part of a larger review of Consumer Credit Agreements called 'Establishing a Transparent Market: Early Settlement, Consumer Credit Advertising, Form and Content of Credit Agreements, APRs on credit cards and On-line Agreements'.[92] This review recommended that it be made 'possible, but not mandatory, to contract electronically' under the Consumer Credit Act.[93] It went on to discuss the detailed proposals allowing for this aim to be achieved, including questions of

---

[89] The Law Commission, *Electronic Commerce: Formal Requirements in Commercial Transactions*, December 2001, para 10.2.

[90] *Ibid*, paras 10.3 and 10.4.

[91] Consultation opened with the publication by the Consumer and Competition Policy Directorate of the consultation document *Review Of The Consumer Credit Act 1974* (No CCP 015/02).

[92] DTI, Establishing a Transparent Market: Early Settlement, Consumer Credit Advertising, Form and Content of Credit Agreements, APRs on credit cards and On-line Agreements, TSO, London, December 2003.

[93] *Ibid*, p 26.

legibility, record keeping and receipt of documentation. At the end of this discussion it asked a further two consultative questions,[94] and asked that responses to these questions be made by 15 March 2004. Only after this process was complete did the DTI draft The Consumer Credit Act 1974 (Electronic Communications) Order 2004;[95] the enabling legislation made under the Electronic Communications Act 2000 which allows for electronic completion of Consumer Credit Agreements. The Order was finally laid before Parliament on 9 December 2004, and took effect on 31 December 2004. The ECD provisions were to have been enacted by 17 January 2002. On that date, the provisions of Article 9, if enacted would have created legal equivalence for electronic Consumer Credit Act agreements. By instead using the Electronic Communications Act route, the introduction of electronic Consumer Credit Act agreements was thus delayed by nearly three years, and was only introduced following a costly and lengthy evaluation and consultative process, which did not yield any substantive amendments to the enabling legislation.

Is there anything citizens can do about this failure? Well, Directives can be directly effective under European Law. In order to be so they must be clear and unambiguous, and there must be a failure to implement the directive. Is the relevant Article clear and unambiguous? When we look at Article 9 its terms seem clear: the Government shall ensure that no formal requirements impede electronic contracting. Failure to adequately modify UK Law to ensure compliance with Article 9 by 17 January 2002 is arguably then a breach of the Directive. These factors would suggest that the Directive is of direct effect. But the direct effect of a Directive is not an absolute entitlement to every member of the public to freely enter into electronic consumer credit agreements. Instead, direct effect of Directives is limited. It is of a vertical nature, not a horizontal nature which means that the direct effect of a Directive is between a member of the public and the state (or an emanation of the state).[96] This means that the terms of the Directive are only enforceable by a member of the public against the state or a public authority. This is clearly of very limited value as the vast majority of effected agreements will be of a horizontal nature, but in the few cases where individuals contract with an emanation of the state, for instance the purchase of property from a local authority, the provisions of Article 9 could be brought to bear.

It is a shame that in 2005 we should be considering whether or not Article 9 of the ECD is directly effective within the UK. There is no good reason why the UK

---

[94] These were: 'What additional costs will lenders incur as a result of implementing these changes to allow agreements to be concluded electronically?' and 'Will costs be different for different types of businesses?'

[95] Now enacted as SI 2004/3236.

[96] *Marshall v Southampton and South West Hampshire Area Health Authority* [1986] ECR 723. This reasoning is based on the terms of the EU Treaty where Art 249 of the EC Treaty makes clear that Directives are directed at member states.

Government could not have simply introduced a blanket equivalence for these few remaining formal contracts that could not be concluded by electronic means. By this time the UK should have been one of the leading e-economies. In 1998 the Government set out its vision for the UK as a 'knowledge driven economy'. Therein it was stated that the role of Government was to 'create the right environment for business success by providing an economic framework which is stable and enterprising [by putting] in place policies and programmes to help businesses innovate and succeed as we all face the challenge of the knowledge driven economy.'[97] We were told by the Prime Minister that, 'old-fashioned state intervention did not and cannot work.'[98] With this in mind the obvious question to be tabled is why the DTI has, in breach of its duties under the ECD, made a conscious decision to continue to pursue its blinkered policy of case-by-case equivalence for e-documents? To do so puts Britain out of step with the rest of Europe, undoubtedly adversely effecting the ability of UK businesses to fully enter the world of European e-commerce. Further it continues a policy of unnecessary state intervention which, as conceded by the Prime Minister, cannot work.

[97] 'Our Competitive Future: Building the Knowledge Driven Economy' (Cmnd 4176) December 1998.
[98] *Ibid*, Foreword by the Prime Minister.

4

Articles 12–15 ECD: ISP Liability The Problem of Intermediary Service Provider Liability

LILIAN EDWARDS[1]

A. Introduction: The E-Commerce Directive (ECD) and ISPs, IAPs, ISSPs and Intermediary Service Providers

The problem of liability for intermediaries on the Internet was one of the earliest problems in the cyberspace environment to grab headlines, worry the fledgling Internet industry and demand the serious attention of lawyers.[2] Early cases mainly originated in the USA and focused on the liability of large Internet Service Providers (ISPs) such as AOL or CompuServe for hosting, transmitting and publishing material that was in some way criminal or civilly actionable: notably libellous, defamatory or pornographic content.[3] The problematic content might be content originated by a party with whom the ISP had a contractual relationship, eg, where a website was hosted by the ISP for a monthly sum; content provided by a third party with no contractual nexus with the ISP, eg, a newsgroup posting transmitted by the ISP as part of its standard 'feed' to customers; or content originated by the ISP itself.

---

[1] Co-Director, AHRC Centre for Research into Intellectual Property and Technology, School of Law, University of Edinburgh; email L.Edwards@ed.ac.uk.

[2] *Cubby v CompuServe* 766 F Supp 135 (SDNY, 1991), for example (see discussion below at n 16) was one of the earliest cyberlaw cases of any kind to be decided. A Dutch prosecution of an ISP for hosting copyright material was also reported in 1991, see DTL Oosterbaan, *et al*, 'eCommerce 2003: Netherlands' in *Getting the Deal Through: eCommerce 2003 in 25 Jurisdictions Worldwide* (Law Business Research Ltd, 2003).

[3] For historical context, see earlier discussion of these issues by this writer in L Edwards, 'Defamation and the Internet' and 'Pornography and the Internet' in L Edwards and C Waelde (eds), *Law and the Internet: A Framework for Electronic Commerce* (Hart Publishing, 2000). An earlier version of the defamation chapter appeared in L Edwards and C Waelde, *Law and the Internet: Regulating Cyberspace* (Hart Publishing, 1997).

The different issues of policy raised by these different classifications of authorship and types of content were largely not teased out systematically in the early jurisprudence, leading to widely differing regimes being imposed both in different legal systems and within the same legal system but in differing scenarios. This lack of harmonisation in the emerging case law led to calls from industry for some form of rescuing certainty in the form of special statutory regimes from as early as the mid 1990s. As discussed below, over time the liability regime debate came to be seen less as tied to different types of content—libel, pornography, material infringing copyright—and more as a holistic problem of whether intermediaries on the Internet should in general be made responsible for the content they make accessible to the public. At the same time, the issue of liability for content became a major worry not just for the relatively small traditional ISP community, but also for a wide spectrum of Internet hosts, eg, universities, traditional media organizations going 'digital', software providers like Microsoft and Sun, libraries and archives, chatrooms and 'webblog' sites, individuals setting up personal Web 'home pages'— and also affected a wider range of Internet communications intermediaries than traditional telcos, such as Internet backbone providers, cable companies, and mobile phone communications providers.

The early sharp distinction drawn between Internet Access Providers (IAPs)— who merely provided 'fundamental communications services such as access, information storage etc', and Internet Service Providers (ISPs), who provided 'some additional service which facilitates a transaction between end users, eg identifying one of the parties, providing search facilities etc'[4] became less and less meaningful as the ISP sector expanded during the boom years of the Internet to provide portal services giving access to large amounts of both in-house and third party produced content, while providers of what might be seen as 'pure' telecommunications services, like mobile phone companies, also became deeply involved in both the 'content business' and in providing 'value added' services such as locational data handling. It is almost impossible in 2004 to identify an IAP pure and simple. All this has had serious implications, as we shall see, for the development of an on-line intermediary liability regime which is practical, uniform, acceptable to industry and yet protective of both consumer and citizen needs.

Articles 12–15 of the EC E-Commerce Directive[5] (ECD) introduced throughout Europe a harmonised and relatively sophisticated regime dealing with the liability of intermediaries. The regime affects not just 'ISPs' but 'ISSPs': 'information society services providers'[6] or, as the title of Section 4 of the ECD also calls them, 'intermediary service providers'. An 'information society service' is defined[7]

---

[4] C Reed, *Internet Law: Text and Materials* (Butterworths, 2000) ch 4, p 78.

[5] 2000/31/EC, passed 8 June 2000.

[6] Art 2(b), ECD. These providers can be natural or juristic persons.

[7] Art 2(a) of the ECD refers back to the definition in Art 1(2) of Directive 98/34/EC as amended by Directive 98/48/EC. The definition is discussed further in Recs 17 and 18 of the ECD.

as 'any service normally provided for remuneration, at a distance, by means of electronic equipment for the processing (including digital compression) and storage of data, and at the individual request of a recipient of a service.' 'Recipient of a service' is defined[8] as 'any natural or legal person who . . . uses an information society service . . .'. Thus, broadly, the ECD intermediary service provider liability regime covers not only the traditional ISP sector, but also a much wider range of actors who are involved in selling goods or services on-line (eg, e-commerce sites such as Amazon and Ebay); offering on-line information or search tools for revenue (eg, Google, MSN, LexisNexis or WestLaw); and 'pure' telecommunications, cable and mobile communications companies offering network access services. However the requirement that an information society service be offered 'at the individual request of the recipient' means that TV and radio broadcasters do not fall within the remit of the ECD liability regime, although sites which offer individually on-demand services such as video-on-demand or email are included. In particular spammers and other 'providers of commercial communications'[9] are included as providers of information society services.

Importantly, Recital 18 of the ECD notes explicitly that although a service may be free to the recipient, this does not mean the provider of that service need fall outside the scope of the ECD if the service broadly forms part of an 'economic activity': so, arguably, providing non-commercial services on-line, such as the delivery of e-government services by state departments, falls within the ECD regime if the state will be making economic gains out of the activity (eg, if they are cutting costs by putting service delivery on line). It would be more difficult to say if, to give another example, the provision of free political and lobbying information on sites such as FaxYourMP.com (which tells UK citizens how to email their MP and is run by volunteer labour) should be included. Since the liability regime is designed on the whole to benefit rather than burden the service provider, it seems right to argue it should be defined extensively. It seems uncontroversial that a search engine company such as Google, which provide its engine free to the public, but which service has helped it to create an extremely successful business which makes revenue in other ways,[10] should fall within the ECD regime. Given that one of the dominant successful models of e-business is to give away a major product or service but then make money out of it in lateral ways (the 'Netscape' effect) it would be foolish if the ECD definition of a service provider was to be interpreted in any more restrictive way.

Some relationships are however clearly excluded by Recital 18 as not provided wholly 'at a distance': an employer, for example, is not a provider of an 'information society service' in terms of his employment relationship with his workers, it

---

[8] Art 2(d), ECD.

[9] See further Rec 18, ECD, and Chapter 2 of this volume.

[10] Google's IPO announcement in August 2004 put a preliminary valuation on the business of over $30 billion and aroused 'IPO auction fever'.

seems (even if they work for him exclusively down a broadband line from home and were hired after a video-conferenced interview?); a doctor is not a provider of such a service even if he bills his private clients and sends them their prescriptions by email, so long as his advice even partially requires the 'physical examination of a patient'. The Directive as a whole also excludes certain activities from its remit,[11] including taxation, competition law, the activities of notaries and gambling. Thus, although there is increasing European concern at the unregulated nature of off-shore gambling sites,[12] in principle those who operate them do not fall with the definition of information society service provider and do not fall within the intermediary liability regime.

Before going on to look in detail at the rules of the EC liability regime, we will first consider the context and policy background to this area of regulation.

B. Key Areas of Concern in Internet Intermediary Liability

1. Pornography

The reputation of the Internet as 'the biggest dirty bookshop in the world' is well known, if sometimes overstated. Because ISPs effectively act as gatekeepers regulating access to Internet content, and because porn tends to be warehoused on sites in a relatively small number of countries with lax legal enforcement or (like the USA) strong constitutional protection of free speech, it is always going to be tempting for authorities in other states to deem ISPs to be 'importers' or similar of foreign originated illicit material, and therefore responsible for preventing its 'entry' or circulation within that state. In one of the most infamous incidents in Internet legal history, in May 1998, a court in Bavaria, Germany, found Felix Somm, the Chief Executive Officer of CompuServe Europe, guilty of distributing child pornography and other adult content. This rested on the fact that CompuServe, as most ISPs do as a normal part of their business, had circulated within Bavaria news-groups, including some which were deemed to contain such illegal content under Bavarian law.[13] Pleas that CompuServe had neither

---

[11] See Art 1(5).

[12] See the concerns, eg, of the UK children's charity NCH, for example, that off-shore gambling sites lack basic age validation checks—see http://www.nch.org.uk/page.asp?auto=783.

[13] Local Court, Munich, 12 May 1998. An English language version of the case is available at http://www.cyber-rights.org/isps/somm-dec.htm. See also G Bender, '*Bavaria v Felix Somm*: the Pornography Conviction of the Former CompuServe Manager' (1998) *IJCLP* Web-Doc 14–1–1998 at http://www.digital-law.net/papers/index.html.

originated this content nor could exercise effective monitoring of it, or control over it (news-group feeds taken by ISPs usually run to millions of individual news items[14]) failed to prevent the original prosecution succeeding; however an appeal in November 1999 did eventually reverse the decision, to somewhat less publicity.[15]

The case (to adapt the usual free speech cliché) had an undeniably chilling effect on ISPs (and their chief executives) everywhere. The Somm affair is also interesting as a graphic illustration of the public interest in providing immunity to ISPs as a freedom of speech issue. Because of technical restraints at the time, when CompuServe sought to remove the offending newsgroups from Germany they had to be excluded from Europe as a whole. This was despite the fact that in some European states some of the content in question was probably legal—thus demonstrating that fixing liability on ISPs tends to encourage them in the interests of simplicity to restrict content hosted or delivered to the level of the lowest common denominator of national content laws, and may thus globally restrict free speech.

2. Defamation

The role of ISPs as 'publishers' for the purposes of liability or immunity in respect of defamatory comments originated by third parties was extensively discussed in case and statute law in both the US and the UK in the mid to late 1990s, especially in the key US cases of *CompuServe v Cubby*[16] and *Stratton Oakmont v Prodigy*.[17] This was probably partly because in Anglo-American jurisprudence (and elsewhere), it had always been clear that anyone who republished a libel was as culpable in damages as the original author of the libelous comment. Potential scope for ISP liability was thus much more of an initially obvious threat here, than it was in respect of, say, copyright infringement, where difficult questions as to whether an ISP hosting pirate material was a direct infringer, a contributory to infringement, or authorising infringement, put liability (at least in the late 1990s before the advent of peer-to-peer technologies had wholly inflamed the copyright lobby) at a slightly safer distance. In the UK, the case of *Godfrey v Demon*[18] alarmed the Internet industry and stirred the civil liberties debate about how free speech should operate on the net, how notice and take down regimes should operate and whether ISPs should be treated differently from conventional publishers.

---

[14] BT Internet estimated in 1999 that just to effectively monitor news-group traffic alone, they would have to hire 1500 new employees working 24 hours a day. See *WIPO Workshop on Service Provider Liability*, Geneva, 9–10 December 1999, paper by Janet Henderson, Rights Strategy Manager, BT Internet. One's mind boggles to think what the figure would be today.

[15] See 'Germany clears Net chief of child porn charges' *The Independent*, 18 November 1999.

[16] (1991) 766 F Supp 135.

[17] 1995 NY Misc LEXIS 229 (NY Sup Ct Nassau Co, 1995). Both cases are discussed at p 102 below.

[18] *Godfrey v Demon Internet* [1999] 4 All ER 342. See discussion at p 115 below.

3. Hate Speech

The key case in this area has been the globally reported French prosecution of the US auction site Yahoo! for hosting and making access available to French citizens of sales of Nazi memorabilia, contrary to French anti-Holocaust legislation. Yahoo! US asserted that (a) the French courts did not have jurisdiction over their activities conducted on and published from US soil (where they were legal); (b) a finding against them would infringe their US First Amendment-guaranteed constitutional rights of free speech; and (c) it was not reasonably possible for them using available technologies to block access to the US website so that French citizens could not reach the offending parts of the auction site. The French court repelled all these defences (the technical issue after some further months of deliberation by a panel of experts) and, finding Yahoo! US in breach of French criminal law, ordered them to take all possible measures to prevent access in France to the relevant US hosted web pages.[19] Subsequently however a US court refused to enforce the French decree against Yahoo! on much the same grounds of freedom of speech that had been rejected in Paris.[20]

The interest of the Yahoo! case lies mainly in its stark illustration of the difficulties (i) for national authorities who seek to impose their laws relating to Internet hosts and Internet content in a global and transnational market for content and access and (ii) for ISPs and hosts in their turn, of servicing a global market when every country has its own plethora of dithering national laws relating to content, especially in polarised moral areas constructed by national history and culture such as hate speech and obscene content. As Reidenberg notes, the Yahoo! decision was widely seen as a misguided, futile or token attempt to impose national sovereignty and rules on to the global playing field of the Internet; but it can also be seen as an attempt to reassert respect for local democratic values on the Internet which are neither necessarily American nor those espoused by a global technological elite.[21]

4. Material Infringing Copyright

There have been no reported UK cases to date, and surprisingly few global ones[22] (those few often involving the Church of Scientology as vigilant plaintiffs) dealing

---

[19] TGI Paris, Ordonnance de refere du 20 November 2000. This order confirmed the earlier decision issued on 22 May 2000.

[20] *Yahoo! v La Ligue Contre Le Racisme et L'Antisemitisme* 169 F Supp 2d 1181 (ND Cal, 2001).

[21] See J Reidenberg, 'The "*Yahoo*" Case and the International Democratisation of the Internet', Fordham University, Research Paper 11, April 2001. See also C Penfold, 'Nazis, Porn and Politics: Asserting Control over Internet Content' 2001(2) *JILT* at http://elj.warwick.ac.uk/jilt/01–2/penfold.html.

[22] See notably the early US cases *Playboy Enterprises v Frena* 839 F Supp 1552 (MD Fla,1993); and *Religious Technology v Netcom* 923 F Supp 1231 (ND Cal 1995).

directly with Internet intermediary liability for hosting or distributing infringing material.[23] However the potential risk for hosts is so great given the volume of pirate material distributed and hidden on the Internet, that this is now perhaps the main issue driving the development of ISP liability law worldwide. In the 1990s, the main worry ventilated for ISPs relating to intellectual property (IP) infringement was potential liability for 'caching'—a ubiquitous technical process whereby local copies of remote web pages are made by hosts when requested, in order to speed up delivery of those pages on subsequent request. It was initially uncertain if such activity would be construed as making unauthorised copies of copyright work. To some extent, WIPO-lead activity has since resolved this particular question;[24] but anxiety about caching has given way to general concern about liability for the vast amount of pirate music, software and movies which is available on the Internet. Such content often exists without the knowledge either of the ISPs who give access to it, but more pressingly, the host whose servers it sits on. The explosion in illegal downloading and filesharing via peer-to-peer (P2P) networks such as the (now defunct) pre-commercialised Napster, KaaZaa/Morpheus, EMule and AudioGalaxy,[25] has only exacerbated the concerns of intermediaries at their exposure to risk. Not only do ISPs and hosts now have to consider if they may be held liable for hosting pirate material of whose existence they may be entirely ignorant, but also if they potentially may be liable for hosting or giving access to software used to enable illegal file-sharing and downloading by third parties. The controversial US Digital Millennium Copyright Act (DMCA) introduced a detailed code in Title 512 which largely exempts ISPs in the USA from liability for hosting copyright infringing material, but only on certain terms, such as the disclosure of the identity of infringers on request, and subscription to a detailed code of practice relating to notice, 'take-down' and 'put-back';[26] this enactment is of especial interest here as the DMCA liability provisions have something of a family resemblance to the liability regime of the ECD.

---

[23] 'Indirect' copyright infringement cases involving the liability of sites distributing peer-to-peer software which assists in illegal downloading are, as discussed below, a slightly different kettle of fish, though they do clearly have some relevance in the domain. See the discussion of global trends and cases relating to ISP and P2P liability below, at p 135.

[24] See in Europe, EC Copyright Directive 2001/29/EG of the European Parliament and the Council of 22 May 2001, Art 5(1) which includes as an exemption from the exclusive right of reproduction of the author, 'temporary acts of reproduction which are transient or incidental and part of a technological process whose sole purpose is to enable (a) a transmission in a network between third parties by an intermediary and (b) a lawful use of a work or other protected material). There are still doubts that the provisions of the EC Copyright Directive and the ECD on caching are entirely reconcilable: see C van der Net, 'Civil Liability of Internet providers following the Directive on Electronic Commerce' in H Snijders and S Weatherill (eds), *E-commerce Law* (Kluwer, 2003) 53.

[25] See as a brief introduction to P2P technologies, downloading and the law, A Guadamuz, 'Music Downloading: the Basics' at http://www.law.edac.uk/ahrb/publications/online/downloads.htm and accompanying Powerpoint presentation at http://www.law.edac.uk/ahrb/publications/online/musicdownloads.ppt.

[26] See further p 112ff below.

It can be seen from this brief overview that the issue of intermediary liability is not a simple one. In the examples above, we see that ISPs run the risk of being held liable both when providing access to illicit content originated by other content providers (*Felix Somm* case, *Godfrey v Demon*); and when hosting their own local content (*CompuServe* and *Prodigy*); when providing access to their own sub-scribers or publishing to the Internet at large. Furthermore the growth of concern around music and film piracy and P2P networks has exposed ISPs and hosts to potential risk in ways quite different from conventional anticipated forms of 'pub-lication' liability. Some issues, such as P2P liability for ISPs (as opposed to for those who write and distribute P2P software, or those who are end users of P2P networks) are so far both under under-explored in European case law although some, not entirely consistent US case law does exist;[27] another key grey area is whether liability exists when an intermediary makes a hyperlink to a site where illicit content is available, or when such a hyperlink is generated automatically by a locational tool such as a search engine.[28]

As the examples above also suggest, liability issues extend across many different types of content and may raise different issues depending on the type of content. As well as those discussed above, disputes have been reported involving material which is in contempt of court;[29] material to which privacy rights apply (for exam-ple, the *Estelle Halliday* case in France[30]); and material which is blasphemous.[31] As we shall see below, legislation has sometimes been introduced to deal with par-ticular types of content (the UK Defamation Act 1996, the US Digital Millennium Copyright Act) while other legislation is intended to provide immunity in respect of all, or at least a range, of different types of content liability.

[27] See in the US *UMG Recordings, Inc v MP3.Com*, 92 F Supp 2d 349 (SDNY, 2000); and *Universal City Studios, Inc v Reimerdes*, 111 F Supp 2d 294 (SDNY, 2000), both of which roughly suggest that under the DMCA at least ISPs may be liable for hosting and giving access to programmes such as (but not restricted to) P2P software which enable illegal acts by their party users. However by contrast, there *is* case law finding that a P2P software author itself does *not* benefit from ISP immunity under the DMCA—see *A & M Recordings, Inc v Napster, Inc*, 2000 WL 573136 (ND Cal, 12 May 2000).

[28] The early Scottish case of *Shetland Times v Wills* broadly explored the question of whether hyperlinking constituted copyright infringement, but failed to reach a determinative conclusion.

[29] See *R v Barnardo* [1995] Ont CJ Lexis. In the UK in 2001 the ISP Demon successfully asked the courts to grant them an exemption from strict liability for contempt of court; this arose in relation to their fear that they would inevitably be involved in illegal pre trial publicity relating to the 'Jamie Bulger' Thompson and Venables murder trial: see http://www.guardian.co.uk/Archive/Article/0,4273,4222156,00.html.

[30] Tribunal de Grande Instance de Paris, 9 June 1998. See summary at http://www.kahnlaw.com/usa/newsjob/publications/french_isp_cag_dg.htm.

[31] See unreported 1997 UK case involving gay poem found illegal as blasphemous in the UK courts; a host in the UK subsequently linked to that poem (which was hosted physically on a server abroad) and was reported to the police for so doing. A police investigation followed but no charges were to this author's knowledge ever brought. Details at http://www.xs4all.nl/~yaman/linkpoem.htm.

C. Policy Issues in Constructing Legal Regimes for Intermediary Liability

The obvious starting point when exploring intermediary liability is to note that the Internet is a unique medium where no content author or provider can, in general, publish or distribute material on the Net without the aid of an Internet access provider. This immediately put the emerging industry sector of ISPs on the spot as star defenders in early Internet liability cases. In the UK and the US, the attractions for a claimant in libel or defamation of suing an ISP as publisher rather than the actual author of a defamatory comment speedily became apparent—since the ISP was likely to be locatable, with a registered place of business, and probably with significant liquid assets. By contrast, the original defamer might have vanished, acted under the cover of anonymity or pseudonymity,[32] be living in another country where judgements for damages were difficult or impossible to get recognised and enforced, or simply have no attachable assets. As a result, ISPs by virtue of their role as gatekeepers to the Internet, have long felt themselves to be sitting on a liability time-bomb.[33]

This would be unfortunate enough without going on to consider the nature and quantity of the content which ISPs distribute. A commercial ISP typically allows its subscribers access both to read and write to newsgroups or local forums, chatrooms, mailing lists and the millions of Web home pages. This content is not static but may change from minute to minute. This is simply far too much material to be manually checked and supervised for potentially defamatory comment. In comparison a newspaper editor (or that newspaper's lawyer) can generally check over the entire paper each day. Furthermore the content ISPs handle is in the main supplied by persons out of the control of the ISP, whereas a conventional publisher such as a newspaper can limit its risk, for example, issuing acceptability guidelines to its employees, or putting indemnity clauses into contracts with the freelancers who contribute columns. Software filtering technologies, which usually depend on searching for and blocking certain notorious sites by their address, or sites containing certain key-words or images, can be helpful to ISPs which seek to block access to criminal content such as child pornography images, or particularly offensive words but are of no use at all in relation to libel where legal risk may

---

[32] This is true of many well known Internet libel cases. See eg *Godfrey v Demon*, discussed below, and *Zeran v AOL* 1997 US Dist Lexis 3429 (ED Va, 21 March 1997).

[33] The best known case which has provided grounds for such fears is the *Felix Somm* case discussed above n 13, in the Bavarian courts (Germany) where Somm in his capacity as chief executive of CompuServe Europe was sentenced to a jail sentence for distributing obscene material in Bavaria in the form of newsgroups handled routinely by CompuServe. After criticism in both Germany and abroad, the conviction was reversed on appeal on 17 November 1999.

arise as much from a discussion of poetry publishing as a discussion forum on sex or paedophilia.

From the mid 1990s therefore, in the US, the UK, and elsewhere, ISPs made vigorous claims that they should be exempted from liability on the basis of some kind of innocent dissemination defence—essentially claiming that had no effective control over the material they re-distributed, and thus should not be held legally liable in respect of it as publishers. To some extent this argument rested on whether ISPs were seen as more akin to conventional hard copy publishers, or TV and radio broadcasters—who have control over what they publish, and a corresponding duty to check that the material they publish is *not* defamatory—or whether they should be seen as more like 'common carriers' such as the phone company—who are seen as 'mere passive conduits' for information, with no effective control over it, and who are thus usually not held liable for whatever material they carry. Somewhere between the two a third analogy or metaphor can be drawn, to news-stands or bookstores—persons who are responsible for distributing large quantities of potentially defamatory material and have some chance to examine it, but who cannot reasonably be expected to check it all in detail if they are to stay in business.[34]

Two early, widely discussed US cases failed to settle for US law the issue of whether ISPs should have the benefit of an innocent dissemination defence.[35] In *Cubby v CompuServe*,[36] CompuServe were sued in respect of a message appearing in a local forum hosted by them, called 'Rumorville USA'. CompuServe had employed a third party specifically to edit and control the content of this forum. The third party posted the information on the Internet once it was edited, with no intervening opportunity for CompuServe to review the material prior to publication. CompuServe argued that they were merely a distributor of the information, not a publisher, and should therefore not be held liable. The New York District Court agreed, holding that CompuServe was here acting in a way akin to a news-stand, book store or public library, and that to hold it to a higher standard of liability than these distributors, would place undue restrictions on the free flow of electronic information.

But in *Stratton Oakmont Inc v Prodigy Services*,[37] the decision went the opposite way. On similar facts, Prodigy was sued in respect of comments posted to a local discussion forum it hosted. Again, Prodigy had employed persons known as 'board leaders' to monitor and edit the content of the forum and had empowered

---

[34] While this three category analysis is commonly accepted in US law and has by extension penetrated global Internet law, it should be noted that it has been rejected in English law, albeit in the context of hard copy magazine publishing: see *Goldsmith v Sperrings* [1977] 1 WLR 478.

[35] But see now *Zeran v AOL*, discussed below at n 67.

[36] 766 F Supp 135 (SDNY, 1991).

[37] LEXIS 229 (NY Sup Ct, Nassau Co, 1995).

these board leaders to remove material, although only after it was posted. The crucial difference from the CompuServe case (such as there was) was that Prodigy had explicitly marketed itself as 'a family oriented computer network', which as part of its 'value added' services, would control and prevent the publication of inappropriate messages. This seems to have been enough to lead the court to regard Prodigy as the publisher of the libels in question, rather than as a mere distributor, and accordingly they were held liable.[38]

The most unfortunate aspect of the *Prodigy* and *CompuServe* decisions was that the ratio that could most easily be extracted from the two contrasting results was that to avoid liability, an ISP should do as little as possible to monitor and edit the content of the messages or other material it carries. This, it was argued, would make it seem more like a newsstand, and less like a publisher. But such a strategy (which can be labelled the 'put your head in the sand' approach) has unfortunate results both for ISPs and the public interest in the development of the Internet.

For ISPs, the *Prodigy* principle equated any attempt to exercise control over even some of the content the ISP carries, with risk. Yet commercial ISPs, and host sites who double as intermediaries, largely *wish* to provide large amounts of local edited content as a key part of their business strategy. ISPs make some of their money from subscriptions, but increasingly revenue is derived from sponsorship, advertising, and a cut from the business acquired via the ISP by e-commerce sites like Amazon.com. These revenues depend on hit rates and other audience indices, and audiences are gathered partly by providing unique local editorial content; but also by providing easier, faster, more convenient or more sanitised access to key information which is ubiquitously available (such as weather, comment, horoscopes, financial information, news headlines and so forth). ISPs also increasingly gain market share (just as Prodigy was intending to) by offering editorial control and filtering. BT Internet operating in the UK has recently become the first major ISP in the Western world to offer a service which claims to filter out all child pornographic material in advance,[39] while AOL in the UK offer customers a choice of a 'family friendly' filtered service or an 'adult' unfiltered service, and make their filtering services the focus of an expensive advertising campaign. ISPs also of course routinely filter email for spam messages; AOL, for example, reportedly filter out some 80% of the mail which it receives for its customers. However if ISPs

---

[38] *Prodigy* was in fact overruled by the US Supreme Court in a subsequent case, *Lunney v Prodigy Services Co*, on 5 February 2000 (available at http://www.courts.state.ny.us/ctapps/decisions/164opn.htm). However by that time, as discussed below, the force of the decision had been overtaken by the immunity provisions for ISPs introduced in the Communications Decency Act 1996. The case does however confirm that in US law an ISP is now officially regarded as not a publisher at common law.

[39] See 'BT to block access to child porn sites', http://www.out-law.com, 8 June 2004. BT subsequently announced that in the first three weeks of blocking they had already blocked 230,000 attempts to access child pornography sites; one wonders how effective this makes it as a marketing strategy.

do decide to exercise editorial control over *some* content, they will then, following the *Prodigy* reasoning, perhaps enter the class of publishers rather than distributors, and find themselves liable for *all* illegal or actionable material they do 'publish', host or deliver, no matter who originated it and however little actual control the ISP has over it. The ISP industry complain, with some reason therefore, that if they are made to take responsibility for checking every item of content they carry, they will be unable to fulfil this duty due to the volume of traffic,[40] and faced with unquantifiable risk, will either have to go out of business, leave the jurisdiction for one with more helpful laws, or pass the potential insurance costs on to the consumer, thus raising the costs of Internet access.

As well as ISPs, the public and the state have interests at stake in the debate over liability. The public's interest is complex. First, as noted above, ISPs are seen as the natural gatekeepers to the Internet and are unarguably in the best position to filter out and stop the distribution of illegal and offensive content throughout the Internet. If the Internet is truly the information superhighway of ancient cliché (albeit now clogged with spam), then the ISPs are the toll stations at its entrance— the obvious place to stop and inspect the traffic. The EC has had a strong interest in ISPs taking up the role of 'cleaning up the Internet' since the early days of EC Internet policy,[41] not just as might be assumed, to promote public morality and decency and the protection of vulnerable groups such as children, but also so as to allow Europe to catch up with the US in development e-commerce. Europe perceived itself as worryingly lagging behind the USA in the glory days of dot.com boom in developing and exploiting the lucrative e-commerce market[42]—and one of the reasons most often cited for that lag in uptake of e-commerce in Europe was lack of public confidence that the Internet was a safe, secure and respectable medium for commercial transactions. The Net, with its baggage of spam, porn, hate speech, libel and general weirdness, is something of a sleazy downtown in commercial terms: full of loan sharks, dirty magazine stalls and wide boys—certainly not somewhere the average punter would happily leave his or her credit card details. Cleaning up the Net was thus not a matter of mere squeamishness, but a

---

[40] See n 14 above. The UK industry association, the ISPA, continues to protest this vociferously: see www.ispa.org.uk/html/media/content_liability.html, 'It is not possible or practical for an ISP to monitor the content held on their servers because . . . ISPs deal with a vast amount of articles.' They also cite the dynamic quality of Internet content, and how it can be 'changed by the website owner in a matter of seconds'.

[41] See Rec 40 of the ECD which gives the smooth functioning of the Internal Market and prevention of distortions in competition as the first reason for the Directive to concern itself with ISP liability; the prevention of illegal activities is a secondary concern. See also the EC Action Plan on Illegal and Offensive Content which ran from 1999 to 2002, was extended to 2004, and has since been further extended under the name 'Safer Internet Plan' as part of the eEurope 2005 initiative. See now http://europa.eu.int/information_society/eeurope/2005/all_about/action_plan/index_en.htm   and http://www.saferinternet.org/.

[42] For example, in 1998, 7000 US companies were conducting business on-line compared to only 2000 in the EU.

business priority. However public access to the Internet, both for private and public, commercial, personal or e-governmental purposes, was, and is, predicated on
a healthy, cheap and competitive ISP market, which placing unreasonable or
impossible to fulfil burdens on ISPs will not foster (especially as, compared to
most industries, it is not that difficult for ISPs physically to up and move to a more
supportive legal environment).

So the question becomes how best to encourage ISPs to take up an active role in
the control of Internet content without reducing their business efficiency. There is
a general consensus that market forces—the desire to gain and retain market share
in a competitive market for Internet services—will lead ISPs, left to their own
devices, to naturally take on an editorial and filtering role. The most obvious
example of this relates to spam. ISPs which deliver large amounts of unfiltered
spam to its clients are unpopular and rapidly lose market share; hence ISPs have
taken the leading role both in prosecuting spammers and developing anti-spam
technology.[43] Thus the task of legislatures, it seems, is to *protect* ISPs from liability
as content hosts or transmitters, so that they can fulfil their role as editors and
monitors to the extent they find commercially enticing—a self regulatory strategy.
In particular, legislatures should refrain from imposing impossible demands on
hosts and ISPs that they monitor all traffic they carry or all content they host.

If this were not a difficult enough balance, finally there are the interests of what
might be called the 'victims'. The victims of libelous content on the Net, for example, arguably have a right to take action against ISPs who distribute the remarks
that besmirch their reputation to the world, as much as they have against the
original libeler, since it is the ISP after all who is likely to magnify the damage to
reputation by spreading the comments far and wide.[44] Institutional owners of
intellectual property rights—principally the recording, film, software and publishing industries—have also put this side of the argument very strongly indeed.
Authors in particular surely have some kind of moral entitlement to action against
intermediary hosts who give access to the world to pirate copies of their works
even after they have been notified of the problem.[45] Since 2000 or so, the rough
emerging consensus that ISPs should be left as free from liability as possible, has
been substantially shaken by the cash-backed demands of rights-holders in the
content industry that ISPs be somehow compelled to assist them in preventing
copyright piracy. In their eyes, ISPs (particularly since the advent of broadband,
which is the *sine qua non* for effective downloading of films and games) know fine
well that they are making money out of extensive illicit downloading[46] and should

---

[43] See further Chapter 2 in this volume.
[44] See *Zeran v AOL*, above n 32 and discussed below at n 67.
[45] See *Ellison v AOL* 189 F Supp 2d 1051 (CD Cal, 2002), discussed below.
[46] Some commentators have estimated that up to 80% of ISP traffic is now used for P2P downloading. 'P2P packets have been said to comprise up to 80% of some ISP traffic volumes, and these applications are essentially the only ones driving widespread residential broadband deployment.' See
http://www.boardwatch.com/techchannels/oss/.

not be simply allowed to turn a blind eye on the grounds that they are only the 'messenger' and not the actual promoter of piracy, when it is known that many hosted sites and newsgroups are warehouses for illegal copies of software and music files, or repositories from which P2P software can be downloaded. (ISPs themselves on the other hand point out that high bandwidth downloading on fixed rate bandwidth connections tends to loss rather than profit making.)[47] Jack Valenti, former President of the Motion Picture Industry association of America, has spearheaded an onslaught on ISPs intended to prevent them being granted full immunity in respect of downloadable pirate content in the hearings prior to the DMCA.[48] Although Valenti has now moved on, the rights-holders lobby may yet have the potential to unsettle a global consensus on intermediary liability which at the time of drafting of the ECD seemed to be on the point of crystallizing.

D. Approaches to Regulating ISP Liability

Three approaches can be identified as emerging globally:

(i) The '*direct approach*': Broadly this suggests that ISPs be directly threatened with criminal sanctions until they agree to take up their role as gatekeepers, and cleanse the Internet of undesirable content. Such an approach is not uncommon in certain non Western countries where the Internet may be seen as a conduit for dissemination of subversive, seditious and politically unsettling material and ISPs are encouraged forcibly to act as an arm of state censorship.[49] However in the West such an approach has usually been regarded as both practically unworkable, and dangerously likely to impede freedom of speech. An interesting attempt at legislating to this effect recently took place in Australia however, in the form of the early version of the Broadcasting Services Amendment (On Line Services) Act 1999, discussed below.

(ii) The '*self regulation/total immunity*' approach: This, on the other hand, views the market as the best tool for encouraging ISPs to regulate and remove unwanted content. It rests on the belief that ISPs left to their own devices will,

---

[47] Some commentators have estimated that up to 80% of ISP traffic is now used for P2P downloading. 'P2P packets have been said to comprise up to 80% of some ISP traffic volumes, and these applications are essentially the only ones driving widespread residential broadband deployment.' See http://www.boardwatch.com/techchannels/oss/.

[48] See in particular *On-Line Copyright Liability Limitation Act and WIPO Copyright Treaties Implementation Act: Hearing on HR 2280 and HR 2281 Before the House Judiciary Committee, Courts and Intellectual Property Subcommittee*, 105th Cong (1997) (statement of Jack Valenti, President, Motion Picture Industry Association of America).

[49] Reed notes, for example, that in China a form of strict liability is imposed on ISPs who are enjoined *inter alia* to refrain from 'producing, posting or disseminating pernicious information that may jeopardise state security and disrupt social stability, contravene laws and regulations and spread superstition and obscenity'. See C Reed, 'Liability of Online Information Providers—Towards a Global Solution' (2003) 17(3) *International Review Law Computers and Technology* 255 at n 4.

for commercial reasons, naturally take on an editorial and filtering role, if they are not afraid that by taking any kind of control of content they are putting themselves in a position of risk as publishers, distributors or the like. It also recognises sensibly that approach (i) will fail since hosts and ISPs cannot actually physically monitor or control all the content they distribute or host. To facilitate the market-driven approach then, ISPs must be guaranteed total immunity from liability in respect of content they carry—the 'common carrier' ideal. This approach also fits well within the currently dominant liberal paradigm that markets, including the e-commerce and Internet access markets, flourish best with minimum state interference. Thus this paradigm also tends to involve rhetoric about co-decision making of state with industry, and semi official governmental recognition of Codes of Practice issued by industry bodies.[50] What may be given short shrift in this market-driven paradigm is the protection of minority voices in society who actually want mandatory filtering to remove eg racist or pornographic content; and the rights of 'victims' as characterised earlier. Furthermore, total immunity can easily be abused by ISPs, as seen in two US cases discussed below.[51] There are two leading examples of 'total immunity' regulation in global legislation— the US regime for ISPs in respect of all content other than that covered by the DMCA, and the Australian regime in its 'amended' mode, as discussed below.

(iii) The '*limitation of liability/notify and take down*' approach: This is currently the most prevalent approach. It is the approach taken in both the US DMCA and the ECD, Articles 12–15, as well as in numerous other national laws such as the German Multimedia Act 1998, Article 5, and the Japanese law of 2001.[52] This roughly takes the same view as (ii), namely that ISPs will generally be unable to control all content they host or give access to, and so should not be treated as publishers or distributors; but on the other hand it recognises that the gift of total immunity should be balanced against other policy factors, such as the need to protect 'victims' (including, especially, holders of intellectual property rights) and the public interest in controlling the growth in undesirable speech on-line.

---

[50] See discussion of both the practice and the rhetoric of self regulation and codes of practice in the Oxford University Centre for Socio-Legal Studies, Programme in Comparative Media Law and Policy (PCMLP) and IAPCODE joint research paper *Self-Regulation of Digital Media Converging on the Internet: Industry Codes of Conduct in Sectoral Analysis*, April 2004, available at http://www.selfregulation.info/iapcoda/0405–iapcode-final.pdf. The work was commissioned by the European Commission.

[51] See *Zeran v AOL and, Blumenthal v Drudge*, discussed below pp 111–2

[52] Law No 137 of 2001. See I Yamaguchi, 'Beyond de Facto Speech: Digital Transformation of Free Speech Theory in Japan' (2002) 38(1) *Stanford J Intl L* 109 at 114.

1. The 'Direct' Approach

As noted, this involves the direct application of criminal sanctions to ISPs and Internet content hosts where they host, or (sometimes) give access to, illegal or undesirable content. The Australian experience with the Broadcasting Services Amendment (On Line Services) Act 1999, which, after a chequered legislative history, came into force on 1 January 2000[53] is instructive here. This complicated enactment will here only be addressed in outline[54] from the perspective of ISP liability, ignoring many issues relating to Internet hosts who are not also ISPs (eg, the whole question of censorship of private material on home PCs.)

The Australian scheme was much vilified on its introduction to the public in Bill form, by all ISPs, some lawyers, and most anti censorship activists. A representative quote from Brendan Scott of Gilbert and Tobin, Solicitors gives a flavour. The Bill was described as:

> A totally unworkable administrative process to implement regulation that internet users do not want and it casts its net so broadly as would serve quite adequately as the groundwork for a totalitarian state. It is the sort of legislation that Voltaire would have railed against at the dawn of the Age of Reason and it is just this sort of legislation that should be vigorously opposed.[55]

The controversial legal regime ushered in by this Act was largely seen as a political gesture indicating the government's commitment to cleaning up both Internet content hosted and physically held in Australia, and content physically held abroad but accessible in Australia via Australian ISPs. When originally introduced, the shape of the scheme was broadly that Australian ISPs were required either to remove 'prohibited content'[56] if they physically hosted the offending material within Australia (by order of a 'take-down' notice); or to block access to it if it was physically held abroad (by order of an 'access-prevention' notice). The sanctions for failing to do so were draconian: a scale fine of A$27,500 per day was imposed for failure to meet these duties, accumulating on a daily basis.

---

[53] See at http://scaleplus.law.gov.au/html/comact/10/6005/0/CM000060.htm.

[54] There is a great deal of literature on the Australian scheme, although care has to be taken to separate criticism written at different stages of the Bill as the content changed under pressure applied. Good sites critiquing the proposals are Electronic Freedom Australia *passim* (http://www.efa.org.au) and the CSIRO media release on the ineffectiveness of the government proposals (http://www.csiro.au/news/mediarel/mr1999/mr9975.html). The Second Reading Speech for the Bill which outlines the governmental policy behind the Bill is at http://www.dcita.gov.au/nsapi-text/MIval=dca_dispdoc&ID=3761. The Act has been analysed cogently by C Penfold, 'Nazis, Porn and Politics: Asserting Control over Internet Content' (2001) 2 *JILT* at http://elj.warwick.ac.uk/jilt/01–2/penfold.html; and C Penfold, 'The Content Control that Wasn't: Two Years of the Online Services Amendment' (2002) 11 *Inf Comm Tech L* 141.

[55] B Scott, 'The Dawn of a New Dark Age—Censorship and Amendments to the Broadcasting Services Act' at http://ww.gtlaw.com.au/pubs/newdarkage.html.

[56] 'Prohibited content' was that classified as Refused Classification (RC) or X by the National Classification Board.

Appalled reaction met this scheme both from the Australian ISP industry and the global cyber rights community. The main practical complaint was that it was simply not possible to block access to foreign content effectively. Blocking could be evaded if the foreign site changed its URL, or merely changed its underlying IP address (which would not require a change of URL and hence not confuse existing customers.) Foreign proscribed sites could also still be accessed by using a foreign proxy server site as an anonymiser. A change to the wording of the then Bill which allowed ISPs only to take steps which were 'technically and commercially feasible' did not assuage the flood of complaints. Furthermore if access-prevention was impossible, it was said, then take-down of domestic content was also largely futile. Internet content is extremely portable, and any domestic site served with a take-down notice could fairly easily transfer itself to a foreign site simply by signing on with a foreign ISP; which would then be equally accessible by the Australian public.

Faced with a potentially very embarrassing situation, the Australian government appeared to retreat to a compromise solution. A late draft of the Bill had introduced the concept that some ISPs who agreed to comply with a Code of Practice formulated by agreement between the ABA and an ISP industry body might be exempted from access-prevention notices. This had first been thought of as an exceptional provision, to exempt only ISPs which already provided a high standard of content filtering (for example ISPs providing services to schools), and thus had no need of being served with access-prevention notices as well. By the time the Bill was finally passed however, compliance with a Code, if one was accepted by the ABA, had entirely replaced the issue of access-prevention notices.[57] When the Internet Industry of Australia's (IIA) Code of Practice was finally accepted by the ABA, it required only that ISPs undertake to make software filtering tools from an approved list available to their subscribers (and, if they wished, at the expense of the subscriber).[58] These tools would filter out URLs of sites which had been classified as illicit by the Classification Board and those URls would be regularly updated. Subscribers, however, could not be compelled to take delivery of these filtering tools, nor to use them, make their children use them, or keep them updated. As a result, the IIA's own *Guide for Internet Users* in December 1999 shortly before the coming into force of the Act pronounced that: 'We anticipate that industry developed code alternatives will entirely circumvent ABA action in respect of internationally sourced content.'[59]

In other words, a legal regime aimed at exerting direct censorship over ISPs decayed almost without notice to a regime which was in essence totally self

[57] See s 40(1)(b) of the 1999 Act.
[58] See Internet Industry Code of Practice, draft 6.0, December 1999, para 6.2, at http://www.iia.net.au/code6.html. Note the current version of the code is 7.2, available at http://www.iia.net.au/contentcode.html.
[59] See http://www.iia.net.au/guide.html.

regulatory (at least in relation to foreign content). In all cases where foreign content is classified as 'prohibited' according to Australian law, a public access-prevention notice need not be served—which would at least provide transparency and potentially arouse global publicity and international concern—but instead the URL of the offending site will merely be passed to the makers of the approved software filtering tools so these can be updated to block those sites.[60] Essentially the Australian system has moved from one of overt censorship imposed by publicly debated legislation, to covert filtering backed by industry developed 'soft law', an acceptably moderate self regulatory regime. As predicted, furthermore, the still-extant domestic 'direct effect' regime is now entirely circumventible. In the first three months of the Act coming into operation, out of 45 foreign sites that were deemed 'prohibited content', 17 were originally Australian hosted.[61] Domestic Australian content hosts coming under fire by direct criminal sanction thus, it seems, merely relocated abroad. Unless all states in the world can be persuaded at once to sign up for a 'direct effect' regime then, it seems unlikely to be highly effective, as sites hosting illicit material will simply vote with their electronic feet and domestic ISPs are unlikely to be able to effectively block that content. As Penfold summarises: 'There is no evidence that objectionable Internet content is any less accessible than two years ago or that individuals or families now have better ability to manage access to Internet content for themselves.'[62]

2. The 'Total Immunity/Self Regulation' Approach

The Australian experience provides a remarkable example of a regime which was initially one of the most radical in the world in applying direct penalties to secure removal of undesirable content from the Internet, being diluted to the point where, taking into account that Australian ISPs were also guaranteed total immunity in respect of all laws other than the Broadcasting Offences Act,[63] it is one of the most self-regulatory in the world. So long as ISPs supply the required filtering technology to customers and abide by the Code of Practice, they are immune from liability for foreign-hosted content.

---

[60] See the ABA report, *Internet content complaints scheme—the first 3 months* at http://www.aba.gov.au/about/public_relations/newrel_2000/27nr2000.htm, which reveals that in the first 3 months of operation, take down was ordered in respect of 31 items of Australian-hosted content, 45 items of content hosted outside Australia were referred to the makers of filtering software products and 7 items of content were referred to law enforcement agencies. See also the EFA assessment of the working of the 1999 Act issued in November 2002 at http://www.efa.org.au/Publish/efasubm_bsa2002.html.

[61] *Ibid,* Table 2. See also 'Down Under Smut Goes Up and Over', *Wired*, 2 February 2000, at http://www.wired.com/news/politics/0,1283,34043,00.html, which describes the move of www.teenager.com.au (an Australian teen sex site) to a US server after a take down notice was issued.

[62] C Penfold, n 57 above, 'The Content Control that Wasn't', p 154.

[63] 1999 Act, Sch 5, s 91.

The Australian regime was mainly aimed at obscene or pornographic material. The other main extant example of a total immunity/self regulation regime was also mainly aimed at pornography, and also, interestingly, arrived on the scene almost by legislative accident. The Communications Decency Act 1996 ('the CDA') was the first federal US attempt at controlling obscene or indecent content in cyber-space in a long line of Acts which have foundered on the rock of the First Amendment.[64] The CDA's primary goal was to prohibit the publication of obscene or indecent speech in cyberspace wherever it might be known to be acces-sible by a minor child—unfortunately, given the inherently un-zoned nature of most of the Internet, this was everywhere it appeared. The legislature took the view that the Act would only be enforceable if ISPs, in return for their co-operation in monitoring and filtering content, were granted the *quid pro quo* of absolute immu-nity as publishers, in respect of civil, criminal and statutory liability for all content originated by a third party.[65] Effectively, the *Prodigy* case (discussed above) was being reversed by statute. These main provisions of the CDA were however later struck down by the US Supreme Court as being unreasonably in breach of the con-stitutional rights of freedom of speech of adults.[66] Meanwhile however the statu-tory "safe harbor" for ISPs remained in force, and has operated, as was held in the case of *Zeran v AOL*,[67] to wholly suspend actions in common law (including actions for negligence and defamation) against ISPs for publishing material origi-nated by another content provider. In *Zeran,* the Eastern Virginia District Court found that the existence of the CDA pre-empted the right of the court to hear an action for libel and negligent mis-statement brought against AOL.[68] Imposition of common law liability on AOL would have frustrated the objective of section 230(c), which was to encourage ISPs to put in place monitoring and blocking con-trols so as to restrict circulation on the Internet of offensive material. Accordingly the action was struck out.

The US experience provides interesting insight into why a 'total immunity' regime is not entirely a good idea. In the case of *Zeran,* above, for example, Mr Zeran was libelled by an anonymous prankster who posted a message to an AOL forum offering t-shirts for sale glorifying the infamous Oklahoma bomber, and giving Mr Zeran's real name and address as the contact for the sales. Mr Zeran then

[64] See also the Children's Online Protection Act (COPA) and the Child Obscenity and Pornography Prevention Act (COPPA). By contrast, the Children's Internet Protection Act (CIPA), which mandates filtering in libraries, has been adjudged constitutional: see *US v ALA,* US Supreme Court, No 02–361 (23 June 2003).

[65] See s 230 (c) which provides 'No provider or user of an interactive computer service shall be treated as the publisher or speaker of any information provided by another content provider.' See fur-ther judicial interpretation in *Zeran v America On-Line* 1997 US Dist Lexis 3429 (ED VA, 21 March 1997); *Blumenthal v Drudge* 1998 BNA EC&L 561.

[66] Supreme Court decision in *Reno v ACLU,* 1997 2 BNA EPLR 664, available at http://www.aclu.org/court/renovacludec.html.

[67] 1997 US Dist Lexis 3429 (ED VA, 21 March 1997).

[68] See also *Doe v America Online Inc,* Fla Cir Ct, Palm Beach Cty, No CL 97–631 AE, 13 June 1997.

suffered extreme harassment from persons incensed at his apparent bad taste. He asked AOL to remove the posting but they refused. When he sued them as publishers of a libel, they relied on section 230(c) and were accordingly exculpated. Total immunity had given them carte blanche to ignore the legitimate demands of victims.

Another significant US case is *Blumenthal v Drudge*.[69] AOL paid Drudge, a well known political hack, $36,000 a year to provide them with an on line political gossip column. Blumenthal, a Clinton aide, sued AOL for publishing an item libelling him within Drudge's column. Although AOL clearly benefited from the content Drudge supplied in terms of audience capture, since the content was provided by a third party not AOL, they were immune from any suit. Since AOL gained profit from Drudge's willingness to recklessly defame others, this was a clearly unjust result. Interestingly there has recently been some retrenchment in US case law against the high water mark of immunity achieved in *Zeran* and *Blumenthal*—see discussion at p 129 below—but this has not so far reached the stage of a consistent reversal of the general 'total immunity' granted by section 230(c).

So far we have seen that the 'direct approach' is something of an unworkable solution and invidious to the prosperity of the Internet industry, while the 'total immunity' approach is open to abuse from ISPs and poor at protecting the interests of 'victims' and incentivising ISPs to take an active role in removing illicit content from the Internet. What then of the third, middle ground approach?

3. The 'Limitation of Liability/Notify and Take Down' Approach: The ECD Rules and the DMCA

The ECD takes a horizontal approach to ISP liability—in other words it deals with all kinds of content issues, whether intellectual property, criminal obscenity, libel, etc—rather than focusing on a single area. Furthermore, rather than giving a blanket immunity to ISPs in all circumstances where the content is provided by a third party other than the ISP, as the US CDA section 230(c) does, it takes a more subtle approach in which the various activities of ISPs are addressed separately. Where ISPs act as a 'mere conduit'—ie, as a relay station transmitting content originated by and destined for other parties—the Directive, in the form of Article 12, regards them as basically absolved from all liability. To maintain immunity, the ISP must not initiate the transmission, select the receiver of the transmission or modify the information contained in the transmission.[70] This is very much in line

---

[69] See n 65 above.

[70] Art 12. Transmission includes automatic, intermediate, and transient storage. Presumably 'information' excludes header information which ISPs routinely and automatically add to through traffic they forward. Such header information is vital to the routing of packets through the Internet to their destination, but does not form part of the message information actually read by the recipient.

with the position as to liability for 'common carriers' such as the post office and the phone company. The Directive also makes it clear[71] that ISPs will not be held liable simply because they cache material. Caching, as noted above, is a common practice whereby ISPs and hosts (such as universities and large businesses with their own servers) store a local copy of a Web page that has been retrieved from a remote server at a user's request, so that any future requests for that page by other users can be met more quickly. The effect of caching is to speed up the Web for all users since traffic is reduced. It is therefore important that caching not be legally discouraged lest the Internet slow to a crawl. As with the 'mere conduit' provision, immunity is subject to the requirement the information not be modified by the ISSP and also that the cached copy be updated regularly according to industry practice. More controversially, immunity is also subject to the ISSP taking down cached copies once they obtain actual knowledge that the original source of the information has been removed or access to it disabled, or removal or blocking of access has been ordered by a competent court or authority. These provisions may be a serious concern for some hosts, notably search engines, who sometimes maintain copies of material locally to assist searchers even when they have moved on the original site, and mirror sites set up to reduce the demand on a single site offering popular pages.[72] These ECD rules are largely replicated verbatim in the UK implementation of Articles 12 and 13 in the Electronic Commerce (EC Directive) Regulation 2002, Regulations 17 and 18.[73]

E. Hosting, Notice and Take Down: The Self Regulation Conundrum

The main controversy in the EC regime has centred on the hosting provisions in Article 14, which deals with circumstances where ISPs host or store more than transiently content originated by third parties. These rules most, typically,

---

[71] In Art 13. Worries that the European Parliament had introduced provisions incompatible with Art 13 at the draft stage of another EC Directive, on copyright and related rights, were partially allayed by the final text. See further discussion below n 24.

[72] See further discussion on notice and take down in relation to Art 14 below. Immunity for caching is most obviously relevant to content copied by an ISP *prima facie* in breach of copyright. However it is conceivable that a cached copy of a page containing libellous or obscene material might be deemed to be 'published' by an ISP or host since it can still be retrieved by other subscribers to that ISP seeking that particular page until the cache is purged. In the US, cease and desist letters under the DMCA demanding 'take down' of material infringing the copyright of the rights-holder are now frequently being received by the search engine Google, which maintains cached copies for a short period of material even after it has been removed from the original host site. See, as sample, report of such request from Church of Scientology to Google at http://chillingeffects.org/dmca512/notice.cgi?NoticeID=1352 and request for removal of a 'collection of recipes' at http://chillingeffects.org/dmca512/notice.cgi?NoticeID=1327.

[73] SI 2002 No 2013.

perhaps, apply to the situation where an ISP physically finds space on its server for files (HTML or otherwise) belonging to each of its subscribers as part of its core commercial operations. But they may also extend to a chatroom hosting conversations in real time by its nick-named participants; a pornographic website which encourages its subscribers to post pictures of their wives in compromising positions; a university which gives every student an electronic place to store their essays, email and research; a 'weblog' site where millions of users contribute daily the details of their intimate private lives in the expectation of confidentiality and often anonymity; the BBCi site where vast amounts of information about news, culture, the media and the arts is updated every day for the public good; the Google search engine site which is more and more the key to looking for information in the giant information ant-heap that is the modern Internet; and an aggregator site which collates news stories from multiple different news sites without originating any content of its own at all. As might be imagined, these very different types of intermediaries pose different types of challenges to the basic rules. One important point is that Article 14(2) provides that content is not to be treated as originating from a third party if that recipient acts 'under the authority ot control of the [ISSP]'—thus the ECD avoids the difficulties found in Blumenthal above, where Drudge would almost certainly have been found to be acting under the 'authority' of AOL and hence AOL would not have benefited from immunity.

Under Article 14, information society service providers (ISSPs) are declared exempt from liability in respect of the storage of information provided by a recipient of their services, so long as they have no 'actual knowledge' of 'illegal activity or information' (criminal liability); and, as regards claims for damages (civil liability) are immune as long as they have no such actual knowledge *and* are not aware of 'facts and circumstances from which the illegal activity or information is apparent'. Although this implies that ISSPs may be liable in civil though not in criminal law for constructive as well as actual knowledge, it is made very clear that they do not have to go out and actively *seek* this awareness in Article 15. This provides that EC states are not to impose any general monitoring requirement on ISSPs, although ISSPs may be asked to inform the authorities of allegedly illegal activities they do happen to come across. Some commentators have expressed confusion at this proviso on the grounds that it is unreasonable to expect an ISSP to avoid liability under the 'constructive knowledge' provisions relating to civil liability of Article 14 if it cannot be asked to monitor proactively under Article 15, especially given that Recital 48 provides that it is still possible for states to require ISSPs 'to apply duties of care which can reasonably be expected from them and which are specified by national law, in order to detect and prevent certain types of illegal activities'.[74] The best solution here seems to be to take the purposive inter-

---

[74] See R Bagshaw, 'Downloading Torts: An English Introduction to On-Line Torts' in H Snijders and S Weatherill (eds), *E-Commerce Law* (Kluwer, 2003).

pretation that both the caveat to the prohibition on monitoring in Article 15 and Recital 48 refer to duties of care in a public national security context only, even though neither in fact uses that terminology. For example, in the UK, ISPs might still be (and indeed are) asked to monitor and intercept transmissions under the Regulation of Investigatory Powers Act 2000 for purposes of crime prevention and national security. The 'duties of care' however should not be read as extending to ordinary duties under private law since that would negate the point of Article 15 in the context of the Directive's hosting provisions generally. In practice, the main debate around Articles 14 and 15 has concerned not constructive knowledge but actual knowledge, and its implications in the forms of 'notice and take down'.

What if an ISP is told by an aggrieved member of the public that a Web site the ISP hosts contains material defaming him or her and will the ISP please take it down immediately? Does the ISP become liable immediately since they now have actual 'knowledge' or 'awareness' that the content may be illegal? Article 14(1)(b) in response provides specifically that so long as the ISP 'acts expeditiously to remove or to disable access to the information', they will retain their protection from liability, even after notice. No guidance is given in the Directive as to what 'expeditious' means, however, and whether it allows enough time to, for example, consult an in house lawyer, find an external lawyer or request counsel's opinion. In large ISPs it may take some time for a take-down request to find the appropriate employee while in small ISPs it may be difficult to identify an employee with the resources to take charge of the request; and how these indoor management issues affect 'expedience' is also unclear. Article 14, furthermore, seems to imply that once notice has been given and the expedient period of grace expired, liability is strict even if take-down presents technical or administrative problems. A better alternative might be, as the German Multimedia Act and indeed, the Australian legislation discussed above provide, for liability to arise only after the ISP has failed to take some kind of 'reasonable steps'. As discussed above, this problem of whether mere fulfilment of a reasonable level of duty or actual removal/blocking of content should be demanded, is exacerbated further when we talk of access-prevention, but it is also relevant to ordinary hosting liability.

This issue of 'notice and take down' has become the key object of controversy in the EC regime, and has so far only been explored once in UK case law, in *Godfrey v Demon Internet*,[75] a decision which preceded implementation of the ECD but was dealt with under a similar set of rules in the UK Defamation Act 1996, section 1. The case involved allegations by a British physicist, Lawrence Godfrey, that an anonymous hoax message posted in a newsgroup, soc.culture.thai, in 1997, was libelous and damaging to his reputation. Godfrey asked the ISP Demon, who carried the newsgroup in question, to remove the offensive posting. When Demon did not comply, Godfrey raised an action against them for publishing a libel.

[75] Above n 18.

Demon claimed the benefit of the section 1 defence under the Defamation Act 1996, which provided, in substance much as Article 14 now does, that an ISP loses its claim to immunity as a host if it can no longer claim that it 'did not know and had no reason to believe what [it] did contributed to the publication of a defamatory statement'.[76] Because Demon *had* been notified of the allegedly libellous posting and not removed it, the judge held that they clearly fell foul of section 1(1)(c) and thus could not take advantage of the section 1 defence.[77]

The message forcibly sent by *Godfrey* to ISPs was that, in the interest of avoiding litigation, they would be best served by removing or blocking access to any item of content hosted by them which was brought to their notice without too much fuss, however unfounded or trivial the objection might seem to be. Cyberliberty groups protested that this had serious implications for freedom of expression since in effect, any crank caller or pressure group could now censor text posted on the Internet simply by complaining that it was illegal to the ISP. ISPs may thus be forced into taking part in what has been termed 'privatised censorship' even though they do not have the constitutional authority or legal knowledge of a court or lawyer, nor, in general, the desire to take on the role of a court. (Small or free ISPs may not even have anyone on staff who is legally qualified, or even if so, still may not be knowledgeable in the niceties of Internet law, libel, copyright, privacy and obscenity law).[78] One constraining factor on an ISP's willingness to take down might be that if access to a Web site is removed as containing illegal material, but it is later exculpated in court, the ISP might conceivably suffer a breach of contract claim from the content provider whose material was taken down. In this worst case scenario, an ISP might fairly consider itself hard done to: damned if it does take down and damned if it doesn't. In the US under the regime of the DMCA Title 512, by contrast, when an ISP 'takes down' on request of a rights-holder in good faith it benefits from a safe harbor which protects it from any liability arising from that take down. No such equivalent protection exists in the ECD or in the UK rules implementing it (although as the Directive is a minimum harmonisation there is no reason states cannot introduce such). It seems likely from anecdotal evidence, though, that ISPs in any case regard the easiest way out of a difficult situation as to take down first and hope not to be in breach of

---

[76] 1996 Act, s 1(1)(c).

[77] The case was subsequently settled. Demon originally publicly stated their intention to appeal on the s 1 defence point, but later dropped the appeal, ostensibly because they were anticipating legislative change, but probably because of the adverse publicity they received as at the time they were going through a takeover battle.

[78] See discussion in C Ahlert, C Marsden and C Yung, 'How Liberty Disappeared from Cyberspace: the Mystery Shopper Tests Internet Content Self-Regulation' ('*Mystery Shopper*') cited at http://pcmlp.socleg.ox.ac.uk/text/liberty.pdf. In a survey of Dutch ISPs, out of 5 who responded, none said they would involve a lawyer in examining take down requests. The overall impression given is that ISPs regarded dealing with take down requests as a time sink which did not contribute to their core business goals.

contract second. Well drafted terms of the subscriber contract can probably control the latter risk, and consumer-oriented ISPs may also rely on the inertia of consumers in relation to litigation, while the former risk of being held liable for illegal material not removed expeditiously is one which cannot easily be avoided by private mechanisms[79] and may attract the attention of efficient public or industry law enforcement authorities where obscenity and copyright infringement are concerned. Empirical research conducted by Oxford researchers for the EU into the mechanism of notice and take down in the ISP industry concluded in 2004 that 'the current regulatory settlement has created an environment in which the incentive to take down content from the Internet is higher than the potential costs of not taking it down.'[80]

It is useful to take the *Godfrey* case and change the facts a little. What if the libel Godfrey complained of related to matters which were in fact potentially privileged in English libel law, as there was a public duty to reveal those facts?[81] What duty if any would the ISSP come under either to check the facts or consider the law relating to the potential defence? Would they, in practice, be likely to engage in any checks at all? As already noted, the time available for verification for an ISSP is already likely to be limited given the vagueness of the term 'expediently'. The wording 'illegal activity or information' is also unhelpfully loose here. It can be argued that until an ISSP has checked if a defence is indeed relevant and operable, it does not have knowledge of 'illegal activity'—merely of alleged illegality.[82] The earlier version of the ECD in draft was more supportive of such an interpretation than the final text. In practice, there is little constraint on an ISP—and little incentive—to do any investigation at all. In research carried out at Oxford known as the 'Mystery Shopper' test,[83] a major UK ISP was asked to take down a web page which was alleged to be a pirate copy being hosted in breach of the copyright of the complaining rights-holder. In fact the web page contained Chapter II of John Stuart

---

[79] In fact to some extent it can be: this writer has earlier recommended (see Edwards, 'Defamation and the Internet' (2000), above n 3) that ISPs could take out liability insurance against potential risk, as other commercial operations do when specific legal challenges about their activities are brought to their attention; or could insert into contracts with their own subscribers clauses which require such subscribers to indemnify them if the ISP subsequently incurs legal liability as a result of content originated by that subscriber. However it seems that the market has not developed support for either suggestion. See *Rightswatch* report conducted by the MCPS-PRS Alliance, on behalf of the European Community, November 2002–January 2003 (www.Rightswatch.com), s 9.10 (on insurance) and 9.2 (on indemnities). Consumer indemnity clauses might also be challengeable as unfair under European and UK consumer protection legislation such as the EC Unfair Terms Directive and the Unfair Contract Terms Directive 1977.

[80] *Mystery Shopper*, above n 80, at 12.

[81] This claim was made in an English Internet libel case not concerned with ISP liability, *Loutchansky v Times Newspapers* [2001] 4 All ER 115, where the alleged libel related to claims that Russian businessmen living in London were connected to the mob activities, a matter of public interest.

[82] See earlier comments to this effect in Edwards, 'Defamation and the Internet', 2000, above n 3. See also Bagshaw, above n 74, pp 72–73.

[83] See '*Mystery Shopper*', above n 80.

Mill's 'On Liberty' which was published in 1869 and had long been in the public domain. Nonetheless the webpage was removed without demur.[84]

Another issue around notice and take-down relates to who has or should have authority to demand take-down, and what should happen if take-down is disputed. What if Godfrey had complained to his ISP that his children could access a site where men and women were having sex in some grossly indecent way? Should the ISP remove (or disable access to) the site for fear Godfrey would complain to the police and they might become liable, having been put on notice, for distributing pornography? It is quite likely given the state of UK law that obscenity involving adults as opposed to children might not actually be illegal at all. While Godfrey at least had 'locus' to complain in relation to material allegedly libeling him, and a rights-holder such as a music publisher has clear interest in the take-down of pirate material, here we might ask who made Godfrey the agent of enforcement of public morality? Godfrey's dislikes may not correspond to what is legal under UK law and certainly not what might be legal in the place where the offending site's server is located (the 'country of origin' rather than the 'country of destination'—considered below).[85] Again an ISP's instinct is probably however to take down and attempt to minimise both irritation to customer base, the possibility of damaging publicity (no ISP likes to be seen as the distributor of pornography) and potential criminal legal risk.

Continuing the previous example, what if the owners of the porn site complained about wished to deny that their site was illegal and wished it to stay up or remain accessible from the ISP in question (given that pornography is mostly not given away for free, but is a very lucrative business)? Nothing in the EC regime even requires notification to the site whose content is taken down and largely this would be a matter for each ISP's contractual rules and internal procedures. The requirement of 'expedient' take-down of course again encourages an ISP even further to take down now, and notify later, if at all. Yet arguably until content has been proven illegal by a court or at least authoritatively labelled as such by a relevantly authorised professional such as a prosecutor (the approach taken in the Belgian implementation of the ECD) it should remain in place, otherwise administrative prior restraint is effectively operating to 'chill' freedom of speech and restrict the reasonable contractual expectations of content providers. Again, in the US, the DMCA has on the whole been widely applauded for its more sophisticated

---

[84] Similar results were found in a similar experiment carried out subsequently by Sjoera Nas at Bits of Freedom, a digital human rights group based in the Netherlands. Nas, posing as copyright owner and complainant, asked 10 Dutch ISPs to remove works by Multatuli, a Dutch writer who died in 1860 and hence was in the public domain. 7 providers took down the text without apparently checking it out at all; one failed to respond to the complaint; one examined the text complained of and noted it was in the public domain (xs4all, a small ISP with a history of digital rights activism) and one forwarded the complaint to the website owner. Her 'takedown hit rate' was thus 70%. See further http://www.bof.nl/docs/researchpaperSANEpdf.

[85] Infra, p 126.

treatment of some of these difficult issues. Broadly, the same attitude to notify and take down is implemented as in the ECD, Article 14 and the Defamation Act 1996, section 1, except that there is provision that a take-down notice *must* be notified to the 'owner' of the material which is to be taken down, who then has the opportunity to intervene and protest that the material should not be removed. If that person disputes that there is copyright infringement then the material in question is 'put back' by the ISP. If the original notifier then continues to dispute the legality of the content, the argument can be moved fairly rapidly into the courts and away from the 'privatised' extra-judicial control of ISPs, who may not understand the finer detail of copyright defences such as fair use nor even know what works are indeed copyright and which in the public domain. While dispute is under way, the ISP is given 'safe harbor' to keep the content up, free from liability even if in the end a court does decide the content was illicit or actionable. The DMCA also has strict rules that the person demanding take-down must properly identify themselves as the rights-holder with locus to demand take-down (using digital signature identification if requesting take-down by email); however this is of course an easier issue to deal with in the context of copyright and rights-holders, than obscenity where every member of the public arguably has an interest to complain.

If these issues raised by notice and take-down seem perplexing, the scenario becomes even more complex when one considers the growing tend toward notice and take-down being organized on an institutional rather than a mere *ad hoc* individual basis. In the area of child pornography in the UK, a non-governmental organization, the Internet Watch Foundation,[86] has since 1996 existed to provide a means by which the ISP industry as a whole can receive directions as to whether allegedly illegal content complained about by the public should be taken down or have access to it blocked. The IWF provides a free hot-line channel and a website, so that the public can report by phone, email or fax offensive material they encounter on the Internet. The IWF, which has a membership largely drawn from the ISP industry, law enforcement and children's charities, but is not a court or tribunal with legal standing or training, then vets these reports of objectionable content and takes action if appropriate, which can consist of some combination of making a report to the UK police (if the item appears to have originated within the UK), reporting to the National Crime Intelligence Service (NCIS) (who organise liaison with foreign police forces), or recommending removal of the item from the servers of UK ISPs (which may be the only way to deny access in the UK where the item is of foreign origin, which overwhelmingly most often it is). The IWF was initially conceived as a way to stop ISPs being prosecuted by the police for failing to take an active role in removing pornography from their servers, following threatened action by the London Metropolitan force.[87] In essence it is primarily an

---

[86] http://www.iwf.org.uk.
[87] See D Wall, 'Policing and the Regulation of the Internet' [1998] *Criminal L Rev, Special Edition on Crime, Criminal Justice and the Internet* 79.

industry self-regulatory body and freedom of expression is, understandably, not one of its main priorities (though according to the rhetoric of its annual reports, child protection is). The IWF, it can be argued, is actually good news for free speech since it means take down requests will at least be mediated rather than simply complied with on a casual basis by individual ISPs lacking time and legal resources; and IWF decision making is also to some small extent transparent as statistics are issued about types of complaints and action taken. By contrast the Oxford research[88] clearly seems to suggest that individual ISPs when considering complaints may be neither accountable, transparent nor necessarily applying the relevant legal rules. On the other hand, the IWF at one point very strongly took the view that they would only adjudicate on child pornography complaints since they indicated material which was (a) illegal without, in practice, any complicated legal exemptions,[89] and (b) obvious in its character even to the legally untrained eye. However the IWF is now according to its own website dealing with complaints of hate and racist speech.[90] The legal niceties of these are far more challenging for laypersons, with obviously worrying consequences of the 'chilling effects' variety.

The IWF is largely regarded by the public (and the EU) as a success story, its possibly deleterious effects on free speech mostly seen as less important than the public service it provides in suppressing access to illegal content, especially to children. It is questionable if the same public interest justification can be applied to a body designed to rationalise take-down in respect of illegal *copyright* material. Copyright infringement was once rarely imagined as directly involving issues of public freedom of speech and covert censorship. However the persuasive forces of the Creative Commons lobby have very successfully focused attention on the power that 'cease and desist' letters have to silence public debate and lock up the public domain.[91] In the UK, ISPA research from 2002 found that over half of all take-down requests to UK ISPs concerned copyright material;[92] the figure is now probably much higher. Should take-down requests by IP rights-holders be funneled via a single non-judicial institutional body which would then be in a position to exert considerable influence over ISPs in relation to take-down of

---

[88] See 'Mystery Shopper', above n 80.

[89] Although see for the claim that possession of child pornography was for the purposes of scientific research, *Whitelaw* case, Paisley Sheriff Court, Scotland, February 2003. Whitelaw's defence was that the material was intended for the database of files created by his firm to help companies combat inappropriate use of the Internet by staff.

[90] See IWF Annual Report for 2003 at http://www.iwf.org.uk/about/annual_report/, which reports that racial abuse complaints in 2003 were up 101%.

[91] See especially the 'Chilling Effects Clearinghouse' at http://www.chillingeffects.org/, a joint project of the Electronic Frontier Foundation and Harvard, Stanford, Berkeley, University of San Francisco, University of Maine, and George Washington School of Law clinics, which gives notice to the public of 'cease and desist' take-down letters received by a wide variety of host including, notably, the search engine Google. Creative Commons operate at http://www.creativecommons.org in the USA and at http://creativecommons.org/projects/international/uk/ in the UK See further n 74 above.

[92] *'Mystery Shopper'*, above n 80 at n 39.

alleged pirate material, just as the IWF does in relation to obscene material? This was one of the initial suggestions considered by the Rightswatch project funded by the EC from 2002–03. In the end however the project members could not reach agreement on what the role of such an institution would be: whether it should merely act as a 'postbox', should investigate and validate complaints, or should actively search for hosted pirate material. Most significantly, the Rightswatch project revealed substantial dissensus between the interests of the various stakeholders in the market. Four stakeholder groups were identified: ISPs, rights-holders, content providers and 'users' or the public. 'Trusted' major rights-holders such as music companies had their own legal staff and procedures in place and saw no advantage in a mediating third party. Smaller 'non-trusted' rights-holders feared that they would be given less rights and less hearing than major rights-holders in an institutional scheme. The ISP sector's main concern was not for improved validation of the legal substance of take-down requests—indeed their overwhelming wish was to avoid making difficult, time consuming, unpopular and costly[93] decisions about take-down—but for a legally enforceable safe harbour to protect them from suit if and when they responded to take-down notices. For them, a new self regulatory scheme involving a copyright 'IWF' had little improvement to offer over the current status quo. 'High levels of mutual hostility' were, furthermore, identified between ISPs and rights-holders. Groups representing content providers and users were mainly concerned with citizen access to information and freedom of speech issues, and felt they had no real involvement and representation in the current process. For them, there was a 'strong view that civil liberties are being replaced by consumer rights and judicial due process is being replaced by industry self regulation'.[94] The Rightswatch project thus produced no clear way forward, and has to be deemed not only a failure, but a strong indication that a self regulatory code of practice or institutional scheme that meets the needs of all parties simply cannot be put in place without the imprimatur of law.

It is odd, to make an unusual comparison, that privatized notice and take down by institutions like the IWF largely receives such a good press from all quarters except freedom of speech campaigners, when the Australian scheme discussed above has had such a bad press. Notice and take down schemes have undeniable appeal to a public who mostly want objectionable content—whether pictures of adults having sex with children, or pirate MP3s—removed or blocked as swiftly as possible without having to wait for the weary ways of the law to grind on. Leaving aside its many admitted flaws, the Australian scheme at least allows for a regime which is (a) entirely complaint led from the public and yet (b) allows for immediate examination *before* take down of the legality of material complained about, by

---

[93] The ISPA's own research in 2002 suggested that every take-down notice costs an ISP up to £1000 to process. See 'ISP Liability Update: Notice and Take Down' (2003) (April) *Electronic Business Law* 16.
[94] Rightswatch Final Report, above n 81, para 5.5.

a Classification Board who are democratically empowered, resourced, and trained to deal with exactly this issue. Even after classification, review can be sought and the matter eventually taken to the courts. The one thing the Australian scheme cannot be accused of is private covert censorship. Indeed, if the alternative to a complaint driven notice and take down scheme is covert control by filtering enabled either by ISPs or end users—as the 'amended' Australian scheme and indeed the EC Safer Action Plan[95] promote—it might be asked which is worse— *post* publication removal or blocking of Internet content on the demand of a properly empowered quasi-tribunal or court; or *prior* restraint on Internet content by the operation of invisible constraints in filtering software.[96] It is clearly one of the weaknesses of 'notice and take down' schemes in relation to these types of content, as we have seen in *Godfrey* and may yet see in the UK via the IWF and a potential 'Rightswatch', that such mechanisms may be used by partisan factions such as (i) 'moral majorities' who want to bury content they find personally objectionable; or (ii) vexatious complainants who are trying to silence rivals, attack hate objects, maximize profit by suppressing the public domain or just cause trouble.[97]

The issue of what body (if any) should adjudicate on notice and take-down— judicial or administrative, self-regulatory or with a more public oversight, industry funded or state funded, open or acting behind closed doors—is one which is opening up significant differences across industry sectors, and between the various member states of the EU. As we have seen, the UK has effectively developed an intermediary institution in the shape of the IWF to protect the ISP industry and (arguably) to minimize the exposure of the UK public to hard core obscene material; yet content providers whose material is taken down have no *locus standi* there to argue their case. They can of course go to court; but all the usual factors of cost, time, ignorance of the law and inertia operate to make this an implausible option for most individual consumers and citizens. Natural justice might suggest that a mirror ADR institution for content providers and users to air complaints and requests for 'put-back' should develop.[98] In Belgium, take down of content by an ISP must be authorized not by a full court but by a state prosecutor. In Italy and Spain, their implementation regulations demand that 'a competent body' deter-

---

[95] Above n 42.

[96] Another point to consider here is that Internet content, more than hard copy content, basically becomes invisible in a world of prior restraint. There are few hard copy indices or abstracts of Internet content to alert the public that the material has been covertly censored; not does banned Internet content, at least so far, seem to attract the same mass public attention as banned books such as *Spycatcher*.

[97] Clive Feather of Demon suggested after the *Godfrey* case was decided in March 1999 that it would mean that complaints would have to be taken seriously 'even if written in crayon on tissue paper.'

[98] ISPs of course can provide alternative dispute resolutions themselves to deal with such complaints, and since the passing of the Communications Act 2003 are in fact under an obligation to provide access to an external dispute resolution scheme to deal with customer complaints. Aggrieved ISP customers can go to Otelo, the Office of the Telecommunications Ombudsman, or to CISAS, an approved scheme backed by the ISP industry.

mine the legality of disputed content.[99] In the UK, the EC Directive regulations (as ever) add little to the bare bones of the Directive. Regulation 22, added after substantial lobbying by the ISP industry, provides merely that in determining if an ISSP has 'actual knowledge', the court shall take into account all matters which seem relevant to it including whether a notice had been received, and the extent to which that notice adequately identified the complainant, the location of the information complained about, and the nature of the unlawful activity or information. The Publisher's Association, interestingly for a rights-holders organisation, have proposed a scheme whereby as soon as 'take-down' is opposed by the provider of the disputed content, the matter must go to the courts and the content meanwhile remain in the public view.[100] Across Europe, only Finland, Iceland and Hungary have enacted full legal provisions dealing with notice and take-down rather than relying on industry self-regulation and codes of conduct. The Finnish provisions controversially provide for mandatory notice of take-down to the content provider who is the subject of complaint; and for mandatory 'put-back' if the content provider challenges the take-down request. The content provider must also be directly approached by the complainant before the ISSP can be asked to take down. Furthermore complainants who perjure themselves (eg by complaining work is theirs when it is in the public domain) are liable to indemnify the ISSP for any loss suffered as a result. Thus ISSPs are not offered a DMCA style safe harbor but are offered some relief from risk.[101]

What the 'Mystery Shopper' and associated Oxford research, as well as the US experience recounted on the 'Chilling Effects' site,[102] certainly seem to establish is that neither the interest of legal control of content nor of freedom of speech nor of transparency and natural justice will be well met by leaving take down entirely to the whims of the ISP industry. The European Commission's own view, expressed rather anodynely in the First Report on implementation of the ECD,[103] is that there is little practical experience of how the hosting provisions in Article 14 are so far operating but that self regulatory practice in this area, as advocated by Recital 40 and Article 16, is approaching some consensus on 'the essential elements which should be taken into account' and generally, that 'the approach taken in the Directive appears to have wide reaching support from stakeholders'. It is difficult to square this conclusion with the results of the (EU-funded) Rightswatch project discussed above. The EU is however under an obligation to re-examine the provisions on notice and take down every two years under Article 21(2) of the ECD and

---

[99] See *Reporters sans Frontieres* news Report, 5 April 2004.

[100] Oral presentation by PA representative, *Not-Con*, London, 5 June 2004.

[101] Unofficial translation of Ch 5 of the Finnish Act on Offering of Information Society Services provided by Martin von Willebrand of HH Partners, Attorneys at Law, Helsinki. My sincere thanks for this information. The US DMCA also provides for sanctions for perjury on wrongful requests for take-down.

[102] Above n 91.

[103] COM (2003) 702 final, at paras 4.7–4.8.

it will be interesting to see how the law in this area develops now substantial research input is available. The Oxford PCMLP–IAPCODE research identifies a number of essential requirements for a self regulatory dispute resolution system to work effectively and in the public interest in the digital media/content area. *Inter alia* such schemes should be:

• Beneficial to consumers
• Accessible to members of the public
• Independent from interference by interested parties
• Adequately funded and staffed
• Provide effective and credible sanctions
• Provide for auditing and review by the relevant independent regulatory authority (IRA)
• Be publicly accountable
• Provide for an independent appeals mechanism.[104]

Self evidently, existing bodies making decisions on take-down such as the IWF, and individual ISSPs, do not currently meet most or all of these criteria. The Oxford research suggests[105] that codes of conduct developed by industry bodies in this area—such as the ISPA—should be accredited by the relevant IRA, which for the digital media sector in the UK is now Ofcom. Accreditation could be indicated by kite marking as with the successful tScheme.[106] The IRA should also then continue to audit such self regulatory schemes in some co-regulatory paradigm, in order to assess how they are impacting fundamental rights such as freedom of speech, via a 'Fundamental Rights Impact Assessment'. A 'national resource audit of ISP and content sectors' should also be undertaken to see if ISPs have the resources sustainably to devote to effective self regulation. Structures should be assessed to see if and how they incorporate independent representation, external monitoring of compliance, public accountability and adequate publicity and transparency functions. Performance indicators (such as time taken to address complaints) should also be set so that regular review could be conducted against such benchmarks. Some ISSPs—especially in Accession countries—may also need technical assistance to set up effective self regulation. In relation to notice and take-down in particular, the Oxford study recommends legislative backing for a 'put-back' scheme, presumably accompanied by some form of safe harbour for ISPs. These are useful, practical and detailed suggestions and it is to be hoped that when the next review of notice and take-down by the EU is due in 2005, they will be re-examined carefully by both the DTI and the Commission.

---

[104] PMCLP-IAPCODE, above n 52, para 12.1.
[105] *Ibid*, S 12: Watching the Watchdogs: Accreditation of Self-regulatory Codes and Institutions.
[106] See http://www.tscheme.org/.

F. Hosting and Linking

Another issue expressly dealt with by the DMCA but left out the ECD is the question of linking liability. This is a particularly crucial matter to consider for search engines sites, which as their raison d'etre create links to unknown material. The question of linking liability is most obviously a worry in relation to copyright infringement,[107] but remains a problem in relation to other types of content liability as well, such as for defamatory[108] and criminal[109] content. 'Hosting' as dealt with in Article 14 requires storage, undefined in either the ECD or the UK Regulations, which seems to imply that merely making a hyper-link to content cannot constitute 'hosting'—therefore any liability which may arise in relation to a hyper-link under national law is not excluded by Article 14. The DMCA by contrast expressly grants immunity[110] under certain conditions where a link is made to infringing material. The question of whether specific provision should be made concerning linking liability is another point the Commission is specifically instructed to investigate on an ongoing basis by Article 21(2). So far, Spain, Austria, Lichtenstein and Portugal have all chosen to extend intermediary immunities to cover linking liability, while all other states have so far not, creating a perhaps unhelpful cross-Europe disharmony. Linking is of ever greater significance as the Internet becomes manageable only via search engines and as noted above, these are already becoming the frequent target of cease and desist letters and thus must be uncomfortably conscious of their position of globally uncertain legal immunity. Since the drafting of the ECD, aggregators have also become important intermediaries—sites which provide links to a variety of sites so that, say, a user can read the headlines from multiple news sites conveniently on one page. Such aggregators are technically making links to a wide variety of 'upstream' content over which they may or may not have technical control to remove individual items, depending on how their software code is implemented.[111] Similarly price

---

[107] See for example *Intellectual Reserve Inc v Utah Lighthouse Ministry* 75 F Supp 2d 1290 (DUtah, 1999) and comment thereon in M Landau, 'Silencing Content Providers: They're Coming from Everywhere and Under Every Theory' (2003) 17 *Intl Rev L, Computers & Technology* 285.

[108] See Sandburg 'The Great Linking Debate: Finding Defamation in Cyberspace' which reported that a San Francisco professor was suing a student web site which has *linked to* allegedly defamatory remarks about the plaintiff's teaching style posted on a Teacher Review Web Site. (The latter site was also being sued.) See http://www.lawnewsnetwork.com/practice/techlaw/news/A15559–2000Feb7.html.

[109] See the UK blasphemy case noted above n 31.

[110] S 512 (d) Information Location Tools.

[111] As an example, Lawrence Lessig, the well known cyber-lawyer, maintains a popular weblog site at http://www.lessig.org/blog/. The site can be accessed directly via the Web but it can also be delivered as an 'RSS feed' to other sites, ie, as text in XML form, which can be aggregated by any other content providing site. Thus, this writer can say, read Lessig's blog along with Eugene Volokh's blog, several friends' blogs, and sundry news headlines all on one page at (say) http://www.livejournal.com, a blogging site, as her start to the day. Suppose Lessig declares (untruthfully) that all of Edwards's work is

comparison sites generate links to a wide variety of sites ranked by factors such as price and availability and are an important feature for the Internet in promoting consumer choice. It would seem logical, both for reduction of business risk, harmonisation within Europe and harmony with the US DMCA scheme, to incorporate immunity from linking liability into the ECD intermediary scheme in future.

G. Local Rules, Global Publication: The EC Intermediary Regime and 'Country of Origin' Rules

Although notice and take-down may exercise the minds of policymakers and civil liberties groups, for commercial ISPs themselves their principal worry is how to deal with doing business globally in a world where every country has different rules relating to liability for content. This was of course the problem Yahoo! US faced in its well publicised dispute with the French authorities: while US law emphasised freedom of expression and immunity for publishers, French law focused on suppression of pro Nazi materials in French sovereign territory. ISSPs also therefore need not only worry about the details of the on-line intermediary liability/immunity regime of their own home country, which at least is certain, known and can be complied with, but about the need to deal with multiple differing liability regimes in multiple countries. Their choice is then to restrict their business operation to a small number of countries where they feel confident they can comply with the law—which seems rather futilely to diminish the opportunity the Intenet gives to trade and publish globally—or to trade globally and run the risk of running foul of local laws which they may not only not know, but even if every effort is made, find difficult to access in a language they can understand. Reed[112] gives the example of the Mongolian Banking Law—although two English translations can be found of it on the Internet, they contradict each other—and it is unlikely (though not impossible) that a translation into Icelandic (say) can be found. The only reliable way to find out if commercial activities meet local laws is

---

plagiarised from her students on his blog. I demand that LiveJournal.com remove the item from their RSS feed delivered to many other thousands of users who read the Lessig blog via LiveJournal. LiveJournal's technical ability to do so depends on the format of the original XML text supplied. Although it will normally be possible to remove a single item, as a worst case scenario, it might conceivably not be possible for them to take down the alleged libellous item without disabling the entire feed. The administrative overhead of such take-down for aggregators, who often offer this service for free, will also be not inconsiderable. (My thanks to Simon Bisson and Andrew Ducker for technical assistance on this point.)

[112] Above n 4.

to consult a local lawyer—and for small ISSPs or content providers this may be prohibitively difficult or expensive.

The ECD is partially helpful in this regard in the form of its 'internal market' clause in Article 3.[113] This provides that ISSPs shall have to comply only with the laws of the state in which they are established ('country of origin' regulation—see further Waelde in Chapter 1.) Thus in principle a French ISSP need only comply with French rules on misleading advertising (say) and not those of Italy, Belgium, the UK etc. This rule is however subject to significant exceptions, notably in relation to the protection of consumers and consumer contracts. Here, the 'country of destination' rules may still prevail. So a French ISSP might still need to take account of Italian, Belgian, UK etc rules protecting consumers from misleading adverts. Within the EU, so much consumer legislation is in fact already harmonised that this is not such a problem as it was in some jurisdictions made out to be during the progress of the ECD. However for ISSPs the major problem continues to be that in the nature of their activities they deliver content not just to EU countries but also to those beyond. How can this risk be managed?

In essence the problem is one of international private law (IPL). Practice varies between countries but the dominant approach in relation to information/ publication liability is that the law applied is the law of the place of publication ('country of destination') not the law of the place from which publication originates ('country of origin'). Reed[114] suggests that the way forward is via a new international convention on liability of 'on-line information providers'. These are defined as any publishers of information on-line, where a 'publisher' is a person who 'controls access to that information by persons other than the publisher'. Reed, drawing on his experience as part of the group attempting to re draft the Hague Convention IPL rules on jurisdiction and judgments, asserts that a harmonised 'country of origin' choice of law rule will only be internationally acceptable[115] where domestic rules are already closely harmonised—as is the case in the EU in relation to ISSP liability rules (as well of course as other aspects of consumer, Internet and commercial law). Outside the EU, this is largely not the case, and the country of origin solution is politically impossible to achieve. Instead of harmonising the choice of law rule, therefore, he suggests that states should be left free to refer issues of liability to whatever law is appropriate according to their existing choice of law rules—which will usually refer to the law of the country of 'publication'—*but*, that the *'place of publication'* should be redefined by treaty to solely mean the place of origin of the published material (the fixed establishment

---

[113] Implemented in the UK in the Electronic Commerce (EC Directive) Regs SI 2002 No 2013, Regs 4 and 5.

[114] Above n 113.

[115] But compare MF Kightlinger, 'A Solution to the Yahoo! Problem? The EC E-Commerce Directive as a Model for International Co-operation on Internet Choice of Law' (2003) 24 *Mich J Intl L* 719.

of the publisher from which the information was published). In other words, 'place of publication' would become the country of origin of the publisher. Reed also suggests adopting a single publication rule akin to that found in US law: so information would be deemed to be published in one place only, as above, and at one time only (the time when it is first accessible at the server side, ie time of upload), thus preventing publishers being exposed to multiple suit for multiple publications in multiple jurisdictions.[116] This solution is ingenious but it is also disingenuous in terms of global politics. If states will not go for a harmonised international treaty solution which involves harmonising their *choice of law* rules on liability for publication, they are equally unlikely, it seems to this writer, to go for a backdoor method of reaching the same solution via harmonisation of the interpretation of the *connecting factor*.[117]

An alternative approach might be to abandon the idea of globally harmonising national IPL rules as unworkable, and focus instead on information provision to ISSPs. As Reed has noted, what is most pressingly needed to allow ISSPs to manage local legal risk is speedy and comprehensible access to relevant local laws. The EC currently benefits from a Transparency Directive[118] which requires member states to give prior notice to the Commission of any laws they promulgate relating to information society services. The Commissioner for the Information Society, Erkki Likanen, recently commented on how this had helped engender a genuine culture of dialogue and transparency between member states.[119] Could an international treaty not be drafted which would merely impose on signatory states the obligation to provide an authoritative copy of laws relevant to liability for ISSPs, on an official website, perhaps run by the UN or WIPO, with authorised translations in (say) English, French, Spanish, German and Mandarin? The website might also provide contact details of a local civil servant who could help for free with interpretation of the local law. Within the EC, a transposition status page for the ECD does exist[120] which provides a starting point for finding out how the ECD has been implemented locally in the 25 Member states. However the page merely links to legislation in the local language which, when this is Finnish or Hungarian (for example) may not be entirely helpful to all EU ISSPs. It would be a good example for the EU itself to take the initiative to publish all transposition legislation in at least the two working languages of the Community as well as simply linking to the original text.

---

[116] See *Gutnick v Dow Jones* [2002] HCA 305 (High Court of Australia) for a recent rejection of the 'single publication rule' in a Commonwealth jurisdiction in relation to Internet publications. This writer wholeheartedly endorsed the Reed proposal on this point: see L Edwards, '*Caveat* Uploader? Recent Developments in Cyberspace Jurisdiction' (2003) E L@w Review 9–1.

[117] See AE Anton and P Beaumont, *Private International Law*, 2nd edn, (W Green, 2003) on this issue further.

[118] Directive 98/34/EC as extended by Directive 98/48/EC.

[119] Press release, 23 May 2003, ref IP/03/739.

[120] See http://europa.eu.int/comm/internal_market/en/ecommerce/transposition_en.pdf.

H. The Fall and Rise of Intermediary Liability

The discussion above has described how the competing interests of the stakehold-ers in the Internet content industry—ISSPs, content providers, rights-holders and other 'victims', and the public interest or 'users'—had led to a broad consensus at the turn of the millennium that the best solution to on-line intermediary immun-ity was the 'limited liability/notice and take-down' approach. This was the approach espoused by the ECD and the DMCA. However, if it is accepted that the level and extent of ISP duties is a matter of balancing policy needs, and not simply a matter of historical accident, or natural justice, then it becomes plausible that as the Internet industry matures and policy interests change, so the imposition of ISP liability—or immunity from such—may also fluctuate.

We are seeing something of a quiet retrenchment on the current level of ISP immunities, pursued on the whole via *ad hoc* case law not prominent public leg-islative activity. In the US, a series of court cases such as *Batzel v Smith*,[121] *Barrett v Rosenthal*,[122] and, most recently, *Grace v EBay*[123] have begun to successfully attack the 'total immunity' granted to on-line service providers by the CDA in respect of publication liability not to do with copyright infringement.[124] These cases circumvent the 'publisher' immunity granted by Congress in section 230 (c) of the CDA in a number of ways, eg, by categorising ISPs as distributors rather than publishers.[125] So far these decisions merely restore what might be seen as a natural balance; as suggested above, the CDA 'total immunity' regime, itself some-thing of a historical accident, is over-protective of ISPs and under-protective of 'victims', and out of step with the general duty of take-down expected of ISPs in receipt of 'actual knowledge' in other jurisdictions.[126]

But other current jurisprudence goes further in threatening the accepted status of global intermediary immunities. Outside of the Australian experience recounted

---

[121] 2003 333 F3d 1018.

[122] 114 Cal App 4th 1379 (Cal App 1st Dist, 2003), Cal Sup Ct review granted.

[123] 2004 WL 1632047 (Cal App 2nd Dist, 22 July 2004). EBay were sued for defamatory remarks made on its auction site by a disgruntled bidder in respect of another user of the site. But note that although EBay lost on CDA immunity, having been found not to be a publisher of information but a distributor, they still were held not liable because their contractual terms successfully excluded liabil-ity. The message to ISP lawyers is clearly to review their subscriber terns and conditions and not rely on legislative immunities.

[124] See below, pp 111–2.

[125] Another approach to attacking 'total immunity' is to construct ISPs as themselves the content provider rather than merely the publisher. This has so far largely been unsuccessful however: see *Carafano v Metrosplash.com Inc* US Central District of California Court of Appeals, DC No CV–01–00018–DT, 13 August 2003, reversing the earlier decision. Such an approach could, it is sug-gested, have been usefully taken in *Blumenthal v Drudge*, above n 65.

[126] See for an excellent article suggesting that there are no longer cogent reasons for the CDA regime to subject ISPs in the US to a lower standard of duty of care than under the DMCA regime, M Reisler, 'Differing Statutes', *New York LJ*, 19 March 2004.

above, there had until recently been little or no attempt by Western states to hold ISPs (or ISSPs) responsible for providing *access* to illicit material, as opposed to actually *hosting* it. As a result, while the ECD grants near total immunity in Article 12 where an ISSP acts as 'mere conduit', and limited liability in Article 14 when it acts as a host, it is unhelpfully silent on the connected question of linking liability, which is really just another form of access-provision as opposed to local hosting or storage. Yet in Germany recently, as in France in the *Yahoo!* case, ISPs have been successfully ordered to block access to sites abroad and at home offering access to hate speech.[127] This is a trend which can be discerned across Continental Europe, where states are perturbed to find that their post-WW II anti-Nazi laws forbidding glorification of Fascist and racist speech are being overwhelmed by a deluge of hate speech content stored, legally, on US servers.[128] They then have no way to attack the phenomenon except by demanding that local ISPs play their part and block access.

Meanwhile back in the US, in *Ellison v AOL*[129] the science fiction author Harlan Ellison fought for two years to stop ISPs including AOL providing *access*—as opposed to local hosting—to pirated copies of his fiction. Although the case finally settled before full adjudication, the message was clearly that, even in the area of copyright regulated by the DMCA, an ISP could no longer completely rely on being treated as a 'mere conduit' when it continually and knowingly provided access to known pirated material, even though it was not a local host.[130] In still another development, attempts have been made using the subpoena provisions of the DMCA to bring an Internet access provider, Verizon, into the same 'notice and take-down' regime as 'ordinary' ISPs hosting illegal material, even though Verizon was merely providing *access* to that material and *not* local hosting. Although these attempts were in the end repelled,[131] considerable consternation broke out in the telecommunications, free speech and academic communities in the interim

---

[127] See PH Schumacher, 'Fighting Illegal Content—May Access Providers be Required to Ban Foreign Websites? a Recent German Approach' (2004) 8 *Intl J Comm L & Policy*, available at http://www.ijclp.org/8_2004/pdf/schumacher-paper-ijclp.pdf.

[128] N Ryan, 'Fear and Loathing', *The Guardian*, Online Section, 12 August 2004 at http://www.guardian.co.uk/online/story/0,3605,1,280,992,00.html.

[129] Above n 45.

[130] See account of settlement reached between Ellison and AOL at http://www.authorslawyer.com/c-ellison.shtml. The litigation apparently leaves open the possibility that although AOL would have benefited from the 'mere conduit' immunity of the DMCA, they could still be found liable alternately as a contributory infringer of copyright.

[131] See for the initial decision upholding the subpoena against Verizon sought by the RIAA, *In re Verizon Internet Services*, 2003 US Dist LEXIS 681 (DDC 2003). That decision was successfully appealed by Verizon on February 2004: see http://www.eff.org/legal/cases/RIAA_v_Verizon/opinion–20031219.pdf. The RIAA are now seeking to appeal to the US Supreme Court. The EFF amicus brief explaining why Verizon should not be regarded as a 'service provider' for the purpose of the DMCA can be found at http://www.eff.org/legal/cases/RIAA_v_Verizon/20030516_eff_amicus.pdf.

period.[132] We are thus seeing attempts to deconstruct existing immunities for ISPs in relation to 'traditional' publication liability immunities, attempts to bring 'mere conduits' into the same legal category as 'service providers' and, most importantly, attempts to impose liability for access-provision as well as actual local hosting of illegal content.

Why this apparent onslaught on on-line intermediary immunity? A number of reasons can be teased out. First, the reasoning which led to ISP limited liability described at p 101ff above may simply no longer hold. The liberal market ideology which surmised that ISPs left to their own devices would adopt a filtering and monitoring strategy to maximize market share does not seem to be transpiring, or at least not on a consistent basis. ISPs have taken an active role in suppressing and filtering out spam, yes, as it is a heavy business cost to them, swallows bandwidth, and prejudices their entire business model. But for every BT Internet and AOL who decide that it is a positive market strategy to be seen to try to remove and block access to child pornography, there are many others who see no advantage in publicising themselves on the one hand as censors or on the other as warehousers or distributors of obscene material.[133] As already noted, European governments are also extremely worried about the growth in 'import' of hate speech and child porn, and the perceived need to block access to it is not a challenge that is willingly being taken up by ISPs. As the Oxford PCMLP research suggests, most ISPs would far rather be seen as anonymous middle-men and consider a filtering, monitoring and adjudicatory role as merely an extra cost and an activity which is peripheral and diverting from their core business.

The incentive to put heavier liability burdens on ISPs to encourage them to take their part in 'cleaning up the Internet' may also be growing as the problem of illicit content gets worse, and the other, more user-focused solutions for solving the 'content problem' look less and less helpful. The EU recently assessed its Internet Action Plan[134] which originally ran from 1999 to 2002, and which was explicitly designed in the wake of the striking down of the CDA in the US, to find ways of using extra legal strategies rather than 'direct effect' laws to help rid European users of the Internet of undesirable content. Broadly, the EU's findings were that European hotlines of the IWF variety—which of course put the major onus on ISPs to remove content, albeit once notified—have been the only successful way forward found. Filtering tools for adoption by users continue to be poor at their job and little used or understood by adult users. Rating tools, designed to allow websites to self-rate for adult content, have also failed to reach critical mass of

---

[132] See for example J Hilden, 'Anonymity v Law Enforcement: the Fight Over Subpoenaing Alleged Downloader's Names from ISPs', at http://findlaw.com, 1 October 2003.

[133] See Tony Blair's recent speech in which he implored other ISPs to follow BT Internet's example and take an active role in removing and blocking pornographic material. 'Blair urges ISPs to block porn sites' *The Guardian*, 22 July 2004.

[134] Renamed Safer Internet Action Plan in 2002. See above n 42.

adoption. Awareness programmes promoting safe Internet use at school level may make an impact in the future, but are not solving current problems. All this makes the option of asking the Internet industry to grit their teeth and take on a more hands-on 'gatekeeper' role ever more attractive.

Furthermore, the ISP industry sector is now rather more established and also more ubiquitous than it was in the times which spawned the ECD and the DMCA. It no longer seems plausible that major ISPs like Yahoo!, AOL and Freeserve/Wanadoo, faced with the imposition of less limited liability would give up doing business, or up sticks, exercise regulatory arbitrage and move to (say) Vanuatu. Even if they did there are plenty of alternative Internet access providers in the market now, such as cable companies; the growth in wireless Internet and Internet services via mobile phone providers is also significant here. It may be time for the ISP industry to recognise (or be forced to recognise), like other industry sectors, that certain legal risks simply have to be accepted as part of the costs of doing business and that their own business interests have to be balanced against the needs of both 'victims' and the public interest. Of course this is a somewhat sweeping statement, and not necessarily applicable to all Internet intermediaries in every role they play. Search engines, for example, are vital both to doing business on the Internet, to scholarship and creativity, and to digital access and freedom of expression; it seems crucial to put as few content-related burdens on them as possible. On the other hand, as Hilden notes,[135] Google News—a service which provides an aggregated list of news headline links to users according to prior user-selected criteria—is essentially doing the same editorial job as traditional newspapers; and yet benefits, as they do not, from freedom from possible liability for libel as a result of the CDA. It seems unreasonable for an on-line news service to have this economic advantage over an off-line news service just because the media of distribution is different. Future legislators and judges may need to consider if omnibus and horizontal 'intermediary service provider' regimes covering all types of intermediaries and all types of content[136] are really the best way to proceed. A subtler, more industry-sectoral content-specific approach may be needed (although of course it will have the drawback of being less immediately clear and applicable to lay industry professionals and users).

The straw which may break the camel's back, as already discussed,[137] is the uncontroversial fact that ISPs are, possibly without 'actual knowledge' but with a great deal of 'constructive knowledge', providing the broadband access essential to

---

[135] J Hilden, 'Why You Can't Sue Google', http://findlaw.com, 25 May 2004. Hilden notes that although Google News is driven by customer—selected criteria, it effectively offers searchers what they know the searchers are likely to be interested in—'thereby serving the very same function that newspapers and other traditional media publishers seek to achieve'.

[136] See also the discussion above that 'notice and take-down' rules which are appropriate to copyright and libel may not be so suitable in relation to obscenity and hate speech where no complainant has the authoritative 'agency' to complain.

[137] See pp 105–6 below.

the efficient downloading of pirate copyright material by millions of users. Many of the US cases discussed above which try to limit ISP immunities, such as *Ellison* and *Verizon,* have been driven by the rights-holders lobby exerting pressure on ISPs and hosts to help them catch illegal downloaders and remove pirate copies. The content industry lobby has already secured in their own interest laws relating to technological copy-protection measures and anti-circumvention which have been widely criticized as bad for freedom of expression, fair use and the public domain. Given this degree of sectoral self interest, disregard for impact on fundamental liberties, and lobbying power, it does not seem implausible that at some point they may try to extend the current regime as found in the ECD and DMCA from one where liability arises after notice and failure to take-down as *host,* to one where liability is imposed on notice and failure to block *access.* Once upon a time the ISP industry might successfully have claimed (as indeed they did in 1999 in the Australian debate) that such an access-prevention requirement would impose an impossible burden on them—but technologies have improve since 2000, and this excuse may no longer run. In the *Yahoo!* case, the court, presented with the defence that it was technically impossible for Yahoo! US to block access to its Nazi memorabilia auction pages to all persons from France, did not make a decision based on law or rhetoric but instead remitted the question to a technical sub-committee to investigate. They reported back that, in fact, Yahoo! had the capacity (already used to serve up adverts in the relevant language to users from whatever country of origin) to identify and thus block access to 90% of French citizens.[138] Accordingly, Yahoo! were instructed to block access.[139]

Looking further forward still, there may be pressures to extend on-line intermediary liability to new types of behaviour, and to new types of intermediary. One key area of concern currently is 'cyber insecurity'. Internet hosts are often hacked and used as 'zombie hosts' from which all kinds of badness can be perpetrated by remote control: they may be used to send out deluges of spam, to participate in distributed denial of service (DDOS) attacks, and to 'page jack' traffic legitimately directed at other sites. Chandler has suggested that hosts from which such attacks were launched might be put on their guard by potential liability if they should have suspected the possibility of hackers invading their server and yet failed to put adequate security in place.[140] (This has been evocatively described as 'making the

---

[138] See *LICRA et UEJF vs Yahoo! Inc and Yahoo France,* (20 November 2000, Tribunal de Grande Instance de Paris, Superior Court of Paris) p 14. <http://www.gigalaw.com/library/france-yahoo–2000–11–20–lapres.html>. Around 70% of user's country of origin could be established from IP address and the remaining 20% or so could be made up by asking users to fill in a form declaring country of origin. Some degree of evasion would always be possible however because of use of foreign ISPs, proxy servers and anonymising services. See discussion in C Penfold, 'Nazis, Porn and Politics', above n 21.

[139] Although see the US refusal to enforce this decree: above n 20.

[140] J Chandler, 'Security in Cyberspace: Combating DDOS Attacks' [2004] *U Ottawa L & Technology J* available at http://www.innovationlaw.org/lawforum/pages/chandler-final.pdf.

victims liable'.[141]) In her analysis, although this may seem hard on the 'innocent' host which is hacked, the most economically effective solution to a major societal problem may be to make just such hosts liable. If, as is already more or less the case, our national security, commerce, finance and health provision infrastructure is so entirely digitally based now that it is intensely vulnerable to denial of service attacks, then the public interest in protection is so overwhelming that this might become a serious option. There have already been a scattering of unreported cases in which private companies have attempted to sue hosts for cyber-insecurity leading to damage to the plaintiff's business. If this is the scenario we are looking forward to, then could existing on-line intermediary immunities be interpreted to protect such 'innocent' hosts from liability for cyber-insecurity? And should they be?

Another area where the state interest in finding an intermediary to blame is high is illegal off shore Internet gambling. It is very tempting for states to penalise ISPs that allow access to gambling sites when the ISPs are within state control while the gambling sites are effectively untouchable. In an early German case in 1999, the Court of Appeal in Hamburg found an ISP liable for providing 'technical assessibility' to a foreign illegal gambling site. The case was seen as particularly radical in that the ISP was not hosting content but acting basically as a 'mere conduit'.[142] More recently, a class action suit was brought in California against Google, Yahoo! and 12 other major hosts and search engines for providing links (in adverts) to out of state gambling businesses which are illegal in California.[143]

Gambling is also a major force encouraging states to look for new intermediaries other than the traditional ISP sector to act as 'gatekeepers'. A US Bill has been launched attempting to prohibit credit card companies from processing payments in respect of off- shore Internet gambling sites.[144] Similar calls have been made in the UK for credit card companies and banks to blacklist transfers of funds to child pornography sites.[145] The Association of Payment Clearing Services (Apacs) is, interestingly, already engaged in self regulation here: its guidelines suggest that Internet businesses which include websites trading in 'child pornography, racism or terrorism and violence against persons, including scenes of sexual violence' should not be allowed to use credit cards[146] although actual practice varies from

[141] See J Roehmer, 'The Hack Attacks: Are the Victims Liable?' at http://www.thestandard.com, 15 February 2000.

[142] Global ITC report at www.bakernet.com/itc; case heard 4 November 1999. Though this would now seem to contravene Art 12 of the E-Commerce Directive, gambling is excluded in Art 1 from that Directive's scope.

[143] 'Google and Yahoo! sued over gambling ads', http://www.out-law.com, 5 August 2003.

[144] 'US votes to ban credit card payments for Internet gambling', http://www.out-Law.com, 12 June 2003.

[145] 'Banks urged to ban credit card use for Internet porn', *The Guardian*, 3 July 2004.

[146] See Apacs press release at http://www.apacs.org.uk/downloads/CHIS&IWFpr.pdf, 14 March 2003.

card supplier to card supplier: American Express, for example, claim they do not allow their cards to be used to buy adult pornography, but clearly other card providers are less scrupulous. In the US, Christian right groups have been making similar calls for finance companies to ostracise adult pornographic sites. As ever, the same issues are already arising in relation to financial intermediaries as have been ventilated in the traditional ISSP sector. Apacs have already protested that although they are not censors and do not wish to be 'moral arbiters' they 'have to be sure we are doing all we can about preventing the spread of such extreme images'.[147] One wonders more cynically if their concern is less for their part in the war on Internet porn than a prudent self regulatory step by the finance intermediary industry to fend off direct government intervention.

And finally on 'new' on-line intermediaries, of course we have already seen the great witch-hunt against P2P software providers as 'evil intermediaries' *par excellence* in the *Napster*[148] and *MGM v Grokster*[149] litigation. Although there are global trends which seem to indicate that the second generation post-Napster wave of P2P intermediaries—KaZaa *et al*—will not be found liable as intermediaries for copyright infringement[150] because of their lack of effective control over illegal content due to a more distributed architecture, this trend might still be reversed whether by case law or statute,[151] especially if P2P becomes used routinely to distribute content more heinous than mere pirated music and films. P2P software companies were recently warned in an open letter from US state attorneys of the consequences if they did not improve security and filtering so as to deter the use of their services to share not only pirate material, but also child pornography, spamware and spyware.[152] The letter reports 'serious concerns that P2P software is replacing Internet chatrooms and email as a medium of choice for the dissemination of pornography, especially child pornography' and that 'cyber networks like

---

[147] 'Credit cards and extreme websites—APACS revamps guidelines' http://www.out-law.com, 6 July 2004.

[148] *A&M Records, Inc v, Napster Inc*, 239 F3d 1004 (9th Cir, 2001).

[149] See *MGM v Grokster* 380F 3d 1154 (9th Cir 2004). Grokster's case was upheld on appeal to 9th Cir on 19 August 2004. See http://www.eff.org/IP/P2P/MGM_v_Grokster/20040819_mgm_v_grokster_decision.pdf. For background detail see http://www.eff.org/IP/P2P/MGM_v_Grokster/. Grokster however finally lost their case in the Supreme Court on June 27 2005. This defeat to the legality of P2P systems may take the heat off some of the potential vulnerability of ISPs highlighted here.

[150] See in Canada, *Society of Composers, Authors and Music Publishers of Canada v Canadian Assn of Internet Providers* [2004] SCJ No 44, 30 June 2004, which upholds the immunity of Canadian ISPs for content they cache, and broadly defends them from P2P liability; in Holland, KaZaa was found not liable for copyright infringement in the Amsterdam Court of Appeals on 28 March 2002. See discussion of the latter in MR Just, 'Internet File Sharing and the Liability of Intermediaries for Copyright Infringement: A Need for International Consensus' 2003(1) *JILT* at http://elj.warwick.ac.uk/jilt/03–1/just.htm.

[151] The Inducing Infringement of Copyrights Act of 2004 (s 2560) is pending in the US Senate at time of writing. It would create a new category of copyright infringement for 'intentionally' inducing copyright infringement, making it easier to file suit against file sharing software services.

[152] See letter from National Association of Attorneys General, 5 August 2004, linked from http://www.out_law.com, 'Attorneys general warn P2P companies', 9 August 2004.

KaZaa and Morpheus—have become the Mexican border of virtual sexual exploitation.' If not full imposition of liability, we may well soon see attempt to impose obligations on P2P networks not to actively impede law enforcement activity, for example, by bundling encryption with their software.

At the end of 2000, as the dust settled on Articles 12–15 of the ECD, the DMCA and the Australian government's climb down on the Broadcasting Services Act, it was a commonly held belief that global intermediary immunity had reached some kind of tentative harmony. In 2004, it now seems that this may only have been a momentary blip of consensus. For European ISSPs, the next two years may be a time of worrying anticipation, as they wait to see both what pressures national governments, transnational law enforcement authorities,[153] moral lobbying groups and the content industry may bring to bear upon them; and what recommendations if any will come out of the next European Commission review of Articles 12–15, especially in relation to notice and take down, and linking liability. In the meantime, this writer would predict that ways of circumventing ISP immunity which are already allowed under the ECD—eg the seeking of injunctive relief[154] and demands to reveal the identity of anonymous or pseudonymous content providers[155]—will be utilised more and more by rights-holders and other 'victims'; that in terms of hosting liability, renewed attempts will be made to find ISSPs liable on the basis of 'constructive' as well as 'actual' knowledge;[156] that pressure on non-traditional intermediaries such as credit card companies and banks to at least self-regulate to help control illicit content will increase; and that technical methods of access prevention may be more and more put into operation by ISPs, again seeking to forestall legislative action requiring them to utilise such technologies. We may also see serious attempts to promote greater transparency and concern for the rule of law and free speech rights in notice and take-down schemes; but as these are concerns mainly for content providers, users and citizens, not for the well-resourced lobbies of rights-holders and ISSPs, perhaps not. For on-line intermediaries generally though, these are, in the Chinese sense, once again interesting times.[157]

---

[153] Issues for ISSPs here include new obligations of data retention and monitoring imposed in interests of national and international security post 9/11.

[154] Art 14(3).

[155] Nothing in the ECD provides a framework for when disclosure of the identity of a user of an ISSP is legal, although other EC legislation such as the Data Protection Directive is of course relevant. See further in the *UK, Totalise v Motley Fool* [2001] EMLR 29.

[156] G Sutter, 'Don't Shoot the Messenger? The UK and Online Intermediary Liability' (2003) 17 *Intl Rev L, Computers and Technology* 73 gives the good example of an ISP delivering access to a newsgroup such as alt.pictures.youngteen.bondage. Should this not imply constructive knowledge of illegal content?

[157] As this volume went to press, the DTI launched a consultation on whether the provisions of Arts 12–14 of the ECD should be extended to hyperlinkers, location tool providers (search engines) and content aggregators. See DTI Consultation Document, June 2005 at http://www.dti.gov.uk. This illustrates the folly of writing on Internet law.

5

Article 17 ECD: Encouragement of Alternative Dispute Resolution

On-line Dispute Resolution: A View From Scotland

PAUL MOTION[1]

My Lords, when I first became a member of your Lordship's House I was unacquainted with the niceties of the Scots system of pleadings. Since then my acquaintance has grown; so has my disenchantment.

Lord Diplock in *Gibson v BICC*[2]

1. Introduction

Alternative dispute resolution (ADR) is an increasingly popular means of settling national and especially transnational disputes. ADR mechanisms provide private, creative, speedy and cost-effective techniques of dispute resolution, while court based litigation throughout the globe is increasingly slow, cumbersome and expensive. The advantages of ADR in terms of speed and cheapness become even more pronounced when new technologies are added into the mix, to produce a new hybrid, on-line ADR, or ODR. While ODR techniques can be applied to both on-and off-line disputes, they are particularly relevant to e-commerce disputes, where both the initial transaction and any dispute resolution arising can both take

---

[1] Solicitor-Advocate and Partner, Ledingham Chalmers; Chair of the Law Society of Scotland E-Commerce Committee. My thanks to Ashley Theunissen for her help with research.
[2] 1973 SC 15 (HL) 27.

place exclusively via the Internet medium.[3] The European Union has addressed the growth in ADR and ODR in Article 17 of the EC Electronic Commerce Directive[4] (the 'ECD'), by providing that member states must encourage out of court or ADR schemes. According to Article 9 of the ECD, furthermore, member states must amend any rules that currently exclude or restrict the use of electronic documents by including terms like 'writing', 'paper document' or 'presence of both parties'.[5] Taken together, these articles are a significant step towards the promotion of ODR in Europe. This chapter will examine the phenomenon of ADR and ODR in Europe, and aim to give some insights into how these dispute resolution methods can aid in the growth of e-commerce, what their defining characteristics are, and, perhaps most importantly, what institutional hurdles may inhibit their uptake.

2. European Initiatives in Alternative Dispute Resolution (ADR) and On-line Dispute Resolution (ODR)

The ECD was followed swiftly by a strategy paper from the business sector in the form of the International Chamber of Commerce, *ICC and Business to Consumer ADR in E-Commerce.*[6] This provides recommendations separately to companies involved in e-commerce, to business to consumer ('B2C'), ADR providers, and to governments and other regulatory bodies. Unless otherwise specified by contract between merchant and consumer, consumers should have the choice between going to court and making use of B2C ADR. The document also advocates limited government intervention and the endorsement of ADR and ODR.[7] Additionally,

---

[3] The leading texts on ODR and arbitration in cyberspace are C Rule, *ODR for Business* (Wiley, 2002); and E Katsch and J Rifkin, *ODR* (Jossey-Bass, 2001). Useful UK articles include J Hornle, 'Online Dispute Resolution in Business to Consumer E-commerce Transactions' (2002) *Journal of Information, Law and Technology (JILT)* <http://elj.warwick.ac.uk/jilt/02-2/hornle.html>; and J Hornle, 'ODR: the Emperor's New Clothes?' (2003) 17 *Intl Rev L, Computers & Technology* 27 (on B2B ODR). A very perceptive analysis of the potential due process weaknesses of ODR and ADR in the context of consumer e-commerce and click-wrap contracts can be found in EG Thornburg, 'Fast, Cheap, and Out of Control: Lessons from the ICANN Dispute Resolution Process' (2002) 6(1) *J Small & Emerging Business L & W* 191. Finally, a fascinating assessment of eBay's initial pilot use of ODR on its virtual auction site can be found in E Katsh, J Rifkin and A Gaitenby, 'E-Commerce, E-Disputes, and E-Dispute Resolution: In the Shadow of "eBay Law"' (2000) 15 *Ohio State J Dispute Resolution* 706, available at: <http://www.umass.edu/cyber/katsh.pdf>.

[4] The Electronic Commerce Directive ('ECD') (2000/31/EC) was adopted on 8 June 2000 and published in the Official Journal of the European Communities on 17 July 2000.

[5] For exceptions to this rule, see Art 9(2).

[6] 22 June 2001.

[7] Paper presented by C Kuner at forum on legal aspects of ODR, Muenster 22 June 2001.

the European Consumers Association (BEUC) published comments on the Commission's communication on E-Commerce and Financial Services in 2000, stating that the BEUC favoured ADR for consumer contracts, provided that access to the courts remained open.[8]

The European Commission, when working to implement Article 17, have taken the view that, although the number of cross-border consumer transactions are still relatively low, they are expected to grow as the full potential of the Internal Market is realised (see further, Chapter 1 of this volume). In turn, this will increase the number of cross-border disputes. It is therefore important to ensure that ADR schemes are able to handle such cases. To make this possible, the Commission together with Member States have established a network of contact points with national 'Clearing Houses' which provides consumers with information on available ADR schemes, as well as legal advice and practical help in pursuing a complaint by this means. This has thus created a communication and support structure available to all EU/EEA consumers that can be used to settle their commercial disputes with traders in any member states. The aim of the EEJ-Net is to facilitate access to justice for EU/EEA consumers in particular for cross-border e-commerce disputes. EEJ-Net aims to achieve this by linking together the various out-of-court consumer dispute settlement bodies in the EU and EEA member states. This network covers all 15 Member States as well as Norway and Iceland. The Commission launched this network, the European Extra-Judicial Network or EEJ-NET,[9] in May 2000. The tasks of EEJ-NET are:

- to co-ordinate out-of-court-settlement procedures for consumers throughout Europe;
- to provide consumers with easy and informed access to such procedures cross-border;
- to facilitate the solution of cross-border consumer disputes.

The network deals with any dispute between a consumer and a business over goods and services, such as problems over deliveries, defective products, or products or services that do not fit their description. EEJ-NET is complemented by FINNET[10] which is a dedicated network dealing exclusively with consumer complaints about financial services (credit, investments, loans etc).

Closer to home in the UK, the Government welcomed the European Commission's proposals for establishing EEJ-Net in the UK in May 2000. Billed as a low cost, user-friendly alternative to the courts, ADR has seen great success in the

---

[8] Bureau Europeen des Unions de Consommateurs; see http:/www.beuc.org/public/xfiles2000/x2000/x167e.htm.

[9] See http://www.eejnet.org.

[10] Launched on 1 February 2001 as 'an out of courts complaints network for financial services to help businesses and consumers resolve disputes in the internal market fast and efficiently where possible by avoiding, where possible lengthy and expensive legal action'.

UK in recent years.[11] The body responsible for this success is the Citizens Advice Bureau ('CAB'), an independent and impartial consumer organization with established standing in both legal and consumer circles. Originally, chosen to be the clearinghouse in the UK because of this reputation, CAB EEJ-Net is designed to be an additional option for a consumer with a cross border dispute and not a replacement to his/her statutory rights and options.[12] CAB has extended its accessibility to consumers by launching an online European Consumer Centre to help shoppers who have problems with goods or services they have bought in another EU country in June 2004. The site is available in five European languages and contains information on solving your problem, avoiding future problems, as well as fact sheets on common areas of complaint.[13] Key figures complied previous to the launch of the website from the European Consumer Centre in 2003 include:

1. Two thirds of people complaining to the European Consumer Centre in 2003 were based in the UK, 40% of them complaining about Spanish traders.[14]
2. Half the queries in 2003 related to goods or services bought on the trader's premises but the rest were on purchases made via the internet, fax or by phone.[15]

As seen, the UK ADR scheme has evolved to meet the growing needs of consumers. Today, the future of CAB EEJ-Net looks quite promising.

Most recently, the European Commission has been progressing a programme of work on the harmonisation of standards for mediation, in particular, and ADR in general. A wide-ranging Green Paper on ADR in civil an commercial law[16] was issued in 2002 which noted the pivotal role of ADR in e-commerce especially, and sought responses on whether Community action was necessary to guarantee the quality and due process standards of ADR. The question of whether standards should be set equivalently for both ADR and ODR, or whether ODR was so fast developing and specialised as to need its own regulatory framework was also highlighted. In particular, the validity of contractual consumer consent to ADR, and the impact of ADRs on access to justice via clauses excluding the jurisdiction of the courts, were raised as crucial issues; these are discussed later in the ODR context in more detail in this Chapter. One intriguing idea was the extension of the idea of the 'cooling off' period from distance selling and consumer credit legislation to the domain of ADR clauses in consumer contracts. The accreditation, training and liability of ADR service providers were also explored. It will be interesting to see to

---

[11] See: European Consumer Centre (ECC) and Clearing House: the point of view of a Member State at: http://europa.eu.int/comm/consumers/topics/bond.pdf.

[12] In the UK, the EEJ-Net Clearing House is based at the Specialist Support Unit within Citizens Advice. See: Citizen Advice Organisation http://www.citizensadvice.org.uk/docks/EEJ_Net_2003.pdf.

[13] See: http://www.euroconsumer.org.uk/index/news/launch.htm.

[14] *Ibid.*

[15] *Ibid.*

[16] Brussels, 19 April 2002, COM(2002) 196 final.

what extent following this consultation paper the EU is prepared to take on the e-commerce industry, especially that originating from the US, and rein in their freedom to impose mandatory ADR clauses In the meantime the EU has also launched a European Code of Conduct for Mediators[17] and is preparing a draft Directive on common standards for mediation which addresses *inter alia* the problem of enforceability of mediation agreements in courts.[18] European harmonising activity around ADR and ODR, especially in the consumer protection area, can only be expected on current indications to increase.

Outside the EC institutions, perhaps the most significant European contribution on ODR in recent years has been the ODR Forum held in Geneva by the United Nations Economic Commission for Europe in June 2002.[19] The message sent by the Geneva forum was clear. The development of a variety of systems of ODR to meet the range of disputes that can arise on-line is vital. ODR itself has a role in reducing the dependence on the jurisdictional based court systems in a wider sense, and can provide alternative mechanisms for all manner of disputes, not just those created on-line. Trust is an important element to be engendered both via technological security but also, more importantly, via respect for the outcomes of ODR processes.

Overall, the recommendations of the Geneva Forum were:

1. ODR was to be encouraged.
2. Greater awareness was needed at large of the availability of ODR systems and greater awareness of ODR systems.
3. The development of trust marks and self-regulatory guarantees was necessary to instil consumer confidence.
   Transparency was essential for effective ODR
5. More co-operation and standardisation on the IT framework, such as with use of XML and other facilities to enable cross communication between systems. (When data is collected and stored as evidence, and communicated from site to site, issues of standard exchange systems arise—these are the so-called exchange mark up languages or XML.[20]
6. Outcomes of ODR need to be respected and acted upon.
7. Caution is needed in relation to the development of strict rules, and there is a fear of simply developing alternative judicial systems.

---

[17] Available at http://europa.eu.int/comm/justice_home/ejn/adr/adr_ec_code_conduct_en.pdf and made final 2 July 2004.

[18] Available at http://www.cpradr.org/pdfs/Intl_EC_directive_draft_Apr04.pdf. The draft was issued for a brief consultation period in April 2004.

[19] Forum on Online Dispute Resolution (ODR), Conference Room XXVI, Palais des Nations, Geneva, 6–7 June 2002 organised under the auspices of the United Nations Economic Commission for Europe (UNECE) Team of Specialists on Internet Enterprise Development (TSIED) in cooperation with the Centre for Trade Facilitation and Electronic Business (CEFACT).

[20] The Joint Research Commission of the European Commission is currently working on the development of an ODR XML language. See, below, p 158.

Globally, the United Nations Centre for Trade Facilitation and Electronic Business (UN/CEFACT) Legal Working Group (LG) has taken a lead role in looking for global implementations and models for ODR for both B2B and B2C transactions, and researched issues relevant to this domain such as electronic signatures, jurisdiction, enforcement of contracts, and other issues.[21] UN/CEFACT was established in 1996 in response to new technological developments, and the need to make better use of available resources. The LG was requested to work particularly on ODR, because as a dispute settlement mechanism it was seen by the UN as having the potential of facilitating global trade. UN/CEFACT is open to participation from Member States, intergovernmental organizations, and sectoral and industry associations recognized by the Economic and Social Council of the United Nations (ECOSOC). The Centre's objective is to be 'inclusive' and it actively encourages organizations to contribute and help develop its recommendations and standards.[22] UNCITRAL, the UN body responsible for international trade, has, more generally, issued a Model Law on International Commercial Conciliation[23]—however recent legislative activity in the EU seems to be diverging quite significantly from the UN model.[24]

3. On-line Dispute Resolution (ODR)

ODR offers ways to resolve a case definitively (ie, with certainty that the result is binding and enforceable), and swiftly, whilst avoiding the high cost of court-based litigation. In the USA, on average, an insurance company pays $75 a month in administrative overhead for every claim in its database. The average third-party bodily injury claim in the United States takes two to three years to settle. However an ODR pilot project in the USA involving one of the top 15 property/casualty insurers found that within 72 hours of uploading the claims into an ODR system, 40% were settled. Within another 72 hours another 55% settled offline.

This section examines the nature of ODR, the types of ODR on offer, and the issues that affect attempts to translate terrestrial dispute resolution institutions to the Internet. The Scottish *Intersettle* website[25] is described in detail below as a case study of a typical small scale commercial ODR system.

---

[21] The CEFACT web page is: http://www.unece.org/cefact/.

[22] Current UNCEFACT ODR projects are—CEFACT/2001/LG14 [Draft Recommendation on Online Dispute Resolution]; CEFACT/2002/LG04 [Comments Concerning Draft ODR Recommendation] CEFACT/2002/LG07 [ICC Comments on the Online Dispute Resolution Draft].

[23] See UN Resolution 57/18, 52nd Plenary Meeting, Official Records of the General Assembly, A/RES/57/18, available at http://www.uncitral.org/stable/res5718–e.pdf.

[24] See E van GInkel, 'Transatantic Dispute Resolution', *Mediate.com*, October 2004, at http://www.mediate.com/articles/vanGinkelE1.cfm#5.

[25] www.intersettle.co.uk.

ODR takes place in an environment characterised by interconnection and dematerialisation. Using ODR, parties no longer travel to meet in courtrooms or in front of arbiters or mediators. The parties stay behind their computers, communicate by electronic means, and try to resolve their disputes by an agreement reached online or by submitting their dispute to an online arbitration tribunal or a cybercourt. The first recorded experience of ODR dates from May 1996 when a joint venture of academics and business lawyers rendered a decision after having communicated with the parties exclusively by electronic means. This cyber-tribunal was the Virtual Magistrate,[26] a joint project of the Cyberspace Law Institute, the American Arbitration Association, the National Centre for Automated Information Research, and the Villanova Centre for Information Law and Policy. The case was *Tierney and E-Mail America.*[27] Here, the defendant had placed an advertisement on a website belonging to AOL, offering to sell millions of e-mail addresses for bulk mailings. After four days the Virtual Magistrate rendered a decision stating that in the advertisement was a harmful or offensive activity according to AOL's terms of service agreement, internet custom and practice, and customer complaints. AOL, although not one of the parties, complied with the award and removed the advertisement. This is the only Virtual Magistrate decision to date, although the project did later form the basis for a commercial UDRP dispute resolution provider (see p 148 below).

Early articles on ODR reflected the optimistic 'dot.com' climate in which they were written. A report released by Forrester Research in 2001[28] on the auto insurance industry found that most of the insurance companies it interviewed were investing in claims reporting systems. 'Insurance companies really are the ones that have the ability to run the (claims) process,' said Todd Eyler, the Forrester analyst who authored the report. 'The customer wants to go to them and trusts them. The insurance company is the one that's in a position to manage the whole claims process. That being said, they're not very good at developing the solutions for each part of that process.'[29]

4. Forms of ADR

The traditional forms of ADR are negotiation, mediation and arbitration. In ODR the environment of negotiation is very different than the traditional off-line domain, hence the traditional forms are to some extent mutating (as in the

---

[26] See: http://www.vmag.org/.

[27] See: http://www.vmag.org/docs/press/52,196.html.

[28] See: http://www.forrester.com/ER/Research/Report/Summary/0,1338,10837,00.html.

[29] G Crawford, 'KMPG Analysis: Online Claims Settlement Grows Despite Dot-Com Meltdown' *Insurance Insider*, 3 April 2001.

WIPO/UDRP domain name dispute resolution forums discussed below). ODR is used for mechanisms as different as dispute prevention, ombudsman programmes, conflict management, assisted negotiation, early neutral evaluation, mediation/conciliation, mediation-arbitration (binding and/or non-binding). So a first distinction has to be drawn between actual dispute resolution which covers procedures intending directly to resolve conflicts and, on the other hand, services that should rather be considered as satellite functions seeking to prevent disputes or to facilitate or improve their resolution without actually resolving them.

(a) Automated Negotiation

Here, usually a claimant contacts an institution and presents its request. The Automated Negotiation provider then contacts the other party, which can accept or refuse to submit to the jurisdiction of the institution. The parties then enter a 'blind bidding' procedure. Each of them in turn offers or demands a certain amount of money. The proposed figures are confidential; they are neither made public nor communicated to the other party. When the amounts of the offer and the demand are sufficiently close, the case is settled for the arithmetic mean of the two figures. Often the proposed amounts are usually considered close enough for settlement when the difference narrows to 30%, but some mechanisms require 10% or even 5%. The number of bids varies between three and unlimited. Most sites offering automated negotiation also impose a time limit for the parties to reach an agreement, ranging from 15 days to 90 day and up to a year. Automated Negotiation ODR is most applicable to monetary disputes. The parties are very diverse, from insurance companies and consumers to law firms and government agencies. Most automated websites use blind bidding eg, Intersettle.co.uk, Cybersettle.com, and The ClaimRoom.[30]

(b) Assisted Negotiation

Here, the ODR provider supplies only a secure site and possibly a storage means and other facilities of this nature, but no actual negotiation service. Parties have to reach an agreement without any external entity deciding for them. The main service provided is thus software for setting up the communication, assistance in developing agendas, engaging in productive discussions, identifying and assessing potential solutions, and writing agreements. Some institutions also provide trust marks or certification programmes as a means for leading the parties towards

---

[30] Cybersettle states that its Automated Negotiation system was used in 2003 to settle a US $12.5 million product liability claim.

negotiation. The Internet auction website eBay[31] has a business relationship with *squaretrade.com*[32] which has successfully settled over 1 million cases and has over 50 million active users (according to its own website, as at November 2004). Assisted Negotiation providers are often linked to a trust mark or seal programme, as is Square Trade. Some ODR providers offer negotiations to various categories of party[33] whilst others limit themselves to consumer transactions.[34]

So far, it would seem that the major advantage of negotiation through electronic means is simplicity. The procedure requires almost nothing from the parties but goodwill and an Internet connection. No one needs to travel or agree a venue or pay a mediator because there is no meeting either in space or in time. It is sufficient to leave messages on a communication software platform. This simplicity also brings cost savings. However, these advantages also highlight the major drawback of such systems. Generally, they are not suited to more complex negotiations. In particular, and this is perhaps why on-line sites have done relatively poorly in the UK, they lack an important human touch. There are no face-to-face meetings. It is impossible to observe body language, to glean hints or other subtle indications during breaks. Generally, and perhaps more than solicitors actually realise, body language plays a major role in understanding one party's interests and aspirations and can greatly enhance settlement prospects in the right situation. This is perhaps why solicitors are so keen on the telephone.

(c) Mediation

It is often said that solicitors mediate disputes all the time by writing letters and making telephone calls to their opposite numbers. This is to misunderstand the process of mediation. Mediation is based on the activity of a neutral third party, the mediator. The third party helps the main parties in dispute come to an agreement to resolve their differences. The mediator has no decision making power. He never imposes a solution, makes no findings in fact, nor any legal determinations. His intervention can range from the lightest possible touch to so-called 'muscle' mediation where the third party in effect tries to force an agreement on to the parties in dispute.

Off-line mediation is usually organised along three major steps or sessions. First, there is an opening joint session where parties put their cards on the table. Then come a series of private meetings in which the mediator discusses each party's case in turn, in private. Most who have participated in mediation agree that it is these sessions that drive the process to a successful conclusion. Finally, there

[31] www.ebay.com.
[32] www.squaretrade.com.
[33] *Ibid.*
[34] www.bbbonline.com.

comes a closing joint session during which the parties speak with each other again and verify the terms of the settlement reach or at least the progress they have made. These latter two steps can repeat several times.

In on-line mediation, real space is replaced by cyberspace. However, to be effective, ODR providers must be able to offer common and private discussion rooms. In one study[35] researchers found that only one mediation provider actually applied the same standards that were developed by large institutions for off-line mediation.[36] In addition, instead of being organised into the three types of sessions just described, on-line procedures are sometimes over-simplified. In particular, real time discussion is virtually never offered and common and private communication rooms are not always available. One rule however is of prime importance to make the procedure effective—mediation must always be without prejudice and confidential.

Mediation is the most common form of ODR. However, it relies extensively on confidentiality. Many institutions offer mediation for any kind of dispute. Examples range from e-commerce transactions and medical claims to employment matters, personal injuries and verbal abuse on the web. The quality of justice is arguably much better than in negotiation because of the intervention of a third party. The main challenge in conducting on-line mediation is the need that parties have to 'vent'. Highly developed technology and software is needed. Getting this right means that 'the use of the screen can enhance convenience, build trust and raise expectations that the process will provide value.'[37]

(d) Arbitration

'The gist of the notion of arbitration, as regulated by most laws on arbitration, is that it is conceived as a substitute for court litigation'.[38] Even more forcefully, it has been said, 'The functions of the arbitrator and judge are exactly the same. Only the origin differs.'[39]

---

[35] University of Geneva—'Online Dispute Resolution—The State of the Art and the Issues, December 2001'. This report is the first milestone of a research project conducted by the Private International Law Department of the Geneva University Law School. The project is financed by a grant of the Swiss National Research Fund. The project aims at evaluating both legally and technologically the first experiments in online dispute resolution and to formulate on this basis recommendations for the improvement of dispute settlement mechanisms using information technology. It involves a review of existing practice; an identification of the problem areas; the formulation of possible solutions.

[36] http://www.onlineresolution.com, formerly http://www.onlinemediators.com.

[37] E Katsh and J Rifkin, *On Line Dispute Resolution—Resolving Conflicts in Cyberspace* (John Wiley and Sons, 2001) (full text searchable on Amazon.com).

[38] AJ van den Berg, *The New York Arbitration Convention of 1958*, (Kluwer, 1994) p 44.

[39] E Jarrosson, *La Notion d'Arbitrage*, LGDJ, 1987, p 101.

The most powerful advantage of arbitration is the worldwide enforceability of arbitral awards provided certain formalities are met. This is the effect of the New York Convention 1958.[40] The relevant provisions state that—

Article 3 Each contracting state shall recognise arbitral awards as binding and enforce them in accordance with the rules of procedure of the territory where the award is relied upon, under the conditions laid down in the following Articles.

Article 4 To obtain the recognition and enforcement mentioned in the preceding Article, the party applying for recognition and enforcement shall, at the time of the application, supply (a) the duly authenticated original award or a certified copy; (b) the original agreement under which the parties undertake to submit their difference to arbitration.

Approximately 20 ODR websites offer arbitration services. There is virtually no limit to the type of dispute handled. Online arbitration is available for relationships involving businesses or consumers. However, arbitration is the form of ODR that applies legal rules with the highest regularity. It is the most formal method of ODR. Offline, it is a common procedure in international disputes. Effectively it is the private equivalent of a court. Online arbitration providers have to make sure that their mechanisms conform to the formal rules, particularly to achieve enforceability under the New York Convention of 1958.

Agreements to arbitrate online face problems concerning their validity, their evidence and their enforceability. If agreements to arbitrate are to be entered into online, many national laws and international conventions still require the arbitration agreement to be in writing.[41] The current wording and interpretation of the New York Convention (Article 2 (2)), for instance, do not envisage the agreement being recorded by electronic means. There is also the problem that, under the New York Convention, Article 4(1), as traditionally interpreted, the party moving for enforcement must provide an award that is in 'writing', signed by a majority of the arbitrators, and that is either the authenticated original or a duly certified copy thereof. Technically, these conditions could be met if electronic documents were recognised as constituting writing[42] and if digital signatures were used—because these can authenticate the sender and the content of the message—but these solutions do not correspond to the current wording of the New York Convention, nor to its common interpretation. One obvious solution would be to use an

---

[40] See http://www.hartwell.demon.co.uk/nyc_text.htm for full text.

[41] Only the UNCITRAL Model Law (Art 7(2)), the German Arbitration Act (§ 1031(1)), the English Arbitration Act (s 5(6)), and the Swiss Private International Law Act (Art 178(1)) consider that the agreement is in writing when recorded by electronic means.

[42] See the Electronic Communications Act 2000, s 7.

'E-watermarked' printed version of the arbitral award,[43] which could be signed by the arbiter, and the signed print-out would clearly constitute the original award.

(e) UDRP

Perhaps the best-known and most successful example of ODR is the Uniform Domain Name Dispute Resolution Policy ('UDRP'), which is a procedure for online resolution of disputes that concern trademarks, and domain names. It was drafted under the auspices of the World Intellectual Property Organisation (WIPO) to be a multinational privatized solution to the endemic problem of cyber-squatting and is regulated by the Internet Corporation for Assigned Names and Numbers (ICANN),[44] a private California based non-profit organisation, which manages Internet domain names and Internet Protocol (IP) addresses. Four ICANN-approved bodies operate actual dispute resolution under the UDRP. The procedure established by the UDRP does not exactly match any of the previously defined forms of alternative dispute resolution. It is neither negotiation nor mediation, but it is also unlike arbitration. It cannot be termed as arbitration for many reasons notably that its decisions are not binding and the procedure is not exclusive for proceedings before courts.

The institutions approved by ICANN are WIPO,[45] National Arbitration Forum,[46] CPR Institute for Dispute Resolution,[47] and the Asian Domain Name Dispute Resolution Centre.[48] Together they have processed more than 4000 cases in less than two years. We can identify the following reasons for the success of the UDRP, reasons that all ODR providers should learn from.

1. The participation of WIPO adds credibility to the process.
2. Transparency of the procedure—decisions available online immediately in full text.
3. Self-executing—two months after filing, the case is closed. Foreign authorities cannot block the outcome.
4. The UDRP clause is imposed on every dot.com registrant. Trademark owners can force registrants to undergo the procedure.
5. The subject matter of domain names is publicity sensitive, hence press interest, which imposes a degree of public accountability.
6. All interaction is electronic. This forces people to deal with the matter by electronic means solely, quickly and efficiently.

---

[43] See: http://www.watermarkingworld.org; http://www.abathorn.com.
[44] See: http://www.icann.org/udrp/.
[45] See: http://arbiter.wipo.int/domains/filing/index.html.
[46] See: http://www.arbforum.com/domains/.
[47] See: http://www.cpradr.org/ICANN_Menu.htm.
[48] http://www.adndrc.org/adndrc/index.html.

5. Features of ODR: Due Process, Enforceability, Security, Confidentiality and Costs

The Quality of Justice On-line

Solving disputes requires communication. Be it in court litigation or other forms of dispute resolution, the existence of rights and obligations has to be expressed, arguments have to be uttered, and reality has to be described to apply a fair process. The right and the capacity of the parties to communicate with the deciding body and the other party is an issue of due process, or at least of quality of justice. Offline, due process and quality of justice often depend on questions of time: there has, for instance, to be a proper time-period for evidence and argumentation and the global length of the procedure has to be neither too short nor too long.[49]

One of the characteristics of cyberspace is the worship of speed. In the field of law, however, speed induces mixed feelings. As courts become slower, demands arise for a better access to justice. A mechanism that is too fast may not be felt to provide quality justice.[50] In negotiation and mediation, there is no 'hearing' of the parties as lawyers understand it, but they both have to be able to express themselves. This is the argument of natural justice. Of course, there is nothing to stop parties contracting for a blind bidding system. Haynes states: 'In mediation language is almost all we have to work with'.[51] He further argues that communication in mediation, as in any communication, is full of subtleties and these can often determine the chances of settlement.[52] Parties often go into mediation in an entrenched position. The mediator has to get each party off its perch and towards negotiating. He has to understand what the parties want which is not always money. It could be an apology or it could be an acknowledgement of blame. The mediator has to build up trust between himself and the parties and between the parties themselves. For this he must observe body language, and vocal cues because these indicate the degrees of trust and willingness to reach agreement. Therefore, on-line institutions providing mediation must offer the equivalent of common private discussion rooms, and real time communication facilities. Even here there is a risk—people with good typing skills and a high-speed computer

---

[49] V Bonnet, K Boudaoud, J Harms, (Centre Universitaire Informatique University of Geneva Switzerland) and T Schultz, G Kaufmann-Kohler and D Langer, (Faculty of Law, University of Geneva, Switzerland) *Electronic Communication Issues Related To Online Dispute Resolution Systems.*

[50] In *Walkinshaw v Diniz* [2002] Lloyd's Rep 165 (Court of Appeal) the High Court in England reflected on the 'number of meetings that justice required'. In ODR the problem is not so much the number of meetings but what happens during them. For instance, is e-mail contact enough?'

[51] J Haynes, 'Metaphors of Mediation', excerpts found at http://mediate.com/articles/metaphor.cfm.

[52] *Ibid.*

connection can easily dominate a forum such as a chat room. Occasionally however slow typing and the resulting time lag can cause people to pay more attention to the contents of messages. Furthermore, assisted negotiations are usually conducted only by e-mail.[53]

(a) Enforceability of ODR Clauses

It is trite to state that in common law, courts will regard a contractual agreement to resolve disputes by arbitration as highly persuasive[54] and also as good reason to sist their own proceedings, provided the motion to do so is made sufficiently early on. The law does not oust the jurisdiction of the Court in general terms from consideration of contracts containing arbitration clauses but 'where the claim or dispute in question falls firmly within the terms of the arbitration clause it will only be in the most exceptional cases that the Court will interfere to prevent the matter being resolved by arbitration'.[55] Many Internet contracts, especially the many whose choice of law is in the USA, contain onerous dispute resolution provisions, requiring arbitration in a particular US state or place. Frequently the terms and conditions of contract on a website, or for downloaded materials are 'clicked through' unread. In the cause of EU consumer contracts, this hazardous approach at least may run foul of the statutory cooling off period under the Distance Selling Regulations.[56] Mandatory arbitration clauses in consumer contracts may, one imagines, also be challenged under UK or EC legislation relating to unfair contractual terms such as the UK Unfair Contract Terms Act 1977—although no such challenges have yet been to the relevant court. This lack of precedent is a serious concern for European ODR suppliers.

At present there are no reported UK cases dealing with arbitration in the context of Internet contracts. But an indication of the sort of issues that may in future arise in these situations can be found in the recent USA class action case against PayPal.[57] Here the plaintiffs sought injunctive relief on behalf of a purported nationwide class for alleged violations of state and federal law by PayPal, Inc. PayPal filed a motion to compel individual arbitration pursuant to the arbitration

---

[53] Where parties can sometimes leave messages in a common discussion room effectively without real time communication (onlineresolution.com). Some mediation sites offer both common and private communication possibilities: 123settle.com [note past tense] offered confidential and 'open' e-mail correspondence; theResolutionForum.com allows private and public communication.

[54] *Hamlyn & Company v Talisker Distillery* [1894] R 21 (HL).

[55] Orkney Island Council, Petitioners [2002] SLT 10.

[56] The Consumer Protection (Distance Selling) Regulations 2000 (SI 2000 No 2334) transpose into UK law the EU Directive 97/7/EC on the protection of consumers in respect of distance contracts—see further Nordhausen, Chapter 8.

[57] *Comb and Toher v PayPal, Inc* (US District Court, ND Cal, San Jose Div).

clause contained in its standard User Agreement and the US Federal Arbitration Act ('FAA')[58]

(i) *The* PayPal *Case*

PayPal[59] is an on-line payment service that allows a business or private individual to send and receive payments via the Internet. A PayPal account holder sends money by informing PayPal of the intended recipient's e-mail address and the amount to be sent and by designating a funding source such as a credit card or bank account. PayPal accesses the funds and immediately makes them available to the intended recipient. PayPal generates revenues from transaction fees and the interest it derives from holding funds until they are sent. As of 1 January 2001, approximately 10,000 account holders had registered with PayPal.[60] But Paypal then experienced a sudden increase in its popularity, attracting 10.6 million accounts (of which private individuals held 8.5 million) by 30 September 2001.

The plaintiffs alleged, in short, that Paypal had grown too fast, so that it was making damaging errors with transactions whilst failing to deal with complaints. Plaintiff Comb, not even a PayPal customer, alleged that without his knowledge, consent or authorisation, PayPal removed the sums of $110.00 and $450.00 from his bank account. This caused Comb's bank account to have insufficient funds, and the bank charged Comb $208.50 for failing to maintain his required balance. Co-plaintiff Roberta Toher alleged that she opened a PayPal account sometime in 2000. PayPal failed to provide her with the name, address, and telephone number of a person she should notify in the event of an unauthorized electronic transfer. On 24 February 2002, Toher discovered that PayPal had transferred funds from her cheque account to four individuals without her knowledge, consent or authorisation. Her attempts to contact PayPal were largely unsuccessful. Co-plaintiff Resnick alleged that he registered an account with PayPal and linked his e-mail address resnickjeff@hotmail.com (with two 'f's) to that account. A third party appropriated Resnick's PayPal user name and password and linked an e-mail account resnickjefff@hotmail.com (with three 'f's) to Resnick's PayPal account. The third party sold two Apple Computers on eBay, and the buyers deposited their payment into the fraudulent account. When the buyers did not receive their product, they filed a complaint with PayPal, which without notice or explanation then restricted Resnick's—legitimate—account.

PayPal's User Agreement contained the following arbitration clause:

> Arbitration. Any controversy or claim arising out of or relating to this Agreement or the provision of Services shall be settled by binding arbitration in accordance with the

---

[58] 9 USC § 1, *et seq.*

[59] See: http://www.paypal.com (and http://www.papyal.co.uk), and discussed further in Guadamuz and Usher, Chapter 6 in this volume.

[60] See *Comb v PayPal, Inc*, above n 57.

commercial arbitration rules of the American Arbitration Association. Any such controversy or claim shall be arbitrated on an individual basis, and shall not be consolidated in any arbitration with any claim or controversy of any other party. The arbitration shall be conducted in Santa Clara County, California, and judgment on the arbitration award may be entered in any court having jurisdiction thereof . . .

In California, contractual defences, such as fraud, duress, or unconscionability, may be applied to invalidate arbitration agreements. And although California has a strong policy favouring arbitration, '[i]t is beyond cavil that arbitration is a matter of contract and a party cannot be required to submit to arbitration any dispute which he has not agreed so to submit.'[61]

The plaintiffs argued that they had not agreed to PayPal's User Agreement, and that even if the court found that they had, the User Agreement and the arbitration clause were unconscionable. The judge agreed with their submission that unconscionability in the USA has both procedural and substantive components. The procedural component is satisfied by the existence of unequal bargaining positions and hidden contractual terms. The substantive component is satisfied by 'overly harsh or one-sided results that shock the conscience.' The two elements operate on a sliding scale, so that the more significant one is, the less significant the other need be.

Was the Mandatory Arbitration Clause Unconscionable?

The concept of unconscionability is as familiar to English lawyers as in the US, notably in the area of estoppel.[62] Unconscionability normally arises in disputes about contractual terms that are so oppressive as to amount to a penalty clause, which as such is unenforceable. In *City Inn v Shepherd Construction*,[63] the Scottish courts in discussing the nature of a penalty clause held that a such a clause 'does not constitute a genuine pre-estimate of the loss likely to be suffered by the latter party as a result of the relevant breach of contract, but is instead unconscionable in respect that it is designed to operate *in terrorem*, or oppressively or punitively'. This language clearly echoes the "shock the conscience" terminology adopted in the PayPal case.

PayPal argued that their arbitration clause was not procedurally unconscionable because it did not concern essential items such as food or clothing and because the plaintiffs had meaningful alternative sources for the subject services.[64] However the District Court rejected this, noting that the party asserting uncon-

---

[61] *Ajida Tech, Inc, v Roos Instruments, Inc*, 87 Cal App 4th 534 (2001) 541.

[62] Scots law has recently also restated the existence of a doctrine of estoppel in *City Inn v Shepherd Construction* [2002] SLT 781.

[63] *Ibid.*

[64] Relying upon *Dean Witter Reynolds, Inc v Superior Court*, 211 Cal App 3d 758, 769 (1989).

scionability was not here as in previous jurisprudence 'a sophisticated investor'; in the PayPal case, the amount of the average transaction was $55.00, the vast majority of PayPal customers were private individuals who were not 'sophisticated,' and there was at least a factual dispute as to whether PayPal's competitors offer their services without requiring customers to enter into arbitration agreements.

In the USA an unconscionable clause can still be enforced if its terms are overall reasonable.[65] The Court in *PayPal* therefore assessed reasonableness by looking at (a) lack of mutuality in the User Agreement (b) and the practical effects of the arbitration clause with respect to consolidation of claims, (c) the costs of arbitration, and (d) forum.

Section V (3) of the User Agreement, stated that in the event of a dispute, PayPal 'at its sole discretion' may restrict accounts, withhold funds, undertake its own investigation of a customer's financial records, close accounts, and procure ownership of all funds in dispute unless and until the customer is 'later determined to be entitled to the funds in dispute.' PayPal alone makes the final decision with respect to a dispute. The User Agreement 'is subject to change by PayPal without prior notice (unless prior notice is required by law), by posting of the revised Agreement on the PayPal website.' PayPal argued that the User Agreement did not lack mutuality because nothing in the agreement precludes a customer from using the court system to seek relief. This argument failed: PayPal could not show that 'business realities' justified such one-sidedness.

Prohibition Against Consolidation of Claims

The arbitration clause prohibited PayPal customers from consolidating their claims. But in *Szetela v Discover Bank*,[66] the court had determined that a large credit card company could not enforce a prohibition with respect to consumer claims, because in practice most claims were likely to involve consumers seeking the return of small amounts of money, and any remedy obtained by the few consumers who would not be dissuaded from pursuing their rights would pertain only to those consumers without collateral estoppel effect. The court concluded that such circumstances raise '[t]he potential for millions of customers to be overcharged small amounts without an effective method of redress'. PayPal's prohibition against consolidation was held unreasonable.

The plaintiffs in *Paypal* claimed that the cost of an individual arbitration under the User Agreement was likely to exceed $5000. Further, because the arbitration clause was silent as to who bore the cost of arbitration, under California law each party was required to pay a *pro rata* share of costs.[67] The Court concluded that

[65] *Craig v Brown & Root, Inc,* 2000 84 Cal App 4th 416, 422–23 where arbitration clause enforced.
[66] 2002 97 Cal App 4th at 1094.
[67] Cal Code Civ P § 1284.2.

these aspects of the arbitration clause were so harsh as to be substantively uncon-scionable.

Forum

The User Agreement required that any arbitration must take place in Santa Clara County, California. The judge was scathing, holding that ' limiting the venue to PayPal's back yard appears to be yet one more means by which the arbitration clause serves to shield PayPal from liability instead of providing a neutral forum in which to arbitrate disputes'.

In conclusion therefore, Paypal's motion to compel individual arbitration in California was denied: a welcome victory for the consumer and a decision of significance for consumers in the UK and EC also seeking to overturn mandatory consumer arbitration clauses.

(a) Confidentiality

Most ODR sites offer some or all of the following:

- E-mail
- Web posting
- Telephone calls or tele-conferencing
- Real time chat, instant messaging, online conferencing
- Video conferencing
- Fax and sometimes, voicemail[68]

ODR providers have to strike a balance between the privacy desired by the parties using these technologies, and the transparency, accountability and building of trust, which is engendered by publishing the decisions of the ODR provider. ODR providers must provide clear policies on how they deal with confidentiality. All blind bidding websites provide that the figures negotiated are unknown to any party except the bidder.[69] Most ODR blind bidding sites provide that the submit-ted figures will not be revealed to anybody.[70] In Assisted Negotiation, the usual position is that all information gathered during proceedings is confidential.[71] Mediation is almost always confidential and without prejudice. The agreement to

---

[68] Surprisingly found on only one site—http://www.OnlineDisputes.com.

[69] TheClaimRoom.com can display offers and demands on a website accessible to both parties.

[70] www.Allsettle.com reserves the right to publish outcomes in the future. www.TheClaimRoom.com on special request will provide bidding statistics.

[71] At www.webtrader.com its trust mark programme requires the merchants to post comments of the customers on its website.

mediate usually includes specific provisions that the mediator is not allowed to give evidence or produce documents or other information in a court or in arbitration. In on-line mediation, the proceedings are always private and confidential; outsiders are never allowed to participate in the sessions; and most ODR providers address confidentiality on their website.

Confidentiality is usually expected in arbitration. However, a general obligation of confidentiality cannot be said to exist as a matter of law in national arbitration, so that 'arbitration rules should be drafted so as to create an explicit, positive duty on the part of the participants in the arbitration'.[72] In on-line arbitration, the practice universally seems to be that the proceedings are confidential and private according to all the providers.

A dispute resolution provider operating under the UDRP must publish all its decisions in full text on the Internet. However it is not clear how far this unusual degree of transparency as to ODR outcomes has actually resulted in greater consistency and user confidence in UDRP decisions. Mueller argues in *Rough Justice—An Analysis of ICANN's Uniform Dispute Resolution Policy*, published in late 2000, that, after analyzing the first 500 completed disputes under the UDRP,[73] there was decisive statistical evidence that certain arbitrators take a preliminary view as to whether or not a registrant has acted in bad faith.[74] The 'bad faith' condition required by the UDRP for a claimant to obtain or cancel a disputed domain name has, the report found, become the crucial part of the test in practice.[75] The report further referred to a number of specific decisions, which it criticised.[76] In principle, however, the transparency and publication of decisions espoused by the UDRP is to be recommended.

(c) Security

ODR systems have to balance accessibility against security. They must avoid long delays in communication, be simple to follow and use, and must adapt to new user profiles without collecting excessive data and overuse of cookies. In the United Kingdom, the seventh data protection principle of the Data Protection Act 1998[77] requires data controllers to use appropriate levels of security in respect of data which identifies living individuals, whilst prohibiting the gathering of excessive amounts of data, or excessive retention of data.

---

[72] J Paulsson and N Rawding ('The Trouble with Confidentiality', 1995) 11 *Arbitration International* 303.

[73] The report is available at: http://dcc.syr.edu/roughjustice.htm.

[74] *Ibid.*

[75] See J Warchus, 'Domain Name', practice note at: http://www.itconstructionforum.org.uk/uploadedFiles/DomainNames.pdf.

[76] Crew.dom and Barcelona.com as noted on:http://www.itconstructionforum.org.uk/uploadedFiles/DomainNames.pdf.

[77] 1998 Act, s 29.

Unprotected e-mails and web-based communications are more vulnerable than communications by paper documents, although electronic messages can of course be protected by encryption. Electronic communication and the access to data should ideally be secured before, during and after ODR procedure. Methods of securing e-mail include:

- secure multi-purpose Internet mail exchange protocol S/MIME Pretty Good Privacy (PGP) and digital signatures;
- digital signatures, ie, cryptographic instruments backed up by certificates from trusted third parties (Effectively a digital signature verifies the origin and integrity of a message. If the key of the apparent sender has been used in order to create the signature, a dispute resolver is most likely to hold that the message is attributable to the sender/holder of the private key that was used.)[78]

Most ODR providers do not however in fact use secure e-mail or secure authentication to their websites. This area may be taken as developing. It may be necessary to distinguish between small disputes with low amounts at stake and larger disputes with high financial stakes.

Issues of security, integrity, authentication and verification become crucial if electronic communications may constitute evidence to be submitted to an arbitral tribunal or a court. If no specific tools are used, the parties may easily argue that e-mail was forged or the information of a web page has been altered since the conclusion of the contract. Technological means must be used to rule out any reasonable doubt that data produced as evidence has been altered.

In summary, ODR providers must recognise the risks implied by the technology they use. They must take necessary measures to reduce them and have a clear policy regarding the remaining risks. The customer must be informed about the risks. ODR providers must address issues specific to dispute resolution such as data integrity and protection, system simplicity and accessibility. They must also ensure compatibility of their systems with both merchants and customers. They must agree on a standard of documents (data record and data exchange models).[79] In principle it can be argued that it is the sender's responsibility to secure the information he or she sends. If the validity of the message depends upon its reception by the addressee, the sender bears the risk of late or non-delivery and has interception by third parties. However, if a cosumer pays by giving his credit card data the general rules place the burden of proof for establishing his order was so placed on the credit card company.[80]

---

[78] See regulation in the EC Electronic Signatures Directive 1999/93.

[79] See the XML discussion later in this chapter.

[80] Art 8 of the EC Directive 1997/7/CE on Distance Selling states that clauses that put the risk of fraud on customers are void.

(d) Cost and Duration of ODR

Cost is often cited along with speed as the major reason to prefer ODR to traditional litigation or ADR. Costs generally vary according to the type of ODR service provided. ODR blind bidding sites generally charge a registration fee per claim according to value, and a settlement fee when the case settles.[81] Fees for Assisted Negotiation are usually per party per hour.[82] Some sites levy a percentage of settlement amounts.[83]

The fees for on-line mediation are lower than off-line. Most institutions determined their fees by the hour.[84] Some institutions offer mediation as part of a trust mark programme.[85] Many B2C sites offer mediation free to customers, or at a highly subsideised rate, so as to build consumer trust in transacting on their site: for example, eBay bought Square Trade, an established ADR provider to provide such services, and now offer ODR including mediation services to their clients either free, or at a highly reduced rate. For on-line B2B arbitration, most institutions charge by the hour. Two institutions provide arbitration for a flat fee.[86] There are numerous other variations on the theme in relation to arbitration.

For the UDRP, there is one global flat fee defined according to the number of domain names to be decided by a single panellist. For a dispute to be decided by a panel of three, the fee is doubled. The charges after February 2002 were $1150 or $2800 for between 1 and 5 names and according to whether there were one or three panellists.[87] For 6 domain names up to 10 domain names, the fees are $1750 and $3500.[88]

The duration of ODR proceedings is generally limited in Automated Negotiation, either by a maximum number of submissions or by agreement between the parties. In Assisted Negotiation, no time limit is usually set. In ODR Mediation, and ODR Arbitration, there are usually two time limits, those for submissions and replies, and those that relate to the conclusion of the transaction. Four websites provide a time limit, which sets a maximum duration for the procedure of between four hours and sixty days.

---

[81] Intersettle, Cybersettle, The Claim Room.
[82] OnlineResolution.com.
[83] Claimchoice.com.
[84] WebMediate, Online Resolution, NewCourtCity.
[85] http://www.novaforum.com.
[86] MARS, and Webdisputes.com.
[87] Effective 1 February 2002, found at: http://www.arb-forum.com/domains/UDRP/fees.asp.
[88] See: http://www.arb-forum.com/domains/UDRP/fees.asp.

(e) Interoperability: Standard Setting and XML

If ODR systems are to talk with each other, interoperable standards must be developed. Such technologies will be vital, particularly when data needs to be exchanged between institutions such as the courts or brokerage firms and ADR providers. The most promising candidate mechanism for such standardization is XML, or eXtensible Mark-up Language. XML is a globally recognized open standard used to tag information on web pages, forms and free flowing text documents. XML[89] is 'a simplified subset of the Standard Generalized Markup Language (SGML) which allows construction of structured data (trees) which rely on composition relationships'.[90] XML will allow a currently static Web page to function like a database, but without requiring the resources now required to put a database on the Web. Because of this value to the commercial sector, Microsoft and all the major software companies have encouraged the development of XML. Some features for browsing XML sites are already contained in Internet Explorer. XML is being investigated as a potential technology for filing court documents.[91] In 2003, UNCEFACT announced that the latest completed versions of XML specifications have been endorsed by the 2003 plenary session of UN/CEFACT meeting in Geneva.[92] UNCEFACT is actively considering the application to ODR of XML to enable the exchange of information (data) between different applications and data sources on the World Wide Web.

6. ODR vs Traditional Litigation: The View from Scotland

Legal professionals, and the traditional civil dispute resolution methods that hitherto have been applied by them, have historically been trammelled by, and yet paradoxically also comforted by, the necessity of operating within physical and temporal constraints. Scottish civil court procedures undergo changes in matters of detail from time to time[93] but the core processes would be quite recognisable to practitioners of two centuries ago. The modern form of summons used in the Court of Session was introduced in 1850. In Scotland, arbitration is still regulated

---

[89] *Per* UNCEFACT's definition.

[90] See: www.pisces.co.uk. PISCES is also concerned with XML standards in UK property transactions.

[91] http://www.oasis-open.org/committees/tc_home.php?wg_abbrev=legalxml-courtfiling.

[92] See: http://xml.coverpages.org/UNCEFACT-Endorse-ebXMLhtml.

[93] Court of Session rule changes were made in 1994 to introduce 'fast track' Commercial Court procedures; new fast track procedure specific to asbestosis cases was introduced in 2002; and simplified personal injury procedures came into force in April 2003.

by the Arbitration (Scotland) Act 1894. Courts and ADR processes, including not only traditional arbitration but the more recent advent of third-party mediation, each rely for their ultimate effectiveness upon the physical presence of parties and their representatives, usually at a particular geographical location, and between particular hours of the day. Time also equates to expense, both in terms of payment for professional representation as well as the disruptions to business and lifestyle inherent in conducting a traditional adversarial process. These factors perhaps explain why in Scotland some 96% of all civil cases that are set down for proof (trial) ultimately settle out of court, the majority at the last moment 'at the door of the court'. However, it seems professionals have become somewhat too comfortable with, or at least somewhat reluctant to question, the numerous ways in which delay and inertia can detract from the attainment of justice. Procedures are followed, postures adopted, and advice is given using familiar reference points and cues discovered, learned and subsequently instilled upon the next generation. Criticism of delay is frequent yet pressure for change is not commensurately overwhelming. The last word on the matter perhaps ought to be left to the working party on Court of Session Procedure, established at the request of the Lord President on 9 October 1997, whose Report[94] commences with the following indictment:

> Like all of those who have thought about the way [personal injury] actions are presently dealt with, the Working Party has been impressed by the inconvenience caused by the large number of cases which settle either on the day of the proof (trial) or during the preceding week. Substantial numbers of witnesses are compelled to attend court unnecessarily, or are subjected to the inconvenience of being cited and then told that they need not attend. In the case of professional witnesses, substantial fees may be incurred in relation to cases that never start . . . [P]ursuers may feel under last minute pressure to accept sums less than the full value of their claims, particularly in view of their fear of the sanction of a crippling award of expenses. The mere fact that there is a risk that, if the case is not called and no settlement is reached, there will be further extensive delay may create pressure to settle, particularly for a pursuer. It does seem quite inappropriate for so many actions to be settled in a pressure situation . . . which may, to the litigant experiencing his first Tuesday morning there, appear chaotic.[95]

Commercial and consumer disputes in Scotland have therefore historically been settled using adversarial techniques. For example the Supreme Civil Court, the Court of Session, based in Edinburgh has served the needs of the community since the early 16th century. Claims of lesser value in Scotland are habitually referred to local Sheriff Courts. The governing statute in respect of Sheriff Courts disputes is still the Sheriff Court (Scotland) 1907. A Small Claims procedure for amounts under £750 was introduced in 1986. Most consumer disputes are not resolved

---

[94] http://www.scotcourts.gov.uk/index1.asp.
[95] *Ibid.*

through this procedure for reasons associated with delay and the public's general wariness of the court process. The Court of Session is principally regulated by delegated legislation known as Act of Sederunt. The most recent incarnation of the Court of Session rules was laid down in 1994.[96] The modern rules of the Sheriff Court were written in 1993.[97] Although both sets of rules were a welcome improvement upon their predecessors, Scottish litigation procedures today are still couched in adverserial terms, ranging the 'pursuer' against the 'defender'. Generally, formal encouragements to resolve litigation by means of ADR are non-existent in Scotland. The dramatic rewriting of the civil procedure rules that occurred in 1996 in England and Wales known colloquially as the Woolf reforms[98] have not been replicated in Scotland. The Court of Session has had special provisions for dealing with commercial actions for many years. New much-revised fast track arrangements have been operating since September 1994, replacing the earlier procedure that had fallen into desuetude. New fast track procedures were also introduced on 1 April 2003 for personal injury claims. In 2002, a dedicated, fast track procedure was established solely for asbestosis claims. Mediation in Scotland is in its infancy, enjoying a small but dedicated following.[99] In family cases however, mediation has been more successful[100] however, for the general body of Scottish litigation, mediation has yet to become accepted as a mainstream technique. Unlike in England and Wales, judicial sanction has never been visited upon a party to the Scottish action who refuses to mediate, or who reaches an agreement to go to mediation. This position contrasts somewhat starkly with decisions with England where the courts have penalised such conduct by declining to follow tradition and award expenses (costs) to a successful party.[101] At present, therefore, the only two alternatives to outright litigation available in Scotland are arbitration; and, in relation to construction contracts, adjudication procedure.[102] Adjudication can frequently be an inquisitorial process.

Where the parties have contracted for arbitration, the Scottish courts have long held that the arbitration clause must be given effect and litigation is regularly assisted (stayed) to enable arbitration.[103] One of the key advantages, particularly in disputes having an international element, stems from the provisions of the New York Convention of 1958, which in effect gives decrees arbitral global

---

[96] Rules of the Court of Session 1994.

[97] Ordinary Cause Rules 1993.

[98] SI 1998 No 3132 L17, The Civil Procedure Rules 1998, came into force on 26 April 1999.

[99] For example, http://www.core-mediation.co.uk.

[100] Ordinary Cause Rules, Rule 32.22.

[101] As in *Dunnett v Railtrack* [2002] EWCA Civ 303; and *Cow v Plymouth Council* [2002] Fam Law 265. However recent cases have suggested that initial enthusiasm for this approach may be cooling: see *Hurst v Leeming* [2002] EWHC 1051; and *Corenso (UK) Ltd v The Burnden Group plc*, LTL [2003] EWHC 1805 (QB).

[102] Under the Housing Grants, Construction and Regeneration Act 1996.

[103] *Hamlyn v Talisker Distillery* (1894) 2 SLT 12.

enforceability.[104] This Convention, in summary, enables the party in whose favour arbitration is determined to register the Award in the courts of each country that is a signatory to the 1958 convention. Having taken this step, the successful party achieves the equivalent of a Court judgement in the relevant jurisdiction, which may be enforced according to the ordinary procedures of the territory concerned. It is however, a fair and relevant criticism of arbitration that the cost of the procedure can be prohibitive, particularly if both parties engage learned legal representation. In addition, funding requires to be provided not only for a venue but also for the services of the arbiter(s). Procedure within arbitration is habitually, though not necessarily, unstructured. Arbitration is unashamedly an adversarial procedure.

Leaving to one side, therefore, the processes of arbitration and adjudication, and also the limited application of mediation to family disputes, the general observation may be made that Scottish Court Procedure in the early part of the twenty-first century looks little different to the situation obtaining the end of the nineteenth century. Overall, Scottish litigation practitioners and conveyancing solicitors (being by definition those first likely to need to learn new processes with the advent of changes in technology outlined above) have been for rather too long accustomed to the traditional 'rhythm' of court cases and land transactions, each being in essence a recurring sequence of postures built around the exchange of large amounts of paper. The incentive for change is low. Whilst external pressure—including it would seem client pressure—upon lawyers to use technology other than for basic email, document creation and 'back office' is not yet intolerable, changes are in the pipeline. Automated Registration of Title to Land (ARTL) is well advanced in Scotland,[105] and when the system goes live, probably in early 2006, Recording Dues and Stamp Duty will automatically be debited from a solicitor's account as soon as the Property Register is amended by the on-line registration of title deeds and security documentation.[106] Also, in relation to solicitor and client banking services, changes to the BACS clearing system[107] were announced in September 2002. By the end of 2005, these changes mean that anyone wishing to transfer funds using the BACS system will be able to do so only using Public Key Infrastructure (PKI), that is to say, someone in a suitable position of authority within solicitors and client firms, or perhaps many such individuals, will need to have digital signatures and encryption installed on their desktop PCs. The new

---

[104] Convention on the Recognition and Enforcement of Foreign Arbitral Awards, New York, 1 June 1958, discussed elsewhere in this chapter.

[105] http://www.ros.gov.uk/pdfs/artlbrochure.pdf.

[106] For the situation in England & Wales see the Property Information System Common Exchange Standard ['PISCES'] project, or visit http://www.pisces.co.uk.

[107] BACS Ltd previously known as Bankers Automated Clearing Service. Established in 1968, BACS is owned by the major banks and building societies. BACS' business encompasses the Electronic Funds Transfer (EFT) processing of Direct Debit, Direct Credit, Standing Order, information advice and the management of inter-bank network services.)

programme will implement an upgrade to BACSTEL, the existing, telecoms-based customer delivery channel to BACS and its payment services, fully utilising PKI and the latest cryptographic methods.[108]

7. Intersettle: A Case Study from Scotland[109]

Scotland's ODR website, www.intersettle.co.uk was born in late 2000, co-funded by eight of the major Scottish litigation firms.[110] Intersettle provides parties who are in dispute with an opportunity to settle financial claims with the help of an on-line system for making bids. The process is consensual. It can be invoked before or during litigation and is most commonly used for personal injury cases. Liability need not have been admitted, though most frequently recourse to the Intersettle website occurred when liability was not in dispute.

The Intersettle process is not a means of deciding liability. Individuals or agents acting on their behalf can register, register a new 'case', and make a figure as a settlement bid which will then be sent via email to the other party. By default, the bidding is undertaken blind (ie, neither party is aware of the figures submitted by the other), although users can alter this if they so choose. The protocol employed by the site settles the claim automatically at the mid-point of the difference between bids that fall within 15% of each other (or a percentage less than 15% as specified by the initiating party).[111] The parties to a claim are required to complete the negotiation within a 90–day period from the initiation of the case with Intersettle. If no settlement is reached, then the parties must resort to traditional means of settling the case—hence the default position of blind bids so as not to prejudice either side's position should no settlement be reached.[112]

The germ of Intersettle came from the revolutionary progress being made in the negotiation of blind-bidding claim settlements on-line in the US. Scotland was an ideal marketplace for such a system, partly as a result of the existence of an extra-judicial settlement fee scale. This provides that where claims are settled entirely outside the court process in Scotland, the solicitor's fee is determined not by how much time he or she has spent on the claim, but purely on how much the claim has actually settled for. This system of, effectively, fixed scale rather than per hour

---

[108] See http://www.bacs.co.uk/services/BACSTEL-IP_whatis.php.

[109] The author hereby discloses an interest as a non-executive director of and shareholder in, Intersettle. Intersettle was the brainchild of a Glasgow trainee solicitor, Stephen Moore, now in business in his own right as a freelance IT consultant. The following section is largely based upon a draft contributed by him, and I am grateful for his contribution.

[110] Anderson Strathern, Balfour & Manson, Digby Brown, Drummond Miller, HBM Sayers, Ledingham Chalmers, Macroberts, Thompsons.

[111] http://www.intersettle.co.uk/how_it_works/.

[112] *Ibid.*

fees provided an incentive for solicitors and insurers alike to use a system, which sped up, rather than span out the lengthy and frustrating negotiation process. Settlement negotiation of low value claims is, furthermore, in the main a straightforward process. Rarely does a claims handler or solicitor with a moderate degree of experience come across a situation where they are ready to negotiate without having a figure in mind as to what would be a reasonable settlement. However, and without exception, both parties, aware of what they would ultimately accept, habitually started off the process at opposite extremes of the settlement scale. A wasteful and lengthy negotiation process nearly always ensues.[113] ODR, it seemed, had the potential to short-circuit this lengthy and ritualised process. The involvement of a variety of leading industry parties in backing the ODR system, furthermore, would result in the creation and implementation of a truly impartial system rather than a proprietary one which would lead to increased market uptake as well as a fairer process.

The Intersettle system was designed and developed following extensive consultation with the eight participating litigation practices and subsequent testing proved very successful. The product was launched; insurers were approached and before long trials of the site had been initiated involving founder member firms, recently joined firms and claims departments. On a functionality level all companies who used the system were happy and found that claims settled more quickly than they had done using traditional methods. The cost savings, on a volume scale, would be considerable.

Intersettle's flying start did not last. The website found it extraordinarily hard to attract a sufficient volume of claims necessary to enable an effective cost benefit analysis. Without this, the company was unable to persuade the major claims departments to commit to its service and without that commitment and caseloads of the major insurers we found we could not rely on solicitors to load sufficient cases to persuade them to adopt the necessary new working practices. This created a circular effect making it more difficult to sign up new user organisations.

In retrospect one can identify the key problems:

Autonomy in law firms. The relative autonomy of high fee-earning partners in legal firms means that those who bring in large fees, but oppose the use of technology, are under no obligation to use systems being proposed. A minority of influential partners retain an enormous caseload of slow moving files, which seem to be forced into court for reasons other than client focused settlement resolution.

Focus of law firms on fees earned not costs. Law firms generally focus on fee income as opposed to cost. Where a firm requires to increase profitability, it looks first at increasing fee income and reducing staff costs, as opposed to

---

[113] This has been referred to in Intersettle presentations and literature as the 'Litigation Dance'.

identifying areas where costs can be reduced by way of more efficient work processes and technology. This attitude is only slowly changing.

Integration into litigation support technology. The Intersettle system perhaps placed too much emphasis on the negotiation aspect of the claim. In reality, settlement negotiation is one aspect of an otherwise lengthy and convoluted process. If the fee earner or claims handler were able to progress the whole claim on their desktop via an integrated litigation support solution, then a negotiation engine like Intersettle would be far more viable and useful as an integrated part of this system. The fee earner would be able to click to settle, as opposed to bringing out their paper file, consulting paper based reference materials and textbooks, dictating a letter to their client requesting their permission to settle, and finally, logging onto Intersettle (or any other ODR system) as only the concluding part of the litigation process. Fee earners would access their own branded collaboration tool to post documents, share medical reports, discuss progress with counsel and opponents, initiate negotiation—all while reducing costs and fee-earner time.

Intersettle's experience largely mirrors that of the majority of blind-bidding ODR websites. Embedded practices within law offices and insurance providers have kept user numbers low. In June 2003, Intersettle formed a commercial association with TheClaimRoom,[114] itself a partnership with ODR International (ODRI) who distribute ODR and Online Collaboration (OC) systems. But Intersettle is not the only website to experience difficulty in persuading professionals to adopt to new methods. Of 38 websites offering ODR as their main product in early 2001, only 20 are still active.[115] Most of these providers offer assisted negotiation for B2B, B2C and C2C disputes.[116] Websites currently still offering automated 'blind bidding' negotiation include: Cybersettle,[117] Intersettle,[118] MARS,[119] Settlement Online Systems (SOS),[120] The Claim Room,[121] and WebMediate.[122] The UK-based WeCanSettle site remains up but appears dormant.[123] Websites currently offering assisted negotiation include Online Resolution,[124] The Resolution

---

[114] http://www.theclaimroom.com.
[115] See: T Schultz, 'The Current State of Play in ODR' at http://www.online-adr.org/2ndCCform_Talk.pdf.
[116] *Ibid.*
[117] http://www.cybersettle.com/.
[118] http://www.intersettle.co.uk/homepage/.
[119] http://www.sonomacountybar.org/public/pub_mars.htm.
[120] www.settlementonlinesystems.com.au The only Australian ODR website—experiences very similar to those of Intersettle according to its founder.
[121] http://www.theclaimroom.com/.
[122] http://www.webmediate.com/.
[123] https://www.wecansettle.com/.
[124] http://www.onlineresolution.com/.

Forum,[125] SquareTrade,[126] The Claim Room,[127] and TRUSTe.[128] Websites currently offering on-line mediation include: e-Mediator,[129] Internet Neutral,[130] MARS,[131] NovaForum,[132] the Resolution Forum,[133] SquareTrade,[134] WebAssured.com,[135] and WebMediate.[136] Website institutions offering online arbitration include: MARS, NovaForum.com, Online Resolution, the Resolution Forum, SquareTrade, WebAssured.com, and WebMediate. In interesting contradistinction to this somewhat moribund state of affairs in general ODR, the numbers of providers for on-line domain name dispute resolution (UDRP providers) has increased overall since 2001 as noted elsewhere in this chapter, although their case load is also now dropping, arguably as a result of a general decline in cybersquatting as the market in domain names cools down since the dot.com fever retreated. (Another factor is that pin-point accurate search engines such as Google have reduced the pressing need to obtain by fair means or foul the right domain name for one's business.)

8. Conclusions: What Future for Lawyers and ODR?

(a) The 'Settlement' Genre

Why do lawyers in all jurisdictions take up certain postures, interact in certain ways, and ultimately settle disputes the way the do? Davenport and Horton have proposed that these intuitive responses are a product of what is called the Settlement Genre.[137] Claims settlements in Scotland are characterised by a specific timeframe, a specific division of labour, and established sequences of interaction. As a branch of legal activity, settlement is undertaken by means of a number of different types of interaction, in different modalities: paper documents, meetings and phone conversations. These interactions have been conceptualised as a communicative type, the

---

[125] http://www.resolutionforum.org/services.html.
[126] http://www.squaretrade.com/cnt/jsp/index.jsp.
[127] http://www.theclaimroom.com/.
[128] http://www.truste.org/about/watchdog.php.
[129] http://www.consensusmediation.co.uk/e-mediator.html.
[130] http://www.internetneutral.com/.
[131] http://www.sonomacountybar.org/public/pub_mars.htm.
[132] http://www.novaforum.com/.
[133] http://www.resolutionforum.org/.
[134] http://www.squaretrade.com/cnt/jsp/index.jsp.
[135] http://www.webassured.com/.
[136] http://www.webmediate.com/.
[137] E Davenport, K Horton, P Motion, 'Exploring Hybrid Genres: Online Dispute Resolution (ODR) and the Scottish Legal System', Proceedings of the Hawaii International Conference on System Sciences (HICSS–37), January 2004.

'settlement' genre.[138] Genre analysis may help unravel resistance to ODR systems like Intersettle. Yates and Orlikowski[139] identify three characteristic elements of 'genres': a recurrent situation, substance ('social motives ... themes ... topics'), and form (structural features, communication medium, and symbolism). Genres have dual status as (1) an articulation of what has emerged as appropriate behaviour (their role as a 'categorizing' device) and (2) as a prescription for activity in a community of practice (their role as a 'regulatory' device). Genres, say Yates and Orlikowski, are thus structurational devices.[140]

Davenport and Horton say that ADR can be described in these terms. The 'recurrent situation' is the agreement to honour claims by means of negotiated settlement without contesting them in court. The 'substance' is the set of settlements and agreements (based on precedents and norms) that constitute the 'settlement' genre: the fees that are paid by the client, for example, are in many cases index-linked to a scale that associates levels of awards and injuries. 'Form' refers to the sequence of communicative acts and texts (oral, and written) that constitute the sociability of the genre. The 'rules' that link these elements reflect the strong ties and equally strong norms that bind professionals who operate within a small jurisdiction such as the Scottish legal system. It is thus likely that a change in any one of these elements will affect the others. Once established, a genre repertoire serves as a powerful social template for shaping, how, why and with what effort members of a community interact to get their work done.

In Scots legal practice, it often appears that 'the common aim is to create or maintain patterns of social relations (the business relationship), which is in turn achieved through social interaction—ie, the organisation of the discourse of the negotiation'[141] The negotiation of the settlement and the placing of bids rely on what Loos calls 'tyings' (references to what has gone before and will follow any point in the conversation) and 'cues', picked up by the speakers by means of intuitive conversation analysis, sensitive to nuances in tone and pitch, and to the rhythm of the conversation.[142] Davenport and Horton argue that, viewed from this perspective, resistance to Intersettle is not perplexing. A process articulated in a complex business genre that is strongly embedded in social and professional norms will pose a challenge for any designer who wishes to entice practitioners to

---

[138] J Swales, *Genre Analysis: English in Academic and Research Settings* (Cambridge, CUP, 1990).

[139] J Yates and W Orlikowski, 'Genres of Organizational Communication: a Structurational Approach to Studying Communication and Media' (1992) 17(2) *Academy of Management Rev* 99–326.

[140] J Yates, W Orlikowski and J Rennecker, 'Collaborative Genres for Collaboration: Genre Systems in Digital Media' in R Sprague (ed), Proceedings of the 30th Hawaii International Conference on System Sciences (HICSS–30) Digital Documents Track, vol VI, (Los Alamitos, CA, IEEE Computer Society Press, 1997) pp 50–59.

[141] C Mirjliisa, 'Business Negotiations: Interdependence between Discourse and the Business Relationship' (1996) 15(1) *English for Specific Purposes* 19–36.

[142] E Loos, *Intertextual Networks in Organisations: the Use of Written and Oral Business Discourse in relation to Context* (Pearson Education Ltd, 1999) pp 315–32.

undertake the process on-line. They query whether in relation to ODR the social element was given due attention. This is seen as immensely important in the close-knit world of Scots law, which is less competitive than its US or even English counterpart. In Scotland, social networks and ethos are different. In addition, the initial digitisation was partial and only extended to the final component of the settlement genre—financial settlement bidding. This disrupted the social rhythm, or social flow that characterises the transaction sequence.

In addition to sociability, there is the issue of disruption of work practice. If practitioners undertake most of the steps of a process by traditional means, but are invited to migrate to a new modality at the final stage, there is little incentive to do so.

Davenport and Horton suggest that adoption of ODR is more likely to benefit from moves at the macro level, than at the micro level. This has happened, for example, in relation to EDI's acceptability. The Scottish legal world is characterised by a relatively small and closely-knit group of professionals whose interactions are embedded in a local social matrix where tacit knowledge and opportunism are important factors in achieving professional objectives. By making more explicit and 'up front' these factors, online mediation disrupts the micro level political arena. In addition, ODR requires a stricter adherence to timeliness than ordinary settlement practice, and physical effort in terms of keyboarding or comparable input. If such factors contribute to institutional resistance to ODR, what macro-factors may overcome them?

(b) Does ODR Have a Future in Scotland?

There were some 8422 solicitors in Scotland as at the year 2003.[143] It is not possible to practice as a solicitor in Scotland[144] unless one is admitted to the Roll of Solicitors and holds a practicing certificate. The Law Society of Scotland[145] is the sole body with the requisite legal status enabling it to issue practicing certificates. As at April 2003, the Law Society of Scotland's records indicated that only some 6500 Solicitors had notified an email address to the Society. Insofar as any trend could be detected from the notifications, it appeared that medium to large organisations possessed the highest numbers of email users whereas smaller firms, sole practitioners, and particularly criminal firms, rarely used email. This is however is an increase on the situation in April 2001, at which stage only about 50% of Scottish solicitors had notified an email address to the Society. The situation in relation to websites reflects these statistics. Whilst one or two smaller firms have

---

[143] These numbers as of Summer 2003: http://www.prospects.ac.uk/cms/ShowPage/Home_page/ Explore_job_sectors/Legal_services/As_it_is/p!eadcig.

[144] Pursuant to Solicitors Scotland Act 1980, s 4.

[145] www.lawscot.org.uk.

embraced the Internet as a marketing tool, large numbers of small firms still do not possess a website or, if they do, maintain a bare presence on the Web.

Scottish solicitors currently find themselves under no pressure whatsoever to adopt an innovative or even marginally different approach to litigation. The Law Society of Scotland embarked upon a project during 2002 to design and evaluate a system of PKI for use by Scottish solicitors and their clients.[146] This was to follow the model envisaged by the Electronic Communications Act 2000 and the EC E-Commerce Directive. Essentially, the Law Society of Scotland would by virtue of its exclusive right to issue practicing certificates and regulate the profession in Scotland, act as a trusted third party of registration authority. By cross referring applications against the role of Solicitors, the Society was in a unique position to issue digital certificates to persons entitled to hold themselves as Scottish Solicitors. Solicitors would be able to communicate with each other, with government institutions, and with their clients, in a way that would put beyond doubt the identity of the Solicitor. Further, in a fashion somewhat analogous to the steps already undertaken by Solicitors under the money laundering regulation, solicitors would be entitled to issue their clients with digital certificates. The project underwent its pilot stage in 2003, which was successful, but at the eleventh hour the project was cancelled in December 2003 upon the basis that insufficient solicitor or client demand existed.

There is undoubtedly reticence on the part of the Scottish legal profession to acquire digital certificates. Advocates of digital signatures point to the manner in which the approach of the profession to the use of email matured in a relatively short time. A practice note introduced by The Law Society of Scotland in 1997 when email was in its infancy, equated the use of an email message to something along the lines of a telephone call. Solicitors were obliged to confirm the contents of the email with their client before acting upon it. Such an arrangement is regarded as completely impractical today. This rule, if it is observed at all, is so observed more in the breach and by observance.[147]

A second example of a technical application that on the face of it ought to succeed but which in practice has attracted interest mainly from the IT enthusiasts is Scottish Legal Voice.[148] This was established in 2002 and was backed again by the Law Society of Scotland. Scottish Legal Voice is a web based discussion forum designed to enable Scottish Solicitors to share problems and views on a multitude of issues. In practice, only those practitioners interested in the field of information technology, as well as Law Society representatives have used the service.

---

[146] 'Lawseal' PKI, developed in conjunction with the Royal Bank of Scotland and Trustis.

[147] The Law Society of England and Wales published comprehensive new guidelines for the use of email in mid–2004: http://lawsocietyinternetp.aspective.com/documents/downloads/emailguidelines.pdf.

[148] http://www.scottishlegalvoice.com.

A third initiative that may have the effect of requiring Scottish solicitors to embrace digital technology with more relish than is presently the case, involves automated registration of title to land.[149] This initiative, backed by the Registers of Scotland[150] is well advanced. A pilot project was run in 2001. Registration of title involves remote alteration (subjective verification by the Registers staff) of the Register. Inherent in the system is the requirement that solicitors using it should authenticate themselves securely using PKI or digital certificates. PKI will also be required for the introduction in 2005 of the NEWBACS and BACSTEL-IP funds transfer systems. The Scottish Legal Aid Board[151] is also moving towards a portal-based application system, having received funding from the Modernising Government Intitiative to develop this.

It seems therefore that change will finally be visited upon the Scottish legal profession. If so, lawyers may finally have to adapt to new methods and ODR may, at last, emerge as the beneficiary of all this new enlightenment.

---

[149] http://www.ros.gov.uk/solicitor/artlwhatis.html.
[150] www.ros.gov.uk.
[151] www.slab.org.uk.

Part II
Other European and UK
E-Commerce Legislation

6

The EC Electronic Money Directive 2000

Electronic Money: The European Regulatory Approach

ANDRES GUADAMUZ AND JOHN USHER[1]

Introduction

Electronic money has yet to become as familiar to consumers as cash, cheques and credit and debit cards, but may yet have the potential to be the greatest revolution in payment systems since the development of money itself. Financial services practices and new technology are coming together to change the way in which we conduct our everyday life. The potentially universal acceptance of electronic or 'e-money' for commercial transactions may have wide-ranging effects in our lives—not least, for consumers: electronic money could serve as the tool that finally eases the pervasive consumer apprehension regarding online transactions.[2]

This chapter deals with the recently passed European Directive regulating Electronic Money Institutions (the 'E-Money Directive'[3]), which has granted legal recognition to electronic money, and has also provided an authorising foundation to financial institutions eager to deploy this payment method. Economists, regulators, government institutions and businesses are now gearing themselves up for the possibilities of electronic money in everyday life. Nevertheless, despite such recognition and plans for commercial exploitation, there are still very palpable concerns about the eventual implementation of e-money. Tests, trials and pilot schemes seem to come and go, yet no dates are given when we can expect to see permanent development in this area. The introduction of e-money requires

---

[1] Respectively, Co-Director, AHRC Centre for Intellectual Property and Technology Law, and Professor of European Law, University of Exeter.

[2] See further throughout this volume, especially C Waelde, ch 1.

[3] Directive 2000/46/EC of the European Parliament and of the Council of 18 September 2000 on the taking up, pursuit of and prudential supervision of the business of electronic money institutions. OJEC L275/39, 27 October 2002.

caution, not least because the security issues have not been put to rest. There are also questions about the commercial viability of electronic money schemes, and whether or not consumers will buy into the new technology. Although the promptness with which the regulatory framework has been put in place is in some respects to be welcomed, this chapter will ask if the EU may have jumped the gun and mis-read current trends in electronic key payment systems in its push to put new regulations in place in this area. We will begin by analysing the European regulatory scheme implemented so far (along with its UK implementation), with the goal of providing a better understanding of the type of payment schemes that it covers. We will look at the technology behind electronic money schemes, in order to determine if the Directive and the UK Regulations really address the practical issues in this domain.

1. Electronic Money

1.1 The Definition

In the simplest terms, electronic money is the replacement of physical cash in the shape of coins and banknotes with an electronic equivalent. According to Webopedia, digital cash is:

> A system that allows a person to pay for goods or services by transmitting a number from one computer to another. Like the serial numbers on real dollar bills, the digital cash numbers are unique. Each one is issued by a bank and represents a specified sum of real money. One of the key features of digital cash is that, like real cash, it is anonymous and reusable.[4]

This definition makes it clear that electronic money is very much like physical money for all practical purposes. It is anonymous; it is given value by a financial institution; and it must be used to pay for goods and services in any sort of transaction. The Electronic Money Institutions European Directive (EMI Directive) also defines electronic money for the purpose of the legal regime that will regulate this emerging sector. It states that:

> ... 'electronic money' shall mean monetary value as represented by a claim on the issuer which is: (i) stored on an electronic device; (ii) issued on receipt of funds of an amount not less in value than the monetary value issued; (iii) accepted as means of payment by undertakings other than the issuer.[5]

---

[4] Webopedia, *Digital Cash*, <http://www.webopedia.com/TERM/D/digital_cash.html>.

[5] Directive 2000/46/EC of the European Parliament and of the Council of 18 September 2000 on the taking up, pursuit of and prudential supervision of the business of electronic money institutions. OJEC L275/39, 27 October 2002, Art 1.3(b).

This definition is a very comprehensive, with the added advantage that it attempts to be technology neutral—this is to say that it is written without a specific type of technology in mind. According to this definition, a payment system will be considered electronic money if it fulfils the following requirements:

a) The electronic cash must have monetary value, which assumes that schemes such as store reward points will not apply to this definition (Nectar points, airmiles, Boots points). It is important to point out that monetary value is not the same as having mere value. The draft Uniform Money Services Business Act (UMSBA)[6] in the United States defines monetary value as 'a medium of exchange, whether or not redeemable in money. This definition does not include value that is only redeemable by the issuer in the issuer's goods and services or is only redeemable within a limited geographic area.' This definition would therefore exclude so-called 'Internet cash' payment systems, such as Beenz, Flooz or Digicash, because these systems use a proprietary currency useable only with participating merchants.[7]

b) The fact that it presents a '*claim on the issuer*' means that the money issuer must accept it and provide the equivalent of the monetary value back to the bearer. This is equivalent to physical money, in particular banknotes, in which the issuing bank offers to pay the bearer the face value inscribed in the note.[8]

c) The main difference between electronic money and physical money is that the latter must be stored by some electronic method. Presumably this means any sort of electronic storage medium, such as cards, PDAs, mobile phones, personal computers and any other electronic device.

d) The value stored in an electronic money device must not be any less than the monetary value issued. This means that the value issued should not be superior to the amount paid for. If this was the case, then the electronic money would be considered a credit device, and thus subject of an entirely different regulatory system.[9] The practical effect of this requirement is that it reduces the possibilities of the card issuer to profit from the cards from the consumer. This must imply that the issuer will have to profit in another way, which will be discussed in more detailed later.

---

[6] An annotated version of the draft can be found here: <http://www.law.upenn.edu/bll/ulc/moneyserv/msb0620.htm>.

[7] The complexity of these systems and the lack of universality doomed these schemes, and most of these systems no longer exist. For more on the Internet money collapse, see: J Kornblum, 'Internet Currency: You Flooz, You may Lose', *USA Today*, 22 August 2001, <http://www.usatoday.com/life/cyber/tech/2001–08–22–ebrief.htm>.

[8] This promise to pay is often misunderstood with legal tender. Legal tender is not a payment method that must be accepted by all merchants, but it is simply a legal term that specifies that banknotes will not be refused by a creditor in satisfaction of a debt. For more on the issue of money, banknotes and legal tender, see: Bank of England, *Bank Notes: Legal Tender and the Promise to Pay*, March 2003, p 2.

[9] For some of the regulatory regimes for credit cards, see: EP Ellinger, E Lomnicka and R Hooley, *Modern Banking Law* (Oxford, OUP, 2002) 532–36.

1.2 The Technology

Because the definition of electronic money is so broad as to include any sort of electronic device to store monetary value, the methods of electronic money are only limited to the existing technology. At present there are three main storage methods for electronic money: by software, by cards, and by accounts.

a) The method of storing money in *software* is a payment system where monetary value is stored in a computer hard drive by means of a proprietary software program.[10] The program creates an electronic wallet that is charged with money from a bank account, and then the user can purchase goods or services by sending the information via this electronic method. The transaction is encrypted and the identity of the user is kept hidden from the merchant.[11] There are several companies offering software like this, but these systems have failed to catch the public interest so far and would appear to be dead at the time of writing. One of the main players in the software electronic money was DigiCash, a company that offered the customer a small downloadable computer program that allowed the user to store money in their computers. DigiCash proved to be a disappointment, and has been purchased by another company called Ecash, but the scheme appears to be either stalled or in its early development stages.[12] Other software money schemes exist, but suffer from the same lack of interest by consumers.[13]

b) The most viable and promising electronic money system is that of storing monetary value in secure cards with microchips, known as *smart-cards.* The smart-card is simply put, 'a plastic rectangle containing an electronic chip, and holding a certain amount of readable data.'[14] This technology is not only circumscribed to electronic payment systems, it is also to be found in several other areas such as digital television boxes and Subscriber Identity Module (SIM) cards for mobile phones. Smart-cards for electronic payments use the chip to store certain amount of value, which can be charged in any configured card reader—including public phones and Automated Teller Machines (ATM).[15] For security reasons, the information in the card must be stored

---

[10] J Chuah, 'The New EU Directives to Regulate Electronic Money Institutions—A Critique' (2000) 15 *J Intl Banking L* 181–82.

[11] P Robertson, 'Internet Payments' in M Brindle and R Cox (eds), *Law of Bank Payments*, (London, Sweet & Maxwell, 1999) 251–53.

[12] <http://www.ecash.com/online/>.

[13] Some other software money schemes are CyberCash: <http://www.cybercash.com> and NetCash <http://www.netbank.com/~netcash>.

[14] S Newman, 'Introduction: Smart Cards' in S Newman (ed), *Smart Cards*, (ECLIP II, IST Project Report, 1999) 3.

[15] L Edgar, 'Electronic Money' in C Reed, I Walden and L Edgar (eds), *Cross Border Electronic Banking: Challenges and Opportunities*, 2nd edn, (London, LLP, 2000) 203.

using encryption algorithms that can only be decoded by an adequate reader; otherwise the value from the card cannot be unlocked. The bearer will present the card to a retailer that has a card reader, and the value will be then unlocked and transferred to their account. This value is then redeemable by the card issuer. Smart-cards can also be used for Internet transactions if the consumer has a card reader attached to their computer. This reader will unlock the value in the card and send the information to the online retailer, facilitating an anonymous e-commerce transaction.

c) *Account-based programmes* operate without ties to a specific technological solution, but rely on consumers having access to an account by means of user authentication—such as passwords, vouchers, unique identification numbers, non-smart-cards or even biometric identification.[16] The idea behind this is that the user will have the responsibility of maintaining the means to access the account data by secure means—much in the same way that users are responsible for keeping their bank-issued PIN number secure. The user can therefore transact by any of the accepted means, be it via e-mail (such as PayPal),[17] a non-smart-card (such as Splash Plastic or PrePay),[18] or even by SMS messaging or a printed piece of paper (such as Smart Voucher).[19] The problem with account-based payment systems is that while they may not be proprietary, users will very likely become confused with so many electronic payment systems. Some of these will certainly survive, but it is still too early to tell exactly which will make the cut.

1.3 The Schemes

As it has been explained, there are several electronic payment methods competing for a share of the growing online payment market.[20] This section will explore some of the systems that are most likely to be subject to the electronic money regulations.

1.3.1 Stored Value or Smart Card Payment Schemes

There are a growing number of smart-cards schemes under development, such as Proton, Mondex, and VisaCash; each trying to take the initiative in this competitive new market. The common feature of these programmes is that they intend to present themselves as real alternatives for physical money. To achieve this goal, the

---

[16] H Allen, 'Innovations in retail payments: e-payments' [2003] *Bank of England Q Bulletin* 429–30.
[17] See PayPal: <http://www.paypal.co.uk>.
[18] Located at <http://www.splashplastic.com/>.
[19] More on this scheme can be found at: <http://www.smartvoucher.com/>.
[20] For a comprehensive list of different electronic payments systems, see: P Hallam-Baker, *Electronic Payment Schemes*, World Wide Web Consortium, < http://www.w3.org/ECommerce/roadmap.html>.

cards must have wide recognition and be subject to be used to pay for goods and services by parties other than the issuer, so they need to build a network of agreements with retailers and service providers to make sure that they will accept electronic money. These agreements are often called multi-party, tripartite,[21] or even 'four-party'[22] payment systems (see Diagram 1). The names for these schemes evidently comes the number of parties involved in the transactions. In tripartite schemes, the parties are the card holder, the card-issuer and the dealer. In four-party schemes, the parties are the payer, the paying intermediary, the receiving intermediary, and the recipient.[23] In a traditional credit card scheme, the paying intermediary would be the company issuing the card, and the receiving intermediary would be the recipient's bank. Electronic money schemes are more likely to be four-party, but this is not necessary, as the banking issuing the electronic money card could very well be the same payee's bank.

DIAGRAM 1: *Multi-Party Scheme*

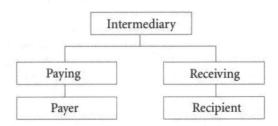

The multi-party scheme that was first into the UK market was Mondex, which started as an initiative of the National Westminster Bank (NatWest), and later received the support of the credit card company Master Card. This scheme already had a large number of affiliates in several countries around the world, and the companies involved originally claimed that Mondex would become the next e-money standard around the world. In fact however, pilot schemes seem to have come and gone, without any sign of a more comprehensive and permanent roll out, at least in the UK.[24]

Mondex is (or was) a multi-party scheme where Mondex served as a payment intermediary between the seller and the buyer. The stated objective of the scheme

---

[21] For more on these, see Ellinger, *et al*, above, pp 529–43.

[22] HM Treasury, *Competition in Payment Systems: Consultation Report*, (2000), <http://www.hm-treasury.gov.uk/media//870B7/54.pdf>.

[23] *Ibid.*

[24] For more on the Mondex scheme, see: J Finlayson-Brown, 'Mondex: Structure of a New Payment Scheme' (1997) 12 *J Intl Banking L* 362–66. Further details were once available at <http://www.mondex.com>. However that page was no longer active as of January 2005 and visitors were redirected to the main Mastercard site.

was to have as wide a market acceptance around the world as possible. To achieve this, Mondex International offered to provide different franchise, technology and originator agreements to participating companies in the target territory. These agreements give separate rights to the participators in the scheme, such as the right to issue cards, manage local agreements with merchants, or provide hardware (such as card readers). There appeared to be no restriction to one undertaking in each market taking all of the above responsibilities.[25]

A typical Mondex monetary transaction would then look like this: The buyer obtains a Mondex cash card by any means, with the most likely source being issued by a bank. The buyer can transfer value to this card at authorised locations—such as ATM machines, bank tellers, authorised merchants or even public telephones. The buyer would then take the card to a participating store, which would likely be identified with the Mondex logo, just as merchants identify debit and credit card acceptance with visible stickers. The value would then be deducted from the card and transferred into the recipient's cash purse. This value will then be redeemable in 'real currency' to the card issuer, but in effect what may happen is that the value will be entered automatically into the seller's bank account.

1.3.2 Account-based Schemes

One of the most promising account-based schemes is the popular consumer payment system called PayPal, a company founded in 1998.[26] PayPal has often been called 'email money', and its business model warrants such name. A customer can open a PayPal account by giving credit card or bank information in a simple transaction that can take less than five minutes. However, the account will not be activated until the customer has validated the bank account or credit card used. This is usually performed by a small charge being made by PayPal to that account (the amount varies). The consumer then checks the amount and goes back to PayPal to verify it. Another way of verification is a code that shows up on the monthly credit card report, which must be then verified back in PayPal's account management site.

Once this user account is created, the customer can send money to any person giving their email address and placing a monetary sum in an on-line form. Once the recipient receives the email, he or she must in turn open a PayPal account; the money is then taken from the sender's bank account or credit card and deposited into a new account in PayPal. As can be seen, the effect is an almost viral like growth in uptake in PayPal acounts, which explains the incredible growth of PayPal accounts since its inception in 1998.[27] Each PayPal consumer can choose

[25] *Ibid.*

[26] A Cohen, *The Perfect Store: Inside eBay*, (Boston, Little Brown Co, 2002) 229–30.

[27] J Sansford, 'PayPal Sees Torrid Growth with Money-Sending Service', *Wall Street Journal*, 16 February 2000, <http://www.paypal.com/html/wsj3.html>. See also evidence in *Comb v PayPal, Inc* 218 FSupp 2d 1165 that PayPal went from having 10,000 accounts to 10 million in 9 months in 2001

to keep their money in an account with the company for further use, or can choose to have that amount of money credited to their bank or credit card account (see Diagram 2). It is important to point out that PayPal does not disclose the account information of either party to the other in any payment, ensuring the security of the transaction and enabling user trust.[28]

DIAGRAM 2: *PayPal*

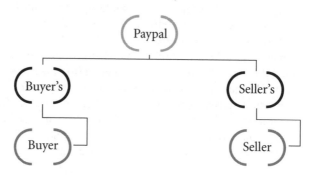

The key question is whether PayPal can or should be considered an electronic money institution (EMI) for the purposes of the EMI Directive. At first glance at the definition of electronic money noted earlier, the answer seems to be negative. PayPal does not issue value in the sense that the Directive seems to indicate; it draws monetary value from an existing bank account or credit card and stores it in a user PayPal account, which can then be transferred to other users with PayPal accounts, regardless of whether they are transferring the money to pay for goods or services, although they often are. This would appear to negate the main requirement for the definition of PayPal as an electronic money issuer. Instead, it looks more as if PayPal acts as a credit institution, which would subject it to an altogether separate regulatory regime. Nevertheless, PayPal Europe made a request to be accredited as an EMI in June 2003,[29] and was granted that status by the UK's Financial Services Authority (FSA) in February 2004.[30] Because this is such an important regulatory issue, it will be dealt with in detail in a later section.[31]

(see P Motion, ch 5 of this volume). As of January 2005, PayPal claimed to have 56 million account holders in 45 countries worldwide. PayPal was bought by eBay in September 2002, which has probably further stimulated its growth as the payment method of choice for eBay buyers and sellers.

[28] D Sorkin, 'Payment Methods for Consumer-to-Consumer Online Transactions' (2001) 35 *Akron L Rev* 1, 11–12.

[29] N Naraine, PayPal Europe, 'PayPal Readies European Subsidiary', *Internet News*, 5 January 2004, <http://www.internetnews.com/ec-news/article.php/3295181>.

[30] R Kavanagh, 'PayPal Launch European Service', *ITVibe*, 11 February 2004, <http://itvibe.com/default.aspx?NewsID=1270>. It is rather ironic that the author of this small news item calls PayPal an 'electronic bank'.

[31] See below, s 4.

Simpay is another promising account-based payment system that is set to explode on to the European mobile telephone payments scene. The company is part of the Mobile Payments Services Association (MPSA), founded by Orange, Telefónica Móviles, T-Mobile and Vodafone, the four major European mobile networks.[32] Simpay is attempting to ride on the popularity of mobile phones in Europe[33] by helping users to pay for goods and services directly over their phones ('m-commerce') but as a plus, also using the built-in identification and security technology of mobile phones, Such a technique is particularly appropriate to micro-payment type purchases such as individual MP3 files, and ring-tones, where transaction costs for credit card purchase would be prohibitively high. Simpay admit thjeir main focus is on the under 10 Euros market. It is also targeting transactions such as movie and theatre tickets, parking tickets, vending machines and flowers (for example) commonly bought in a hurry over the phone by consumers on the move. Simpay works by the customer entering into a transaction with an authorised provider through their mobile phone by the use of SMS messaging or WAP interfaces. The amount is then credited to the user's phone bill, which is paid at the end of the month with the other mobile phone charges.

DIAGRAM 3: *Simpay*

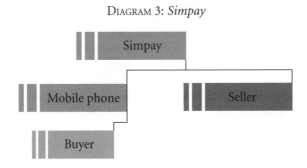

Although mobile phones have a smart-card incorporated in the shape of a SIM card, it seems clearly arguable that Simpay should not be considered an electronic money scheme under the EMI Directive definition. The key point is that no value is issued and stored into the mobile, which is one of the requirements for an electronic money scheme. Simpay therefore acts more like a credit token provider[34]— using Simpay is akin to using a credit card, as the payment will actually be billed

---

[32] 'Mobile firms offer payment service', *BBC News*, 23 June 2003, <http://news.bbc.co.uk/1/hi/technology/3,012,914.stm>.

[33] It is however expanding outside of Europe, eg into South Africa as of February 2004.

[34] Credit token is defined in s 14 of the Consumer Credit Act 1974 as any card, check, voucher, coupon, stamp, form, booklet or other document that is given to an individual, who will be able to purchase goods and services when shown to the issuer or to an authorised third party.

to the user and then paid at a later occasion. Allen[35] argues that as they are not EMI's, mobile payment providers are not regulated at this moment, at least not under EMI rules, and he also considers them in a different category than more conventional e-commerce account-based systems, such as PayPal. Many of the arguments regarding the status of PayPal as an EMI (or not) can however fairly clearly also be applied to mobile phone payment systems. In traditional contract law, SimPay would seem most easily characterised as an agent which collects money for a variety of principals—the vendors of the m-commerce items purchased by Simpay users—rather than the issuer of any kind of money, whether real or virtual.

2. Reasons for Implementation

Before considering how electronic money is regulated, it is important to understand what the commercial advantages behind their introduction are, and to whom these advantages accrue. Customers (payers), merchants (recipients) and issuers (usually banks or other credit institutions) often have very different stakes in or worries about electronic money or payment systems. Physical currency has existed for millennia in one shape or another, and has been proven to work as a widely circulated and universally acceptable payment method. Why the sudden push to transfer monetary value to electronic systems? What are the advantages of electronic money replacing physical money, and for whom? And do these advantages apply to off-line as well as on-line transactions?

2.1 Issuers

The parties perhaps most interested in the implementation of electronic money schemes are the issuing banks. The reason for this enthusiasm is the possibility of obtaining considerable profits from the schemes. The credit card and debit card payment systems that already exist are costly, as they require a complex system of contractual and operational interactions between consumers, retailers and issuers. Another factor that elevates the cost of this system—and in particular in credit card payments—is that consumers have to be credit-worthy in order to receive credit. This means that costs are incurred checking out potential customers for credit worthiness, or alternately where credit checking goes wrong, by parties defaulting on credit card payments. These high operational costs have several consequences. For example, the number of credit card users is limited to those with

---

[35] Allen, above, p 438.

acceptable credit rating. Another result is that the credit card payment system is not efficient for micro-payments, which are increasingly important in the context of the Internet where pay-per-use or pay-per-download schemes in relation to digital music, e-books, ring-tones and Internet performances are increasingly common.[36]

In contrast to this, electronic money works in a much simpler and cheaper way, which makes it ideal for micro-payments. The low cost of electronic money is based on the fact that the value in a card is transferred by the card-owner in advance of purchase, from existing funds, such as a bank account. In other words, paying by e-money is in principle a debit not a credit transaction. Hence funds can be transferred using e-money without the need to contact a network facility to corroborate, as with credit card payment, that the credit payment has been properly authorised. The transaction can instead be performed locally.[37]

If electronic money schemes reduce costs and a large enough number of consumers will use it as a service, then the feasibility of the system hinges on finance. Will electronic money schemes make enough money to engage the investment of financial institutions? This is a more difficult question to answer, but the amount of interest in implementing electronic money schemes that has been displayed by several major players in financial markets seems to indicate that these institutions at least believe that this is going to be a profitable exercise. It is possible that the profits will be obtained by the issuer charging a small transaction fee to the merchant and not to the consumer. This would be similar to what already exists in the area of debit cards, where there are no immediate charges or interest rates per transaction to the consumer—as happens with credit cards—but there is a small transaction charge to the merchant.[38] Although it is not yet clear just how small this charge will be, it is apparent that typical transaction charges from electronic money will be smaller than 1% of the total transaction cost,[39] which is still smaller than that paid by merchants in debit and credit card transactions.

Issuers have to balance the advantages of e-cash with two main problems. One is the regulatory maze around the issue of e-money. The EMI Directive and the implementing UK rules are unclear on some vital points. In particular, there is considerable doubt about which e-schemes should be subject to these regulations. As mentioned before, there is doubt as to whether the EMI Directive excludes some of the most popular electronic payment schemes available at present.[40] This could certainly put off some potential investors and issuers.

---

[36] S Miller, 'Payment in an Online World' in L Edwards and C Waelde (eds), *Law & the Internet: a Framework for Electronic Commerce Law* (Oxford, Hart Publishing, 2000) 74–75.

[37] T Tether, 'Payment systems for E-commerce' in C Reed, I Walden and L Edgar (eds), *Border Electronic Banking: Challenges and Opportunities*, above, pp 194–95.

[38] Ellinger, *et al*, above, pp 529–43.

[39] Finlayson-Brown, above, p 364.

[40] See above s 1.3.

The other main concern for issuers is the security of electronic money. As happens with physical cash, widespread counterfeiting of electronic currency could have deeply worrying implications both for the issuers and indeed for the economy in general, similar to those that would rise from widespread counterfeiting of physical money.[41] If the security of an electronic money scheme was breached, and fraudsters could insert value into the electronic storage device without actually debiting any real world funds, obviously the issuer would very likely be bankrupted or at best, the particular scheme destroyed. The problem of security cannot be underestimated when talking about e-money, both or commerce and governments. With e-money schemes rolled out around the world, security concerns for the issuer who is liable to global hack attacks have only increased.

Security experts have warned since the early trials of e-money that storing value on smart-cards was vulnerable to hacking attacks.[42] This threat was dismissed originally as scaremongering, but it was only a short while before a security-consulting firm broke the embedded encryption security of the Mondex card. The story was first made public in a leaked memorandum from the National Bank of New Zealand about the time of one of the Mondex trials in England. In this memo, officials at the Bank expressed concerns about a report by the Dutch security consultancy firm TNO, which specified that the encryption had been broken by mapping the card and identifying the process used to manufacture it. The report was immediately made public on the Internet and was later corroborated by the Bank.[43] Rumours of security vulnerabilities flew around the web, including several apocryphal stories involving using a microwave oven and a calculator to charge the cards with hundreds of pounds.[44] Although some of these stories may seem laughable, there are several well documented cases of smart-card vulnerability, such as a widespread attack by Dutch hackers that found a way of re-charging German phone cards protected with smart-card technology.[45] A very telling indication that there are real fears about the potential vulnerability of electronic money is that most of the trials have been run in very small communities where a cancellation of the program would be easier if security has been compromised.[46]

---

[41] In fact, counterfeiting has been shown to be such an economic worry that it receives some of the strictest law enforcement in the world, as it has the potential of creating runaway inflation and to generally reduce the value of money in a country. For more about counterfeiting, see: E Groseclose, *America's Money Machine: Story of the Federal Reserve* (New York, Crown Publishing, 1980).

[42] D Bank, 'Smart Cards Are Open to New Attack by Hackers, Say Israeli Researchers', *Wall Street Journal*, 21 October 1996, p A17.

[43] R Brown, 'Leaked National Bank memo confirms pilot version of Mondex broken', *Computerworld News Wire*, 15 September 1997, <http://insight.mcmaster.ca/org/efc/pages/media/nz-computerworld.15sep97.html>.

[44] For one of these reports, see <http://www.s-t.com/daily/10–96/10–20–96/f05bu035.htm>.

[45] L Karppinen, *Attacks Related to the Smart Card used in Electronic Payment and Cash Cards*, Seminar on Network Security, Helsinki University of Technology, Fall 2000, <http://www.tcm.hut.fi/Opinnot/Tik–110.501/2000/papers/karppinen.pdf>.

[46] For more details about the trials, see: BA Good, *Electronic Money*, Federal Bank Reserve of Cleveland Working Paper, 96/17, <http://www.clev.frb.org/research/workpaper/1997/wp9716.pdf>.

Security concerns remain, as chip hackers assert that they can probably hack any sort of technology thrown at them. Strong encryption can be used to protect smartcards, but it is possible that large criminal organisations could afford to employ cryptographers to break the security systems. Even if security risks are in reality relatively remote, consumer perception of security is also a crucial issue. If consumers are afraid of using the system because of worries about security, e-money systems in their entirety are unlikely to reach critical mass.[47]

Account based systems such as PayPal cannot be hacked in the same way as smartcard technology, but they do suffer from other security threats, for example, a type of online fraud known as 'phishing'.[48] Phishing is the distribution of unsolicited messages resembling a legitimate communication from a bank, credit card company or even an account-based payment system like PayPal. The message requires the user to disclose some information, usually bank account details, credit card numbers or passwords, which are then misused by the fraudster to draw money or make purchases in the name of the user. Phishing is a hugely growing threat: in May 2004, it was estimated that 57 million phishing emails were sent to users in the USA and that around 20% of recipients responded as if those communications were genuine.[49] A UK APACS study in October 2004 revealed that at least 4% of users would respnd to a 'phishing' email giving away the personal details to the relevant bank or other account. Widespread phishing aimed especially at account based systems could destroy consumer trust in them and consequent uptake fairly effectively.[50]

2.2 Consumer

What are the advantages and disadvantages of e-money for consumers? One of the main advantages is their availability to a wider sector of the public than is true of credit cards. At present, credit card usage rates vary from one economy to another, but in developed countries only around 50–60% of the population tend to have access to credit cards.[51] Considerable numbers of consumers would thus benefit from a payment system that does not involve credit checking. Electronic money schemes usually involve the issue of value from existing funds in the consumer's

---

[47] This was another problem faced by the Swedish cashcard trial; see Holmström and Stadler, *infra* n 59.

[48] For more on the subject of phishing, see: <http://www.antiphishing.org/>.

[49] Figures courtesy of Struan Robertson, editor of OUT-Law, Masons and Pinsent, Solicitors, Glasgow.

[50] Anti-Phishing Working Group, *Phishing Attack Trends Report* (January 2004), <http://www.antiphishing.org/APWGPhishing.Attack.Report.Jan2004.pdf >.

[51] It is difficult to talk about percentages of people with credit cards because a significant amount of users tend to have two or more cards. In the UK, there are an estimated 71 million cards in 2002, covering a total of 60% of the population. See: Association for Payment Clearing Services, Association for Payment Clearing Services (APACS), *UK Payment Markets Trends and Forecasts* (2003), <http://www.apacs.org.uk/downloads/APACSInBrief2003.pdf>.

own bank account; so almost anybody, of whatever age or credit worthiness, whether transient or foreign, could be supplied with a smart-card because there is little risk to the issuer.[52] However the utility of e-money smart cards to consumers is closely dependent on how widely they can be charged up, and redeemed. One of the reasons Mondex trials appeared to fail was because only a limited number of merchants accepted payment by Mondex. At present, consumers have to draw money from ATMs, while smart cards could possibly be charged in a wider number of locales, including, importantly, the point of sale itself.[53]

Electronic money may also appeal to consumers, because a smart-card, like conventional bank notes, only represents the amount of money that the bearer has stored in it, and does not—as a credit card (or its number and other details) does—unlock access to far greater amounts of liability. Consumers, it is hoped, will be more willing to purchase goods and services over the Internet if they are unafraid of fraudsters, hackers or unscrupulous merchants misusing personal data as a result. Studies show that the fear of having credit card details abused is the number one reason consumers cite for not buying more goods and services on-line. Some smartcard schemes are also issuing cards with a built in 'locking code', which will make sure that if the card gets lost or stolen no other person will be able to use the money.[54]

A third advantage for consumers is that electronic money, like real world cash, has to date usually been designed to be an anonymous payment system. A smart-card, for example, is in principle an anonymous purse that is made redeemable by the bearer, so there is no need to identify the payer. With account-based systems too, transactions can take place anonymously. When PayPal is used to by a purchaser to buy an item on eBay, for example, neither party to the sale needs to find out the other's bank details or true name, though they will have access to an email address. Given the general insecurity of the Internet medium, and the pervasive abuse of personal data collected, this is a very attractive feature. Electronic cash was originally designed to be as analogous to physical money as possible: like money bills, it was thought it would be anonymous, passable from bearer to bearer and untraceable. Compare the identifying and tracing potential of credit card payments. This has two drawbacks however. First, if the user loses their electronic purse, they will also lose the value stored in it, just as if one lost a wallet. By contrast, fraudulent use of credit cards which are lost or stolen can usually be recouped so the consumer suffers no loss. Secondly, in the post 9/11 world, anonymity and untraceability are no longer seen as uncontrovertible good things. It is possible that a new generation of e-money may be developed under government pressure that lends itself less well to anonymous transactions.

---

[52] Miller, above, p 75.

[53] S Newman and G Sutter, 'Electronic Payments: The Smart Card' (2002) 18(5) *Computer Law & Security Report* 307–13.

[54] Newman and Sutter, above.

Key problems still remain with electronic money. At the moment there are several competing electronic money systems that may lead to consumer confusion. From the consumer point of view, cash (albeit of different currencies) and credit cards are pretty much accepted everywhere, while different e-money schemes compete, each with a limited network of accepting merchants and places of operation. Interoperability and universal acceptance may be targets to aim for but we are nowhere near that point yet. Initial indications are that users are slow to take up new payment systems; the European Central Bank calculated that only 0.3% of transactions conducted in 1999 used electronic money.[55] It is hard nowadays given the diversification of payment system architectures—store cards, mobile payments, smart cards etc—to name figures but it is clear anecdotally that cash and credit cards are still by far the dominant ways to pay, even on the Internet.

Consumers also have concerns about the protection they will be entitled to if something goes wrong using e-money. In the UK, credit cards and debit cards[56] are subject to a comprehensive protection regime enacted by the Consumer Credit Act (CCA),[57] which includes protection if users lose their cards, or if they are subject to fraud or misuse of their cards. This protection has not been implemented into the EMI Directive, arguably because there is less potential for misuse in a non-credit system, but also creating another reason for consumer inertia in moving over to the new technology. It will be interesting to see if electronic money issuers will be willing to address this shortcoming by offering some sort of self-regulated protection of electronic money (just as Amazon.com, for example, offer a guarantee against credit card fraud if a customer is defrauded when purchasing using that card on their site). PayPal do offer consumer protection schemes to accompany their payment systems, perhaps in order to alleviate negative consumer perception of electronic payment systems.[58]

Consumer inertia is a general problem in the uptake of new e-commerce methods and indeed new technology in general. Consumers generally need strong reasons to change from their tried and tested methods of payment, particularly if these methods work quite well and the replacement does not offer any immediate advantages. In short, electronic money has to prove that it is a killer application for consumers, and the promised convenience may not prove enough. From the consumer's standpoint, debit cards fulfil almost all of the same functions as most

---

[55] European Central Bank, above, p 29.

[56] Although debit cards are not protected by the CCA, financial institutions have decided to apply this regime to debit cards by self-regulation via the Bank Code.

[57] G Bamodu, 'The Regulation of Electronic Money Institutions in the United Kingdom' (2003) 2 *JILT* <http://elj.warwick.ac.uk/jilt/03–2/bamodu.html>.

[58] PayPal Europe now offers a scheme called PayPal Buyer Protection, which protects users up to £250 GBP in selected transactions for a number of irregularities, including protection if the purchased goods do not arrive, or if they are not the goods described. For more on this programme, see: <http://www.paypal.com/>.

electronic money schemes—particularly card-based systems. Even widely publicised implementations have failed as a result of lack of interest from the public. Three major Swedish banks rolled-out an ambitious electronic cashcard system between 1997 and 1998. The system failed to capture the interest of the public and merchants. It was felt that '*neither them [merchants] nor the customers had anything to gain from the cashcard as it was presented by the banks.*'[59] Electronic money will have to challenge consumer apathy before it can succeed. At present it is the mobile payments and account based methods which seem most likely to achieve that goal as they offer immediate advantages to users over using credit or debit cards.

2.3 Merchants

Merchants, like issuers, especially small and medium enterprises (SMEs) merchants, have clear financial gains to make from persuading consumers to adopt e-money. As noted above, companies providing low value or micro-payment goods or services, such as MP3s, ringtones, pay per view documents, etc. have high transaction costs compared to total transaction value if they accept payment by credit card (or worse still, cheque). In traditional multi-party payment systems, the issuer usually recoups costs by charging merchants and/or consumers for each transaction in the shape of a percentage transaction fee. For credit cards, this can be a very high percentage because of the high costs of maintaining the credit card network and because there is always an element of risk involved in providing credit. To be able to take credit cards, an SME has to apply for a merchant account with a bank, which implies a tripartite agreement.[60] This agreement almost universally includes the charge by the bank of the transaction fee to the merchant, which will vary depending on the transaction volume and on the merchant's credit history. These rates vary from one market to another, but they tend to stay in the range of 1.5–5%, with the average for a SME being about 3%.[61] Debit card transactions are also subject to variable transaction fees depending on the issuing bank. Because costs associated are lower with debit than with credit cards, these usually involve a flat rate per transaction (generally £0.50 GBP). Because of this flat rate, debit cards are more appropriate for micro-payments than credit cards, but they are still not ideal for transactions under £5 GBP. Other intermediary payment systems also involve transaction charges to the merchant. PayPal charges from 2.2–2.9%, while WorldPay, another intermediary payment service for SMEs, charges as much as 4.5%.

---

[59] J Holmström and F Stalder, 'Drifting Technologies and Multipurpose Networks: The Case of the Swedish Cashcard' (2001) 11 *Information and Organization* 187–206.

[60] Ellinger, *et al*, above, pp 532–35.

[61] F Wilson, 'Unravelling the Mysteries of Merchant Credit Card Accounts for Web Commerce', *Web Commerce Today*, 15 August 1997.

Any payment system that charges considerably less than these rates per transaction is extremely attractive to merchants. As already noted, electronic money transactions are considerably cheaper than any of the systems described, which allows for much smaller transaction fees.

The other great advantage to merchants of moving on from the credit card schemes is escaping the problem of credit card chargeback. 'Chargeback' happens when a credit card issuer bills back the cost of a purchase made on credit to the merchant. There are a number of reasons for this but the main example is where a customer cancels a transaction because it was made by a fraudster or because it was unsatisfactory in some way eg damaged goods.[62] The contracts merchants enter with credit card issuers invariably bind them to accept chargebacks as a condition of membership of the scheme. As a result when credit cards are fraudulently misuses, eg, it is the merchant in the end not the issuer (or consumer) who usually bears the risk. Chargeback is thus a major cost to most merchants who accept credit cards of doing business. With electronic money, on the other hand, if (say) a smartcard or electronic purse is stolen or misused, it is the consumer, not the issuer, who suffers the loss of stored value, and so there will be no liability to the issuer to pass on to the merchant by chargeback.

The main potential disadvantage for merchants, such as it is, is the possible multiple costs of signing-up to competing incompatible e-money schemes. But if such a competitive market in e-money issuers were actually to arise (it does not yet exist), it would likely be good news for merchants, as competition would probably drive down the charges levied by such schemes.

3. Regulatory Framework

3.1 European Regulation

The Electronic Money Directive 2000/46/EC[63] is intended to prepare the way for the eventual rollout of electronic money schemes across the European Union. The main purpose of the Directive is to provide clear guidelines about the type of financial institutions that will be able to issue electronic money, and to establish a set of rules that will attempt to provide proper supervision of such institutions. The rationale behind it is to provide electronic money institutions with 'prudent limitations of their investments aimed at ensuring that their financial liabilities

---

[62] For more on chargebacks, see: D Bruggink, 'Card Payments: New Online Security Solutions' (2003) 4(3) *World Internet Law Report* 3–5.
[63] Above n 3.

related to outstanding electronic money are backed at all times by sufficiently liquid low risk assets.'[64]

The EMI Directive starts, as we have seen,[65] by defining electronic money, stating that electronic money is monetary value stored on an electronic device issued on receipt of funds and accepted as means of payment by third parties.[66] The directive then defines an electronic money institution (EMI) as 'an undertaking or any other legal person, other than a credit institution as defined in Article 1(1)(a) of Directive 2000/12/EC, which issues means of payment in the form of electronic money'.[67]

EMIs are thus defined as institutions concerned with the issuing of 'electronic money' which we have already considered earlier (see 1.1). 'Credit institutions' meanwhile are defined in Directive 2000/12/EC (otherwise known as the First Banking Directive (FBD)[68] as amended[69] to include the concept of EMIs. Article 1 of the FBD accordingly now reads:

1. Credit institution shall mean:

(a)   an undertaking whose business is to receive deposits or other repayable funds from the public and to grant credits for its own account; or
(b)   an electronic money institution within the meaning of Directive 2000/46/EC of the European Parliament and of the Council of 18 September 2000 on the taking up, pursuit and prudential supervision of the business of electronic money institutions.

This is an entire circular definition. The EMI Directive defines electronic money institutions in accordance to the FBD definition of credit institution, which in place defines credit institutions as those who issue electronic money in accordance to the EMI Directive. The policy behind this definition of EMIs as a sub-set of credit institutions is that the EMI Directive should not apply to deposit-taking or credit-giving institutions already adequately regulated by existing European banking directives in place prior to the EMI Directive.[70] Thus Article 2(3) of the EMI Directive specifies that receiving money for the purpose of exchanging it for electronic money will not be considered a deposit for the purposes of the FBD, which would turn these institutions into credit institutions. The effect of this complicated setup is that the provisions in the EMI Directive apply only to EMIs that are

---

[64]   EMI Directive, Preface (12).

[65]   Art 1.1.

[66]   EMI Directive, Art 1.3(b).

[67]   Art 3(b), EMI Directive.

[68]   Directive 2000/12/EC of the European Parliament and of the Council of 20 March 2000 relating to the taking up and pursuit of business of credit institutions; OJ L126/1.

[69]   As last amended by Directive 2000/28/EC, generally known as the Second Banking Directive (SBD).

[70]   Deposit has been defined by the Directive 94/19/EC as a credit balance that results from funds entered into an account and which the credit institution must pay back. This definition appears in the Directive 94/19/EC of the European Parliament and of the Council of Europe of 16 May 1994 on deposit-guarantee schemes, OJ L 135, 1994, Art 1.1.

not traditional credit institutions, while credit institutions that in addition issue electronic money are covered by the general banking directives.

Finally, and most importantly, the EMI Directive then *specifies* that member countries are to forbid any person or undertaking that is not a credit institution from issuing electronic money.[71]

DIAGRAM 4

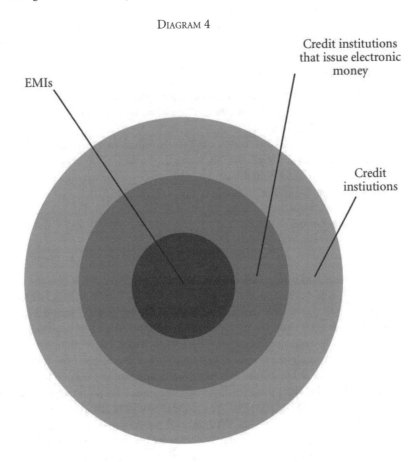

EMIs

Credit institutions that issue electronic money

Credit instiutions

The definition of EMIs as a sub set of credit institutions has the useful side benefit of allowing EMIs to benefit from the single passport license rule that exists in the First Banking Directive and other banking regulations, which allows banks to operate throughout the European Union if they are licensed by any one member state.[72] For example, PayPal Europe, applied to be recognised by the UK FSA as an

---

[71] EMI Directive, Art 1(4).
[72] Chuah, above, p 182.

EMI, and therefore it can now operate as such throughout the EU without further applications to national regulatory authorities. However, it is odd that Article 2(2) of the EMI Directive already grants EMIs with a limited version of the European single market passport when it states that 'The mutual recognition arrangements provided for in Directive 2000/12/EC shall not apply to EMI's business activities other than the issuance of electronic money.'

The EMI Directive goes on to state what an EMI is allowed to do other than issuing electronic money, which amount mostly to administrative or operational functions.[73]

Other important provisions include that:

- The electronic money must be redeemable from the issuer at any time in bank notes or coins, and the contracts should always be clear about the conditions of redemption (Article 3).
- Electronic money institutions must have an initial capital of one million EUR, and their own funds shall not fall below that amount. At any time, the institution must own funds that are equal or above 2% of the average total amount of their financial liabilities for the previous six months (Article 4).
- These institutions should have investments of an amount of no less than their financial liabilities in electronic money, and the operation of the institution should be sound and prudent (Articles 5–6).
- Electronic money institutions will be subject to money laundering regulations.

An important and interesting omission of the EMI Directive is that the subject of liability for loss or misuse of e-money is not covered and hence is left to the disparate domestic laws and codes of practice of the various EC states. The original recommendations from the European Commission contained several rules about responsibilities and liabilities that were not included in the final version of the Directive.[74] Among these recommendations was the suggestion that the cardholder would be liable for the loss of the card, and would be liable for an amount of up to €150 for the misuse of the card. The issuer would however be liable for any security breach or failure in the card that would result in loss of value attributable to the issuer. In the UK, the relevant rules may be found in the Banking Code, the self-regulation code of practice for British financial services which states that the liabilities of the holder of any electronic purse will not exceed £50. Newman and Sutter argue that this rule should be interpreted to apply to all electronic money schemes.[75] It is not at all clear how this rule might apply to an account based system such as PayPal, and some of these problems will clearly need

---

[73] Chuah, above, p 183.

[74] Commission Recommendation (97/489/EC) of 30 July 1997 concerning transactions by electronic payment instruments and in particular the relationship between issuer and holder; OJEC L208/52, 02 August 1997.

[75] Newman and Sutter, above.

to be sorted out if use of electronic money is to become widespread, but as it has been mentioned already, losing value in an electronic purse could be consider an equivalent of losing one's wallet.

Another interesting result of the EMI Directive is that it seems difficult for EMIs to profit directly from the schemes they offer. Very strict limits are placed on the type of charges that an EMI will be able to pass onto the consumer. As mentioned earlier, part of the definition of electronic money specifies that this monetary value will be 'issued on receipt of funds of an amount not less in value than the monetary value issued'. In practice, this means that the issuer cannot have a 'money offer', such as offering to charge an electronic purse with more value than that which has been paid for. The reason for this is that if this took place, then this action would be the issuing of credit, and then the electronic money would be a credit token.

Another result of the directive that affects profit is the redeemability rule, which makes it difficult for an issuer to charge a consumer for the service of placing the stored value onto an electronic device. This rule exist in Article 3(1) which states: 'A bearer of electronic money may, during the period of validity, ask the issuer to redeem it at par value in coins and bank notes or by a transfer to an account free of charges other than those strictly necessary to carry out that operation.'

If the EMI cannot offer credit when it issues the money, and cannot charge when it redeems the electronic value, then how will it make a profit? The question has to be answered by assuming that the issuer will attempt to make its profits from charges on merchants who agree to accept the electronic money in question (for as we saw earlier, the charge per transaction is likely to be lower than that currently levied by credit card issuers). There is nothing in the EMI Directive that stops EMIs charging merchants for accrediting them as part of an electronic money scheme. However it logically follows that the only type of electronic money schemes that are likely to be commercially viable will be those involved in tripartite or multi-party schemes, where the main cost of the transaction is passed onto sellers and suppliers. On first brush, this seems to indicate that the Directive is not technology or scheme-neutral and is in fact favouring a specific type of electronic money scheme. The Directive itself appears to assume that all electronic money systems as defined are necessarily tripartite, as there are clearly three parties involved at all times: the issuer, the bearer and the provider of goods and services.

Another possible means for profit is to charge consumers for hardware, such as additional cards for children or spouses, or to sell readers or proprietary software to both consumers and merchants; but this seems unlikely, as it would probably alienate potential customers and be a counter-productive strategy in a new and competitive market for e-money.

3.2 United Kingdom

The United Kingdom has recently adopted the EMI Directive in the Electronic Money (Miscellaneous Amendments) Regulations 2002.[76] The main bulk of the implementation is done by the Electronic Money Regulations 2002 (EMR), amending a number of existing pieces of legislation. However, some of the most interesting amendments are found in the Financial Services Regulated Activities Amendment Order 2002 (RA Amendment Order),[77] which amends existing delegated legislation[78] made under the Financial Services and Markets Act 2000 (FSMA).[79]

The first important change performed by the RA Amendment Order is that the implementation adds the definition of electronic money to the existing list of regulated activities contained in the FSMA, this is done with very similar wording to that of the EMI Directive.[80] However, there is one considerable change in the UK version of the definition. The EMI Directive clearly specifies that the value in the electronic money will be stored with no less value than the amount of money issued. The UK version of the article simply says that electronic money is 'issued on receipt of funds'. The FSA has clearly accepted that this was done on purpose to stop firms attempting to circumvent the regulations by issuing money at a discount, that is, issuing more value than the one paid for.[81] This would appear to be a mistake from the FSA, as it could be argued that an electronic money institution that attempts to give money in this way would possibly be incurring in credit-giving operations, which are more heavily regulated than the issuing of electronic money, so there would be no benefit in doing this.

The next important amendment is that the RA Amendment Order creates an exception to what will be considered a deposit taking activity, much in line with the EMI Directive. Specifically, Article 9A specifies that accepting money which will be then exchanged into electronic money value will not be considered to be a deposit-taking activity, hence exempting electronic money issuers from the strictest parts of the regulations directed towards credit institutions.

Another vital amendment performed by the RA Amendment Order is that it adds a new chapter to the existing FSMA RA Order in which electronic money institutions will be included in the list of regulated activities.[82] This brings it in line

[76] SI 2002 No 765.

[77] The Financial Services and Markets Act 2000 (Regulated Activities) (Amendment) Order 2002, SI 2002 No 682.

[78] The order is the Financial Services and Markets Act 2000 (Regulated Activities) Order 2001, SI 2001 No 544.

[79] For a detailed description of the UK implementation of the EMI Directive, see: Bamodu, above.

[80] RA Amendment Order, Art 3(1).

[81] Financial Services Authority, *The Regulation of Electronic Money Issuers: Feedback on CP117*, Policy Statement, April 2002. Available at <http://www.fsa.gov.uk/pubs/policy/ps117.pdf>.

[82] FSMA, Ch IIA.

with the EMI Directive requirements that define electronic money institutions as a regulated activity. The effect of this inclusion is that the regulatory regime in the UK will be the responsibility of the FSA, which will have the power to decide when an institution is to be considered an issuer of electronic money.

The FSA will have to implement a complex regime of exclusion certificates, which will be issued by this regulator to certain institutions that issue electronic money under certain circumstances. These certificates will allow these institutions to operate outside of the requirements of the EMI Directive. An issuer of electronic money will be able to apply for this certificate by fulfilling a number of complex requirements set out by the FSMA RA Order. An electronic money institution will only be exempt if the undertaking fulfils one of the requirements listed in paragraphs (4), (5) or (6) of section 9.2 of Chapter IIA of the amended FSMA RA Order. These paragraphs are:

(3) The authority must, on the application of such a person ('A'), give A a certificate if it appears to the Authority that paragraph (4), (5) or (6) applies.

(4) This paragraph applies if—(a) A does not issue electronic money except on terms that the electronic device on which the monetary value is stored is subject to a maximum storage amount of not more than 150 euro; and

(b) A's total liabilities with respect to the issuing of electronic money do not (or will not) usually exceed 5 million euro and do not (or will not) ever exceed 6 million euro.

This is the most straightforward of the paragraphs, and it is intended to limit the application of the Directive to small enterprises. This is because the strict requirements could become too burdensome to new and small undertakings with interest in establishing new electronic money schemes. The following paragraphs are considerably more complex. Paragraph 5 reads:

(5) This paragraph applies if—(a) the condition in paragraph (4)(a) is met;

(b) A's total liabilities with respect to the issuing of electronic money do not (or will not) exceed 10 million euro; and

(c) electronic money issued by A is accepted as a means of payment only by—

(i) subsidiaries of A which perform operational or other ancillary functions related to electronic money issued or distributed by A; or

(ii) other members of the same group as A (other than subsidiaries of A).

This is a more specific rule than that expressed in the previous paragraph. The amount of liabilities accepted has increased from €5 million to €10 million, with the caveat that the electronic money is only accepted by subsidiaries or associates or the issuer, or by companies within the same group of companies. This exception is designed to exclude from the regulation electronic payment systems that only apply to a limited number of participants, because the objective of the regulation is to authorise only wide-ranging schemes. This exception will appear to exclude the application of some smaller electronic payment systems, such as store cards and award points schemes within a group of companies. Paragraph (6) is even more precise, it says that:

> (6) This paragraph applies if—(a) the conditions in paragraphs (4)(a) and (5)(b) are met; and
>
> (b) electronic money issued by A is accepted as a means of payment, in the course of business, by not more than one hundred persons where—
>
>> (i) those persons accept such electronic money only at locations within the same premises or limited local area; or
>>
>> (ii) those persons have a close financial or business relationship with A, such as a common marketing or distribution scheme.

This set of rules are even more restrictive, and are designed to rule out very limited payment card schemes, even if those receiving payment are not related in any way to the electronic money issuer. It would appear that the term 'persons' in this paragraph refers to natural and legal persons. This would rule out even some wider schemes such as Nectar points,[83] which are only accepted by less than 100 undertakings.

The Treasury criticised the definition of electronic money in the EMI Directive as being too narrow, and not technologically neutral enough back in 2001.[84] As a result, the Treasury recommended that the FSA should have the power to decide in an *ad hoc* basis whether a payment scheme should be considered as an electronic money institution and be subject to the regulation contained in it regardless of the regulatory framework described above.

4. Case Study: PayPal as an EMI

One of the key problems with the EMI Directive may be that, although very recently implemented in most EU states, it may still require almost immediate and substantial revision in order to regulate the newer non-stored value or smart card payment systems. As matters stand, a strong argument can be made that the EMI is not designed to regulate them.

In the payments market, card-based electronic money schemes appears to be faltering to the point of extinction, while account-based schemes are the fastest growing sector in the electronic payment world. Should account-based schemes

---

[83] More about Nectar points can be found at <http://www.nectar.com/NectarHome.nectar>.
[84] HM Treasury, *Implementation of the Electronic Money Directive: A Consultation Document*, (October 2001), <http://www.hm-treasury.gov.uk/mediastore/otherfiles/e_money.pdf>.

therefore be considered electronic money,[85] or should they fall into a different regulatory regime, such as that for credit institutions. Even a perfunctory glance at PayPal's business operation makes the similarity with the functions performed by a credit institution become immediately apparent. The First Banking Directive defines a credit institution as 'an undertaking whose business is to receive deposits or other repayable funds from the public and to grant credits for its own account.'[86] Are PayPal's functions a deposit-taking exercise in the sense of the Directive?

A deposit is defined[87] as a credit balance that results from funds entered into an account and which the credit institution must pay back.[88] This is rather straightforward definition of what a deposit is, but differs slightly from the definition in effect in the UK through the Regulated Activities Order 2001 (RAO), which defines a deposit in two different ways:

> (a) money received by way of deposit is lent to others; or(b) any other activity of the person accepting the deposit is financed wholly, or to a material extent, out of the capital of or interest on money received by way of deposit.[89]

This is interesting because of the 'or'. If an undertaking accepts deposits and uses them to finance any of its activities, the letter of the law clearly implies that this would be considered as a regulated deposit-taking activity. The question then is whether PayPal takes deposits and uses those deposits to finance any other activity. The answer to this is uncertain, as there are contradicting statements coming from PayPal in this regard. In 2000, Peter Thiel, PayPal's chief executive commented that, 'The PayPal account doesn't provide interest, so PayPal can invest any money left there until the user wants to spend it.'[90] This would seem like a clear-cut admission that PayPal acts as a deposit-taking institution, and therefore should be considered as a bank for all regulatory purposes. However, PayPal now claims that it does not make any use of the deposits in the user accounts it holds. In fact, PayPal's user agreement states that 'PayPal will at all times hold your funds separate from its corporate funds, will not use your funds for its operating expenses or any other corporate purposes, and will not voluntarily make funds available to its creditors in the event of bankruptcy or for any other purpose.'[91] This paragraph poses an interesting conundrum, as PayPal claims not to use the funds in the accounts held by the customers for operational expenses, and therefore could not be considered a bank.

---

[85] For a more detailed argument about the legal status of PayPal, see: A Guadamuz, 'PayPal: Legal Implications of a C2C Electronic Payments System' (2004) 20 *Computer Law and Security Report* 1.

[86] 2000/12/EC, Art 1, above.

[87] Directive 94/19/EC of the European Parliament and of the Council of Europe of 16 May 1994 on deposit-guarantee schemes, OJ L 135, 1994,

[88] *Ibid*, Art 1.1.

[89] ROA, s 5(1).

[90] P Thiel, cited by Sapsford, above.

[91] PayPal user agreement, para 2.1.

Another consideration that lends credence to the argument that PayPal is not a bank is that the EMI Directive clearly states that the storing of funds into an electronic device (or account in this case) should not be considered a deposit for the purposes of the FBD.[92] The United States Federal Deposit Insurance Corporation (FDIC) decided that PayPal was not a bank in accordance with US bank regulations because it did not physically handle or hold the money placed in the customer's accounts. The FDIC also ruled that PayPal should not be considered a bank because it did not have a bank charter, which is one of the legal requirements in US legislation.[93] However, there appears to be some discrepancy in the FDIC's opinion, as they have also held that deposits made to PayPal will be subject to federal deposit insurance, which is usually given only to banking institutions.[94]

However, if PayPal is not a bank, then is it an EMI? As briefly discussed above, PayPal Europe was recognised as an EMI by the UK FSA in February 2004. PayPal has since changed their user agreement to state that:

> The Service is an e-money payment service rather than a banking or escrow service, and we are not acting as a trustee with respect to balances that you choose to keep in your account. We are acting only as an issuer of electronic money (stored value). You are not required to maintain a balance in order to use the Service to make payments although a balance will be created whenever you use the Service to make a payment funded from your bank or card.[95]

The problem here is that even if one argues that PayPal is only storing electronic value into an account, this is almost undistinguishable from what takes place in a bank, other than the fact that the deposited money does not gain interest. The fact also remains that an electronic money scheme is surely a scheme which is mainly about the *issuing* of money. Yet in the case of PayPal, the usefulness of the account is not only to make payments, but very often, even exclusively, to *receive* them from other users with a PayPal account.

The conclusion that account-based payment systems should not be considered (solely?) electronic money institutions seems compelling, but the FSA evidently disagrees. Unfortunately, the reasoning behind the FSA's decision has not been made public.

The main reasons behind the decision may simply be of politics and pragmatism. One of the stated goals of the EMI Directive was to present a technology neutral definition of electronic money in order to accommodate future technological

---

[92] EMI Directive, Art 2(3).

[93] T Wolverton, 'PayPal Not a Bank', *CNet News*, 12 March 2002, <http://news.com.com/2100–1017–858264.html?tag=bplst>.

[94] Bureau of National Affairs, 'Electronic Payments: Paypal Funds Eligible for Pass-Through Insurance From FDIC as Deposits by Agent' (2002) 7(12) *BNA Newsletter*, 20 March 2002, p 254.

[95] PayPal Europe User Agreement, s 2.

innovations and new payment systems. In fact, the Directive's preamble clearly says:

> Within the wider context of the rapidly evolving electronic commerce it is desirable to provide a regulatory framework that assists electronic money in delivering its full potential benefits and that avoids hampering technological innovation in particular. Therefore, this Directive introduces a technology-neutral legal framework that harmonises the prudential supervision of electronic money institutions to the extent necessary for ensuring their sound and prudent operation and their financial integrity in particular.[96]

This objective, to be technology neutral, would be clearly defeated if the dominant payment methods in the market which were analogous or as near as damn it to electronic money were exposed as not covered by the supposedly 'technology-neutral' definitions. The EMI Directive seems clearly to have been drafted with smart-card technology in mind, as the dominant paradigm at the time of drafting. The UK Treasury expressed serious concerns with the definition of an electronic money institution included in the Directive when consulting for UK implementation, and decided to favour as wide an interpretation of an EMI as possible. They stated that:

> There is a wide range of schemes that could be considered as e-money and whether the Directive catches any given scheme will depend on the application of the definition to the details of a particular case. Given the emergent nature of the e-money industry, we do not believe it is possible to elaborate on this definition in such a way as to legislate explicitly for all the different types of scheme that might be developed.[97]

The FSA appears to have taken this recommendation to heart.[98] The FSA reached the decision that an account-based payment scheme could be electronic money,[99] but that this would have to be determined on a case-by-case basis, otherwise all electronic storage of monetary value ever devised would have to be considered electronic money, including banks. A set of questions was designed to test whether or not an account is a deposit-taking scheme or electronic money. These include:

---

[96] EMI Directive, para (5).

[97] HM Treasury, *Implementation of the Electronic Money Directive: A Consultation Document*, above n 84.

[98] In particular they drew on the Treasury assertion (*ibid*) that 'The Treasury believes the Directive's definition includes both e-money schemes in which value is stored on a card that is used by the bearer to make purchases, and account-based e-money schemes where value is stored in an electronic account that the user can access remotely.'

[99] Financial Services Authority, *Guidance on the scope of the regulated activity of issuing e-money* (2004), Appendix 3.3.20, <http://www.fsa.gov.uk/handbook/BL3AUTHpp/AUTH/Appendix_3.pdf>.

An account is a **deposit-taking** account if:	An account is an **electronic money** scheme if:
– monetary value can be drawn by non electronic means (cheques)	– it is designed as means of savings
– it has features that are not necessary for payment (overdraft, direct debit)	– the account operates even without money in it
– there are incentives to leave the money in the account (interest rates)—it is designed to pay for goods and services	– the service is advertised and offered as an electronic money system

Furthermore, the FSA added that 'a deposit involves the creation of a debtor-creditor relationship under which the person who accepts the deposit stores value for eventual return. E-money, in contrast, involves the purchase of a means of payment.'[100] It would seem that the FSA believes that PayPal's main use is for making not receiving payments, hence their decision. Unfortunately, the European Commission does not appear to share this opinion. In a statement about future development in payment systems in Europe,[101] the Commission considered the perceived lack of regulation of new payment schemes, and considered the need for a possible new Directive. With regards to PayPal, the Commission considered that PayPal was closer to a credit token than to electronic money. In fact, the paper states:

> However, payment services do exist, which may be regarded as not being covered by the E-Money Directive and which could have a potential to become EU-wide schemes in fulfilling some payment needs, such as micro payments in the internet or in wireless communication services. Some payment products on the market, such as mobile operator accounts and virtual accounts (eg, PayPal), are closer to credit transfers in a centralised account system than real bearer instruments.

It is perhaps unfortunate that the Commission decided to regulate electronic money before other methods of consumer-to-consumer electronic payment had evolved, which would have solved some of the inconsistencies highlighted in this section. Nevertheless, with the FSA's decision to grant PayPal EMI status, this debate is now, at it stands, in the UK at least, academic.

---

[100] Financial Services Authority, *Guidance on the scope of the regulated activity of issuing e-money* (2004), Appendix 3.3.20, <http://www.fsa.gov.uk/handbook/BL3AUTHpp/AUTH/Appendix_3.pdf>.

[101] Commission of the European Community, Communication from the Commission to the Council and the European Parliament concerning a New Legal Framework for Payments in the Internal Market, COM(2003) 718 final, 2 December 2003.

5. Conclusion

There is no doubt that electronic money has enormous potential. It may bolster the market for e-commerce as well as be a tool for real world transactions. It may one day even eventually replace physical currency. Is European law taking e-money regulation seriously enough? It is encouraging that the EU has already lead the world in making regulatory efforts in this direction. It is unfortunate however that the EMI Directive may have jumped the gun, by orienting itself towards one set of technologies, despite pleas of 'technology neutrality', when the market was already turning in a different direction. We must wait now to see if practical as opposed to potential problems do arise from the ambiguities of the EMI Directive, and if national implementations do fall short of reassuring merchants, issuers and consumers that e-money can work. The proof will, in the end, be in how vigorously the real world of consumers takes up virtual payment mechanisms. The carrot of new rules of consumer protection may yet be needed, as was the case with credit cards, or it may not. Concerns such as security and hacking, meanwhile, will remain crucial but are not easily solved by legislation. The consequences of insecurity in a major e-payment mechanism could be disastrous not just for issuers but for entire economies. It remains to be seen what new regulation, if any, we may yet require to make the world of electronic money a reality.

7

VAT on Electronic Services Directive 2002/38/EC

Amending VAT Law for Electronic Transactions: A Simple Choice for a Simple Tax?

A. Introduction

In a simple world, VAT would be a simple tax. Each time a good or service is supplied, the supplier collects tax from the purchaser and pays to the tax authorities the difference between the tax collected on the sale and the VAT he paid in the course of production. Eventually the good or service ends up with a final consumer—along with the whole tax burden simply because he will not be able to claim credit for the tax he paid on purchase. However, we no longer inhabit a simple world and VAT is not a simple tax. In the well known words of Lord Justice Sedley, 'Beyond the everyday world . . . lies the world of VAT, a kind of fiscal theme park in which factual and legal realities are suspended or inverted.'[1]

As we shall see, there is no fantasy world which more effectively achieves the standards of Byzantine complexity than the VAT rules on supplies of international services.

The whole edifice of tax rests on building blocks which are place specific: we need to know in which country certain things happen or where someone belongs for tax purposes. Fundamental to VAT, for example, is the concept of 'the place of supply'. The default position is that this is the place of the 'fixed establishment' of

---

[1] *Royal & Sun Alliance Insurance Group plc v Commissioners of Customs and Excise* [2001] STC 1476.

the supplier although sometimes one needs to know where the consumer belongs or where the services are actually consumed. Notions developed in the days when the world was largely material have had to adapt, sometimes rather ill-fittingly, to the electronic world.

This chapter discusses the VAT issues arising out of the transmission of electronic content and the provision of the content itself. In particular it discusses the new EU rules concerning telecom services, broadcasting services and other electronic services introduced to provide a more level playing field for the providers of such services, with focus on the implementation of these rules in the UK. It is not pretended that these rules are simple or capable of short exposition.[2] Potentially, answers to all the following questions have to be answered before it can be determined whether VAT has to be imposed on a supply and, if so, at what rate:

- Am I making a supply from outside the EU?
- Am I making a supply to someone in the EU?
- Is the person receiving the supply a registered trader in the EU?
- Am I making a supply of goods or of services?
- If I am supplying services, how should they be classified? In particular, are they telecom services, broadcasting services or electronic services?
- If I am required to account for VAT on the goods or services, how and to whom should I do this?

Before we consider how to approach these questions, a brief reminder of how VAT operates in relation to goods and services which cross borders might be helpful.

B. The Nature of VAT on Cross Border Supplies of Goods and Services

The backbone of the VAT system operating in the member states of the EU is the Sixth VAT Directive, dating from 1977. Although the tax is designed to be borne by the ultimate consumer, it is a 'fractionated' tax, ie it is collected at each stage in the process of production through the system of input and output tax, rather than a single stage tax which operates at the point of sale. Any VAT paid out by a registered trader on goods and services used in that trader's business, the input tax credit, is allowed as a deduction against the VAT the trader collects in the same tax period on the goods and services he or she produces, the output tax. Eventually, someone (usually, but not always, the final consumer) pays a sum that includes VAT for goods or services but is not permitted to set off the VAT as a deduction.

---

[2] Indeed it is virtually impossible to discuss the application of VAT on international services without appearing to have some form of obsessive disorder.

It is at this point that the person who purchases the good or service from the supplier ends up actually *bearing* the tax, even though the person who accounts for the tax to the authorities will be the supplier.

There is an important point about economic neutrality to be made here. A person who can get full deduction of the input tax on the goods and services purchased for business use is more or less indifferent as to whether, or at what rate, VAT is paid, as it is fairly quickly reflected in the amount of VAT he or she is required to account for to the tax authorities. In contrast, those for whom input credit is *not* or is only partially available will prefer to pay as little VAT as possible. So, which persons do not receive the full input tax credit? Most obviously, the ultimate consumers: those who are using the goods or services for personal rather than business purposes. Also included are persons who are not registered for VAT at all because they do not make sufficient supplies to reach the minimum limit for registration—the small trader. More importantly, persons who make *exempt* supplies are not entitled to a full deduction[3] and, as exempt supplies include financial services, all banks and other financial institutions fall into this group. Finally, the list also includes persons who receive supplies other than for the purposes of a business, for example governments and the public sector.

As a matter of terminology, I shall in this paper refer to all persons who do not get the benefit of an input tax credit as 'consumers', except when I am specifically referring to exempt suppliers.

VAT is a tax on consumption and as a general principle VAT on a supply should end up with the jurisdiction where consumption takes place. As it can be difficult to determine the actual place of consumption, as discussed below, most jurisdictions operate on the basis of some more clearly identifiable proxy. The next sections consider how VAT currently operates within the EU, dealing first with supplies of goods (business to business(B2B)), then business to consumer (B2C)), followed by a similar consideration of the VAT treatment of cross border services.

1. VAT on Goods—B2B Supplies

Where the supplier and the consumer are in the same tax jurisdiction, the place of consumption is unlikely to be problematic. But once goods are transferred across borders, there are two main difficulties with allowing the VAT chain to continue unbroken. To understand these difficulties, it is first necessary to examine the way in which VAT works at present in a cross border transaction. Imagine that A finds driftwood on the beach in northern Scotland, cleans it up, and sells it for 100 to B, an entrepreneur in Edinburgh. B sells the driftwood to C for 200, a retailer of

---

[3] A person making only exempt supplies will get no credit for input tax. Those who make both exempt and taxable supplies will get only a proportion of input tax as a set-off against output tax.

curiosities situated in another member state. The rate of VAT in the UK is 17.5% and is 25% in the other member state. Assuming A is registered for VAT, he will charge B VAT of 17.50 which A will then pay to his own tax authorities. B will pay 117.50 to A, representing the price of the wood plus VAT. B has an 'input tax credit' of 17.50, which he can set off against any VAT he collects on his own supplies, or if he doesn't make enough taxable supplies in the VAT quarterly accounting period, he can claim it back as a refund from the tax authorities.

When B supplies the wood to C, because C is in another country, the supply is 'zero-rated'. This means two things—first, B charges no VAT on the good, and second, B has an input tax credit for the VAT he paid out to A which he can claim as a refund from the UK tax authorities. In turn, this means that B does not have to increase the price he charges for the good to reflect the VAT he paid out. Effectively, VAT is 'washed out' of the good as it leaves the country: it carries with it no vestiges of UK VAT, either directly as a charge of VAT, or indirectly as a cost incurred in its production.

When C receives the wood, because he is in another member state, he is required to account for VAT at 25% to his tax authorities on the wood's acquisition, or 50. This is an inversion of the normal rule that it is the supplier rather than the person acquiring the good who accounts for VAT but is necessary to ensure a level playing field between goods C acquires from his own member state, which would have borne VAT, and those he acquires from abroad, which are zero-rated. However, the liability to account is normally matched by an identical deduction, as the VAT he is supposed to account for on acquisition in turn is given to him as an input tax credit. (If this seems odd, imagine C had purchased the wood from a supplier in his own state. C would have paid VAT to the supplier and had a matching deduction as an input tax credit. All that is happening on an acquisition from overseas is that instead of C paying the VAT to the supplier, he accounts for it to his own tax authority and gets a matching deduction. Economically they are identical.)

This system has certain strengths. First, it insulates against variations in VAT rates between member states. It is of no advantage/disadvantage to acquire goods from a member state with a low/high rate of VAT if you are a VAT registered person. The same amount of VAT is being paid on the acquisition whether the goods are acquired from a local supplier or from an overseas supplier and, apart from a slight cash flow advantage in acquiring goods from another member state,[4] the location of the supplier is irrelevant from a tax point of view.

Second, it ensures that the whole of the VAT on a good is paid to the country of consumption.

---

[4] There can be a slight cash-flow advantage in acquiring the goods from overseas as the VAT will not be payable alongside the price for the goods but in the first VAT return made after the acquisition.

However, one disadvantage of the 'destination system' as the system described above is called, is that goods cross borders with no VAT on them which makes the system vulnerable to fraud. Accordingly, the long term goal of the EU is to shift to a system whereby the VAT chain stretches across borders, which will reduce the opportunities for fraud, and also gain the advantage that suppliers no longer have to differentiate between domestic and cross border supplies. Both symbolically and administratively this is perceived as an improvement on the current system. However, as mentioned above, there are difficulties of allowing VAT to cross borders. First, under the alternative system, B would charge C VAT of 35 (17.5% of 200) and the total amount of VAT accounted for to the UK tax authorities would be 35 even though no consumption has taken place there. Part of the tax ends up with the country of export rather than the place of final consumption, which would be likely to give rise to claims for redistribution of tax revenue between states. The second problem is one of administration: that of persuading one tax authority to grant recognition of the foreign tax credit, necessary to avoid discrimination against imports in comparison with domestic supplies.

Where goods leave the EU, whether to a business or a consumer, they are also zero rated and whether the person who receives the supply is required or not to account for VAT depends on his or her domestic system.

2. VAT on Goods—B2C Supplies

An EU supply of a good to an EU consumer carries with it the VAT of the country of the supplier. This is in breach of the destination principle, which is that the revenue should accrue to the state of consumption. The main reason for this is simplicity as EU suppliers do not need to adjust the VAT on their supplies by reference to the place of residence of the customer, as long as the customer is within the EU. The potential for economic distortion caused by cross border shopping from states with lower rates of VAT is limited by a number of special rules, for example, the rules which apply to distance selling and cars. A supply to a customer outside the EU is, as noted above, zero-rated.

Where goods are being acquired by an EU consumer from outside the EU, the customer is required to account for the VAT on import, again with some exceptions, for example small value imports. It is relevant to note that this is the only situation in which a consumer is personally required to account for the tax directly to tax authorities.

3. VAT on Services—B2B Supplies

The most important question in relation to cross border services is to determine where the supply is made. The default position is that a supply of services is made where the supplier belongs, although there are many special rules in Article 9(2) of the Sixth VAT Directive, many of which apply to services which are typically supplied cross border.[5] Of particular significance is Article 9(2)(e), which shifts the place of supply to the place of the customer where a EU supplier supplies certain services to either:

a) a customer established outside the EU or
b) a business in another member state within the EU.

The economic effect of these special rules is similar to that achieved by the zero-rating of goods. In relation to (a), the shift effectively relieves the supply of any VAT. In relation to (b), the obligation to account for the tax is shifted from the supplier to the person receiving the supply. This is known as the reverse charge, where the person *receiving* rather than the person *making* the supply accounts for the tax. This might sound odd and indeed convoluted but in practice it works well. First, it means that the person receiving the supply is, as with goods, largely indifferent from the tax point of view as to whether the supplies are made from a supplier in his own member state, another EU state or elsewhere in the world, so the reverse charge achieves economic neutrality. Furthermore, there is a distinct administrative advantage to the recipient in the use of the reverse charge in the context of cross border supplies: input tax credits do not cross borders under the present tax regime, so any overseas VAT paid has to be reclaimed from the overseas tax authority. Where refund is available, it is often a tedious and drawn out process.[6] As an example, a UK business which engages French legal services would, in the absence of the reverse charge, be required to pay legal fees including French VAT but would not be permitted a tax credit for this VAT in the UK. The UK business would have to seek recovery of the French VAT from the French tax authorities. Under the reverse charge, the UK business pays no French VAT on the supply, but accounts for VAT to the UK as if it had made the supply itself. At the same time, it gets a matching input tax credit which will normally cancel out the obligation to pay.[7] In practice, the reverse charge is used widely around the world and has proved 'feasible, effective and carries a low compliance and administrative burden.'[8]

---

[5] Sixth VAT Directive 77/388/EEC Art 9(2) is reproduced below at p 430. Examples of 9(2)(e) services include advertising, consultancy, legal and accountancy. To this list was added telecom, radio and broadcasting and electronic services. See the discussions below at pp 214–216.

[6] If a business incurs VAT in a member state of the EU in which the business is not registered, repayment under the 8th or 13th Directive is supposed to be made within six months of the claim. This is by no means a deadline which is always achieved.

[7] The point of accounting for VAT and making a claim for a tax credit, which may seem a longwinded way of achieving nothing, is that such a process is necessary where the person receiving the supply makes some exempt supplies, which means that the full input tax credit will not be available.

[8] 'Consumption Tax Aspects of Electronic-Commerce' (OECD) Report from Working Party 9 to the Committee for Fiscal Affairs, February 2001, para 43, http://www.oecd.org/dataoecd/37/19/2673667.pdf.

4. VAT on Services—B2C Supplies

Originally, the proxy chosen as the place of consumption of services in relation to supplies of services in the EU was the place where the service was provided,[9] but this proved difficult to operate in practice, and the default position for the place of supply was soon changed to the supplier's place of business.[10] Here it remains as Article 9(2)(e), discussed above, does not apply in relation to supplies made to EU consumers by EU suppliers. In the early days of VAT most services were consumed close to the place of supply and this rule successfully allocated most of the tax-take to the country of consumption.[11] The 1993 distance selling rules[12] ensure that suppliers of goods across borders with in the EU are required to register in the member state to which supplies are made (except where supplies are insignificant) which ensures that the rate of tax charged on goods is the rate of tax applicable in the country of the customer. However, at the time these were introduced, cross border services were not regarded as sufficiently significant.[13] Now, with the increased availability of cross border services it is of obvious benefit to consumers to acquire services from a jurisdiction where lower rates, or preferably zero rates of VAT apply.[14] This distortion of competition in relation to supplies from else-where within the EU is limited by the existence of minimum EU VAT rates, but more significant problems arise when the services are being supplied from outside the EU to a consumer within the EU where in principle *no* VAT is charged. Similarly, a consumer outside the EU will be less inclined to buy services from a EU supplier if similar services can be acquired from someone else who is not required to charge VAT. As we shall see later, in order to deal with these non-neutralities, the place of supply of certain services is often shifted.

C. Potential for Distortion

Overall, where does the potential for distortion in supplies lie? In relation to the biggest category of supplies, those which are business to business, there is limited

[9] Second VAT Directive (67/228/EEC) Art 6(3).

[10] Sixth VAT Directive (77/388/EEC) Art 9(1).

[11] Hairdressing services are often used as an example of services which are consumed close to the place of supplier. However, even this apparently mundane example can be problematic: take an artiste who has his or her hair done in the morning in Germany and flies to Paris for an awards ceremony which is beamed around the world that evening: where is the service consumed?

[12] Now in the Sixth VAT Directive Art 28b.

[13] As the EU are currently working out how to cut down on the administrative burdens on suppliers, the introduction of the distance selling rules to services is not under consideration. This is discussed later at p 232.

[14] Sixth VAT Directive (77/388/EEC) Art 9(1).

scope for the VAT system to influence the choice of location of supplier. Businesses within the EU have to account for tax on goods and most services received from abroad, whether from the EU or elsewhere. Persons (businesses and consumers) outside the EU who acquire *goods* from an EU supplier will benefit from the rules on zero-rating and bear no EU VAT. Although there may be local tax on a supply to a non-EU customer, this provides for a level playing field locally. The major exception to this is the group of businesses which do not receive full credit for their input tax. As discussed earlier, this group includes some big players, including most financial institutions.[15]

This leaves supplies (of goods and services) to consumers in the EU and supplies of services to those outside the EU to be considered. Supplies of goods to an EU consumer are in principle always subject to VAT: at home rates where goods are imported from outside the EU or where the distance selling rules apply, and at local rates where goods are purchased from another member state. The capacity for distortion here is limited as, although the variation in rates within the EU from 15% to 25% will provide a certain amount of incentive to cross border shop, the associated travel costs mean that any differential in rates is unlikely to create distortions at a significant level.

This leaves supplies of services as the area where the problems of distortion really start to arise and there are two main non-neutralities. First, in relation to EU consumers, they have an obvious price incentive to acquire services tax-free from outside the EU, or at least from a member state which imposes a lower rate of tax than the consumer's state of residence. Second, in relation to EU suppliers, if they are required to charge VAT even if they are making supplies to consumers outside the EU, they will be at a serious competitive disadvantage in comparison with suppliers from a jurisdiction, for example the USA, where no equivalent tax is charged.

There are only two ways in which a level playing field can be established in relation to the supply of intangible goods and services under the current VAT system: all such goods and services consumed within a jurisdiction must either bear *no* tax or bear the *same* tax. The first involves loss of revenue and increased distortion between tangibles and intangibles. The second involves difficulties of collection where the supply is made from outside the tax jurisdiction of the consumer. Either tax must be collected from the consumer under some kind of reverse charge, with the attendant difficulties of enforcing compliance, or the tax must be collected from the supplier or intermediary. It is unrealistic to expect any tax authority to enforce another's tax obligations, so essentially one is looking to require the supplier to fulfil its tax collection function through the tax authorities of the consumer. Given that the supplier of electronic goods or services may have no business presence apart from a few rented wires in the consumer's jurisdiction,

---

[15] See p 205.

enforcement issues arise. As the Technology TAG of the OECD noted 'the ability of a tax jurisdiction to enforce such a tax regime beyond their borders will be spotty at best, leading to market distortions and inequalities'.[16]

It is against this background that the new EU rules emerged, first, on telecommunication services and subsequently, on broadcasting and electronic services and it to these we now turn.

D. The Response of the EU

Until deregulation in the 1980s, telecom services were supplied by public bodies under state monopoly but once private bodies began to compete with both the public sector and each other to supply telecom services, the two main non-neutralities identified in the last section were brought into sharp focus.[17] Telecom services were at this point still operating under the normal place of supply rule and, at a critical point in its development in a deregulated environment, the telecoms business in the EU was facing competitive disadvantage.[18] US based telecom companies were not slow to exploit their advantage by the use of various 'callback' schemes which gave the EU consumer access to the US provider's network free of VAT. Faced with unilateral action by member states to correct this distortion, the EU promulgated first a derogation[19] (backdated to homologate the action already taken) and subsequently a directive, which amended the Sixth VAT Directive by adjusting the place of supply of telecom services.[20] First, telecom services were added to the list in Article 9(2)(e), which relieved EU suppliers from charging VAT on supplies to persons outside the EU, and brought supplies received by EU businesses within the reverse charge. More controversially, it also shifted the place of supply by non–EU telecom providers to consumers within the EU to the place where the services are 'used and enjoyed'.[21] This placed non-EU providers under an obligation to register for VAT in each member state once their supplies in each state reached that state limit for registration.

But this only provided a solution to the telecoms industry and providers of other electronic services were struggling under continued economic imbalance. In

---

[16] Report by the Technology Technical Advisory Group (OECD) December 2000, http://www.oecd.org/dataoecd/46/2/1,923,248.pdf.

[17] Referred to above at p 210.

[18] As telecom services were not originally subject to the reverse charge, businesses acquiring supplies from outside the EU also paid no VAT This is only of significant advantage to businesses making exempt supplies as other businesses will get full credit for an input VAT paid.

[19] Issued under Art 27 of the Sixth VAT Directive, granted with retrospective effect from 1 January 1997.

[20] 97/209/EC, amended by 1999/59/EC.

[21] Sixth VAT Directive, Art 9(4).

addition there was considerable uncertainty about the operation of Article 9(2)(c) which taxes various services, including scientific, educational and entertainment services, where they are physically carried out. With electronic delivery of such services becoming possible, determining the place where they are physically carried out was becoming increasingly difficult.[22] Furthermore, the distinction which had been created between telecom services and other electronic services was proving difficult to operate in practice, with many Internet Service Providers (ISPs) providing composite supplies.

The continuing debate eventually resulted in a proposal in 2000 which broadly recommended that broadcasting services should be brought under the telecoms regime and that similar rules be applied to electronic services.[23] The proposal was contentious both within and outside the EU, primarily on the basis that the introduction of such a scheme should wait until the technological support existed to operate it without imposing significant administrative burdens on businesses required to use it.

An acknowledgement of the difficulties likely to be faced by electronic service suppliers, of which there are likely to be many, including some small businesses, is reflected in the (temporary) special scheme for registration.[24] Suppliers of electronic services to EU consumers are to be permitted to operate a simplified registration scheme, registering in just one member state.[25] Two further provisions in the original proposals were also designed to alleviate the administrative burden for non-EU suppliers. First, it was proposed that suppliers should apply just one rate of VAT, the rate of the member state of registration, irrespective of the location of the customer. Second, it was suggested that there should be a de minimis level of 100,000 Euro worth or supplies under which registration was not required. There was considerable disquiet about these two suggestions: first, in relation to the single rate of VAT, the member states charging higher rates of VAT pointed out that there was considerable advantage for a non-EU supplier to register in a low member state. In relation to the de minimis limit, it was felt that this still discriminated against EU suppliers to an unacceptable extent. Eventually both proposals were dropped. With the addition of an intra-member state clearing house to redistribute the VAT according to place of customer, in 2002 the VAT on

---

[22] As an example, *British Sky Broadcasting Group Plc v Customs and Excise Commissioners* [2001] STC 437 (LON/94/7 8A), the taxpayer argued that it was providing 'entertainment' services under Art 9(2)(c), rather than falling under the default rules of Art 9(1). This argument was unsuccessful. Today such services would fall within Art 9(2)(e).

[23] COM (2000) 349.

[24] Discussed below at pp 226–29. In contrast, suppliers of telecom services are typically large enterprises and are more able to absorb the costs of registration in each member state into which supplies are made.

[25] The use of simplified registration procedures was also recommended by the OECD's Working Party 9 in the report 'Consumption Tax Aspects of Electronic Commerce' above n 8.

Electronic Services Directive was approved, with an implementation date of 1 July 2003.[26]

E. Place of Supply

So VAT, which is such a simple tax in conception, operates internationally on a complex matrix of variables: the place of supply, which is critical because it determines which tax jurisdiction governs the supply,[27] depends on the nature of supply, the tax status and place of the person receiving the supply and, sometimes, where the services are consumed.

The EU position in relation to the place of supply from 2003 is summarised in the following table.

PLACE OF SUPPLY OF INTERNATIONAL SERVICES

Category of service Supplied	Supplier/ Customer	Place of supply	Can the 'effective use and enjoyment' rules apply?
Normal rule (default position)	All customers	Place where the supplier belongs Article 9(1)	No
Telecom and broadcasting Services	B(EU)2B(EU)	Place where customer belongs Article 9(2)(e)	Yes (permissive) Article 9(3)
	B(nonEU)2B(EU)	Place where customer belongs Article 9(2)(e)	Yes (permissive) Article 9(3)
	B(EU)2C (EU)	Place where the supplier belongs Article 9(1)	Yes (permissive) Article 9(3)
	B(nonEU)2C(EU)	Place of use and enjoyment	Yes (Compulsory) Article 9(4)
	Customer outside the EU	Place where customer belongs Article 9(2)(e)	Yes (permissive) Article 9(3)
Electronic services	B(EU)2B(EU)	Place where customer belongs Article 9(2)(e)	Yes (permissive) Article 9(3)

[26] Directive 2002/38/EC and Regulation No 792/2002.
[27] And thus the rate of charge, the characterisation of the supply, the reporting requirements, which jurisdiction receives the tax.

PLACE OF SUPPLY OF INTERNATIONAL SERVICES (*continued*)

Category of service Supplied	Supplier/ Customer	Place of supply	Can the 'effective use and enjoyment' rules apply?
Electronic services	B(nonEU)2B(EU)	Place where customer belongs 9(2)(e)	Yes (permissive) Article 9(3)
	B(EU)2C(EU)	Place where the supplier belongs Article 9(1)	No Article 9(3)
	B(nonEU)2C(EU)	Place where customer belongs Article 9(2)(f)	No Article 9(3)
	Customer outside the EU	Place where customer belongs Article 9(2)(e)	Yes (permissive) Article 9(3)

The following sections discuss the key concepts used in this table.

1. Nature of Supply

(a) Goods or Services

The VAT treatment of supplies is determined in part by whether the supply is of goods or services and from an early stage in the discussions of taxation of electronic commerce, internationally agreed policy has been that the supply of dematerialised goods should in general be treated as a supply of services. This policy was included in the Taxation Framework Conditions,[28] developed at the OECD Ministerial conference in Ottawa in 1998 and has been recognised by the VAT authorities of member states. There may still be problems with bundled goods (see below).

(b) Classification of Services

The default position for the place of supply of services is the place where the supplier belongs and it is only if the services come within one of the special provisions in Article 9(2) that the place of supply is shifted. Although telecom, radio and broadcasting services and electronic services are all listed in Article 9(2)(e), it is

---

[28] OECD (1998) 'Electronic Commerce: Taxation Framework Conditions' Committee of Fiscal Affairs, http://www.oecd.org/dataoecd/46/3/1923256.pdf.

necessary for two purposes to distinguish between electronic services and the others First, only supplies of electronic services fall under the special scheme for registration, discussed later. Second, the use and enjoyment provisions do not operate identically for the two groups of services.

(i) Telecom, Radio and Broadcasting

The Directive defines telecoms services as services relating to 'the transmission, emission or reception of signals, writing, images or sounds or information of any nature by wire, radio, optical or other electromagnetic systems, including the transfer or assignment of the right to use capacity for such transmission emission or reception'. They also include 'access to global information networks.'

Radio and television broadcasting services, which are not further defined, were originally excluded from Article 9(2)(e) and the main distinction between telecom services and broadcasting services was the one between the means of delivery and delivery of the content: a subscription TV company provides broadcasting services but a company supplying access to satellite or cable TV provides telecom services.[29] The rules now apply to all these services across the board and no further distinction between them is necessary.

(ii) Other Electronic Services

A new annex was added to the Sixth Directive outlining the type of services which are regarded as electronically supplied services.[30] This is reproduced in functionally identical form in the VAT Act 1994 Schedule 5 paragraph 7C:

Electronically supplied services, for example—

(a) website supply, web-hosting and distance maintenance of programmes and equipment;
(b) the supply of software and the updating of software;
(c) the supply of images, text and information, and the making available of databases;
(d) the supply of music, films and games (including games of chance and gambling games);
(e) the supply of political, cultural, artistic, sporting, scientific and entertainment broadcasts (including broadcasts of events);
(f) the supply of distance teaching.

But where the supplier of a service and his customer communicate via electronic mail, this shall not of itself mean that the service performed is an electronically supplied service.'

---

[29] Example from VAT Information Sheet 01/03 para 3.2. See also *R (on the application of Freeserve.com plc) v C & E Commissioners* [2004] STC 187.
[30] Annex L inserted by Council Directive 2002/38.

The list is clearly illustrative and does not purport to include all electronic services. It brings Article 9(2)(c) services[31] within the scope of Article 9(2)(e) when these services are supplied by electronic means, although the use of electronic communication methods to deliver a traditional service will not in itself make that service electronic for the purposes of the Act. So, whilst distance teaching will be an electronic service where it is entirely automated, interactive teaching using electronic methods of communication will remain within Article 9(2)(c) and thus supplied where the teaching is actually carried out.

The VAT Committee of the EU drafted more detailed guidance on the context of electronic services in the context of Annex L, reproduced as an appendix hereto. Although, as 'soft law', this has no legal force, the guidance has been published by the tax authorities of each member state as part of their advice to taxpayers, an approach designed to achieve consistency without the necessity of getting the agreement necessary for hard law. The precise dividing line is likely to be elusive at the margins and depend to a degree on the amount of human involvement: the more human involvement, the less likely the service is to be 'electronic'.

(c) Bundled Supplies

The correct classification of a supply becomes rather more difficult when more than one type of supply is being made in the same transaction, for example the supply of a computer will usually come with software already installed or the sale of software may also include follow up support or a package which provides access to the internet includes interactive facilities such as access to chat forums. Another example is the sale of a book with password protected access to an on-line version. The issue of the treatment of such bundled services was very much more significant in the period between the implementation of the Telecoms Directive and the VAT on E-Commerce Directive, as in this period telecom supplies to the EU from outside the EU had to bear VAT whilst other e-services did not.[32] As most supplies of electronic services into the EU will now bear VAT the issue is not so pronounced, although the distinction is still relevant for the use and enjoyment provisions and access to the special scheme. For example, if a telecom company provides access to a phone network but also allows the customer to download content, is this a telecom service to be taxed where the service is used or an electronic service to be taxed where the customer is resident? In most cases it will not make any difference as services are usually used in the country of residence but it does matter where the customer uses the services outside the country of residence.

---

[31] For present purposes, the most relevant services are those in the first indent of 9(2)(c): cultural, artistic, sporting, scientific, educational, entertainment or similar activities.

[32] In *R (on the application of Freeserve.com plc) v C & E Commissioners* [2004] STC 187, Freeserve unsuccessfully sought judicial review of the decision of Customs and Excise to treat the package provided by AOL to its UK customers as falling outside the Telecoms Directive 99/59/EC.

It will be necessary to determine whether there is a single supply, identified in character by the main supply, or whether there is more than one supply made as part of the same service. For example, the supply of an electronic game with an email address or phone number to access for tips in playing the game will be a supply of electronic services, rather than a supply of electronic services and provision of information. Following the guidance of the ECJ in *Card Protection Plan Ltd v C & E Commissioners*,[33] the test to determine whether there is a single service or a multiple supply of services involves the following consideration:

> There is a single supply in particular in cases where one or more elements are to be regarded as constituting the principal service, whilst one or more elements are to be regarded, by contrast, as ancillary services which share the tax treatment of the principal service. A service must be regarded as ancillary to a principal service if it does not constitute for customers an aim in itself, but a means of better enjoying the principal service supplied *(C & E Commrs v Madgett (t/a Howden Court Hotel)* (Joined Cases C–308/96 and C–94/97) [1998] BTC 5,440; [1998] ECR I–0000, para 24). In those circumstances, the fact that a single price is charged is not decisive.[34]

Ultimately it is a question of fact in each case which has to be determined by national courts and, in some circumstances, it will become necessary to apportion a single price according to the separate elements. The test is not always going to be easy to apply in practice, as is evidenced by the continuing litigation over whether listing magazines supplied by cable TV companies are zero-rated as magazines, or standard rated as part of a package of telecom services.[35]

2. Place where the Supplier Belongs

So far, we have discussed the place of supply as being the place where the supplier or customer 'belongs'. This is the UK shorthand[36] for the formula used in the Sixth VAT Directive, which is 'the place where the supplier [or customer] has established his business or has a fixed establishment from [or to] which the service is supplied or, in the absence of such a place of business or fixed establishment, the place where he has his permanent address or usually resides.'[37]

The UK's provision is contained in section 9 of the VAT Act 1994. In relation to the supplier, section 9(2) provides:

---

[33] C–349/96 [1996] 2 AC 601.

[34] Para 30.

[35] Most recently, *Telewest Communications plc v Customs & Excise Commissioners* [2005] ECWA Civ 102.

[36] VAT Act 1994 s 7(10).

[37] Sixth VAT Directive Arts 9(1), 9(2)(e), 9(2)(f), 9(4).

The supplier of services shall be treated as belonging in a country if

he has there a business establishment or some other fixed establishment and no such establishment elsewhere; or

he has no such establishment (there or elsewhere) but his usual place of residence is there; or

he has such establishments both in that country and elsewhere and the establishment of his which is most directly concerned with the supply is there.

Section 9(5) provides that a 'branch or agency' shall be regarded as a business establishment.

A clear hierarchy between the EU tests of 'business establishment' and that of 'other fixed establishment' emerged some years ago in the ECJ case of *Berkholz*, in which it was held that the place of business establishment is the primary point of reference.[38] Regard is only to be had to some 'other establishment' if using the place of business establishment 'does not lead to a rational result for tax purposes or creates a conflict with another member state',[39] so it is not just a question of determining the place which is most closely economically connected with the supply.[40] This hierarchy casts some doubt on the compatibility of section 9(2)(c) of the VAT Act 1994 with Article 9 of the Sixth VAT Directive to the extent that section 9(2)(c) provides in the event of the existence of a business establishment and a fixed establishment in different jurisdictions, one looks to the one most directly concerned with the supply, rather than turning to the fixed establishment only in the last resort.[41]

Neither place of business/business establishment nor fixed establishment are defined in either the Sixth Directive or UK legislation and, unlike the concept of permanent address/usual place of residence, neither have much in the way of common sense content. At the level of the EU, the place of business appears to be regarded as the place where the company has its registered office,[42] although guidance issued by Customs and Excise indicates their view that the 'business establishment' (of which there can only be one) is the principal place of business but that this is not necessarily the place where the company is registered.[43] UK guidance suggests that it is usually the 'head office, headquarters or "seat" from which the business is run'.[44]

---

[38] C–168/84 *Berkholz v Finanzamt Hamburg-Mitte-Altstadt* [1985] ECR 2251.

[39] *Berkholz, ibid,* para 17; C–231/94 *Faaborg-Gelting Linien A/S v Finanzamt Flensburg* [1996] All ER (EC) 656; [1996] ECR I–2395; C–260/95 *C & E Commissioners v DFDS A/S* [1997] ECR I–1005.

[40] *C&E Commissioners v Chinese Channel (HK) Ltd* [1998] BTC 5073 per Moses J at 5081.

[41] The doubt was expressed in *Chinese Channel* above per Moses J at 5081. However, the view as expressed by Customs and Excise in VAT Notice 741 is still expressed in terms of the UK statutory provisions.

[42] Eg Advocate General in *Berkholz* above n 31 at 2255 para 2.

[43] See VAT Notice 741 example 2.4 (second example).

[44] *Ibid,* para 2.3.

The ECJ has had several opportunities to consider the meaning of 'fixed establishment'. There are broadly two issues which need to be addressed. The first
might be regarded as a question as to whether there is *too much* presence in a jurisdiction and asks whether the establishment through which the supplies are made
is actually an independent supplier making its own supplies rather then being a
fixed establishment of another operation. At the opposite end of the spectrum lies
the issue as to whether there is *sufficient* presence in the member state in question
to constitute a fixed establishment.

The first issue usually involves a determination as to whether the person
through which the main supplier is operating is independent or dependent of the
main supplier. The significance of the supply being made through an independent
supplier is that this fixes the place of supply as being the place of the independent
supplier. If A (registered in country Y) makes supplies in country X through a
fixed establishment in X, there may be a debate over which establishment is
making the supply. If A makes a supply to an independent supplier in X, which in
turn makes onward supplies, there are now two supplies, and no doubt where the
supply to the final consumer takes place. The question of whether a supplier is
independent is one of degree involving an assessment of issues such as ownership
of capital, contractual relationship between the parties, degree of independence of
the agent and the economic risk undertaken by the principal.[45]

In relation to the second issue, whether there is sufficient presence to constitute
a 'fixed establishment', it is evident that the presence of a machine on its own, with
no human support, will not constitute an establishment.[46] Before there can be a
fixed establishment there must be a presence of reasonable size with permanent
human and technical resources.[47] In *ARO Lease*,[48] the question was whether a car
leasing company which used an intermediary in another member state could be
regarded as operating through a fixed establishment. The intermediary was paid
on commission and negotiated the terms of the car leases with the customers. The
ECJ held that the intermediary was not a fixed establishment of the leasing company on the basis that the leasing company did not possess 'either its own staff or
a structure which has a sufficient degree of permanence to provide a framework in
which agreements may be drawn up or management decisions taken and thus to
enable the services in question to be supplied on an independent basis.' In contrast, in *DFDS*,[49] a UK company which acted as an agent for a Dutch company,
selling holidays and taking commission, with a significant staff in the UK, was

---

[45] *DFDS* above n 32; C–266/93 *Bundeskartellamt v Volkswagen AG and VAG Leasing GmbH* [1995]
ECR I–3477.

[46] *Berkholz*, above n 38.

[47] C–190/95 *Berkholz, ARO Lease BV v Inspecteur der Belastingdienst Grote Ondernemingen
Amsterdam* [1997] ECR I–4383; [1997] STC 1272.

[48] *Ibid.*

[49] Above, n 39.

regarded as a fixed establishment of the Dutch company. Factors which were relevant to the determination in this case included where the contracts with the eventual consumers were made, where the service was offered and in which currency payment was made. The UK case of *Customs and Excise Commissioners v Chinese Channel (HK) Ltd*[50] provides a further relevant example. The taxpayer was a Hong Kong based company operating a satellite television station under licence, broadcasting Chinese language television programmes to the Chinese community in the UK and Europe. The taxpayer company bought programmes which it transmitted by satellite to a related UK company (CCUK), which edited and scheduled these programmes for the European service. The issue was, was CCUK a fixed establishment of the taxpayer? If so, it becomes possible to put forward the argument that the services were made from the UK and thus were subject to UK tax. (This case concerned supplies made prior to the change in the place of supply of broadcasting services.) If CCUK was not a fixed establishment of the taxpayer, then this argument could not be even be attempted and there should be no charge to VAT on the supplies. On the facts, notwithstanding that there was considerable disparity in size between the Hong Kong operation (4 persons were employed there) and the UK operation where 40 persons were employed, the High Court felt that they could not overturn the decision of the VAT Tribunal that there was no fixed establishment in the UK. 'It is not just a matter of comparing the activities of the two companies, it is more important, as the tribunal recognised, to consider the significance of those activities and the part they play in their contribution to the service supplied.' The main contribution to the supply (making contracts, making arrangements for transmission and selecting programmes) took place in Hong Kong.

The significance of this case today, after the implementation of the 1999 Telecoms Directive, is not whether or not VAT should be charged (because telecoms services from outside the EU are no longer supplied from the place of the supplier) but where the place of supply takes place for the purposes of registration. If the supplier is outside the EU, the place of supply of broadcasting services to a consumer is the place where the services are used and enjoyed. If the supplier is making supplies to a consumer within the EU, the place of supply is the place where the supplier belongs.

An agent will not constitute a fixed establishment where the only services performed consist of bringing the client and provider together, so for example the host of a website would not without more amount to a fixed establishment of the supplier. It is the view of the UK tax authorities that the services of the agent must supply more than incidental services, giving as examples of incidental services, clerical and typing.[51]

---

[50] Above, n 40.
[51] HMRC information sheet: 'Place of Supply of Services' (Notice 741) para 2.5.

3. Place where the Customer Belongs

The place of supply of certain services is shifted from the place where the supplier 'belongs' to the place where the customer 'belongs'.

This shift occurs where Article 9(2)(e) services are supplied either to an EU business by a supplier from a different jurisdiction, whether within or outside the EU (the reverse charge) or are supplied by an EU business to a customer (business or private) outside the EU. It also applies where electronic services are supplied from outside the EU to a consumer in the EU.[52] The shift is to the place where the 'customer has established his business or has a fixed establishment to which the service is supplied or, in the absence of such a place, the place where he has his permanent address, or usually resides.'[53]

(a) Supplies to a Business

Where the recipient is a business, again the question may arise as to which establishment is receiving the service where there is more than one and each establishment is in a different country. Again, the UK rules may be slightly out of kilter with the provisions of Article 9, providing as they do that in the event of there being more than one establishment in different countries, the place of the establishment is the one where the services are 'most directly used'. However, any attempt to operate the test must refer back to the Sixth Directive which has direct effect in UK law.[54] The VAT and Duties tribunal has been asked to consider the use of accountancy and other similar services supplied to a UK registered office of a company with no other business operation in the UK and have concluded that the UK registered office was an 'other fixed establishment' to the extent that it was that establishment which most directly used the services, accountancy services being particularly relevant to the head office.[55] However, in a case concerning advertising services, it was held that a UK registered office did not constitute a fixed establishment of a company for the purposes of receiving this supply as it had no other offices in the UK and no other business presence, which meant that it did not have, adapting the *Berkholz* test, 'sufficient minimum strength to enable it to receive and use the specific services in question'.[56] So it appears that the UK test at least involves a consideration of the *use* of services which is not apparent in the EU legislation.

---

[52] Art 9(2)(f).

[53] Art 9(2)(e), (f) and (4).

[54] VAT Act 1984 s 9(4)(b). See the discussion above at p 218.

[55] *Binder Hamlyn v Commissioners of Customs and Excise* [1983] VATTR 171; *Vincent Consultants Ltd v Commissioners of Customs and Excise* [1989] CMLR 374; *Singer and Friedlander Ltd v Commissioners of Customs and Excise* [1989] VATTR 27. Note these cases might require reconsideration in light of the doubt cast on VAT Act 1984 s 9(2)(c) by recent cases: see text at n 41.

[56] *BUPA Ltd v Commissioners of Customs and Excise* [2002] CMLR 300, 328.

(b) Supplies to a Consumer

Where the recipient is a consumer, the place of the supply is not altered from the default position (the place where the supplier belongs) where the supply is intra-EU. In relation to electronic services, where the recipient is outside the EU[57] or inside the EU but receiving services from outside the EU,[58] the place of supply shifts to the place where the consumer has a permanent address or usually resides according to the Sixth VAT Directive, translated by the VAT Act into 'usual place of residence'.[59] Where the services are telecom or broadcasting, the place of supply is overlaid by the use and enjoyment rules, considered next.

4. Effective Use and Enjoyment Rules

The 'use and enjoyment' rules have been in place since 1984, but have come to prominence recently particularly in the context of telecom and broadcasting services. They give member states the option (and in one case, impose a requirement) to shift the place of supply of Article 9(2)(e) services to the place where services are actually used or enjoyed.

The main purpose of the rule is to prevent obvious avoidance techniques, such as establishing a related non-EU company in a low tax jurisdiction to receive services which are then used on behalf of a business within the EU.[60] The principle behind the rule itself is without criticism: it discards proxies for the place of consumption and uses the actual test. However, there are difficulties with the application of the provision in practice.

The rules are contained in Article 9(3) and (4) of the Sixth Directive:

3. In order to avoid double taxation, non-taxation or the distortion of competition, the Member States may, with regard to the supply of services referred to in 2(e), [ie including telecom and broadcasting services and electronic services] except for the services referred to in the last indent [ie electronic services] when supplied to non-taxable persons, and also with regard to the hiring out of forms of transport consider:

(a) the place of supply of services, which under this Article would be situated within the territory of the country, as being situated outside the Community where the *effective use and enjoyment* of the services take place outside the Community;
(b) the place of supply of services, which under this Article would be situated outside the Community, as being within the territory of the country where the effective use and enjoyment of the services take place within the territory of the country.

---

[57] Sixth VAT Directive Art 9(2)(e).
[58] *Ibid* Art 9(2)(f) in relation to electronic services.
[59] VAT Act 1984 s 9(3).
[60] This not be especially advantageous if the business makes chargeable or zero-rated supplies, as the VAT paid out would be given as an input tax credit, It would be advantageous for businesses making exempt supplies.

4. In the case of telecommunications services and radio and television broadcasting services referred to in paragraph 2(e) when performed for non-taxable persons who are established, have their permanent address or usually reside in a member state, by a taxable person who has established his business or has a fixed establishment from which the service is supplied outside the Community, or in the absence of such a place of business or fixed establishment, has his permanent address or usually resides outside the Community, member states shall make use of paragraph 3(b).' [words in brackets added]

In its original form, the use of Article 9(3) was entirely at the option of member states, but from 1 July 2003, paragraph 9(4) was added to make its use compulsory for telecom and broadcasting services supplied to EU consumers from suppliers outside the EU where the VAT position would otherwise be distorted.[61] In addition, it is made clear that the use and enjoyment rules may not be used to shift the place of supply of electronic services supplied to a consumer. The combined effect of these rules are as follows:

• Supplies of telecom and broadcasting services: use and enjoyment rule *may* be used in relation to all supplies and *must* be used when supplied to a consumer from a supplier outside the EU.
• Supplies of electronic services: place of supply *may* be shifted to the place of use and enjoyment when supplies are made to a business, but the rules *shall not* be used where the supply is made to a consumer.

It may seem odd that the use and enjoyment rules are compulsory for supplies to EU customers by non-EU suppliers in relation to telecom and broadcasting services, whilst they are prohibited between the same parties in relation to electronic services. The explanation lies in what it is reasonable for the supplier to know about his customer and in particular seeks to protect the subjection of suppliers of electronic services against onerous requirements to seek information from their customers. Telecoms and broadcasting companies are not only both larger and better resourced than many of the firms supplying electronic services (with some obvious exceptions) but also have a greater capacity to know where their services are being used.

It is important to note that the use and enjoyment rules are only to be used where there would otherwise be distortion and the test for distortion is made at EU level. For example, the rules would not apply to shift the place of supply where a UK resident uses the supplies in France because tax is being accounted for somewhere in the EU.[62]

Despite the existence of mandatory elements to the use and enjoyment rules, there remains a significant amount of variation in their application between member states, with the UK applying them to the fullest extent, even when the supply is made to another business.[63] This can cause uncertainty for those who supply

---

[61] Council Directive 2002/38/EC Art 1, inserting para 4, effective for 3 years from 1 July 2003.
[62] See Customs Information Sheet 04/03 for examples.
[63] VAT (Place of Supply of Services) Order 1992 [1992/3121] Arts 17 and 18 [1992/3121].

services from outside the EU and is likely to lead to double or non-taxation. The test can be clumsy to apply in practice—to apply it literally would mean that a US phone company providing phone services to a US tourist visiting the EU and making phone calls home would be treated as making a supply in each member state from which a call is made.[64] Furthermore, it is not always easy for a supplier to determine where its customer is intending to use services supplied. The difficulty may be even greater in the case where a non-EU company head-office receives services which are then used by branches in several EU member states. In such a case, each branch will be required to account for VAT under the reverse charge in accordance with the proportion of use of those services. All these difficulties remind us of the reasons for the use of proxies for the place of actual consumption in the first place.

5. UK Guidance on Ascertaining the Necessary Information about the Customer

Acquiring the information necessary to make a determination of the correct VAT treatment is potentially an onerous requirement. The supplier needs to know the status of his customer (business or non-business), the location of his customer (in the EU or elsewhere and, if in the EU, whether in the supplier's own jurisdiction or elsewhere) and, sometimes, where the service is actually going to be used. The Sixth VAT Directive is silent on this issue but guidance has been issued by Customs and Excise in the UK on the use of appropriate evidence of customer status and location.[65]

(a) Customer Status—Business or Consumer?

The situations in which the status of the customer is relevant are:

- supplies by a EU business to someone elsewhere in the EU; and[66]
- supplies by a non-EU business to someone in the EU.[67]

---

[64] Indeed, the UK expressly provide a concession for the situation where a telecom service is used in the UK as an incidental part of a contract held by a non-EU customer who is temporarily in the K: VAT Notice 741 para 14.7.

[65] VAT Information Sheet 05/2003. This is in accordance with the guidance issued by the OECD to tax authorities on the type of evidence they can reasonably expect businesses to acquire about their customers in the identification of the place of consumption for business to business supplies and the verification of customer status and jurisdiction: available at http://www.oecd.org/dataoecd/25/31/17,851,117.pdf.

[66] Supplies by an EU business to someone in the same jurisdiction will be subject to VAT, whether to a business or a consumer. Supplies made to a person outside the EU will either carry VAT or not, depending on whether the place of supply is shifted, but irrespective of the status of the non-EU customer.

[67] There is no requirement of registration where supplies are made to a taxable person in the EU, as the reverse charge will operate.

It is moderately easy for the EU supplier to check whether the person who is being supplied is a registered person in the EU by using the VIES (VAT Information Exchange System)[68] VIES allows a supplier to check a VAT reference number against a name and address, although at present such a check has to be done separately and not as part of any automated transaction. The only information which VIES can confirm is that number corresponds (or not) with a name and address of someone registered within the EU. It does not, for example, allow to supplier to know whether the supply will be used for business purposes or not.

Except where the customer is known to the supplier, Customs and Excise will expect a check through VIES to be made when electronic services are supplied and where the VAT in a single transaction or in a quarter exceeds £500. It also suggests that the use of the number should be 'challenged' where the content of supply suggests that it is not supplied for business purposes (for example where the supply is of music or games). In the absence of a VAT number, other evidence is acceptable, for example contracts, business letterheads, digital certificates etc.[69]

(a) Customer Location

In determining the location of the customer, Customs and Excise have indicated that, in addition to customer self-declaration, the use of one of five further checks is acceptable:

• postal address where actual deliveries are made;
• matching home address with billing address of credit/debit card;
• matching country of issuing bank with country of residence;
• using geo-location software; or
• where business are already supplying services which require identification of the place of used and enjoyment of those services (ie telecom services), Customs will, by concession, accept the place of use and enjoyment as a proxy for the place of residence in relation to other supplies.

If the use of any one of these checks creates doubt in the supplier's mind as to the location of the customer, additional checks must be made.

No advice has yet been issued in the UK on the steps which must be taken to verify the place of use and enjoyment.

The combination of these rules places an onerous requirement on the supplier, depending on whether its tax jurisdiction intends to proceed with a light touch or not and, in particular, automated transactions become difficult to operate.

---

[68] Available at http://europa.eu.int/vies. VIES is also the method by which traders report cross border B2B supplies of goods, and the reporting aspects of VIES are widely recognised as not working entirely effectively: Com 2004 728. There are no plans to require those supplying cross border services to operate an unreformed VIES reporting system although they may in the longer term be brought in.
[69] VAT Information Sheet 05/2003 para 3.

F. Obligation to Register in the EU

1. Normal Registration Requirements

A person who is in business and either makes or intends to make taxable supplies within a member state may be required to register within that member state once supplies have exceeded the de minimis level operated in each state. In the UK, registration is not required, broadly, until taxable supplies have exceeded £58,000 in a year.[70] In certain circumstances registration may be made voluntarily. Because of the reverse charge, suppliers from outside the EU will only be subject to local registration requirements where they make supplies to consumers (or other businesses which are not registered for VAT): supplies of services within Article 9(2)(e) made to a business in the EU are treated as supplied by the recipient rather than the supplier.

The consequences for a supplier from outside the EU of services to EU consumers is that, potentially, registration must be made in each of 25 member states, involving considerable inconvenience and expense.

2. Special Scheme for the Supply of Electronic Services

Whilst the operation of registration in relation to telecom service providers appeared to be working relatively well, the suppliers are a relatively small group of large companies who, for a variety of reasons, will be inclined to conform to the legal requirements of the EU. Accordingly, broadcasting services, the suppliers of which share similar characteristics, have been brought under the same umbrella by the 2003 Directive. In contrast, the diverse nature of persons supplying 'electronic services' meant that further thought had to be given to making the administrative requirements less burdensome. A special scheme, initially to operate for three years from 1 July 2003, has been devised to this end.[71] The hope (rather than necessarily the expectation) is that by 2006 technology will have found answers to the problems it caused in the first place and that the special rules will no longer be necessary.

The main advantage of the special scheme is that the supplier only registers in one member state in the EU. Initially it was proposed that the rate of VAT of the state of registration would be charged on all services made by that supplier made within the EU, irrespective of the place of the customer. Several member states objected to this on the basis that it would clearly encourage suppliers to register in

---

[70] Or where supplies in the next 30 days will exceed £58,000: VATA 1994 Sch 1 para 1.
[71] Sixth VAT Directive Art 26c, VAT Act 1994 s 3A and Sch 3B.

the member state with the lowest VAT rates and the proposal was withdrawn. Now under the special scheme, the supplier must identify the place of residence of the consumer within the EU and charge the appropriate rate of tax. The tax is accounted for to the state of registration, who then passes it on to the state of residence of the consumer.

However, small suppliers, whose supplies to each member state are less than the registration limit operational in that state, are still better off by not using the special scheme: once a supplier has registered under the special scheme, all supplies in the EU are subject to tax, irrespective of the level of supply into each member state whereas if a supplier makes supplies under the registration limit is not required to account for VAT on the supply.

The supplier of electronic services is required to register with one member state only—called the member state of identification. There is no requirement of a physical presence and only electronic communication between the supplier and the member state of identification will be required.

The special regime will only apply to a 'non-established taxable person' who is 'a taxable person who neither has established his business nor has a fixed establishment within the EU.' In other words, it applies to those who make supplies of electronic services to consumers within the EU and who are not already registered or required to be registered under normal EU rules for registration. Registration will not be necessary for those who only provide services to EU businesses in the EU as in this case, VAT will be accounted for by the recipient under the reverse charge. Neither will the special scheme apply to suppliers who are already registered in the EU in respect of other supplies, including telecom or broadcasting services. If there is already a point of registration in the EU, the supplies will be treated as having been made from that place of registration.

The administrative responsibilities placed on the supplier are supposed to be pared down to a minimum. The supplier must provide the member state with information concerning his name, postal address, electronic address including web sites, national tax number if any and a statement that the person is not identified for VAT purposes within the EU. This can be done electronically via the websites of the tax authorities of the member states, who will, on registration, issue a VAT identification number which will be in a format specific to the special scheme. Each calendar quarter, within 20 days of the end of the quarter, an electronic return must be made, even if no supplies have been made in that quarter. The return must provide information on the value of services and VAT relative thereto supplied to each member state, normally in Euros,[72] and must be accompanied by electronic payment of the VAT due. The VAT authorities of the

---

[72] Where this is not the currency of the member state, the return shall be in the relevant currency unless returns in Euros are also permitted. The UK for example does not permit returns in Euros. For conversion rates the European Central Bank's rates are used: see http://www.ecb.int.

member state of identification will then account to the member state of consumption for the VAT due on supplies made to consumers in each member state.

Some concern has been expressed about the potential number of audits as, in addition to the state of registration, the member state of the consumer is entitled to carry out an audit. However it is understood that the member state of the consumer will normally liaise with the member state of identification.

There are no penalties which apply specifically under the special scheme, so the normal penalties for failing to register, failure to make declarations, underpayment of tax, dishonestly evading tax etc will apply. However, persistent default will render the supplier ineligible for the special scheme, in which case normal registration will be required,[73] although if there is persistent default under the special scheme, the chances of getting the recalcitrant supplier to register and make returns in each member state under the normal regime seem slim.

It is understood from informal sources that, just over a year after the special scheme was introduced, 135 special scheme registrations in the UK had been made.[74] Language is one reason why the UK might be an attractive place for US businesses to register.

3. Special Scheme or Normal Registration?

In general the administrative convenience of the special scheme will suggest that this is the better option for most businesses, although there are some advantages of setting up a base in the EU through which supplies are made and then accounting for VAT using standard procedures. If this choice is made, it is important that this is done properly, with sufficient presence to support the claim that the supplies are being made through a business establishment or fixed establishment in that state otherwise the trader will render himself liable to penalties for failing to register in each member state in which supplies over the *de minimis* limit have been made.

The first advantage of setting up an establishment in one member state and registering there is that the place of supply to consumers is not shifted from the place where the supplier belongs, although there are suggestions for changes currently being mooted.[75] At the moment this means that the rate of tax on supplies within the EU is determined according to the rate of tax of the state of registration, which

---

[73] VAT Act 1994 Sch 3B para 9.

[74] This information was supplied in August 2004. In October 2004 the Commission stated that 'well under' 1000 registrations have been made in the EU as a whole: COM 2004 728 http://europa.eu.int/eur-lex/lex/LexUriServ/site/en/com/2004/com2004_0728en01.pdf.

[75] See p 232.

can be deliberately chosen for its low rates. AOL, for example, registered in Luxembourg which applies a VAT rate of 15%.[76]

Second, normal registration procedures enable credit for any VAT incurred by the supplier to be given instantly. Under the special scheme, no credit for VAT incurred on expenditure within the EU is given and a claim for recovery of input VAT will have to be submitted under the 13th VAT Directive, sometimes a cumbersome and slow process. Realistically, the amount of VAT incurred in the EU by distance sellers is likely to be small so this is unlikely to be a significant factor.

A third advantage of making supplies through an establishment in one member state is that the supplier need only apply one rate of VAT, the rate of the state of registration, and can avoid the administrative burden of determining the member state in which his customers reside.

G. Problems with the Above Arrangements

We might use the following criteria to judge the operation of a particular set of tax arrangements—neutrality (including fairness), administrative feasibility and robustness. On each of these, the present arrangements receive rather low marks.

Whilst the position is more neutral than it was prior to the Telecom and VAT on E Commerce Directives, when supplies of services were always taxed according to the place of residence of the supplier, a number of non-neutralities remain.

First, an incentive remains for a supplier of telecom and electronic services to consumers to register in the member state where the VAT rate is lowest. The absence of the operation of the destination principle in relation to services to consumers encourages cross-border sourcing of supplies of services from suppliers *within* the EU and, once supplies from outside the EU are considered, further distortions arise. The existence of a special scheme for non-EU suppliers of e-services, which *does* effectively seek to implement the destination principle, creates a distortion in comparison with suppliers from within the EU. Under the special scheme, the rate of tax applicable in the consumer's place of residence will apply, whereas an identical supply from an EU supplier will bear the rate of tax applicable to the place where the supplier belongs. For example, a supplier registered in Luxembourg under the normal registration procedures making a supply to a customer in Denmark will apply VAT at a rate of 15% (the rate applicable in

---

[76] Ironically, the same UK ISPs who had earlier lobbied so hard to have AOL subjected to UK VAT on telecoms services made to UK customers have since set up establishments in Madeira where the VAT rate is a mere 12% In the last two years, Freeserve, Virgin.net, Btopenworld have all been moved to Madeira. Despite both Freeserve and Virgin each having only a handful of employees each in Madeira, executives are regularly flown out to make business decisions in order to satisfy the requirement that the companies have a business establishment in the jurisdiction.

Luxembourg) whereas a non-EU supplier registered there under the special scheme will impose tax at 25% (the Danish rate). If the country of supply and destination are reversed, the competitive advantage shifts to the non-EU supplier. There have been suggestions that there may be WTO issues in relation to the differential treatment of suppliers from outside the EU as customers in Denmark will have a continued incentive to source their supplies from a supplier registered under normal procedures within a low VAT rate member state within the EU.

A further neutrality issue concerns the differential treatment of goods and their dematerialised equivalents. Treating intangibles as services rather than goods can affect their tax treatment. For example provision of books and newspapers are often charged at reduced rates in contrast to their electronic versions.

A lack of consistent application and enforcement between member states creates the risk of double taxation, a major concern expressed by businesses to the OECD.[77] The problem can be more serious in the context of VAT than in direct taxation where the problems are often fixed by double taxation agreements. Double VAT may be caused by conflicting place of supply rules. For example, inconsistent application of the 'use and enjoyment' provisions may have the result that two member states seek to tax the same supply.[78] If one member state regards the supply as coming within the default rules and supplied where the supplier belongs, whilst the member state of the recipient regards the supply as falling within Article 9(2)(e) and thus subject to the reverse charge, both states will impose VAT. Double VAT may also be caused by conflicting definitions, conflicting results arising from the application of different verification criteria in relation to both jurisdiction and status, and incompatible treatment of bundled supplies.

Turning to the administrative burden to be faced by suppliers, it should be now be clear from the raft of questions have to be answered about the nature of the supply, the place of the customer and perhaps where the use of the supply takes place, that the suppliers are faced with significant difficulties. It is not clear how answers are to be achieved in the context of supplies which are made electronically, requiring an instantaneous decision to be made in the absence of any face to face relationship and, in many cases, with no previous trading relationship. US suppliers in particular are incensed that they are required to apply VAT on sales outside the EU when the US Supreme Court has already decided that it is unconstitutional to require them to apply consumption taxes on sales to persons in other US states.[79]

In terms of robustness, one of the issues which led the UK to consistently oppose the special scheme proposals was that of enforceability. Whilst telecom

---

[77] 'Consumption Tax Aspects of Electronic Commerce' Report from Working Party No 9 on Consumption Taxes to the Committee on Fiscal Affairs February 2001.

[78] Because at least part of the 'use and enjoyment provisions' are permissive rather than compulsory, it means that the ECJ are unable to fix this problem as it is up to Member States as to whether to apply them to a large extent. See further the discussion at pp 222–223.

[79] *Quill Corp v North Dakota* (91–0194), 504 US 298 (1992).

services are usually offered by the big players who for several reasons are likely to comply with registration requirements, at present there is no method that the member states can realistically employ to identify or enforce tax liabilities incurred by companies outside the EU who, for example, sell software or music over the internet. Registration in the UK is likely to be attractive to US businesses for language reasons and, as indicated earlier, there have already been 135 registrations in the UK under the special scheme although under 1000 overall.[80] However, we cannot judge whether this is indicates success of the special scheme or failure as we simply have no way of telling whether this is a high or low proportion of businesses supplying e-services into the EU. Experience suggests that this is likely to be a small percentage of the businesses making electronic supplies into the EU and it is likely that those who are registering are simply the bigger players who have not already registered in the EU and who are unwilling to fall foul of local compliance laws or have significant outstanding unpaid VAT debts showing on their balance sheets. It seems likely that it is the elephants rather than the mice who are registering.[81]

H. Are Things Likely to Get Better?

Many of the difficulties that currently exist have arisen because of the piecemeal approach to services involved in the adaptation of the original rules: inevitably, carving out certain types of supply for special treatment leads to problems of definition and economic distortion. Guidance on categorisation can be issued by the Commission to improve consistency of treatment but has no legally binding effect and needs constant revision if it is not to become outdated. The addition of electronic services to Article 9(2)(e) has been declared to be the last before the outcome of the review on the place of supply of services in the EU by the Commission.[82] So far, only B2B supplies have been fully considered by the Commission and draft proposals to modify the 6th VAT Directive have recently been published which, if implemented, would move the default place of B2B supplies to the place where the recipient of services belongs.[83] The main benefit of this is that, in relation to most services, it removes the necessity of distinguishing

---

[80] See n 74.

[81] See P Swire and E Litan, *None of Your Business: World Data Flows, Electronic Commerce, and the European Privacy Directive* (Brookings Institution Press, 1998).

[82] 'VAT—The Place of Supply of Services' TAXUD/C3/May 2003, available at http://europa.eu.int/comm/taxation_customs/taxation/consultations/supply/consultation_supply_en.pdf. The summary report of the outcome of the consultation issued 12 September 2003 (TAXUD/C3/2357) is at http://europa.eu.int/comm/taxation_customs/taxation/consultations/ vat_supply_results_en.pdf.

[83] The proposed Directive is Com (2003) 822.

between different types of services supplied to businesses, thus avoiding problems of classification, and utilises the advantages of the reverse charge for supplies from both within and outside the EU. Not only is compliance likely to be high, as recipients benefit from the input tax deduction as well as the deduction of the cost in the computation of profits, but there are also significant administrative advantages as a non-EU supplier avoids any registration requirements if supplies are restricted to business customers within the EU.

Consultation on the place of supply of B2C services, a much more difficult undertaking, is taking place at the time of writing.[84] The preliminary view of the Commission is that as consumers cannot reasonably be required to self-assess on the receipt of taxable services, the administrative difficulties of changing the place of B2C supplies to the place of consumption are such as to leave the general rule unchanged. However, they do suggest extending the principle of using the place where the customer is established as the place of supply of *all* telecom, broadcasting and electronic services, rather than, at present, using this rule only in relation to supplies from outside the EU.

There are broadly two ways in which the EU supplier could account for VAT to the state of the consumer at the appropriate rates. First, registration could be required in each member state in which services are supplied. There is already a model for this in the current distance selling rules and in the registration requirements on non-EU telecoms and broadcasting supplies. However this option is not under consideration as the Commission is trying to reduce administrative obligations on traders, including reducing the number of cross border registrations required.

However, there is another possibility: to introduce a system that allows a supplier to satisfy all his EU VAT obligations through dealings with his own member state. With a view to achieving a reduction in registrations in other member states, there have been recent discussions culminating in a proposal for a 'One Stop Shop' for EU traders who make supplies to consumers in another member state.[85] The introduction of the special scheme for electronic services provided from outside the EU has broken the traditional link between accounting for tax to a jurisdiction and complying with the administrative rules of the jurisdiction through registration there and has provided the impetus for further bold proposals. The 'One Stop Shop' would allow a trader to fulfil his reporting obligations to another member state through a single portal from his own jurisdiction, without local registration. The return would then be transmitted automatically to the member state of the

---

[84] February 2005: Consultation Paper 'VAT—the place of supply of services to non-taxable persons', available at http://europa.eu.int/comm/taxation_customs/resources/documents/vat_place_of_supply_en.pdf. A recent report of the OECD Consumption Tax TAG concluded that there is no single option for B2C supplies which is 'without significant difficulties', para 60.

[85] The idea was canvassed in Com 2003 614 (final) and a consultation of businesses followed. The proposals for the necessary modifications to the 6th Directive are contained in Com 2004 728 (final).

consumer, although it is not proposed that tax should similarly be transmitted. Neither can the trader pay all EU VAT due to his member state of registration and expect it to be passed on: whilst this is a feature of the special scheme for non-EU providers of e-services, it is proving to be a complex arrangement which member states are not prepared to take on in a significantly larger context. In the absence of a shift in the place of supply for most services,[86] the scheme would most likely to be useful for those who are currently within the distance selling regulations for goods which, at the moment, require registration in each member state once supplies of goods into that member state exceed a limit. If telecom, broadcasting and electronic services are also brought within this regime, its scope would be significantly extended.

Stepping back for a moment to assess the combined effect of the proposed changes in the place of supply of services, one would conclude that the position of the B2B trader will be made somewhat easier as a result of the default place of supply position being the place of the recipient, although there remain exceptions of which he must be aware. Economically it makes no difference to member states, as VAT between traders in principle gets washed out anyway.

However, the EU B2C supplier of services will carry a significantly increased administrative burden. Before, all it required to know was whether the consumer was within the EU or not. After it will be required to know in which member state the consumer resides. Before, it only required to charge one rate of VAT. After it will be required to charge multiple rates of VAT. Before, it only had to account for VAT to its own member state. After, it will be required to account for VAT to each member state in which it supplies services to consumers. A level playing field for supplies within the EU market has been achieved in the sense that VAT will be charged at the rate of tax operational in the jurisdiction of consumption. Furthermore, the principle that VAT should accrue to the state of consumption is more closely satisfied, although at increased administrative burden to the trader.

Consultation with business has led to issues of simplification emerging as an important theme and there are some initiatives within the EU facilitating this. First there is the Invoice Directive which means that a trader in the EU will now only have to comply with one set of rules for all the invoices he issues, irrespective of where the goods or services he is supplying are taxable. Any invoice complying with these rules will be acceptable for VAT purposes throughout the EU by all tax administrations.[87] This Directive also creates a legal framework for electronic transmission and storage of invoices. There were also proposals to amend the

---

[86] The One Stop Shop proposal pre-dates the consultation exercise on B2C services and the kind of services which are likely to be subject to this proposed scheme are those where the place of supply is shifted from the place of the supplier by Art 9(2), for example installation or assembly services, or services to immoveable property. It could apply to electronic services and telecoms if extended.

[87] Council Directive 2001/115/EC, in force from 1 January 2004 in existing EU Member States and from 1 May 2004 in the Accession Countries.

operation of the Eighth VAT Directive, to the effect that instead of seeking a refund of VAT paid in another member state, a taxable person may set off this VAT in his own member state, leaving adjustment to be made at national level,[88] although member states have been unable to agree this and the proposal is now watered down to a 'one-stop shop' for refunds through an electronic portal.[89] It is worth explaining the main reason why member states were not prepared to recognise cross border deductions: where the member state of registration has more generous rules for deduction of VAT, it would be required to reduce its own VAT by recognising the input tax that the member state of supply would not have recognised.[90] Given that the base of VAT is significantly harmonised, this could be no more than a very minor transfer of funds and the cost to individual member states has to be dwarfed by the combined benefit to cross border traders.

The Commission is also engaged in a project to get guidelines on common interpretation issued by the VAT Committee of the European Union and have proposed that the Council will have authority to transfer these interpretations into law. At present any guidelines have no legal status and are not published at Community level. Member States are therefore not legally bound by them, and neither can they be relied upon before a court, be it a national court or the Court of Justice, leaving both traders and national administrations without any legal certainty. To be able to ensure uniform application of existing VAT provisions, it is necessary to find a way of giving the guidelines agreed by the VAT Committee legal status.

I. Conclusion

Even though the above list contains merely edited highlights of some of the proposals currently afoot, all these do not mask the fact that the operation of VAT on cross border services is a complex and expensive operation for traders. The most recent proposals, for example, will improve neutrality in the application of VAT on services to consumers but at increased cost to business. It is likely that eventually technological changes will facilitate automated collection and transmission of tax although real progress appears to be painfully slow.[91] At present, technology is capable of calculating tax using multiple rates and is used by distance sellers of

---

[88] Com 1998 377 final.
[89] Com 2004 728 final.
[90] *Ibid.*
[91] Discussions are continuing within the OECD as well as within the EU: see the OECD Report 'Electronic Commerce: Facilitating Collection of Consumption Taxes on B2C Cross-border E-commerce Transactions, (February 2005), http://www.oecd.org/dataoecd/51/33/34422641.pdf where the primary focus is the development of some kind of tax agent to act on behalf of the supplier, and certification of software.

goods, tax can be added to the cost by automated process and programmes exist that will remit tax automatically to tax authorities. The question is whether these functions can be brought together to form an integrated process, who should pay for their development, and how they will be given recognition by tax authorities in individual member states. Development of software is expensive and becomes more so the more complex the rules to be operated and the more administrative functions to be performed. And, 'ambiguity cannot be automated'.[92]

One thing at the moment at least is sure: the member states are not going to contribute to the expense of the development of appropriate software. In contrast, in the United States where the Streamlined Sales Tax Project is in the process of implementation, states are contributing towards the cost of the development of appropriate technology, as well as agreeing to operate considerably simplified and harmonised systems.[93] Compare this to the attitude of the member states who are even not prepared to recognise cross border VAT credits. It is appropriate to recollect that businesses currently act as unpaid collectors of VAT, income tax, national insurance contributions and student loans as well as administering certain tax credits on behalf of their respective states. If the member states of the EU are serious about achieving a competitive playing field for EU businesses, they should look to the example of the USA where there is evidence of a much greater willingness of those participating to act to mitigate the impact of the burdens that revenue collection impose on business.

---

[92] 'Automating Consumption Tax Collection Mechanisms': report to the CFA of the OECD, 12 June 2003, http://www.oecd.org/dataoecd/51/42/17995301.pdf.
[93] See the website http://www.streamlinedsalestax.org/ for more information.

APPENDIX—VAT COMMITTEE GUIDELINES

TABLE 1

Annex L Reference	Supplies covered by the legal text	Example of a service that is an electronically supplied service
Item 1	A. Web site supply, web-hosting and distance maintenance of programmes and equipment	Web-site hosting and web-page hosting Automated, on-line distance maintenance of programmes Remote systems administration On-line data warehousing (i.e., where specific data is stored and retrieved electronically) On-line supply of on-demand disc space
Item 2	A. Software and updating thereof	Accessing or downloading software (e.g. procurement/accountancy programmes, anti-virus software) plus updates Bannerblockers (software to block banner adverts showing) Download drivers, such as software that interfaces PC with peripheral equipment (e.g., printers) On-line automated installation of filters on web-sites On-line automated installation of firewalls
Item 3	A. Images B. Text and information C. Making databases available	Accessing or downloading desktop themes Accessing or downloading photographic or pictorial images or screensavers The digitised content of books and other electronic-publications Subscription to on-line newspaper and journals Weblogs and website statistics On-line news, traffic information and weather reports On-line information generated automatically by software from specific data input by the customer, such as legal and financial data (e.g., continually updated stock market data) The provision of advertising space (e.g., banner ads on a web site/web page) Use of search engines and Internet directories
Item 4	A. Music B. Films C. Broadcasts and cultural, artistic, sporting, scientific and entertainment D. Games, including games of chance and gambling games	Accessing or downloading of music onto PCs, mobile phones, etc. Accessing or downloading of jingles, excerpts, ringtones, or other sounds Accessing or downloading of films Web-based broadcasting that is only provided over the Internet or similar electronic network and is not simultaneously broadcast over a traditional radio or television network, as opposed to Item 4, Table 2 Downloads of games onto PCs, mobile phones, etc. Accessing automated on-line games which are dependent on the Internet, or other similar electronic networks, where players are remote from one another

| Item 5 | A. *Distance teaching* | Teaching that is automated and dependent on the Internet or similar electronic network to function, including virtual classrooms, as opposed to Item 2(b), Table 2 Workbooks completed by pupil on-line and marked automatically, without human intervention |
| Item 6 Other services included: | A. *Those not explicitly listed in Annex L* | On-line auction services (to the extent that they are not already considered to be web-hosting services under Item 1) that are dependent on automated databases and data input by the customer requiring little or no human intervention (e.g., an on-line market place or on-line shopping portals), as opposed to Item 3(f), Table 2 Internet Service Packages (ISPs) in which the telecommunications component is an ancillary and subordinate part (i.e., a package that goes beyond mere Internet access comprising various elements (e.g., content pages containing news, weather, travel information; games for a; web-hosting; access to chat-lines etc.)) |

TABLE 2

Example of a transaction not considered to be a supply of an 'electronically supplied service'	Rationale
1) A supply of . . .	These are supplies of goods
(a) A good, where the order and processing is done electronically	
(b) A CD-ROM, floppy disc and similar tangible media	
(c) Printed matter such as a book, newsletter, newspaper or journal	
(d) A CD, audio cassette	
(e) A Video cassette, DVD	
(f) Games on a CD-ROM	
2) A supply of . . .	This is a supply of service that relies on substantial
(a) services of lawyers and financial consultants, etc. who advise clients through e-mail	human intervention and the Internet or electronic network is only used as a means of communication
(b) interactive teaching services where the course content is delivered by a teacher over the Internet or an electronic network (i.e., via remote link)	

TABLE 2 *(cont.)*

Example of a transaction not considered to be a supply of an 'electronically supplied service'	Rationale
3) A supply of . . . (a) Physical repair services of computer equipment (b) Off-line data warehousing services (c) Advertising services, such as in newspapers, on posters and on television (d) Telephone helpdesk services (e) Teaching services involving correspondence courses such as postal courses (f) Conventional auctioneers' services reliant on direct human intervention, irrespective of how bids are made (e.g., in person, Internet or telephone), as opposed to Item 6(a), Table 1	These are supplies of services that are not delivered over the Internet and rely on substantial human intervention
4) A supply of a radio and television broadcasting service provided over the Internet or similar electronic network simultaneous to the same broadcast being provided over traditional radio or television network, as opposed to Item 4(c), Table 1	This is a supply of a radio and television broadcasting service, which is covered by the penultimate indent of Article 9(2)(e)
5) A supply of . . . (a) Videophone services (i.e., telephone services with a video component) (b) Access to the Internet and World Wide Web (c) Telephony (i.e., telephone service provided through the Internet)	These are supplies of telecommunication services and are covered by the place of supply rules for such services under the ninth indent of Article

8

Distance Selling Directive 1997; Distance Marketing of Financial Services Directive 2002

Distance Marketing in the European Union

ANNETTE NORDHAUSEN[1]

A. Introduction

With modern technologies, contracts can be concluded not only in writing or orally, but also electronically. In contrast to electronic transmission through telephone or fax, the relevant declarations do not have to be oral or in writing first to be transferred by electronic means later on. Instead, using an Internet terminal device (eg computer, mobile phone or hand held device) offers and acceptances can be made by electronic means (text or click). Although the Electronic Commerce Directive (ECD)[2] introduced special regulations for contracts concluded by electronic means, it is crucial to note that such contracts are invariably also distance contracts, and thereby follow the general rules for distance sales, in particular the Distance Selling Directive ('the Directive') 1997/7/EC.[3]

Distance selling is an important and growing market within the European Union. The sales figures are constantly increasing[4] and apart from the employees directly and indirectly working for distance sales, telecom companies profit remarkably from the trade sector. Most distance marketing companies currently

---

[1] Lecturer, Department of Law, University of Sheffield.

[2] Of 8 June 2000, OJ L178, 17 July 2000, p 1.

[3] Of 20 May 1997, OJ L 144, 4 June 1997, p 19.

[4] EMOTA, Comparative Study on the Implementation of Directive 97/7/EC of 20 May 1997 on the Protection of Consumers in Respect of Distance Contracts, p 2; P Vittet-Philippe, 'Europe in the E-Economy: Challenges for EU Enterprises and Policies' (2002) *Computer Law and Security Report* 24.

offer a multi-channel approach in their contacts with consumers, using post, phone and the Web or email. In contrast to a few years ago, today almost all goods[5] and services sold at a distance can be obtained on-line.[6]

Imperative to the acceptance of distance marketing aimed at consumers, whether e-commerce[7] or traditional mail order, is consumer confidence.[8] Consumers need to be convinced that they are dealing with reliable companies in terms of offering, delivery, privacy protection and secure payment. Mutual trust must exist between all parties involved, the businesses as well as consumers, and this is the objective for legislative measures.

The main barriers for businesses which wish to trade across the European Single Market, have traditionally been taxation (VAT),[9] distribution (postal services) and international payment.[10] Another important issue are differences in legislation as well as in implementation and interpretation of European Directives. Following these difficulties most companies have set up subsidiaries in different Member States.[11]

There are two types of distance selling: contracts between businesses, business-to-business contracts (B2B), and contracts between a business or trader and a consumer (B2C). Depending on the contracting parties, different rules apply. The Distance Selling Directive applies only to consumer contracts. Consumer protection is one of the crucial issues in the European Union. The EC Treaty itself

---

[5] Including software, music or other goods or services delivered electronically: see BP Aalberts and HB Banniak, 'Muziekgebruik op internet' (2000) *Nederlands Juristenblad* 1868; P Meads, 'E-Consumer Protection—Distance Selling' (2002) *International Company and Commercial Law Review*, 179, 181.

[6] H-W Moritz, 'Quo vadis elektronischer Geschäftsverkehr?' (2000) *Computer und Recht* 61.

[7] J Nazerali and D Cowan, 'E-Commerce and Cross-Border Shopping—Can the EU Untangle the Web?' (2000) *Business Law Review* 117; R Nimmer, 'Electronic Commerce Fundamentals—The US Perspective' (2000) *Computer und Recht International* 97; A Youngerwood and S Mann, 'Extra Armoury for Consumers: The new Distance Selling Regulations' (2000) *Jourbnal of Information Law and Technology* 3; R Azim–Khan, 'Keeping online in line' (2001) *Lawyer* 45; S Sidkin and J Elliot, 'Coming to terms with the new regime' (2001) *E-Commerce Law and Policy* 10; TMJ Möllers, 'Europäische Richtlinien zum Bürgerlichen Recht' (2002) *Juristenzeitung* 121.

[8] For consumer confidence in E-Commerce and its economic analysis, S Grabner-Kräuter, 'Konsumentenverhalten im E-Commerce' in P Horster (ed), *Elektronische Geschäftsprozesse* (IT-Verlag fur Informationstechnik, 2001) 303; J Kaufman Winn, 'Open Systems, Free Markets, and Regulation of Internet Commerce' (1998) *Tulane L Rev* 1177; G Smith, 'Legislating for Electronic Transactions' (2002) *Computer and Telecommunications Law Review* 58; J Dickie, 'Consumer Confidence and the EC Directive on Distance Contracts' (1998) *Journal of Consumer Policy* 217; M Fallon, 'La protection internationale de l'acheteur sur l'intéresseau dans le contente communautaire' in B Stauder (ed), *La protection des consommateurs acheteuts à distance* (Schultess Verlag, Bruylant, 1999) 241; IE Vassilaki, 'Das Prinzip Vertrauen für Informationsdienste' (2002) *Computer und Recht* 742.

[9] See further S Eden, Chapter 7 in this volume. See also P Howitt, 'Sales Tax on Distance Selling in the US and Europe' (2002) *E-Commerce Law and Policy* 10; B Baldwin, *EC Tax Journal* 1995/96, 2003.

[10] For this issue the introduction of the Euro in many Member States was a step forward.

[11] EMOTA, Comparative Study on the Implementation of Directive 97/7/EC of 20 May 1997 on the Protection of Consumers in Respect of Distance Contracts, p 2.

requires in its Article 153 a high level of consumer protection[12] and the Single European Market requires a certain level of harmonisation of consumer protection regulation especially for distance sales. Distance selling allows the consumers to take part in the Single Market to a wider extent, and thus benefit from wider availability of choice and price. However buying across EU borders has drawbacks too. The inherent risks lie mainly in the differing legal regulations, doubts as to the applicable law, different requirements for the conclusion of contracts, and different levels of consumer protection.[13] These drawbacks have been (and maybe still are) a significant reason for the lack of acceptance of cross border contracts and the incompleteness of the Single European Market for consumers.

B. The Distance Selling Directive

The main problem in distance sales, especially in electronic transactions lies in the anonymity of the contracting parties and the difficulty of verifying the territorial jurisdiction.[14] The Distance Selling Directive does not only regulate the traditional distance selling methods as orders by mail, telephone or fax but also includes means of electronic communication. Annex 1 of the Directive, replicating the first draft of 1992,[15] mentions in addition to more traditional distance communication methods, explicitly videotext, video telephone, telefax, teleshopping and electronic mail. The Directive is thus in theory technically neutral and covers electronic communications such as online transactions as well as allowing for future developments.

One aim of the Directive is to obtain a high level of consumer protection; consumers are recognized as a fundamental part of the Internal Market and due to the technical possibilities can participate in the Internal Market and cross-border trade to a significant share. The consumer's participation in cross-border trade can be beneficial for consumers and suppliers, combined with probably the most important prerequisite for a functioning of cross-border consumer trade which is

---

[12] N Reich, 'Verbraucherschutz und Verbraucherpolitik' im *Vertrag von Amsterdam*, (Verbraucht und Recht, 1999) 3; generally E Steindorff, *EG-Vertrag und Privatrecht* (Nomos, 1996); BW Harvey and DL Parry, *The Law of Consumer Protection and Fair Trading*, 6th edn, (Butterworths, 2000) 39ff.

[13] A Pützhoven, 'Harmonisierung des europäischen Verbraucherschutzrchts' (1999) *Europaisches Wirtschafts-und Steurrecht* 447. But See for a contrary view C Waelde, ch 1 of this volume.

[14] H-W Moritz, 'Quo vadis elektronischer Geschäftsverkehr?' (2000) *Computer und Recht* 61, 66; N Reich, *Europäisches Verbraucherrecht* (Nomos, 1996) No 167.

[15] OJ C 156/14 of 23 June 1992; JG Meents, *Verbraucherschutz bei Rechtsgeschäften im Internet*, (Ort Schmidt Verlag, 1998) p 173; S Grundmann, *Europäisches Schuldvertragsrecht* (Walter de Gruyter, 1999) p 225f; N Reich, 'Die neue Richtlinie 97/7EG über den Verbraucherschutz bei Vertragsabschlüssen' im *Fernabsatz*, (1997) *Europaische Zeitschrift fur Wirtschaftsrecht*, 581.

of course, consumer confidence. Hence one of the main aims of the Directive is to increase consumer confidence in cross-border transactions.[16]

It is questionable whether this can be reached by legislation or if legislative measures can be supportive to reach this aim. The existence of at least common minimum standards everywhere in the EU enable the consumer to predict roughly how the process will work and what are his or her rights. A common standard makes distance sales and the especially cross-border distance sales more familiar to consumers. Some knowledge about the mechanisms in practice and their rights will certainly increase consumer confidence in the market.

Are consumers best protected by a minimum or maximum harmonisation approach[17]? The approach chosen for the Directive was minimum harmonisation, which allows Member States the possibility to maintain or introduce a higher level of consumer protection than that guaranteed by the Directive. It has been questioned if this approach in practice leads to a higher level of consumer protection, or if, especially in a domain such as distance sales online, businesses may chose a Member State with a minimum standard of consumer protection from which to operate, thereby exploiting the minimum harmonisation approach in a 'race to the bottom'.[18] Following reviews of the Directive on Distance Selling,[19] the maxi-

---

[16] A Willingmann, 'Auf dem Weg zu einem einheitlichen Vertriebsrecht für Waren und Dienstleistungen in der Europäischen Union?—Die Richtlinie über den Verbraucherschutz bei Vertragsabschlüssen im Fernabsatz (97/7/EG)', 1998 *Verbraucher und Recht* 395; J Newton, 'Distance Selling: Keeping the Customer in the Know' (2001) *Electronic Business Law* 16; K Henderson and A Poulter, 'The Distance Selling Directive: Points for Future Revision' (2002) *International Review of Law, Computers and Technology* 289; P Dobson, *Sale of Goods and Consumer Credit*, 6th edn, (Sweet & Maxwell, 2000) ch 16–05; N Reich, 'Die neue Richtlinie 97/7/EG über den Verbraucherschutz bei Vertragsabschlüssen' im Fernabsatz' (1997) *Europaische Zeitschrift fur Wirtschaftsrecht* 581.

[17] A Pützhoven, 'Harmonisierung des europäischen Verbraucherschutzrechts' (1999) *Europaische Wirtschafts- und Steurrecht S* 447 argues for a comprehensive European Consumer Law; W-H Roth, 'Europäischer Verbraucherschutz und BGB' (2001) *Juristenzeitung* 475; G Howells, 'European Consumer Law—The Minimal and Maximal Harmonisation Debate and Pro Independent Consumer Law Competence' in S Grundmann and J Stuyck (eds), *An Academic Green Paper on European Contract Law* (2002); E Hondius, 'Niederländisches Verbraucherrecht—vom Sonderrecht zum integrierten Zivilrecht' (1996) *Verbraucher und Recht* 295; A Sanders, 'Die japanische Rezeption des europäischen Zivilrechts—Ein Modell für die europäische Rechtsvereinheitlichung?' (2002) *Zeitschrift fur Europaisches Privatrecht* 96; H-P Schwintowski, 'Auf dem Wege zu einem Europäischen Zivilgesetzbuch' (2002) *Juristenzuetung* 205; D Staudenmeyer, 'Wie soll es mit dem Europäischen Vertragsrecht weitergehen?' (2002) *Euroaisches Zeitschrift fur Wirtschaftrecht* 481; G-P Callies, 'The Limits of Electicism in Consumer Law: National Struggles and the Hope for a coherent European Contract Law. A Comment on the ECJ's and FCJ's "Heininger" decisions' 3 *German Law Journal* 8; H Kötz, 'Savigny v Thibaut und das gemeineuropäische Zivilrecht' (2002) *Zeitschrift fur Europaisches Privatrecht* 431; M Cremona, 'The distance selling directive' (1998) *Journal for Business Law* 613, 615.

[18] EMOTA, Comparative Study on the Implementation of Directive 97/7/EC of 20 May 1997 on the Protection of Consumers in respect of Distance Contracts', p 6; N Reich, 'Competition between Legal Orders: a New Paradigma of EC Law?' (1992) *CML Rev* 861.

[19] Like the EMOTA study 'Comparative Study on the Implementation of Directive 97/7/EC of 20 May 1997 on the Protection of Consumers in respect of Distance Contracts'. In the commentary section of the review a maximum harmonisation approach is clearly favoured for all distance sales, as it would create 'a more level legal playing field on a EU wide level', p 5.

mum harmonisation approach has come into favour. Whereas the E-Commerce Directive also follows the minimum harmonisation approach, the more recent Directive on Distance Marketing of Financial Services (see in detail p 263 below) follows the maximum harmonisation approach.

Article 13 of the Directive states that it shall only apply insofar as there are no particular EU provisions governing certain special types of distance contracts.[20] In any conflict, those special rules take precedence. Article 14 makes it explicit that Member States may introduce or maintain more stringent provisions to ensure a higher level of consumer protection.[21] This may include a ban on the marketing of certain goods or services, eg medicinal products, in the general interest.[22]

1. Legislative Competence

The Directive is based on Article 100a (now Article 95) of the Treaty,[23] the power to adopt harmonisation measures in the course of the establishment and functioning of the Internal Market. Motive 3 and 4 of the Directive read:

(3) Whereas, for consumers, cross-border distance selling could be one of the main tangible results of the completion of the internal market, as noted, *inter alia*, in the communication from the Commission to the Council entitled 'Towards a single market in distribution'; whereas it is essential to the smooth operation of the internal market for consumers to be able to have dealings with a business outside their country, even if it has a subsidiarity in the consumer's country of residence;

(4) Whereas the introduction of new technologies is increasing the number of ways for consumers to obtain information about offers anywhere in the Community and to place orders; whereas some Member States have already taken different or diverging measures to protect consumers in respect of distance selling, which has had a detrimental effect on competition between businesses in the internal market; whereas it is therefore necessary to introduce at Community level a minimum set of common rules in this area.

This however does not mean that the Directive shall only be applicable within the Internal Market. Included are also national transactions as well as cross-border transactions with third countries.[24]

---

[20] Art 13(1).

[21] But this again, causes problems due to the lack of harmonisation as experienced in previous directives on consumer law; for the Unfair Contract Terms Directive: I Klauer, 'General Clauses in European Private Law and "Stricter" National Standards: The Unfair Contract Terms Directive' (2000) *ERPL* 187.

[22] C Koenig, E Müller and A Trafkowski, 'Internet-Handel mit Arzneimitteln und Wettbewerb' im EG-Binnenmarkt (2000) *Europaisches Wirtschaft- und Steuerrecht* 97.

[23] S Grundmann, *Europäisches Schuldvertragsrecht* (Walter de Gruyter, 1999) 227.

[24] H-W Micklitz, in H-W Micklitz and N Reich, *Die Fernabsatzrichtlinie im deutschen Recht* (Nomos, 1998) 2; P Groeschke and K Kiethe, 'Die Ubiquität des europäischen Verbraucherleitbildes— Der europäische Pass des informierten und verständigen Verbrauchers' (2001) *WRP* 230.

The Directive was to be implemented into the laws of the Member States by 5 June 2000. Only a few Member States met this deadline; however the Directive has now been implemented in all Member States.[25]

2. Scope of Application—Definition Consumer and Supplier

The scope of application as regards the person affected is regulated by the definition of the terms 'consumer' and 'supplier'. Consumer is, according to Article 2(2) 'any natural person who, in contracts covered by this Directive, is acting for purposes which are outside his trade, business or profession'; the term supplier is defined in Article 2(3) as 'any natural or legal person who, in contracts covered by this Directive, is acting in his commercial or professional capacity'.

(a) Consumer

The consumer is defined in the usual way as in other Directives,[26] especially the Unfair Contract Terms Directive 93/13. As the transactions are carried out over distance and without a personal contact between the supplier and the consumer it will often be very difficult to ascertain the object of the contract, but it governs the applicability of the Directive. Many goods or services can be used for private or commercial and professional purposes. As all actions are carried out over distance, the person and the purpose of contract will in most cases not be known to the supplier who is obliged to comply with the special requirements for consumer contracts according to the Distance Selling Directive. The Directive itself does not provide a suitable solution for these cases. It seems appropriate, as it has been suggested, to gear for everyday goods (and services) to the usual purpose, and in any doubt define the contract as a consumer contract. The scope of application of the Directive must, following the aim of the Directive to further cross-border transactions, be interpreted broadly. The occasional use of the contractual goods for professional purposes does not oppose the applicability of the Directive. If however, it is obvious from the amount of the transaction or the speciality of the goods or services, that the use is mainly for commercial or professional purposes, the Directive does not apply.

---

[25] See below.

[26] Generally on the consumer definition in European Law: P Groeschke and K Kiethe, 'Die Ubiquität des europäischen Verbraucherleitbildes—Der europäische Pass des informierten und verständigen Verbrauchers' (2001) *WRP* 230; generally on the concept of consumer law: J Keßler, 'European Consumer Law—zu den dogmatischen und didaktischen Konzepten des europäischen Verbraucherrechts' (1999) *Verbraucher und Recht* 415; M Lehmann, 'Electronic Commerce und Verbraucherschutz in Europa' (2000) *Europaisches Zeitschrift fur Wirtschaftrecht* 517; R Sack, 'Die Präzisierung des Verbraucherleitbildes durch den EuGH' (1999) *WRP* 399; R Bradgate, 'The EU Directive on distance selling' (1997) *Web JCLI* 4; N Reich in N Reich and A Nordhausen, *Verbraucher und Recht im europäischen Geschäftsverkehr (eG)* (Nomos, 2000) 126; S Niemöller, *Das Verbraucherleitbild in der Deutschen und Europäischen Rechtsprechung* (München, 1999).

(b) Supplier

The Directive is only applicable in contracts between a consumer and a supplier but not applicable in contracts between two consumers or between businesses. The definition of a supplier, however, is rather wide. It includes all representatives or agents of the supplier[27] of goods or services. For the scope of application it is irrelevant if the transaction carried out is legal or if restrictions for distance sales apply, i.e. for legal advice or pharmaceuticals. If however, special regulations for distance transactions are in force, these are not overruled by the Directive and stay in force.[28]

Distance communication means may often be used not only by businesses or consumers who are clearly identifiable as a business or a consumer but also by suppliers who are not running a business in the traditional sense but using the distance selling methods occasionally this might not be recognizable for the consumer. As this is a situation like the one described the other way round above the solution ought to be the same. Here again it can be presumed that it is *prima facie* a business to consumer transaction if means of distance communication are used for the transaction. The supplier, if he or she is a private supplier, can easily avoid the consequence of applicability of the Directive by informing the consumer about his status.

(c) Scope of Application

The Directive defines in Article 2(1), the scope of application as regards to the subject matter. According to this definition a distance contract:

> means any contract concerning goods or services concluded between a supplier and a consumer under an organized distance sales or service-provision scheme run by the supplier, who, for the purpose of the contract, makes exclusive use of one or more means of distance communication up to and including the moment at which the contract is concluded.

Means of distance communication includes all channels that can be used for the conclusion of a contract without simultaneous physical presence of the contracting parties.

An exclusive use means that it must be possible that all steps necessary for the conclusion of the contract are done by means of distance communications (these include telephone and e-mail!).[29] If only information or advertisement is

---

[27] Although, other than in the Doorstep-selling Directive this is not mentioned explicitly here; H-W Micklitz and N Reich, *Die Fernabsatzrichtlinie im Deutschen Recht* (Nomos, 1998) 14.

[28] See Art 14(2).

[29] For contracts between solicitors and their clients: M Bürger, 'Das Fernabsatzrecht und seine Anwendbarkeit auf Rechtsanwälte' (2002) *Neue Juristischen Wochenschrift* 465; AG Wiesloch, 'Zum Widerrufsrecht bei Abschluss eines Anwaltvertrages durch Fernkommunikation' (16 November 2001) 1 C 282/01, (2002) *Juristen Zeitung* 671.

communicated by means of distance communication and the contract itself can only be concluded with simultaneous physical presence of the contracting parties, the Directive does not apply. In practice, in most cases the advertisement or information will offer one, or other way, to contracting over distance as this will mostly be the purpose of the information or advertisement. The term 'exclusive use' does not imply that only one method of communication could be used during the negotiations and the conclusion of the contract. Consumer and supplier can use different methods of distance communication during their contact. Certain channels may only be offered for specific communications, for example, enquiries by phone, fax or e-mail, and contractual offers only by phone or fax. As a rule, so long as distance selling is generally offered the Directive is applicable.[30]

It is not necessary that the supplier makes a binding contractual offer when contacting the consumer in the first instance. It is sufficient if the communication from the supplier aims towards the conclusion of a contract and becomes irrelevant if the contract is actually concluded by means of distance communication or with both parties present or not at the end.

The distance sales or service-provision scheme has to be run by the supplier as an organized scheme. This restrictive provision aims only to exclude the occasional use of distance communications for a contract and therefore has to be interpreted narrowly. To fulfil this requirement it is necessary that the supplier aims to do all or a part of his business by means of distance communication. It does not matter if the distance sales are a remarkable part of all transactions or not, whenever it is not rather unusual and the supplier has got some sort of organisation for distance sales the Directive shall apply. The organisation does not need to be a sophisticated system for distance orders or anything of the sort, the general offer of one or more methods is sufficient. Relevant is the view of the average consumer: if the supplier apparently uses distance sales mechanisms but in fact does not, the Directive still applies.

(d) Exemptions

The Directive excludes a number of transactions for various reasons, the most important being financial services as these are now regulated in a different directive, the Directive 2002/65 on distance marketing of financial services.[31]

Other exemptions are according to Article 3(1), contracts

- concluded by means of automatic vending machines or automated commercial premises;
- concluded with telecommunications operators through the use of public payphones;

---

[30] M MacDonald, 'Defining Distance Contracts' (2002) *JLSS* 34.
[31] See detailed below; VK Bange, 'The impact of Distance Selling Directive' (2000) *IT & CLJ* 3.

- concluded for the construction and sale of immovable property or relating to other immovable property rights, except for rental;
- concluded at an auction.

Contracts concluded by using an automatic vending machine are distance sales contracts following the definition of the directive but it would not be possible or at all useful to apply the provisions of the Directive to these contracts. The contract is fulfilled immediately with the use of the machine. As they are mostly used for everyday goods the consumer is familiar with consumer protection would not be increased.[32]

As regards the use of public payphones a similar argument applies. It would be neither necessary nor practical to apply the Directive to those contracts.

Regarding immovable property the situation is different. In most Member States contracts on immovable property or rights therein have to be concluded in person, in writing or through a notary. With these requirements contracts on immovable property are not eligible for distance sales means and the Member States ought not to be required to allow distance sale of immovable property.

Contracts concluded at an auction are exempted as well. With a growing number of Internet auctions this seems problematic. Two issues are important here, firstly the term 'auction' itself and secondly the requirements for the conclusion of a contract. The term auction is not defined in the Directive, it is defined in the laws of the Member States but these definitions may differ slightly, with European Law having to be interpreted autonomously. Usually at Internet auctions the highest bid is accepted automatically after lapse of time. As distinct from 'traditional' auctions the on-line auctioneer does not play an active role in the conclusion of the contract, the only function in Internet auctions is the provision of the platform. It follows then, that on-line auctions are typically not auctions, no matter what they are called.

The conclusion of the contract itself is not regulated in the Directive. For Internet auctions one contract (on the provision of a service) is concluded between the provider of the platform and the supplier of the goods, and another between the provider of the platform and the customer who wishes to purchase the goods. The actual sales contract is concluded between the offeror and the purchaser. Only the latter contract is a contract concluded at an auction and therefore exempted from the Directive, the contracts between the service provider and seller or purchaser, are not concluded at an auction. In many cases the offeror will be a private rather than a business supplier and the Directive would not be applicable on this ground either.

---

[32] P Barrat, 'The EC Distance Selling Directive' (1993) *International Company and Commercial Law Review* 304, 306.

Other types of contracts are partly exempted from the Directive. For these contracts the information requirements and the right of withdrawal (Article 4, 5, 6 and 7(1) of the Directive) shall not apply. The exempted contract types are:

- contracts for the supply of foodstuffs, beverages or other goods intended for everyday consumption supplied to the home of the consumer, to his residence or to his workplace by regular roundsmen;
- contracts for the provision of accommodation, transport, catering or leisure services, where the supplier undertakes, when the contract is concluded, to provide these services on a specific date or within a specific period; exceptionally, in the case of outdoor leisure events, the supplier can reserve the right not to apply Article 7(2) in specific circumstances.

With foodstuffs and beverages, everyday goods are exempted which the consumer generally knows well and as the shelf-life of these products is limited, a longer withdrawal period would make these contracts practically impossible.

Following this wording package tours are also excluded, but for those the package tour Directive[33] applies and secures certain consumer rights. For the other exempted contracts it would be too restrictive for the supplier as these require special arrangements for the specified date or period and the possible grounds for withdrawal are grounds that lay only in the sphere of the consumer and not in the service itself.

3. Pre-contractual Information

Whenever the Directive is applicable and the contract is not explicitly exempted the supplier has to provide the consumer with certain specified information.[34]

The general principle *emptor curiosus esse debet* (that it is up to contracting parties to acquire all relevant information before concluding the contract) although rooted in all continental European jurisdictions,[35] has not been preserved in the recent developments of European law.[36] The reasons for this are various.

---

[33] Directive 90/314 on Package Travel, Package Holidays and Package Tours.

[34] AR Lodder and MB Voulon, 'Intelligent Agents and the Information Requirements of the Directives on Distance Selling and E-Commerce' (2002) *International Review of Law Computers and Technology* 277; A Rose, *Distance Selling and the Internet* (Paisner Intellectual Property Briefing, 1997) 12; R Lawson, 'E-Commerce and Distance Selling' (2002) *Computer Security Report* 94; J Hornle, 'Germany—Distance Selling—Information Requirements and Withdrawal Right' (2002) *European Business Law* 14; J Newton, 'Distance Selling: Keeping the Customer in the Know' (2001) *European Business Law* 16; OLG Frankfurt/M, 'Pflichtangaben beim Fernabsatz, judgement of 17 April 2001, 6 W 37/01' (2001) *Multimedia und Recht*, 529.

[35] TMJ Möllers, 'Europaische Richtlinien zum Burgerlichen Recht' (2002) *Juristen Zeitung* 121, 129.

[36] H Fleischer, 'Vertragsschlussbezogene Informationspflichten im Gemeinschaftsprivatrecht' (2000) *Zeitschrift fur Europaisches Privatrecht* 772; S Grundmann, 'Privatautonomie' im 'Binnenmarkt' (2000) *Juristen Zeitung* 1133; G Howells and T Wilhelmsson, 'EC Consumer law: has it Come of Age?' (2003) 28 *European Law Review* 370, 380; generally on information duties in EU law: S Kind, *Die*

Foremost is the development and integration of consumer protection in the Treaty, and technical developments which generally make it more difficult to understand products and their possible impacts, as well as the possibilities and restrictions of distance and electronic marketing.

Article 4 of the Directive requires this information to be given 'in good time prior to the conclusion of any distance contract'. The latest possible point of time for providing this information is just before the last step necessary for the binding conclusion of the contract, depending on national laws.

The information required is as following:

a. The identity of the supplier (and additionally the address if prior payment is required): This is particularly important for contracts concluded over the Internet. Unfortunately the address is only required if prior payment is required and not in all cases. For contracts concluded over the Internet usually payment by credit card is offered (or required). Even if the supplier promises to charge the amount only after delivery, this has to be considered as prior payment as it is completely at the discretion of the supplier.

b. The main characteristics of the goods or services: This requirement is fairly obvious and will in most Member States be essential for the contract (*essentialia negotii*) but this information has also to be given prior to the conclusion of the contract.

c. The price of the goods or services including all taxes: The price is also an essential issue for the consumer and needs to be as detailed as possible. As the price has to be mentioned including all taxes, the taxes have to be added to the price of the goods or services and cannot be noted separately or as a percentage rate. If a supplier is contracting with consumers as well as businesses he may show the taxes separately.

d. Delivery costs, where appropriate: Delivery costs are another crucial issue in distance contracts and depending on the goods or services and their origin may be a high percentage of, or even higher than, the value of the goods.

e. The arrangement for payment, delivery or performance: Payment and delivery arrangements are also important at the pre-contractual stage. In an extreme case an arrangement for delivery could be that the consumer has to collect the goods at the suppliers premises—and the consumer ought to be informed about this before he enters into a contract.

Grenzen des Verbraucherschutzes durch Information—aufgezeigt am Teilzeitwohnrechtegesetz (Duncker & Humblot, 1997); N Reich, 'Verbraucherpolitik und Verbraucherschutz' im 'Vertrag von Amsterdam' (1999) *Verbraucher und Recht* 3, 5ff; P Rott, 'Informationspflichten in Fernabsatzverträgen als Paradigma für die Sprachenproblematik' im 'Vertragsrecht' (1999) *Zeitschrift fur Vergleichende Rechtswissenschaft* 98, 382; P Mankowski, 'Fernabsatzrecht: Information über das Widerrufsrecht und Widerrufsbelehrung bei Internetauftritten' (2001) *Computer und Recht* 767; P Rees and M Hargreaves, 'EU and US Regulation of Electronic Commerce: Converging Approaches in a Changing World' (1999) *International Company and Commercial Law Review* 176; G Howells and T Wilhelmsson, *EC Consumer Law* (Brookfield USA, Aldershot, 1997) 9 ff.

f. The existence of a right of withdrawal, except in the cases referred to in Article 6(3): The right of withdrawal is one of the main issues of the Directive and the consumer has to be informed about the existence prior to the conclusion of the contract. The information about the existence does not include the information about the details of the right and also not the information that a right of withdrawal does not exist for the particular contract. The cases referred to in Article 6(3) are cases in which the consumer may not exercise the right of withdrawal unless the parties have agreed otherwise for example goods made to the consumer's specification, products dependant on fluctuations in the financial market, or, if performance of a service contract has begun with the consumer's consent.

g. The cost of using the means of distance communication, where it is calculated other than at the basic rate: The normal communication costs (i.e. telephone) are foreseeable for the consumer and beyond the suppliers knowledge and control, whereas about all other costs (i.e. special telephone numbers or costs for using databases which will be charged through the telephone companies) the consumer needs information to enable him or her to decide if they wish to enter into the contract in question.

h. Where appropriate, the minimum duration of the contract in the case of contracts for the supply of products or services to be performed permanently or recurrently: This ensures that the consumer is informed about the fact that the contract runs over a longer period as well as the length of the period itself. Where other provisions exist (i.e. for standard contract terms) and the minimum length is generally restricted, these provisions remain in force. The notice period does not necessarily have to be mentioned at the pre-contractual stage.

All information has, according to Article 4(2), to be given in a clear and comprehensible manner, appropriate according to the means of distance communication used. This means that the information can, and shall, be given differently on a website than in a telephone conversation.[37] The language in which this information has to be given is not specified[38] and therefore it must not necessarily be the first language of the consumer but the information must also be given with due regard to the principles of good faith in commercial transactions.[39] Information given in a language other than the first language of the consumer (or his country of residence), the language of the origin of the supplier, a commonly understood language or the language of the advertisement, or the contract will be against these principles.

[37] P Meads, 'E-Consumer Protection—Distance Selling' (2002) *International Company and Commercial Law Review* 179, 180.

[38] N Downes and H Heiss, 'Sprachregulierungen im Vertragsrecht: Europa—und internationalprivatrechtliche Aspekte' (1999) *Zeitschrift für Vergleichende Rechtswissenschaft* 98, 28.

[39] P Mankowski, 'Verbraucherschutzrechtliche Widerrufsbelehrung und Sprachrisiko' (2001) *Verbraucher und Recht* 359.

Article 5 of the Directive requires that a written confirmation of the information has to be provided to the consumer.[40] This does not necessarily require a written document. The information can either be given 'in writing', commonly interpreted as 'hard copy', or in another 'durable medium' available and accessible to the consumer. What is a durable medium has been controversial. This certainly includes more than paper, such as text delivered on floppy disc, or compact disc. Presentation of the information solely by a website link, will, however, arguably not be sufficient, as the consumer must have an opportunity to read the information once the contract is concluded. The wording of the Directive 'the consumer must receive' should be interpreted as meaning that it is the supplier's duty to ensure that the consumer receives the information. It would therefore not be sufficient if the supplier only allows or asks the consumer to download the information from the website and save it on his computer. The statement that the consumer has to receive the information also does not allow exclusive presentation on the website, and it is also questionable whether a website is a durable medium.

Email (and email attachments) however may be a different matter. The UK DTI guidance on 'durable medium' states that it includes email—as it can be printed out, and is in any case, once received, stored on the consumer's local hard disc or other device for email receipt. An email attachment is indeed sent to the consumer and available, but the accessibility is dependent on the capacity of the server on which the consumer's e-mails are stored. The term 'durable medium' is also, interestingly, used in the Directive on Distance Marketing of Financial Services[41] where, unlike in the 1997 version, it is explicitly defined to include email. The E-Commerce Directive (ECD) requires in Article 10(3) that contract terms and general conditions to be provided to the recipient must be made available in a way that allows him to store and reproduce them. As the ECD aims to encourage distance selling and rapid legal transactions, this seems to recognise belatedly that for some contracts, it may be a major obstacle to traders if the information has to be send by post—therefore it should be sufficient to send the information by e-mail or as an e-mail attachment. The consumer's interests may still however require that the information be sent to him individually; it is very easy to ignore, delete or 'lose' in the general electronic deluge information sent be email. In most distance sales, as delivery of the goods will still be necessary, and the deadline for the provision of information is the time of delivery at the latest, there should not be a real problem. The issue arises most crucially in contracts for the delivery of wholly or potentially virtual goods such as music or software or computer games. It would help if this issue was at some point clarified.

The information to be provided is the pre-contractual information required in Article 4(1)(a) to (f) and:

---

[40] E Madden, 'A Safe Distance?' (2002) *GLSI* 14.
[41] 2002/65/EC See below, pp 265ff.

- the conditions and procedures for exercising the right of withdrawal, including possible exemptions;
- the geographical address of the place of business of the supplier to which the consumer may address any complaints;
- information on after-sales services and guarantees;
- the notice period for contracts for unspecified duration or a duration exceeding one year.

Excluded are services supplied on only one occasion which are performed through a means of distance communication and invoiced by the operator of the communication means but the consumer must still be able to obtain the geographical address of the place of business to which he can address any complaints.

This information shall enable the consumer to exercise the right of withdrawal without further investigation.

4. Right of Withdrawal

The right of withdrawal in Article 6 is the key part of the Directive.[42] The consumer can withdraw from all distance contracts to which the Directive is applicable within a period of, as a minimum, seven working days, without incurring any charges.

(a) The Right of Withdrawal and the Time Limit

Following the wording of the Directive, the right of withdrawal is only granted *once* a contract is concluded. Should a consumer change his mind before the contract is concluded and withdraw from his declaration the usual mechanisms in force in the national laws will apply, so depending on the national laws the consumer may be bound by his declaration and can only withdraw from the contract upon conclusion. This will probably not become relevant very often in practice, but, if it does, the declaration of withdrawal of the consumer should be interpreted as a withdrawal from the contract immediately after its conclusion.

The right of withdrawal can be exercised without stating any reasons and shall not lead to the consumer incurring any charges.[43] The only charge that may be made to

---

[42] P Rott, 'Widerrufsrechte ernst genommen—eine Botschaft zur rechten Zeit' (2001) *Verbraucher und Recht* 389; R Lawson, 'E-Commerce and Distance Selling' (2002) *Computer Security Report* 94; CT Steins, 'Distance Selling and German Law' (2000) *Computers & Law* 37; B Klingsporn, 'Zum Widerruf telefonisch angebahnter Haustürgeschäfte' (1997) *Neue Juristischen Wochenschrift* 1546; OLG Frankfurt, 'Widerruf eines darlehnsfinanzierten Computerkaufs im Fernabsatzhandel', judgement of 28 November 2001' 9 U 148/01, (2002) *Computer und Recht* 638; K Tonner, 'Probleme des novellierten Widerrufsrechts: Nachbelehrung, verbundene Geschäfte, Übergangsvorschriften' (2002) *BKR* 856.

[43] A Arnold and W Dötsch, 'Verschärfte Verbraucherhaftung beim Widerruf?' (2003) *Neue Juristischen Wochenschrift* 187.

the consumer is the direct cost of returning the goods. This not only excludes damages for breach of contract, penalties, but also imposed lump-sums under penalty clauses. The consumer shall not be confronted with any other cost than the direct costs for returning the goods, therefore is not liable for any other costs or compensation, i.e. for loss of value due to the opening of the packaging or the possibility to use the goods. As the right of withdrawal is granted generally for all distance contracts it does not matter if the consumer has paid for the goods in advance or by credit card. The way the money has to be refunded is not regulated in the Directive and therefore follows the national laws of the individual Member States.

(b) Commencement of the Time Limit

The commencement of the period for the exercise of the right of withdrawal is also subject to very detailed regulation. For contracts for goods it commences if:

- the consumer has received the confirmation of information either in writing or on another durable medium—and
- the consumer has received the goods.

This ensures that the consumer has got the goods in his or her hands and can test them and also has got all relevant information needed for the exercise of the right of withdrawal.

Contracts for services commence:

- either from the day of the conclusion of the contract; or
- if later, from the day on which the information requirements were fulfilled and the written confirmation received.

If the supplier fails to fulfil the information requirements, the period will be three months beginning for contracts on goods from the day of receipt of the consumer and for contacts on services from the day of the conclusion of the contract.

(c) Exemptions from the Right of Withdrawal

Following Article 6(3) some contracts are exempted from the right of withdrawal. For these contracts the consumer may not exercise the right of withdrawal unless the parties have agreed otherwise.

These are:

- For the provision of services if performance has begun, with the consumer's agreement, before the end of the withdrawal period.
- For the supply of goods made to the consumer's specifications or clearly personalised or which cannot be returned[44] or are liable to deteriorate or expire

---

[44] OLG Dresden, 'Unzulässiger Ausschluss des Widerrufsrechts nach FernabsG für elektronische Bauteile, judgement of 23 August 2001' 8 U 1535/01, (2002) *Computer und Recht*, 180.

rapidly; as well as the supply of newspapers, periodicals or magazines:
for newspapers, periodicals or magazines some Member States require a
right of withdrawal in other provisions (ie in Germany in the
Verbraucherkreditgesetz—VerbrKrG). These provisions can remain in force, as
the Directive only requires minimum harmonisation.

- For the supply of audio or video recordings or computer software, which were
  unsealed by the consumer: Unsealing of these goods constitutes an implied
  waiver of the right of withdrawal. The consumer may not be aware of this as he
  does not have to be informed about the fact before the conclusion of the contract
  but only with the written confirmation of the information and these can be sent
  at the latest together with the delivery of the goods. It is very unlikely that the
  consumer will read the information before inspecting the goods and although
  the purpose of this provision, to prevent the consumer copying the data and
  thereafter exercising the right of withdrawal, is well founded, however the aim of
  the Directive can only be achieved if the consumer is reasonably well informed.
  The supplier therefore has to make sure that the average consumer is likely to
  take notice of this information before unsealing the goods. This can be achieved
  by either informing the consumer in good time before the conclusion of the contract, together with the other pre-contractual information, or by ensuring that
  the consumer is likely to take notice of the information when he gets the goods,
  ie by a sticker with the information on the goods. This cannot apply to software
  or data sent online as it cannot be sealed. Regularly these contracts will however
  be service contacts performed (with the consumer's agreement) before the end
  of the withdrawal period and following exempted from the right of withdrawal
  on this ground.
- For the supply of goods or services the price of which is dependent on fluctuations in the financial market which cannot be controlled by the supplier: The
  field of application for this provision remains unclear as financial services are
  generally exempted from the Directive[45] and prices other than for financial services are not dependent on the fluctuations in the financial market.
- For gaming and lottery services as these would otherwise become impossible to
  market through means of distance communication.

(d) Credit Cards

Although the right of withdrawal regulations are very detailed the exercise of the
right will be problematic in practice in many cases.[46] Whenever the consumer pays
by credit card, a payment method generally appropriate to all means of distance
communication, the payment involves a third party, the provider of the credit

---

[45] Now regulated in the Directive 2002/65/EC on distance marketing of financial services.
[46] Payment Systems, J Dickie, *Internet and Electronic Commerce Law in the European Union* (Hart
Publishing, 1999) 15 ff.

card. The Directive, or other EU law, does not provide the possibility for any recourse to the provider of the credit card, the Consumer Credit Directive allows a recourse only for linked transactions and not if the card is used for payment. For claims on the repayment will—other than for the sales contract itself—mostly the law of the seat of the business be applicable and which may cause complications for the consumer.[47]

Most credit card providers nowadays offer charge-back systems allowing quick and efficient refunds without any costs for the consumer,[48] although the Directive does not require this apart from Article 8, which regulates the cases of fraudulent use of the card.

Fraudulent use does not exclusively mean fraud in the definition of criminal law but has to be interpreted widely as a private law term for the purposes of the Directive as all use that is not approved by the bearer of the card. In case of fraudulent use, the consumer shall have a right to request cancellation of a payment and be recredited or have the money returned.

5. Performance

Entirely new to EU legislation is the provision on performance in Article 7. Up to the Distance Selling Directive, regulation on performance had always been left to the law of the Member States.[49]

Article 7 of the Directive requires performance within a maximum of 30 days from the day following that on which the consumer forwarded his order to the supplier. The parties can agree otherwise. If the supplier cannot perform because the goods or services ordered are not available, he must inform the consumer about this and refund any sums the consumer has already paid as soon as possible but in any case within 30 days. To avoid these consequences, the supplier has to ensure that they offer realistic times for performance although this might often be difficult to achieve as the supplier is usually dependent on punctual performance of his suppliers as well. The performance period does not have to be individually negotiated but can also be in standard terms if the clause is in line with the regulations on unfair contract terms (see Directive 93/13/EEC). However, a clause that would leave the performance to the discretion of the supplier would not meet the requirements of Article 7 of the Directive.

---

[47] R Pichler, 'Kreditkartenzahlung im Internet' (1998) *Neue Juristischen Wochenschrift* 3234; P Rott, 'Electronic Payment by Consumers—The German Law' (1998) *Consumer Law Journal* 227; S Singleton, 'The Distance Selling Directive' (1999) *Consumer Law Today* 9; T Needing, *Distance Selling in a Digital Age* (1998) *Communications Law* 85; X Favre-Bulle, 'Les paiement à distance et les consommateurs' in *Jahrbuch des schweizerischen Konsumentenrechts (JKR)*, (Bern, 1999) 113.

[48] J Rothchild, 'Making the Market Work' (1998) *Journal of Consumer Policy* 279, 296.

[49] M Cremona, 'The Distance Selling Directive' (1998) *Journal of Business Law* 613, 619.

The Member States can, however lay down that the supplier may provide the consumer with goods or services of equivalent quality and price, provided the consumer was informed about this possibility in a clear and comprehensible manner. This information shall be given prior to the conclusion of the contract but in the contract at the latest. In this case the costs for returning the goods must be borne by the supplier; again the consumer must be informed of this. Only in this case and for goods or services of equivalent quality and price the supply of goods or services which had not been ordered by the consumer is not deemed to constitute inertia selling according to Article 9.

Strictly interpreted, generous performance instead of the originally ordered goods of higher quality or price (but without demanding the higher price) would be inertia selling, with the consequence that the supplier would lose their claim for payment completely.

Inertia selling is defined as 'supply of goods or services to a consumer without their being ordered by the consumer beforehand, where such supply involves a demand for payment' and is prohibited.[50] The consumer is protected as the unsolicited supply of goods or services cannot result in the conclusion of a contract and therefore create any duties for the consumer.

6. Restrictions on the Use of Certain Means of Distance Communication

New technologies like e-mail and SMS, are of course a very cheap, and therefore popular, means to market goods or services.[51] The use of distance communications for commercial purposes is, in B2C relations, only permitted, under general EC data protection law, if the consumer did not object to such use. Data protection law did not however originally require *prior consent*; merely that the consumer had an opportunity to 'opt out' of, or object to, the use of unsolicited communica-

---

[50] Art 9.

[51] J Worthy and N Graham, 'Electronic Marketing—New Rules for Electronic Marketing—and Obstacle to M-Commerce?' (2002) *Computer Law and Security Report* 106; A Günther, 'Erwünschte Regelung unerwünschter Werbung?' (1999) *Computer Recht* 172; P Heermann, 'Vertrags—und wettbewerbsrechtliche Probleme bei der e-mail Nutzung' (1999) *K&R* 6; T Hoeren, 'Cybermanners und Wettbewerbsrecht—Einige Überlegungen zum Lauterkeitsrecht im Internet' (1997) *WRP* 993; A Leupold, P Bräutigam and M Pfeiffer, 'Von der Werbung zur kommerziellen Kommunikation: Die Vermarktung von Waren und Dienstleistungen im Internet' (2000) *WRP* 575; J Taeger, 'Rechtlicher Regelungsrahmen des Elektronischen Geschäftsverkehrs' in P Horster (ed), *Elektronische Geschäftsprozesse* (IT-Verlag fur Informationstechnik, 2001) p 459, 465; JM Schmittmann, 'Kosten beim Empfänger unerwünschter E-Mail–Werbung' (2002) *K&R* 135; N Reich, 'Rechtsprobleme grenzüberschreitender irreführender Werbung im Binnenmarkt' (1992) 56 *Rabels Zeitschrift fur auslandisches und internationals Privatrecht* 444.

tions.[52] Prior consent was required only for the use of automated calling systems without human intervention and fax.[53] 'Cold calling' by phone, and 'spamming' by email, thus remained legal under the DSD. As some member states chose nonetheless to go further and ban these practices, difficulties of non-harmonisation across Europe arose.[54] These issues have however at least to some extent been resolved in the Privacy and Electronic Communications Directive 2002, which is discussed more fully in Chapter 2 of this volume, and which bans unsolicited commercial communications without prior consent, for (*inter alia*) phone, email and electronic texts, albeit with some significant exceptions.

7. Redress

The Directive was the first consumer related directive introducing an obligation for the Member States not only to implement the Directive, but also to ensure that a remedy be provided for breach of the provisions of the Directive in national law. The Directive also regulates judicial or administrative redress, but not jurisdiction.[55]

---

[52] See further L Edwards, Chapter 2 in this volume, on spam and cookies. See also N Dethloff, 'Europäisches Kollisionsrecht des unlauteren Wettbewerbs' (2000) *Juristischen Zeitung* 179; N Dethloff, 'Marketing im Internet und Internationales Wettbewerbsrecht' (1998) *Neue Juristische Wochenschrift* 1596; P Ayad and T Schafft, 'Einwilligung ins Direktmarketing—formularmäßig unwirksam?' (2002) *BB* 1711; R Azim-Khan, 'Cross-Border Sales Promotions' (2002) *European Business Law* 16; A Joint, 'Regulating the Message' (2002) *IT Law Today* 20; G Gardiner, 'Unsolicited Communications—Are They a Thing of the Past?' (2001) JECL & P 14; O Das, 'Spam—the Legal Regime in the United Kingdom' (2001) *IBL* 435; G Howells, 'The privatisation of justice' (2000) *NLJ* 972.

[53] If these means are used nevertheless the sanctions are different in the Member States, they may include criminal sanctions; JM Schmittmann, 'Sachbeschädigung (§ 303 StGB) durch Telefaxübermittlung von Werbung' JurPC Web-Dok 45/2002; R Winter, 'Zur Mitstörerhaftung bei unverlangter 0190–Telefaxwerbung' JurPC Web-Dok 254/2002; R Winter, 'Unverlangte E-mail Werbung: Gedanken zur Wiederholungsgefahr' JurPC Web-Dok 177/2002; Berlin, Beweislast für Zustimmung zum Empfang von Werbe-E-Mails, judgement of 16 May 2002, 16 O 4 and 02, *Computer Recht* 2002, 606; KG, Unzulässigkeit unaufgefordert zugesandter E-Mail–Werbung, judgement of 8 January 2002, 5 U 6727/00, *Computer Recht* 2002, 759.

[54] J Glöckner, '"Cold Calling" und Europäische Richtlinie zum Fernabsatz—ein trojanisches Pferd im deutschen Lauterkeitsrecht' (2000) *GRUR Int* 29; ECJ, ECR [1995], 141, *Alpine Investments* C–384/93; ECJ, [2002], 2 *Common Market Law Review* 3 *De Agostini*; N Reich in H-W Micklitz and N Reich, 'Die Fernabsatzrichtlinie im deutschen Recht' (Nomos, 1998) 85ff; HJ Sonnenberger, 'Privatrecht und Internationales Privatrecht im künftigen Europa: Fragen und Perspektiven' (2002) *RIW* 489.

[55] This problem becomes even more important for contracts concluded over the Internet: D Langer, 'Vertragsanbahnung und Vertragsschluß im Internet—Rechtswahl und Verbraucherschutz' (2000) *EuLF* 117; B Lurger, 'Internet, Internationales Privatrecht und europäische Rechtsangleichung' in M Gruber (ed), *Die rechtliche Dimension des Internet—Antrittsvorlesungen an der Rechtswissenschaftlichen Fakultät der Universität Salzburg im Wintersemester 2000/2001* (Wien, 2001) 69; F Regaldo, 'Cyberspace—Recht und Nationales Recht' (2000) *EuLF* 112, 114f; N Reich and A Gambogi Carvalho, 'Gerichtsstand bei internationalen Verbrauchervertragsstreitigkeiten im E-Commerce—Die EG-Verordnung 44/2001 und der Haager Konventionsentwurf über die gerichtliche Zuständigkeit und die Anerkennung und Vollstreckung ausländischer Entscheidungen in Zivil- und Handelssachen' (2001) *Verbracher und Recht* 269; H Rubin, 'Jurisdictional Risk Management in Cyberspace' (2000) *CRi* 33; H Rüßmann, 'Verbraucherschutz im Internet' (1998)

The provisions of the Directive are binding for the consumer and the businesses. The consumer can, following Article 12(1) of the Directive, not waive any of the rights conferred on him by the Directive and its transposition into the national laws.[56] Additionally, Article 12(2) requires the Member States to ensure that the consumer does not lose the protection granted by virtue of the choice of the law of a non-member country whenever the contract has a close connection with the territory of one or more Member States. This provision restricts the choice of law in consumer contracts and shall prevent avoidance of the Directive. Following the wording of the Directive the choice of the law of another Member State, no matter if there is a close connection, should be possible as the law of all Member States have to grant a minimum standard of protection for consumers. The international private law of the Member States may, however, forbid or restrict choice of law clauses in consumer contracts generally.

However, Article 12(2) only restricts the choice of law. If the law of a non-member country is applicable on objective grounds, the minimum standard is not granted. Especially in e-commerce where it is relatively easy to construct an objective connection to a non-member state or any off shore jurisdiction this is a severe gap in the legal protection and opens the possibility for avoidance of the provisions of the Directive.[57]

Article 11(1) of the Directive requires the Member States to ensure adequate and effective means to ensure compliance with the Directive in the interests of consumers. This general rule goes further than the general obligation to implement the provisions of the Directive into national law and creates an obligation for the Member States to introduce or maintain effective redress systems in the interests of consumers. This general rule is specified in the following paragraphs.

K&R 129; O Sandrock, 'Neue Herausforderungen an das Internationale Wirtschaftsrecht' (1999) *Zeitschrift fur Vergleichende Rechtswissenschaft* 98, 227; I Walden, 'Regulating Electronic Commerce: Europe in the Global E-conomy' (2001) *European Law Review* 529, 539; A Fenner and A Farquharson, 'Where Can We be Sued?' (2002) *New Law Journal* 152; M Martin, 'Constitutional Review of Foreign Law in English and German Courts: a Comparative Study' (2002) *Oxford University Commonwealth Law Journal* 5; H Rowe, 'Legal Implications of Consumer-Orientated Electronic Commerce' (1998) *CLSR* 232; generally on jurisdiction and arbitration issues and conflicts in German and English decisions: N Reich, 'Zur Wirksamkeit von Schiedsklauseln bei grenzüberschreitenden Börsentermingeschäften' (1998) *Zeitschrift fur Europaisches Privatrecht* 981.

[56] In case of insufficient transposition the Member State may be liable, N Reich, 'Bürgerrechte in der EU' (Nomos, 1999) 142 ff.

[57] M Seidel, 'Erstreckung des Verbraucherschutzes der EG auf Drittstaaten?' (2002) *Europaisches Zeitschrift fur Wirtschaftsrecht* 449; S Briskman, 'A Year's Review of the Distance Selling Regime' (2002) *European Consumer Law and Policy* 13; W-H Roth, 'Angleichung des IPR durch sekundäres Gemeinschaftsrecht' (1994) *Praxis des Internationalen Privat- und Verfahrensrecht* 165; S Leible, 'Kollisionsrechtlicher Verbraucherschutz im EVÜ und EG-RiLi' in R Schulze and H Schulte-Nölke (eds), *Europäische Rechtsangleichung und Nationale Privatrechte* (Nomos, 1999) 353; M Nettesheim, 'Effektive Rechtsschutzgewährleistung im Arbeitsteiligen System Europäischen Rechtsschutzes' (2002) *Juristen Zeitung* 928.

Article 11(2) requires that these means include the possibility for at least one of the specified bodies to take action under national law before the courts or the competent administrative bodies. The specified bodies are

• public bodies or their representatives;
• consumer organisations having a legitimate interest in protecting consumers; or
• professional organizations having a legitimate interest in acting.

Following the wording it would be sufficient to allow only one of these bodies to take action, but most of the Member States allowed at least two of these. As the wording says 'include', these enumerated means cannot be the only means for redress. The other important one is individual redress. These mechanisms can, and do in most Member States, follow the normal procedural system for individual claims if the provisions of the Directive are implemented into national law. Problems arise if the Directive generally, or one or more provisions, are not implemented or not properly implemented into national law, but these are problems not specific to this Directive.

It has been discussed if the Member States ought to be obliged to introduce complaints systems. The provision in Article 17 is a result of these discussions and a compromise. The Commission will study the feasibility of establishing effective means to deal with consumers' complaints and present a report within two years after the entry into force of the Directive. This report was presented on the 10 March 2000[58] but in the meantime discussions have continued and for e-commerce contracts, complaint systems shall be introduced; these systems are not restricted to consumer contracts any more.[59]

The Member States may following Article 11(3) (a) stipulate that the burden of proof concerning the existence of prior information, written confirmation, compliance with time limits or consumer consent can be placed on the consumer. This provision has been used, or was already in force, following the procedural rules in some Member States and can be very important for the consumer as it is mostly to proved negative. For example, it might be difficult for the consumer to prove that information has not been supplied whereas it is relatively easy for the supplier to ensure proof that it was provided.

The Member States are, according to Article 11(3) (b), obliged to take the measures needed to ensure that suppliers and operators of means of communication comply with the provisions adopted pursuant to this Directive. This provision seems redundant but it ensures the implementation of the provisions of the Directive in practice.

---

[58] COM (2000) 127 final of 10 March 2000.
[59] M Odams De Zylva, 'Effective Means of Resolving Distance Selling Disputes' (2001) *Arbitration* 230.

Article 11(4) allows the Member States to provide for voluntary supervision by self-regulatory bodies and recourse to such bodies for the settlement of disputes. This provision mainly affects the Member States with a tradition of self-regulatory bodies like the UK and allows fitting the Directive into the existing systems. On the EU-level the Extra-Judicial-Network (EEJ-NET) has been introduced in the meantime. This is a voluntary dispute settlement system, designed for consumer complaints intended to work cross-border (see further discussion in Motion P, Chapter 5 in this volume).

C. Implementation

The measures imposed by the Directive only become effective through implementation in the Member States. All Member States have now implemented the Directive into their national laws[60] although not by the date set in the Directive.

---

[60] Austria: Fernabsatz-Gesetz BGBl; I Nr 185/1999; Belgium: Loi modifiant la loi du 14 juillet 1991 sur les pratiques du commerce et sur l'information et la protection du consommateur; Loi du 02/08/2002 relative à la publicité trompeuse et à la publicité comparative, aux clauses abusives et aux contrats à distance en ce qui concerne les professions libérales ref: MB du 20/11/2002 p 51,704 (C–2002/09820)(SG(2003)A/00473 du 20/01/2003); Denmark: Act 442, 31.5.2000; Finland: Laki kuluttajansuojalain muuttamisesta, 15/12/2000 ref: Suomen säädöskokoelma 2000 n 1072 (p 2809), SG(2001)A/868 du 22/01/2001 Laki sopimattomasta menettelystä elinkeinotoiminnassa annetun lain 2:n muuttamisesta, 15/12/2000 ref: Suomen säädöskokoelma 2000 n 1073 (p 2817), SG(2001)A/868 du 22/01/2001; France: Ordonnance n 2001–741 du 23 août 2001 portant transposition de directives communautaires et adaptation au *droit* communautaire en matière de *droit* de la consommation ref: JORF 196 du 25 août 2001 p 13,645–NOR ECOX100,083R (SG(2001)A/11,576 du 22/10/2001 et 11,790 du 25/10/2001) LOI n 2001–1062 du 15 novembre 2001 relative à la sécurité quotidienne (Art 36) ref: JORF du 16 novembre 2001; Germany: Fernabsatzgesetz of 27.6.2000; Greece: Arrêté ministériel conjoint: Z1 496/2000 du 07/12/2000 (N2251/94) ref: FEK 1545/A du 18/12/2000, p 20,693 (idem SG(2001)A/2876 du 08/03/2001); Ireland: European Communities (Protection of Consumers in Respect of Contracts made by Means of Distance Communication) Regulations 2001; 15/5/2001 ref: SI 207 of 2001 Sale of Goods and Supply of Services Act, 1980 ref: SI No 16 of 1980; Italy: Decreto legislativo 22 maggio 1999, n 185. Attuazione della direttiva 97/7 relativa a la protezione dei consumatori in materia di contratti a distanza; Luxembourg: Loi du 16 avril 2003 concernant la protection des consommateurs en matière de contrats à distance. ref. Memorial A n 61 du 8 mai 2003 pg.1026; Netherlands: Wet van 21/12/2000 tot aanpassing van Boek 7 van het Burgerlijk Wetboek aan richtlijn nr. 97/7/EG van het Europees Parlement en de Raad van de Europese Unie van 20 mei 1997 betreffende de bescherming van de consument bij op afstand gesloten overeenkomsten (PbEG L 144)(21/12/2000) ref: Staatsblad van het Koninkrijk der Nederlanden 2000 617; Portugal: Decreto-Lei n 143/2001 de 26 de abril 2000 ref: Diário da Repùblica I série A n 97, 26/04/2001, p 2360; Spain: Ley 47/2002, de 19 de diciembre, de reforma de la Ley 7/1996, de 15 de enero, de Ordenacion del Comercio Minorista, para la transposicion al Ordenamiento juridico espanol de la Directive 97/7/CE, en materia de contratos a distancia, y para la adaptacion de la Ley a diversas Directivas comunitarias ref: BOE n 304 de 20/12/2002 p 44,759; Sweden: Transposée par loi SFS 2000:274 sur les contrats à distance; United Kingdom: Reg 2000 SI 2000/2334. Changes may be made following consultation by the DTI in January 2005; see http://www.dti.gov.uk/ccp/consultations.htm#distsell.

The different dates of implementation create problems for businesses[61] but fortunately are only for a transitional period, due to the structure of the EU and the EU law.

The implementation of the Directive in the Member States shows some remarkable differences, not all of them based on the minimum harmonisation approach giving the Member States some scope for discretion.[62]

Commencing with the definitions from Article 1 of the Directive, some Member States have not implemented the definitions for all terms,[63] but have included other or widened the definitions.[64] The same applies to exemptions from the Directive, enumerated in Article 3 of the Directive, where some Member States did not implement all exemptions[65] while others excluded some other types of contracts as well.[66] As with the definitions, not all implementation measures may be in line with the Directive.

Although measures for the information requirements from Article 4 show some differences in the Member States they do, to a large extent, follow the Directive.[67] Regarding written confirmation of the information required in Article 5 of the Directive, certain Member States either include the possibility of confirmation by e-mail explicitly[68] whereas other Member States do not mention e-mail confirmation explicitly[69] but the general definition ought to include e-mail confirmations. In Sweden, a website alone is considered satisfactory; it is doubtful if a website should be considered as satisfactory following the Directive as a website can be amended very easily and therefore cannot be seen as durable. Furthermore Article 5 requires that the consumers receipt of the information, which might have to be proved by the supplier, and the presentation of the information on a website, requires that the consumer actively accesses the information and ensures receipt of information through downloading. The Directive, however, requires the confirmation in writing, or on a durable medium, and this enumeration requires that the methods have to be comparable.[70] A website cannot fulfil these requirements.

---

[61] As the EMOTA study points out, p 55; G Brooks, 'Compliance: Avoiding the Pitfalls' (2002) *European Consumer Law and Policy* 8.

[62] For a comprehensive analysis see: H-W Micklitz and N Reich, *Die Fernabsatzrichtlinie im deutschen Recht* (Nomos, 1998); H-W Micklitz, and N Reich, 'Umsetzung der EG-Fernabsatzrichtlinie' (1999) *BB* 2093; S Sidkin and J Elliot, 'Coming to Terms with the New Regime' (2001) *European Consumer Law and Policy* 10; S Briskman, 'A Year's Review of the Distance Selling Regime' (2002) *European Consumer Law and Policy* 13.

[63] Austria, Denmark, Finland and Sweden for 'means of distance communication'.

[64] Belgium, Great Britain, Greece and Portugal.

[65] Austria, Belgium, Denmark, Finland, Greece, Italy, Luxemburg, Netherlands and Sweden.

[66] Germany and Great Britain.

[67] Detailed analysed in the EMOTA study, p 60.

[68] Austria, Denmark, Finland, Germany, Great Britain, Ireland, Luxembourg and Sweden.

[69] Belgium, France, Greece, Italy, Portugal and Spain.

[70] Generally on formal requirements for online transactions: P Graf Fringuelli and M Wallhäuser, 'Formerfordernisse beim Vertragsschluß im Internet' (1999) *Computer und Recht* 93; P Dobson, 'Distance Selling Regulations' (2001) *SL Rev* 12.

The cooling-off periods are either, following the minimum requirements in Article 6, seven working days[71] or 14 calendar days.[72] Seven working days can extend to a maximum of 14 calendar days in any Member State. Only Italy and Greece have 10-day periods. The cooling-off period of 10 working days in Italy is certainly in line with the requirement of at least seven working days in the Directive but as it can extend the withdrawal period to more than 14 calendar days, this can be problematic for suppliers. A supplier could fulfil all different requirements in all Member States with a 14-calendar-day withdrawal period. Setting the withdrawal period in calendar days is, especially in cross-border contracts, generally preferable for suppliers as well as consumers as it is a provision clearly understood and defined without need for knowledge of regional differences. It also avoids the problem of different withdrawal periods within one Member States as some Member States have different public holidays in different parts of the country.[73] The regulation in Greece of 10 days does not meet the requirements of the Directive, as this period may be less than the required seven working days. For the cost to return the goods the regulations vary, in most Member States the consumer has to bear the cost of returning the goods,[74] only in Finland and Germany the supplier generally has to bear the costs for the return. In practice, however, and in the interests of an increase in consumer confidence, many suppliers bear the costs for returns voluntarily.

For the performance of the contract, the implementation of Article 7 of the Directive, the regulations in the Member States also vary following the sphere for discretion granted for their implementation. Most Member States, however, allow substitution,[75] although it may depend on the contract or agreement between the parties.[76] Only Austria and Luxembourg do not provide any possibility of substitution in the implementing legislation.

All Member States have implemented the prohibition of inertia selling following the clear requirement in Article 9 of the Directive.

Regarding the restrictions in the use of certain means of distance communication as regulated in Article 10 of the Directive, all Member States require an opt-in system for automated calling machines and faxes. For other types of communication, regulations differ. Some Member States have extended the opt-in requirement to other means,[77] whereas other Member States allow the use of other

---

[71] Austria, Belgium, France, Great Britain, Ireland, Luxembourg, Netherlands and Spain.

[72] Denmark, Finland, Germany, Portugal and Sweden.

[73] Ie, in Germany for the 16 Federal States and in Great Britain for England, Scotland and Wales.

[74] Austria, Belgium, Denmark, France, Great Britain, Greece, Ireland, Luxembourg, Netherlands. Portugal, Spain and Sweden.

[75] Finland, France, Germany, Great Britain, Greece, Ireland, Italy, Netherlands, Portugal and Spain.

[76] Denmark and Sweden, Belgium allows substitution implied at the risk of the supplier.

[77] Denmark for e-mail and some phone marketing to private households; Finland for e-mail and SMS; Germany for e-mail, SMS and telephone communications for advertising purposes; Greece for telephone communications, e-mail and other forms of electronic communication; Italy for telephone and e-mail; Luxembourg for telephone communications.

communication (apart from automated calling machines and faxes) if there is no opposition from the consumer (opt-out),[78] occasionally with the requirement that the advertisements have to be clearly recognizable as such.[79]

Regarding the implementation of Article 12, extra-territorial application, all Member States apart from Portugal follow the provision of the Directive strictly; in Portugal there are no provisions that guarantee extra-territorial application.

D. Distance Marketing of Financial Services, Directive 2002/65/EC of 23 September 2002

The Distance Marketing of Financial Services Directive (DMFSD) introduces, unsurprisingly, a specialist framework for the distance marketing of financial services.[80] The aim of the DMFSD is to ensure consumer protection in financial services. Financial services had been excluded from the general Distance Selling Directive because of political wrangles and the complexity of financial services, and when the exclusion was agreed upon the planning process for a separate directive on financial services had already started. The first draft was adopted in October 1998, however long discussions followed until the final proposal was adopted in Summer 2002. The DMFSD had to be implemented before 9 October 2004 and some though not all Member States, like the UK,[81] met (or almost met[82]) this deadline for implementation.

---

[78] Belgium; Denmark for all means apart from e-mail and some phone calls to private households; Finland for all means apart from e-mail and SMS; France; Great Britain for telephone communications; Ireland; Italy for all means apart from telephone and e-mail; Luxembourg for all means apart from telephone communications; Netherlands; Portugal; Spain; Sweden.

[79] Belgium, Luxembourg and Spain for e-mails.

[80] R Zwitser, 'Internetbankieren met Pay Pal' (2000) *NJB* 1479; G Spindler, 'Internet, Kapitalmarkt und Kollisionsrecht unter besonderer Berücksichtigung der E-Commerce—Richtlinie' (2001) *Zeitschrift des gesamte Handelsrecht und Wirtschaftrecht* 165, 324; F Heinemann and M Jopp, 'Der vergessene Konsument: Nachteile eines unvollendeten Binnenmarktes ûfr Finanzdienstleistungen' (2002) *Integration*, 200; M Kunz, 'Switzerland: Home or Host Country for Cross-Border Electronic Finance Services?' (2002) *JIFM* 32; for the legal problems general see G Vandenberghe, 'Rechtliche Aspekte verbraucherorientierter Telebanking—und Teleshopping—Dienste in der Europäischen Gemeinschaft' in J Scherer (ed), *Nationale und Europäische Perspektiven der Telekommunikation* (Nomos, 1987); M Anassutzi, 'E-Commerce—Directive 00/31' (2002) *International Company and Commercial Law Review* 337, 341; R Metz, 'Der Fernabsatz von Finanzdienstleistungen—verbraucherpolitische Defizite' in L Kramer, H-W Micklitz and K Toumer (eds), *Law and Diffuse Interests in the European Legal Order/Recht und diffuse Interessen in der Europaischen Rechtsordnung, Liber Amicorum Norbert Reich* (Nomos, 1997) 603; N Härting and M Schirmbacher, 'Finanzdienstleistungen im Fernabsatz' (2002) *Computer und Recht* 809; G Mai, 'Wertpapierhandel im Internet' (2002) *Computer und Recht* 200.

[81] SI 2004 No 2095, The Financial Services (Distance Marketing) Regulations 2004.

[82] The UK implementation came into force on 31 October 2004.

Although the DMFSD is a specialised regulation for financial services it interplays with the Distance Selling Directive as well as the E-Commerce Directive, and it builds on and overlaps with the measures found in these two Directives.[83] The similarities can mainly be found in areas such as information requirements, cooling-off periods and the restrictions on inertia selling. Some differences exist, but these are mainly founded on the different nature of the services. One of the most important differences lies in the harmonisation approach. In contrast to the Distance Selling Directive, the DMFSD follows the maximum harmonisation approach. As a result the Member States have less scope when implementing and the level of harmonisation will be higher than for general distance selling.

1. Imperative Nature

The DMFSD is binding, as a consumer may, as Article 12(1) states, not waive the rights conferred on them by the Directive. Additionally, Article 12(2) requires that Member States take the measures needed to ensure that the consumer does not lose the protection granted by the Directive by virtue of the choice of law of a non-member country as applicable law whenever the contract has a close link with the territory of one or more Member States. This provision restricts the choice of law for consumer contracts significantly and requires corresponding provisions in the private international law of the Member States, which are already known for consumer contracts in the law of most of the Member States.

2. Scope of Application

The DMFSD applies to any contract concerning financial services between a supplier and a consumer under an organised distance sales scheme run by the supplier, which makes exclusive use of a means of distance communication up to and including the time that the contract is concluded. The definitions of the terms used in the DMFSD are the same as used in the general Distance Selling Directive, apart from the fact that in this directive the term 'financial service' is defined in addition. The interpretations found for the terms used in the Distance Selling Directive can thus be transferred to the Financial Services Directive. The interpretations from the national laws of the Member States cannot be transferred, as EU law requires an independent interpretation, but within EU law the definitions ought to be generally the same.

'Financial service' is defined in Article 2(b) as 'any service of a banking, credit, insurance, personal pension, investment or payment nature'.

---

[83] J Coffey, 'E-Commerce Directive and Financial Services' (2002) *Solicitors Journal* 504.

3. Information Duties

As with the Distance Selling Directive, the DMFSD requires certain information to be provided to the consumer in good time prior to conclusion of the contract. Compared to the general Directive, far more information has to be provided and all information has to be given in good time before the conclusion of the contract in a way appropriate to the means of distance communication used. All the information has, as Article 5(1) requires, to be given 'in writing or in another durable medium' before the consumer is bound by any contract or offer. This, due to the complexity of the services, is considerably earlier than for the general Distance Selling Directive. The wording 'before the consumer is bound by any distance contract or offer' seems to imply that the information has to be communicated before the consumer can make a binding offer and it could be argued that this communication of information is a necessary pre-requisite for the conclusion of a contract. This argument would be very much in favour of the consumer but it would make Article 11 of the DMFSD redundant, which requires the Member States to provide appropriate sanctions in the event of non-compliance with provisions pursuant to the Directive. One sanction suggested in Article 11 is the right for the consumer to cancel the contract at any time. As this is only one possible option for sanctions, it does not exclude the possibility for Member States to turn the information duties into essential requirements for a contract (*essentialia negotii*) but it does not require it either. In certain cases it might also be disadvantageous for the consumer and therefore doubtful if compatible with the aim of the Directive.

At any time during the contractual relationship the consumer shall be entitled to receive, on his request, the contractual terms and conditions on paper. Additionally, Article 5(3) gives the consumer a choice of the means of distance communication used, unless it is incompatible with the contract or the nature of the financial service.

4. Information Prior to the Conclusion of the Contract

(a) General Requirements

Article 3 requires the consumer to be provided with information 'in a clear and comprehensible manner' in any way appropriate to the means of distance communication used, concerning the supplier, the financial service, the distance contract and redress. The commercial purpose of the contract must always be made clear and all communication must follow the principles of good faith in commercial transactions and the principles governing the protection of persons unable to give consent, such as minors.

(b) Telephony Communications

Article 3(3) regulates the special information duties for voice telephony communications. The information supply shall generally follow the special requirements of the means of distance communication used but as in the general Distance Selling Directive, use of the telephone is regulated. This is particularly necessary as fulfilment of the information requirements over the telephone is especially difficult, as fulfilling all information requirements by reading the information out to the consumer would, especially with the amount of information required for financial services, be rendered senseless for the consumer and would likely in practice exclude telephony communications completely, a result that would be contrary to the aim of the DMFSD.

Nevertheless the information requirements shall be independent from the means of distance communication used. Consequently the DMFSD regulates the information duties separately for telephony communications.

On the occasion of telephony communications the supplier has to provide the consumer with the following information:

The supplier has to make his identity and the commercial purpose of the call explicitly clear at the beginning of any conversation with the consumer. The consumer has to agree upon the use of the telephone for the communication. This provision allows the use of telephony communications generally, but requires that the consumer is informed about the commercial purpose and the identity of the supplier. As noted above, the DMFSD, like the DSD, originally allowed cold-calling for the marketing of financial services. However unsolicited commercial communications of whatever kind, including phone and email, are now banned without prior consent by the Privacy and Electronic Communications Directive 2002, save in certain exceptional circumstances—see further L Edwards, Chapter 4 in this volume.

If the consumer consents to the communication generally and the use of the telephone explicitly, only the specified information below has to be given:

- The identity of the person calling and his link with the supplier;
- The main characteristics of the financial service;
- The total price to be paid by the consumer, including all taxes paid via the supplier. (When the calculation of the exact price is not possible the basis for the calculation of the price has to be given to enable the consumer to verify it.)
- Notice of the possibility that other taxes and/or costs may exist which are not paid via the supplier;
- The existence or absence of a right of withdrawal. If a right of withdrawal exists the consumer also has to be informed about its duration and the conditions to exercise it, including the information on any payment for services, which have already been provided before the withdrawal.

Furthermore, the supplier has to inform the consumer about other information, its nature and that it is available on request.

In any case the supplier has to provide full information according to Article 5 on paper or another durable medium, either in good time before the consumer is bound by any contract or offer or, if the contract has, on the consumers request, been concluded before these requirements could possibly be fulfilled, immediately after the conclusion of the contract.

5. The Individual Information Duties

For all means of distance communication other than telephony communication, the full information requirements have to be fulfilled. The consumer has to be provided with detailed information by the means of distance communication used and which is confirmed on paper or another durable medium. The information required includes information about the supplier, the financial service itself, the distance contract and redress mechanisms. This individual information required is as follows:

(a) Information about the Supplier

The information to be given about the supplier includes the following:

- The identity and the main business of the supplier, the geographical address at which the supplier is established and any other geographical address relevant for the customer's relations with the supplier. For the geographical address a post box address alone will not be sufficient, although the supplier can of course use a post box address for correspondence.
- The identity of any representative of the supplier established in the consumer's Member State of residence and the relevant geographical addresses.
- If the supplier is registered in a trade or similar public register the registration number and the public register.
- If the activity is subject to an authorisation scheme, the particulars of the relevant supervisory authority.

(b) Information about the Financial Service

The information about the financial service itself requires:

- A description of its main characteristics.
- The total price to be paid by the consumer. This must include all fees, charges and expenses as well as all taxes, including the taxes paid via the supplier. If it is not possible to name the exact amount, the basis for the calculation of the price has to be indicated to enable the consumer to verify the price.

- If special risks are involved in specific features or instruments or if the price is dependent on fluctuations in the financial markets outside the supplier's control, these risks have to be mentioned expressly.
- A notice of the possibility that other taxes or costs may exist that are not paid via the supplier or imposed by him.
- Any limitations of the period for which the information is valid.
- The arrangements for payment and for performance.
- If any specific additional cost is charged for using the means of distance communication, these costs have to be specified.

(c) Information about the Distance Contract

The information to be given about the distance contract is as follows:

- The existence or absence of a right of withdrawal according to Article 6 of the Directive. If such a right exists, its duration and the conditions for exercising it, including the information on the amount, which the consumer may be, required paying for services provided before withdrawal. The conditions for this payment are specified in Article 7(1). Information has also to be given about the non-exercise of the right of withdrawal. In contrast to the general Distance Selling Directive the consumer has to be informed not only about the existence of a right of withdrawal but also if for the special contract, a right of withdrawal does not exist. This ensures that the consumer cannot be misled by any general information he or she might have about a right of withdrawal and assuming that a right of withdrawal exists whereas it is excluded for the specific contract.
- If the financial services to be performed permanently or recurrently, the minimum duration of the distance contract has to be specified.
- If the parties have any rights to terminate the contract early or unilaterally by virtue of the terms of the distance contract, the terms and conditions, including any penalties imposed by the contract have to be notified. This covers the right of termination for the parties, the consumers as well as the suppliers.
- Practical instructions for the exercise of the right of withdrawal, including the address to which the notification of a withdrawal should be sent.
- The Member State or States whose laws are a basis for the establishment of relations with the consumer prior to the conclusion of the distance contract.
- The law applicable to the distance contract and/or the competent court.
- The language or languages, in which the contractual terms and conditions, and the pre contractual information are supplied. Furthermore the language or languages in which the supplier undertakes to communicate during the duration of the distance contract. The latter needs the agreement of the consumer.

(d) Information about Redress

The information about redress includes the following:

- Whether or not there is an out-of-court complaint and redress mechanism for the consumer as well as the methods for having access to it.
- The existence of guarantee funds or other compensation arrangements other than required by the EU-law on deposit guarantee schemes and on investor compensation schemes.

6. Additional Information Requirements

Article 4(1) requires additional information for the cases in which other EU-law provisions require prior information additional to the information requirements of the Directive. In these cases the supplier has to comply with the full information requirements following the Directive on distance marketing of financial services as well as any other information requirements.

Article 4(2) allows the Member States to maintain or introduce more stringent provisions on prior information requirements as long as these requirements are in conformity with Community law.[84] The Member States have to communicate any provisions requiring additional information to the Commission and the Commission shall communicate this information to suppliers and consumers to enable them to comply with these requirements. This provision is an exemption from the general maximum harmonisation approach of the Directive, but the exemption is restricted only to more stringent information requirements and pending further harmonisation. This stresses the maximum harmonisation approach and has to be read in conjunction with Article 20, which requires a review following the implementation of the directive and a report to be presented before April 2006. This review and the report shall examine the impact of the directive and in particular the effect of the information requirements and the right of withdrawal.

7. Burden of Proof

Article 15 of the Directive allows the Member States to place the burden of proving that the seller has met the obligations of the Directive in certain cases on the consumer. However, the onus of proof that the consumer consented prior to

---

[84] Ie, for German law see the comprehensive analysis: S Abegglen, *Die Aufklärungspflichten in Dienstleistungsbeziehungen, Insbesondere im Bankgeschäft* (Stampfli, 1995); regarding Standard Contract Terms: P Derleder and A Pallas, 'Vertragsschluss und AGB—Einbeziehung im Kreditwirtschaftlichen Distanzgeschäft' (1999) *ZIP* 1285.

conclusion of the contract, and especially, whenever performance shall begin before the end of the withdrawal period, also to performance, is on the supplier. This is appropriate, as the consumer would have to prove the non-performance of the information duties or the consent, which can be rather difficult or impossible whereas the supplier can without extraordinary expenses ensure the positive—the performance of information duties or the consent of the consumer. As the supplier of financial services is only obliged to provide the information and communicate them on paper or another durable medium it does not create an undue hardship to impose the burden of proof on the supplier.

Any contractual term or condition imposing the burden of proof in these areas on the consumer will, following the second paragraph of Article 15, be regarded as an unfair contract term[85] within the meaning of the Directive on Unfair Terms in Consumer Contracts 93/13/EEC.[86]

8. Right of Withdrawal

Article 6 regulates the right of withdrawal, which is generally a similar regulation as the right of withdrawal in the general Distance Selling Directive. The withdrawal period, however, is 14 calendar days and not 7 working days as in the general Distance Selling Directive. This is not only due to the complexity of financial services but also to the different periods in the national laws which not only result from the minimum harmonisation approach that allows Member States to establish longer withdrawal periods but also from the different definition of working days and different public holidays. All this causes a lack of harmonisation and remarkable barriers for cross-border trade.

The withdrawal period is prolonged to 30 calendar days for contracts on life insurances and personal pensions. This prolonged withdrawal period is based on the nature of these services due to which they only take effect a considerably long time after the conclusion of the contract.

The period for withdrawal shall, similar to regulation for services in the general Distance Selling Directive, begin either from the day of the conclusion of the contract or from the day on which the consumer receives the contractual terms and condition and the required information. Again contracts on life insurances, for which the withdrawal period only begins when the consumer is informed that the contract has been concluded, are exempted.

---

[85] P Derleder and A Pallas, 'Vertragsschluss und AGB—Einbeziehung im Kreditwirtschaftlichen Distanzgeschäft' (1999) *ZIP* 1285; S Kamanabrou, 'Vorgaben der E-Commerce—Richtlinie für die Einbeziehung von AGB bei Online—Rechtsgeschäften' (2001) *Computer und Recht* 421; M Löhnig, 'Die Einbeziehung von AGB bei Internet—Geschäften' (1997) *Neue Juristische Wochenschrift* 1688; J Mehrings, 'Verbraucherschutz im Cyberlaw: Zur Eibeziehung von AGB im Internet' (1998) *BB* 2373; P v Wijk, 'Protection against Unfair Contracts: An Economic Analysis of European Regulation' (2000) *European Journal of Law and Economics* 89, 73.

[86] 5 April 1993, OJ L95 of 21 April 1993, p 29.

Article 6(2) excludes a number of contracts from the right of withdrawal. This list is exclusive and following the maximum harmonisation approach has to be incorporated by all Member States. The services excluded are:

Financial services whose price depends on fluctuations in the financial market outside the supplier's control, which may occur during the withdrawal period. This provision has to be interpreted narrowly as the price of most financial services somehow depends on fluctuations in the financial market which will usually be outside the supplier's control. It is important that these fluctuations may occur during the withdrawal period. To ensure predictability these have to be understood as occurrence within the regular or normal developments of the markets, not the developments during the individual withdrawal period for a contract. The Directive lists services to which this applies:

- Foreign exchange
- Money market instruments
- Transferable securities
- Units in collective investment undertakings
- Financial-future contracts, including equivalent cash-settled instruments
- Forward interest-rate agreements (FRAs)
- Interest-rate, currency and equity swaps
- Options to acquire or dispose of any instruments referred to in the list of exemptions including equivalent cash-settled instruments, which includes in particular options on currency and on interest rates.
- Travel and baggage insurance policies or similar short-term insurance policies of less than one month's duration;
- Contracts whose performance has been fully completed by both parties at the consumer's express request before the consumer exercises his right of withdrawal.

Despite the maximum harmonisation approach, Article 6(3) allows the Member States to exempt further exclusively specified services from the right of withdrawal. If the Member States make use of this possibility they have to communicate this to the Commission and the Commission shall ensure that this information is available to consumers and suppliers requesting it. The possible exemptions are:

- any credit intended primarily for the use on immovable property as acquiring or retaining rights in land or buildings, renovating or improving a building;
- any credit secured either by mortgage or immovable property or by a right related to immovable property;
- declarations by consumers using the services of an official, provided that the official confirms that the consumer is guaranteed receipt of the full information on paper or another durable medium.

The consumer shall, in exercising of the right of withdrawal, before the expiry of the withdrawal period, notify the withdrawal following the practical instructions given to him by means, which can be proved in accordance with the national law. The deadline shall be deemed to have been observed if the notification is dispatched before the deadline expires. In contrast to the general regulation in most Member States, but the same as in the general Distance Selling Directive, the relevant point of time is here the dispatch and not the receipt of the notification.

9. Payment

When the consumer withdraws from the contract he or she may, according to Article 7(1) only be required to pay for the service actually provided by the provider in accordance with the contract. The performance of the contract shall only begin after the consumer has given his approval. The payment shall be proportionate to the full coverage of the contract and not be such that it could be construed as a penalty.

For insurance contracts Article 7(2) allows the Member States to provide that the consumer is free from any payment when upon withdrawal of the contract.

If the supplier cannot prove that the consumer was duly informed about the amount payable in case of withdrawal, or if the supplier commenced the performance of the contract before the expiry of the withdrawal period without the consumer's consent, Article 7(3) excludes the requirement of any payment from the consumer.

Article 7(4) requires the supplier to return any sum the consumer has paid in advance without undue delay and no later than within 30 calendar days from the day on which the supplier receives the notification of withdrawal.

As well as the supplier the consumer is obliged to return any sums and/or property he has received from the supplier without undue delay and no later than 30 calendar days from the dispatch of the notification of withdrawal.

Article 8 requires the Member States to ensure that a consumer can request cancellation of a payment and be re-credited with the sum paid or have them returned in the event of fraudulent use of his payment card in connection with distance contracts. As Article 8 only regulates the rights in case of a fraudulent use of a card, this regulation does not apply to refunds in case of withdrawal or any other grounds for refunds.

10. Unsolicited Services

Article 9 of the Directive prohibits the supply of unsolicited financial services. Unsolicited services are all financial services, which are supplied to a consumer without a prior request from the consumer for which payment is required, no matter if the payment is required immediately or deferred. Should the consumer nevertheless be supplied with an unsolicited service, the consumer shall be free from any obligation and the absence of a reply cannot constitute consent. This means the consumer has no obligation regarding unsolicited services. If a consumer receives unsolicited services no reaction at all is required. The consumer does not have to refuse the service or inform the supplier. This means for suppliers that they have to bear the risk if they send unsolicited services intentionally but also for services which, for one or another reason are sent to the wrong person, or if it emerges that the contract had not been concluded properly.

Generally the renewal of distance contracts shall not be deemed as unsolicited. The rules on the renewal and especially the tacit renewal of distance contracts are not regulated in the Directive but remain the responsibility of the Member States and therefore follow the provisions of the national laws of the Member States.

11. Unsolicited Communications

Article 10 of the Directive restricts the use of unsolicited communications for certain distance communication techniques. For the use of automatic calling machines and fax machines, Article 10(1) requires prior consent from the consumer.[87] As noted above, a general ban on all unsolicited commercial communications now exists in EC law, following the implementation of the Privacy and Electronic Communications Directive 2002 (see Chapter 9 in this volume).

12. Sanctions

Article 11 of the DMFSD requests appropriate sanctions for non-compliance with the implemented provisions of the Directive. The sanctions must be effective, proportional and dissuasive. The DMFSD does not specify these terms but gives non-specific examples as the Member States may provide for this purpose in particular that the consumer may cancel the contract at any time, free of charge and without penalty. The requirement of sanctions for non-compliance with the provisions arising from the directives is relatively new in consumer law directives and the provisions have become more and more elaborated over time. Whereas the general Distance Selling Directive in Article 11 under the heading 'judicial or administrative redress' only required the Member States to ensure that adequate and effective means exist to ensure compliance with the Directive in the interests of consumers, the ECD requires sanctions for non-compliance and the DMFSD is even more elaborate about sanctions.

Unlike the corresponding provision in the Distance Selling Directive and also unlike the corresponding provision in the ECD, this states a clear obligation to the Member States to ensure practical compliance with the provisions of the Directive.

---

[87] A Gkoutzinis, 'The Promotion of Financial Services via the Internet—a Comparative Study of the Regulatory Framework' (2002) *BJIB & FL* 29.

13. Redress

Article 13 and 14 of the Directive deal with redress, Article 13 deals with judicial and administrative redress and Article 14 with out-of-court redress. This is more elaborate, unlike previous Directives, and shows the development in the EU law towards a higher level of consumer protection and generally a higher level of harmonisation. But again, the question of jurisdiction is not regulated.[88]

(a) *Judicial and Administrative Redress*

Article 13(1) and (2) use basically the same wording as used in the Distance Selling Directive for the requirement of judicial and administrative redress, with only one small difference. The wording of Article 13(3) seems to indicate its aim more clearly than the corresponding provision in the DSD:

> Member States shall take the measures necessary to ensure that operators and suppliers of means of distance communication put an end to practices that have been declared to be contrary to this Directive, on the basis of a judicial decision, an administrative decision or a decision issued by a supervisory authority notified to them, where those operators or suppliers are in a position to do so.

This again, like the provisions on sanctions for non-compliance with the implemented provisions of the Directives, shows a clear obligation to the Member States to ensure the practical compliance with the provisions of the Directive.

The reasons for the slightly different regulations in the three Directives related to distance marketing cannot be found in different requirements of the regulated areas, as these Directives do have great overlaps in their scope of application and there is no need for different treatment resulting from the different areas regulated. The reasons lie more in the different time at which the Directives were adopted, and experience with the practical application of previous Directives.

(b) *Out-of-Court Redress*

Out-of-court redress is a mechanism that has been promoted within the EU only recently. Disputes on cross-border consumer contracts are very often not of high value but seeking redress can be very difficult, long and expensive for the consumer and could in practice restrict the consumer's rights and affect consumer participation in the Internal Market. As this result would be contrary to the aims of the EU law and the Internal Market in general and consumer law in particular, the Commission launched out-of-court dispute settlement systems especially aimed at consumer contracts.

---

[88] Jurisdiction in contracts and consumer contracts is however harmonised in the EU via the Brussels Regulation—see further C Waelde, ch 1 in this volume.

Article 14 of the DMFSD, like Article 17 of the ECD, encourages Member States to promote the setting up or development of out-of-court dispute settlements for consumer complaints concerning financial services provided at distance. If any bodies responsible for out-of-court dispute settlement exist, the Member States shall encourage these bodies to cooperate in the resolution of cross-border disputes. In addition to these requirements, the European Commission has encouraged the development of a voluntary electronic dispute settlement system as well as a network of existing out-of-court dispute settlement bodies specialising in financial services in the Member States (FIN-NET).

E. Implementation

In the UK, the Directive has been implemented by the Financial Services (Distance Marketing) Regulations 2004,[89] which came into force on 31 October 2004. Most of the provisions of the DMFSD were directly transposed into the Regulations, with no-or only very small amendments-to the text of the Directive. The amendments are mainly due to a slightly different use of terminology in the national law but do not result in any substantial change. Only the provisions on unsolicited communications in Article 10 of the Directive were not included in the Regulations; as these provisions are already covered more extensively by regulations 19–26 of the Privacy and Electronic Communications (EC Directive) Regulations 2003.[90]

Regulations 3–5 identify the transactions to which the substantive provisions of the Regulations apply and implement the definitions of Article 2 of the DMFSD. Regulation 6 sets out how the Regulations apply if financial services are marketed through an intermediary. Regulations 7 and 8 and the Schedules deal with the information obligations and require suppliers of financial services to provide consumers with all information listed in the Schedules. This information generally has to be provided before the consumer is bound by a distance contract. Regulation 9 contains the right to cancel, specifying the means by which the right can be exercised and defining the effect of cancellation as termination of the contract at the time at which the notice of cancellation is given. Regulation 10 defines the period during which the cancellation right can be exercised; this follows the requirements of the Directive. Regulation 11 lists certain types of contracts to which the cancellation right does not apply. Regulation 12 provides that, where a contract is cancelled under regulation 9, certain other subsidiary distance

---

[89] SI 2004 No 2095, implementing the Privacy and Electronic Communications Directive 2002: see further Edwards, ch 4.

[90] SI 2003 No 2426.

contracts connected with that contract are automatically cancelled too. Regulation 13 provides for the consequences of cancellation of distance contracts and requires the supplier to refund any sums received from the consumer under the contract, less a proportionate charge for any services already supplied. Regulation 14 gives the consumer the right to cancel payment made fraudulently with a plastic card and have all sums paid re-credited or returned by the card issuer.

Regulation 15 prevents consumers from being bound by any obligation in respect of financial services supplied to them if they have not asked for it. Regulation 16 is designed to prevent the Regulations being undermined. The final regulations contain or provide for enforcement mechanisms in relation to the substantive provisions of the Regulations.

9

Telecommunications (Lawful Business Practice) (Interception of Communications) Regulations 2000

Workplace Surveillance, Privacy and New Technologies

JANE FRASER[1]

Surveillance in the workplace has become a topical subject within employment law in recent years. However, the monitoring of employees at work is hardly a new phenomenon. Traditionally employers have always monitored workers to check on their conduct and performance. Employees tended only to be monitored by supervisors of the human variety. There were obvious limits to the amount of information that could be obtained and used by management.

The advent of new technology over the years has brought increasingly more sophisticated means by which employers may track their employees. There is now a healthy market in products and services designed to maximise the information that businesses can obtain and use for its personnel purposes. Software packages are routinely used to monitor email and Internet use, which are now common in UK workplaces, for example. Law in this area has had to develop to draw the boundary between lawful tracking and unlawful intrusion. This chapter will look at these new forms of workplace monitoring and the extent to which the law presently operates as a restraint to employers.

---

[1] Solicitor, Maclay Murray & Spens, Solicitors.

A. The Scope of Monitoring At Work

A plethora of tracking devices are now available. Employees may be monitored by CCTV cameras, active badges/ location trackers,[2] their emails can be read, their telephone conversations can be listened to and recorded, logs can be made of the telephone numbers they call or receive calls from, and the addresses of the websites that they visit can also be logged. In doing all this, employers have various choices to make as to the style of monitoring they wish to pursue, such as whether to monitor on a continuous or occasional basis or a combination of both. Whatever the means and methods of monitoring used, what is clear is that more and more employers are engaging in some form of monitoring. The most common kind is probably monitoring the use of email and Internet facilities and employers commonly issue policies making it clear that they reserve the right to monitor use of the company systems.

B. Why Do Employers Monitor?

Why do employers feel the need to use the technology available to monitor their staff? Would there not be a better environment if employees felt that they were trusted? Employers monitor for a variety of reasons. One reason is to retain control and to protect themselves from potential legal liabilities. The fact is that many employers simply want to know what is going on. Employers monitor to check on the performance and the conduct of their employees; they want to know about their staff's efficiency and productivity.

The introduction into the workplace of Internet and email facilities was originally hailed as bringing improved efficiency to the workplace. However, providing access to such facilities can result in lost working time as employees are engaged in sending private emails or looking at web pages when they should be working. There are also various other risks associated with providing such facilities to employees. One issue is that of security; this covers both the prevention of viruses entering the system and the protection of trade secrets or confidential information. The damage caused to businesses by viruses introduced to their systems is regularly documented in the media. Firewalls are commonly used to block inappropriate or suspect files finding their way onto business systems. Other operational issues include the need to back up emails or other important files to allow recovery in the event of loss or destruction.

---

[2] These are worn like normal security tags and emit below-red signalling allowing the monitor to track the location of the wearer.

However, the main risk perhaps arises in relation to inappropriate use of the facilities by employees. Contracts or damaging admissions can easily be made by emails that can have unintended consequences. Expensive actions for defamation have followed embarrassing emails sent by employees criticising products and services offered by competitors. Recent discrimination cases have also highlighted the ease with which bullying or harassing emails can be recovered by technical means. In August 2003 a company of financial advisers paid a former employee £10,000 in order to settle a sexual harassment case that she had brought against them. The case had arisen out of the discovery by the former employee that nine of her colleagues were circulating obscene email about her.[3] Viewing or circulating pornography has also emerged as a particular workplace problem for employers to deal with in recent years.[4] At the extreme end of this scale, there is the risk that facilities could be used for illegal purposes such as downloading child pornography or committing fraud.

CCTV cameras are common in certain workplace environments for security reasons. Banks, building societies, petrol stations, retail stores, jewellery stores, casinos and other such establishments make use of surveillance cameras. Even outdoor workers may find themselves caught on security camera in their local high street, for example. Whilst most are used for security purposes, there can also be other uses, such as companies employing mystery shoppers with hidden cameras as part of evaluating customer care standards and performance.

There is no doubt that many employers have good business reasons for carrying out some form of monitoring. Equally, however, employers need to be aware that monitoring inevitably brings varying degrees of intrusion into the lives of their workers. The law on employee monitoring has developed to recognise and try to deal with the tension that exists here. The key for any business is to keep their monitoring within the law and find the right balance for them.

C. Unlawful Monitoring: Overview of the Pitfalls

The law that currently applies to employee monitoring is far from straightforward and comes from a variety of sources. First of all, the common law implies a fundamental term into every contract of employment that each party owes a duty of mutual trust and confidence to the other. An employer must not take steps to damage or destroy this relationship without reasonable or proper cause.[5] Whilst

---

[3] *Workplacelaw Network*, http://www.workplacelaw.net, Law Centre Resources, 22 August 2003.

[4] A recent UK survey indicated that disciplinary cases for email and internet abuse exceeded those for dishonesty, violence and health and safety breaches put together—European Industrial Relations Observatory On-line: www.eiro.eurofound.eu.int.

[5] *Woods v WM Car Services* [1982] Com L Rev 208.

there is little case law in the context of employee monitoring to date, it is thought that this contractual duty may operate as an important restraint on employers not to subject workers to disproportionate monitoring.[6] Breach of this term allows an employee to resign from employment and claim unfair constructive dismissal under the Employment Rights Act 1996.

Monitoring will also usually need to comply with legislation such as the Human Rights Act 1998 (HRA) and the Data Protection Act 1998 (DPA). The HRA impacts on employee monitoring because it provides the right of the employee to a private life. This has been found to extend to the workplace, although the right is qualified rather than absolute. It also impacts on the admissibility of evidence that employers have gathered through unlawful monitoring at work. As public bodies, courts and tribunals must consider the HRA when considering the admissibility of evidence. The DPA is mainly concerned with the gathering and use of personal information in relation to individuals and in practice operates as the main restraint upon employee monitoring.

Whilst the HRA and the DPA will generally apply to most forms of monitoring that employers carry out, there are additional restrictions which are specific to monitoring communications, such as telephone calls or emails. The Regulation of Investigatory Powers Act 2000 (RIPA) and the Telecommunications (Lawful Business Practice) (Interception of Communications) Regulations 2000 (LBP Regulations)[7] operate to allow the interception of communications only for certain specified purposes.

1. The Human Rights Act 1998

The Human Rights Act 1998 incorporated the European Convention on Human Rights ('the Convention'), into our domestic legislation and its provisions came into force on 2 October 2000, heralded as a landmark change to the UK constitution.

In relation to monitoring at work, the main interest lies in Article 8 of the Convention which guarantees the respect for private and family life:

Article 8: Respect for Private and Family Life

Everyone shall have the right to respect for his private and family life, his home and his correspondence.

There shall be no interference by a public authority with the exercise of this right except such as in accordance with the law and is necessary in a democratic society in the interests of national security, public safety or the economic well-being of the country, for

---

[6] In one recent case an employee was unsuccessful in arguing that a drugs test carried out after an office Christmas party was intended to damage his good character without good reason: EAT/1140/01 *Dolby Hotel Liverpool v Farley* (30 October 2002).

[7] SI 2000/2699.

the prevention of disorder or crime, for the protection of health or morals, or the protection of the rights and freedoms of others.

Cases before the European Court of Human Rights (ECHR) have shown that Article 8 does provide employees with a degree of privacy in the workplace, but that this right to privacy is qualified.[8] This means that it is possible to interfere with an employee's right to privacy but only lawfully in the circumstances prescribed by Article 8(2).

One of the seminal cases in this area is *Halford v UK*.[9] Alison Halford was the Assistant Chief Constable of Merseyside Police. In her role, she had been given two telephones, one for business use and the other for personal use. She was assured that the calls made on the personal telephone would not be monitored or recorded. This was important to her as she used this telephone to contact her solicitor during working hours, in relation to a discrimination complaint she was pursuing against the police force. When she found out that her calls had indeed been intercepted on this telephone, she brought an action claiming a breach of Article 8(1) of the Convention. The ECHR agreed that she had been given a reasonable expectation of privacy and that her rights under Article 8 had thereby been infringed by the Police.

The importance of this case, now that the HRA is in force, is to highlight that workers may take direct legal action against public authorities where they feel their privacy at work has been violated. This arguably extends beyond telephone calls to any other area where workers have been given, or otherwise have a reasonable expectation of, privacy. Many employers responded to the case by making clear that all calls made or emails sent using company systems are not private and may be intercepted by the business. However, the effectiveness of a blanket 'no privacy' position is open to challenge, given that it runs against both the contractual duty of trust and confidence, as well as the recent recognition within data protection law that workers are entitled to a degree of privacy within their workplace.

Direct claims under the HRA however only lie against public authorities.[10] If the employer is not a public authority then generally it is not bound directly by the HRA. The Convention however does have an important indirect effect on all other employers, because all primary and secondary legislation will so far as possible be interpreted in a way which is compatible with the HRA.[11] Employment tribunals and courts therefore have to make sure that statutory concepts such as unfair dismissal are interpreted in light of Convention rights. Any breach of Convention rights is therefore highly relevant to litigation involving private as well as public authority employers.

---

[8] Eg, *Niemietz v Germany* (1993) 16 EHRR 97; and *Halford v UK* (1997) 24 EHRR 523.
[9] Above, n 8.
[10] S 6, HRA—discussion of the definition of a 'public authority' is beyond scope of this chapter.
[11] S 3(1), HRA.

It is probably fair to say that the extent to which a right to privacy at work is recognised under Article 8 remains to be seen. More cases are certain to come before courts and tribunals which challenge the legality of employer monitoring and consider how far reasonable expectations of privacy at work should actually extend. The concept of proportionality is firmly enshrined in Convention jurisprudence and is likely to be influential in relation to arguments as to lawful interferences under Article 8(2). It would not be surprising to see other applicable legislation (such as data protection law) play an important role here by setting some boundaries in relation to privacy at work.

Article 6(1) of the Convention is also relevant to the question of whether an employer may be able to lead evidence which has been obtained through unlawful monitoring:

Article 6: Right to a Fair Trial

In the determination of his civil rights and obligations or of any criminal charge against him, everyone is entitled to a fair and public hearing within a reasonable time by an independent and impartial tribunal established by law. Judgement shall be pronounced publicly but the press and public may be excluded from all or part of the trial in the interests of orals, public order or national security in a democratic society, where the interests of juveniles or the protection of the private lives of the parties so require, or to the extent strictly necessary on the opinion of the court in special circumstances where publicity would prejudice the interests of justice.

There has been recent controversy over the extent to which evidence obtained by way of unlawful monitoring may be admissible before courts and tribunals. The cases to date indicate that unlawful monitoring, including breaches of Article 8(1), will not necessarily result in the evidence being inadmissible.

In *Jones v University of Warwick*[12] the Court of Appeal allowed evidence consisting of covertly filmed footage of a personal injury claimant obtained by an insurance agent who had gained access into her home whilst posing as a market researcher. Whilst the Court was clearly uncomfortable with the methods that had been used to obtain the evidence, they took the view that it would breach the right of the defendant to a fair trial under Article 6 of the Convention, not to allow the evidence to be shown.[13]

This case was recently followed by the Employment Appeal Tribunal (EAT) in the case of *Avocet Hardware v Morrison*.[14] In that case a telesales operator was dismissed for gross misconduct and raised a claim for unfair dismissal. The critical evidence that the employer had was a tape recording of the operator making inappropriate comments to a client. The call was made during business hours, on the

---

[12] [2003] 1 WLR 954 (CA).

[13] The court reflected its disapproval in the order for costs in connection with the admissibility of evidence question against the defendant.

[14] [2003] All ER (D) 126.

employer's telephone, in the course of employment. The employer however had not informed the operator his calls could be monitored. The EAT referred to *Jones* and held that the employment tribunal below had been wrong to disallow the evidence on the basis that this might breach Article 8. Although the respondent had obtained the evidence unlawfully in terms of RIPA and Article 8, the principal duty of the employment tribunal under Article 6(1) was to ensure a fair trial took place. In that case there was no dispute that the comments were made; rather the dispute was around context and intent and the best evidence was the tape.

Despite these cases, it would be dangerous for any employer to assume that unlawfully obtained evidence will always be admissible. The more intrusive the surveillance has been the less likely a court is to allow it to be heard. Much will depend on the facts and circumstances of each case but a challenge to admissibility should always be expected.

2. The Data Protection Act 1998

The DPA is a complex piece of legislation which deals with how 'personal data' is obtained and otherwise processed in relation to living individuals. The Act does not apply to pure monitoring itself (such as viewing by means of a CCTV camera) but will apply whenever information is recorded by automated means (so for example would apply to any CCTV camera recording). For this reason, it will usually apply to any information obtained or held by an employer by monitoring communications.

The main requirement under the DPA is for the information to be obtained, held and otherwise processed fairly and lawfully.[15] Other provisions add that the information must be processed only for the stated purposes, must not be excessive or irrelevant in relation to these purposes, must not be kept for longer than is necessary, and must be kept securely.[16] Individuals are entitled to seek access to this information by making a subject access request.[17] This clearly places a number of restrictions on monitoring employees.

Compliance will usually require, as a minimum, that employees are told what information may be held and processed on them, the circumstances in which monitoring may take place and the purposes for which this information will be used. Unless there are genuinely exceptional circumstances, employers must therefore tell their workers what monitoring will take place.[18] This can be done by way of warnings in staff communications policies or for example by displaying prominent signs near CCTV cameras. In addition, the employer needs to be able

---

[15] Para 1, Pt 1, Sch 1, DPA.
[16] Pt 1, Sch 1, DPA.
[17] S 7, DPA.
[18] See below for discussion of covert surveillance.

to demonstrate either that (a) the employee has consented or (b) that the processing is necessary for one of the conditions set out in the Act.[19] It is thought however that 'consent' is difficult to rely on, since it needs to be 'freely given, specific and informed'.[20] Employers should therefore ensure that all monitoring is conducted proportionately and only for legitimate business interests.

In order for monitoring to be proportionate it must be a response to the actual risks faced by the business and not excessive. For example, it is not enough for a company to decide that, in order to ensure that email and Internet policies are being complied with, it will routinely open and read personal emails sent or received by its employees. Similarly, whilst restricted use of CCTV cameras is acceptable for security purposes, it is likely to be excessive to use similar cameras for performance management purposes. Even where express consent has been given, such processing is likely to be excessive in relation to the legitimate business purposes.

The information obtained or accessible to the company from the monitoring activities must not be kept longer than is necessary for the business purpose. Employees should be advised on the likely amount of time the information will be kept for.

Personal data also needs to be processed lawfully. This means that all other requirements (including under RIPA or the LBP Regulations) must be complied with otherwise there will be a breach of the DPA and potentially the HRA. The scope of the term 'personal data' was addressed in *Durant v FSA* in which it was held that the qualifying data will be 'biographical in a significant sense' and have the 'data subject as its focus'.[21]

3. The Code of Practice

A Code of Practice is being published by the Information Commissioner in four parts, which provides guidance or 'benchmarks' for employers to meet, in order to comply with the DPA. Part 3 of this Code of Practice focuses specifically on 'Monitoring at Work'.[22] Whilst the Code is not legally binding, it is likely to be influential when considering whether a breach of the Act has taken place. The

---

[19] See Sch 2, DPA: one condition is for legitimate business purposes which do not have unwarranted interference with rights of individuals. Note that the processing of 'sensitive personal data' also needs to satisfy more limited conditions in Sch 3.

[20] This 'consent' difficulty comes from the parent Data Protection Directive 95/46 from which the DPA is derived.

[21] *Durant v FSA* [2004] FSR 28. See further L Edwards, 'Taking the "Personal" Out of Personal Data: *Durant v FSA* and its Impact on the Legal Regulation of CCTV' (2004) 1:2 *SCRIPT-ed*, <http://www.law.edac.uk/ahrb/script-ed/issue2/durant.asp>.

[22] The Information Commissioner is the government agency responsible for publishing guidance and taking enforcement action in relation to data protection. The Employment Practices Data Protection Code is being issued under s 51 of the DPA and is available to download at www.dataprotection.gov.uk.

Code is detailed and represents the best guidance available to employers on how to meet requirements of data protection law.

The Code sets out the following core principles for employers on the subject of monitoring:

- It is usually intrusive to monitor workers;
- Workers have legitimate expectations that they can keep their personal lives private and that they are also entitled to a degree of privacy in the work environment;
- If employers wish to monitor workers, they should be clear about the purpose and satisfied that the particular monitoring arrangement is justified by real benefits that will be delivered;
- Workers should be aware of the nature, extent and reasons for any monitoring, unless (exceptionally) covert monitoring is justified;
- In any event, workers' awareness will influence their expectations.[23]

The Code makes clear that the DPA does not prevent monitoring from taking place. Its main purpose is to ensure that any adverse impact of monitoring on individuals is outweighed by the benefits to employers and others. It states that in all but the most straightforward cases employers should carry out an impact assessment in order to consider the business need for monitoring against the adverse impact this may have on individuals. This assessment should also look at whether the same or similar benefits could be achieved by less intrusive means and should ultimately conclude whether the monitoring is justified or not in the circumstances. One specific example given is that it is less intrusive to use content analysis software to check compliance with email and Internet policies rather than personally randomly reading emails. Impact assessments should be retained for future use in case the basis for monitoring is later challenged.

The Code confirms that the proper carrying out of an impact assessment will generally allow monitoring that does not require individual consent unless sensitive personal data is being processed.[24] There is also detailed guidance in the Code on monitoring communications. In particular, the Code emphasises that any clearly personal communications should not be monitored, save in exceptional circumstances. The safest view is therefore that any monitoring of personal email folders would require a specific reason, perhaps for example to investigate a specific complaint of harassment.

The Code states that covert monitoring should not normally be considered unless there are grounds for suspecting criminal activity or malpractice, where

---

[23] Pt 3.2.
[24] Sensitive personal data is defined in s 2 of the DPA and includes your racial or ethnic origins, your political opinions, your religious beliefs or other beliefs of a similar nature, your membership or otherwise of a trade union, your physical or mental health or condition or the commission or alleged commission by you of any offence.

notification to individuals about the monitoring would prejudice its prevention or detection. It suggests that the police should be involved in all such cases.[25]

It is unclear to what extent workers may be filmed by mystery shoppers. As a minimum, employees will have to be told in advance by employers that this might happen. The more frequent and intrusive the surveillance, however, the less likely it is to comply with the DPA. Restricting monitoring to genuine business need is therefore vital.[26]

The Code has been criticised for being too complex and going too far towards recognising a right of privacy at work not warranted by the DPA. This remains to be seen as cases emerge which test the legislation. Nevertheless, in the meantime the Code stands as an extremely helpful document looking at all the various issues which surround employee monitoring, and represents guidance which employers ignore at their peril.

4. The Regulation of Investigatory Powers Act 2000 (RIPA)

As outlined earlier, RIPA and the LBP Regulations (discussed below) apply only to the interception of communications, whether on private or public systems. The legislation sets out the lawful conditions under which such interceptions may take place. Failure to comply gives rise to both criminal and civil liability on the part of the person making the interception.[27] Networks which are entirely self-contained, such as office Intranets, are not subject to this legislation. Interception is defined as the modifying or interfering or monitoring of a communication, so 'as to make some or all of the contents of the communication available, while being transmitted, to a person other than the sender or intended recipient of the communication'.[28]

The effect of RIPA is that employers may only lawfully intercept communications in the following two situations:

- where the interception is carried out with the permission of all the parties involved in the communication; or
- where the interception complies with one of the exceptions provided for in the Telecommunications (Lawful Business Practice) (Interception of Communications) Regulations 2000 (LBP Regulations).[29]

The primary concern for employers is whether they should seek consent from their employees to monitor their communications, or whether they should rely on

---

[25] Pt 3.5.1.

[26] The Information Commissioner has also published a specific Code of Practice on the use of CCTV cameras under s 51(3)(b) of the DPA, which is available to download at www.dataprotection.gov.uk.

[27] S 1(2), RIPA.

[28] S 2(2), RIPA.

[29] SI 2000/2699.

the LBP Regulations. The difficulties of obtaining effective consent have already been discussed above in relation to data protection law. This is compounded here by the requirement that 'all parties' to the communication consent, which may include all parties outside the business who may telephone or email its employees.[30] For this reason, the safest route for employers is thought to be to proceed by way of complying with the LBP Regulations.

5. The LBP Regulations

The Regulations state that in order for an employer to intercept an employee's communications the employer must make all reasonable efforts to inform every person who may use the telecommunication system in advance that their communications may be intercepted.[31] The information must therefore be brought to the attention of all employees who use the system in such a way that everyone will be aware that monitoring will take place. This must be done before any monitoring of the system takes place. If suitable notice is not drawn to the fact that monitoring is likely to take place then all monitoring will be unlawful under RIPA. The DTI guidelines suggest that businesses should place a note in staff contracts or in other readily available literature informing staff that interceptions may take place.[32] Electronic warnings might also assist with this.

Interception may only take place for the following limited reasons:

- To establish the existence of facts relevant to the business (eg archiving and examining business related emails in future);
- To ascertain compliance with regulatory or self-regulatory practices or procedures relevant to the business (eg legal obligations or industry wide practices or procedures);
- To ascertain or demonstrate standards which are or ought to be achieved by persons using the system (eg quality control or staff training purposes);
- To prevent or detect crime (eg monitoring or recording to detect fraud or corruption);
- To investigate or detect the unauthorised use of systems (eg monitoring to ensure that employees do not breach company email and Internet policy); or
- To ensure the effective operation of the system (eg monitoring for viruses or other threats to the system).

---

[30] There has been a discussion as to whether the word 'user' goes beyond that of 'employee', eg, see Baigent, 'Your Call May be Recorded' (2001) 7(5) *CTLR* 104; however the DTI in Annex C: Notes for Business The Telecommunications (Lawful Business Practice) (Interception of Communications) Regulations 2000 at pt 4 do not think that it does.

[31] S 3(2)(c), LBP Regulations. This leads to many companies advising callers at the outset of calls that they may be recorded and placing similar warnings in email disclaimers.

[32] Annex C: Notes for Business The Telecommunications (Lawful Business Practice) (Interception of Communications) Regulations 2000, pt 4.

The LBP Regulations also permit monitoring (but not recording) to determine whether communications are relevant to the business. This would allow an employee's email or voicemail to be checked if they were on holiday or off sick.

An additional control that the Regulations place on all interceptions is that they must be relevant to the business. If it is not relevant to the business then it will not be permitted under the LBP Regulations. The term 'relevant' is defined broadly however and includes any communication which relates to the business or takes place in the course of carrying out that business. A private email sent 'out of hours' which breaches company email and Internet use policy is therefore likely to be 'relevant' to the business. Whilst businesses need to be aware of RIPA and the LBP Regulations, the main requirement is clearly that of advising employees that monitoring shall take place. The grounds on which interception may take place have been criticised as so vague as to generally allow any monitoring which is in some way connected to the business. However, the various limitations of the DPA discussed above will also usually apply to such monitoring.

If businesses need to intercept outside the scope of the Regulations then they must get the consent of the sender and the recipient as prescribed under RIPA.

D. Method of Monitoring

Once it has been established that a certain type of monitoring is justified within these limitations, it may be a salutary exercise to consider how the monitoring will be achieved. A surfeit of content-scanning technologies and software packages are available for employers to choose from, but recent data from the US suggests that many employers are not confident that such software fulfils its job description.[33] Up to 40% of the firms surveyed employ or intend to employ staff specifically to monitor outbound email content. This of course raises its own issues not only in terms of appropriate training and awareness of the issues already outlined here, but also in terms of who will monitor those individuals.

However, employers have reason to question the efficacy and even desirability of software solutions. The rise of the internet as a day-to-day business medium and resource has led to prolific numbers of PCs being infected with spyware technology, through workers downloading seemingly innocuous and legitimate applications or even through software applications such as those used to monitor employees. Spyware is to be feared, not only for its ability to destroy entire hard drives, but also for its potential use in industrial espionage and fraud or the increased risk of breaches in client confidentiality. Businesses must look to their IT

---

[33] Survey conducted by Forrester Consulting on behalf of Proofpoint (a security software firm). Reported on www.out-law.com, 14 July 2004.

security infrastructure to ensure they are adequately protected through the anti-spyware products available. Employers too may experience the discomfort of being watched.

E. Conclusion

It can be see that there are various limitations placed on the means by which employers can monitor the workplace. At the centre of these restrictions lie the concepts of fairness, transparency and proportionality. Employers who carefully consider why they need to monitor, the means by which they monitor and the impact it will have upon employees, and clearly explain to workers the extent of any monitoring that will take place, will thereby comply with many of the legal requirements, which are designed to protect against secretive and invasive information-gathering in the workplace. There is arguably no need to be daunted by the legislation that applies in this area if these basic principles can be followed. The best means to achieve this is by way of impact assessment backed up by clear policy statements on any proposed monitoring. Taking on board any views expressed by workers or trade unions would also amount to good industrial relations practice and may avoid disputes later. Many argue that increased monitoring will lead to drops in morale and satisfaction at work and this has been borne out in workplace surveys.[34] Careful thought should therefore be given to the sensitive introduction of any new systems. Ultimately, maintaining a happy and productive workforce is just as important as keeping an eye on them.

---

[34] M McGrath, 'Video Surveillance' 18 May 2000, *Source Public Management Journal*, www.sourceuk.net; M Whitty, 'Should Filtering Software be Utilised in the Workplace?' (2004) 2(1) *Surveillance & Society* 39.

10

Disability Discrimination Act 1995
Web Access and Disability

MARTIN SLOAN[1]

Whilst risk management is becoming increasingly important in modern commerce, businesses appear to be continually ignoring one issue in their quest to establish an online presence. The introduction of Part III of the Disability Discrimination Act 1995 in 1999 led to a raft of new duties on service providers. Most notable are the requirements to make adjustments to buildings, which came into force in October 2004. However, the reach of this Act is far wider. Duties extend to the virtual world as well as the physical world and this arguably includes Internet websites.

A. What is Web Accessibility?

1. An Evolving Web

The World Wide Web has become something of a modern phenomenon, having started as a relatively simple text-based way of sharing academic information in the early 1990s. Today, the Web known to most members of the public is arguably one of the strongest marketing tools available, being a convergence of various forms of media and allowing easy access to a vast array of information never previously thought possible. Estimates suggest that around 934 million people worldwide now have access to the Internet[2] and having started as a closed academic network, 'the Web' has now become an integral part of modern society.

---

[1] Solicitor and Member of the Technology and Information Group, Brodies LLP. See http://www.brodies.co.uk.
[2] According to 2004 estimates by Computer Industry Almanac Inc See Clickz Stats website: http://www.clickz.com/stats/big_picture/geographics/article.php/5911_151151.

Tim Berners-Lee, a British physicist working at the CERN research centre in Switzerland,[3] developed the World Wide Web in 1992. Berners-Lee's original vision was of a platform-independent way of sharing information between users across the world, linked together by hypertext and accessible to everyone:

The power of the Internet is in its universality. Access by everyone regardless of disability is an essential aspect.[4] This original design meant that anyone with a computer running a browser capable of interpreting a simple mark-up language (HyperText Mark-up Language or HTML) could access the network and the information available on it. As the system was purely textual and keyboard-based, the pages were as accessible to those with visual impairments, using screen-reading software, as they were to able-bodied users.

As the Web has evolved, this has changed. The ability to add video and audio content to a webpage has transformed the way that we access information, with up to the minute news sites able to stream video clips within minutes of journalists posting reports. The advent of the Web as a marketing tool has also led to the use of proprietary technologies and applications such as Flash movies and Java applets to add to the multimedia experience. However, as these technologies have been introduced, and the original tenets of the internet departed from, access has been limited to "those that have". This has resulted in the exclusion of a small, but significant community.

2. Disability and the Net

Disability can lead to several problems when accessing the Internet. Aside from visual impairments, hearing, dyslexia and motor problems can also cause a person to encounter difficulties when using a computer. However, 'assistive technologies' can often be used to overcome these problems. For example, a visually impaired person can use a web browser and a screen reader to 'speak' the text that appears on screen or a refreshable Braille display to 'feel' the text; and a person with motor problems (who is unable to use a mouse) might navigate his way around the screen using the keyboard or a special input device.

The use of these assistive technologies relies on coding webpages in compliant HTML and providing accessible alternatives where proprietary technologies are used. In recent years, Web designers have increasingly ignored these standards and used proprietary technologies without any accessible alternatives.

Examples of instances that cause problems include using images for navigation without providing an 'ALT' attribute (descriptive text that a screen reader can read); using Java based navigation applets where information is only revealed by

---

[3] http://www.cern.ch.
[4] http://www.w3c.org/WAI/.

moving the mouse over text and the exclusive use of inaccessible formats such as Flash, Shockwave and Adobe Acrobat (PDF).[5] Basic coding errors such as stipulating the formatting of text rather than referring to style sheets (such as Cascading Style Sheets) and incorrectly coded HTML can also lead to accessibility problems. Whilst modern web browsers can cope with errors in coding semantics, such errors can render a page unreadable when using assistive technologies. If style sheets are used for formatting text a user who finds a specific font size or colour scheme easier to read can choose to ignore the provided style sheet in favour of his own personal settings. Captioning or transcripts of audio and video can make content accessible to people with hearing impairments, as can descriptions of video for the visually impaired.

In recognition of this problem, the World Wide Web Consortium (W3C),[6] the body that sets and develops HTML standards, introduced its Web Accessibility Initiative (WAI) in 2000. This led to the introduction of a set of guidelines for website designers, aimed at providing guidance on developing accessible websites. However, whilst awareness of these guidelines has increased marginally since a survey in 2000 by CNN,[7] many sites still contain accessibility barriers to disabled people and breach the guidelines.[8]

Perhaps the biggest irony is that the disabled community has arguably the most to reap from embracing the Internet. For example, a supermarket's home shopping service could provide an invaluable service to a visually impaired and housebound person, who is unable to visit a supermarket, or who can only do so with the assistance of a friend. Yet if the supermarket's website is inaccessible, the people who could benefit the most will potentially be unable to use it.

3. Commercial Benefits

The issue of accessibility does not just affect users with disabilities. By alienating those without the latest technology, or who have not downloaded the latest proprietary technology plug-ins, websites are also alienating those who access the Web using older computers and software and those using Web-enabled mobile phones and PDAs. Accessible sites are often more economical in file size and faster

---

[5] Although recent versions of Macromedia's Flash technology and Adobe's popular Acrobat file format claim to be accessible, only the most recent versions of the creating software and browser plug-ins can use the accessibility features. This still leaves a huge legacy of inaccessible material on the Web.

[6] http://www.w3.org.

[7] Out of a survey of 30 blue-chip websites, only a handful admitted any interest in the issue of Web Accessibility, with far less having taken any action. CNNcom, 'Analysis: websites are locking out the disabled' (7 August 2000 11:27am EDT) http://www.cnn.com/2000/TECH/computing/08/07/web.site.accessibility.idg/index.html.

[8] The W3C's WAI Site contains advice on accessibility problems and how to fix them: http://www.w3.org/WAI/.

to download. It is no coincidence that following the tragedies of September 11 online news providers such as the BBC and CNN stripped their sites down to the bare minimum. The huge surge in demand for information led to congested servers and choked bandwidth. Only by removing graphics and unnecessary textual formatting were the services able to cope.

One also only needs to look at the most successful sites on the Net to see that good (and often accessible) site design is major factor. Sites such as Amazon.com, the BBC and in particularly Google have become major successes due to their fast, simple and easy to use websites. Yet for every Google, there are 100 Boo.coms— slow, bloated, unintuitive websites doomed to a rapid death.

Combining these benefits with the spending power of the disabled community (estimated at £40 billion in the UK alone[9]), it is clear that in addition to the legal argument, there is also a compelling commercial argument for considering website accessibility.

B. The American Approach

The United States was one of the first jurisdictions to introduce anti-disability discrimination legislation and, until the past 18 months, it seemed clear that an inaccessible website would be a breach of anti-disability discrimination legislation. However, a recent rash of cases has muddied the waters and conflicting judgments now sit uneasily with each other.

The Americans with Disabilities Act of 1990 (the ADA), Title III, introduced obligations that require the providers of 'public accommodations' to make their services accessible to disabled people by providing 'effective communication'. In defining a physical accommodation, the ADA gives a list of example situations that ranges from shops and motels to gymnasiums, museums and zoos. All the examples given share one common theme: they are all physical bricks and mortar businesses.

1. A Developing Case Law

An early case analogous to Web accessibility, considered access to telephone based mail order services by disabled people. In the 1994 case of *Carparts Distribution Center Inc v Automotive Wholesaler's Association of New England Inc*,[10] the Court

---

[9] Bob Niven, Chief Executive of the Disability Rights Commission, quoted in '"Smiles" all round as bank changes rules over access to Internet accounts' (1 June 2002) http://www.drc-gb.org/newsroom/newsdetails.asp?id=251&section=1.

[10] No 93–1954 37 F3d 12; 1994 US App LEXIS 28319; 131 ALR Fed 637; 3 Am Disabilities Cas (BNA) 1237. The Judgment also available online at http://www.harp.org/carparts.txt.

of Appeals for the 1st Circuit held that 'public accommodations' were not limited to physical structures such as shops and offices. The Court held that:

It would be irrational to conclude that persons who enter an office to purchase services are protected by the ADA, but persons who purchase the same services over the telephone or by mail are not. Congress could not have intended such an absurd result.[11]

The commonly held conclusion from the case of *Carparts* was that a clear corollary exists between telephone and mail based services and those provided over the Internet. *Carparts* has accordingly been referred to on several occasions. In the first action to have been brought relating to accessibility and the Internet, in 2000 the National Institute for the Blind sued AOL[12] on the grounds that the software provided by AOL as part of their Internet Service Provider subscription service was not compatible with screen reading software. However, the parties settled the case out of court, before the court could rule on whether web site services came within the realm of a public accommodation, with AOL agreeing to introduce screen reader compatibility in later versions of its browser software.[13]

Several months later, another action came to court, this time involving an individual who used a service providing web-based Bridge tournaments. In the case of *Hooks v OKBridge Inc*,[14] the US Department of Justice ('DOJ') submitted an *amicus curiae* or 'friend of the court' brief arguing that the ADA applied to websites.[15]

The District court had originally ruled that a website was not a public accommodation as there was 'no physical structure of facility'. However, on appeal to the Court of Appeals for the 5th circuit, the DOJ formalised its position by arguing that it was not the website itself that was the public accommodation, but rather the place where the servers are physically located was the public accommodation and the online tournaments a service of that place of public accommodation. The DOJ further argued that to say that Congress had not intended the ADA to apply to the Internet because it had not existed at the time would be akin to arguing that the First Amendment did not apply to films, as the movie industry post-dated the drafting of the Constitution.[16] The DOJ went on to point out that the ADA applies to the services 'of' a public accommodation, rather than 'at', clearly including services such as websites. Unfortunately, although the Court of Appeal found

---

[11] Web version at p 7.

[12] *National Federation of the Blind, Inc v AOL Time Warner, Inc*, Civil Action No 99–12303 (D Mass) complaint filed 16 November 1999.

[13] See CD Waddell, 'Will the National Federation for the Blind Renew their ADA Web Complaint against AOL?' (2000) 18(5) *Disability Compliance Bulletin and National Disability Reporter* 9.

[14] 1999 232 F3d 208.

[15] The *amicus curiae* are available from the US DOJ website: http://www.usdoj.gov/crt/briefs/hooks.htm.

[16] M Mason, 'Does the ADA Apply to the Web?' (2000) 15(13) *Washington Technology*. Also available from: http://www.wtonline.com/vol15_no13/federal/1815–1.html.

favour with this argument, once again the court did not reach a conclusion on the issue as it threw out Mr Hooks' action on another ground.

The next case in the building of what seemed like a coherent argument involved the American version of the TV quiz show 'Who Wants to Be a Millionaire?' In *Rendon v Valleycrest Productions Limited*,[17] individuals with hearing and mobility impairments alleged that the use of a 'Fastest Finger First' telephone-based quali-fying process for appearing on the show constituted a breach of Title III of the ADA. A telephone based quiz clearly presents problems for those with limited mobility and hearing and there was no option to use a reasonable alternative such as a text based TDD telephone.

At first instance, the District Court rejected the claim on the grounds of the interpretation of a public accommodation. The Court held that as the TV studio was the 'place' of the public accommodation the discrimination would need to take place at the studio. As the alleged discrimination in this case took place over the telephone, the Court concluded that there was no 'place' of public accommo-dation at which discrimination could have occurred. In overturning this ruling, the Court of Appeal (11th Circuit) considered this argument unpersuasive holding that the telephone-based quiz was effectively a barrier, or screen, to access to the TV studio. The ADA did not contain any wording requiring that such discrimination must take place 'on site' for a breach to occur:

Defendants urge us to hold, in effect, that so long as discrimination occurs off site, it does not offend Title III. We do not believe this is a tenable reading of Title III; indeed, off-site screening appears to be the paradigmatic example contem-plated in the statute's prohibition of 'the imposition or application of eligibility criteria that screen out or tend to screen out an individual with a disability . . .'. Furthermore, the fact that the plaintiffs in this suit were screened out by an auto-mated telephone system, rather than by an admission policy administered at the studio door, is of no consequence under the statute; eligibility criteria are fre-quently implemented off site-for example, through the mail or over the telephone. The DOJ submitted a similar *amicus curiae* in the *Rendon* case[18] and in reaching its conclusion, the 11th Circuit Court of Appeal clearly seems to have accepted the DOJ's assertion that the ADA applies to services 'of' a public accommodation, rather than 'at'. In finding in the plaintiffs' favour the Court, as in the *Carparts* case (although the plaintiff in *Rendon* did not cite it), again used its judicial inter-pretation to apply the ADA to situations outside the original list of physical accommodations.[19]

---

[17] 294 F 3d 1279 (11th Cir, 2002), reh'g denied en banc, 2002 US App LEXIS 27593 (25 October 2002).

[18] Available from http://www.usdoj.gov:80/crt/briefs/rendon.pdf.

[19] For a more detailed discussion of the *Hooks* and *Rendon* cases see the National Council for the Disabled's paper discussing the application of the ADA to websites: 'Application of the ADA to the Internet and the World Wide Web' published 10 July 2003 and available from the NCD website at: http://www.ncd.gov/newsroom/publications/adainternet.html.

2. The *Southwest Airlines* Case

The most recent and controversial case involved America's fourth largest airline, Southwest Airlines. In the case of *Access Now Inc and Robert Gumson* v *Southwest Airlines Co*,[20] Mr Gumson brought an action under Title III of the ADA. Mr Gumson and the disability rights organisation Access Now alleged that Southwest Airline's 'virtual ticket counter' operated through its website 'southwest.com' was inaccessible to blind persons and as such in breach of the ADA, relying in the main on the *Carparts* and *Rendon* cases. Southwest argued that the website was not a 'place of public accommodation' and was therefore outside the scope of Title III.

In her judgment issued on 18 October 2002, Judge Seitz found in favour of Southwest. In distinguishing the *Carparts* and *Rendon* cases, Judge Seitz noted that the concept of 'cyberspace' had been discussed in both the Court of Appeal and the Supreme Court. Both courts had agreed that cyberspace was a unique medium, which did not exist in any particular geographical location. Therefore, as Southwest.com (the place at which the discrimination took place) did not exist in any particular location it could not be a concrete physical space or public accommodation in the same way as a travel agent could.

This judgment can be criticised on a number of levels, not least Judge Seitz's fundamental misunderstanding of the concept of cyberspace and W3C guidelines. Judge Seitz dismissed the W3C guidelines because they were over three years old and there was no indication that the Guidelines were a generally accepted authority.[21] In reply to this, the W3C has issued an amicus curiae itself defending the authority of the guidelines and pointing to the continuing work carried out by it in this field.[22] That Australian case law has specifically referred to the guidelines (see below) shows that Seitz's conclusion is questionable.

More important is the discussion of the definition of 'public accommodation'. The wider interpretation shown in the *Carparts* case was rejected on two grounds: firstly, that the decision was by a different Circuit of the Court of Appeal (there are various circuits which cover four or five States) which has historically taken a wider interpretation of the ADA and secondly because *Rendon* did not even cite it. On these grounds, and its interpretation of *Rendon*, the Court dismissed the action.

The plaintiff appealed the decision. However, as expected, the Court of Appeals for the 11th Circuit dismissed the appeal on procedural grounds and did not have an opportunity to consider the greater question of the application of the ADA to

---

[20] Case No 02–21734–CIV-SEITZ/BANDSTRA (Unreported). The judgment is available in PDF format from the Florida Southern District Court website: http://www.flsd.uscourts.gov/default.asp?file=cases/index.html.

[21] *Ibid*, p 3.

[22] W3C Brief available from http://www.w3.org/2003/03/17–brief.html.

the Internet.[23] Unfortunately, public accommodations under Title III of the ADA do not include commercial airplanes. This is because separate legislation, the Air Carrier Access Act of 1986, covers access to air travel. On this basis, the Court of Appeal was bound to dismiss the action. However, it is important to note that the Court of Appeal did not uphold the ruling of the lower court and in giving its judgment highlighted the importance of the issues before it:

In declining to evaluate the merits of this case, we are in no way unmindful that the legal questions raised are significant. The Internet is transforming our economy and culture, and the question whether it is covered by the ADA—one of the landmark civil rights laws in this country—is of substantial public importance. Title III's applicability to web sites—either because web sites are themselves places of public accommodation or because they have a sufficient nexus to such physical places of public accommodation—is a matter of first impression before this Court. Unfortunately, this case does not provide the proper vehicle for answering these questions.[24]

It is clear that the Court of Appeal recognises that there are a number of outstanding questions and that interpretation of Title III of the ADA is still far from unsettled. Whilst, in the long-term, the decision in *Southwest Airlines* may be considered irrelevant, the current position is an unhappy situation where a bad case has led to bad law.[25]

3. Title II of the ADA and Section 508

Whilst Title III of the ADA relates to public accommodations, Title II of the ADA deals with State, local government bodies and commuter authorities. In the case of *Vincent Martin v Metro Atlanta Rapid Transit Authority (MARTA)*[26] an action was filed in November 2001 against a commuter authority. Title II requires that disabled people are not excluded from participation in or denied the benefits of the services, programs, or activities of a public entity, or subject to discrimination by any such entity[27]

The plaintiff alleged that MARTA was breaching its obligations under the ADA Title II by not providing timetable information on its website in an accessible

---

[23] *Access Now Inc v Southwest Airlines Company* 2004 US App LEXIS 20060; 17 Fla L Weekely Fed C 1064; No 02–16163 (11th Cir, 24 September 2004). The judgment is available in PDF format from the Findlaw website at: http://caselaw.lp.findlaw.com/data2/circs/11th/216163ppdf.

[24] *Ibid*, p 27.

[25] A recent investigation by the Attorney General in New York into Ramada and Priceline.com's websites resulted in settlements being reached between the Attorney General and the two companies involved. However, once again, a potential action has been settled prior to reaching court. See OAG's press release dated 19 August 2004: http://www.oag.state.ny.us/press/2004/aug/aug19a_04.html.

[26] No 1:01–CV–3255–TWT (ND Ga, 7 October 2002). The judgment is available in PDF format from http://www.haledorr.com/pdf/marta.pdf.

[27] ADA Title II s 202.

format. Judge Thomas W Thrash, Jr, found in favour of the plaintiff. He concluded that, as a disabled person cannot adequately use the service if the scheduling accessible information is not provided in a form accessible, MARTA were in breach of the ADA mandate of requiring that adequate communications capacity is made through accessible formats and technology.[28] Judge Seitz did discuss the case of *MARTA* in *Southwest Airlines* but ultimately rejected its relevance as it related to Title II rather than Title III under which Access Now brought their action.

In addition to Title II of the ADA, section 508 of the Rehabilitation Act of 1973 requires that Federal agencies' information technology is accessible to disabled people. Section 508 has lead to specific guidelines on website accessibility and seen a drive to require accessible websites not only for Federal agencies, but also for suppliers with whom agencies contract.

These guidelines are largely similar to the W3C WAI content guidelines. Importantly however, by applying to contractors of Federal agencies many of America's largest companies are now required to provide accessible websites under legislation other than the ADA. Section 508 has also had the interesting knock-on effect of requiring companies such as Adobe and Macromedia to make their proprietary formats such as Acrobat and Flash accessible in order that they can sell their software to Federal agencies. The effect of this has been to improve the accessibility of these proprietary formats for everyone.[29]

The case of *MARTA* and specific requirements of section 508 seem to contradict the current interpretation of Title III of the ADA following Judge Seitz's decision. The Court of Appeal for the 11th Circuit, which heard the appeal in *Rendon* (and ruled in favour of broadening the scope of the ADA), also heard the appeal in *Southwest Airlines*. Much of the current problems in the US stem from the interpretation of the term 'public accommodations' and whether Senate intended this to be interpreted beyond the ADA. It perhaps unfortunate that the Court of Appeal for the 11th Circuit was not, therefore, given the Court of Appeal to interpret its own judgment, especially in light of the strong case put forward by the DOJ through their briefs to the court. Ultimately, an unfortunate choice of wording in drafting the legislation and an unfortunate choice of defendant for a test case has led to confusion as to where the law stands.[30]

---

[28] *Ibid*, p 34.
[29] For more information on the s 508 guidelines see the Access Board's website: http://www.section508.gov.
[30] Interestingly, two previous actions brought by Access Now (against Claire's Accessories and the bookstore Barnes & Noble) both settled out of court prior to the judgment in *Southwest Airlines*. See *Wired News* 'Man sues airline for fare access' 14 October 2002, available from http://www.wired.com/news/print/0,1294,55708,00.html.

C. Australia—*Maguire v SOCOG*

Arguably, the most important case regarding Web accessibility and the law took place in Australia in spring 2000. Australia's Human Rights and Equal Opportunities Commission (HREOC), heard an action brought by Bruce Maguire, an Australian who had been blind since birth, who has become something of a warrior for disability rights in Australia. Mr Maguire brought a series of complaints against the Sydney Organising Committee for the Olympic Games (SOCOG).[31] Two of these related to the provision of ticket booklets and souvenir programs in Braille were set and the third to the inaccessibility of the SOCOG official website.

1. The Claim

Mr Maguire, a highly experienced computer user who accessed the Web using a web browser and refreshable Braille display, found that he was unable to access the Olympics website and along with his other complaints filed an action under the Commonwealth Disability Discrimination Act 1992 (the Cth DDA). He claimed that by not providing an accessible website SOCOG were discriminating against him because of his disability and as such were in breach of their duties under the Cth DDA.

Unable to resolve the issue, a hearing was set for 3 and 4 July 2000 before the HREOC. On 29 April 2000, the Mr Maguire delivered a statement in compliance with the directions of the earlier hearing before the Commission. This stated that although SOCOG had made some changes to the site it was still inaccessible on 17 April 2000. Mr Maguire requested that the Commission order that:

• SOCOG include ALT attributes on all graphics and image map links on the website;
• SOCOG ensure access from the Schedule page to the Index of Sports was provided in an accessible form; and
• that SOCOG ensure access to the Results Tables on the website during the Olympic Games was provided in an accessible form[32]

In its defence, SOCOG stated that further changes to the site had cured the lack of ALT attributes on graphics and image maps and that access to the Index of Sports had always been possible by entering the Uniform Resource Locator (URL—ie the

---

[31] H99/115 *Maguire v SOCOG* Judgment available online at http://www.hreoc.gov.au/disability_rights/decisions/comdec/2000/DD000120.htm.
[32] *Ibid*, p 3.

webpage address) for each sport directly into the web browser. In defence of the third crave, SOCOG argued that compliance would result in unjustifiable hardship and therefore it had a defence under the Cth DDA.

The statutory provisions under the Cth DDA are very similar to those contained in the UK DDA. Under section 24 of the Cth DDA, it is unlawful for a person who provides goods, facilities or services to discriminate on the grounds of disability by:

a) refusing to provide the other person with those goods or services or to make those facilities available to the other person; or

b) in the terms or conditions on which the first-mentioned person provides the other person with those goods or services or makes those facilities available to another person; or

c) in the manner in which the first-mentioned person provides the other person with those goods or services or makes those facilities available to the person

Mr Maguire alleged that as the website, the service, was only completely accessible by a fully sighted person SOCOG were discriminating on the grounds of disability and therefore breaching section 24.

In response, SOCOG claimed that to comply with Mr Maguire's request it would encounter 'unjustifiable hardship' in terms of section 24(2). 'Unjustifiable hardship' is determined by considering:

a) the nature of the benefit or detriment likely to accrue or be suffered by any persons concerned;

b) the effect of the disability of a person concerned;

c) the financial circumstances and the estimated amount of expenditure required to be made by the person claiming unjustifiable hardship; and

d) in the case of the provision of services, or the making available of facilities an action plan given to the Commission under section 64[33]

2. The Commission's Findings

The Commission dealt first with the question of whether an act of discrimination had taken place. In doing so, the Commission referred to the W3C Content Accessibility Guidelines and SOCOG's argument on 18 June 1999 that when the W3C released the Guidelines on 5 May 1999 the website had already undergone 'substantial implementation' and planning. SOCOG claimed that to apply these guidelines retrospectively would lead to unjustifiable hardship given the advanced stage of site design and construction.

---

[33] S 11.

The Commission noted however that the website had been, and indeed at the time of the hearing was still, under continual development. In evidence of this, the Commission pointed to the alterations introducing ALT attributes to the graphics which IBM, SOCOG's technology partner, expected to complete by 8 August.

The Commission further noted that SOCOG's assertion in relation to the Index of Sports links that the user could simply enter the URL for each sport went against the way that the Internet worked. One of the basic concepts of webpages and HTML is that links between pages can be coded allowing the user to jump from one page to another without having to know what the actual URL is. Indeed, the URLs used on the SOCOG website did not even follow a coherent and predictable structure: the URL for the canoe/kayak slalom page was '.../sports/CS/home.html' whereas the URL for the canoe/kayak sprint page was '.../sports/CF/home.html.' Despite this cryptic method of page identification, SOCOG and IBM actually tried to advance it as a realistic alternative to simple clickable links.[34]

The Commission therefore concluded that discrimination had taken place with respect to each of Mr Maguire's three particular accessibility issues. The Commission also held that by creating a website accessible by Internet users across Australia and the World, SOCOG was 'intending to offer a service to the public'. In this case, the Commission held the service to be the provision of a wide body of information related to the Games to Internet users across the globe. Due to the way in which SOCOG had made this information available, whilst it was perfectly accessible to a sighted person the information, and hence the service, was not available to a blind person such as Mr Maguire. As the service was not available to Mr Maguire for reasons related to his disability it therefore followed that he as a blind person received less favourable treatment and thus SOCOG was in clear breach of its obligations under the Act.

The Honourable William Carter QC, the Commissioner who chaired the hearing, went on to add further sociological reasons to his findings by stating that the Olympic Games were a unique event of great cultural significance:

It is a primary consideration that as far as possible all Australians should have the capacity to share equally in an event of this significance; an alternative source which makes available the same amount or body of information is simply not available. And finally, it is clear that the complainant is not nor is he able to comply with the relevant requirement or condition.[35]

---

[34] For further examples of the URLs used see Joe Clark's Weblog at http://www.contenu.nu/socog.html.
[35] *Maguire v SOCOG*, p 11.

3. Unjustifiable Hardship

The Commissioner considered the question of unjustifiable hardship to be a question of fact between the assessments of the work involved by expert witnesses on either side. Unsurprisingly, there were large differences between the views of the witnesses called by SOCOG and those of Mr Maguire. SOCOG called Mr Brand and Mr Smeal, two IT consultants based in Sydney, who estimated that the work required to make the website accessible would cost Au$2.2m and take 368 working days. In contrast, Mr Maguire's expert witnesses, Ms Treviranus (an academic and W3C Chair) and Mr Worthington (an architect of the Commonwealth Government's Internet and Web strategy) argued that the cost of compliance would be modest and take a small team about four weeks. Ms Treviranus further suggested that a fully accessibly site could have been achieved within 1% of the total time taken to create the website to date, had accessibility been considered from the start.

In favouring the evidence of Mr Maguire's expert witnesses, the Commission noted that SOCOG had engaged its witnesses only days before the hearing, when SOCOG realised that it would have to form a case for the defence. Due to their late appointment, Mr Brand and Mr Smeal had only limited access to both the site and information. By contrast, Mr Maguire's witnesses had been engaged in the issue for several months. The Commission also held the experience and authority carried by Mr Maguire's witnesses to be highly persuasive in favouring their evidence.

In light of these facts, the Commission went on to consider the test of unjustifiable hardship under section 11. This test could be reduced to the measuring of the potential benefit to the complainant compared to the detriment and hardship that the defendant would incur following compliance with the Act. In this case, there was immense potential benefit to Mr Maguire, whilst the detriment suffered by SOCOG would be moderate and, had it considered the issue of accessibility throughout the design, potentially negligible.

On these grounds, the Commission concluded that the unjustifiable hardship claim to be unfounded. Further comment regarding SOCOG's constant procrastination in attempting to delay or stop proceedings at every possible opportunity by suppressing information about the site on the grounds of 'confidentiality' also helped to undermine SOCOG's defence.[36] The Commission felt that this effectively acted as a bar against the use of the section 11 defence. Had SOCOG attended to the accessibility issues when Mr Maguire first raised his complaint in June 1999, the time taken to implement the changes would be irrelevant and the costs would have

---

[36] *Ibid* p 5. Mr Maguire sought this information following a submission made on behalf of SOCOG that to comply with the W3C Guidelines on accessibility it would 'have to retrain many of its staff and redraw its entire development methodology . . . such expense would be an unjustifiable financial imposition' under s 11.

been absorbed over a greater period. The suggestion is therefore that even if the Commission had not accepted Mr Worthington and Ms Treviranus' evidence it would still have rejected SOCOG's defence under section 11.

D. The Disability Discrimination Act

The Disability Discrimination Act 1995 (the DDA) forms the basis for disability-discrimination legislation in UK. The DDA is very similar to the Cth DDA in both its requirements and application and, in the absence of any test case thus far in the UK,[37] this similarity of legislation could be of critical importance in establishing a legal obligation on service providers to provide their Web presence in an accessible form.

1. The Act and its Obligations

The Disability Discrimination Bill was introduced to Parliament by the then Minister for Social Security and Disabled People, William Hague, following 14 previous backbench attempts to provide disabled people with similar rights to those contained in the sex and race relations legislation. The Bill received Royal Assent in November 1995 and the Disability Discrimination Act 1995 came into force gradually over the next few years.

Part III (Discrimination in other areas) of the Act relates to the provision of Goods, Facilities, Services and Premises and is:

> A universal, all embracing right of non-discrimination against disabled people
> ... applicable to all providers of goods, facilities and services to the general public, with the specific exclusions of transport and education[38] [and] will not only prohibit discriminatory behaviour but also require positive action which is reasonably and readily achievable to overcome physical and communication barriers that impede disabled people's access.[39]

As with Part II of the DDA (Employment), a Code of Practice accompanied the introduction of Part III on 1 October 1999 ('the Code').[40] The Code's primary function is to provide guidance to both service providers and disabled people.

---

[37] Recent reports have suggested that the RNIB will soon be launching a test case; however, at the time of writing, the RNIB are unable to confirm this, or the parties involved, for legal reasons. See *The Guardian* 'Access All Sights', 4 September 2003, available from: http://www.guardian.co.uk/online/story/0,3605,1034801,00.html.

[38] Minister for Social Security and Disabled People, *Hansard*, HC Standing Committee E col 290.

[39] White Paper, *Ending all discrimination against disabled people*, Cm 2729(1995) para 4.4.

[40] The Code is now in its second edition. Current version: Disability Rights Commission *Code of Practice: Rights of Access: Goods, Facilities, Services and Premises* (2002).

Whilst the Code is not an authoritative statement of the law, there is a requirement that a court consider any part of the Code which seems to be relevant to the case before it. However, the intention of the Code is to prevent the need to resort to legal action in the first place by suggesting and encouraging good practice and early or alternative dispute resolution.[41]

The DDA also led to the establishment of the Disability Rights Commission ('the DRC') under the Disability Discrimination Act 1999. The DRC[42] has taken over the duties of the National Disability Council and is now responsible for drafting the various Codes of Practice. In addition to this, the DRC is responsible for the advancement of disability rights and has limited powers to seek compliance with the DDA.

Part III of the DDA sets out four ways in which a provider of services can discriminate against a disabled person, three of which are relevant to the issue of Web accessibility:

a) in refusing to provide, or deliberately not providing, to the disabled person any service which he provides, or is prepared to provide, to members of the public;
b) in failing to comply with any duty imposed on him by section 21 in circumstances in which the effect of that failure is to make it impossible or unreasonably difficult for the disabled person to make use of any such service;
c) in the standard of service which he provides to the disabled person or the manner in which he provides it to him.[43]

Under the DDA, anyone considered a 'disabled person' can claim protection from alleged discrimination. The definition of 'disability' is set out under sections 1–2 and schedules 1–2 and the Code defines this as 'someone who has a physical or mental impairment which has an affect on his or her ability to carry out normal day-to-day activities.'[44] This impairment must be substantial, adverse and long term. It is therefore clear that the majority of disabilities associated with Web accessibility problems come within the scope of the DDA. The DDA may even protect a person with learning difficulties who struggles to read long and complicated passages of text in certain circumstances.

The DDA defines discrimination as a two-part test. Under section 20, the provider of services discriminates against a disabled person if

a) for a reason which relates to the disabled person's disability, he treats him less favourably than he treats or would treat others to whom that reason does not or would not apply; and
b) he cannot show that the treatment in question is justified

---

[41] *Ibid*, para 10.14.
[42] http://www.drc-gb.org.
[43] S 19.
[44] Para 2.9. For a further discussion of the meaning of 'disability' see A Samuels, 'Disability Defined' (2000) 144(17) *Solicitors Journal* 424.

2. What is a Service Provider?

Much like the equivalent terminology in the ADA, the definition of a 'service provider' is vague and there is no specific mention of the Web as a service. This is unsurprising, given that the Web was still in its infancy in 1995. The latest draft of the Code does now refer to a website as an example of service that would be subject to the DDA. In this instance, the code gives an example of an airline's online booking service (much like that in the *Southwest Airlines* case).[45]

Using the rationale in the *Carparts* case, this seems entirely logical. As with the ADA, it is illogical that Parliament intended the DDA to apply to services offered by, for example, a travel agent in a branch, but not to the chain's website.[46]

However, whilst the Code indicates that a website such as an online booking facility comes within the definition of a service, and will therefore subject to the DDA, it is unclear as to how far this applies. For instance, what of a newspaper's website or a promotional website operated by a drinks company to run alongside a marketing campaign? To answer this one needs to look at the wording of the DDA.

The DDA defines a service by example, rather than definitively, and includes services provided for free as well as those that are charged for.[47] Amongst the eight non-exhaustive examples given is the 'access to and use of information services'.[48] Reference to *Hansard* for enlightenment as to the intention of this term is of little help. If anything, this perhaps confuses the reader even further as this term and a reference to 'communications systems' has been included to 'reflect the importance of communication and information services to disabled people.'[49] Given that the few people had heard of the Web in 1995, it is not clear what information services the Minister had in mind here. It could be that the intention was to cover telephone-based services or perhaps even closed networks such as Compuserve, the latter of which, unlike the Internet, has a clear service provider-customer relationship. However, whilst it may be possible to infer that online information services such as railway timetables and e-government sites will come within the scope of the DDA, this is complicated by further reference to *Hansard*. The DDA explicitly states that it only applies to the *provision* of goods, facilities and services and premises, not the actual product itself. Lord Mackay (the then Minister for State) further qualified this in the House of Lords when he stated that:

---

[45] For a discussion of the new Code of Practice, introduced in 27 May 2001, see M Sloan, 'Disability Laws and the Internet: an Update' (2002) 4(4) *Electronic Business Law* 5.

[46] Of course this is at odds with the position taken in the *Southwest Airlines* case discussed above, but this is of course subject to appeal.

[47] S 19(2).

[48] S 19(3)(c).

[49] Minister for Social Security and Disabled People, 16 February 1995, *Hansard* HC Standing Committee E, col 291.

This is the case even where the product could be regarded as 'information'; for example, newspapers books and television programmes. There will therefore be no requirement for those items to be made available in an accessible format.[50]

The reasons for this are clear. To extend the scope of the DDA to cover products would create an overbearing and at times completely unattainable burden on service providers. However, requiring that the service or mechanism of delivering the product be accessible is a realistic target that will make a difference to disabled people.

This however raises the question of whether a website is a service or a product. Whilst it now seems clear that an e-commerce operation is a service (in that it is the online equivalent of a shop), what of the online version of a newspaper— which in its off-line equivalent is quite definitely a product?

One can consider this question on two levels. On the one hand, a newspaper's website provides information and stories, chosen on demand by the user by clicking on the relevant link. This would seem to be an 'information service'. However, does this then mean that the actual news page delivered is then a product? Considering the design of a website from a technical point of view, there should be two distinct aspects to a correctly designed site: the content itself—i.e. the basic text contained in the page—and style applied to the page—i.e. the font and colour scheme used. The latter causes the majority of accessibility problems when designers either do not use style sheets or use them incorrectly. It is arguable that the product is the text, whereas the styles that apply to the website are part of the service delivering the product.

However, the present writer would argue that all websites come within the grouping of 'Information Services'. This is substantiated by the view of the Commission in the *SOCOG* case. As is discussed above, the Commission held that the Olympic Games website, which gave news and information on the Games, was a service that came within the scope of the Cth DDA:

> The respondent in creating its own website sought to include in it a considerable body of information to which any person could have access. The provision of the website was a *service* relating to the provision by the respondent of information relating to the largest and most significant entertainment or recreation event in the history of this country.[51]
> [emphasis added]

In addition to providing similar content to a newspaper's website, the SOCOG site also contained promotional material and information on venues. It is therefore clear that, in Australia at least, the courts will interpret the definition of service widely when considering websites.

---

[50] *Hansard* vol 566 col 251. But see ss 303–10 of the Communications Act 2003, which now require OFCOM to produce Codes of Practice setting quotas for the number of programs which are subtitled or captioned and accessibility standards of digital television etc.

[51] *SOCOG v Maguire*, p 6.

Whilst the printed media clearly falls outside the DDA, the differing nature of a website and the additional facilities and services offered by it mean that the online equivalent is likely to a service. Further, there is no reason to suspect that the courts will treat other websites, such as promotional sites, any differently.

3. The Meaning of Discrimination

Having established that most websites are likely to come within the definition of a Service, the next step is to consider whether the provision of an inaccessible site constitutes discrimination under the DDA.

The definition of discrimination is contained in section 20. Under section 20(1), discrimination occurs if for a reason related to his disability the service provider treats a disabled person less favourably than a non-disabled person and it cannot justify this treatment. This less favourable treatment must relate to the disabled person's disability. The Code gives the example of a football supporter with cerebral palsy who is the only visiting fan refused access to a football stadium, where the club can offer no other justification.[52]

To analogise this with a website, if the only people who are unable access to the website are disabled and it is because of the design of the site that they are unable to 'gain access' this less favourable treatment will amount to discrimination.

However, the Code also notes that there is a difference between bad treatment and less favourable treatment.[53] Therefore, returning to the example in the Code, if the football club refuses all the visiting fans access to the football stadium, the football club will not be treating the person with cerebral palsy any differently to his contemporaries and there will be no incidence of discrimination. This is of course subject to the proviso that the reason for turning back all the fans was that one of the fans has cerebral palsy. Developing the website analogy, this means that if the accessibility problems relate to the software or hardware the user is using there is unlikely to be an instance of discrimination. For example, if a website requires a user to have Internet Explorer 4 or higher, a disabled user who's computer only has Internet Explorer 3 will not be able to claim that he is being discriminated against on the grounds of his disability if he cannot access the site.

This question of 'social accessibility' highlights another issue. A website may post content using Adobe Acrobat's proprietary PDF format. The website operator may create the file using the latest version of Adobe Acrobat, utilising the accessibility features that can now be included when creating the file. However, to be able to access these features the latest version of Acrobat reader is required. Unlike the previous example however, earlier versions of Acrobat Reader can still read the file and non-visually impaired users will be able to view the file.

---

[52] The Code, para 3.3.
[53] The Code, para 3.5.

This therefore raises the question of whether any discrimination is taking place. The file is only inaccessible to those disabled people who do not have the latest version of Acrobat Reader, rather than all users who do not have the latest version of Acrobat Reader. The question here is whether there is a corresponding onus on the user to have the latest version of software. This will be a question of reasonableness (as discussed below) and may depend on the circumstances. It would seem unreasonable to require a disabled user to have any higher version of software than that of the 'average user'. Therefore, if most Internet users have Acrobat Reader 4, it would be unreasonable to expect all disabled users to have version 6. The reasoning behind this is that if the content contained within the PDF file has been created by the service provider (ie it is a PDF of a document it has created) it is relatively simple to create a fully accessible HTML version of the same file and host this as well. Indeed this is good practice and is something that website designers often seem to forget.

Arguably, the only occasion where the use of PDFs can be justified as the only format is in cases such as the Hutton Enquiry where scans of all the productions are available on the website. In this case, the PDF reproduces a physical printed page. As the original document would not be in a fully accessible format (i.e. there would not be a Braille version), it is unreasonable to expect that the Enquiry will produce an accessible version of each document for the website. Instead, it is reasonable to expect that a brief synopsis describing the content is available for those that cannot access the PDF version.

4. The Duties Under Sections 19(1)(a) and (C)

(a) Duty Under Section 19(1)(a)

The duty under section 19(1)(a) is the duty not to refuse to provide or deliberately not provide a service to a disabled person which the service provider provides or is prepared to provide to the public. In the case of an inaccessible website, this might include a case where a service provider has considered the issue of accessibility when creating a website, but has decided not to make the site accessible for a particular reason—such as a misguided view that it will 'look better'.[54]

The applicability of this section is however limited, as the sub-section relates to refusal or the deliberate non-provision of a service, both of which are active actions. Therefore, a service provider would at least *consider* have to accessibility before deciding to discriminate. An example here would be the US clothing retailer Gap, who were quoted in August 2000 by CNN.com as saying 'we're aware

---

[54] In reality, very few accessibility problems cannot be surmounted—for instance by creating a parallel site or the correct use of style sheets and HTML Therefore, even if a service provider did hold such a view, it is likely to be unfounded as well as in breach of the Act.

of the technologies but have no plans to implement them' when asked why the company were denying disabled people access to their e-commerce site.[55]

(b) Duty Under Section 19(1)(C)

The duty under section 19(1)(c) is not to discriminate in the standard of service or manner in which the service is offered to a disabled person. The Code gives an interesting example: a bookshop that offers a book ordering service, but refuses to order a large print book for a visually impaired customer.[56] This could be analogous to a retailer who offers an online shopping service which is available outside the normal opening hours of its 'bricks and mortar' store, but which is not accessible by disabled people. Under section 19(1)(c), this is likely to be a case of a disabled person being offered a lower standard of service as they would be unable to take advantage of the convenience and flexibility offered by the website.

Likewise, Web-based financial products such as current and savings accounts often offer preferential interest rates. If the website is inaccessible to a disabled person because of his disability, that person will be unable to use the online account and benefit from the preferential rates. In such a situation, the disabled person would have to use a branch or telephone-based account and this is likely to be a lower standard of service. A similar argument could apply to all sorts of other e-commerce operations where the service provider passes on the cost savings of operating online to the customer.

(c) Justification

Under section 20(3) of the DDA, a service provider can justify its actions under 4 grounds. The first two of these apply to both section 19(1)(a) and (c) and the third and fourth are particular to each duty:

- health and safety
- incapacity to contract
- in the case of a refusal of service under section 19(1)(a), that the service provider would otherwise be unable to provide a service to the public
- in the case of a lower standard of service, that the treatment was required in order to allow the service to be provided.[57]

It is difficult to envisage where these grounds could apply in relation to Web accessibility. There are clearly no health and safety grounds and the majority of disabilities do not affect the person's ability to contract.

---

[55] Gap Spokewoman: Anna Lonergan quoted in 'Analysis: websites are locking out the disabled', see n 7 above.

[56] Para 3.21.

[57] S 20(4).

Again, in relation to the third ground, a site that is an accessible site to disabled users will also be accessible to non-disabled people. In fact, as has already been discussed, the site will become accessible to a far wider community—for instance those using PDAs, Web TV and mobile phones. If properly implemented, an accessible site should still be able to be as visually impressive as an inaccessible site.

This also ties in with the fourth justification—it is difficult to imagine a scenario where an inaccessible site is required in order to offer a service. The requirement of a particular version of web browser for encryption reasons is unrelated to disability; rather it is a social accessibility issue, as discussed above. Indeed the only situation where this justification might apply is where the content of the site is itself intrinsically inaccessible—for instance a music download site, where it would be justifiable to argue that there is no requirement on the service provider to provide transcripts of all the songs that can be downloaded for those with hearing impairments.

The final justification is that of knowledge. The Code states that 'the lawfulness of what a service provider does or fails to do will be judged by what it knew (or could reasonably have known), what it did and why it did it *at the time* of the alleged discriminatory act.'[58] A service provider may claim to have been unaware that its site was inaccessible and thus unaware that it was in breach of its duties under the Act. However, unlike the first edition of Code, following the case of *Rose v Buouchet*[59] there is now a requirement on the service provider to make enquiries, seek advice and come to a considered position in light of the circumstances.[60]

In addition to this subjective test, there is an objective test where the court can also consider whether the service provider's view was reasonable. It is therefore possible that if a service provider failed to take advice on the legal issues regarding its website that a court could consider that it ought to have and that it was therefore in breach of its obligations under the DDA.

On the other hand, if the service provider has sought advice and believed from this that it was not in breach of its obligations under the DDA, or that it did not require to make changes to its website, a court may consider that reasonable efforts had been made. However, even if this were the case, in legal terms this would merely rule out any damages up until the point where the user notified the service provider of the problem. Once it did become aware of its duties, it would have no defence for not fixing the accessibility problems and could still be open to a court making a decree requiring the service provider to make changes.

[58] The Code, para 7.8.
[59] 1999 SCLR (1) 2004; [1999] IRLR (2) 463; 1999 GWD (3)20–958.
[60] The Code, para 6.7.

5. 'Reasonable Adjustments' under Section 21

Section 20(2) of the DDA gives an alternative definition of 'disability'. This section states that a service provider will discriminate against a disabled person if it fails to comply with a duty imposed under section 21 and cannot show that this failure is justified. If the failure to comply with these duties leads to the service being impossible or unreasonably difficult to use by a disabled person then discrimination will take place under section 19(1)(b). In relation to this duty, the Code suggests an interpretation for 'unreasonably difficult' as including regard for the time, inconvenience, discomfort and efforts that may be considered unreasonable by other people.[61]

The duties imposed under section 21 apply to the provision of 'reasonable adjustments'. Reasonable adjustments include making changes to any practice, policy or procedure, the provision of auxiliary aids or services. In answering what a reasonable change would be, the Code reveals that an accessible website is an example of an auxiliary aid or service that a service provider could provide to circumvent an existing accessibility issue.[62] It is also conceivable that a service provider's practice, policy or procedure could inhibit accessibility: for instance if the service provider has a policy regarding the style and content of its website and in practice it adds content to its site which is inaccessible.

However, adjustments need only be made if they can be considered a reasonable step in the particular circumstances and the first two justifications discussed above do not apply. Although the DDA does not define what is reasonable, the Code suggests that service providers should consider several factors:

- the type of services being offered
- the nature of the service provider and its size and resources
- the extent to which taking any particular steps would be effective in overcoming the difficulty in question
- the extent to which such steps are practical
- the financial and other costs of making the adjustment
- the extent to which disruption would be caused
- the amount of any resources already spent on making adjustments.[63]

As has already been discussed, the provisions of the DDA and the Cth DDA are very similar. It is further clear that the main issues here are very similar to those considered by the Commission in the _SOCOG_ case. The SOCOG case is likely to be highly important in any argument before a UK Court and it is

---

[61] The Code, para 4.33.
[62] The Code, paras 5.23 and 5.26.
[63] The Code, paras 4.21 and 4.22.

therefore relevant to consider this case in light of the provisions of the DDA and the corresponding Code.

In *SOCOG,* the evidence of the expert witnesses suggested that compliance costs were modest, even for a website of the size of SOCOG's. In its opinion, the Commission referred to SOCOG's financial backing and concluded that this only increased the duty. Thus, the expectation is far greater on larger organisations with greater resources, even if such an organisation operated many complex websites. SOCOG and IBM's protestations at the high cost of making the website accessible did not persuade the Commission. It is clear that a failure to consider accessibility and consequential higher costs does not excuse a service provider from its duties.

The Commission's judgment also indicates that the fact the site was still in development after the introduction of the W3C accessibility guidelines meant that there was an even higher level of expectation. This is similar to the requirement in the Code that states that there is a continuing duty on service providers to review their duties. Specifically, 'technological developments may provide new or better solutions to the problems of inaccessible services.'[64]

In tandem with this last point, the Code also states that:

> Service providers should not wait until a disabled person wants to use a service which they provide before they give consideration to their duty to make a reasonable adjustments. . . . They should anticipate the requirements of disabled people and the adjustments that may have to be made for them.[65]

These two requirements, to continually review and anticipate problems, indicate that even if the W3C guidelines were introduced following the design of the a website a requirement to 'retrofit' is likely to exist. The evolving nature means that as future drafts of the W3C guidelines are introduced service providers should consider and apply these as necessary.

6. A Non-Web-based Alternative?

An issue often raised is whether an accessible website is the only option available to comply with the DDA. The argument put forward is that if, for example, the service provider also provides a telephone based service then a person with a visual impairment who is unable to use its website could use the telephone-based service instead. This argument is perfectly valid, but only to a point.

In setting out a service provider's obligations, the DDA states that a service provider should not provider a disabled person with a lower standard of service. Therefore, it is also important to consider issues of convenience and equivalence of service. For instance, if a bank offers its best interest rates to its Internet-only

---

[64] The Code, para 4.20.
[65] The Code, para 4.19.

customers, it must offer equivalent rates to a disabled person who is unable to use the website, even though that person operates his account over the phone.

Service providers must also consider issues of convenience. The Web offers 24/7 instantaneous to a vast array of information. If a service provider wishes to provide a non-Web-based alternative means of access to disabled people such service must match the convenience and availability of the website in order for the service provider to meet its obligations under the DDA.

As a third example, a home shopping service may offer the option to telephone in an order. However, if the shopping service carries a wide-range of stock then it is important for the user to know what the service provider is selling, what the various options are and what the price is. Whilst an able-bodied person may browse the site before deciding what to buy, that option is not open to a disabled person if the website is inaccessible. As an analogy, imagine trying to shop at a supermarket without being able to see what products the supermarket sold and whether or not the particular product you wished was in stock. If the service provider required the disabled person to 'guess' what might be in stock it is unlikely that the service would be of an equivalent standard.

Therefore, whilst there are arguably alternatives to providing an accessible website, such alternatives are still unlikely to satisfy the requirements of the DDA in many cases.

7. Remedies and Compliance

The Code of Practice advocates settling disputes without recourse to the Courts and the intention is that the Disability Rights Commission, the organisation tasked with advancing disability rights, will play a part in this. However, in the event that a dispute is irresolvable the Sheriff Court (or County Court in England) will hear the dispute.[66] The DDA gives rise to civil remedies, and a person who alleges that he has been discriminated against by the service provider may bring civil proceedings in the same way as any other claim in tort or reparation for breach of statutory duty.

Although it is the County or Sheriff Court that will hear an action, the remedies available are those that would be available in the High Court or Court of Session.[67] This means that there are essentially two powers available to the court—that to award damages for injury to feelings and economic loss and the power to grant an order of specific implement or specific performance.

---

[66] S 25.
[67] S 25(3)–(5).

(a) Damages

In *SOCOG*, the Commission did not award damages as part of its original determination. However, SOCOG's subsequent failure to comply with the determination in time for the start of the Games led to a hearing for an award of damages on 6 November 2000.[68] At this hearing, the Commissioner considered the award of pecuniary damages under several grounds—in respect of injuries for hurt and feeling, legal expenses and aggravated damages.

In considering the loss or damage suffered, the Commission referred to the complainant's expectations at being able to access the information and the dismissive attitude of such a prestigious body as the respondent when approached by Mr Maguire with his concerns. The Commission held that SOCOG's suggestion that Mr Maguire find a sighted person to aid his access to the website to be 'wholly inconsistent with his own expectations.'

The Commission also held that the public statements made by the respondent after the hearing and its subsequent non-compliance further aggravated the hurt caused. However, after concluding that the purpose was not to punish 'an apparently financially resourceful respondent', but rather to award a figure that was reasonable under the circumstances, the Commission awarded a figure of Au $20,000.

Under Scots law, as in the SOCOG case, a successful pursuer is entitled to damages for pain and suffering (or solatium) and any derivative economic loss. In considering the former, the court may take into account anything which reduces the quality of the pursuer's life or leads to a deprivation of amenity and hurt to feelings. There are many instances where Web Accessibility can lead to a loss of amenity. For instance, the use of a home shopping service for a visually impaired person where he can 'hear' what is on the shelf and have it delivered without having to go through the trauma of visiting the supermarket or arrange for someone to visit on his behalf could be invaluable.[69]

In terms of derivative economic loss, there is a potential for a claim too. For instance, the interest rates offered by Internet banks compare very favourably to those available on the High Street and indeed this forms a key part of the advertising for such accounts. Likewise, the savings offered by other online shopping would also be of relevance when calculating damages. The demonstration of any derivative economic loss would therefore be relatively straightforward to calculate.

---

[68] H99/115 *Bruce Lindsay Maguire v Sydney Organising Committee for the Olympic Games.*

[69] There is a power under sch 3 para 7 for the Minister to set an upper limit to damages for hurt to feeling, but this has so far not been used.

(b) Specific Implement

Perhaps the most desirable remedy from the point of view of the person who against whom the discrimination has been committed is the power of the court to order the service provider to fix the website. As well as considering what type of order a court might grant, it is also interesting to explore this from the point of view of compliance with the Act.

The remedy of granting an order of specific implement, or specific performance in England, is one that orders a defender who is under a legal duty to carry out or perform an act, such as statutory duties, to do so. A court can therefore use this power to order a service provider to comply with the Act by forcing it to make its website accessible. However, due to the punitive sanctions available for non-compliance[70] the decree sought must be suitably specific. Indeed, the case of *Fleming & Ferguson* v *Paisley Magistrates*[71] is particularly analogous to the instance of Web Accessibility. The pursuer in this case was attempting to enforce an alleged obligation that required the defender to maintain a navigable channel. In considering the application for a decree, Lord President Cooper observed:

When the pursuers use in their conclusion the word 'navigable,' they must surely indicate by what the channel is to be navigated, for a specification of the beam and length of the ships to be accommodated is just as important for determining the dimensions of the channel and the radius of the curves as the draught. These are not idle questions. An answer is indispensable to the remedy sought.[72]

It is likely that a simple declaration for a website to be 'made accessible' would be too vague in the sense that request for a channel be 'navigable' was held to be by the Lord President. Accessible by whom? And to what extent? Whilst the duty under the Act is one to the entire disabled community, only the person who against whom the discrimination is committed can bring an action under the DDA[73] and therefore any remedies sought must be specific to him and that discrimination. To return to our maritime analogy, the remedy sought would have to be to allow the complainer's boat to navigate the channel—rather than all boats. For websites, the remedy must specifically fix the pursuer's accessibility problem—although if this is such that it fixes all accessibility problems then that is an added bonus. Here it is useful to turn to the W3C guidelines that the Commission held so important in *SOCOG*. Under these guidelines, there are three levels of conformity:

---

[70] The use of imprisonment is 'an invocation of the power inherent in every civil court to ordain performance of acts within its jurisdiction, and in default to commit the defaulter to prison'—*Wilson v McKellar* (1896) 24 R 254. The Law Reform (Miscellaneous Provisions) (Scotland) Act 1940 s 1 sets out the formal proceedings for this power.

[71] [1948] SC 547.

[72] P 558.

[73] S 25(1)(a).

- Priority 1 or 'A'—which is described as things that *must* be done.
- Priority 2 or 'AA'—things which *should* be done.
- Priority 3 or 'AAA' which is things that *may* be done.[74]

In the *SOCOG* case, there is much reference to the WAI guidelines. As the first time that a court of law had considered the guidelines to have any formal standing, this set a worldwide precedent. In evidence from Ms Treviranus reference is made as to how Level A compliance could be reached in four weeks. With no other statutory accessibility test or benchmark, the Commission opted to propose that Level A should be the accepted standard required for compliance with the Cth DDA. A quote from the Deputy Commissioner, Graeme Innes, reinforces this opinion:

> The view of the Commission is that if you comply with [the W3C guidelines] you'll be complying with the Disability Discrimination Act.[75]

As suggested by *SOCOG*, Level A would be a realistic and clear standard for the UK courts to set as an initial benchmark for DDA compliance. This would also be suitably specific for an order of specific implement. Although complex, these guidelines are very comprehensive and should leave a service provider in no doubt as to what its duties are under the decree.

E. Summary

When the predecessor to this chapter was first written some three years ago,[76] the paper concluded by saying that the RNIB and DRC had highlighted the area of Web accessibility and that a test case would only be a matter of time. There has yet to be a test case in the UK, whilst events in the States have developed a pace in the intervening period. However, instead of settling the law, the most recent case, *Southwest Airlines*, has ruled, albeit under unusual circumstances, that the ADA does not apply to the Web.

As has been explained, it is unlikely that this case will have any bearing on a UK test case. The strong and coherent argument developed in *SOCOG*, together with the similarities in legislation, should mean that UK law takes its lead from the southern hemisphere rather than the US. The European Commission has also begun to issue advice in this area, requiring that all member states ensure that their

---

[74] W3C 'Techniques for Web Content Accessibility Guidelines 1.0' http://www.w3.org/TR/WCAG10–TECHS/.

[75] Fairfax IT 'SOCOG Makes Unflattering History' (21 November 2000) archived at http://theage.au.com.

[76] M Sloan, 'Web Accessibility and the DDA' (2001) 2 *J Information, L & Technology*, http://www2.warwick.ac.uk/fuc/soc/law/elj/jilt/2001-2/sloan/.

public websites are WAI WCAG compliant.[77] It is likely that such advice will develop into legislative requirements for public sector websites and latterly the private sector.

In light of this, it is therefore critical that service providers act now to prevent themselves from exposing themselves to possible claims of discrimination. For those service providers who develop their websites in-house this means proper auditing of their existing websites and establishing guidelines for future websites. As suggested by the HREOC official, by complying with the W3C's guidelines it is likely you will be complying with the law.[78]

For service providers who do not develop their own Web presence, but choose instead to contract this out to a specialist third party, audits of existing sites will also be required. However, service providers will also need to examine contracts for future websites to ensure that a fully WAI WCAG compliant and independently tested site is provided along with the necessary warranties and indemnities.[79]

Whilst it is not possible to contract out of liability under the DDA, in that the service provider will always be the party liable for compliance, a properly drafted contract should enable the service provider to sue for damages in the event of a Web developer providing a site that does not comply with the DDA.[80]

The issue of Web accessibility and potential liability under the DDA is still to grab the headlines in both the newspapers and corporate boardrooms. This is despite a recent Formal Investigation[81] by the DRC, which revealed that over 80% of websites tested failed to comply with the WCAG. The DRC stated that it did not intend to 'name and shame' the worst offenders, but indicated that if service providers failed to take action it would use its enforcement powers to seek the intervention of the courts.

Whilst an increasing number of companies are identifying the risks that they are exposing themselves to, there are a great many still to do so. That there will be a successful test case and accompanying negative media coverage and damage to a blue chip company's good will is not in doubt—it is just a matter of time.[82]

---

[77] 'Accessibility of Public Websites and their Content' Com (2001) 0529, 25 September 2001. This Communication does not, however state which level of WAI WCAG compliance websites should achieve. UK guidance is for websites to be Level A compliant (although recent guidance has changed this to Level AA for local authority websites in England and Wales).

[78] But see n 78 below.

[79] One of the important conclusions to come out of the DRC's investigation (n 79 below) is that simple box-ticking against the WCAG alone is not sufficient and that some degree of human/user testing is also required to ensure a fully accessible website. From a contractual point of view it also therefore important that suitable indemnities are obtained from the website designer regarding DDA litigation.

[80] The issue of a website developer's contractual liability and possible negligence claims is discussed in greater detail in Sloan, 'Web Accessibility & the DDA', n 75 above.

[81] DRC *The Web: Access and Inclusion for Disabled People* (2004). This is the DRC's first formal investigation and was carried out in collaboration with Human Computer Interaction department at University College London.

[82] For more information on Web Accessibility and the DDA and links to all relevant legislation and articles, see the author's website at http://www.web-access.org.uk.

Appendix 1

DIRECTIVE 2000/31/EC OF THE EUROPEAN PARLIAMENT AND OF THE COUNCIL

of 8 June 2000

on certain legal aspects of information society services, in particular electronic commerce, in the Internal Market (Directive on electronic commerce)

THE EUROPEAN PARLIAMENT AND THE COUNCIL OF THE EUROPEAN UNION,

Having regard to the Treaty establishing the European Community, and in particular Articles 47(2), 55 and 95 thereof,

Having regard to the proposal from the Commission ([1]),

Having regard to the opinion of the Economic and Social Committee ([2]),

Acting in accordance with the procedure laid down in Article 251 of the Treaty ([3]),

Whereas:

(1) The European Union is seeking to forge ever closer links between the States and peoples of Europe, to ensure economic and social progress; in accordance with Article 14(2) of the Treaty, the internal market comprises an area without internal frontiers in which the free movements of goods, services and the freedom of establishment are ensured; the development of information society services within the area without internal frontiers is vital to eliminating the barriers which divide the European peoples.

(2) The development of electronic commerce within the information society offers significant employment opportunities in the Community, particularly in small and medium-sized enterprises, and will stimulate economic growth and investment in innovation by European companies, and can also enhance the competitiveness of European industry, provided that everyone has access to the Internet.

(3) Community law and the characteristics of the Community legal order are a vital asset to enable European citizens and operators to take full advantage, without consideration of borders, of the opportunities afforded by electronic commerce; this Directive therefore has the purpose of ensuring a high level of Community legal integration in order to establish a real area without internal borders for information society services.

(4) It is important to ensure that electronic commerce could fully benefit from the internal market and therefore that, as with Council Directive 89/552/EEC of 3 October 1989 on the coordination of certain provisions laid down by law, regulation or administrative action in Member States concerning the pursuit of television broadcasting activities ([4]), a high level of Community integration is achieved.

(5) The development of information society services within the Community is hampered by a number of legal obstacles to the proper functioning of the internal market which make less attractive the exercise of the freedom of establishment and the freedom to provide services; these obstacles arise from divergences in legislation and from the legal uncertainty as to which national rules apply to such services; in the absence of coordination and adjustment of legislation in the relevant areas, obstacles might be justified in the light of the case-law of the Court of Justice of the European Communities; legal uncertainty exists with regard to the extent to which Member States may control services originating from another Member State.

([1]) OJ C 30, 5.2.1999, p. 4.
([2]) OJ C 169, 16.6.1999, p. 36.
([3]) Opinion of the European Parliament of 6 May 1999 (OJ C 279, 1.10.1999, p. 389), Council common position of 28 February 2000 (OJ C 128, 8.5.2000, p. 32) and Decision of the European Parliament of 4 May 2000 (not yet published in the Official Journal).

([4]) OJ L 298, 17.10.1989, p. 23. Directive as amended by Directive 97/36/EC of the European Parliament and of the Council (OJ L 202, 30.7.1997, p. 60).

L 178/2   EN   Official Journal of the European Communities   17.7.2000

(6) In the light of Community objectives, of Articles 43 and 49 of the Treaty and of secondary Community law, these obstacles should be eliminated by coordinating certain national laws and by clarifying certain legal concepts at Community level to the extent necessary for the proper functioning of the internal market; by dealing only with certain specific matters which give rise to problems for the internal market, this Directive is fully consistent with the need to respect the principle of subsidiarity as set out in Article 5 of the Treaty.

(7) In order to ensure legal certainty and consumer confidence, this Directive must lay down a clear and general framework to cover certain legal aspects of electronic commerce in the internal market.

(8) The objective of this Directive is to create a legal framework to ensure the free movement of information society services between Member States and not to harmonise the field of criminal law as such.

(9) The free movement of information society services can in many cases be a specific reflection in Community law of a more general principle, namely freedom of expression as enshrined in Article 10(1) of the Convention for the Protection of Human Rights and Fundamental Freedoms, which has been ratified by all the Member States; for this reason, directives covering the supply of information society services must ensure that this activity may be engaged in freely in the light of that Article, subject only to the restrictions laid down in paragraph 2 of that Article and in Article 46(1) of the Treaty; this Directive is not intended to affect national fundamental rules and principles relating to freedom of expression.

(10) In accordance with the principle of proportionality, the measures provided for in this Directive are strictly limited to the minimum needed to achieve the objective of the proper functioning of the internal market; where action at Community level is necessary, and in order to guarantee an area which is truly without internal frontiers as far as electronic commerce is concerned, the Directive must ensure a high level of protection of objectives of general interest, in particular the protection of minors and human dignity, consumer protection and the protection of public health; according to Article 152 of the Treaty, the protection of public health is an essential component of other Community policies.

(11) This Directive is without prejudice to the level of protection for, in particular, public health and consumer interests, as established by Community acts; amongst others, Council Directive 93/13/EEC of 5 April 1993 on unfair terms in consumer contracts[1] and Directive 97/7/EC of the European Parliament and of the Council of 20 May 1997 on the protection of consumers in respect of distance contracts[2] form a vital element for protecting consumers in contractual matters; those Directives also apply in their entirety to information society services; that same Community acquis, which is fully applicable to information society services, also embraces in particular Council Directive 84/450/EEC of 10 September 1984 concerning misleading and comparative advertising[3], Council Directive 87/102/EEC of 22 December 1986 for the approximation of the laws, regulations and administrative provisions of the Member States concerning consumer credit[4], Council Directive 93/22/EEC of 10 May 1993 on investment services in the securities field[5], Council Directive 90/314/EEC of 13 June 1990 on package travel, package holidays and package tours[6], Directive 98/6/EC of the European Parliament and of the Council of 16 February 1998 on consumer production in the indication of prices of products offered to consumers[7], Council Directive 92/59/EEC of 29 June 1992 on general product safety[8], Directive 94/47/EC of the European Parliament and of the Council of 26 October 1994 on the protection of purchasers in respect of certain aspects of contracts relating to the purchase of the right to use immovable properties on a timeshare basis[9], Directive 98/27/EC of the European Parliament and of the Council of 19 May 1998 on injunctions for the protection of consumers' interests[10], Council Directive 85/374/EEC of 25 July 1985 on the approximation of the laws, regulations and administrative provisions concerning liability for defective products[11], Directive 1999/44/EC of the European Parliament and of the Council of 25 May 1999 on certain aspects of the sale of consumer goods and associated guarantees[12], the future Directive of the European Parliament and of the Council concerning the distance marketing of consumer financial services and Council Directive 92/28/EEC of 31 March 1992 on the advertising of medicinal products[13]; this Directive

---

[1] OJ L 95, 21.4.1993, p. 29.
[2] OJ L 144, 4.6.1999, p. 19.
[3] OJ L 250, 19.9.1984, p. 17. Directive as amended by Directive 97/55/EC of the European Parliament and of the Council (OJ L 290, 23.10.1997, p. 18).
[4] OJ L 42, 12.2.1987, p. 48. Directive as last amended by Directive 98/7/EC of the European Parliament and of the Council (OJ L 101, 1.4.1998, p. 17).
[5] OJ L 141, 11.6.1993, p. 27. Directive as last amended by Directive 97/9/EC of the European Parliament and of the Council (OJ L 84, 26.3.1997, p. 22).
[6] OJ L 158, 23.6.1990, p. 59.
[7] OJ L 80, 18.3.1998, p. 27.
[8] OJ L 228, 11.8.1992, p. 24.
[9] OJ L 280, 29.10.1994, p. 83.
[10] OJ L 166, 11.6.1998, p. 51. Directive as amended by Directive 1999/44/EC (OJ L 171, 7.7.1999, p. 12).
[11] OJ L 210, 7.8.1985, p. 29. Directive as amended by Directive 1999/34/EC (OJ L 141, 4.6.1999, p. 20).
[12] OJ L 171, 7.7.1999, p. 12.
[13] OJ L 113, 30.4.1992, p. 13.

should be without prejudice to Directive 98/43/EC of the European Parliament and of the Council of 6 July 1998 on the approximation of the laws, regulations and administrative provisions of the Member States relating to the advertising and sponsorship of tobacco products (¹) adopted within the framework of the internal market, or to directives on the protection of public health; this Directive complements information requirements established by the abovementioned Directives and in particular Directive 97/7/EC.

(12) It is necessary to exclude certain activities from the scope of this Directive, on the grounds that the freedom to provide services in these fields cannot, at this stage, be guaranteed under the Treaty or existing secondary legislation; excluding these activities does not preclude any instruments which might prove necessary for the proper functioning of the internal market; taxation, particularly value added tax imposed on a large number of the services covered by this Directive, must be excluded form the scope of this Directive.

(13) This Directive does not aim to establish rules on fiscal obligations nor does it pre-empt the drawing up of Community instruments concerning fiscal aspects of electronic commerce.

(14) The protection of individuals with regard to the processing of personal data is solely governed by Directive 95/46/EC of the European Parliament and of the Council of 24 October 1995 on the protection of individuals with regard to the processing of personal data and on the free movement of such data (²) and Directive 97/66/EC of the European Parliament and of the Council of 15 December 1997 concerning the processing of personal data and the protection of privacy in the telecommunications sector (³) which are fully applicable to information society services; these Directives already establish a Community legal framework in the field of personal data and therefore it is not necessary to cover this issue in this Directive in order to ensure the smooth functioning of the internal market, in particular the free movement of personal data between Member States; the implementation and application of this Directive should be made in full compliance with the principles relating to the protection of personal data, in particular as regards unsolicited commercial communication and the liability of intermediaries; this Directive cannot prevent the anonymous use of open networks such as the Internet.

(15) The confidentiality of communications is guaranteed by Article 5 Directive 97/66/EC; in accordance with that Directive, Member States must prohibit any kind of interception or surveillance of such communications by others than the senders and receivers, except when legally authorised.

(16) The exclusion of gambling activities from the scope of application of this Directive covers only games of chance, lotteries and betting transactions, which involve wagering a stake with monetary value; this does not cover promotional competitions or games where the purpose is to encourage the sale of goods or services and where payments, if they arise, serve only to acquire the promoted goods or services.

(17) The definition of information society services already exists in Community law in Directive 98/34/EC of the European Parliament and of the Council of 22 June 1998 laying down a procedure for the provision of information in the field of technical standards and regulations and of rules on information society services (⁴) and in Directive 98/84/EC of the European Parliament and of the Council of 20 November 1998 on the legal protection of services based on, or consisting of, conditional access (⁵); this definition covers any service normally provided for remuneration, at a distance, by means of electronic equipment for the processing (including digital compression) and storage of data, and at the individual request of a recipient of a service; those services referred to in the indicative list in Annex V to Directive 98/34/EC which do not imply data processing and storage are not covered by this definition.

(18) Information society services span a wide range of economic activities which take place on-line; these activities can, in particular, consist of selling goods on-line; activities such as the delivery of goods as such or the provision of services off-line are not covered; information society services are not solely restricted to services giving rise to on-line contracting but also, in so far as they represent an economic activity, extend to services which are not remunerated by those who receive them, such as those offering on-line information or commercial communications, or those providing tools allowing for search, access and retrieval of data; information society services also include services consisting of the transmission of information via a communication network, in providing access to a communication network or in hosting information provided by a recipient of the service; television broadcasting within the meaning of Directive EEC/89/552 and radio broadcasting are not information society services because they are not provided at individual request; by contrast, services which are transmitted point to point, such as video-on-demand or the provision of commercial communications by electronic mail are information society services; the use of electronic mail or equivalent individual communications for instance by natural persons acting outside their trade, business or profession including their use for the conclusion of contracts between such persons is not an information society service; the contractual relationship between an

(¹) OJ L 213, 30.7.1998, p. 9.
(²) OJ L 281, 23.11.1995, p. 31.
(³) OJ L 24, 30.1.1998, p. 1.

(⁴) OJ L 204, 21.7.1998, p. 37. Directive as amended by Directive 98/48/EC (OJ L 217, 5.8.1998, p. 18).
(⁵) OJ L 320, 28.11.1998, p. 54.

L 178/4 [EN] Official Journal of the European Communities 17.7.2000

employee and his employer is not an information society service; activities which by their very nature cannot be carried out at a distance and by electronic means, such as the statutory auditing of company accounts or medical advice requiring the physical examination of a patient are not information society services.

(19) The place at which a service provider is established should be determined in conformity with the case-law of the Court of Justice according to which the concept of establishment involves the actual pursuit of an economic activity through a fixed establishment for an indefinite period; this requirement is also fulfilled where a company is constituted for a given period; the place of establishment of a company providing services via an Internet website is not the place at which the technology supporting its website is located or the place at which its website is accessible but the place where it pursues its economic activity; in cases where a provider has several places of establishment it is important to determine from which place of establishment the service concerned is provided; in cases where it is difficult to determine from which of several places of establishment a given service is provided, this is the place where the provider has the centre of his activities relating to this particular service.

(20) The definition of 'recipient of a service' covers all types of usage of information society services, both by persons who provide information on open networks such as the Internet and by persons who seek information on the Internet for private or professional reasons.

(21) The scope of the coordinated field is without prejudice to future Community harmonisation relating to information society services and to future legislation adopted at national level in accordance with Community law; the coordinated field covers only requirements relating to on-line activities such as on-line information, on-line advertising, on-line shopping, on-line contracting and does not concern Member States' legal requirements relating to goods such as safety standards, labelling obligations, or liability for goods, or Member States' requirements relating to the delivery or the transport of goods, including the distribution of medicinal products; the coordinated field does not cover the exercise of rights of pre-emption by public authorities concerning certain goods such as works of art.

(22) Information society services should be supervised at the source of the activity, in order to ensure an effective protection of public interest objectives; to that end, it is necessary to ensure that the competent authority provides such protection not only for the citizens of its own country but for all Community citizens; in order to improve mutual trust between Member States, it is essential to state clearly this responsibility on the part of the Member State where the services originate; moreover, in order to effectively guarantee freedom to provide services and legal certainty for suppliers and recipients of services, such information society services should in principle be subject to the law of the Member State in which the service provider is established.

(23) This Directive neither aims to establish additional rules on private international law relating to conflicts of law nor does it deal with the jurisdiction of Courts; provisions of the applicable law designated by rules of private international law must not restrict the freedom to provide information society services as established in this Directive.

(24) In the context of this Directive, notwithstanding the rule on the control at source of information society services, it is legitimate under the conditions established in this Directive for Member States to take measures to restrict the free movement of information society services.

(25) National courts, including civil courts, dealing with private law disputes can take measures to derogate from the freedom to provide information society services in conformity with conditions established in this Directive.

(26) Member States, in conformity with conditions established in this Directive, may apply their national rules on criminal law and criminal proceedings with a view to taking all investigative and other measures necessary for the detection and prosecution of criminal offences, without there being a need to notify such measures to the Commission.

(27) This Directive, together with the future Directive of the European Parliament and of the Council concerning the distance marketing of consumer financial services, contributes to the creating of a legal framework for the on-line provision of financial services; this Directive does not pre-empt future initiatives in the area of financial services in particular with regard to the harmonisation of rules of conduct in this field; the possibility for Member States, established in this Directive, under certain circumstances of restricting the freedom to provide information society services in order to protect consumers also covers measures in the area of financial services in particular measures aiming at protecting investors.

(28) The Member States' obligation not to subject access to the activity of an information society service provider to prior authorisation does not concern postal services covered by Directive 97/67/EC of the European Parliament and of the Council of 15 December 1997 on common rules for the development of the internal market of Community postal services and the improvement of quality of service(¹) consisting of the physical delivery of a printed electronic mail message and does not affect voluntary accreditation systems, in particular for providers of electronic signature certification service.

(29) Commercial communications are essential for the financing of information society services and for developing a wide variety of new, charge-free services; in the interests of consumer protection and fair trading, commercial communications, including discounts, promotional offers and promotional competitions or games, must meet a number of transparency requirements; these requirements are without prejudice to Directive 97/7/EC; this Directive should not affect existing Directives on commercial communications, in particular Directive 98/43/EC.

(30) The sending of unsolicited commercial communications by electronic mail may be undesirable for consumers and information society service providers and may disrupt the smooth functioning of interactive networks; the question of consent by recipient of certain forms of unsolicited commercial communications is not addressed by this Directive, but has already been addressed, in particular, by Directive 97/7/EC and by Directive 97/66/EC; in Member States which authorise unsolicited commercial communications by electronic mail, the setting up of appropriate industry filtering initiatives should be encouraged and facilitated; in addition it is necessary that in any event unsolicited commercial communities are clearly identifiable as such in order to improve transparency and to facilitate the functioning of such industry initiatives; unsolicited commercial communications by electronic mail should not result in additional communication costs for the recipient.

(31) Member States which allow the sending of unsolicited commercial communications by electronic mail without prior consent of the recipient by service providers established in their territory have to ensure that the service providers consult regularly and respect the opt-out registers in which natural persons not wishing to receive such commercial communications can register themselves.

(32) In order to remove barriers to the development of cross-border services within the Community which members of the regulated professions might offer on the Internet, it is necessary that compliance be guaranteed at Community level with professional rules aiming, in particular, to protect consumers or public health; codes of conduct at Community level would be the best means of determining the rules on professional ethics applicable to commercial communication; the drawing-up or, where appropriate, the adaptation of such rules should be encouraged without prejudice to the autonomy of professional bodies and associations.

(33) This Directive complements Community law and national law relating to regulated professions maintaining a coherent set of applicable rules in this field.

(34) Each Member State is to amend its legislation containing requirements, and in particular requirements as to form, which are likely to curb the use of contracts by electronic means; the examination of the legislation requiring such adjustment should be systematic and should cover all the necessary stages and acts of the contractual process, including the filing of the contract; the result of this amendment should be to make contracts concluded electronically workable; the legal effect of electronic signatures is dealt with by Directive 1999/93/EC of the European Parliament and of the Council of 13 December 1999 on a Community framework for electronic signatures(²); the acknowledgement of receipt by a service provider may take the form of the on-line provision of the service paid for.

(35) This Directive does not affect Member States' possibility of maintaining or establishing general or specific legal requirements for contracts which can be fulfilled by electronic means, in particular requirements concerning secure electronic signatures.

(36) Member States may maintain restrictions for the use of electronic contracts with regard to contracts requiring by law the involvement of courts, public authorities, or professions exercising public authority; this possibility also covers contracts which require the involvement of courts, public authorities, or professions exercising public authority in order to have an effect with regard to third parties as well as contracts requiring by law certification or attestation by a notary.

(37) Member States' obligation to remove obstacles to the use of electronic contracts concerns only obstacles resulting from legal requirements and not practical obstacles resulting from the impossibility of using electronic means in certain cases.

(¹) OJ L 15, 21.1.1998, p. 14.

(²) OJ L 13, 19.1.2000, p. 12.

L 178/6   EN   Official Journal of the European Communities   17.7.2000

(38) Member States' obligation to remove obstacles to the use of electronic contracts is to be implemented in conformity with legal requirements for contracts enshrined in Community law.

(39) The exceptions to the provisions concerning the contracts concluded exclusively by electronic mail or by equivalent individual communications provided for by this Directive, in relation to information to be provided and the placing of orders, should not enable, as a result, the by-passing of those provisions by providers of information society services.

(40) Both existing and emerging disparities in Member States' legislation and case-law concerning liability of service providers acting as intermediaries prevent the smooth functioning of the internal market, in particular by impairing the development of cross-border services and producing distortions of competition; service providers have a duty to act, under certain circumstances, with a view to preventing or stopping illegal activities; this Directive should constitute the appropriate basis for the development of rapid and reliable procedures for removing and disabling access to illegal information; such mechanisms could be developed on the basis of voluntary agreements between all parties concerned and should be encouraged by Member States; it is in the interest of all parties involved in the provision of information society services to adopt and implement such procedures; the provisions of this Directive relating to liability should not preclude the development and effective operation, by the different interested parties, of technical systems of protection and identification and of technical surveillance instruments made possible by digital technology within the limits laid down by Directives 95/46/EC and 97/66/EC.

(41) This Directive strikes a balance between the different interests at stake and establishes principles upon which industry agreements and standards can be based.

(42) The exemptions from liability established in this Directive cover only cases where the activity of the information society service provider is limited to the technical process of operating and giving access to a communication network over which information made available by third parties is transmitted or temporarily stored, for the sole purpose of making the transmission more efficient; this activity is of a mere technical, automatic and passive nature, which implies that the information society service provider has neither knowledge of nor control over the information which is transmitted or stored.

(43) A service provider can benefit from the exemptions for 'mere conduit' and for 'caching' when he is in no way involved with the information transmitted; this requires among other things that he does not modify the information that he transmits; this requirement does not cover manipulations of a technical nature which take place in the course of the transmission as they do not alter the integrity of the information contained in the transmission.

(44) A service provider who deliberately collaborates with one of the recipients of his service in order to undertake illegal acts goes beyond the activities of 'mere conduit' or 'caching' and as a result cannot benefit from the liability exemptions established for these activities.

(45) The limitations of the liability of intermediary service providers established in this Directive do not affect the possibility of injunctions of different kinds; such injunctions can in particular consist of orders by courts or administrative authorities requiring the termination or prevention of any infringement, including the removal of illegal information or the disabling of access to it.

(46) In order to benefit from a limitation of liability, the provider of an information society service, consisting of the storage of information, upon obtaining actual knowledge or awareness of illegal activities has to act expeditiously to remove or to disable access to the information concerned; the removal or disabling of access has to be undertaken in the observance of the principle of freedom of expression and of procedures established for this purpose at national level; this Directive does not affect Member States' possibility of establishing specific requirements which must be fulfilled expeditiously prior to the removal or disabling of information.

(47) Member States are prevented from imposing a monitoring obligation on service providers only with respect to obligations of a general nature; this does not concern monitoring obligations in a specific case and, in particular, does not affect orders by national authorities in accordance with national legislation.

(48) This Directive does not affect the possibility for Member States of requiring service providers, who host information provided by recipients of their service, to apply duties of care, which can reasonably be expected from them and which are specified by national law, in order to detect and prevent certain types of illegal activities.

(49) Member States and the Commission are to encourage the drawing-up of codes of conduct; this is not to impair the voluntary nature of such codes and the possibility for interested parties of deciding freely whether to adhere to such codes.

17.7.2000 [EN] Official Journal of the European Communities L 178/7

(50) It is important that the proposed directive on the harmonisation of certain aspects of copyright and related rights in the information society and this Directive come into force within a similar time scale with a view to establishing a clear framework of rules relevant to the issue of liability of intermediaries for copyright and relating rights infringements at Community level.

(51) Each Member State should be required, where necessary, to amend any legislation which is liable to hamper the use of schemes for the out-of-court settlement of disputes through electronic channels; the result of this amendment must be to make the functioning of such schemes genuinely and effectively possible in law and in practice, even across borders.

(52) The effective exercise of the freedoms of the internal market makes it necessary to guarantee victims effective access to means of settling disputes; damage which may arise in connection with information society services is characterised both by its rapidity and by its geographical extent; in view of this specific character and the need to ensure that national authorities do not endanger the mutual confidence which they should have in one another, this Directive requests Member States to ensure that appropriate court actions are available; Member States should examine the need to provide access to judicial procedures by appropriate electronic means.

(53) Directive 98/27/EC, which is applicable to information society services, provides a mechanism relating to actions for an injunction aimed at the protection of the collective interests of consumers; this mechanism will contribute to the free movement of information society services by ensuring a high level of consumer protection.

(54) The sanctions provided for under this Directive are without prejudice to any other sanction or remedy provided under national law; Member States are not obliged to provide criminal sanctions for infringement of national provisions adopted pursuant to this Directive.

(55) This Directive does not affect the law applicable to contractual obligations relating to consumer contracts; accordingly, this Directive cannot have the result of depriving the consumer of the protection afforded to him by the mandatory rules relating to contractual obligations of the law of the Member State in which he has his habitual residence.

(56) As regards the derogation contained in this Directive regarding contractual obligations concerning contracts concluded by consumers, those obligations should be interpreted as including information on the essential elements of the content of the contract, including consumer rights, which have a determining influence on the decision to contract.

(57) The Court of Justice has consistently held that a Member State retains the right to take measures against a service provider that is established in another Member State but directs all or most of his activity to the territory of the first Member State if the choice of establishment was made with a view to evading the legislation that would have applied to the provider had he been established on the territory of the first Member State.

(58) This Directive should not apply to services supplied by service providers established in a third country; in view of the global dimension of electronic commerce, it is, however, appropriate to ensure that the Community rules are consistent with international rules; this Directive is without prejudice to the results of discussions within international organisations (amongst others WTO, OECD, Uncitral) on legal issues.

(59) Despite the global nature of electronic communications, coordination of national regulatory measures at European Union level is necessary in order to avoid fragmentation of the internal market, and for the establishment of an appropriate European regulatory framework; such coordination should also contribute to the establishment of a common and strong negotiating position in international forums.

(60) In order to allow the unhampered development of electronic commerce, the legal framework must be clear and simple, predictable and consistent with the rules applicable at international level so that it does not adversely affect the competitiveness of European industry or impede innovation in that sector.

(61) If the market is actually to operate by electronic means in the context of globalisation, the European Union and the major non-European areas need to consult each other with a view to making laws and procedures compatible.

(62) Cooperation with third countries should be strengthened in the area of electronic commerce, in particular with applicant countries, the developing countries and the European Union's other trading partners.

L 178/8 | EN | Official Journal of the European Communities | 17.7.2000

(63) The adoption of this Directive will not prevent the Member States from taking into account the various social, societal and cultural implications which are inherent in the advent of the information society; in particular it should not hinder measures which Member States might adopt in conformity with Community law to achieve social, cultural and democratic goals taking into account their linguistic diversity, national and regional specificities as well as their cultural heritage, and to ensure and maintain public access to the widest possible range of information society services; in any case, the development of the information society is to ensure that Community citizens can have access to the cultural European heritage provided in the digital environment.

(64) Electronic communication offers the Member States an excellent means of providing public services in the cultural, educational and linguistic fields.

(65) The Council, in its resolution of 19 January 1999 on the consumer dimension of the information society (¹), stressed that the protection of consumers deserved special attention in this field; the Commission will examine the degree to which existing consumer protection rules provide insufficient protection in the context of the information society and will identify, where necessary, the deficiencies of this legislation and those issues which could require additional measures; if need be, the Commission should make specific additional proposals to resolve such deficiencies that will thereby have been identified,

HAVE ADOPTED THIS DIRECTIVE:

CHAPTER I

GENERAL PROVISIONS

Article 1

Objective and scope

1.   This Directive seeks to contribute to the proper functioning of the internal market by ensuring the free movement of information society services between the Member States.

2.   This Directive approximates, to the extent necessary for the achievement of the objective set out in paragraph 1, certain national provisions on information society services relating to the internal market, the establishment of service providers,

---

(¹) OJ C 23, 28.1.1999, p. 1.

commercial communications, electronic contracts, the liability of intermediaries, codes of conduct, out-of-court dispute settlements, court actions and cooperation between Member States.

3.   This Directive complements Community law applicable to information society services without prejudice to the level of protection for, in particular, public health and consumer interests, as established by Community acts and national legislation implementing them in so far as this does not restrict the freedom to provide information society services.

4.   This Directive does not establish additional rules on private international law nor does it deal with the jurisdiction of Courts.

5.   This Directive shall not apply to:

(a) the field of taxation;

(b) questions relating to information society services covered by Directives 95/46/EC and 97/66/EC;

(c) questions relating to agreements or practices governed by cartel law;

(d) the following activities of information society services:

— the activities of notaries or equivalent professions to the extent that they involve a direct and specific connection with the exercise of public authority,

— the representation of a client and defence of his interests before the courts,

— gambling activities which involve wagering a stake with monetary value in games of chance, including lotteries and betting transactions.

6.   This Directive does not affect measures taken at Community or national level, in the respect of Community law, in order to promote cultural and linguistic diversity and to ensure the defence of pluralism.

Article 2

Definitions

For the purpose of this Directive, the following terms shall bear the following meanings:

(a) 'information society services': services within the meaning of Article 1(2) of Directive 98/34/EC as amended by Directive 98/48/EC;

(b) 'service provider': any natural or legal person providing an information society service;

(c) 'established service provider': a service provider who effectively pursues an economic activity using a fixed establishment for an indefinite period. The presence and use of the technical means and technologies required to provide the service do not, in themselves, constitute an establishment of the provider;

(d) 'recipient of the service': any natural or legal person who, for professional ends or otherwise, uses an information society service, in particular for the purposes of seeking information or making it accessible;

(e) 'consumer': any natural person who is acting for purposes which are outside his or her trade, business or profession;

(f) 'commercial communication': any form of communication designed to promote, directly or indirectly, the goods, services or image of a company, organisation or person pursuing a commercial, industrial or craft activity or exercising a regulated profession. The following do not in themselves constitute commercial communications:

— information allowing direct access to the activity of the company, organisation or person, in particular a domain name or an electronic-mail address,

— communications relating to the goods, services or image of the company, organisation or person compiled in an independent manner, particularly when this is without financial consideration;

(g) 'regulated profession': any profession within the meaning of either Article 1(d) of Council Directive 89/48/EEC of 21 December 1988 on a general system for the recognition of higher-education diplomas awarded on completion of professional education and training of at least three-years' duration([1]) or of Article 1(f) of Council Directive 92/51/EEC of 18 June 1992 on a second general system for the recognition of professional education and training to supplement Directive 89/48/EEC([2]);

(h) 'coordinated field': requirements laid down in Member States' legal systems applicable to information society service providers or information society services, regardless of whether they are of a general nature or specifically designed for them.

(i) The coordinated field concerns requirements with which the service provider has to comply in respect of:

— the taking up of the activity of an information society service, such as requirements concerning qualifications, authorisation or notification,

— the pursuit of the activity of an information society service, such as requirements concerning the behaviour of the service provider, requirements regarding the quality or content of the service including those applicable to advertising and contracts, or requirements concerning the liability of the service provider;

(ii) The coordinated field does not cover requirements such as:

— requirements applicable to goods as such,

— requirements applicable to the delivery of goods,

— requirements applicable to services not provided by electronic means.

Article 3

Internal market

1.   Each Member State shall ensure that the information society services provided by a service provider established on its territory comply with the national provisions applicable in the Member State in question which fall within the coordinated field.

2.   Member States may not, for reasons falling within the coordinated field, restrict the freedom to provide information society services from another Member State.

3.   Paragraphs 1 and 2 shall not apply to the fields referred to in the Annex.

4.   Member States may take measures to derogate from paragraph 2 in respect of a given information society service if the following conditions are fulfilled:

(a) the measures shall be:

(i) necessary for one of the following reasons:

— public policy, in particular the prevention, investigation, detection and prosecution of criminal offences, including the protection of minors and the fight against any incitement to hatred on grounds of race, sex, religion or nationality, and violations of human dignity concerning individual persons,

— the protection of public health,

([1]) OJ L 19, 24.1.1989, p. 16.
([2]) OJ L 209, 24.7.1992, p. 25. Directive as last amended by Commission Directive 97/38/EC (OJ L 184, 12.7.1997, p. 31).

L 178/10　　[EN]　　Official Journal of the European Communities　　17.7.2000

— public security, including the safeguarding of national security and defence,

— the protection of consumers, including investors;

(ii) taken against a given information society service which prejudices the objectives referred to in point (i) or which presents a serious and grave risk of prejudice to those objectives;

(iii) proportionate to those objectives;

(b) before taking the measures in question and without prejudice to court proceedings, including preliminary proceedings and acts carried out in the framework of a criminal investigation, the Member State has:

— asked the Member State referred to in paragraph 1 to take measures and the latter did not take such measures, or they were inadequate,

— notified the Commission and the Member State referred to in paragraph 1 of its intention to take such measures.

5.　Member States may, in the case of urgency, derogate from the conditions stipulated in paragraph 4(b). Where this is the case, the measures shall be notified in the shortest possible time to the Commission and to the Member State referred to in paragraph 1, indicating the reasons for which the Member State considers that there is urgency.

6.　Without prejudice to the Member State's possibility of proceeding with the measures in question, the Commission shall examine the compatibility of the notified measures with Community law in the shortest possible time; where it comes to the conclusion that the measure is incompatible with Community law, the Commission shall ask the Member State in question to refrain from taking any proposed measures or urgently to put an end to the measures in question.

CHAPTER II

PRINCIPLES

Section 1: Establishment and information requirements

Article 4

Principle excluding prior authorisation

1.　Member States shall ensure that the taking up and pursuit of the activity of an information society service provider may not be made subject to prior authorisation or any other requirement having equivalent effect.

2.　Paragraph 1 shall be without prejudice to authorisation schemes which are not specifically and exclusively targeted at information society services, or which are covered by Directive 97/13/EC of the European Parliament and of the Council of 10 April 1997 on a common framework for general authorisations and individual licences in the field of telecommunications services [1].

Article 5

General information to be provided

1.　In addition to other information requirements established by Community law, Member States shall ensure that the service provider shall render easily, directly and permanently accessible to the recipients of the service and competent authorities, at least the following information:

(a) the name of the service provider;

(b) the geographic address at which the service provider is established;

(c) the details of the service provider, including his electronic mail address, which allow him to be contacted rapidly and communicated with in a direct and effective manner;

(d) where the service provider is registered in a trade or similar public register, the trade register in which the service provider is entered and his registration number, or equivalent means of identification in that register;

(e) where the activity is subject to an authorisation scheme, the particulars of the relevant supervisory authority;

(f) as concerns the regulated professions:

— any professional body or similar institution with which the service provider is registered,

— the professional title and the Member State where it has been granted,

— a reference to the applicable professional rules in the Member State of establishment and the means to access them;

(g) where the service provider undertakes an activity that is subject to VAT, the identification number referred to in Article 22(1) of the sixth Council Directive 77/388/EEC of 17 May 1977 on the harmonisation of the laws of the Member States relating to turnover taxes — Common system of value added tax: uniform basis of assessment [2].

---

[1] OJ L 117, 7.5.1997, p. 15.
[2] OJ L 145, 13.6.1977, p. 1. Directive as last amended by Directive 1999/85/EC (OJ L 277, 28.10.1999, p. 34).

17.7.2000   EN   Official Journal of the European Communities   L 178/11

2.   In addition to other information requirements established by Community law, Member States shall at least ensure that, where information society services refer to prices, these are to be indicated clearly and unambiguously and, in particular, must indicate whether they are inclusive of tax and delivery costs.

Section 2: Commercial communications

Article 6

Information to be provided

In addition to other information requirements established by Community law, Member States shall ensure that commercial communications which are part of, or constitute, an information society service comply at least with the following conditions:

(a) the commercial communication shall be clearly identifiable as such;

(b) the natural or legal person on whose behalf the commercial communication is made shall be clearly identifiable;

(c) promotional offers, such as discounts, premiums and gifts, where permitted in the Member State where the service provider is established, shall be clearly identifiable as such, and the conditions which are to be met to qualify for them shall be easily accessible and be presented clearly and unambiguously;

(d) promotional competitions or games, where permitted in the Member State where the service provider is established, shall be clearly identifiable as such, and the conditions for participation shall be easily accessible and be presented clearly and unambiguously.

Article 7

Unsolicited commercial communication

1.   In addition to other requirements established by Community law, Member States which permit unsolicited commercial communication by electronic mail shall ensure that such commercial communication by a service provider established in their territory shall be identifiable clearly and unambiguously as such as soon as it is received by the recipient.

2.   Without prejudice to Directive 97/7/EC and Directive 97/66/EC, Member States shall take measures to ensure that service providers undertaking unsolicited commercial communications by electronic mail consult regularly and respect the opt-out registers in which natural persons not wishing to receive such commercial communications can register themselves.

Article 8

Regulated professions

1.   Member States shall ensure that the use of commercial communications which are part of, or constitute, an information society service provided by a member of a regulated profession is permitted subject to compliance with the professional rules regarding, in particular, the independence, dignity and honour of the profession, professional secrecy and fairness towards clients and other members of the profession.

2.   Without prejudice to the autonomy of professional bodies and associations, Member States and the Commission shall encourage professional associations and bodies to establish codes of conduct at Community level in order to determine the types of information that can be given for the purposes of commercial communication in conformity with the rules referred to in paragraph 1

3.   When drawing up proposals for Community initiatives which may become necessary to ensure the proper functioning of the Internal Market with regard to the information referred to in paragraph 2, the Commission shall take due account of codes of conduct applicable at Community level and shall act in close cooperation with the relevant professional associations and bodies.

4.   This Directive shall apply in addition to Community Directives concerning access to, and the exercise of, activities of the regulated professions.

Section 3: Contracts concluded by electronic means

Article 9

Treatment of contracts

1.   Member States shall ensure that their legal system allows contracts to be concluded by electronic means. Member States shall in particular ensure that the legal requirements applicable to the contractual process neither create obstacles for the use of electronic contracts nor result in such contracts being deprived of legal effectiveness and validity on account of their having been made by electronic means.

2.   Member States may lay down that paragraph 1 shall not apply to all or certain contracts falling into one of the following categories:

(a) contracts that create or transfer rights in real estate, except for rental rights;

L 178/12   EN   Official Journal of the European Communities   17.7.2000

(b) contracts requiring by law the involvement of courts, public authorities or professions exercising public authority;

(c) contracts of suretyship granted and on collateral securities furnished by persons acting for purposes outside their trade, business or profession;

(d) contracts governed by family law or by the law of succession.

3.   Member States shall indicate to the Commission the categories referred to in paragraph 2 to which they do not apply paragraph 1. Member States shall submit to the Commission every five years a report on the application of paragraph 2 explaining the reasons why they consider it necessary to maintain the category referred to in paragraph 2(b) to which they do not apply paragraph 1.

Article 10

Information to be provided

1.   In addition to other information requirements established by Community law, Member States shall ensure, except when otherwise agreed by parties who are not consumers, that at least the following information is given by the service provider clearly, comprehensibly and unambiguously and prior to the order being placed by the recipient of the service:

(a) the different technical steps to follow to conclude the contract;

(b) whether or not the concluded contract will be filed by the service provider and whether it will be accessible;

(c) the technical means for identifying and correcting input errors prior to the placing of the order;

(d) the languages offered for the conclusion of the contract.

2.   Member States shall ensure that, except when otherwise agreed by parties who are not consumers, the service provider indicates any relevant codes of conduct to which he subscribes and information on how those codes can be consulted electronically.

3.   Contract terms and general conditions provided to the recipient must be made available in a way that allows him to store and reproduce them.

4.   Paragraphs 1 and 2 shall not apply to contracts concluded exclusively by exchange of electronic mail or by equivalent individual communications.

Article 11

Placing of the order

1.   Member States shall ensure, except when otherwise agreed by parties who are not consumers, that in cases where the recipient of the service places his order through technological means, the following principles apply:

— the service provider has to acknowledge the receipt of the recipient's order without undue delay and by electronic means,

— the order and the acknowledgement of receipt are deemed to be received when the parties to whom they are addressed are able to access them.

2.   Member States shall ensure that, except when otherwise agreed by parties who are not consumers, the service provider makes available to the recipient of the service appropriate, effective and accessible technical means allowing him to identify and correct input errors, prior to the placing of the order.

3.   Paragraph 1, first indent, and paragraph 2 shall not apply to contracts concluded exclusively by exchange of electronic mail or by equivalent individual communications.

Section 4: Liability of intermediary service providers

Article 12

'Mere conduit'

1.   Where an information society service is provided that consists of the transmission in a communication network of information provided by a recipient of the service, or the provision of access to a communication network, Member States shall ensure that the service provider is not liable for the information transmitted, on condition that the provider:

(a) does not initiate the transmission;

(b) does not select the receiver of the transmission; and

(c) does not select or modify the information contained in the transmission.

2.   The acts of transmission and of provision of access referred to in paragraph 1 include the automatic, intermediate and transient storage of the information transmitted in so far as this takes place for the sole purpose of carrying out the transmission in the communication network, and provided that the information is not stored for any period longer than is reasonably necessary for the transmission.

3.   This Article shall not affect the possibility for a court or administrative authority, in accordance with Member States' legal systems, of requiring the service provider to terminate or prevent an infringement.

Article 13

'Caching'

1.   Where an information society service is provided that consists of the transmission in a communication network of information provided by a recipient of the service, Member States shall ensure that the service provider is not liable for the automatic, intermediate and temporary storage of that information, performed for the sole purpose of making more efficient the information's onward transmission to other recipients of the service upon their request, on condition that:

(a) the provider does not modify the information;

(b) the provider complies with conditions on access to the information;

(c) the provider complies with rules regarding the updating of the information, specified in a manner widely recognised and used by industry;

(d) the provider does not interfere with the lawful use of technology, widely recognised and used by industry, to obtain data on the use of the information; and

(e) the provider acts expeditiously to remove or to disable access to the information it has stored upon obtaining actual knowledge of the fact that the information at the initial source of the transmission has been removed from the network, or access to it has been disabled, or that a court or an administrative authority has ordered such removal or disablement.

2.   This Article shall not affect the possibility for a court or administrative authority, in accordance with Member States' legal systems, of requiring the service provider to terminate or prevent an infringement.

Article 14

Hosting

1.   Where an information society service is provided that consists of the storage of information provided by a recipient of the service, Member States shall ensure that the service provider is not liable for the information stored at the request of a recipient of the service, on condition that:

(a) the provider does not have actual knowledge of illegal activity or information and, as regards claims for damages, is not aware of facts or circumstances from which the illegal activity or information is apparent; or

(b) the provider, upon obtaining such knowledge or awareness, acts expeditiously to remove or to disable access to the information.

2.   Paragraph 1 shall not apply when the recipient of the service is acting under the authority or the control of the provider.

3.   This Article shall not affect the possibility for a court or administrative authority, in accordance with Member States' legal systems, of requiring the service provider to terminate or prevent an infringement, nor does it affect the possibility for Member States of establishing procedures governing the removal or disabling of access to information.

Article 15

No general obligation to monitor

1.   Member States shall not impose a general obligation on providers, when providing the services covered by Articles 12, 13 and 14, to monitor the information which they transmit or store, nor a general obligation actively to seek facts or circumstances indicating illegal activity.

2.   Member States may establish obligations for information society service providers promptly to inform the competent public authorities of alleged illegal activities undertaken or information provided by recipients of their service or obligations to communicate to the competent authorities, at their request, information enabling the identification of recipients of their service with whom they have storage agreements.

CHAPTER III

IMPLEMENTATION

Article 16

Codes of conduct

1.   Member States and the Commission shall encourage:

(a) the drawing up of codes of conduct at Community level, by trade, professional and consumer associations or organisations, designed to contribute to the proper implementation of Articles 5 to 15;

(b) the voluntary transmission of draft codes of conduct at national or Community level to the Commission;

(c) the accessibility of these codes of conduct in the Community languages by electronic means;

(d) the communication to the Member States and the Commission, by trade, professional and consumer associations or organisations, of their assessment of the application of their codes of conduct and their impact upon practices, habits or customs relating to electronic commerce;

(e) the drawing up of codes of conduct regarding the protection of minors and human dignity.

2.   Member States and the Commission shall encourage the involvement of associations or organisations representing consumers in the drafting and implementation of codes of conduct affecting their interests and drawn up in accordance with paragraph 1(a). Where appropriate, to take account of their specific needs, associations representing the visually impaired and disabled should be consulted.

Article 17

Out-of-court dispute settlement

1.   Member States shall ensure that, in the event of disagreement between an information society service provider and the recipient of the service, their legislation does not hamper the use of out-of-court schemes, available under national law, for dispute settlement, including appropriate electronic means.

2.   Member States shall encourage bodies responsible for the out-of-court settlement of, in particular, consumer disputes to operate in a way which provides adequate procedural guarantees for the parties concerned.

3.   Member States shall encourage bodies responsible for out-of-court dispute settlement to inform the Commission of the significant decisions they take regarding information society services and to transmit any other information on the practices, usages or customs relating to electronic commerce.

Article 18

Court actions

1.   Member States shall ensure that court actions available under national law concerning information society services' activities allow for the rapid adoption of measures, including interim measures, designed to terminate any alleged infringement and to prevent any further impairment of the interests involved.

2.   The Annex to Directive 98/27/EC shall be supplemented as follows:

   '11. Directive 2000/31/EC of the European Parliament and of the Council of 8 June 2000 on certain legal aspects on information society services, in particular electronic commerce, in the internal market (Directive on electronic commerce) (OJ L 178, 17.7.2000, p. 1).'

Article 19

Cooperation

1.   Member States shall have adequate means of supervision and investigation necessary to implement this Directive effectively and shall ensure that service providers supply them with the requisite information.

2.   Member States shall cooperate with other Member States; they shall, to that end, appoint one or several contact points, whose details they shall communicate to the other Member States and to the Commission.

3.   Member States shall, as quickly as possible, and in conformity with national law, provide the assistance and information requested by other Member States or by the Commission, including by appropriate electronic means.

4.   Member States shall establish contact points which shall be accessible at least by electronic means and from which recipients and service providers may:

(a) obtain general information on contractual rights and obligations as well as on the complaint and redress mechanisms available in the event of disputes, including practical aspects involved in the use of such mechanisms;

(b) obtain the details of authorities, associations or organisations from which they may obtain further information or practical assistance.

5.   Member States shall encourage the communication to the Commission of any significant administrative or judicial decisions taken in their territory regarding disputes relating to information society services and practices, usages and customs relating to electronic commerce. The Commission shall communicate these decisions to the other Member States.

Article 20

Sanctions

Member States shall determine the sanctions applicable to infringements of national provisions adopted pursuant to this Directive and shall take all measures necessary to ensure that they are enforced. The sanctions they provide for shall be effective, proportionate and dissuasive.

CHAPTER IV

FINAL PROVISIONS

Article 21

Re-examination

1.   Before 17 July 2003, and thereafter every two years, the Commission shall submit to the European Parliament, the Council and the Economic and Social Committee a report on the application of this Directive, accompanied, where necessary, by proposals for adapting it to legal, technical and economic developments in the field of information society services, in particular with respect to crime prevention, the protection of minors, consumer protection and to the proper functioning of the internal market.

2.   In examining the need for an adaptation of this Directive, the report shall in particular analyse the need for proposals concerning the liability of providers of hyperlinks and location tool services, 'notice and take down' procedures and the attribution of liability following the taking down of content. The report shall also analyse the need for additional conditions for the exemption from liability, provided for in Articles 12 and 13, in the light of technical developments, and the possibility of applying the internal market principles to unsolicited commercial communications by electronic mail.

Article 22

Transposition

1.   Member States shall bring into force the laws, regulations and administrative provisions necessary to comply with this Directive before 17 January 2002. They shall forthwith inform the Commission thereof.

2.   When Member States adopt the measures referred to in paragraph 1, these shall contain a reference to this Directive or shall be accompanied by such reference at the time of their official publication. The methods of making such reference shall be laid down by Member States.

Article 23

Entry into force

This Directive shall enter into force on the day of its publication in the *Official Journal of the European Communities*.

Article 24

Addressees

This Directive is addressed to the Member States.

Done at Luxemburg, 8 june 2000.

For the European Parliament	*For the Council*
The President	*The President*
N. FONTAINE	G. d'OLIVEIRA MARTINS

L 178/16 ┌──────┐ Official Journal of the European Communities 17.7.2000
           │ EN │
           └──────┘

ANNEX

DEROGATIONS FROM ARTICLE 3

As provided for in Article 3(3), Article 3(1) and (2) do not apply to:

— copyright, neighbouring rights, rights referred to in Directive 87/54/EEC (¹) and Directive 96/9/EC (²) as well as industrial property rights,

— the emission of electronic money by institutions in respect of which Member States have applied one of the derogations provided for in Article 8(1) of Directive 2000/46/EC (³),

— Article 44(2) of Directive 85/611/EEC (⁴),

— Article 30 and Title IV of Directive 92/49/EEC (⁵), Title IV of Directive 92/96/EEC (⁶), Articles 7 and 8 of Directive 88/357/EEC (⁷) and Article 4 of Directive 90/619/EEC (⁸),

— the freedom of the parties to choose the law applicable to their contract,

— contractual obligations concerning consumer contacts,

— formal validity of contracts creating or transferring rights in real estate where such contracts are subject to mandatory formal requirements of the law of the Member State where the real estate is situated,

— the permissibility of unsolicited commercial communications by electronic mail.

(¹) OJ L 24, 27.1.1987, p. 36.
(²) OJ L 77, 27.3.1996, p. 20.
(³) Not yet published in the Official Journal.
(⁴) OJ L 375, 31.12.1985, p. 3. Directive as last amended by Directive 95/26/EC (OJ L 168, 18.7.1995, p. 7).
(⁵) OJ L 228, 11.8.1992, p. 1. Directive as last amended by Directive 95/26/EC.
(⁶) OJ L 360, 9.12.1992, p. 2. Directive as last amended by Directive 95/26/EC.
(⁷) OJ L 172, 4.7.1988, p. 1. Directive as last amended by Directive 92/49/EC.
(⁸) OJ L 330, 29.11.1990, p. 50. Directive as last amended by Directive 92/96/EC.

Appendix 2

Statutory Instrument 2002 No. 2013

The Electronic Commerce (EC Directive) Regulations 2002

© Crown Copyright 2002

STATUTORY INSTRUMENTS

2002 No. 2013

ELECTRONIC COMMUNICATIONS

The Electronic Commerce (EC Directive) Regulations 2002

Made	*30th July 2002*
Laid before Parliament	*31st July 2002*
Coming into force	
Regulation 16	*23rd October 2002*
Remainder	*21st August 2002*

The Secretary of State, being a Minister designated[1] for the purposes of section 2(2) of the European Communities Act 1972[2] in relation to information society services, in exercise of the powers conferred on her by that section, hereby makes the following Regulations:—

Citation and commencement

1.—(1) These Regulations may be cited as the Electronic Commerce (EC Directive) Regulations 2002 and except for regulation 16 shall come into force on 21st August 2002.
 (2) Regulation 16 shall come into force on 23rd October 2002.

Interpretation

2.—(1) In these Regulations and in the Schedule—

"commercial communication" means a communication, in any form, designed to promote, directly or indirectly, the goods, services or image of any person pursuing a commercial, industrial or craft activity or exercising a regulated profession, other than a communication—

(a) consisting only of information allowing direct access to the activity of that person including a geographic address, a domain name or an electronic mail address; or

---

[1] S.I. 2001/2555.back
[2] 1972 c. 68.back

(b) relating to the goods, services or image of that person provided that the communication has been prepared independently of the person making it (and for this purpose, a communication prepared without financial consideration is to be taken to have been prepared independently unless the contrary is shown);

"the Commission" means the Commission of the European Communities;

"consumer" means any natural person who is acting for purposes other than those of his trade, business or profession;

"coordinated field" means requirements applicable to information society service providers or information society services, regardless of whether they are of a general nature or specifically designed for them, and covers requirements with which the service provider has to comply in respect of—

(a) the taking up of the activity of an information society service, such as requirements concerning qualifications, authorisation or notification, and

(b) the pursuit of the activity of an information society service, such as requirements concerning the behaviour of the service provider, requirements regarding the quality or content of the service including those applicable to advertising and contracts, or requirements concerning the liability of the service provider,

but does not cover requirements such as those applicable to goods as such, to the delivery of goods or to services not provided by electronic means;

"the Directive" means Directive 2000/31/EC of the European Parliament and of the Council of 8 June 2000 on certain legal aspects of information society services, in particular electronic commerce, in the Internal Market (Directive on electronic commerce)[3];

"EEA Agreement" means the Agreement on the European Economic Area signed at Oporto on 2 May 1992 as adjusted by the Protocol signed at Brussels on 17 March 1993[4];

"enactment" includes an enactment comprised in Northern Ireland legislation and comprised in, or an instrument made under, an Act of the Scottish Parliament;

"enforcement action" means any form of enforcement action including, in particular—

(a) in relation to any legal requirement imposed by or under any enactment, any action taken with a view to or in connection with imposing any sanction (whether criminal or otherwise) for failure to observe or comply with it; and

(b) in relation to a permission or authorisation, anything done with a view to removing or restricting that permission or authorisation;

"enforcement authority" does not include courts but, subject to that, means any person who is authorised, whether by or under an enactment or otherwise, to take enforcement action;

"established service provider" means a service provider who is a national of a member State or a company or firm as mentioned in Article 48 of the Treaty and who effectively pursues an economic activity by virtue of which he is a service provider using a fixed establishment in a member State for an indefinite period, but the presence and use of the

[3] O.J. L178, 17.7.2000, p.1.back
[4] O.J. L1, 3.1.94, p.3 and p.572.back

technical means and technologies required to provide the information society service do not, in themselves, constitute an establishment of the provider; in cases where it cannot be determined from which of a number of places of establishment a given service is provided, that service is to be regarded as provided from the place of establishment where the provider has the centre of his activities relating to that service; references to a service provider being established or to the establishment of a service provider shall be construed accordingly;

"information society services" (which is summarised in recital 17 of the Directive as covering "any service normally provided for remuneration, at a distance, by means of electronic equipment for the processing (including digital compression) and storage of data, and at the individual request of a recipient of a service") has the meaning set out in Article 2(a) of the Directive, (which refers to Article 1(2) of Directive 98/34/EC of the European Parliament and of the Council of 22 June 1998 laying down a procedure for the provision of information in the field of technical standards and regulations[5], as amended by Directive 98/48/EC of 20 July 1998[6]);

"member State" includes a State which is a contracting party to the EEA Agreement;

"recipient of the service" means any person who, for professional ends or otherwise, uses an information society service, in particular for the purposes of seeking information or making it accessible;

"regulated profession" means any profession within the meaning of either Article 1(d) of Council Directive 89/48/EEC of 21 December 1988 on a general system for the recognition of higher-education diplomas awarded on completion of professional education and training of at least three years' duration[7] or of Article 1(f) of Council Directive 92/51/EEC of 18 June 1992 on a second general system for the recognition of professional education and training to supplement Directive 89/48/EEC[8];

"service provider" means any person providing an information society service;

"the Treaty" means the treaty establishing the European Community.

(2) In regulation 4 and 5, "requirement" means any legal requirement under the law of the United Kingdom, or any part of it, imposed by or under any enactment or otherwise.

(3) Terms used in the Directive other than those in paragraph (1) above shall have the same meaning as in the Directive.

Exclusions

3.—(1) Nothing in these Regulations shall apply in respect of—

    (a) the field of taxation;

    (b) questions relating to information society services covered by the Data Protection Directive[9] and the Telecommunications Data Protection Directive[10]

---

  [5] O.J. L204, 21.7.98, p.37.back

  [6] O.J. L217, 5.8.98, p.18.back

  [7] O.J. L19, 24.1.89, p.16. Directive as last amended by Directive 2001/19/EC; O.J. L206, 31.7.2001, p.1.back

  [8] O.J. L209, 24.7.92, p.25. Directive as last amended by Directive 2001/19/EC; O.J. L206, 31.7.2001, p.1.back

  [9] O.J. L281, 23.11.95, p.31.back

  [10] O.J. L24, 30.1.98, p.1.back

and Directive 2002/58/EC of the European Parliament and of the Council of 12th July 2002 concerning the processing of personal data and the protection of privacy in the electronic communications sector (Directive on privacy and electronic communications)[11];

(c) questions relating to agreements or practices governed by cartel law; and

(d) the following activities of information society services—

> (i)   the activities of a public notary or equivalent professions to the extent that they involve a direct and specific connection with the exercise of public authority,
>
> (ii) the representation of a client and defence of his interests before the courts, and
>
> (iii) betting, gaming or lotteries which involve wagering a stake with monetary value.

(2) These Regulations shall not apply in relation to any Act passed on or after the date these Regulations are made or in exercise of a power to legislate after that date.

(3) In this regulation—

"cartel law" means so much of the law relating to agreements between undertakings, decisions by associations of undertakings or concerted practices as relates to agreements to divide the market or fix prices;

"Data Protection Directive" means Directive 95/46/EC of the European Parliament and of the Council of 24 October 1995 on the protection of individuals with regard to the processing of personal data and on the free movement of such data; and

"Telecommunications Data Protection Directive" means Directive 97/66/EC of the European Parliament and of the Council of 15 December 1997 concerning the processing of personal data and the protection of privacy in the telecommunications sector.

Internal market

4.—(1) Subject to paragraph (4) below, any requirement which falls within the coordinated field shall apply to the provision of an information society service by a service provider established in the United Kingdom irrespective of whether that information society service is provided in the United Kingdom or another member State.

(2) Subject to paragraph (4) below, an enforcement authority with responsibility in relation to any requirement in paragraph (1) shall ensure that the provision of an information society service by a service provider established in the United Kingdom complies with that requirement irrespective of whether that service is provided in the United Kingdom or another member State and any power, remedy or procedure for taking enforcement action shall be available to secure compliance.

(3) Subject to paragraphs (4), (5) and (6) below, any requirement shall not be applied to the provision of an information society service by a service provider established in a member State other than the United Kingdom for reasons which fall within the coordinated field where its application would restrict the freedom to provide information society services to a person in the United Kingdom from that member State.

[11] O.J. L201, 31.7.2002, p.37.back

(4) Paragraphs (1), (2) and (3) shall not apply to those fields in the annex to the Directive set out in the Schedule.

(5) The reference to any requirements the application of which would restrict the freedom to provide information society services from another member State in paragraph (3) above does not include any requirement maintaining the level of protection for public health and consumer interests established by Community acts.

(6) To the extent that anything in these Regulations creates any new criminal offence, it shall not be punishable with imprisonment for more than two years or punishable on summary conviction with imprisonment for more than three months or with a fine of more than level 5 on the standard scale (if not calculated on a daily basis) or with a fine of more than £100 a day[12].

Derogations from Regulation 4

5.—(1) Notwithstanding regulation 4(3), an enforcement authority may take measures, including applying any requirement which would otherwise not apply by virtue of regulation 4(3) in respect of a given information society service, where those measures are necessary for reasons of—

> (a) public policy, in particular the prevention, investigation, detection and prosecution of criminal offences, including the protection of minors and the fight against any incitement to hatred on grounds of race, sex, religion or nationality, and violations of human dignity concerning individual persons;
>
> (b) the protection of public health;
>
> (c) public security, including the safeguarding of national security and defence, or
>
> (d) the protection of consumers, including investors,

and proportionate to those objectives.

(2) Notwithstanding regulation 4(3), in any case where an enforcement authority with responsibility in relation to the requirement in question is not party to the proceedings, a court may, on the application of any person or of its own motion, apply any requirement which would otherwise not apply by virtue of regulation 4(3) in respect of a given information society service, if the application of that enactment or requirement is necessary for and proportionate to any of the objectives set out in paragraph (1) above.

(3) Paragraphs (1) and (2) shall only apply where the information society service prejudices or presents a serious and grave risk of prejudice to an objective in paragraph (1)(a) to (d).

(4) Subject to paragraphs (5) and (6), an enforcement authority shall not take the measures in paragraph (1) above, unless it—

> (a) asks the member State in which the service provider is established to take measures and the member State does not take such measures or they are inadequate; and

---

[12] The maximum penalty allowed under paragraph 1(1)(d) of Schedule 2 of the European Communities Act 1972 c. 68.back

(b) notifies the Commission and the member State in which the service provider is established of its intention to take such measures.

(5) Paragraph (4) shall not apply to court proceedings, including preliminary proceedings and acts carried out in the course of a criminal investigation.

(6) If it appears to the enforcement authority that the matter is one of urgency, it may take the measures under paragraph (1) without first asking the member State in which the service provider is established to take measures and notifying the Commission and the member State in derogation from paragraph (4).

(7) In a case where a measure is taken pursuant to paragraph (6) above, the enforcement authority shall notify the measures taken to the Commission and to the member State concerned in the shortest possible time thereafter and indicate the reasons for urgency.

(8) In paragraph (2), "court" means any court or tribunal.

General information to be provided by a person providing an information society service

6.—(1) A person providing an information society service shall make available to the recipient of the service and any relevant enforcement authority, in a form and manner which is easily, directly and permanently accessible, the following information—

    (a) the name of the service provider;

    (b) the geographic address at which the service provider is established;

    (c) the details of the service provider, including his electronic mail address, which make it possible to contact him rapidly and communicate with him in a direct and effective manner;

    (d) where the service provider is registered in a trade or similar register available to the public, details of the register in which the service provider is entered and his registration number, or equivalent means of identification in that register;

    (e) where the provision of the service is subject to an authorisation scheme, the particulars of the relevant supervisory authority;

    (f) where the service provider exercises a regulated profession—

        (i) the details of any professional body or similar institution with which the service provider is registered;

        (ii) his professional title and the member State where that title has been granted;

        (iii) a reference to the professional rules applicable to the service provider in the member State of establishment and the means to access them; and

    (g) where the service provider undertakes an activity that is subject to value added tax, the identification number referred to in Article 22(1) of the sixth Council Directive 77/388/EEC of 17 May 1977 on the harmonisation of the laws of the member States relating to turnover taxes—Common system of value added tax: uniform basis of assessment[13].

[13] O.J. L145, 13.6.77, p.1. Directive as last amended by Directive 2002/38/EC; O.J. L128, 15.5.2002, p.41.back

(2) Where a person providing an information society service refers to prices, these shall be indicated clearly and unambiguously and, in particular, shall indicate whether they are inclusive of tax and delivery costs.

Commercial communications

7. A service provider shall ensure that any commercial communication provided by him and which constitutes or forms part of an information society service shall—

(a) be clearly identifiable as a commercial communication;

(b) clearly identify the person on whose behalf the commercial communication is made;

(c) clearly identify as such any promotional offer (including any discount, premium or gift) and ensure that any conditions which must be met to qualify for it are easily accessible, and presented clearly and unambiguously; and

(d) clearly identify as such any promotional competition or game and ensure that any conditions for participation are easily accessible and presented clearly and unambiguously.

Unsolicited commercial communications

8. A service provider shall ensure that any unsolicited commercial communication sent by him by electronic mail is clearly and unambiguously identifiable as such as soon as it is received.

Information to be provided where contracts are concluded by electronic means

9.—(1) Unless parties who are not consumers have agreed otherwise, where a contract is to be concluded by electronic means a service provider shall, prior to an order being placed by the recipient of a service, provide to that recipient in a clear, comprehensible and unambiguous manner the information set out in (a) to (d) below—

(a) the different technical steps to follow to conclude the contract;

(b) whether or not the concluded contract will be filed by the service provider and whether it will be accessible;

(c) the technical means for identifying and correcting input errors prior to the placing of the order; and

(d) the languages offered for the conclusion of the contract.

(2) Unless parties who are not consumers have agreed otherwise, a service provider shall indicate which relevant codes of conduct he subscribes to and give information on how those codes can be consulted electronically.

(3) Where the service provider provides terms and conditions applicable to the contract to the recipient, the service provider shall make them available to him in a way that allows him to store and reproduce them.

(4) The requirements of paragraphs (1) and (2) above shall not apply to contracts concluded exclusively by exchange of electronic mail or by equivalent individual communications.

Other information requirements
10. Regulations 6, 7, 8 and 9(1) have effect in addition to any other information requirements in legislation giving effect to Community law.

Placing of the order
11.—(1) Unless parties who are not consumers have agreed otherwise, where the recipient of the service places his order through technological means, a service provider shall—

> (a) acknowledge receipt of the order to the recipient of the service without undue delay and by electronic means; and
> (b) make available to the recipient of the service appropriate, effective and accessible technical means allowing him to identify and correct input errors prior to the placing of the order.

(2) For the purposes of paragraph (1)(a) above—

> (a) the order and the acknowledgement of receipt will be deemed to be received when the parties to whom they are addressed are able to access them; and
> (b) the acknowledgement of receipt may take the form of the provision of the service paid for where that service is an information society service.

(3) The requirements of paragraph (1) above shall not apply to contracts concluded exclusively by exchange of electronic mail or by equivalent individual communications.

Meaning of the term "order"
12. Except in relation to regulation 9(1)(c) and regulation 11(1)(b) where "order" shall be the contractual offer, "order" may be but need not be the contractual offer for the purposes of regulations 9 and 11.

Liability of the service provider
13. The duties imposed by regulations 6, 7, 8, 9(1) and 11(1)(a) shall be enforceable, at the suit of any recipient of a service, by an action against the service provider for damages for breach of statutory duty.

Compliance with Regulation 9(3)
14. Where on request a service provider has failed to comply with the requirement in regulation 9(3), the recipient may seek an order from any court having jurisdiction in relation to the contract requiring that service provider to comply with that requirement.

Right to rescind contract
15. Where a person—

> (a) has entered into a contract to which these Regulations apply, and
> (b) the service provider has not made available means of allowing him to identify and correct input errors in compliance with regulation 11(1)(b),

he shall be entitled to rescind the contract unless any court having jurisdiction in relation to the contract in question orders otherwise on the application of the service provider.

Amendments to the Stop Now Orders (E.C. Directive) Regulations 2001
16.—(1) The Stop Now Orders (E.C. Directive) Regulations 2001[14] are amended as follows.
(2) In regulation 2(3), at the end there shall be added—

"(k) regulations 6, 7, 8, 9, and 11 of the Electronic Commerce (E.C. Directive) Regulations 2002.".

(3) In Schedule 1, at the end there shall be added—

"11. Directive 2000/31/EC of the European Parliament and of the Council of 8th June 2000 on certain legal aspects of information society services, in particular electronic commerce, in the Internal Market (Directive on Electronic Commerce)."[15]

Mere conduit
17.—(1) Where an information society service is provided which consists of the transmission in a communication network of information provided by a recipient of the service or the provision of access to a communication network, the service provider (if he otherwise would) shall not be liable for damages or for any other pecuniary remedy or for any criminal sanction as a result of that transmission where the service provider—

    (a) did not initiate the transmission;
    (b) did not select the receiver of the transmission; and
    (c) did not select or modify the information contained in the transmission.

(2) The acts of transmission and of provision of access referred to in paragraph (1) include the automatic, intermediate and transient storage of the information transmitted where:

    (a) this takes place for the sole purpose of carrying out the transmission in the communication network, and
    (b) the information is not stored for any period longer than is reasonably necessary for the transmission.

Caching
18. Where an information society service is provided which consists of the transmission in a communication network of information provided by a recipient of the service, the service provider (if he otherwise would) shall not be liable for damages or for any other pecuniary remedy or for any criminal sanction as a result of that transmission where—

    (a) the information is the subject of automatic, intermediate and temporary storage where that storage is for the sole purpose of making more efficient onward transmission of the information to other recipients of the service upon their request, and
    (b) the service provider—

        (i)　does not modify the information;
        (ii)　complies with conditions on access to the information;
        (iii)　complies with any rules regarding the updating of the information, specified in a manner widely recognised and used by industry;

[14] S.I. 2001/1422.back
[15] O.J. L178, 17.7.00, p.1.back

(iv) does not interfere with the lawful use of technology, widely recognised and used by industry, to obtain data on the use of the information; and
(v) acts expeditiously to remove or to disable access to the information he has stored upon obtaining actual knowledge of the fact that the information at the initial source of the transmission has been removed from the network, or access to it has been disabled, or that a court or an administrative authority has ordered such removal or disablement.

Hosting

19. Where an information society service is provided which consists of the storage of information provided by a recipient of the service, the service provider (if he otherwise would) shall not be liable for damages or for any other pecuniary remedy or for any criminal sanction as a result of that storage where—

(a) the service provider—

(i) does not have actual knowledge of unlawful activity or information and, where a claim for damages is made, is not aware of facts or circumstances from which it would have been apparent to the service provider that the activity or information was unlawful; or
(ii) upon obtaining such knowledge or awareness, acts expeditiously to remove or to disable access to the information, and

(b) the recipient of the service was not acting under the authority or the control of the service provider.

Protection of rights

20.—(1) Nothing in regulations 17, 18 and 19 shall—

(a) prevent a person agreeing different contractual terms; or
(b) affect the rights of any party to apply to a court for relief to prevent or stop infringement of any rights.

(2) Any power of an administrative authority to prevent or stop infringement of any rights shall continue to apply notwithstanding regulations 17, 18 and 19.

Defence in Criminal Proceedings: burden of proof

21.—(1) This regulation applies where a service provider charged with an offence in criminal proceedings arising out of any transmission, provision of access or storage falling within regulation 17, 18 or 19 relies on a defence under any of regulations 17, 18 and 19.

(2) Where evidence is adduced which is sufficient to raise an issue with respect to that defence, the court or jury shall assume that the defence is satisfied unless the prosecution proves beyond reasonable doubt that it is not.

Notice for the purposes of actual knowledge

22. In determining whether a service provider has actual knowledge for the purposes of regulations 18(b)(v) and 19(a)(i), a court shall take into account all matters which appear to it in the particular circumstances to be relevant and, among other things, shall have regard to—

   (a) whether a service provider has received a notice through a means of contact made available in accordance with regulation 6(1)(c), and

   (b) the extent to which any notice includes—

      (i)   the full name and address of the sender of the notice;

      (ii) details of the location of the information in question; and

      (iii) details of the unlawful nature of the activity or information in question.

Alan Johnson,

Minister of State for Employment Relations Industry and the Regions, Department of Trade and Industry

30th July 2002

SCHEDULE

Regulation 4(4)

   1. Copyright, neighbouring rights, rights referred to in Directive 87/54/EEC[16] and Directive 96/9/EC[17] and industrial property rights.

   2. The freedom of the parties to a contract to choose the applicable law.

   3. Contractual obligations concerning consumer contracts.

   4. Formal validity of contracts creating or transferring rights in real estate where such contracts are subject to mandatory formal requirements of the law of the member State where the real estate is situated.

   5. The permissibility of unsolicited commercial communications by electronic mail.

---

[16] Council Directive 87/54/EEC of 16 December 1986 on the legal protection of topographies of semiconductor products; O.J. L24, 27.1.87, p.36.back

[17] Directive 96/9/EC of the European Parliament and of the Council of 11 March 1996 on the legal protection of databases; O.J. L77, 27.3.96, p.20.back

Appendix 3

 COMMISSION OF THE EUROPEAN COMMUNITIES

Brussels, 21.11.2003
COM(2003) 702 final

**REPORT FROM THE COMMISSION
TO THE EUROPEAN PARLIAMENT, THE COUNCIL AND
THE EUROPEAN ECONOMIC AND SOCIAL COMMITTEE**

**First Report on the application of Directive 2000/31/EC of the European Parliament and
of the Council of 8 June 2000 on certain legal aspects of information society services, in
particular electronic commerce, in the Internal Market
(Directive on electronic commerce)**

TABLE OF CONTENTS

1.   INTRODUCTION

This report provides the first assessment of the transposition and application of Directive 2000/31/EC on electronic commerce[1] ("the Directive") and its impact. It is based both on the Commission's experience and on feedback received from Member States, industry, professional and consumer associations and other interested parties of their experience with the Directive. In view of the short period of time since the adoption and transposition of the Directive, such experience is necessarily limited. However, it shows that the Directive has had a substantial and positive effect on e-commerce within Europe. Together with the Directive on transparency for information society services[2], which establishes a mechanism allowing the Commission to assess draft national legislation as to its compatibility with Community law, it creates a straightforward Internal Market framework which allows e-commerce to grow across national borders.

Work at European level aiming to promote the development of e-commerce started at an early stage with the Commission's 1997 Communication "A European Initiative in Electronic Commerce"[3]. This set a clear objective of creating a coherent European legal framework for e-commerce by the year 2000.

Its importance was underlined by the 2000 Lisbon European Council, which set a new strategic goal for the European Union for the next decade: to become the most competitive and dynamic knowledge-based economy in the world. The Lisbon Council underlined that both citizens and business must have access to inexpensive, world-class communications infrastructure and a wide range of services and that realising Europe's full e-potential depended on creating the right conditions for e-commerce and the internet to flourish.

The Directive, which was adopted soon after the Lisbon Council, is fully in line with this objective. It removes obstacles to cross-border online services in the Internal Market and provides legal certainty to business and citizens alike. In so doing it enhances the competitiveness of European service providers, and stimulates innovation and job creation. It also contributes to the free flow of information and freedom of expression in the European Union.

The Directive provides a light and flexible legal framework for e-commerce and addresses only those elements which are strictly necessary in order to ensure the proper functioning of the Internal Market in e-commerce. It is drafted in a technologically neutral way to avoid the need to adapt the legal framework constantly to new developments.[4] It covers a wide variety

---

[1]   Directive 2000/31/EC of the European Parliament and of the Council of 8 June 2000 on certain legal aspects of information society services, in particular electronic commerce, in the Internal Market (Directive on electronic commerce), OJ L 178, 17.7.2000, p. 1.

[2]   Directive 98/34/EC of the European Parliament and of the Council of 22 June 1998 laying down a procedure for the provision of information in the field of technical standards and regulations and of rules on Information Society services, OJ L 204, 21.7.1998, p. 37 as amended by Directive 98/48/EC of the European Parliament and of the Council of 20 July 1998, OJ L 217, 5.8.1998, p. 18. On 13.2.2003 the Commission adopted a report to the European Parliament and the Council which specifically evaluates the application of Directive 98/34/EC in the field of Information Society Services (COM(2003)69). The report underlines the benefits of the procedure, confirming the value of this Directive as an effective internal-market tool in this new economic field.

[3]   COM(97) 157 final, 16.4.1997.

[4]   For instance, technological applications (WAP or PDA-sets) enabling the content to be accessed by a specific device do not constitute "modification of information" within the meaning of Article 12, but merely "technical specification of content".

of services provided online (so-called "information society services") ranging from online newspapers and specialised news services (such as business or financial information), online selling of various products (books, computer hardware and software, pharmaceuticals, etc.) to the online provision of financial services (online banking, online investment). The latter are of particular importance as they are particularly suitable for cross-border delivery, which the Commission has recognized in its Communication on E-commerce and Financial Services[5]. The Directive applies horizontally across all areas of law which touch on the provision of information society services, regardless of whether it is a matter of public, private, or criminal law. Furthermore, it applies equally both to business-to-business (B2B) and business-to-consumer (B2C) e-commerce.

The cornerstone of the Directive is the Internal Market clause which creates the legal certainty and clarity needed for information society service providers to be able to offer their services throughout the entire Community. The provisions on the liability of intermediaries create legal certainty for intermediary service providers and thus help to ensure the provision of basic intermediary services in the internet. At the same time, the Directive's provisions on information and transparency requirements, its rules on commercial communications, and the basic principles regarding electronic contracts provide for high standards in the conduct of online business in all Member States, thus also increasing consumer confidence.

Due to the fact that the Directive was one of the first legal instruments which approached a broad range of legal issues related to several aspects of the development of e-commerce and which provided a coherent set of legal rules for e-commerce as such, it has attracted a considerable amount of attention amongst regulators at international level and is a model for national, regional, or global regulatory initiatives[6].

In parallel with the putting into place of the legal framework, work continues at European level with the aim of stimulating the development of e-business and e-government. In particular, the Commission set out a coherent strategy in its eEurope Action Plan, which was adopted in 2002 in order to continue with the realisation of the goals set by the Lisbon Council.[7]

2.   ECONOMIC   AND   TECHNOLOGICAL   DEVELOPMENTS   IN E-COMMERCE

Despite the downturn that affected the e-economy, e-commerce is steadily increasing in the European Union. Gradually, online success stories are emerging, for example online market-places, business-to-business (B2B) platforms, and online finance. Development in the use of the internet has been rapid. There are estimated to be already 185 million European internet users.[8] Since the adoption of the Directive, growth in internet penetration in EU households has moved from 18% in 2000 to 43% in November 2002. Internet penetration in businesses is naturally much higher. Even amongst small enterprises (0-49 employees), by 2002, 84% had

---

[5]   COM(2001) 66 final, 7.2.2001.

[6]   UNCITRAL refers to the Directive in its on-going work on electronic contracts, cf. most recently the report on the 41st session of the Working Group on e-commerce at http://www.uncitral.org/en-index.htm; Mercosur is in regular dialogue with the Commission on legal issues relating to e-commerce.

[7]   On research and development, see also Information Society Technologies 2003-04 Work Programme of the European Commission, available at http://www.cordis.lu/ist.

[8]   Source: Interactive Advertising Bureau UK, 2002, http://www.iabuk.net. This is estimated to grow to 190 million by the end of this year by eMarketer, http://www.europemedia.net.

access to the internet. Approximately 70% of EU companies have their own website.[9] More than two-thirds of SMEs use the internet as a business tool. The internet is a key factor for them to increase their competitiveness and to create new products and services.

Since the adoption of the Directive, the potential of e-commerce has, in addition, been growing due to the technological development of broadband and multiplatform access i.e. the possibility of connecting to the internet via other means than a PC, such as digital TV and third generation mobile phones.[10] These developments are opening up a large variety of new opportunities for online services. New services, applications and content will create new markets and provide the means for increasing productivity and hence growth and employment throughout the economy. They will also provide both citizens and business with more convenient access to information and communication tools.[11]

Currently e-commerce represents only about 1-2% of retail sales in the EU, but the prospects for growth are promising: for instance, online Christmas shopping in 2002 saw an increase of 86% over the previous year. At present only about 12% of enterprises are selling online with tourism, financial services, publishing and software being the leading sectors, but their online purchasing has developed much faster.[12] However, according to estimates, B2C e-commerce is expected to increase from €10 billion in 2000 to €70 billion in 2003.[13] It is estimated that 54% of European internet users will shop online by 2006.[14]

In addition, online advertising is a fast growing sector. It has been predicted that growth in online advertising spending will outpace growth in total media spending in 2003.[15] Total spending on advertising grew about 2% in 2002, but online advertising has been growing about ten times faster.[16] Given the number of flexible forms which online advertising can take[17], and the relative speed with which marketers can modify the elements used in an online advertising campaign, marketers have been quick to utilise the various online advertising techniques available and to innovate in order to best suit the needs of potential customers, creating a more interactive marketing process.[18] Indeed, the internet has become a powerful tool for consumers to obtain information and compare offers in an efficient and user-friendly way, i.e., to make "pre-sale searches" enabling consumers to rapidly obtain information

---

9   The European e-Business Report 2002/2003 edition, the Business W@tch of the European Commission, either at www.europa.eu.int/comm/enterprise/ict/policy/watch/index.htm or at www.ebusiness-watch.org.

10   Communication of the European Commission "Towards the Full Roll-Out of Mobile Communications", COM(2002) 301 final, 11.6.2002.

11   eEurope 2005: An information society for all, COM(2002) 263 final, 28.5.2002.

12   eBusiness W@tch (reference above). In the UK and Germany, for instance, more than 50% of enterprises say they already use e-procurement.

13   European Information Technology Observatory, http://www.eito.org.

14   Interactive Advertising Bureau UK, 2002, http://www.iabuk.net.

15   eMarketer's Media Spending Outlook white paper, 2002.

16   In France and the UK record levels for online advertising have been noted in the second half of 2002, with a 52% increase in the UK compared with 2001 and a doubling of its size in France from 153 million euros in 2001 to 309 million euros in 2002, see "Europe's marketers switch to on-line", Interactive Advertising Bureau UK, June 2003.

17   E.g. banner ads, pop-up ads, keyword searches.

18   For example, once a contact has been made with a customer (and his consent given), businesses are able to tailor product offers to individual customer requirements allowing for personal 'one to one' offers by e-mail. The gradual switch from the use of pop-up ads to more user-friendly keyword-search related ads reflects the development of user-friendly advertising techniques.

concerning the range and characteristics of products and services available both throughout Europe and globally.[19]

The competitiveness of EU service providers has recently been substantially improved in e-commerce by the entry into force of the Directive relating to VAT on digital services on 1 July 2003[20], which eliminated competitive disadvantages suffered by EU service providers. The rules on electronic VAT compliance such as e-registration, e-filing and e-invoicing were also modernised.

3.   TRANSPOSITION OF THE DIRECTIVE

3.1.   Transposition timetable

The deadline for Member States to transpose the Directive into national law was 17 January 2002, 18 months after the entry into force of the Directive on 17 July 2000. The Council and the European Parliament accepted a relatively short transposition period having agreed that setting up a legal framework for e-commerce was a matter of priority.

There were, however, some delays in transposition, due mainly to the horizontal nature of the Directive, which affects a large variety of legal issues[21]. So far 12 Member States[22] have brought into force implementing legislation. In the remaining 3 Member States[23], work on the transposition of the Directive is well advanced. The Annex to this Report contains a list of national measures transposing the Directive.[24]

3.2.   Characteristics of transposition

In general, national transpositions have closely followed the form and content of the Directive[25]. Member States, with the exception of the Netherlands, decided to transpose the Directive by a horizontal e-commerce law in order to create as clear and user-friendly a national framework as possible. Germany transposed the Directive by modifying its

---

[19]   Online advertising, websites, e-mails, and search engine marketing have a distinct impact on the process of purchasing products even where the product is not sold on-line, see DoubleClick, Touchpoints: Effective Marketing Sequences in the Interactive Media Age, March 2003, http://www.doubleclick.com/us/knowledge/documents/research/dc_touchpoints_0303.pdf.
Sound statistics on the magnitude of the use of internet for pre-sale research is still lacking, however, surveys indicate that the figures are significant, see Research by the Interactive Advertising Bureau UK on the reach of interactive media around Europe.

[20]   Council Directive 2002/38/EC of 7 May 2002 amending and amending temporarily Directive 77/388/EEC as regards the value added tax arrangements applicable to radio and television broadcasting services and certain electronically supplied services, OJ L 128, 15.5.2002, p. 41. See also Council Regulation (EC) 792/2002, OJ L 128, 15.5.2002, p. 1.

[21]   These reasons came out in bilateral contacts with the Member States during the transposition. Many Member States, for instance, needed time to ensure wide national consultations of interested parties.

[22]   Belgium, Denmark, Germany, Greece, Spain, Ireland, Italy, Luxembourg, Austria, Finland, Sweden, United Kingdom. Of those, three Member States (Germany, Luxembourg, and Austria) transposed the Directive by the deadline of 17 January 2002.

[23]   France, Netherlands, and Portugal.

[24]   In addition, the three EEA-countries, Iceland, Liechtenstein and Norway (Norway with the exception of the liability provisions, which will be separately implemented) have passed the implementing legislation. For accession and candidate countries, see section 5.2.

[25]   As regards France, the Netherlands and Portugal, this comparison and other references in this report have been done on the basis of their draft laws, as the final laws were not yet available.

Teleservices Act.[26] The United Kingdom transposed the Directive in two parts: the general aspects and the financial services aspects. Belgium separated the main parts of the Directive and the Article 3(4)-(6) procedure into two separate laws for constitutional reasons.

In most Member States attention at the transposition stage was focused on the Internal Market clause and the provisions concerning liability of intermediary service providers. In addition, the correct transposition of the Directive has required a number of Member States to screen and modify existing national laws, for instance in order to remove obstacles to electronic contracting[27]. Some Member States included certain additional elements not covered by the Directive in their national laws: the liability of providers of hyperlinks and search engines[28], notice and take down procedures for illegal content[29], registration requirements for information society service providers[30], filtering[31], data retention[32], cryptology[33], and additional rules on electronic contracting. Some Member States also included within the scope of their national e-commerce law matters excluded from the scope of application of the Directive, such as online gambling.[34]

Throughout the transposition procedure the Commission services were in close cooperation with all Member States to provide them with assistance in ensuring the correct transposition of the Directive. Moreover, the large majority of the Member States notified their draft laws under the transparency procedure laid down in Directive 98/34/EC[35], since those drafts contained other rules affecting information society services, thus going beyond the mere transposition of the Directive. Both the close bilateral contacts with Member States and the notification procedure gave the Commission services an opportunity to thoroughly analyse and comment on the draft laws prior to their final adoption. This appeared to be a successful means of improving the quality of national transpositions.

3.3.   Follow-up to transposition

According to the Commission's preliminary evaluation, transposition of the Directive is, in general, satisfactory. Nevertheless, analysis of the final laws as adopted by the Member States will need to continue in 2004. The preliminary analysis indicates that one or two adopted laws contain problems related, in particular, to the transposition of the provisions concerning the liability of internet intermediaries. Before taking any formal steps, the Commission services intend to launch a dialogue with the Member States concerned to discuss the different options for solving these problems.

---

[26]   Germany was the only Member State which had already set up a horizontal legal framework at the national level prior to the adoption of the Directive, by virtue of the Teleservices Act (Teledienstegesetz vom 22. Juli 1997).

[27]   Consistent with Article 9.

[28]   Spain, Austria, and Portugal (see the liability section below for further details).

[29]   Finland has a copyright-specific notice and take down procedure laid down by law (as does EEA-country Iceland).

[30]   Spain and Portugal.

[31]   France.

[32]   Spain.

[33]   France and Luxembourg.

[34]   E.g., Spain, Austria, Luxembourg, and EEA-country Liechtenstein excluded gambling from the scope of the Internal Market principle only, with the effect that other parts of the national transposing measures apply fully to the provision of online gambling services.

[35]   Directive 98/34/EC of the European Parliament and of the Council of 22 June 1998 laying down a procedure for the provision of information in the field of technical standards and regulations, OJ L 204, 21.7.1998, p. 37, as modified by Directive 98/48/EC, OJ L 217, 5.8.1998, p. 18.

4.   APPLICATION OF THE DIRECTIVE

4.1.   Internal Market

The borderless nature of e-commerce required that the legal framework put in place for its operation had to provide legal certainty to both business and consumers. This legal certainty is brought about, along with other flanking measures, by the core feature of the Directive, the Internal Market clause.

This provision takes the form of two complementary features: each Member State must ensure that a provider of information society services established on its territory complies with the national provisions applicable in that Member State which fall within the "coordinated field"[36], even when he provides services in another Member State; in turn, Member States may not, for reasons falling within the co-ordinated field, restrict the freedom to provide information society services from another Member State.

The Internal Market clause is subject to some limited derogations which are set out in the Annex to the Directive. There is also a case by case derogation to the Internal Market clause which Member States may use to take measures, such as sanctions or injunctions, to restrict the provision of a particular online service from another Member State where there is a need to protect certain identified interests, e.g. consumers.[37] Any measures taken by a Member State relying on this provision are subject to strict conditions under Article 3(4)-(6).

Contrary to the expectations of some Member States that they would have frequent need to use this derogation, to date this has not been the case. The Commission has received only 5 formal notifications, all coming from the same Member State and all dealing with essentially the same problem (i.e. the fraudulent use of premium rate numbers), two of which made use of the 'emergency' procedure provided for by Article 3(5).[38] In May 2003, the Commission issued a Communication on the application to financial services of Article 3(4) to (6) of the Electronic Commerce Directive[39] providing guidance on the application of this case by case derogation in the area of financial services. This guidance followed expressions of concern by a number of Member States regarding a full application of the Internal Market clause to financial services pending closer convergence in certain financial services areas. The Communication explains in what limited circumstances[40] a Member State which considers that consumers on its territory should be protected against a particular online financial service, may take measures against that particular incoming financial service following notification to

---

[36]   I.e., requirements laid down in Member States' legal systems applicable to information society service providers or information society services, regardless of whether they are of a general nature or specifically designed for them, Art. 2(h).

[37]   The Article 3(4)-(6) derogation.

[38]   In a further case, the authorities of a Member State successfully took action to enforce their law transposing the Directive against a service provider established on their territory as a result of being requested to take appropriate action under national law by the authorities of another Member State. This action was taken pursuant to the co-operation obligation provided for by Article 3(4)(b), with the result that the problem was resolved without the Member State of destination needing to take any measures against the service provider.

[39]   Communication from the Commission to the Council, the European Parliament and the European Central Bank. Application to financial services of Article 3(4) to (6) of the Electronic Commerce Directive, COM(2003) 259 final, 14.5.2003.

[40]   These circumstances are the same as for other information society services.

the Commission. However, to date there have been no notifications from Member States concerning the provision of financial services.[41]

4.2.   Establishment and information requirements

Since Article 4(1) prohibits Member States from making the taking up and pursuit of the activity of an information society service provider subject to prior authorisation (or any other requirement having equivalent effect), no authorisation scheme exists in any of the Member States. Those Member States which had considered introducing such schemes in relation to all or some information society services refrained from doing so and in some cases abolished existing authorisation requirements. This has ensured that establishing as an information society service provider in a Member State is easy and not subject to bureaucratic hurdles.

By contrast, Article 5 ensures transparency and better information regarding a service provider's identity and place of establishment. It requires, amongst other things, that the name of the service provider, his geographic address, details permitting his rapid contact, and relevant entries in trade or similar registers, are provided. This Article has been transposed almost literally by most of the Member States and the EEA countries.

There seems to be a certain lack of awareness regarding these information requirements amongst internet operators in the EU. However, information society service providers in general responded promptly and positively when shortcomings in the fulfilment of the Directive's information requirements were pointed out to them.[42] Member States will need to increase awareness of these requirements in order to make sure that businesses adapt their websites accordingly.

4.3.   Commercial communications

The ability of a firm to advertise its services or products on the internet has several important effects: it not only provides an excellent medium for firms of any size to make themselves known and provides a major source of revenue for many information society service providers, but importantly, also constitutes an excellent source of information for consumers.

The Directive supplements existing Directives in the field of consumer protection[43] by, for example, adding to the transparency requirements in Community law with which online

---

[41]   In his report to the European Parliament on the Commission Communication on e-commerce and Financial services (COM(2001) 66 final, 7.2.2001), Christopher Huhne stressed the importance of a full application of the internal market clause to the area of financial services, given that area's particular suitability for cross border delivery, and also stressed the opportunities and benefits brought by the application of the Internal Market principle to e-commerce in Europe.

[42]   Results of a sampling of websites carried out by VZBV (Verbraucherzentrale Bundesverband - German association of consumer organisations) between October 2002 and February 2003, see http://www.vzbv.de/home/start/index.php?page=themen&bereichs_id=5&themen_id=20&mit_id=164 &task=mit.
See also a study carried out by the European Consumer Centres, "Realities of the European online marketplace", available at http://www.iia.ie/downloads/eec_report.pdf, with a focus on the implementation of the information requirements pursuant to Directive 97/7/EC of the European Parliament and of the Council of 20 May 1997 on the protection of consumers in respect of distance contracts, OJ L 144, 4.6.1997, p. 19.

[43]   E.g., Directive 97/7/EC of the European Parliament and of the Council of 20 May 1997 on the protection of consumers in respect of distance contracts, OJ L 144, 4.6.1999, p. 19; Directive 2002/65/EC of the European Parliament and of the Council of 23 September 2002 concerning the distance marketing of consumer financial services, OJ L 271, 9.10.2002, p. 16; Directive 84/450/EEC

commercial communications, including discounts, promotional offers, competitions and games, must comply. These requirements[44] provide additional protection to consumers and enhance their confidence in e-commerce. This will be further complemented by the proposed Regulation on Sales Promotions[45], the proposed Directive on Unfair Commercial Practices[46] and the proposed Regulation on Enforcement Cooperation[47]; In addition, the requirement to clearly identify commercial communications set out in Article 6(a) of the Directive is similar to the one applicable to broadcasting in Article 10(1) of the Television Without Frontiers Directive[48]. Virtually all Member States have transposed Article 6(a) quasi literally.[49]

The Directive left open to Member States the possibility of allowing or prohibiting unsolicited commercial communications via e-mail by information society service providers established on their territory and limited itself to requiring such unsolicited commercial communications to be clearly identified.

However, unsolicited commercial communications have increasingly become a problem for consumers and business alike. Therefore, the issue of unsolicited commercial communications via e-mail has now been dealt with at Community level by Directive 2002/58/EC on Privacy and Electronic Communications[50], which allows the sending of unsolicited commercial communications via e-mail only after prior consent by the recipient, when the recipient is a natural person, or, within an established commercial relationship. The Commission has, in addition, launched work on complementary measures, in particular as regards technical and international aspects of unsolicited commercial communications.[51] In the latter case, the Commission is focusing its efforts on international co-operation to fight unsolicited commercial communications, as most originate from outside the EU.

4.4. Regulated professions

The Directive obliges Member States to ensure that members of regulated professions may use commercial communications online, subject to compliance with professional rules in particular relating to the independence, honour and dignity of the profession. This means that members of regulated professions may provide information to clients via websites, which was

---

of 10 September 1984 concerning misleading and comparative advertising, OJ L 250, 19.9.1984, p. 17, as amended by Directive 97/55/EC of the European Parliament and of the Council, OJ L 290, 23.10.1997, p. 18; Council Directive 93/13/EEC of 5 April 1993 on unfair terms in consumer contracts, OJ L 95, 21.4.1993, p. 29.

[44] see Articles 5 and 6.

[45] COM(2001) 546 final, 2.10.2001, amended proposal COM(2002) 585 final, 25.10.2002.

[46] COM(2003) 356 final, 18.6.2003.

[47] COM(2003) 443 final, 18.7.2003.

[48] Directive 89/552/EEC on the co-ordination of certain provisions laid down by law, regulation or administrative action in Member States concerning the pursuit of television broadcasting activities, OJ L 298, 17.10.1989, p. 23, amended by Directive 97/36/EC, OJ L 202, 30.7.1997, p. 60, and currently under review. http://europa.eu.int/comm/avpolicy/regul/twf/newint_en.htm.

[49] Two Member States, France and Spain, have added an obligation to mention the word "publicity" in commercial communications

[50] Directive 2002/58/EC of the European parliament and of the Council of 12 July 2002 concerning the processing of personal data and the protection of privacy in the electronic communications sector, OJ L 201, 31.7.2002, p. 37. Article 7(2) of the Directive on electronic commerce, which applies to natural persons only, is now to be interpreted in the light of Directive 2002/58.

[51] For more information see http://europa.eu.int/rapid/start/cgi/guesten.ksh?p_action.gettxt=gt&doc=IP/03/1015|0|RAPID&lg=EN&display=.

previously not possible in a number of Member States.[52] Legislation transposing the Directive in many Member States explicitly sets down the principle that online advertising is permitted for the regulated professions under the conditions set out at Article 8(1)[53].

Associations representing regulated professions at a European level have responded positively to the call launched by the Directive to develop codes of conduct relating to the use of commercial communications. The accountancy profession[54], lawyers[55], the doctors[56], pharmacists[57], and real estate agents[58] have established codes of conduct at a European level specifically designed to deal with online commercial communications. Some codes exclusively address online commercial communications, others cover a wider range of web-based services. A common thread to all codes is the emphasis on the obligation to provide accurate and truthful information and to refrain from advertising which is 'over commercial' so as to preserve the dignity and honourability of the profession.

4.5.   Electronic contracting

The Directive contains three provisions on electronic contracts, the most important of which being the obligation on Member States to ensure that their legal system allows for contracts to be concluded electronically, see Article 9(1). This provision, in effect, required Member States to screen their national legislation to eliminate provisions which might hinder the electronic conclusion of contracts. Many Member States have introduced into their legislation a horizontal provision stipulating that contracts concluded by electronic means have the same legal validity as contracts concluded by more "traditional" means.[59] In particular, as regards requirements in national law according to which contracts have to be concluded "in writing", Member States' transposition legislation clearly states that electronic contracts fulfil such requirement.[60]

The provisions in the Directive are complemented by Directive 1999/93 on Electronic Signatures[61], which aims at ensuring the legal recognition of electronic signatures, thereby allowing for functional equivalence in the conclusion of contracts between traditional paper documentation and electronic communications. Essentially, Article 5(1) of Directive 1999/93 gives a "qualified electronic signature" attached to electronic data the same status as a hand-

---

[52]   For a general overview on Member States' rules on advertising by regulated professions see the study undertaken by the Institut für höhere Studien, Wien for DG Competition, "Economic impact of regulation in the field of liberal professions in different Member States", available at http://europa.eu.int/comm/competition/publications/publications/#liberal.

[53]   Belgium, Greece, Ireland, Italy, Austria, and Portugal in its present draft.

[54]   Model Code of Conduct Governing On-line Commercial Communications by Member Bodies of the Federation des Expert Comptables Europeens (FEE) and their members, available at http://www.fee.be/secretariat/PDFs/Code%20of%20Conduct%20E-Commerce.pdf.

[55]   Electronic Communication and the Internet, available at http://www.ccbe.org/doc/En/e_com_en.pdf.

[56]   European Good Practice Guide for publicity relating to physicians' professional practice on the Net, available at http://www.cpme.be/adopted/CPME_AD_Brd_160302_6_EN_fr.pdf.

[57]   Les indications du GPUE concernant les services pharmaceutiques en ligne, available at http://www.pgeu.org/webdata/docs/01.06.20F%20PGEU11%20code%20de%20conduit.pdf.

[58]   Code of conduct for real estate professionals in the field of e-commerce, available at http://www.cepi.be.

[59]   Belgium, Germany, Spain, France, Luxemburg, Finland.

[60]   Moreover, the Directive has brought about changes in the national interpretation of 'in-writing' requirements, for instance in Germany as regards insurance contracts and the obligation that prior information be given in writing.

[61]   Directive 1999/93/EC of the European Parliament and of the Council of 13 December 1999 on a Community framework for electronic signatures, OJ L 13, 19.1.2000, p. 12.

written signature on a paper document. Article 5(2) of Directive 1999/93 provides that an electronic signature may not be denied legal effect and may not be considered inadmissible as evidence in legal proceedings solely on the ground that it is in electronic form or that it is not a "qualified" electronic signature.

Furthermore, Articles 10 and 11 of the Directive, concerning information to be provided about the electronic conclusion of contracts and the requirement to confirm receipt of an order are transposed almost literally in national legislation. Feedback from the Member States indicates that after some phasing in and initial difficulties, information society service providers quickly adapted their websites to comply with those requirements.[62]

Three Member States have included rules in their transposition legislation dealing with the actual moment of the conclusion of a contract.[63] In the other Member States this issue is governed by general contract law. So far, no case law has come to the attention of the Commission indicating difficulties created by the general contract law rules in determining the moment of conclusion of an electronic contract.

4.6.   Liability of internet intermediaries

Articles 12-14 establish precisely defined limitations on the liability of internet intermediaries providing services consisting of mere conduit, caching and hosting. The limitations on liability in the Directive apply to certain clearly delimited activities carried out by internet intermediaries, rather than to categories of service providers or types of information.[64] The limitations on liability provided for by the Directive are established in a horizontal manner, meaning that they cover liability, both civil and criminal, for all types of illegal activities initiated by third parties.

The Directive does not affect the liability of the person who is at the source of the content nor does it affect the liability of intermediaries in cases which are not covered by the limitations defined in the Directive. Furthermore, the Directive does not affect the possibility of a national court or administrative authority to require a service provider to terminate or prevent an infringement.[65] These questions are subject to the national law of the Member States.

The limitations on the liability of intermediaries in the Directive were considered indispensable to ensuring both the provision of basic services which safeguard the continued

---

[62]   A sampling of e-commerce websites taken in April 2002 in one Member State showed that already four out of five websites complied with the information requirements imposed by the national legislation although it only had been in force for two months. A sampling in another Member State between October 2002 and February 2003 revealed certain deficiencies in the information provided and in the availability of technical means to correct input errors. However, the service providers who were made aware of problems in their web appearance promptly reacted to adapt their websites to the legal requirements,   see
http://www.vzbv.de/home/start/index.php?page=themen&bereichs_id=5&themen_id=20&mit_id=164 &task=mit.

[63]   France, Luxemburg and Portugal (the latter clarifying that the acknowledgement of receipt does not necessarily determine the moment of conclusion of the contract).

[64]   In particular, the limitation on liability for hosting in Article 14 covers different scenarios in which third party content is stored, apart from the hosting of web-sites, for example, also bulletin boards or 'chat-rooms'.

[65]   Nevertheless, a scenario in which large scale use is made of injunctions as part of a general policy to fight against illegal content rather than being used against a specific infringement, may raise certain concerns. For example, in 2002, the authorities of North Rhine-Westphalia ordered around 90 internet access providers to block access to a number of specified sites.

free flow of information in the network and the provision of a framework which allows the internet and e-commerce to develop. Different approaches in the legislation and case law emerging from Member States and the resulting legal uncertainty for cross-border activities gave rise to the risk of obstacles to the free provision of cross-border services. However, Community-level action was limited to what was deemed necessary to prevent such a risk materialising.[66]

Articles 12-14 provide, in a harmonised manner, for situations in which the intermediaries mentioned in these Articles cannot be held liable and Member States may not create additional conditions to be satisfied before an intermediary service provider can benefit from a limitation on liability. It appears that the Member States have, in general, transposed Articles 12-14 correctly. Many Member States opted to transpose Articles 12-14 quasi literally.[67]

In addition to the matters dealt with by Articles 12-14, some Member States[68] decided to provide for limitations on the liability of providers of hyperlinks and search engines.[69] This was motivated by the wish to create incentives for investment and innovation and enhance the development of e-commerce by providing additional legal clarity for service providers. Whilst it was not considered necessary to cover hyperlinks and search engines in the Directive, the Commission has encouraged Member States to further develop legal security for internet in-termediaries. It is encouraging that recent case-law in the Member States recognizes the importance of linking and search engines to the functioning of the internet. In general, this case-law appears to be in line with the Internal Market objective to ensure the provision of basic intermediary services, which promotes the development of the internet and e-commerce. Consequently, this case-law does not appear to give rise to any Internal Market concerns[70].

In a few cases[71] national courts have already interpreted the Directive. However, in these cases, the national implementing measures of the Directive had not yet been adopted in the States concerned.

There is still very little practical experience on the application of Articles 12-14, but the feedback received so far from the Member States and interested parties has, in general, been positive. The approach taken in the Directive appears to have wide reaching support among stakeholders. In any case the Commission will, in accordance with Article 21, continue to

---

[66]   These conclusions were based on careful analysis of existing rules and emerging case law, including a study on "Existing rules in Member States governing liability for information society services" commissioned by the Commission from Deloitte & Touche in 1998.

[67]   So far, the Commission services have identified, on a preliminary basis, 1-2 cases, in which the Member States appear not to have implemented correctly the limitations on liability, but the analysis of these cases continues.

[68]   Spain, Austria and EEA-State Liechtenstein and Portugal in its draft law.

[69]   Spain and Portugal have opted for the model of Article 14 both for search engines and hyperlinks, whereas Austria and Liechtenstein have opted for the model of Article 12 for search engines and of Article 14 for hyperlinks.

[70]   For example in France TGI Paris, référé, 12 mai 2003, Lorie c/M. G.S. et SA Wanadoo Portails, in Germany in the case Verlagsgruppe Handelsblatt v. Paperboy, aus dem Bundesgerichtshof (BGH), Urteil vom 17. Juli 2003 – I ZR 259/00.

[71]   Cases Deutsche Bahn v. XS4ALL, judgement by Gerechtshof te Amsterdam (Court of Appeals), 762/02 SKG, of 7.11.2002, and Deutsche Bahn v. Indymedia, judgement by Rechtbank Amsterdam (District Court), KG 02/1073, of 20.6.2002, in the Netherlands (judgements available at http://www.rechtspraak.nl); and Case Public Prosecutor v. Tele2 in the EEA-country Norway, judgement by Borgarting Lagmannsrett (Court of Appeals), 02-02539 M/01, of 27.6.2003. Tele2 was acquitted when the public prosecutor dropped charges against it.

monitor and rigorously analyse any new developments, including national legislation, case-law and administrative practices related to intermediary liability and will examine any future need to adapt the present framework in the light of these developments, for instance the need of additional limitations on liability for other activities such as the provision of hyperlinks and search engines.[72]

Article 15 prevents Member States from imposing on internet intermediaries, with respect to activities covered by Articles 12-14, a general obligation to monitor the information which they transmit or store or a general obligation to actively seek out facts or circumstances indicating illegal activities. This is important, as general monitoring of millions of sites and web pages would, in practical terms, be impossible and would result in disproportionate burdens on intermediaries and higher costs of access to basic services for users.[73] However, Article 15 does not prevent public authorities in the Member States from imposing a monitoring obligation in a specific, clearly defined individual case.

4.7.   Notice and take down procedures

The conditions under which a hosting provider is exempted from liability, as set out at Article 14(1)(b) constitute the basis for the development of notice and take down procedures for illegal and harmful information[74] by stake-holders. Article 14 applies horizontally to all types of information. At the time when the Directive was adopted, it was decided that notice and take down procedures should not be regulated in the Directive itself. Instead Article 16 and Recital 40 expressly encourage self-regulation in this field.[75]

This approach has also been followed by the Member States in their national laws transposing the Directive. Out of those Member States which have transposed the Directive, only Finland has included a legal provision setting out a notice and take down procedure concerning copyright infringements only.[76] All the other Member States have left this issue to self-regulation[77].

---

[72]   The approach of the Member States who opted to legislate on the hyperlinks and search engines does not seem to give rise to a risk of fragmentation of the Internal Market. The Commission is, however, actively following work in Member States relating to liability issues such as the fundamental work carried out by "Le Forum des droits sur l'Internet" in France, which has published recommendations on hyperlinks called "Hyperliens: Statut Juridique", published 3.3.2003, and "Quelle responsabilité pour les créateurs d'hyperliens vers des contenus illicites, published 23.10.2003, both available at http://www.foruminternet.org/recommandations/.

[73]   In this context, it is important to note that the reports and studies on the effectiveness of blocking and filtering applications appear to indicate that there is not yet any technology which could not be circumvented and provide full effectiveness in blocking or filtering illegal and harmful information whilst at the same time avoiding blocking entirely legal information resulting in violations of freedom of speech.

[74]   Mechanisms run by interested parties aimed at identifying illegal information hosted on the network and at facilitating its rapid removal.

[75]   The European Parliament, when adopting the Directive in 2000, invited the Commission to encourage the establishment of efficient notice and take down procedures by interested parties. European Parliament legislative resolution on the Council common position for adopting a European Parliament and Council Directive on certain legal aspects of Information Society services, in particular electronic commerce, in the Internal Market, 4.5.2000, OJ C 041, 7.2.2001, p. 38.

[76]   Amongst the EEA countries, Iceland has also set out a statutory notice and take down procedure.

[77]   Belgium has set up a horizontal co-regulatory procedure: Cooperation Protocol between the Belgian administration and the Belgian Association of internet Service Providers, http://www.ispa.be/en/c040201.html

In accordance with Article 21(2), which requires the Commission to analyse the need for proposals concerning notice and take down procedures, the Commission has actively encouraged stakeholders to develop notice and take down procedures and has systematically collected and analysed information about emerging procedures.[78] The Commission has participated in European and international fora where notice and take down procedures have been discussed: in particular, in the Global Business Dialogue[79], in the workshops organised by the European Parliamentarians Internet Group (e-Ping)[80], and in the Rights Watch Project[81]. It has also encouraged Member States to actively work with stakeholders and has cooperated with the Spanish presidency, which held discussions with Member States in the information society working group of the Council.

The Council Recommendation on the protection of minors and human dignity[82] adopted in 1998 is the first legal instrument at EU level concerning the content of audiovisual and information services made available on the internet. The Recommendation offers guidelines for the development of national self-regulation regarding the protection of minors and human dignity. In particular, it requests internet service providers to develop codes of good conduct so as to better apply current legislation.[83]

The Commission has also been working, in the context of its Safer Internet Action Plan, to combat illegal and harmful content on global networks.[84] Directive 2001/29/EC on copyright

---

[78]   Different procedures have been analysed and several companies and organisations have been consulted in the Member States, e.g., the Complainants Bureau for Discrimination on the Internet in the Netherlands; XS4ALL (The Netherlands); Telefónica (Spain); Nokia (Finland); Telia (Sweden), BT online (UK); Internet Watch Foundation (UK); eBay; The European Internet Services Association (Euroispa); The European Federation for the Interactive Software Industry; and the Motion Pictures Association of America.

[79]   Work in the Global Business Dialogue (GBDe) has been followed closely by the Commission through contact with the principal companies involved. The GBDe issued a Recommendation in September 2000 on a specific model for a notice and take down procedure for intellectual property rights. With the encouragement of the Commission the GBDe created in 2002 a task force on Combating Harmful Internet Content with the purpose of addressing notice and take down for other harmful content. This task force issued a Recommendation on October 2002 containing suggestions address to internet intermediaries and to the public authorities on how to develop "processes for dealing with harmful content in the internet", http://www.gbde.org.

[80]   Http://www.eping.org.

[81]   The Rights Watch Project is a research project financed by the Commission through its 5th Framework Program for Research. The project was created in order to set up a fully functioning pilot that would facilitate a pan European self regulatory procedure for the removal of material infringing intellectual property rights. It has been the only initiative so far at European level on notice and take-down. Representatives from the Commission have been present all along the negotiations of the project and, in particular, by participating in the two fora that the project has held, where internet service providers, right holders and users associations were represented, http://www.rightswatch.com.

[82]   Council Recommendation of 24 September 1998 on the development of the competitiveness of the European audiovisual and information services industry by promoting national frameworks aimed at achieving a comparable and effective level of protection of minors and human dignity (98/560/EC), OJ L 270, 7.10.1998, p. 48.

[83]   The implementation of the Recommendation was evaluated for the first time in 2000/2001.The report on the application of this Recommendation published in 2001 (COM(2001)106 final) showed that the application of the Recommendation was already then overall quite satisfactory. The Commission is working on a second report on the implementation of the Recommendation, whose adoption is foreseen at the end of 2003 on the basis of a questionnaire, which was sent to both the Member States and the acceding States. The objective of the new report is to establish what progress has been made in comparison to the situation in 2000, when the data was collected for the first application report.

[84]   Safer Internet Action Plan, OJ L 33, 6.2.1999, p. 1, and its follow-up , Decision No 1151/2003/EC of 16 June 2003, OJ L 162, 1.7.2003, p.1.

and related rights[85] requires Member States to ensure that rightholders are in a position to apply for injunctions, under certain conditions, against intermediaries whose services are used by a third party to infringe a copyright or related right. The Commission also presented a proposal on the enforcement of intellectual property rights, which, amongst other issues, provides for appropriate remedies with respect to internet-related infringements of intellectual property, including injunctive relief.[86]

Intermediary service providers have, themselves, in cooperation with national authorities as well as with other stakeholders, such as IP rightholders, been active in fighting against illegal activity on the internet, whilst also seeking to ensure a balance between the legitimate interests of users, other interested parties, and the freedom of speech. In this regard, intermediary service providers have been instrumental in the production of national codes of conduct for internet service providers[87], some of which have also been notified to the Commission[88].

Analysis of work on notice and take down procedures shows that though a consensus is still some way off, agreement would appear to have been reached among stake holders as regards the essential elements which should be taken into consideration. Although some further work among stake holders seems to be necessary to clarify a number of outstanding issues, the Commission at this stage does not see any need for a legislative initiative.

4.8.   Codes of conduct and out-of-court dispute settlement

The Directive calls on trade, professional, and consumer associations to contribute to developing a reliable and flexible framework for e-commerce by drawing up codes of conduct. Very often such codes are associated with what are termed 'trustmark schemes' or 'labels'.[89] Several associations have established sector specific codes and trustmark schemes at European level[90] and many more codes exist at a national level[91]. However, it appears that

---

[85]   Directive 2001/29/EC of the European Parliament and of the Council of 22 May 2001 on the harmonisation of certain aspects of copyright and related rights in the information society, OJ L 167, 22.6.2001, p. 10

[86]   Proposal for a Directive of the European Parliament and of the Council on measures and procedures to ensure the enforcement of intellectual property rights, COM(2003) 46 final, 30.1.2003. Article 2 of the proposed Directive states that it shall not affect Directive 2000/31/EC.

[87]   EuroISPA's members' codes of conduct, available at http://www.euroispa.org.

[88]   For example the Code of Practice and Ethics by the Internet Service Providers Association of Ireland, http://www.ispai.ie.

[89]   BEUC, the European Consumer Organisation, and UNICE, the European Industry and Employer's association, reached an agreement on principles for such trustmark schemes which takes up many of the requirements set out in the Directive and deals with codes of conduct regarding information to be provided, procedures for placing of orders, and the like. The agreement can be found at: http://212.3.246.118/1/PEDMMGECEFLNDAPDCIBCDIKLPDBY9DAWW69LTE4Q/UNICE/docs/DLS/2002-03813-E.pdf.
The European Commission had initiated and financed work to develop a horizontal European trustmark scheme incorporating a code of conduct, called "Webtrader", a project co-financed by DG Enterprise from 2000 until February 2003, see http://europa.eu.int/comm/enterprise/ict/policy/webtrader.htm. However, no agreement on a horizontal, cross-sectorial code could be reached between the participants.

[90]   E.g., for the insurance sector: http://www.cea.assur.org/cea/publ/download/article149.pdf; for direct marketing: http://www.fedma.org/img/db/Code_of_conduct_for_e-commerce.pdf; and for e-commerce retailers: http://www.euro-label.com/euro-label/ControllerServlet.

[91]   E.g., "Chamber-Trust + Web-Trader" in Belgium (http://194.78.225.199/fr/index.html); "TrustedShops" in Germany (http://www.trustedshops.de/de/home); "l@belsite" in France (http://www.labelsite.org); "e-commerce Gütezeichen" in Austria (http://www.guetezeichen.at); "bbbonline" in the UK (http://www.bbbonline.org).

after an initial boom in the establishment of trustmarks and labels immediately following adoption of the Directive in 2000 and 2001, activity in this area slowed down.[92] The Commission therefore appeals to business and consumer organisations as well as to Member States to continue to actively support and promote initiatives in this area.

In B2B e-commerce, the Commission has already established an expert group to promote the elaboration of codes of conduct in B2B internet trading platforms. The expert group has prepared a report with a checklist for the assessment of such codes.[93]

The increase in opportunities and geographical reach brought about by e-commerce also gives rise to a risk of cross border disputes between trading partners. It is in such cases crucial that access to rapid and flexible out-of-court dispute resolution schemes exists. For this reason, the Directive both obliges Member States to allow for the development of out-of-court dispute settlement mechanisms by electronic means and encourages the development of such schemes. In recent years a wealth of out of court dispute resolution initiatives, often in connection with codes of conduct, has appeared.[94] The Commission has supported the development of such schemes and continues to do so.[95]

4.9.   National e-commerce contact points

Pursuant to Article 19, since transposition of the Directive the Commission has worked actively together with the Member States to ensure the setting up of national contact points for e-commerce. These contact points will improve the cooperation between the Member States (Article 19(2) regarding contact points for cooperation between the Member States) and ensure that consumers and business have access to general information on e-commerce issues relevant to the application of the Directive and details of authorities and other bodies providing further information and assistance, (Article 19(4) regarding contact points for consumers and business). A list of these contact points and contact details are available on the e-commerce website of the Internal Market Directorate General.[96]

---

[92]   This might also be a direct consequence of the general downturn in the e-economy.

[93]   Report of the Expert Group on B2B Internet trading platforms. Final Report (http://europa.eu.int/comm/enterprise/ict/policy/b2b/wshop/fin-report.pdf). To further promote the work of the expert group, the Commission will prepare a Communication on fair trade in B2B.

[94]   See, e.g., the overview by the Centre for Socio-Legal Studies at Oxford University, established with funding from the European Commission under the Internet Action Plan at http://www.selfregulation.info/cocon/coc-reviss03-dwc-020510.htm. See also more generally on ADR the Commission's Green paper on alternative dispute resolution in civil and commercial law, COM(2002) 196 final, 19.4.2002, at http://europa.eu.int/eur-lex/en/com/gpr/2002/com2002_0196en01.pdf.

[95]   ECODIR, for instance, is a pilot project carried out by a consortium of university partners and financed by the Commission. Until June 2003 it has provided an easily accessible online system for the resolution of disputes between consumers and e-commerce businesses. It is now in the process of being evaluated with a view to its continuation. See http://www.ecodir.org/about_us/index.htm. The IST project (IST-2000-25464) "E-Arbitration" (Electronic Arbitration Tribunal) provides an alternative dispute resolution system for SMEs. It defines the technological requirements, the necessary infrastructure and the regulatory framework for establishing and coordinating an internationally distributed Arbitration Tribunal using networked computers and intelligent multi-agent systems as their primary means of communication. Project URL: httm://www.e-global.es/arbitration/
With the initiatives EEJ NET and FIN-Net, although not limited to e-commerce, the Commission, together with Member States, has established out-of-court complaints networks to help business and consumers resolve disputes in the Internal Market quickly and efficiently. More information can be found at EEJ-Net's website http://www.eejnet.org and at FIN-Net's website http://finnet.jrc.it.

[96]   http://europa.eu.int/comm/internal_market/en/ecommerce/index.htm.

5. INTERNATIONAL ASPECTS

5.1. International developments in e-commerce

Due to the very nature of e-commerce and the internet, which do not recognise national frontiers, there is an obvious need for the development of some framework at international level. In this context some of the solutions adopted in the Directive, such as the limitations on liability for internet intermediaries, can serve as a model. The Commission has actively worked to raise awareness of the EU's approach and feedback received has been very positive.[97]

The economic downturn experienced in recent years in the area of e-commerce and the "new economy" has obviously had repercussions on a global scale and led to a stagnation in discussions. With the recent recovery of e-commerce a revived interest in international dialogue and cooperation can be expected. The Commission will continue and, where possible, increase its involvement in various multilateral and bilateral fora and will work towards a global e-business friendly environment.

Among the international fora in which the Commission is present are the World Trade Organization's work programme on e-commerce[98], the Organisation for Economic Co-operation and Development's (OECD) work on broadband issues and consumer protection in cross-border commerce, particularly as regards the internet[99], the Council of Europe's work on information and cooperation on information society issues[100], as well as its work on cybercrime, impact of the new technologies on human rights, conditional access services, and data protection[101], the G8's work on safety and security on the internet and the World Intellectual Property Organisation's (WIPO) work on the protection of intellectual property rights on the internet[102]. Work on electronic contracts is furthermore carried out by the United Nations Commission on International Trade Law (UNCITRAL)[103]. Moreover, the

---

[97] An example of successful "model character" of the Directive is the South African Electronic Communications and Transactions Act 25 of 2002, which closely follows the Directive as regards intermediary liability (Articles 12-15), Government Gazette of the Republic of South Africa, Vol. 446, Cape Town, 2 August 2002, No. 23708.

[98] In 1998, the WTO had already developed a Work Programme on Electronic Commerce (available at http://www.wto.org/english/tratop_e/ecom_e/ecom_e.htm), although the follow-up to the Programme did not fulfil all the expectations it had raised. At present, specific e-commerce issues are discussed at 'dedicated meetings' of the General Council, focusing on the question of how to classify electronic deliveries. The European Commission along with the EU Member States and many other WTO members promotes the view that electronic deliveries constitute services and thus come under the existing GATS regime.

[99] See http://www.oecd.org, topic "Electronic commerce".

[100] On 4.10.2001 the Council of Europe adopted the Convention 180 on information and legal cooperation on Information Society services, modelled on Directive 98/34/EC of the European Parliament and of the Council of 22 June 1998 laying down a procedure for the provision of information in the field of technical standards and regulations and of rules on Information Society services, OJ L 204, 21.7.1998, p. 37, as amended by Directive 98/48/EC of the European Parliament and of the Council of 20 July 1998, OJ L 217, 5.8.1998, p. 18, its definition of information society services being exactly the one provided in the Directive. The Commission has formally proposed to the EU Council to adhere to the Convention on behalf of the EU, COM(2003) 398 final, 7.7.2003.

[101] See http://www.coe.int, of particular interest is the Convention on Cybercrime, ETS no. 185, which is available at http://conventions.coe.int/Treaty/EN/CadreListeTraites.htm.

[102] See http://ecommerce.wipo.int/primer/index.html.

[103] See http://www.uncitral.org. UNCITRAL has already done fundamental work in e-commerce by adopting, in 1996, a Model Law on Electronic Commerce with Guide to Enactment and in 2001 a Model Law on Electronic Signatures, which are frequently referred to in international contexts.

Commission is actively involved in cooperation in the context of the Asia-Europe Meeting[104] Trade Facilitation Action Plan on e-commerce[105]. This involves recommendations on e-commerce regulation adopted in September 2002.[106]

The importance of non-governmental fora such as the Global Business Dialogue in e-commerce (GBDe), Transatlantic Consumer Dialogue (TACD), and Transatlantic Business Dialogue (TABD) in e-commerce should not be underestimated.[107] These fora issue recommendations to governments and develop standards for business on issues such as intermediary liability (GBDe[108]), consumer protection in e-commerce (TACD[109]) and digital trade (TABD[110]). Such initiatives are of particular importance in the quickly evolving and innovative area of e-commerce as they can address the latest developments with greater rapidity and flexibility than governmental fora.

Finally, the Commission is involved in a number of bilateral regulatory dialogues on e-commerce related to information society issues, in order to promote the Directive's regulatory approach and to work towards consistency at international level. These bilateral dialogues include the EU/US Information Society Dialogue, the cooperation with Canada in the context of Canada-EU Trade and Investment Sub-Committee (TISC), including an e-commerce work plan in 1999, the EU-Japan dialogue, the EU-Mercosur regulatory dialogue and the dialogue with the Mediterranean countries.

5.2.   Enlargement

A number of accession countries have already transposed the Directive[111], although in some cases only partially. Out of the three[112] candidate countries only Romania has transposed the Directive. The Commission is actively working with the remaining countries to ensure transposition in due course.

6.   EVALUATING THE BENEFITS OF THE DIRECTIVE

Given the lack of experience with the Directive it is difficult to evaluate its impact. When doing so, it is important to note that information society services are not limited to the mere buying and selling of products and services online. They also comprise online commercial communications, online information and entertainment, provision of internet access services, e-mail, search engines, etc. So far, the only complaints which the Commission services have received from companies engaged in cross-border online activities concern matters excluded from the scope of application of the Directive or from the application of the Internal Market clause, such as online gambling[113]. This seems to indicate that the Directive has otherwise

---

[104]   Grouping the EU and 10 Asian ASEM countries.
[105]   http://www.ktm.fi/eng/news/asem2002ecom/.
[106]   http://www.congrex.fi/asem2002ecom/
[107]   http://www.gbde.org, http://www.tacd.org, and http://www.tabd.org.
[108]   Paris recommendation on liability, 13.9.1999, Miami Model IPR-specific notice and take down procedure, 26.10.2000.
[109]   In particular doc. no ECOM-27-02 "Resolution on children and e-commerce" and doc no. Internet-20-02 "Resolution on protecting consumers from fraud and serious deception across borders".
[110]   Report of the TABD meeting in Chicago in 2002,
         http://www.tabd.org/recommendations/Chicago02.pdf.
[111]   Lithuania, Hungary, Malta, Poland, Slovenia.
[112]   Bulgaria, Romania, Turkey.
[113]   Service providers established in one Member State offering online sports betting are required by other Member States to bar access by their citizen's to those online services.

succeeded in providing an adequate legal framework for information society services in the Internal Market.

The Directive appears to have been successful in reducing court proceedings and hence legal uncertainty, in particular as regards liability of internet intermediaries. Emerging disparities in Member States' case-law was one of the driving forces, which lead the Commission to propose the Directive. After the adoption of the Directive, no such case-law has come to the attention of the Commission. Together with the guarantee that internet intermediaries should not be subject to burdensome and costly monitoring obligations, this seems to have contributed to ensuring low-cost provision of basic intermediary services.

When evaluating the effects of the Directive, there are certain indicators which are of particular interest and which have not yet been used in the present measurements of internet usage and online activities, which are often wrongly limited to online sales. For instance, the percentage of internet users searching for online information prior to offline sales, the number of cross-border online information searches as a percentage of total online information searches, productivity gains resulting from lower information search costs in the B2B field, and expenditure by enterprises on online advertising.

The completion of the transposition of the Directive in all the Member States is expected by the end of 2003, two years after the deadline of January 2002 set in the Directive. This will allow evaluation of the impact of the Directive in more detail, in line with the above-mentioned indicators in the second report on the application of the Directive due in 2005.

7. ACTION PLAN FOR THE FOLLOW-UP OF THE DIRECTIVE

7.1. Ensure the correct application of the Directive

The Commission will continue to closely monitor application of the Directive in the Member States, including follow-up and analysis of any relevant case-law, administrative decisions and complaints from citizens and business. Bilateral contacts, which were successfully used during the transposition of the Directive, will be maintained with the Member States, including Accession and Candidate Countries, to address specific problems and ensure continuous exchange of information. The notification procedure pursuant to Directive 98/34/EC[114], which was instrumental in ensuring the correct and consistent transposition of the Directive, will be an important tool in ensuring coherence between the Directive and new national legislative initiatives which affect information society services.

7.2. Enhance administrative cooperation between Member States

After assisting in the setting-up of contact points for administrative cooperation between the Member States, the Commission will focus on ensuring the practical functioning of administrative cooperation and the continuous exchange of information between both the Commission and the Member States and between the Member States themselves.

---

[114] Directive 98/34/EC of the European Parliament and of the Council of 22 June 1998 laying down a procedure for the provision of information in the field of technical standards and regulations and of rules on Information Society services, OJ L 204, 21.7.1998, p. 37, as amended by Directive 98/48/EC of the European Parliament and of the Council of 20 July 1998, OJ L 217, 5.8.1998, p. 18.

7.3.   Raise information and awareness with business and citizens

After ensuring that Member States have nominated contact points for business and citizens pursuant to Article 19(4), the Commission will focus on enhancing close links and a continuous flow of information between national contact points and business and citizens, in particular, including information on administrative and judicial decisions and cases of out of court dispute resolution. In this context, special attention will be given to the correct application of the information requirements provided by the Directive and to the dissemination of information concerning applicable codes of conduct and their enforcement.

The Commission is already funding the establishment and operation of an online information system, managed by a European network of Euro Info Centres, to raise awareness among SME's on the legal aspects of e-business and to collect feedback on the practical problems enterprises are facing when doing business electronically (ELEAS project).[115] This information system will be extended to the Accession and Candidate countries and will become operational in early 2004.

7.4.   Monitor policy developments and identify areas for additional action

In a number of Member States new regulatory initiatives are under way in areas such as online gambling, including online sports betting, e-pharmacies, or the protection of minors. This gives rise to the risk of regulatory fragmentation and/or distortions of competition. The Commission will closely monitor these policy developments in order to identify possible needs for Community action, which will be considered in the second report on the Directive in 2005.

As far as online gambling is concerned, which is currently outside of the scope of the Directive and, in relation to which, the Commission has received a number of complaints concerning cross-border activities[116], the Commission will initiate the appropriate action to deal with these complaints and, in addition, launch a study to provide the information required to examine the need for and scope of a possible new Community initiative. Furthermore, with respect to insurance, which is currently outside of the scope of the Internal Market clause of the Directive, the Commission has launched work with Member States and interested parties in order to explore possible ways of bringing certain insurance activities in line with the Internal Market clause.

The Commission continues to monitor closely technological developments relevant to information society services in order to ensure that the regulatory framework provides the best possible environment for further development of e-commerce.

7.5.   Strengthen international cooperation and regulatory dialogue

Given the cross-border nature of e-commerce and the resulting need for international solutions, the Commission will strengthen its regulatory dialogue with major trading partners and its presence in international fora. Particular attention will be given to the creation of coherent rules at international level on subjects such as liability of internet intermediaries,

---

[115]   http://ebusinesslex.net
[116]   Regarding Denmark, Germany, Italy, and the Netherlands, where authorities demanded online gambling service providers from other Member States to block access to their websites for citizens living in those states.

including notice and take down procedures for illegal content, electronic contracts, information requirements, and the promotion of out of court dispute resolution.

8.   CONCLUSIONS

With the new legal framework for e-commerce created by the Directive being in the process of being put into place in all Member States, it is now necessary to collect information and gain experience on how the new framework works in practice.

To this end, the Commission has launched an open consultation on legal problems in e-business with a view to collecting feedback and practical experience from the market and to identifying remaining practical barriers or new legal problems encountered by enterprises when doing e-business.[117]

The analysis to date has not shown a need to adapt the Directive as yet and, given the lack of practical experience, a revision of the Directive would in any event be premature. However, e-commerce is a quickly evolving area, in which legal, technical, and economic developments need to be constantly monitored and analysed.

This report is a first stage in a continuous process to ensure that Europe stays in the frontline of development and provides the best possible environment for e-commerce with a maximum level of legal certainty both for business and consumers whilst ensuring a minimum of burdens for business and Member States.

The Commission trusts that this report will be of assistance to Member States in ensuring the correct application of the Directive and to citizens and business in informing them of the opportunities and safeguards provided by the new legal framework. The Commission welcomes feedback on the findings of this report in view of its task of ensuring continuous monitoring of the application of the Directive.[118]

The results of the Action Plan in this report will be made public. It will form the basis for the second report on the application of the Directive due in 2005, which will also address possible needs for adaptation of the Directive.

---

[117]   http://europe.eu.int/yourvoice/consultations/index_en.htm. The consultation was open until 10 November 2003. The Commission services will analyse the results of the consultation in a Commission staff working document by January/February 2004 and will discuss them with all relevant stakeholders at a high-level conference to be organised in April 2004, as foreseen in the e-Europe 2005 Action Plan.

[118]   http://europa.eu.int/comm/internal_market/en/ecommerce/index.htm.

ANNEX

TRANSPOSITION OF DIRECTIVE 2000/31/EC

1. Member States:

Belgique/ België	Loi sur certains aspects juridiques des services de la société de l'information visés à l'article 77 de la Constitution – 11 mars 2003/Wet betreffende bepaalde juridische aspecten van de diensten van de informatiemaatschappif als bedoeld in artikel 77 van de Grondwet – 11 maart 2003 Loi sur certains aspects juridiques des services de la société de l'information – 11 mars 2003/Wet betreffende bepaalde juridische aspecten van de diensten van de informatiemaatschappij – 11 maart 2003 Moniteur belge du 17.3.2003 p. 12960 et 12963. http://www.moniteur.be/index_fr.htm http://www.moniteur.be/index_nl.htm
Danmark	Lov om tjenester i informationssamfundet, herunder visse aspekter af elektronisk handel: LOV nr 227 af 22/04/2002 (Gældende) http://www.retsinfo.dk/_GETDOC_/ACCN/A20020022730-REGL
Deutschland	Gezetz über rechtliche Rahmenbedingungen für den Elektronischen Geschäftsverkehr (Elektronischer Geschäftsverkehr-Gesetz (EGG) Bundesgesetzblatt (BGBl) 2001 Teil I Nr. 70 vom 20. Dezember 2001, S. 3721 http://www.iid.de/iukdg/EGG/index.html Mediendienste-Staatsvertrag in der Fassung des sechsten Rundfunkänderungsstaatsvertrags in Kraft seit 1. Juli 2002, u.a. im Gesetz- und Verordnungsblatt für das Land Rheinland-Pfalz vom 12. Juni 2002, S. 255
Ελλάδα	ΠΡΟΕΔΡΙΚΟ ΔΙΑΤΑΓΜΑ ΥΠ'ΑΡΙΘ. 131 Προσαρμογή στην Οδηγία 2000/31 του Ευρωπαϊκού Κοινοβουλίου και του Συμβουλίου σχετικά με ορισμένες νομικές πτυχές των υπηρεσιών της κοινωνίας της πληροφορίας, ιδίως του ηλεκτρονικού εμπορίου, στην εσωτερική αγορά. (Οδηγία για το ηλεκτρονικό εμπόριο). Αρ. Φύλλου 116, 16 Μαΐου 2003, σελ. 1747 [Presidential Decree n°. 131 transposing Directive 2000/31 of the European Parliament and the Council on certain legal aspects of information society services, in particular electronic commerce, in the Internal Market (Directive on electronic commerce) Official Journal n° 116 of 16 May 2003, p. 1747]

23

España	Ley 34/2002, de 11 de julio, de servicios de la sociedad de la información y de comercio electrónico BOE n° 166, 12.7.2002, p. 25388 http://www.setsi.mcyt.es
France	Transposition not yet completed. Draft law notified to the Commission under the Transparency Directive (Directive 98/34). Notification n° 2003/0127 available on the Commission's web-site http://www.europa.eu.int/comm/enterprise/tris
Ireland	European Communities (Directive 2000/31/EC) Regulations 2003 (S.I. No. 68/2003 of 24.2.2003) http://www.entemp.ie/ecd/ebusinfo.htm
Italia	Decreto legislativo 9/04/2003, n. 70 Supplemento ordinario alla Gazzetta Ufficiale della Repubblica Italiana – Serie Generale – n. 87 del 14/04/2003 http://www.senato.it/parlam/leggi/deleghe/03070dl.htm
Luxembourg	Loi du 14 août 2000 relative au commerce électronique modifiant le code civil, le nouveau code de procédure civile, le code de commerce, le code pénal et transposant la directive 1999/93 relative à un cadre communautaire pour les signatures électroniques, la directive relative à certains aspects juridiques des services de la société de l'information, certaines dispositions de la directive 97/7/CEE concernant la vente à distance des biens et des services autres que les services financiers Memorial, Journal Officiel du Grand-Duché de Luxembourg, A – N° 96 du 8 septembre 2000, p. 2176 http://www.etat.lu/memorial/memorial/a/2000/a0960809.pdf
Nederland	Transposition not yet completed.
Österreich	152. Bundesgesetz, mit dem bestimmte rechtliche Aspekte des elektronischen Geschäfts- und Rechtsverkehrs geregelt (E-Commerce-Gesetz – ECG) und das Signaturgesetz sowie die Zivilprozessordnung geändert werden Bundesgesetzblatt 2001 vom 21. Dezember 2001, Teil I S. 1977. http://bgbl.wzo.at

Portugal	Transposition not yet completed.
	Draft law notified to the Commission under the Transparency Directive (Directive 98/34). Notification n° 2003/0134 available on the Commission's web-site http://www.europa.eu.int/comm/enterprise/tris
Suomi/Finland	Laki N:o 458 tietoyhteiskunnan palvelujen tarjoamisesta, 5.6.2002.
	Suomen Säädöskokoelma N:o 458, 11.6.2002, p. 3039.
	http://www.finlex.fi/pdf/sk/02/vihko072.pdf
	In addition, Finland amended three other acts as part of the transposition. These (Suomen Säädöskokoelma Nos. 459-61) are also available via the enclosed link.
Sverige	Lag om elektronisk handel och andra informationssamhällets tjänster av den 6 juni 2002; SFS 2002:562 av den 14 juni 2002
	Electronic version accessible via http://www.regeringen.se, but a direct link is not available.
United Kingdom	The Electronic Commerce (EC Directive) Regulations 2002
	SI n° 2013 of 21.8.2002
	http://www.legislation.hmso.gov.uk/si/si2002/20022013.htm
	For separate implementation in financial services sector: http://www.hm-treasury.gov.uk/Documents/Financial_Services/Regulating_Financial_Services/fin_r sf_edirec.cfm?

2. Countries belonging to the European Economic Area:

Island	Lög um rafræn viðskipti og aðra rafræna þjónustu 2002 nr. 30 16. apríl.
	Lagasafn. Uppfært til október 2002. Útgáfa 127B. Prenta í tveimur dálkum.
	(Act No 30/2002 on Electronic Commerce and other Electronic Service)
	http://www.althingi.is/lagas/127b/2002030.html
Liechtenstein	Gesetz vom 16. April 2003 über den elektronischen Geschäftsverkehr (E-Commerce-Gesetz; ECG)
	Liechtensteinisches Landesgesetzblatt 2003, Nr. 133 am 12. Juni 2003
Norge	Lov 2003-05-23 nr 35: Lov om visse sider av elektronisk handel og andre informasjonssamfunnstjenester (ehandelsloven)
	Publisert: I 2003 hefte 7.
	http://www.lovdata.no/all/hl-20030523-035.html

Appendix 4

DIRECTIVE 2002/58/EC OF THE EUROPEAN PARLIAMENT AND OF THE COUNCIL

of 12 July 2002

concerning the processing of personal data and the protection of privacy in the electronic communications sector (Directive on privacy and electronic communications)

THE EUROPEAN PARLIAMENT AND THE COUNCIL OF THE EUROPEAN UNION,

Having regard to the Treaty establishing the European Community, and in particular Article 95 thereof,

Having regard to the proposal from the Commission (¹),

Having regard to the opinion of the Economic and Social Committee (²),

Having consulted the Committee of the Regions,

Acting in accordance with the procedure laid down in Article 251 of the Treaty (³),

Whereas:

(1) Directive 95/46/EC of the European Parliament and of the Council of 24 October 1995 on the protection of individuals with regard to the processing of personal data and on the free movement of such data (⁴) requires Member States to ensure the rights and freedoms of natural persons with regard to the processing of personal data, and in particular their right to privacy, in order to ensure the free flow of personal data in the Community.

(2) This Directive seeks to respect the fundamental rights and observes the principles recognised in particular by the Charter of fundamental rights of the European Union. In particular, this Directive seeks to ensure full respect for the rights set out in Articles 7 and 8 of that Charter.

(3) Confidentiality of communications is guaranteed in accordance with the international instruments relating to human rights, in particular the European Convention for the Protection of Human Rights and Fundamental Freedoms, and the constitutions of the Member States.

(4) Directive 97/66/EC of the European Parliament and of the Council of 15 December 1997 concerning the processing of personal data and the protection of privacy in the telecommunications sector (⁵) translated the principles set out in Directive 95/46/EC into specific rules for the telecommunications sector. Directive 97/66/EC has to be adapted to developments in the markets and technologies for electronic communications services in order to provide an equal level of protection of personal data and privacy for users of publicly available electronic communications services, regardless of the technologies used. That Directive should therefore be repealed and replaced by this Directive.

(5) New advanced digital technologies are currently being introduced in public communications networks in the Community, which give rise to specific requirements concerning the protection of personal data and privacy of the user. The development of the information society is characterised by the introduction of new electronic communications services. Access to digital mobile networks has become available and affordable for a large public. These digital networks have large capacities and possibilities for processing personal data. The successful cross-border development of these services is partly dependent on the confidence of users that their privacy will not be at risk.

(6) The Internet is overturning traditional market structures by providing a common, global infrastructure for the delivery of a wide range of electronic communications services. Publicly available electronic communications services over the Internet open new possibilities for users but also new risks for their personal data and privacy.

(7) In the case of public communications networks, specific legal, regulatory and technical provisions should be made in order to protect fundamental rights and freedoms of natural persons and legitimate interests of legal persons, in particular with regard to the increasing capacity for automated storage and processing of data relating to subscribers and users.

(8) Legal, regulatory and technical provisions adopted by the Member States concerning the protection of personal data, privacy and the legitimate interest of legal persons, in the electronic communication sector, should be harmonised in order to avoid obstacles to the internal market for electronic communication in accordance with Article 14 of the Treaty. Harmonisation should be limited to requirements necessary to guarantee that the promotion and development of new electronic communications services and networks between Member States are not hindered.

(¹) OJ C 365 E, 19.12.2000, p. 223.
(²) OJ C 123, 25.4.2001, p. 53.
(³) Opinion of the European Parliament of 13 November 2001 (not yet published in the Official Journal), Council Common Position of 28 January 2002 (OJ C 113 E, 14.5.2002, p. 39) and Decision of the European Parliament of 30 May 2002 (not yet published in the Official Journal). Council Decision of 25 June 2002.
(⁴) OJ L 281, 23.11.1995, p. 31.
(⁵) OJ L 24, 30.1.1998, p. 1.

L 201/38   EN   Official Journal of the European Communities   31.7.2002

(9) The Member States, providers and users concerned, together with the competent Community bodies, should cooperate in introducing and developing the relevant technologies where this is necessary to apply the guarantees provided for by this Directive and taking particular account of the objectives of minimising the processing of personal data and of using anonymous or pseudonymous data where possible.

(10) In the electronic communications sector, Directive 95/46/EC applies in particular to all matters concerning protection of fundamental rights and freedoms, which are not specifically covered by the provisions of this Directive, including the obligations on the controller and the rights of individuals. Directive 95/46/EC applies to non-public communications services.

(11) Like Directive 95/46/EC, this Directive does not address issues of protection of fundamental rights and freedoms related to activities which are not governed by Community law. Therefore it does not alter the existing balance between the individual's right to privacy and the possibility for Member States to take the measures referred to in Article 15(1) of this Directive, necessary for the protection of public security, defence, State security (including the economic well-being of the State when the activities relate to State security matters) and the enforcement of criminal law. Consequently, this Directive does not affect the ability of Member States to carry out lawful interception of electronic communications, or take other measures, if necessary for any of these purposes and in accordance with the European Convention for the Protection of Human Rights and Fundamental Freedoms, as interpreted by the rulings of the European Court of Human Rights. Such measures must be appropriate, strictly proportionate to the intended purpose and necessary within a democratic society and should be subject to adequate safeguards in accordance with the European Convention for the Protection of Human Rights and Fundamental Freedoms.

(12) Subscribers to a publicly available electronic communications service may be natural or legal persons. By supplementing Directive 95/46/EC, this Directive is aimed at protecting the fundamental rights of natural persons and particularly their right to privacy, as well as the legitimate interests of legal persons. This Directive does not entail an obligation for Member States to extend the application of Directive 95/46/EC to the protection of the legitimate interests of legal persons, which is ensured within the framework of the applicable Community and national legislation.

(13) The contractual relation between a subscriber and a service provider may entail a periodic or a one-off payment for the service provided or to be provided. Prepaid cards are also considered as a contract.

(14) Location data may refer to the latitude, longitude and altitude of the user's terminal equipment, to the direction of travel, to the level of accuracy of the location information, to the identification of the network cell in which the terminal equipment is located at a certain point in time and to the time the location information was recorded.

(15) A communication may include any naming, numbering or addressing information provided by the sender of a communication or the user of a connection to carry out the communication. Traffic data may include any translation of this information by the network over which the communication is transmitted for the purpose of carrying out the transmission. Traffic data may, *inter alia*, consist of data referring to the routing, duration, time or volume of a communication, to the protocol used, to the location of the terminal equipment of the sender or recipient, to the network on which the communication originates or terminates, to the beginning, end or duration of a connection. They may also consist of the format in which the communication is conveyed by the network.

(16) Information that is part of a broadcasting service provided over a public communications network is intended for a potentially unlimited audience and does not constitute a communication in the sense of this Directive. However, in cases where the individual subscriber or user receiving such information can be identified, for example with video-on-demand services, the information conveyed is covered within the meaning of a communication for the purposes of this Directive.

(17) For the purposes of this Directive, consent of a user or subscriber, regardless of whether the latter is a natural or a legal person, should have the same meaning as the data subject's consent as defined and further specified in Directive 95/46/EC. Consent may be given by any appropriate method enabling a freely given specific and informed indication of the user's wishes, including by ticking a box when visiting an Internet website.

(18) Value added services may, for example, consist of advice on least expensive tariff packages, route guidance, traffic information, weather forecasts and tourist information.

(19) The application of certain requirements relating to presentation and restriction of calling and connected line identification and to automatic call forwarding to subscriber lines connected to analogue exchanges should not be made mandatory in specific cases where such application would prove to be technically impossible or would require a disproportionate economic effort. It is important for interested parties to be informed of such cases and the Member States should therefore notify them to the Commission.

(20) Service providers should take appropriate measures to safeguard the security of their services, if necessary in conjunction with the provider of the network, and inform subscribers of any special risks of a breach of the security of the network. Such risks may especially occur for electronic communications services over an open network such as the Internet or analogue mobile telephony. It is particularly important for subscribers and users of such services to be fully informed by their service provider of the existing security risks which lie outside the scope of possible remedies by the service provider. Service providers who offer publicly available electronic communications services over the Internet should inform users and subscribers of measures they can take to protect the security of their communications for instance by using specific types of software or encryption technologies. The requirement to inform subscribers of particular security risks does not discharge a service provider from the obligation to take, at its own costs, appropriate and immediate measures to remedy any new, unforeseen security risks and restore the normal security level of the service. The provision of information about security risks to the subscriber should be free of charge except for any nominal costs which the subscriber may incur while receiving or collecting the information, for instance by downloading an electronic mail message. Security is appraised in the light of Article 17 of Directive 95/46/EC.

(21) Measures should be taken to prevent unauthorised access to communications in order to protect the confidentiality of communications, including both the contents and any data related to such communications, by means of public communications networks and publicly available electronic communications services. National legislation in some Member States only prohibits intentional unauthorised access to communications.

(22) The prohibition of storage of communications and the related traffic data by persons other than the users or without their consent is not intended to prohibit any automatic, intermediate and transient storage of this information in so far as this takes place for the sole purpose of carrying out the transmission in the electronic communications network and provided that the information is not stored for any period longer than is necessary for the transmission and for traffic management purposes, and that during the period of storage the confidentiality remains guaranteed. Where this is necessary for making more efficient the onward transmission of any publicly accessible information to other recipients of the service upon their request, this Directive should not prevent such information from being further stored, provided that this information would in any case be accessible to the public without restriction and that any data referring to the individual subscribers or users requesting such information are erased.

(23) Confidentiality of communications should also be ensured in the course of lawful business practice. Where necessary and legally authorised, communications can be recorded for the purpose of providing evidence of a commercial transaction. Directive 95/46/EC applies to such processing. Parties to the communications should be informed prior to the recording about the recording, its purpose and the duration of its storage. The recorded communication should be erased as soon as possible and in any case at the latest by the end of the period during which the transaction can be lawfully challenged.

(24) Terminal equipment of users of electronic communications networks and any information stored on such equipment are part of the private sphere of the users requiring protection under the European Convention for the Protection of Human Rights and Fundamental Freedoms. So-called spyware, web bugs, hidden identifiers and other similar devices can enter the user's terminal without their knowledge in order to gain access to information, to store hidden information or to trace the activities of the user and may seriously intrude upon the privacy of these users. The use of such devices should be allowed only for legitimate purposes, with the knowledge of the users concerned.

(25) However, such devices, for instance so-called 'cookies', can be a legitimate and useful tool, for example, in analysing the effectiveness of website design and advertising, and in verifying the identity of users engaged in on-line transactions. Where such devices, for instance cookies, are intended for a legitimate purpose, such as to facilitate the provision of information society services, their use should be allowed on condition that users are provided with clear and precise information in accordance with Directive 95/46/EC about the purposes of cookies or similar devices so as to ensure that users are made aware of information being placed on the terminal equipment they are using. Users should have the opportunity to refuse to have a cookie or similar device stored on their terminal equipment. This is particularly important where users other than the original user have access to the terminal equipment and thereby to any data containing privacy-sensitive information stored on such equipment. Information and the right to refuse may be offered once for the use of various devices to be installed on the user's terminal equipment during the same connection and also covering any further use that may be made of those devices during subsequent connections. The methods for giving information, offering a right to refuse or requesting consent should be made as user-friendly as possible. Access to specific website content may still be made conditional on the well-informed acceptance of a cookie or similar device, if it is used for a legitimate purpose.

376

Appendix 4

(26) The data relating to subscribers processed within electronic communications networks to establish connections and to transmit information contain information on the private life of natural persons and concern the right to respect for their correspondence or concern the legitimate interests of legal persons. Such data may only be stored to the extent that is necessary for the provision of the service for the purpose of billing and for interconnection payments, and for a limited time. Any further processing of such data which the provider of the publicly available electronic communications services may want to perform, for the marketing of electronic communications services or for the provision of value added services, may only be allowed if the subscriber has agreed to this on the basis of accurate and full information given by the provider of the publicly available electronic communications services about the types of further processing it intends to perform and about the subscriber's right not to give or to withdraw his/her consent to such processing. Traffic data used for marketing communications services or for the provision of value added services should also be erased or made anonymous after the provision of the service. Service providers should always keep subscribers informed of the types of data they are processing and the purposes and duration for which this is done.

(27) The exact moment of the completion of the transmission of a communication, after which traffic data should be erased except for billing purposes, may depend on the type of electronic communications service that is provided. For instance for a voice telephony call the transmission will be completed as soon as either of the users terminates the connection. For electronic mail the transmission is completed as soon as the addressee collects the message, typically from the server of his service provider.

(28) The obligation to erase traffic data or to make such data anonymous when it is no longer needed for the purpose of the transmission of a communication does not conflict with such procedures on the Internet as the caching in the domain name system of IP addresses or the caching of IP addresses to physical address bindings or the use of log-in information to control the right of access to networks or services.

(29) The service provider may process traffic data relating to subscribers and users where necessary in individual cases in order to detect technical failure or errors in the transmission of communications. Traffic data necessary for billing purposes may also be processed by the provider in order to detect and stop fraud consisting of unpaid use of the electronic communications service.

(30) Systems for the provision of electronic communications networks and services should be designed to limit the amount of personal data necessary to a strict minimum. Any activities related to the provision of the electronic communications service that go beyond the transmission of a communication and the billing thereof should be based on aggregated, traffic data that cannot be related to subscribers or users. Where such activities cannot be based on aggregated data, they should be considered as value added services for which the consent of the subscriber is required.

(31) Whether the consent to be obtained for the processing of personal data with a view to providing a particular value added service should be that of the user or of the subscriber, will depend on the data to be processed and on the type of service to be provided and on whether it is technically, procedurally and contractually possible to distinguish the individual using an electronic communications service from the legal or natural person having subscribed to it.

(32) Where the provider of an electronic communications service or of a value added service subcontracts the processing of personal data necessary for the provision of these services to another entity, such subcontracting and subsequent data processing should be in full compliance with the requirements regarding controllers and processors of personal data as set out in Directive 95/46/EC. Where the provision of a value added service requires that traffic or location data are forwarded from an electronic communications service provider to a provider of value added services, the subscribers or users to whom the data are related should also be fully informed of this forwarding before giving their consent for the processing of the data.

(33) The introduction of itemised bills has improved the possibilities for the subscriber to check the accuracy of the fees charged by the service provider but, at the same time, it may jeopardise the privacy of the users of publicly available electronic communications services. Therefore, in order to preserve the privacy of the user, Member States should encourage the development of electronic communication service options such as alternative payment facilities which allow anonymous or strictly private access to publicly available electronic communications services, for example calling cards and facilities for payment by credit card. To the same end, Member States may ask the operators to offer their subscribers a different type of detailed bill in which a certain number of digits of the called number have been deleted.

31.7.2002   [EN]   Official Journal of the European Communities   L 201/41

(34) It is necessary, as regards calling line identification, to protect the right of the calling party to withhold the presentation of the identification of the line from which the call is being made and the right of the called party to reject calls from unidentified lines. There is justification for overriding the elimination of calling line identification presentation in specific cases. Certain subscribers, in particular help lines and similar organisations, have an interest in guaranteeing the anonymity of their callers. It is necessary, as regards connected line identification, to protect the right and the legitimate interest of the called party to withhold the presentation of the identification of the line to which the calling party is actually connected, in particular in the case of forwarded calls. The providers of publicly available electronic communications services should inform their subscribers of the existence of calling and connected line identification in the network and of all services which are offered on the basis of calling and connected line identification as well as the privacy options which are available. This will allow the subscribers to make an informed choice about the privacy facilities they may want to use. The privacy options which are offered on a per-line basis do not necessarily have to be available as an automatic network service but may be obtainable through a simple request to the provider of the publicly available electronic communications service.

(35) In digital mobile networks, location data giving the geographic position of the terminal equipment of the mobile user are processed to enable the transmission of communications. Such data are traffic data covered by Article 6 of this Directive. However, in addition, digital mobile networks may have the capacity to process location data which are more precise than is necessary for the transmission of communications and which are used for the provision of value added services such as services providing individualised traffic information and guidance to drivers. The processing of such data for value added services should only be allowed where subscribers have given their consent. Even in cases where subscribers have given their consent, they should have a simple means to temporarily deny the processing of location data, free of charge.

(36) Member States may restrict the users' and subscribers' rights to privacy with regard to calling line identification where this is necessary to trace nuisance calls and with regard to calling line identification and location data where this is necessary to allow emergency services to carry out their tasks as effectively as possible. For these purposes, Member States may adopt specific provisions to entitle providers of electronic communications services to provide access to calling line identification and location data without the prior consent of the users or subscribers concerned.

(37) Safeguards should be provided for subscribers against the nuisance which may be caused by automatic call forwarding by others. Moreover, in such cases, it must be possible for subscribers to stop the forwarded calls being passed on to their terminals by simple request to the provider of the publicly available electronic communications service.

(38) Directories of subscribers to electronic communications services are widely distributed and public. The right to privacy of natural persons and the legitimate interest of legal persons require that subscribers are able to determine whether their personal data are published in a directory and if so, which. Providers of public directories should inform the subscribers to be included in such directories of the purposes of the directory and of any particular usage which may be made of electronic versions of public directories especially through search functions embedded in the software, such as reverse search functions enabling users of the directory to discover the name and address of the subscriber on the basis of a telephone number only.

(39) The obligation to inform subscribers of the purpose(s) of public directories in which their personal data are to be included should be imposed on the party collecting the data for such inclusion. Where the data may be transmitted to one or more third parties, the subscriber should be informed of this possibility and of the recipient or the categories of possible recipients. Any transmission should be subject to the condition that the data may not be used for other purposes than those for which they were collected. If the party collecting the data from the subscriber or any third party to whom the data have been transmitted wishes to use the data for an additional purpose, the renewed consent of the subscriber is to be obtained either by the initial party collecting the data or by the third party to whom the data have been transmitted.

(40) Safeguards should be provided for subscribers against intrusion of their privacy by unsolicited communications for direct marketing purposes in particular by means of automated calling machines, telefaxes, and e-mails, including SMS messages. These forms of unsolicited commercial communications may on the one hand be relatively easy and cheap to send and on the other may impose a burden and/or cost on the recipient. Moreover, in some cases their volume may also cause difficulties for electronic communications networks and terminal equipment. For such forms of unsolicited communications for direct marketing, it is justified to require that prior explicit consent of the recipients is obtained before such communications are addressed to them. The single market requires a harmonised approach to ensure simple, Community-wide rules for businesses and users.

L 201/42 EN Official Journal of the European Communities 31.7.2002

(41) Within the context of an existing customer relationship, it is reasonable to allow the use of electronic contact details for the offering of similar products or services, but only by the same company that has obtained the electronic contact details in accordance with Directive 95/46/EC. When electronic contact details are obtained, the customer should be informed about their further use for direct marketing in a clear and distinct manner, and be given the opportunity to refuse such usage. This opportunity should continue to be offered with each subsequent direct marketing message, free of charge, except for any costs for the transmission of this refusal.

(42) Other forms of direct marketing that are more costly for the sender and impose no financial costs on subscribers and users, such as person-to-person voice telephony calls, may justify the maintenance of a system giving subscribers or users the possibility to indicate that they do not want to receive such calls. Nevertheless, in order not to decrease existing levels of privacy protection, Member States should be entitled to uphold national systems, only allowing such calls to subscribers and users who have given their prior consent.

(43) To facilitate effective enforcement of Community rules on unsolicited messages for direct marketing, it is necessary to prohibit the use of false identities or false return addresses or numbers while sending unsolicited messages for direct marketing purposes.

(44) Certain electronic mail systems allow subscribers to view the sender and subject line of an electronic mail, and also to delete the message, without having to download the rest of the electronic mail's content or any attachments, thereby reducing costs which could arise from downloading unsolicited electronic mails or attachments. These arrangements may continue to be useful in certain cases as an additional tool to the general obligations established in this Directive.

(45) This Directive is without prejudice to the arrangements which Member States make to protect the legitimate interests of legal persons with regard to unsolicited communications for direct marketing purposes. Where Member States establish an opt-out register for such communications to legal persons, mostly business users, the provisions of Article 7 of Directive 2000/31/EC of the European Parliament and of the Council of 8 June 2000 on certain legal aspects of information society services, in particular electronic commerce, in the internal market (Directive on electronic commerce) (¹) are fully applicable.

(46) The functionalities for the provision of electronic communications services may be integrated in the network or in any part of the terminal equipment of the user, including the software. The protection of the personal data and the privacy of the user of publicly available electronic communications services should be independent of the configuration of the various compo-

nents necessary to provide the service and of the distribution of the necessary functionalities between these components. Directive 95/46/EC covers any form of processing of personal data regardless of the technology used. The existence of specific rules for electronic communications services alongside general rules for other components necessary for the provision of such services may not facilitate the protection of personal data and privacy in a technologically neutral way. It may therefore be necessary to adopt measures requiring manufacturers of certain types of equipment used for electronic communications services to construct their product in such a way as to incorporate safeguards to ensure that the personal data and privacy of the user and subscriber are protected. The adoption of such measures in accordance with Directive 1999/5/EC of the European Parliament and of the Council of 9 March 1999 on radio equipment and telecommunications terminal equipment and the mutual recognition of their conformity (²) will ensure that the introduction of technical features of electronic communication equipment including software for data protection purposes is harmonised in order to be compatible with the implementation of the internal market.

(47) Where the rights of the users and subscribers are not respected, national legislation should provide for judicial remedies. Penalties should be imposed on any person, whether governed by private or public law, who fails to comply with the national measures taken under this Directive.

(48) It is useful, in the field of application of this Directive, to draw on the experience of the Working Party on the Protection of Individuals with regard to the Processing of Personal Data composed of representatives of the supervisory authorities of the Member States, set up by Article 29 of Directive 95/46/EC.

(49) To facilitate compliance with the provisions of this Directive, certain specific arrangements are needed for processing of data already under way on the date that national implementing legislation pursuant to this Directive enters into force,

HAVE ADOPTED THIS DIRECTIVE:

Article 1

Scope and aim

1. This Directive harmonises the provisions of the Member States required to ensure an equivalent level of protection of fundamental rights and freedoms, and in particular the right to privacy, with respect to the processing of personal data in the electronic communication sector and to ensure the free movement of such data and of electronic communication equipment and services in the Community.

(¹) OJ L 178, 17.7.2000, p. 1.

(²) OJ L 91, 7.4.1999, p. 10.

31.7.2002   EN   Official Journal of the European Communities   L 201/43

2.   The provisions of this Directive particularise and complement Directive 95/46/EC for the purposes mentioned in paragraph 1. Moreover, they provide for protection of the legitimate interests of subscribers who are legal persons.

3.   This Directive shall not apply to activities which fall outside the scope of the Treaty establishing the European Community, such as those covered by Titles V and VI of the Treaty on European Union, and in any case to activities concerning public security, defence, State security (including the economic well-being of the State when the activities relate to State security matters) and the activities of the State in areas of criminal law.

Article 2

Definitions

Save as otherwise provided, the definitions in Directive 95/46/EC and in Directive 2002/21/EC of the European Parliament and of the Council of 7 March 2002 on a common regulatory framework for electronic communications networks and services (Framework Directive) (¹) shall apply.

The following definitions shall also apply:

(a) 'user' means any natural person using a publicly available electronic communications service, for private or business purposes, without necessarily having subscribed to this service;

(b) 'traffic data' means any data processed for the purpose of the conveyance of a communication on an electronic communications network or for the billing thereof;

(c) 'location data' means any data processed in an electronic communications network, indicating the geographic position of the terminal equipment of a user of a publicly available electronic communications service;

(d) 'communication' means any information exchanged or conveyed between a finite number of parties by means of a publicly available electronic communications service. This does not include any information conveyed as part of a broadcasting service to the public over an electronic communications network except to the extent that the information can be related to the identifiable subscriber or user receiving the information;

(e) 'call' means a connection established by means of a publicly available telephone service allowing two-way communication in real time;

(f) 'consent' by a user or subscriber corresponds to the data subject's consent in Directive 95/46/EC;

(g) 'value added service' means any service which requires the processing of traffic data or location data other than traffic data beyond what is necessary for the transmission of a communication or the billing thereof;

(h) 'electronic mail' means any text, voice, sound or image message sent over a public communications network which

---

(¹) OJ L 108, 24.4.2002, p. 33.

can be stored in the network or in the recipient's terminal equipment until it is collected by the recipient.

Article 3

Services concerned

1.   This Directive shall apply to the processing of personal data in connection with the provision of publicly available electronic communications services in public communications networks in the Community.

2.   Articles 8, 10 and 11 shall apply to subscriber lines connected to digital exchanges and, where technically possible and if it does not require a disproportionate economic effort, to subscriber lines connected to analogue exchanges.

3.   Cases where it would be technically impossible or require a disproportionate economic effort to fulfil the requirements of Articles 8, 10 and 11 shall be notified to the Commission by the Member States.

Article 4

Security

1.   The provider of a publicly available electronic communications service must take appropriate technical and organisational measures to safeguard security of its services, if necessary in conjunction with the provider of the public communications network with respect to network security. Having regard to the state of the art and the cost of their implementation, these measures shall ensure a level of security appropriate to the risk presented.

2.   In case of a particular risk of a breach of the security of the network, the provider of a publicly available electronic communications service must inform the subscribers concerning such risk and, where the risk lies outside the scope of the measures to be taken by the service provider, of any possible remedies, including an indication of the likely costs involved.

Article 5

Confidentiality of the communications

1.   Member States shall ensure the confidentiality of communications and the related traffic data by means of a public communications network and publicly available electronic communications services, through national legislation. In particular, they shall prohibit listening, tapping, storage or other kinds of interception or surveillance of communications and the related traffic data by persons other than users, without the consent of the users concerned, except when legally authorised to do so in accordance with Article 15(1). This paragraph shall not prevent technical storage which is necessary for the conveyance of a communication without prejudice to the principle of confidentiality.

L 201/44 [EN] Official Journal of the European Communities 31.7.2002

2. Paragraph 1 shall not affect any legally authorised recording of communications and the related traffic data when carried out in the course of lawful business practice for the purpose of providing evidence of a commercial transaction or of any other business communication.

3. Member States shall ensure that the use of electronic communications networks to store information or to gain access to information stored in the terminal equipment of a subscriber or user is only allowed on condition that the subscriber or user concerned is provided with clear and comprehensive information in accordance with Directive 95/46/EC, *inter alia* about the purposes of the processing, and is offered the right to refuse such processing by the data controller. This shall not prevent any technical storage or access for the sole purpose of carrying out or facilitating the transmission of a communication over an electronic communications network, or as strictly necessary in order to provide an information society service explicitly requested by the subscriber or user.

Article 6

Traffic data

1. Traffic data relating to subscribers and users processed and stored by the provider of a public communications network or publicly available electronic communications service must be erased or made anonymous when it is no longer needed for the purpose of the transmission of a communication without prejudice to paragraphs 2, 3 and 5 of this Article and Article 15(1).

2. Traffic data necessary for the purposes of subscriber billing and interconnection payments may be processed. Such processing is permissible only up to the end of the period during which the bill may lawfully be challenged or payment pursued.

3. For the purpose of marketing electronic communications services or for the provision of value added services, the provider of a publicly available electronic communications service may process the data referred to in paragraph 1 to the extent and for the duration necessary for such services or marketing, if the subscriber or user to whom the data relate has given his/her consent. Users or subscribers shall be given the possibility to withdraw their consent for the processing of traffic data at any time.

4. The service provider must inform the subscriber or user of the types of traffic data which are processed and of the duration of such processing for the purposes mentioned in paragraph 2 and, prior to obtaining consent, for the purposes mentioned in paragraph 3.

5. Processing of traffic data, in accordance with paragraphs 1, 2, 3 and 4, must be restricted to persons acting under the authority of providers of the public communications networks and publicly available electronic communications services handling billing or traffic management, customer enquiries, fraud detection, marketing electronic communications services or providing a value added service, and must be restricted to what is necessary for the purposes of such activities.

6. Paragraphs 1, 2, 3 and 5 shall apply without prejudice to the possibility for competent bodies to be informed of traffic data in conformity with applicable legislation with a view to settling disputes, in particular interconnection or billing disputes.

Article 7

Itemised billing

1. Subscribers shall have the right to receive non-itemised bills.

2. Member States shall apply national provisions in order to reconcile the rights of subscribers receiving itemised bills with the right to privacy of calling users and called subscribers, for example by ensuring that sufficient alternative privacy enhancing methods of communications or payments are available to such users and subscribers.

Article 8

Presentation and restriction of calling and connected line identification

1. Where presentation of calling line identification is offered, the service provider must offer the calling user the possibility, using a simple means and free of charge, of preventing the presentation of the calling line identification on a per-call basis. The calling subscriber must have this possibility on a per-line basis.

2. Where presentation of calling line identification is offered, the service provider must offer the called subscriber the possibility, using a simple means and free of charge for reasonable use of this function, of preventing the presentation of the calling line identification of incoming calls.

3. Where presentation of calling line identification is offered and where the calling line identification is presented prior to the call being established, the service provider must offer the called subscriber the possibility, using a simple means, of rejecting incoming calls where the presentation of the calling line identification has been prevented by the calling user or subscriber.

4. Where presentation of connected line identification is offered, the service provider must offer the called subscriber the possibility, using a simple means and free of charge, of preventing the presentation of the connected line identification to the calling user.

5. Paragraph 1 shall also apply with regard to calls to third countries originating in the Community. Paragraphs 2, 3 and 4 shall also apply to incoming calls originating in third countries.

6. Member States shall ensure that where presentation of calling and/or connected line identification is offered, the providers of publicly available electronic communications services inform the public thereof and of the possibilities set out in paragraphs 1, 2, 3 and 4.

Article 9

Location data other than traffic data

1.   Where location data other than traffic data, relating to users or subscribers of public communications networks or publicly available electronic communications services, can be processed, such data may only be processed when they are made anonymous, or with the consent of the users or subscribers to the extent and for the duration necessary for the provision of a value added service. The service provider must inform the users or subscribers, prior to obtaining their consent, of the type of location data other than traffic data which will be processed, of the purposes and duration of the processing and whether the data will be transmitted to a third party for the purpose of providing the value added service. Users or subscribers shall be given the possibility to withdraw their consent for the processing of location data other than traffic data at any time.

2.   Where consent of the users or subscribers has been obtained for the processing of location data other than traffic data, the user or subscriber must continue to have the possibility, using a simple means and free of charge, of temporarily refusing the processing of such data for each connection to the network or for each transmission of a communication.

3.   Processing of location data other than traffic data in accordance with paragraphs 1 and 2 must be restricted to persons acting under the authority of the provider of the public communications network or publicly available communications service or of the third party providing the value added service, and must be restricted to what is necessary for the purposes of providing the value added service.

Article 10

Exceptions

Member States shall ensure that there are transparent procedures governing the way in which a provider of a public communications network and/or a publicly available electronic communications service may override:

(a) the elimination of the presentation of calling line identification, on a temporary basis, upon application of a subscriber requesting the tracing of malicious or nuisance calls. In this case, in accordance with national law, the data containing the identification of the calling subscriber will be stored and be made available by the provider of a public communications network and/or publicly available electronic communications service;

(b) the elimination of the presentation of calling line identification and the temporary denial or absence of consent of a subscriber or user for the processing of location data, on a per-line basis for organisations dealing with emergency calls and recognised as such by a Member State, including law enforcement agencies, ambulance services and fire brigades, for the purpose of responding to such calls.

Article 11

Automatic call forwarding

Member States shall ensure that any subscriber has the possibility, using a simple means and free of charge, of stopping automatic call forwarding by a third party to the subscriber's terminal.

Article 12

Directories of subscribers

1.   Member States shall ensure that subscribers are informed, free of charge and before they are included in the directory, about the purpose(s) of a printed or electronic directory of subscribers available to the public or obtainable through directory enquiry services, in which their personal data can be included and of any further usage possibilities based on search functions embedded in electronic versions of the directory.

2.   Member States shall ensure that subscribers are given the opportunity to determine whether their personal data are included in a public directory, and if so, which, to the extent that such data are relevant for the purpose of the directory as determined by the provider of the directory, and to verify, correct or withdraw such data. Not being included in a public subscriber directory, verifying, correcting or withdrawing personal data from it shall be free of charge.

3.   Member States may require that for any purpose of a public directory other than the search of contact details of persons on the basis of their name and, where necessary, a minimum of other identifiers, additional consent be asked of the subscribers.

4.   Paragraphs 1 and 2 shall apply to subscribers who are natural persons. Member States shall also ensure, in the framework of Community law and applicable national legislation, that the legitimate interests of subscribers other than natural persons with regard to their entry in public directories are sufficiently protected.

Article 13

Unsolicited communications

1.   The use of automated calling systems without human intervention (automatic calling machines), facsimile machines (fax) or electronic mail for the purposes of direct marketing may only be allowed in respect of subscribers who have given their prior consent.

2.   Notwithstanding paragraph 1, where a natural or legal person obtains from its customers their electronic contact details for electronic mail, in the context of the sale of a product or a service, in accordance with Directive 95/46/EC, the same natural or legal person may use these electronic contact details for direct marketing of its own similar products or services provided that customers clearly and distinctly are given the opportunity to object, free of charge and in an easy manner, to such use of electronic contact details when they are collected and on the occasion of each message in case the customer has not initially refused such use.

L 201/46 [EN] Official Journal of the European Communities 31.7.2002

3. Member States shall take appropriate measures to ensure that, free of charge, unsolicited communications for purposes of direct marketing, in cases other than those referred to in paragraphs 1 and 2, are not allowed either without the consent of the subscribers concerned or in respect of subscribers who do not wish to receive these communications, the choice between these options to be determined by national legislation.

4. In any event, the practice of sending electronic mail for purposes of direct marketing disguising or concealing the identity of the sender on whose behalf the communication is made, or without a valid address to which the recipient may send a request that such communications cease, shall be prohibited.

5. Paragraphs 1 and 3 shall apply to subscribers who are natural persons. Member States shall also ensure, in the framework of Community law and applicable national legislation, that the legitimate interests of subscribers other than natural persons with regard to unsolicited communications are sufficiently protected.

Article 14

Technical features and standardisation

1. In implementing the provisions of this Directive, Member States shall ensure, subject to paragraphs 2 and 3, that no mandatory requirements for specific technical features are imposed on terminal or other electronic communication equipment which could impede the placing of equipment on the market and the free circulation of such equipment in and between Member States.

2. Where provisions of this Directive can be implemented only by requiring specific technical features in electronic communications networks, Member States shall inform the Commission in accordance with the procedure provided for by Directive 98/34/EC of the European Parliament and of the Council of 22 June 1998 laying down a procedure for the provision of information in the field of technical standards and regulations and of rules on information society services (¹).

3. Where required, measures may be adopted to ensure that terminal equipment is constructed in a way that is compatible with the right of users to protect and control the use of their personal data, in accordance with Directive 1999/5/EC and Council Decision 87/95/EEC of 22 December 1986 on standardisation in the field of information technology and communications (²).

Article 15

Application of certain provisions of Directive 95/46/EC

1. Member States may adopt legislative measures to restrict the scope of the rights and obligations provided for in Article 5, Article 6, Article 8(1), (2), (3) and (4), and Article 9 of this

Directive when such restriction constitutes a necessary, appropriate and proportionate measure within a democratic society to safeguard national security (i.e. State security), defence, public security, and the prevention, investigation, detection and prosecution of criminal offences or of unauthorised use of the electronic communication system, as referred to in Article 13(1) of Directive 95/46/EC. To this end, Member States may, *inter alia*, adopt legislative measures providing for the retention of data for a limited period justified on the grounds laid down in this paragraph. All the measures referred to in this paragraph shall be in accordance with the general principles of Community law, including those referred to in Article 6(1) and (2) of the Treaty on European Union.

2. The provisions of Chapter III on judicial remedies, liability and sanctions of Directive 95/46/EC shall apply with regard to national provisions adopted pursuant to this Directive and with regard to the individual rights derived from this Directive.

3. The Working Party on the Protection of Individuals with regard to the Processing of Personal Data instituted by Article 29 of Directive 95/46/EC shall also carry out the tasks laid down in Article 30 of that Directive with regard to matters covered by this Directive, namely the protection of fundamental rights and freedoms and of legitimate interests in the electronic communications sector.

Article 16

Transitional arrangements

1. Article 12 shall not apply to editions of directories already produced or placed on the market in printed or off-line electronic form before the national provisions adopted pursuant to this Directive enter into force.

2. Where the personal data of subscribers to fixed or mobile public voice telephony services have been included in a public subscriber directory in conformity with the provisions of Directive 95/46/EC and of Article 11 of Directive 97/66/EC before the national provisions adopted in pursuance of this Directive enter into force, the personal data of such subscribers may remain included in this public directory in its printed or electronic versions, including versions with reverse search functions, unless subscribers indicate otherwise, after having received complete information about purposes and options in accordance with Article 12 of this Directive.

Article 17

Transposition

1. Before 31 October 2003 Member States shall bring into force the provisions necessary to comply with this Directive. They shall forthwith inform the Commission thereof.

(¹) OJ L 204, 21.7.1998, p. 37. Directive as amended by Directive 98/48/EC (OJ L 217, 5.8.1998, p. 18).
(²) OJ L 36, 7.2.1987, p. 31. Decision as last amended by the 1994 Act of Accession.

31.7.2002 | EN | Official Journal of the European Communities | L 201/47

When Member States adopt those provisions, they shall contain a reference to this Directive or be accompanied by such a reference on the occasion of their official publication. The methods of making such reference shall be laid down by the Member States.

2. Member States shall communicate to the Commission the text of the provisions of national law which they adopt in the field governed by this Directive and of any subsequent amendments to those provisions.

Article 18

Review

The Commission shall submit to the European Parliament and the Council, not later than three years after the date referred to in Article 17(1), a report on the application of this Directive and its impact on economic operators and consumers, in particular as regards the provisions on unsolicited communications, taking into account the international environment. For this purpose, the Commission may request information from the Member States, which shall be supplied without undue delay. Where appropriate, the Commission shall submit proposals to amend this Directive, taking account of the results of that report, any changes in the sector and any other proposal it may deem necessary in order to improve the effectiveness of this Directive.

Article 19

Repeal

Directive 97/66/EC is hereby repealed with effect from the date referred to in Article 17(1).

References made to the repealed Directive shall be construed as being made to this Directive.

Article 20

Entry into force

This Directive shall enter into force on the day of its publication in the *Official Journal of the European Communities*.

Article 21

Addressees

This Directive is addressed to the Member States.

Done at Brussels, 12 July 2002.

For the European Parliament	*For the Council*
The President	*The President*
P. COX	T. PEDERSEN

Appendix 5

Statutory Instrument 2003 No. 2426

The Privacy and Electronic Communications (EC Directive) Regulations 2003

© Crown Copyright 2003

STATUTORY INSTRUMENTS

2003 No. 2426

ELECTRONIC COMMUNICATIONS

The Privacy and Electronic Communications (EC Directive) Regulations 2003

Made	*18th September 2003*
Laid before Parliament	*18th September 2003*
Coming into force	*11th December 2003*

The Secretary of State, being a Minister designated[1] for the purposes of section 2(2) of the European Communities Act 1972[2] in respect of matters relating to electronic communications, in exercise of the powers conferred upon her by that section, hereby makes the following Regulations:

Citation and commencement

1. These Regulations may be cited as the Privacy and Electronic Communications (EC Directive) Regulations 2003 and shall come into force on 11th December 2003.

Interpretation

2.—(1) In these Regulations—

"bill" includes an invoice, account, statement or other document of similar character and "billing" shall be construed accordingly;

"call" means a connection established by means of a telephone service available to the public allowing two-way communication in real time;

"communication" means any information exchanged or conveyed between a finite number of parties by means of a public electronic communications service, but does not include information conveyed as part of a programme service, except to the extent that such information can be related to the identifiable subscriber or user receiving the information;

---

[1] S.I. 2001/3495.back
[2] 1972 c. 68.back

"communications provider" has the meaning given by section 405 of the Communications Act 2003[3];

"corporate subscriber" means a subscriber who is—

(a) a company within the meaning of section 735(1) of the Companies Act 1985[4];

(b) a company incorporated in pursuance of a royal charter or letters patent;

(c) a partnership in Scotland;

(d) a corporation sole; or

(e) any other body corporate or entity which is a legal person distinct from its members;

"the Directive" means Directive 2002/58/EC of the European Parliament and of the Council of 12 July 2002 concerning the processing of personal data and the protection of privacy in the electronic communications sector (Directive on privacy and electronic communications)[5];

"electronic communications network" has the meaning given by section 32 of the Communications Act 2003[6];

"electronic communications service" has the meaning given by section 32 of the Communications Act 2003;

"electronic mail" means any text, voice, sound or image message sent over a public electronic communications network which can be stored in the network or in the recipient's terminal equipment until it is collected by the recipient and includes messages sent using a short message service;

"enactment" includes an enactment comprised in, or in an instrument made under, an Act of the Scottish Parliament;

"individual" means a living individual and includes an unincorporated body of such individuals;

"the Information Commissioner" and "the Commissioner" both mean the Commissioner appointed under section 6 of the Data Protection Act 1998[7];

"information society service" has the meaning given in regulation 2(1) of the Electronic Commerce (EC Directive) Regulations 2002[8];

"location data" means any data processed in an electronic communications network indicating the geographical position of the terminal equipment of a user of a public electronic communications service, including data relating to—

(f) the latitude, longitude or altitude of the terminal equipment;

(g) the direction of travel of the user; or

(h) the time the location information was recorded;

---

[3] 2003 c. 21; for the commencement of section 405, see section 411(2) and (3) of the same Act.back

[4] 1985 c. 6.back

[5] OJ No L 201, 31.07.02, p. 37.back

[6] For the commencement of section 32, see article 2(1) of S.I. 2003/1900 (C. 77).back

[7] 1998 c. 29; section 6 was amended by section 18(4) of and paragraph 13(1) and (2) of Part 1 of Schedule 2 to the Freedom of Information Act 2000 (c. 36).back

[8] S.I. 2002/2013.back

"OFCOM" means the Office of Communications as established by section 1 of the Office of Communications Act 2002[9];

"programme service" has the meaning given in section 201 of the Broadcasting Act 1990[10];

"public communications provider" means a provider of a public electronic communications network or a public electronic communications service;

"public electronic communications network" has the meaning given in section 151 of the Communications Act 2003[11];

"public electronic communications service" has the meaning given in section 151 of the Communications Act 2003;

"subscriber" means a person who is a party to a contract with a provider of public electronic communications services for the supply of such services;

"traffic data" means any data processed for the purpose of the conveyance of a communication on an electronic communications network or for the billing in respect of that communication and includes data relating to the routing, duration or time of a communication;

"user" means any individual using a public electronic communications service; and

"value added service" means any service which requires the processing of traffic data or location data beyond that which is necessary for the transmission of a communication or the billing in respect of that communication.

(2) Expressions used in these Regulations that are not defined in paragraph (1) and are defined in the Data Protection Act 1998 shall have the same meaning as in that Act.

(3) Expressions used in these Regulations that are not defined in paragraph (1) or the Data Protection Act 1998 and are defined in the Directive shall have the same meaning as in the Directive.

(4) Any reference in these Regulations to a line shall, without prejudice to paragraph (3), be construed as including a reference to anything that performs the function of a line, and "connected", in relation to a line, is to be construed accordingly.

Revocation of the Telecommunications (Data Protection and Privacy) Regulations 1999

3. The Telecommunications (Data Protection and Privacy) Regulations 1999[12] and the Telecommunications (Data Protection and Privacy) (Amendment) Regulations 2000[13] are hereby revoked.

Relationship between these Regulations and the Data Protection Act 1998

4. Nothing in these Regulations shall relieve a person of his obligations under the Data Protection Act 1998 in relation to the processing of personal data.

Security of public electronic communications services

5.—(1) Subject to paragraph (2), a provider of a public electronic communications service ("the service provider") shall take appropriate technical and organisational measures to safeguard the security of that service.

---

[9] 2002 c. 11.back

[10] 1990 c. 42; section 201 was amended by section 148(1) of and paragraph 11 of Schedule 10 to the Broadcasting Act 1996 (c. 55).back

[11] For the commencement of section 151, see article 2(1) of S.I. 2003/1900 (C. 77).back

[12] S.I. 1999/2093.back

[13] S.I. 2000/157.back

(2) If necessary, the measures required by paragraph (1) may be taken by the service provider in conjunction with the provider of the electronic communications network by means of which the service is provided, and that network provider shall comply with any reasonable requests made by the service provider for these purposes.

(3) Where, notwithstanding the taking of measures as required by paragraph (1), there remains a significant risk to the security of the public electronic communications service, the service provider shall inform the subscribers concerned of—

> (a) the nature of that risk;
> (b) any appropriate measures that the subscriber may take to safeguard against that risk; and
> (c) the likely costs to the subscriber involved in the taking of such measures.

(4) For the purposes of paragraph (1), a measure shall only be taken to be appropriate if, having regard to—

> (a) the state of technological developments, and
> (b) the cost of implementing it,

it is proportionate to the risks against which it would safeguard.

(5) Information provided for the purposes of paragraph (3) shall be provided to the subscriber free of any charge other than the cost to the subscriber of receiving or collecting the information.

Confidentiality of communications

6.—(1) Subject to paragraph (4), a person shall not use an electronic communications network to store information, or to gain access to information stored, in the terminal equipment of a subscriber or user unless the requirements of paragraph (2) are met.

(2) The requirements are that the subscriber or user of that terminal equipment—

> (a) is provided with clear and comprehensive information about the purposes of the storage of, or access to, that information; and
> (b) is given the opportunity to refuse the storage of or access to that information.

(3) Where an electronic communications network is used by the same person to store or access information in the terminal equipment of a subscriber or user on more than one occasion, it is sufficient for the purposes of this regulation that the requirements of paragraph (2) are met in respect of the initial use.

(4) Paragraph (1) shall not apply to the technical storage of, or access to, information—

> (a) for the sole purpose of carrying out or facilitating the transmission of a communication over an electronic communications network; or
> (b) where such storage or access is strictly necessary for the provision of an information society service requested by the subscriber or user.

Restrictions on the processing of certain traffic data

7.—(1) Subject to paragraphs (2) and (3), traffic data relating to subscribers or users which are processed and stored by a public communications provider shall, when no longer required for the purpose of the transmission of a communication, be—

(a) erased;

(b) in the case of an individual, modified so that they cease to constitute personal data of that subscriber or user; or

(c) in the case of a corporate subscriber, modified so that they cease to be data that would be personal data if that subscriber was an individual.

(2) Traffic data held by a public communications provider for purposes connected with the payment of charges by a subscriber or in respect of interconnection payments may be processed and stored by that provider until the time specified in paragraph (5).

(3) Traffic data relating to a subscriber or user may be processed and stored by a provider of a public electronic communications service if—

(a) such processing and storage are for the purpose of marketing electronic communications services, or for the provision of value added services to that subscriber or user; and

(b) the subscriber or user to whom the traffic data relate has given his consent to such processing or storage; and

(c) such processing and storage are undertaken only for the duration necessary for the purposes specified in subparagraph (a).

(4) Where a user or subscriber has given his consent in accordance with paragraph (3), he shall be able to withdraw it at any time.

(5) The time referred to in paragraph (2) is the end of the period during which legal proceedings may be brought in respect of payments due or alleged to be due or, where such proceedings are brought within that period, the time when those proceedings are finally determined.

(6) Legal proceedings shall not be taken to be finally determined—

(a) until the conclusion of the ordinary period during which an appeal may be brought by either party (excluding any possibility of an extension of that period, whether by order of a court or otherwise), if no appeal is brought within that period; or

(b) if an appeal is brought, until the conclusion of that appeal.

(7) References in paragraph (6) to an appeal include references to an application for permission to appeal.

Further provisions relating to the processing of traffic data under regulation 7

8.—(1) Processing of traffic data in accordance with regulation 7(2) or (3) shall not be undertaken by a public communications provider unless the subscriber or user to whom the data relate has been provided with information regarding the types of traffic data which are to be processed and the duration of such processing and, in the case of processing in accordance with regulation 7(3), he has been provided with that information before his consent has been obtained.

(2) Processing of traffic data in accordance with regulation 7 shall be restricted to what is required for the purposes of one or more of the activities listed in paragraph (3) and shall be carried out only by the public communications provider or by a person acting under his authority.

(3) The activities referred to in paragraph (2) are activities relating to—

    (a) the management of billing or traffic;

    (b) customer enquiries;

    (c) the prevention or detection of fraud;

    (d) the marketing of electronic communications services; or

    (e) the provision of a value added service.

(4) Nothing in these Regulations shall prevent the furnishing of traffic data to a person who is a competent authority for the purposes of any provision relating to the settling of disputes (by way of legal proceedings or otherwise) which is contained in, or made by virtue of, any enactment.

Itemised billing and privacy

9.—(1) At the request of a subscriber, a provider of a public electronic communications service shall provide that subscriber with bills that are not itemised.

(2) OFCOM shall have a duty, when exercising their functions under Chapter 1 of Part 2 of the Communications Act 2003, to have regard to the need to reconcile the rights of subscribers receiving itemised bills with the rights to privacy of calling users and called subscribers, including the need for sufficient alternative privacy-enhancing methods of communications or payments to be available to such users and subscribers.

Prevention of calling line identification—outgoing calls

10.—(1) This regulation applies, subject to regulations 15 and 16, to outgoing calls where a facility enabling the presentation of calling line identification is available.

(2) The provider of a public electronic communications service shall provide users originating a call by means of that service with a simple means to prevent presentation of the identity of the calling line on the connected line as respects that call.

(3) The provider of a public electronic communications service shall provide subscribers to the service, as respects their line and all calls originating from that line, with a simple means of preventing presentation of the identity of that subscriber's line on any connected line.

(4) The measures to be provided under paragraphs (2) and (3) shall be provided free of charge.

Prevention of calling or connected line identification—incoming calls

11.—(1) This regulation applies to incoming calls.

(2) Where a facility enabling the presentation of calling line identification is available, the provider of a public electronic communications service shall provide the called subscriber with a simple means to prevent, free of charge for reasonable use of the facility, presentation of the identity of the calling line on the connected line.

(3) Where a facility enabling the presentation of calling line identification prior to the call being established is available, the provider of a public electronic communications service shall provide the called subscriber with a simple means of rejecting incoming calls where the presentation of the calling line identification has been prevented by the calling user or subscriber.

(4) Where a facility enabling the presentation of connected line identification is available, the provider of a public electronic communications service shall provide the called

subscriber with a simple means to prevent, without charge, presentation of the identity of the connected line on any calling line.

(5) In this regulation "called subscriber" means the subscriber receiving a call by means of the service in question whose line is the called line (whether or not it is also the connected line).

Publication of information for the purposes of regulations 10 and 11

12. Where a provider of a public electronic communications service provides facilities for calling or connected line identification, he shall provide information to the public regarding the availability of such facilities, including information regarding the options to be made available for the purposes of regulations 10 and 11.

Co-operation of communications providers for the purposes of regulations 10 and 11

13. For the purposes of regulations 10 and 11, a communications provider shall comply with any reasonable requests made by the provider of the public electronic communications service by means of which facilities for calling or connected line identification are provided.

Restrictions on the processing of location data

14.—(1) This regulation shall not apply to the processing of traffic data.

(2) Location data relating to a user or subscriber of a public electronic communications network or a public electronic communications service may only be processed—

> (a) where that user or subscriber cannot be identified from such data; or
>
> (b) where necessary for the provision of a value added service, with the consent of that user or subscriber.

(3) Prior to obtaining the consent of the user or subscriber under paragraph (2)(b), the public communications provider in question must provide the following information to the user or subscriber to whom the data relate—

> (a) the types of location data that will be processed;
>
> (b) the purposes and duration of the processing of those data; and
>
> (c) whether the data will be transmitted to a third party for the purpose of providing the value added service.

(4) A user or subscriber who has given his consent to the processing of data under paragraph (2)(b) shall—

> (a) be able to withdraw such consent at any time, and
>
> (b) in respect of each connection to the public electronic communications network in question or each transmission of a communication, be given the opportunity to withdraw such consent, using a simple means and free of charge.

(5) Processing of location data in accordance with this regulation shall—

> (a) only be carried out by—
>
> > (i)   the public communications provider in question;
> >
> > (ii) the third party providing the value added service in question; or

(iii) a person acting under the authority of a person falling within (i) or (ii); and

(b) where the processing is carried out for the purposes of the provision of a value added service, be restricted to what is necessary for those purposes.

Tracing of malicious or nuisance calls

15.—(1) A communications provider may override anything done to prevent the presentation of the identity of a calling line where—

(a) a subscriber has requested the tracing of malicious or nuisance calls received on his line; and

(b) the provider is satisfied that such action is necessary and expedient for the purposes of tracing such calls.

(2) Any term of a contract for the provision of public electronic communications services which relates to such prevention shall have effect subject to the provisions of paragraph (1).

(3) Nothing in these Regulations shall prevent a communications provider, for the purposes of any action relating to the tracing of malicious or nuisance calls, from storing and making available to a person with a legitimate interest data containing the identity of a calling subscriber which were obtained while paragraph (1) applied.

Emergency calls

16.—(1) For the purposes of this regulation, "emergency calls" means calls to either the national emergency call number 999 or the single European emergency call number 112.

(2) In order to facilitate responses to emergency calls—

(a) all such calls shall be excluded from the requirements of regulation 10;

(b) no person shall be entitled to prevent the presentation on the connected line of the identity of the calling line; and

(c) the restriction on the processing of location data under regulation 14(2) shall be disregarded.

Termination of automatic call forwarding

17.—(1) Where—

(a) calls originally directed to another line are being automatically forwarded to a subscriber's line as a result of action taken by a third party, and

(b) the subscriber requests his provider of electronic communications services ("the subscriber's provider") to stop the forwarding of those calls,

the subscriber's provider shall ensure, free of charge, that the forwarding is stopped without any avoidable delay.

(2) For the purposes of paragraph (1), every other communications provider shall comply with any reasonable requests made by the subscriber's provider to assist in the prevention of that forwarding.

Directories of subscribers

18.—(1) This regulation applies in relation to a directory of subscribers, whether in printed or electronic form, which is made available to members of the public or a section of the public, including by means of a directory enquiry service.

(2) The personal data of an individual subscriber shall not be included in a directory unless that subscriber has, free of charge, been—

> (a) informed by the collector of the personal data of the purposes of the directory in which his personal data are to be included, and
>
> (b) given the opportunity to determine whether such of his personal data as are considered relevant by the producer of the directory should be included in the directory.

(3) Where personal data of an individual subscriber are to be included in a directory with facilities which enable users of that directory to obtain access to that data solely on the basis of a telephone number—

> (a) the information to be provided under paragraph (2)(a) shall include information about those facilities; and
>
> (b) for the purposes of paragraph (2)(b), the express consent of the subscriber to the inclusion of his data in a directory with such facilities must be obtained.

(4) Data relating to a corporate subscriber shall not be included in a directory where that subscriber has advised the producer of the directory that it does not want its data to be included in that directory.

(5) Where the data of an individual subscriber have been included in a directory, that subscriber shall, without charge, be able to verify, correct or withdraw those data at any time.

(6) Where a request has been made under paragraph (5) for data to be withdrawn from or corrected in a directory, that request shall be treated as having no application in relation to an edition of a directory that was produced before the producer of the directory received the request.

(7) For the purposes of paragraph (6), an edition of a directory which is revised after it was first produced shall be treated as a new edition.

(8) In this regulation, "telephone number" has the same meaning as in section 56(5) of the Communications Act 2003[14] but does not include any number which is used as an internet domain name, an internet address or an address or identifier incorporating either an internet domain name or an internet address, including an electronic mail address.

Use of automated calling systems

19.—(1) A person shall neither transmit, nor instigate the transmission of, communications comprising recorded matter for direct marketing purposes by means of an automated calling system except in the circumstances referred to in paragraph (2).

(2) Those circumstances are where the called line is that of a subscriber who has previously notified the caller that for the time being he consents to such communications being sent by, or at the instigation of, the caller on that line.

(3) A subscriber shall not permit his line to be used in contravention of paragraph (1).

---

[14] 2003 c. 21; for the commencement of section 56(5), see article 2(1) of S.I. 2003/1900 (C. 77).back

(4) For the purposes of this regulation, an automated calling system is a system which is capable of—

(a) automatically initiating a sequence of calls to more than one destination in accordance with instructions stored in that system; and
(b) transmitting sounds which are not live speech for reception by persons at some or all of the destinations so called.

Use of facsimile machines for direct marketing purposes

20.—(1) A person shall neither transmit, nor instigate the transmission of, unsolicited communications for direct marketing purposes by means of a facsimile machine where the called line is that of—

(a) an individual subscriber, except in the circumstances referred to in paragraph (2);
(b) a corporate subscriber who has previously notified the caller that such communications should not be sent on that line; or
(c) a subscriber and the number allocated to that line is listed in the register kept under regulation 25.

(2) The circumstances referred to in paragraph (1)(a) are that the individual subscriber has previously notified the caller that he consents for the time being to such communications being sent by, or at the instigation of, the caller.

(3) A subscriber shall not permit his line to be used in contravention of paragraph (1).

(4) A person shall not be held to have contravened paragraph (1)(c) where the number allocated to the called line has been listed on the register for less than 28 days preceding that on which the communication is made.

(5) Where a subscriber who has caused a number allocated to a line of his to be listed in the register kept under regulation 25 has notified a caller that he does not, for the time being, object to such communications being sent on that line by that caller, such communications may be sent by that caller on that line, notwithstanding that the number allocated to that line is listed in the said register.

(6) Where a subscriber has given a caller notification pursuant to paragraph (5) in relation to a line of his—

(a) the subscriber shall be free to withdraw that notification at any time, and
(b) where such notification is withdrawn, the caller shall not send such communications on that line.

(7) The provisions of this regulation are without prejudice to the provisions of regulation 19.

Unsolicited calls for direct marketing purposes

21.—(1) A person shall neither use, nor instigate the use of, a public electronic communications service for the purposes of making unsolicited calls for direct marketing purposes where—

(a) the called line is that of a subscriber who has previously notified the caller that such calls should not for the time being be made on that line; or

(b) the number allocated to a subscriber in respect of the called line is one listed in the register kept under regulation 26.

(2) A subscriber shall not permit his line to be used in contravention of paragraph (1).

(3) A person shall not be held to have contravened paragraph (1)(b) where the number allocated to the called line has been listed on the register for less than 28 days preceding that on which the call is made.

(4) Where a subscriber who has caused a number allocated to a line of his to be listed in the register kept under regulation 26 has notified a caller that he does not, for the time being, object to such calls being made on that line by that caller, such calls may be made by that caller on that line, notwithstanding that the number allocated to that line is listed in the said register.

(5) Where a subscriber has given a caller notification pursuant to paragraph (4) in relation to a line of his—

(a) the subscriber shall be free to withdraw that notification at any time, and

(b) where such notification is withdrawn, the caller shall not make such calls on that line.

Use of electronic mail for direct marketing purposes

22.—(1) This regulation applies to the transmission of unsolicited communications by means of electronic mail to individual subscribers.

(2) Except in the circumstances referred to in paragraph (3), a person shall neither transmit, nor instigate the transmission of, unsolicited communications for the purposes of direct marketing by means of electronic mail unless the recipient of the electronic mail has previously notified the sender that he consents for the time being to such communications being sent by, or at the instigation of, the sender.

(3) A person may send or instigate the sending of electronic mail for the purposes of direct marketing where—

(a) that person has obtained the contact details of the recipient of that electronic mail in the course of the sale or negotiations for the sale of a product or service to that recipient;

(b) the direct marketing is in respect of that person's similar products and services only; and

(c) the recipient has been given a simple means of refusing (free of charge except for the costs of the transmission of the refusal) the use of his contact details for the purposes of such direct marketing, at the time that the details were initially collected, and, where he did not initially refuse the use of the details, at the time of each subsequent communication.

(4) A subscriber shall not permit his line to be used in contravention of paragraph (2).

Use of electronic mail for direct marketing purposes where the identity or address of the sender is concealed

23. A person shall neither transmit, nor instigate the transmission of, a communication for the purposes of direct marketing by means of electronic mail—

(a) where the identity of the person on whose behalf the communication has been sent has been disguised or concealed; or

(b) where a valid address to which the recipient of the communication may send a request that such communications cease has not been provided.

Information to be provided for the purposes of regulations 19, 20 and 21

24.—(1) Where a public electronic communications service is used for the transmission of a communication for direct marketing purposes the person using, or instigating the use of, the service shall ensure that the following information is provided with that communication—

(a) in relation to a communication to which regulations 19 (automated calling systems) and 20 (facsimile machines) apply, the particulars mentioned in paragraph (2)(a) and (b);

(b) in relation to a communication to which regulation 21 (telephone calls) applies, the particulars mentioned in paragraph (2)(a) and, if the recipient of the call so requests, those mentioned in paragraph (2)(b).

(2) The particulars referred to in paragraph (1) are—

(a) the name of the person;

(b) either the address of the person or a telephone number on which he can be reached free of charge.

Register to be kept for the purposes of regulation 20

25.—(1) For the purposes of regulation 20 OFCOM shall maintain and keep up-to-date, in printed or electronic form, a register of the numbers allocated to subscribers, in respect of particular lines, who have notified them (notwithstanding, in the case of individual subscribers, that they enjoy the benefit of regulation 20(1)(a) and (2)) that they do not for the time being wish to receive unsolicited communications for direct marketing purposes by means of facsimile machine on the lines in question.

(2) OFCOM shall remove a number from the register maintained under paragraph (1) where they have reason to believe that it has ceased to be allocated to the subscriber by whom they were notified pursuant to paragraph (1).

(3) On the request of—

(a) a person wishing to send, or instigate the sending of, such communications as are mentioned in paragraph (1), or

(b) a subscriber wishing to permit the use of his line for the sending of such communications,

for information derived from the register kept under paragraph (1), OFCOM shall, unless it is not reasonably practicable so to do, on the payment to them of such fee as is, subject to paragraph (4), required by them, make the information requested available to that person or that subscriber.

(4) For the purposes of paragraph (3) OFCOM may require different fees—

(a) for making available information derived from the register in different forms or manners, or

(b) for making available information derived from the whole or from different parts of the register, but the fees required by them shall be ones in relation to which the Secretary of State has notified OFCOM that he is satisfied that they are designed to secure, as nearly as may be and taking one year with another, that the aggregate fees received, or reasonably expected to be received, equal the costs incurred, or reasonably expected to be incurred, by OFCOM in discharging their duties under paragraphs (1), (2) and (3).

(5) The functions of OFCOM under paragraphs (1), (2) and (3), other than the function of determining the fees to be required for the purposes of paragraph (3), may be discharged on their behalf by some other person in pursuance of arrangements made by OFCOM with that other person.

Register to be kept for the purposes of regulation 21

26.—(1) For the purposes of regulation 21 OFCOM shall maintain and keep up-to-date, in printed or electronic form, a register of the numbers allocated to individual subscribers, in respect of particular lines, who have notified them that they do not for the time being wish to receive unsolicited calls for direct marketing purposes on the lines in question.

(2) OFCOM shall remove a number from the register maintained under paragraph (1) where they have reason to believe that it has ceased to be allocated to the subscriber by whom they were notified pursuant to paragraph (1).

(3) On the request of—

(a) a person wishing to make, or instigate the making of, such calls as are mentioned in paragraph (1), or
(b) a subscriber wishing to permit the use of his line for the making of such calls,

for information derived from the register kept under paragraph (1), OFCOM shall, unless it is not reasonably practicable so to do, on the payment to them of such fee as is, subject to paragraph (4), required by them, make the information requested available to that person or that subscriber.

(4) For the purposes of paragraph (3) OFCOM may require different fees—

(a) for making available information derived from the register in different forms or manners, or
(b) for making available information derived from the whole or from different parts of the register,

but the fees required by them shall be ones in relation to which the Secretary of State has notified OFCOM that he is satisfied that they are designed to secure, as nearly as may be and taking one year with another, that the aggregate fees received, or reasonably expected to be received, equal the costs incurred, or reasonably expected to be incurred, by OFCOM in discharging their duties under paragraphs (1), (2) and (3).

(5) The functions of OFCOM under paragraphs (1), (2) and (3), other than the function of determining the fees to be required for the purposes of paragraph (3), may be discharged on their behalf by some other person in pursuance of arrangements made by OFCOM with that other person.

Modification of contracts

27. To the extent that any term in a contract between a subscriber to and the provider of a public electronic communications service or such a provider and the provider of an

electronic communications network would be inconsistent with a requirement of these Regulations, that term shall be void.

National security

28.—(1) Nothing in these Regulations shall require a communications provider to do, or refrain from doing, anything (including the processing of data) if exemption from the requirement in question is required for the purpose of safeguarding national security.

(2) Subject to paragraph (4), a certificate signed by a Minister of the Crown certifying that exemption from any requirement of these Regulations is or at any time was required for the purpose of safeguarding national security shall be conclusive evidence of that fact.

(3) A certificate under paragraph (2) may identify the circumstances in which it applies by means of a general description and may be expressed to have prospective effect.

(4) Any person directly affected by the issuing of a certificate under paragraph (2) may appeal to the Tribunal against the issuing of the certificate.

(5) If, on an appeal under paragraph (4), the Tribunal finds that, applying the principles applied by a court on an application for judicial review, the Minister did not have reasonable grounds for issuing the certificate, the Tribunal may allow the appeal and quash the certificate.

(6) Where, in any proceedings under or by virtue of these Regulations, it is claimed by a communications provider that a certificate under paragraph (2) which identifies the circumstances in which it applies by means of a general description applies in the circumstances in question, any other party to the proceedings may appeal to the Tribunal on the ground that the certificate does not apply in those circumstances and, subject to any determination under paragraph (7), the certificate shall be conclusively presumed so to apply.

(7) On any appeal under paragraph (6), the Tribunal may determine that the certificate does not so apply.

(8) In this regulation—

> (a) "the Tribunal" means the Information Tribunal referred to in section 6 of the Data Protection Act 1998[15];
> (b) Subsections (8), (9), (10) and (12) of section 28 of and Schedule 6 to that Act apply for the purposes of this regulation as they apply for the purposes of section 28;
> (c) section 58 of that Act shall apply for the purposes of this regulation as if the reference in that section to the functions of the Tribunal under that Act included a reference to the functions of the Tribunal under paragraphs (4) to (7) of this regulation; and
> (d) subsections (1), (2) and (5)(f) of section 67 of that Act shall apply in respect of the making of rules relating to the functions of the Tribunal under this regulation.

Legal requirements, law enforcement etc.

29.—(1) Nothing in these Regulations shall require a communications provider to do, or refrain from doing, anything (including the processing of data)—

---

[15] 1998 c. 29.back

(a) if compliance with the requirement in question—

(i)   would be inconsistent with any requirement imposed by or under an enactment or by a court order; or

(ii) would be likely to prejudice the prevention or detection of crime or the apprehension or prosecution of offenders; or

(b) if exemption from the requirement in question—

(i)   is required for the purposes of, or in connection with, any legal proceedings (including prospective legal proceedings);

(ii) is necessary for the purposes of obtaining legal advice; or

(iii) is otherwise necessary for the purposes of establishing, exercising or defending legal rights.

Proceedings for compensation for failure to comply with requirements of the Regulations

30.—(1) A person who suffers damage by reason of any contravention of any of the requirements of these Regulations by any other person shall be entitled to bring proceedings for compensation from that other person for that damage.

(2) In proceedings brought against a person by virtue of this regulation it shall be a defence to prove that he had taken such care as in all the circumstances was reasonably required to comply with the relevant requirement.

(3) The provisions of this regulation are without prejudice to those of regulation 31.

Enforcement—extension of Part V of the Data Protection Act 1998

31.—(1) The provisions of Part V of the Data Protection Act 1998 and of Schedules 6 and 9 to that Act are extended for the purposes of these Regulations and, for those purposes, shall have effect subject to the modifications set out in Schedule 1.

(2) In regulations 32 and 33, "enforcement functions" means the functions of the Information Commissioner under the provisions referred to in paragraph (1) as extended by that paragraph.

(3) The provisions of this regulation are without prejudice to those of regulation 30.

Request that the Commissioner exercise his enforcement functions

32. Where it is alleged that there has been a contravention of any of the requirements of these Regulations either OFCOM or a person aggrieved by the alleged contravention may request the Commissioner to exercise his enforcement functions in respect of that contravention, but those functions shall be exercisable by the Commissioner whether or not he has been so requested.

Technical advice to the Commissioner

33. OFCOM shall comply with any reasonable request made by the Commissioner, in connection with his enforcement functions, for advice on technical and similar matters relating to electronic communications.

Amendment to the Telecommunications (Lawful Business Practice) (Interception of Communications) Regulations 2000

34. In regulation 3 of the Telecommunications (Lawful Business Practice) (Interception of Communications) Regulations 2000[16], for paragraph (3), there shall be substituted—

---

[16] S.I. 2000/2699.back

" (3) Conduct falling within paragraph (1)(a)(i) above is authorised only to the extent that Article 5 of Directive 2002/58/EC of the European Parliament and of the Council of 12 July 2002 concerning the processing of personal data and the protection of privacy in the electronic communications sector so permits.".

Amendment to the Electronic Communications (Universal Service) Order 2003

35.—(1) In paragraphs 2(2) and 3(2) of the Schedule to the Electronic Communications (Universal Service) Order 2003[17], for the words "Telecommunications (Data Protection and Privacy) Regulations 1999" there shall be substituted "Privacy and Electronic Communications (EC Directive) Regulations 2003".

(2) Paragraph (1) shall have effect notwithstanding the provisions of section 65 of the Communications Act 2003[18] (which provides for the modification of the Universal Service Order made under that section).

Transitional provisions

36. The provisions in Schedule 2 shall have effect.

Stephen Timms,

Minister of State for Energy, E-Commerce and Postal Services, Department of Trade and Industry

18th September 2003

SCHEDULE 1

Regulation 31

Modifications for the purposes of these Regulations to Part V of the Data Protection Act 1998 and Schedules 6 and 9 to that Act as extended by Regulation 31

1. In section 40—

(a) in subsection (1), for the words "data controller" there shall be substituted the word "person", for the words "data protection principles" there shall be substituted the words "requirements of the Privacy and Electronic Communications (EC Directive) Regulations 2003 (in this Part referred to as "the relevant requirements")" and for the words "principle or principles" there shall be substituted the words "requirement or requirements";

(b) in subsection (2), the words "or distress" shall be omitted;

(c) subsections (3), (4), (5), (9) and (10) shall be omitted; and

(d) in subsection (6)(a), for the words "data protection principle or principles" there shall be substituted the words "relevant requirement or requirements."

---

[17] S.I. 2003/1094.back
[18] 2003 c. 21; for the commencement of section 65, see article 2(1) of S.I. 2003/1900 (C. 77).back

2. In section 41(1) and (2), for the words "data protection principle or principles", in both places where they occur, there shall be substituted the words "relevant requirement or requirements".

3. Section 42 shall be omitted.

4. In section 43—

(a) for subsections (1) and (2) there shall be substituted the following provisions—

"(1) If the Commissioner reasonably requires any information for the purpose of determining whether a person has complied or is complying with the relevant requirements, he may serve that person with a notice (in this Act referred to as "an information notice") requiring him, within such time as is specified in the notice, to furnish the Commissioner, in such form as may be so specified, with such information relating to compliance with the relevant requirements as is so specified.

(2) An information notice must contain a statement that the Commissioner regards the specified information as relevant for the purpose of determining whether the person has complied or is complying with the relevant requirements and his reason for regarding it as relevant for that purpose."

(b) in subsection (6)(a), after the word "under" there shall be inserted the words "the Privacy and Electronic Communications (EC Directive) Regulations 2003 or";

(c) in subsection (6)(b), after the words "arising out of" there shall be inserted the words "the said Regulations or"; and

(d) subsection (10) shall be omitted.

5. Sections 44, 45 and 46 shall be omitted.

6. In section 47—

(a) in subsection (1), for the words "an information notice or special information notice" there shall be substituted the words "or an information notice"; and

(b) in subsection (2) the words "or a special information notice" shall be omitted.

7. In section 48—

(a) in subsections (1) and (3), for the words "an information notice or a special information notice", in both places where they occur, there shall be substituted the words "or an information notice";

(b) in subsection (3) for the words "43(5) or 44(6)" there shall be substituted the words "or 43(5)"; and

(c) subsection (4) shall be omitted.

8. In section 49 subsection (5) shall be omitted.

9. In paragraph 4(1) of Schedule (6), for the words "(2) or (4)" there shall be substituted the words "or (2)".

10. In paragraph 1 of Schedule 9—

(a) for subparagraph (1)(a) there shall be substituted the following provision—

" (a) that a person has contravened or is contravening any of the requirements of the Privacy and Electronic Communications (EC Directive) Regulations 2003 (in this Schedule referred to as "the 2003 Regulations") or";

and

(b) subparagraph (2) shall be omitted.

11. In paragraph 9 of Schedule 9—

(a) in subparagraph (1)(a) after the words "rights under" there shall be inserted the words "the 2003 Regulations or"; and
(b) in subparagraph (1)(b) after the words "arising out of" there shall be inserted the words "the 2003 Regulations or".

SCHEDULE 2

Regulation 36

Transitional provisions

Interpretation

1. In this Schedule "the 1999 Regulations" means the Telecommunications (Data Protection and Privacy) Regulations 1999 and "caller" has the same meaning as in regulation 21 of the 1999 Regulations.

Directories

2.—(1) Regulation 18 of these Regulations shall not apply in relation to editions of directories first published before 11th December 2003.

(2) Where the personal data of a subscriber have been included in a directory in accordance with Part IV of the 1999 Regulations, the personal data of that subscriber may remain included in that directory provided that the subscriber—

(a) has been provided with information in accordance with regulation 18 of these Regulations; and
(b) has not requested that his data be withdrawn from that directory.

(3) Where a request has been made under subparagraph (2) for data to be withdrawn from a directory, that request shall be treated as having no application in relation to an edition of a directory that was produced before the producer of the directory received the request.

(4) For the purposes of subparagraph (3), an edition of a directory, which is revised after it was first produced, shall be treated as a new edition.

Notifications

3.—(1) A notification of consent given to a caller by a subscriber for the purposes of regulation 22(2) of the 1999 Regulations is to have effect on and after 11th December 2003 as a notification given by that subscriber for the purposes of regulation 19(2) of these Regulations.

(2) A notification given to a caller by a corporate subscriber for the purposes of regulation 23(2)(a) of the 1999 Regulations is to have effect on and after 11th December 2003 as a notification given by that subscriber for the purposes of regulation 20(1)(b) of these Regulations.

(3) A notification of consent given to a caller by an individual subscriber for the purposes of regulation 24(2) of the 1999 Regulations is to have effect on and after 11th December 2003 as a notification given by that subscriber for the purposes of regulation 20(2) of these Regulations.

(4) A notification given to a caller by an individual subscriber for the purposes of regulation 25(2)(a) of the 1999 Regulations is to have effect on and after the 11th December 2003 as a notification given by that subscriber for the purposes of regulation 21(1) of these Regulations.

Registers kept under regulations 25 and 26

4.—(1) A notification given by a subscriber pursuant to regulation 23(4)(a) of the 1999 Regulations to the Director General of Telecommunications (or to such other person as is discharging his functions under regulation 23(4) of the 1999 Regulations on his behalf by virtue of an arrangement made under regulation 23(6) of those Regulations) is to have effect on or after 11th December 2003 as a notification given pursuant to regulation 25(1) of these Regulations.

(2) A notification given by a subscriber who is an individual pursuant to regulation 25(4)(a) of the 1999 Regulations to the Director General of Telecommunications (or to such other person as is discharging his functions under regulation 25(4) of the 1999 Regulations on his behalf by virtue of an arrangement made under regulation 25(6) of those Regulations) is to have effect on or after 11th December 2003 as a notification given pursuant to regulation 26(1) of these Regulations.

References in these Regulations to OFCOM

5. In relation to times before an order made under section 411[19] of the Communications Act 2003 brings any of the provisions of Part 2 of Chapter 1 of that Act into force for the purpose of conferring on OFCOM the functions contained in those provisions, references to OFCOM in these Regulations are to be treated as references to the Director General of Telecommunications.

EXPLANATORY NOTE

(This note is not part of the Regulations)

These Regulations implement Articles 2, 4, 5(3), 6 to 13, 15 and 16 of Directive 2002/58/EC of the European Parliament and of the Council of 12 July 2002 concerning the processing of personal data and the protection of privacy in the electronic communications sector (Directive on privacy and electronic communications) ("the Directive").

The Directive repeals and replaces Directive 97/66/EC of the European Parliament and of the Council of 15 December 1997 concerning the processing of personal data and the protection of privacy in the telecommunications sector which was implemented in the UK by the Telecommunications (Data Protection and Privacy) Regulations 1999. Those Regulations are revoked by regulation 3 of these Regulations.

Regulation 2 sets out the definitions which apply for the purposes of the Regulations.

[19] For the commencement of section 411, see section 411(2) and (3) of the Communications Act 2003 (c. 21).back

Regulation 4 provides that nothing in these Regulations relieves a person of any of his obligations under the Data Protection Act 1998.

Regulation 5 imposes a duty on a provider of a public electronic communications service to take measures, if necessary in conjunction with the provider of the electronic communications network by means of which the service is provided, to safeguard the security of the service, and requires the provider of the electronic communications network to comply with the service provider's reasonable requests made for the purposes of taking the measures ("public electronic communications service" has the meaning given by section 151 of the Communications Act 2003 and "electronic communications network" has the meaning given by section 32 of that Act). Regulation 5 further requires the service provider, where there remains a significant risk to the security of the service, to provide subscribers to that service with certain information ("subscriber" is defined as "a person who is a party to a contract with a provider of public electronic communications services for the supply of such services").

Regulation 6 provides that an electronic communications network may not be used to store or gain access to information in the terminal equipment of a subscriber or user ("user" is defined as "any individual using a public electronic communications service") unless the subscriber or user is provided with certain information and is given the opportunity to refuse the storage of or access to the information in his terminal equipment.

Regulations 7 and 8 set out certain restrictions on the processing of traffic data relating to a subscriber or user by a public communications provider. "Traffic data" is defined as "any data processed for the purpose of the conveyance of a communication on an electronic communications network or for the billing in respect of that communication". "Public communications provider" is defined as "a provider of a public electronic communications network or a public electronic communications service".

Regulation 9 requires providers of public electronic communications services to provide subscribers with non-itemised bills on request and requires OFCOM to have regard to certain matters when exercising their functions under Chapter 1 of Part 2 of the Communications Act 2003.

Regulation 10 requires a provider of a public electronic communications service to provide users of the service with a means of preventing the presentation of calling line identification on a call-by-call basis, and to provide subscribers to the service with a means of preventing the presentation of such identification on a per-line basis. This regulation is subject to regulations 15 and 16. Regulation 11 requires the provider of a public electronic communications service to provide subscribers to that service with certain facilities where facilities enabling the presentation of connected line identification or calling line identification are available.

Regulation 12 requires a public electronic communications service provider to provide certain information to the public for the purposes of regulations 10 and 11, and regulation 13 requires communications providers (the term "communications provider" has the meaning given by section 405 of the Communications Act 2003) to co-operate with reasonable requests made by providers of public electronic communications services for the purposes of those regulations.

Regulation 14 imposes certain restrictions on the processing of location data, which is defined as "any data processed in an electronic communications network indicating the geographical position of the terminal equipment of a user of a public electronic communications service, including data relating to the latitude, longitude or altitude of the terminal equipment; the direction of travel of the user; or the time the location information was recorded."

Regulation 15 makes provision in relation to the tracing of malicious or nuisance calls and regulation 16 makes provision in relation to emergency calls, which are defined in regulation 16(1) as calls to the national emergency number 999 or the European emergency call number 112.

Regulation 17 requires the provider of an electronic communications service to a subscriber to stop, on request, the automatic forwarding of calls to that subscriber's line and also requires other communications providers to comply with reasonable requests made by the subscriber's provider to assist in the prevention of that forwarding.

Regulation 18 applies to directories of subscribers, and sets out requirements that must be satisfied where data relating to subscribers is included in such directories. It also gives subscribers the right to verify, correct or withdraw their data in directories.

Regulation 19 provides that a person may not transmit communications comprising recorded matter for direct marketing purposes by an automated calling system unless the line called is that of a subscriber who has notified the caller that he consents to such communications being made.

Regulations 20, 21 and 22 set out the circumstances in which persons may transmit, or instigate the transmission of, unsolicited communications for the purposes of direct marketing by means of facsimile machine, make unsolicited calls for those purposes, or transmit unsolicited communications by means of electronic mail for those purposes. Regulation 22 (electronic mail) applies only to transmissions to individual subscribers (the term "individual" means "a living individual" and includes "an unincorporated body of such individuals").

Regulation 23 prohibits the sending of communications by means of electronic mail for the purposes of direct marketing where the identity of the person on whose behalf the communication is made has been disguised or concealed or an address to which requests for such communications to cease may be sent has not been provided.

Regulation 24 sets out certain information that must be provided for the purposes of regulations 19, 20 and 21.

Regulation 25 imposes a duty on OFCOM, for the purposes of regulation 20, to maintain and keep up-to-date a register of numbers allocated to subscribers who do not wish to receive unsolicited communications by means of facsimile machine for the purposes of direct marketing. Regulation 26 imposes a similar obligation for the purposes of regulation 21 in respect of individual subscribers who do not wish to receive calls for the purposes of direct marketing.

Regulation 27 provides that terms in certain contracts which are inconsistent with these Regulations shall be void.

Regulation 28 exempts communications providers from the requirements of these Regulations where exemption is required for the purpose of safeguarding national security and further provides that a certificate signed by a Minister of the Crown to the effect that exemption from a requirement is necessary for the purpose of safeguarding national security shall be conclusive evidence of that fact. It also provides for certain questions relating to such certificates to be determined by the Information Tribunal referred to in section 6 of the Data Protection Act 1998.

Regulation 29 provides that a communications provider shall not be required by these Regulations to do, or refrain from doing, anything if complying with the requirement in question would be inconsistent with a requirement imposed by or under an enactment or by a court order, or if exemption from the requirement is necessary in connection with legal proceedings, for the purposes of obtaining legal advice or is otherwise necessary to establish, exercise or defend legal rights.

Regulation 30 allows a claim for damages to be brought in respect of contraventions of the Regulations.

Regulations 31 and 32 make provision in connection with the enforcement of the Regulations by the Information Commissioner (who is the Commissioner appointed under section 6 of the Data Protection Act 1998).

Regulation 33 imposes a duty on OFCOM to comply with any reasonable request made by the Commissioner for advice on technical matters relating to electronic communications. Regulation 34 amends the Telecommunications (Lawful Business Practice) (Interception of Communications) Regulations 2000 and regulation 35 amends the Electronic Communications (Universal Service) Order 2003.

Regulation 36 provides for the transitional provisions in Schedule 2 to have effect.

A transposition note setting out how the main elements of the Directive are transposed into law and a regulatory impact assessment have been placed in the libraries of both Houses of Parliament. Copies are also available from the Department of Trade and Industry, Bay 202, 151 Buckingham Palace Road, London SW1W 9SS and can also be found on www.dti.gov.uk.

ISBN 0 11 047594 1

Appendix 6

DIRECTIVE 2000/46/EC OF THE EUROPEAN PARLIAMENT AND OF THE COUNCIL
of 18 September 2000
on the taking up, pursuit of and prudential supervision of the business of electronic money institutions

THE EUROPEAN PARLIAMENT AND THE COUNCIL OF THE EUROPEAN UNION,

Having regard to the Treaty establishing the European Community, and in particular the first and third sentences of Article 47(2) thereof,

Having regard to the proposal from the Commission (^{1}),

Having regard to the opinion of the Economic and Social Committee (^{2}),

Having regard to the opinion of the European Central Bank (^{3}),

Acting in accordance with the procedure laid down in Article 251 of the Treaty (^{4}),

Whereas:

(1) Credit institutions within the meaning of Article 1, point 1, first subparagraph (b) of Directive 2000/12/EC (^{5}) are limited in the scope of their activities.

(2) It is necessary to take account of the specific characteristics of these institutions and to provide the appropriate measures necessary to coordinate and harmonise Member States' laws, regulations and administrative provisions relating to the taking up, pursuit and prudential supervision of the business of electronic money institutions.

(3) For the purposes of this Directive, electronic money can be considered an electronic surrogate for coins and banknotes, which is stored on an electronic device such as a chip card or computer memory and which is generally intended for the purpose of effecting electronic payments of limited amounts.

(4) The approach adopted is appropriate to achieve only the essential harmonisation necessary and sufficient to secure the mutual recognition of authorisation and prudential supervision of electronic money institutions, making possible the granting of a single licence recognised throughout the Community and designed to ensure bearer confidence and the application of the principle of home Member State prudential supervision.

(5) Within the wider context of the rapidly evolving electronic commerce it is desirable to provide a regulatory framework that assists electronic money in delivering its full potential benefits and that avoids hampering technological innovation in particular. Therefore, this Directive introduces a technology-neutral legal framework that harmonises the prudential supervision of electronic money institutions to the extent necessary for ensuring their sound and prudent operation and their financial integrity in particular.

(6) Credit institutions, by virtue of point 5 of Annex I to Directive 2000/12/EC, are already allowed to issue and administer means of payment including electronic money and to carry on such activities Community-wide subject to mutual recognition and to the comprehensive prudential supervisory system applying to them in accordance with the European banking Directives.

(7) The introduction of a separate prudential supervisory regime for electronic money institutions, which, although calibrated on the prudential supervisory regime applying to other credit institutions and Directive 2000/12/EC except Title V, Chapters 2 and 3 thereof in particular, differs from that regime, is justified and desirable because the issuance of electronic money does not constitute in itself, in view of its specific character as an electronic surrogate for coins and banknotes, a deposit-taking activity pursuant to Article 3 of Directive 2000/12/EC, if the received funds are immediately exchanged for electronic money.

(8) The receipt of funds from the public in exchange for electronic money, which results in a credit balance left on account with the issuing institution, constitutes the receipt of deposits or other repayable funds for the purpose of Directive 2000/12/EC.

(9) It is necessary for electronic money to be redeemable to ensure bearer confidence. Redeemability does not imply, in itself, that the funds received in exchange for electronic money shall be regarded as deposits or other repayable funds for the purpose of Directive 2000/12/EC.

(10) Redeemability should always be understood to be at par value.

(^{1}) OJ C 317, 15.10.1998, p. 7.
(^{2}) OJ C 101, 12.4.1999, p. 64.
(^{3}) OJ C 189, 6.7.1999, p. 7.
(^{4}) Opinion of the European Parliament of 15 April 1999 (OJ C 219, 30.7.1999, p. 415), confirmed on 27 October 1999, Council Common Position of 29 November 1999 (OJ C 26, 28.1.2000, p. 1) and Decision of the European Parliament of 11 April 2000 (not yet published in the Official Journal). Decision of the Council of 16 June 2000.
(^{5}) Directive 2000/12/EC of the European Parliament and of the Council of 20 March 2000 relating to the taking up and pursuit of the business of credit institutions (OJ L 126, 26.5.2000, p. 1). Directive as last amended by Directive 2000/28/EC (see page 37 of this Official Journal).

408

Appendix 6

(11) In order to respond to the specific risks associated with the issuance of electronic money this prudential supervisory regime must be more targeted and, accordingly, less cumbersome than the prudential supervisory regime applying to credit institutions, notably as regards reduced initial capital requirements and the non-application of Directive 93/6/EEC (¹) and Title V, Chapter 2, Sections II and III of Directive 2000/12/EC.

(12) However, it is necessary to preserve a level playing field between electronic money institutions and other credit institutions issuing electronic money and, thus, to ensure fair competition among a wider range of institutions to the benefit of bearers. This is achieved since the abovementioned less cumbersome features of the prudential supervisory regime applying to electronic money institutions are balanced by provisions that are more stringent than those applying to other credit institutions, notably as regards restrictions on the business activities which electronic money institutions may carry on and, particularly, prudent limitations of their investments aimed at ensuring that their financial liabilities related to outstanding electronic money are backed at all times by sufficiently liquid low risk assets.

(13) Pending the harmonisation of prudential supervision of outsourced activities for credit institutions it is appropriate that electronic money institutions have sound and prudent management and control procedures. With a view to the possibility of operational and other ancillary functions related to the issuance of electronic money being performed by undertakings which are not subject to prudential supervision it is essential that electronic money institutions have in place internal structures which should respond to the financial and non-financial risks to which they are exposed.

(14) The issuance of electronic money may affect the stability of the financial system and the smooth operation of payments systems. Close cooperation in assessing the integrity of electronic money schemes is called for.

(15) It is appropriate to afford competent authorities the possibility of waiving some or all of the requirements imposed by this Directive for electronic money institutions which operate only within the territories of the respective Member States.

(16) Adoption of this Directive constitutes the most appropriate means of achieving the desired objectives. This Directive is limited to the minimum necessary to achieve these objectives and does not go beyond what is necessary for this purpose.

(17) Provision should be made for the review of this Directive in the light of experience of developments in the market and the protection of bearers of electronic money.

(18) The Banking Advisory Committee has been consulted on the adoption of this Directive,

HAVE ADOPTED THIS DIRECTIVE:

Article 1

Scope, definitions and restriction of activities

1. This Directive shall apply to electronic money institutions.

2. It shall not apply to the institutions referred to in Article 2(3) of Directive 2000/12/EC.

3. For the purposes of this Directive:

(a) 'electronic money institution' shall mean an undertaking or any other legal person, other than a credit institution as defined in Article 1, point 1, first subparagraph (a) of Directive 2000/12/EC which issues means of payment in the form of electronic money;

(b) 'electronic money' shall mean monetary value as represented by a claim on the issuer which is:

  (i) stored on an electronic device;

  (ii) issued on receipt of funds of an amount not less in value than the monetary value issued;

  (iii) accepted as means of payment by undertakings other than the issuer.

4. Member States shall prohibit persons or undertakings that are not credit institutions, as defined in Article 1, point 1, first subparagraph of Directive 2000/12/EC, from carrying on the business of issuing electronic money.

5. The business activities of electronic money institutions other than the issuing of electronic money shall be restricted to:

(a) the provision of closely related financial and non-financial services such as the administering of electronic money by the performance of operational and other ancillary functions related to its issuance, and the issuing and administering of other means of payment but excluding the granting of any form of credit; and

(b) the storing of data on the electronic device on behalf of other undertakings or public institutions.

Electronic money institutions shall not have any holdings in other undertakings except where these undertakings perform operational or other ancillary functions related to electronic money issued or distributed by the institution concerned.

(¹) Council Directive 93/6/EEC of 15 March 1993 on the capital adequacy of investment firms and credit institutions (OJ L 141, 11.6.1993, p. 1). Directive as last amended by Directive 98/33/EC (OJ L 204, 21.7.1998, p. 29).

27.10.2000 | EN | Official Journal of the European Communities   L 275/41

Article 2

Application of Banking Directives

1. Save where otherwise expressly provided for, only references to credit institutions in Directive 91/308/EEC (¹) and Directive 2000/12/EC except Title V, Chapter 2 thereof shall apply to electronic money institutions.

2. Articles 5, 11, 13, 19, 20(7), 51 and 59 of Directive 2000/12/EC shall not apply. The mutual recognition arrangements provided for in Directive 2000/12/EC shall not apply to electronic money institutions' business activities other than the issuance of electronic money.

3. The receipt of funds within the meaning of Article 1(3)(b)(ii) does not constitute a deposit or other repayable funds according to Article 3 of Directive 2000/12/EC, if the funds received are immediately exchanged for electronic money.

Article 3

Redeemability

1. A bearer of electronic money may, during the period of validity, ask the issuer to redeem it at par value in coins and bank notes or by a transfer to an account free of charges other than those strictly necessary to carry out that operation.

2. The contract between the issuer and the bearer shall clearly state the conditions of redemption.

3. The contract may stipulate a minimum threshold for redemption. The threshold may not exceed EUR 10.

Article 4

Initial capital and ongoing own funds requirements

1. Electronic money institutions shall have an initial capital, as defined in Article 34(2), subparagraphs (1) and (2) of Directive 2000/12/EC, of not less than EUR 1 million. Notwithstanding paragraphs 2 and 3, their own funds, as defined in Directive 2000/12/EC, shall not fall below that amount.

2. Electronic money institutions shall have at all times own funds which are equal to or above 2 % of the higher of the current amount or the average of the preceding six months' total amount of their financial liabilities related to outstanding electronic money.

3. Where an electronic money institution has not completed a six months' period of business, including the day it starts up, it shall have own funds which are equal to or above 2 % of the higher of the current amount or the six months' target total amount of its financial liabilities related to outstanding elec-

tronic money. The six months' target total amount of the institution's financial liabilities related to outstanding electronic money shall be evidenced by its business plan subject to any adjustment to that plan having been required by the competent authorities.

Article 5

Limitations of investments

1. Electronic money institutions shall have investments of an amount of no less than their financial liabilities related to outstanding electronic money in the following assets only:

(a) asset items which according to Article 43(1)(a) (1), (2), (3) and (4) and Article 44(1) of Directive 2000/12/EC attract a zero credit risk weighting and which are sufficiently liquid;

(b) sight deposits held with Zone A credit institutions as defined in Directive 2000/12/EC; and

(c) debt instruments which are:

    (i) sufficiently liquid;

    (ii) not covered by paragraph 1(a);

    (iii) recognised by competent authorities as qualifying items within the meaning of Article 2(12) of Directive 93/6/EEC; and

    (iv) issued by undertakings other than undertakings which have a qualifying holding, as defined in Article 1 of Directive 2000/12/EC, in the electronic money institution concerned or which must be included in those undertakings' consolidated accounts.

2. Investments referred to in paragraph 1(b) and (c) may not exceed 20 times the own funds of the electronic money institution concerned and shall be subject to limitations which are at least as stringent as those applying to credit institutions in accordance with Title V, Chapter 2, Section III of Directive 2000/12/EC.

3. For the purpose of hedging market risks arising from the issuance of electronic money and from the investments referred to in paragraph 1, electronic money institutions may use sufficiently liquid interest-rate and foreign-exchange-related off balance-sheet items in the form of exchange-traded (i.e. not OTC) derivative instruments where they are subject to daily margin requirements or foreign exchange contracts with an original maturity of 14 calendar days or less. The use of derivative instruments according to the first sentence is permissible only if the full elimination of market risks is intended and, to the extent possible, achieved.

4. Member States shall impose appropriate limitations on the market risks electronic money institutions may incur from the investments referred to in paragraph 1.

5. For the purpose of applying paragraph 1, assets shall be valued at the lower of cost or market value.

(¹) Council Directive 91/308/EEC of 10 June 1991 on prevention of the use of the financial system for the purpose of money laundering (OJ L 166, 28.6.1991, p. 77).

6. If the value of the assets referred to in paragraph 1 falls below the amount of financial liabilities related to outstanding electronic money, the competent authorities shall ensure that the electronic money institution in question takes appropriate measures to remedy that situation promptly. To this end, and for a temporary period only, the competent authorities may allow the institution's financial liabilities related to outstanding electronic money to be backed by assets other than those referred to in paragraph 1 up to an amount not exceeding the lower of 5 % of these liabilities or the institution's total amount of own funds.

Article 6

Verification of specific requirements by the competent authorities

The competent authorities shall ensure that the calculations justifying compliance with Articles 4 and 5 are made, not less than twice each year, either by electronic money institutions themselves, which shall communicate them, and any component data required, to the competent authorities, or by competent authorities, using data supplied by the electronic money institutions.

Article 7

Sound and prudent operation

Electronic money institutions shall have sound and prudent management, administrative and accounting procedures and adequate internal control mechanisms. These should respond to the financial and non-financial risks to which the institution is exposed including technical and procedural risks as well as risks connected to its cooperation with any undertaking performing operational or other ancillary functions related to its business activities.

Article 8

Waiver

1. Member States may allow their competent authorities to waive the application of some or all of the provisions of this Directive and the application of Directive 2000/12/EC to electronic money institutions in cases where either:

(a) the total business activities of the type referred to in Article 1(3)(a) of this Directive of the institution generate a total amount of financial liabilities related to outstanding electronic money that normally does not exceed EUR 5 million and never exceeds EUR 6 million; or

(b) the electronic money issued by the institution is accepted as a means of payment only by any subsidiaries of the institution which perform operational or other ancillary functions related to electronic money issued or distributed by the institution, any parent undertaking of the institution or any other subsidiaries of that parent undertaking; or

(c) electronic money issued by the institution is accepted as payment only by a limited number of undertakings, which can be clearly distinguished by:

(i) their location in the same premises or other limited local area; or

(ii) their close financial or business relationship with the issuing institution, such as a common marketing or distribution scheme.

The underlying contractual arrangements must provide that the electronic storage device at the disposal of bearers for the purpose of making payments is subject to a maximum storage amount of not more than EUR 150.

2. An electronic money institution for which a waiver has been granted under paragraph 1 shall not benefit from the mutual recognition arrangements provided for in Directive 2000/12/EC.

3. Member States shall require that all electronic money institutions to which the application of this Directive and Directive 2000/12/EC has been waived report periodically on their activities including the total amount of financial liabilities related to electronic money.

Article 9

Grandfathering

Electronic money institutions subject to this Directive which have commenced their activity in accordance with the provisions in force in the Member State in which they have their head office before the date of entry into force of the provisions adopted in implementation of this Directive or the date referred to in Article 10(1), whichever date is earlier, shall be presumed to be authorised. The Member States shall oblige such electronic money institutions to submit all relevant information to the competent authorities in order to allow them to assess within six months from the date of entry into force of the provisions adopted in implementation of this Directive, whether the institutions comply with the requirements pursuant to this Directive, which measures need to be taken in order to ensure compliance, or whether a withdrawal of authorisation is appropriate. If compliance is not ensured within six months from the date referred to in Article 10(1), the electronic money institution shall not benefit from mutual recognition after that time.

Article 10

Implementation

1. Member States shall bring into force the laws, regulations and administrative provisions necessary to comply with this Directive not later than 27 April 2002. They shall immediately inform the Commission thereof.

When Member States adopt these measures, they shall contain a reference to this Directive or shall be accompanied by such reference on the occasion of their official publication. The methods of making such a reference shall be laid down by the Member States.

2.   Member States shall communicate to the Commission the text of the main provisions of national law, which they adopt in the field covered by this Directive.

Article 11

Review

Not later than 27 April 2005 the Commission shall present a report to the European Parliament and the Council on the application of this Directive, in particular on:

— the measures to protect the bearers of electronic money, including the possible need to introduce a guarantee scheme,

— capital requirements,

— waivers, and

— the possible need to prohibit interest being paid on funds received in exchange for electronic money,

accompanied where appropriate by a proposal for its revision.

Article 12

Entry into force

This Directive shall enter into force on the day of its publication in the *Official Journal of the European Communities*.

Article 13

This Directive is addressed to the Member States.

Done at Brussels, 18 September 2000.

For the European Parliament	For the Council
The President	*The President*
N. FONTAINE	H. VÉDRINE

Appendix 7

Statutory Instrument 2002 No. 682

The Financial Services and Markets Act 2000 (Regulated Activities) (Amendment) Order 2002

© Crown Copyright 2002

STATUTORY INSTRUMENTS

2002 No. 682

FINANCIAL SERVICES AND MARKETS

The Financial Services and Markets Act 2000 (Regulated Activities)
(Amendment) Order 2002

Approved by both House of Parliament

Made	*14th March 2002*
Laid before Parliament	*14th March 2002*
Coming into force in accordance	
with article 1(2)	

ARRANGEMENT OF ORDER

PART I

PRELIMINARY

PART II

ELECTRONIC MONEY

Amendments of the principal Order

Supplemental and transitional provisions

7. Amendment of the Financial Services and Markets Act 2000 (Professions) (Non-Exempt Activities) Order 2001
8. Variation of threshold condition
9. Transitional provisions for persons issuing electronic money at commencement
10. Anticipatory consultation on rules

PART III

MISCELLANEOUS AMENDMENTS OF THE PRINCIPAL ORDER

11. Specified activities: disapplication of exclusions in relation to investment firms
12. Accepting deposits: sums received in consideration for the issue of debt securities
13. Sending dematerialised instructions

Whereas, in the opinion of the Treasury, one of the effects of the following Order is that an activity which is not a regulated activity (within the meaning of the Financial Services and Markets Act 2000[1]) will become a regulated activity (within the meaning of that Act);

The Treasury, in exercise of the powers conferred on them by sections 22(1) and (5) and 428(3) of, and paragraph 25 of Schedule 2 to, that Act, hereby make the following Order:

PART I

PRELIMINARY

Citation, commencement and interpretation
1.—(1) This Order may be cited as the Financial Services and Markets Act 2000 (Regulated Activities) (Amendment) Order 2002.

(2) This Order comes into force—

(a) on 11th April 2002, for the purpose of making rules under articles 9G and 9H of the principal Order (as inserted by article 4 of this Order);
(b) on 27th April 2002, for all other purposes.

(3) In this Order—

(a) "the Act" means the Financial Services and Markets Act 2000;
(b) "the principal Order" means the Financial Services and Markets Act 2000 (Regulated Activities) Order 2001[2].

[1] 2000 c. 8.back
[2] S.I. 2001/544, amended by S.I. 2001/3544.back

PART II

ELECTRONIC MONEY

Amendments of the principal Order

Definition of "electronic money"
2. In article 3(1) of the principal Order (interpretation), after the definition of "deposit" insert—

" 'electronic money' means monetary value, as represented by a claim on the issuer, which is—

(a) stored on an electronic device;
(b) issued on receipt of funds; and
(c) accepted as a means of payment by persons other than the issuer;".

Sums received in exchange for electronic money not to constitute deposits
3.—(1) In paragraph (2) of article 5 of the principal Order (accepting deposits), for "articles 6 to 9" substitute "articles 6 to 9A".

(2) After article 9 of the principal Order insert—

" Sums received in exchange for electronic money

9A. A sum is not a deposit for the purposes of article 5 if it is immediately exchanged for electronic money."

Issuing electronic money: the specified activity
4. After article 9A insert—

" CHAPTER IIA

ELECTRONIC MONEY

The activity

Issuing electronic money
9B. Issuing electronic money is a specified kind of activity.

Exclusions

Persons certified as small issuers etc.
9C.—(1) There is excluded from article 9B the issuing of electronic money by a person to whom the Authority has given a certificate under this article (provided the certificate has not been revoked).

(2) An application for a certificate may be made by—

(a) a body corporate, or
(b) a partnership,

(other than a credit institution as defined in Article 1(1)(a) of the banking consolidation directive) which has its head office in the United Kingdom.

(3) The authority must, on the application of such a person ("A"), give A a certificate if it appears to the Authority that paragraph (4), (5) or (6) applies.

(4) This paragraph applies if—

(a) A does not issue electronic money except on terms that the electronic device on which the monetary value is stored is subject to a maximum storage amount of not more than 150 euro; and

(b) A's total liabilities with respect to the issuing of electronic money do not (or will not) usually exceed 5 million euro and do not (or will not) ever exceed 6 million euro.

(5) This paragraph applies if—

(a) the condition in paragraph (4)(a) is met;

(b) A's total liabilities with respect to the issuing of electronic money do not (or will not) exceed 10 million euro; and

(c) electronic money issued by A is accepted as a means of payment only by—

(i) subsidiaries of A which perform operational or other ancillary functions related to electronic money issued or distributed by A; or

(ii) other members of the same group as A (other than subsidiaries of A).

(6) This paragraph applies if—

(a) the conditions in paragraphs (4)(a) and (5)(b) are met; and

(b) electronic money issued by A is accepted as a means of payment, in the course of business, by not more than one hundred persons where—

(i) those persons accept such electronic money only at locations within the same premises or limited local area; or

(ii) those persons have a close financial or business relationship with A, such as a common marketing or distribution scheme.

(7) For the purposes of paragraph (6)(b)(i), locations are to be treated as situated within the same premises or limited local area if they are situated within—

(a) a shopping centre, airport, railway station, bus station, or campus of a university, polytechnic, college, school or similar educational establishment; or

(b) an area which does not exceed four square kilometres;

but sub-paragraphs (a) and (b) are illustrative only and are not to be treated as limiting the scope of paragraph (6)(b)(i).

(8) For the purposes of paragraph (6)(b)(ii), persons are not to be treated as having a close financial or business relationship with A merely because they participate in arrangements for the acceptance of electronic money issued by A.

(9) In this article, references to amounts in euro include references to equivalent amounts in sterling.

(10) A person to whom a certificate has been given under this article (and whose certificate has not been revoked) is referred to in this Chapter as a "certified person".

Applications for certificates

9D. The following provisions of the Act apply to applications to the Authority for certificates under 9C (and the determination of such applications) as they apply to applications for Part IV permissions (and the determination of such applications)—

    (a) section 51(1)(b) and (3) to (6);

    (b) section 52, except subsections (6), (8) and (9)(a) and (b); and

    (c) section 55(1).

Revocation of certificate on Authority's own initiative

9E.—(1) The Authority may revoke a certificate given to a person ("A") under article 9C if—

    (a) it appears to it that A does not meet the relevant conditions, or has failed to meet the relevant conditions at any time since the certificate was given; or

    (b) the person to whom the certificate was given has contravened any rule or requirement to which he is subject as a result of article 9G.

(2) For the purposes of paragraph (1), A meets the relevant conditions at any time if, at that time, paragraph (4), (5) or (6) of article 9C applies.

(3) Sections 54 and 55(2) of the Act apply to the revocation of a certificate under paragraph (1) as they apply to the cancellation of a Part IV permission on the Authority's own initiative, as if references in those sections to an authorised person were references to a certified person.

Revocation of certificate on request

9F.—(1) A certified person ("B") may apply to the Authority for his certificate to be revoked, and the Authority must then revoke the certificate and give B written notice that it has done so.

(2) An application under paragraph (1) must be made in such manner as the Authority may direct.

(3) If—

    (a) B has made an application under Part IV of the Act for permission to carry on a regulated activity of the kind specified by article 9B (or for variation of an existing permission so as to add a regulated activity of that kind), and

    (b) on making an application for revocation of his certificate under paragraph (1), he requests that the revocation be conditional on the granting of his application under Part IV of the Act,

the revocation of B's certificate is to be conditional on the granting of his application under Part IV of the Act.

Obtaining information from certified persons etc.

9G.—(1) The Authority may make rules requiring certified persons to provide information to the Authority about their activities so far as relating to the issuing of electronic money, including the amount of their liabilities with respect to the issuing of electronic money.

(2) Section 148 of the Act (modification or waiver of rules) applies in relation to rules made under paragraph (1) as if references in that section to an authorised person were references to a certified person.

(3) Section 150 of the Act (actions for damages) applies in relation to a rule made under paragraph (1) as if the reference in subsection (1) of that section to an authorised person were a reference to a certified person.

(4) The Authority may, by notice in writing given to a certified person, require him—

> (a) to provide specified information or information of a specified description; or
> (b) to produce specified documents or documents of a specified description.

(5) Paragraph (4) applies only to information or documents reasonably required for the purposes of determining whether the certified person meets, or has met, the relevant conditions.

(6) Subsections (2), (5) and (6) of section 165 of the Act (Authority's power to require information) apply to a requirement imposed under paragraph (4) as they apply to a requirement imposed under that section.

(7) Section 166 of the Act (reports by skilled persons) has effect as if—

> (a) the reference in subsection (1) of that section to section 165 included a reference to paragraph (4) above; and
> (b) the reference in section 166(2)(a) of the Act to an authorised person included a reference to a certified person.

(8) Subsection (4) of section 168 of the Act (appointment of persons to carry out investigations in particular cases) has effect as if it provided for subsection (5) of that section to apply if it appears to the Authority that there are circumstances suggesting that a certified person may not meet, or may not have met, the relevant conditions.

(9) Sections 175 (information and documents: supplemental provisions), 176 (entry of premises under warrant) and 177 (offences) of the Act apply to a requirement imposed under paragraph (4) as they apply to a requirement imposed under section 165 of the Act (the reference in section 176(3)(a) to an authorised person being read as a reference to a certified person).

(10) In this article—

> (a) "specified", in paragraph (4), means specified in the notice mentioned in that paragraph;
> (b) a certified person ("A") meets the relevant conditions at any time if, at that time, paragraph (4), (5) or (6) of article 9C applies.

Supplemental

Rules prohibiting the issue of electronic money at a discount
9H.—(1) The Authority may make rules applying to authorised persons with permission to carry on an activity of the kind specified by article 9B, prohibiting the issue of electronic money having a monetary value greater than the funds received.

(2) Section 148 of the Act (modification or waiver of rules) applies in relation to rules made under paragraph (1).

False claims to be a certified person

9I. A person who is not a certified person is to be treated as guilty of an offence under section 24 of the Act (false claims to be authorised or exempt) if he—

      (a) describes himself (in whatever terms) as a certified person;

      (b) behaves, or otherwise holds himself out, in a manner which indicates (or which is reasonably likely to be understood as indicating) that he is a certified person.

Exclusion of electronic money from the compensation scheme

9J. The compensation scheme established under Part XV of the Act is not to provide for the compensation of persons in respect of claims made in connection with any activity of the kind specified by article 9B.

Record of certified persons

9K. The record maintained by the Authority under section 347 of the Act (public record of authorised persons etc.) must include every certified person."

Agreeing to issue electronic money not to be a regulated activity

5. In article 64 of the principal Order (agreeing to carry on specified kinds of activity), after "article 5," insert "9B,".

Electronic money: the specified investment

6. After article 74 of the principal Order insert—

    " **Electronic money**

      74A. Electronic money."

Supplemental and transitional provisions

Amendment of the Financial Services and Markets Act 2000 (Professions) (Non-Exempt Activities) Order 2001

7.—(1) In the Financial Services and Markets Act 2000 (Professions) (Non-Exempt Activities) Order 2001[3], after sub-paragraph (a) of article 4(1) (activities to which exemption from the general prohibition does not apply), insert—

    "(aa) article 9B (issuing electronic money);".

    (2) In article 8 of that Order, after "article 4(a)," insert "(aa),".

Variation of threshold condition

8. In paragraph 1(2) of Schedule 6[4] to the Act (threshold conditions: legal status of deposit-takers), after "accepting deposits" insert "or issuing electronic money".

Transitional provisions for persons issuing electronic money at commencement

9.—(1) Where, immediately before commencement, a credit institution with Part IV permission to accept deposits was carrying on by way of business in the United Kingdom the

---

[3] S.I. 2001/1227, amended by S.I. 2001/3650.back

[4] Schedule 6 was amended by S.I. 2001/2507.back

activity of issuing electronic money, the institution's permission is to be treated as including, for a period of six months beginning at commencement, permission to carry on an activity of the kind specified by article 9B of the principal Order.

(2) Where, immediately before commencement—

(a) an EEA firm of the kind mentioned in paragraph 5(b) or (c) of Schedule 3 to the Act qualified for authorisation under that Schedule, and
(b) the activities which were treated as permitted activities for the purposes of paragraph 13 or 14 of that Schedule as it applied to that firm included the issuing of electronic money,

the firm's permission under paragraph 15 of that Schedule is to be treated, at commencement, as including permission to carry on that activity.

(3) Where an existing issuer having his head office in the United Kingdom is, after commencement, granted a Part IV permission to carry on an activity of the kind specified by article 9B (and hence becomes a UK firm, within the meaning of Schedule 3 to the Act, in relation to that activity)—

(a) if, immediately before commencement, the existing issuer was carrying on the activity of issuing electronic money from a branch established in another EEA State, the conditions in paragraph 19(2) to (5) of that Schedule are to be treated as satisfied with respect to that branch;
(b) if, immediately before commencement, the existing issuer was carrying on the activity of issuing electronic money by providing services in another EEA State, the conditions in paragraph 20(1) of that Schedule are to be treated as satisfied with respect to the provision of those services in that EEA State.

(4) An existing issuer having his head office in an EEA State other than the United Kingdom who, after commencement, becomes authorised (within the meaning of Article 1 of the banking consolidation directive) by his home state regulator (and hence becomes an EEA firm)—

(a) is to be treated as having complied with the establishment conditions (within the meaning of paragraph 13 of Schedule 3 to the Act) where, immediately before commencement, he was carrying on the activity of issuing electronic money from a branch established in the United Kingdom;
(b) is to be treated as having complied with the service conditions (within the meaning of paragraph 14 of that Schedule) where, immediately before commencement, he was carrying on the activity of issuing electronic money by providing services in the United Kingdom.

(5) Where paragraph (4)(a) or (b) applies, the existing issuer is to be treated as having permission to carry on the activity mentioned in that paragraph through its United Kingdom branch or (as the case may be) by providing services in the United Kingdom.

(6) There is excluded from article 9B of the principal Order any activity carried on by an existing issuer before 27th October 2002, unless he has been granted a Part IV permission to carry on that activity, or has permission to carry on that activity as a result of paragraph (5).

(7) There is also excluded from article 9B of the principal Order any activity carried on by an existing issuer after the beginning of 27th October 2002, provided—

(a) he has made an application before 27th June 2002 under section 40 of the Act for permission to carry on that activity, and has not withdrawn it; and
(b) the application has not been finally determined.

(8) For the purposes of paragraph (7), an application is to be treated as finally determined—

(a) in a case where the Authority gives permission to carry on the activity and does not exercise its power under section 42(7)(a) or (b) or section 43(1) of the Act, on the date on which the permission takes effect;
(b) in a case where the Authority refuses permission, or gives permission but exercises its power under section 42(7)(a) or (b) or section 43 of the Act, at the time when the matter ceases to be open to review (within the meaning of section 391(8) of the Act).

(9) In this article—

(a) "commencement" means the beginning of 27th April 2002;
(b) "credit institution" means a credit institution as defined in Article 1(1)(a) of the banking consolidation directive;
(c) an "existing issuer" means a body corporate or partnership (other than one falling within paragraph (1) or (2)) which, immediately before commencement—

(i)   has its head office in the United Kingdom, and is carrying on by way of business in the United Kingdom the activity of issuing electronic money; or
(ii)   has its head office in an EEA State other than the United Kingdom, and is carrying on such an activity by way of business in the United Kingdom without contravening the law of that other EEA State;

(d) in paragraph (1) and in sub-paragraph (c) of this paragraph, the references to carrying on an activity in the United Kingdom are to be construed without reference to section 418 of the Act (carrying on regulated activities in the United Kingdom).

Anticipatory consultation on rules

10. If—

(a) before 11th April 2002 any steps were taken in relation to a draft of rules which the Authority proposes to make under article 9G(1) or 9H of the principal Order (as inserted by article 4 of this Order), and
(b) those steps, had they been taken after that day, would to any extent have satisfied the requirements of section 155 of the Act,

those requirements are to that extent to be taken to have been satisfied.

PART III

MISCELLANEOUS AMENDMENTS OF THE PRINCIPAL ORDER

Specified activities: disapplication of exclusions in relation to investment firms
11. In article 4(4)(b) of the principal Order, for "articles 15, 68, 69 and 70" substitute "articles 15, 16, 19, 22, 23, 29, 38, 68, 69 and 70".

Accepting deposits: sums received in consideration for the issue of debt securities
12. For article 9(3) of the principal Order substitute—

" (3) In paragraph (2), "commercial paper" means an investment of the kind specified by article 77 or 78 having a maturity of less than one year from the date of issue."

Sending dematerialised instructions
13.—(1) In paragraph (1) of article 45 of the principal Order—

(a) after "security" insert "or a contractually based investment";
(b) for "1995" substitute "2001".

(2) In paragraph (2) of that article, after "security" insert "or a contractually based investment".

(3) In paragraph (3) of that article—

(a) for sub-paragraph (a) substitute—

" (a) "the 2001 Regulations" means the Uncertificated Securities Regulations 2001[5];";

(b) in sub-paragraph (b), for "1995" substitute "2001".

(4) In articles 46, 49 and 69(8) of the principal Order, for "1995" substitute "2001".

Nick Ainger

John Heppell
Two of the Lords Commissioners of Her Majesty's Treasury

14th March 2002

EXPLANATORY NOTE

(This note is not part of the Order)

This Order amends the Financial Services and Markets Act 2000 (Regulated Activities) Order 2001 ("the principal Order"). It gives effect to Directive 2000/46/EC of the European Parliament and of the Council of 18 September 2000 on the taking up, pursuit of and prudential supervision of the business of electronic money institutions (OJ L275, 27.10.2000, p.39); and Directive 2000/28/EC of the European Parliament and of the Council of 18 September 2000 amending Directive 2000/12/EC relating to the taking up and pursuit of the business of credit institutions (OJ L275, 27.10.2000, p.37).

---

[5] S.I. 2001/3755.back

Part II of the Order provides for the issuing of electronic money to be a regulated activity under the Financial Services and Markets Act 2000 ("the Act").

Article 2 inserts a definition of "electronic money" into the principal Order. Article 3 amends that Order to provide that a sum is not a "deposit" for the purposes of that Order if it is immediately exchanged for electronic money.

Articles 4 to 6 insert provisions into the principal Order relating to the regulated activity of issuing electronic money. They include provisions excluding from the scope of that activity certain persons whose operations are on a limited scale, and to whom the Financial Services Authority ("the Authority") has issued a certificate. The Authority is given powers to obtain information from such "certified persons", and to make rules prohibiting the issue of electronic money at a discount. Provision is made excluding the issuing of electronic money from the Financial Services Compensation Scheme established under Part XV of the Act, and providing for details of "certified persons" to be included in the public record maintained by the Authority under section 347 of the Act.

Articles 7 and 8 of the Order make supplemental amendments to provide that the issuing of electronic money is not an exempt activity for the purposes of Part XX of the Act (provision of financial services by members of the professions); and to provide that persons seeking permission under the Act to carry on the regulated activity of issuing electronic money must comply with the threshold condition in paragraph 1(2) of Schedule 6 to the Act (i.e. they must be either bodies corporate or partnerships). Article 9 makes transitional provisions relating to persons who were issuing electronic money immediately before 27th April 2002. Article 10 makes provision about anticipatory consultation on rules to be made under the new powers conferred by articles 9G(1) and 9H of the principal Order.

Part III of the Order makes further, miscellaneous amendments to the principal Order. Article 11 makes additions to the list, in article 4(4) of the principal Order, of those exclusions which must be disregarded for the purposes of giving proper effect to the investment services directive (93/22/EEC). Article 12 makes a clarificatory amendment to article 9 of the principal Order, which provides an exclusion from the activity of accepting deposits for sums received in consideration for the issue of debt securities. Article 13 provides for article 45 of the principal Order (sending dematerialised instructions) to apply to instructions relating to contractually based investments as well as those relating to securities. It also replaces references to the Uncertificated Securities Regulations 1995 with references to the corresponding 2001 Regulations.

ISBN 0 11 039854 8

Appendix 8

COUNCIL DIRECTIVE 2002/38/EC
of 7 May 2002

amending and amending temporarily Directive 77/388/EEC as regards the value added tax arrangements applicable to radio and television broadcasting services and certain electronically supplied services

THE COUNCIL OF THE EUROPEAN UNION,

Having regard to the Treaty establishing the European Community, and in particular Article 93 thereof,

Having regard to the proposal from the Commission ([1]),

Having regard to the opinion of the European Parliament ([2]),

Having regard to the opinion of the Economic and Social Committee ([3]),

Whereas:

(1) The rules currently applicable to VAT on radio and television broadcasting services and on electronically supplied services, under Article 9 of the sixth Council Directive 77/388/EEC of 17 May 1977 on the harmonisation of the laws of the Member States relating to turnover taxes — Common system of value added tax: uniform basis of assessment ([4]), are inadequate for taxing such services consumed within the Community and for preventing distortions of competition in this area.

(2) In the interests of the proper functioning of the internal market, such distortions should be eliminated and new harmonised rules introduced for this type of activity. Action should be taken to ensure, in particular, that such services where effected for consideration and consumed by customers established in the Community are taxed in the Community and are not taxed if consumed outside the Community.

(3) To this end, radio and television broadcasting services and electronically supplied services provided from third countries to persons established in the Community or from the Community to recipients established in third countries should be taxed at the place of the recipient of the services.

(4) To define electronically supplied services, examples of such services should be included in an annex to the Directive.

(5) To facilitate compliance with fiscal obligations by operators providing electronically supplied services, who are neither established nor required to be identified for tax purposes within the Community, a special scheme should be established. In applying this scheme any operator supplying such services by electronic means to non-taxable persons within the Community, may, if he is not otherwise identified for tax purposes within the Community, opt for identification in a single Member State.

(6) The non-established operator wishing to benefit from the special scheme should comply with the requirements laid down therein, and with any relevant existing provision in the Member State where the services are consumed.

(7) The Member State of identification must under certain conditions be able to exclude a non-established operator from the special scheme.

(8) Where the non-established operator opts for the special scheme, any input value added tax that he has paid with respect to goods and services used by him for the purpose of his taxed activities falling under the special scheme, should be refunded by the Member State where the input value added tax was paid, in accordance with the arrangements of the thirteenth Council Directive 86/560/EEC of 17 November 1986 on the harmonisation of the laws of the Member States relating to turnover taxes — arrangements for the refund of value added tax to taxable persons not established in Community territory ([5]). The optional restrictions for refund in Article 2(2) and (3) and Article 4(2) of the same Directive should not be applied.

(9) Subject to conditions which they lay down, Member States should allow certain statements and returns to be made by electronic means, and may also require that electronic means are used.

(10) Those provisions pertaining to the introduction of electronic tax returns and statements should be adopted on a permanent basis. It is desirable to adopt all other provisions for a temporary period of three years which may be extended for practical reasons but should, in any event, based on experience, be reviewed within three years from 1 July 2003.

(11) Directive 77/388/EEC should therefore be amended accordingly,

([1]) OJ C 337 E, 28.11.2000, p. 65.
([2]) OJ C 232, 17.8.2001, p. 202.
([3]) OJ C 116, 20.4.2001, p. 59.
([4]) OJ L 145, 13.6.1977, p. 1. Directive as last amended by Council Directive 2001/115/EC (OJ L 15, 17.1.2002, p. 24).

([5]) OJ L 326, 21.11.1986, p. 40.

L 128/42　　　　[EN]　　　　Official Journal of the European Communities　　　　15.5.2002

HAS ADOPTED THIS DIRECTIVE:

Article 1

Directive 77/388/EEC is hereby temporarily amended as follows:

1. in Article 9:

   (a) in paragraph (2)(e), a comma shall replace the final full stop and the following indents shall be added:

   '— radio and television broadcasting services,

   — electronically supplied services, *inter alia*, those described in Annex L.'

   (b) in paragraph 2, the following point shall be added:

   '(f) the place where services referred to in the last indent of subparagraph (e) are supplied when performed for non-taxable persons who are established, have their permanent address or usually reside in a Member State, by a taxable person who has established his business or has a fixed establishment from which the service is supplied outside the Community or, in the absence of such a place of business or fixed establishment, has his permanent address or usually resides outside the Community, shall be the place where the non-taxable person is established, has his permanent address or usually resides.'

   (c) in paragraph 3, the introductory phrase shall be replaced by the following:

   '3. In order to avoid double taxation, non-taxation or the distortion of competition, the Member States may, with regard to the supply of services referred to in paragraph 2(e), except for the services referred to in the last indent when supplied to non-taxable persons, and also with regard to the hiring out of forms of transport consider:'

   (d) paragraph 4 shall be amended as follows:

   '4. In the case of telecommunications services and radio and television broadcasting services referred to in paragraph 2(e) when performed for non-taxable persons who are established, have their permanent address or usually reside in a Member State, by a taxable person who has established his business or has a fixed establishment from which the service is supplied outside the Community, or in the absence of such a place of business or fixed establishment, has his permanent address or usually resides outside the Community, Member States shall make use of paragraph 3(b).'

2. in Article 12(3)(a), the following fourth subparagraph shall be added:

'The third subparagraph shall not apply to the services referred to in the last indent of Article 9(2)(e).'

3. the following Article shall be added:

'*Article 26c*

Special scheme for non-established taxable persons supplying electronic services to non-taxable persons

A. Definitions

For the purposes of this Article, the following definitions shall apply without prejudice to other Community provisions:

(a) "non-established taxable person" means a taxable person who has neither established his business nor has a fixed establishment within the territory of the Community and who is not otherwise required to be identified for tax purposes under Article 22;

(b) "electronic services" and "electronically supplied services" means those services referred to in the last indent of Article 9(2)(e);

(c) "Member State of identification" means the Member State which the non-established taxable person chooses to contact to state when his activity as a taxable person within the territory of the Community commences in accordance with the provisions of this Article;

(d) "Member State of consumption" means the Member State in which the supply of the electronic services is deemed to take place according to Article 9(2)(f);

(e) "value added tax return" means the statement containing the information necessary to establish the amount of tax that has become chargeable in each Member State.

B. Special scheme for electronically supplied services

1. Member States shall permit a non-established taxable person supplying electronic services to a non-taxable person who is established or has his permanent address or usually resides in a Member State to use a special scheme in accordance with the following provisions. The special scheme shall apply to all those supplies within the Community.

2. The non-established taxable person shall state to the Member State of identification when his activity as a taxable person commences, ceases or changes to the extent that he no longer qualifies for the special scheme. Such a statement shall be made electronically.

The information from the non-established taxable person to the Member State of identification when his taxable activities commence shall contain the following details for the identification: name, postal address, electronic addresses, including websites, national tax number, if any, and a statement that the person is not identified for value added tax purposes within the Community. The non-established taxable person shall notify the Member State of identification of any changes in the submitted information.

3. The Member State of identification shall identify the non-established taxable person by means of an individual number. Based on the information used for this identification, Member States of consumption may keep their own identification systems.

The Member State of identification shall notify the non-established taxable person by electronic means of the identification number allocated to him.

4. The Member State of identification shall exclude the non-established taxable person from the identification register if:

(a) he notifies that he no longer supplies electronic services, or

(b) it otherwise can be assumed that his taxable activities have ended, or

(c) he no longer fulfils the requirements necessary to be allowed to use the special scheme, or

(d) he persistently fails to comply with the rules concerning the special scheme.

5. The non-established taxable person shall submit by electronic means to the Member State of identification a value added tax return for each calendar quarter whether or not electronic services have been supplied. The return shall be submitted within 20 days following the end of the reporting period to which the return refers.

The value added tax return shall set out the identification number and, for each Member State of consumption where tax has become due, the total value, less value added tax, of supplies of electronic services for the reporting period and total amount of the corresponding tax. The applicable tax rates and the total tax due shall also be indicated.

6. The value added tax return shall be made in euro. Member States which have not adopted the euro may require the tax return to be made in their national currencies. If the supplies have been made in other currencies, the exchange rate valid for the last date of the reporting period shall be used when completing the value added tax return. The exchange shall be done following the exchange rates published by the European Central Bank for that day, or, if there is no publication on that day, on the next day of publication.

7. The non-established taxable person shall pay the value added tax when submitting the return. Payment shall be made to a bank account denominated in euro, designated by the Member State of identification. Member States which have not adopted the euro may require the payment to be made to a bank account denominated in their own currency.

8. Notwithstanding Article 1(1) of Directive 86/560/EEC, the non-established taxable person making use of this special scheme shall, instead of making deductions under Article 17(2) of this Directive, be granted a refund according to Directive 86/560/EEC. Articles 2(2), 2(3) and 4(2) of Directive 86/560/EEC shall not apply to the refund related to electronic supplies covered by this special scheme.

9. The non-established taxable person shall keep records of the transactions covered by this special scheme in sufficient detail to enable the tax administration of the Member State of consumption to determine that the value added tax return referred to in paragraph 5 is correct. These records should be made available electronically on request to the Member State of identification and to the Member State of consumption. These records shall be maintained for a period of 10 years from the end of the year when the transaction was carried out.

10. Article 21(2)(b) shall not apply to a non-established taxable person who has opted for this special scheme.'

Article 2

Article 22, contained in Article 28h of Directive 77/388/EEC, is hereby amended as follows:

1. in paragraph 1, point (a) shall be replaced by the following:

'(a) Every taxable person shall state when his activity as a taxable person commences, changes or ceases. Member States shall, subject to conditions which they lay down, allow the taxable person to make such statements by electronic means, and may also require that electronic means are used.'

2. in paragraph 4, point (a) shall be replaced by the following:

'(a) Every taxable person shall submit a return by a deadline to be determined by Member States. That deadline may not be more than two months later than the end of each tax period. The tax period shall be fixed by each Member State at one month, two months or a quarter. Member States may, however, set different periods provided that they do not exceed one year. Member States shall, subject to conditions which they lay down, allow the taxable person to make such returns by electronic means, and may also require that electronic means are used.'

3. in paragraph 6, point (a) shall be replaced by the following:

'(a) Member States may require a taxable person to submit a statement, including all the particulars specified in paragraph 4, concerning all transactions carried out in the preceding year. That statement shall provide all the information necessary for any adjustments. Member States shall, subject to conditions which they lay down, allow the taxable person to make such statements by electronic means, and may also require that electronic means are used.'

4. in paragraph 6, the second paragraph in point (b) shall be replaced by:

'The recapitulative statement shall be drawn up for each calendar quarter within a period and in accordance with procedures to be determined by the Member States, which shall take the measures necessary to ensure that the provisions concerning administrative cooperation in the field of indirect taxation are in any event complied with. Member States shall, subject to conditions which they lay down, allow the taxable person to make such statements by electronic means, and may also require that electronic means are used.'

Article 3

1. Member States shall bring into force the laws, regulations and administrative provisions necessary to comply with this Directive on 1 July 2003. They shall forthwith inform the Commission thereof.

428

When Member States adopt these measures, they shall contain a reference to this Directive or shall be accompanied by such reference on the occasion of their official publication. Member States shall determine how such reference is to be made.

2.   Member States shall communicate to the Commission the text of the provisions of domestic law which they adopt in the field covered by this Directive.

Article 4

Article 1 shall apply for a period of three years starting from 1 July 2003.

Article 5

The Council, on the basis of a report from the Commission, shall review the provisions of Article 1 of this Directive before 30 June 2006 and shall either, acting in accordance with Article 93 of the Treaty, adopt measures on an appropriate electronic mechanism on a non-discriminatory basis for charging, declaring, collecting and allocating tax revenue on electronically supplied services with taxation in the place of consumption or, if considered necessary for practical reasons, acting unanimously on the basis of a proposal from the Commission, extend the period mentioned in Article 4.

Article 6

This Directive shall enter into force on the day of its publication in the *Official Journal of the European Communities*.

Article 7

This Directive is addressed to the Member States.

Done at Brussels, 7 May 2002.

For the Council
The President
R. DE RATO Y FIGAREDO

ANNEX

'ANNEX L

ILLUSTRATIVE LIST OF ELECTRONICALLY SUPPLIED SERVICES REFERRED TO IN ARTICLE 9(2)(e)

1. Website supply, web-hosting, distance maintenance of programmes and equipment.

2. Supply of software and updating thereof.

3. Supply of images, text and information, and making databases available.

4. Supply of music, films and games, including games of chance and gambling games, and of political, cultural, artistic, sporting, scientific and entertainment broadcasts and events.

5. Supply of distance teaching.

Where the supplier of a service and his customer communicates via electronic mail, this shall not of itself mean that the service performed is an electronic service within the meaning of the last indent of Article 9(2)(e).'

Appendix 9

I

(Acts whose publication is obligatory)

COUNCIL REGULATION (EC) No 792/2002
of 7 May 2002
amending temporarily Regulation (EEC) No 218/92 on administrative cooperation in the field of indirect taxation (VAT) as regards additional measures regarding electronic commerce

THE COUNCIL OF THE EUROPEAN UNION,

Having regard to the Treaty establishing the European Community, and in particular Article 93 thereof,

Having regard to the proposal from the Commission [1],

Having regard to the opinion of the European Parliament [2],

Having regard to the opinion of the Economic and Social Committee [3],

Whereas:

(1) Council Directive 2002/38/EC of 7 May 2002 amending and amending temporarily Directive 77/388/EEC as regards the value added tax arrangements applicable to radio and television broadcasting services and certain electronically supplied services [4] provides for the framework for taxing electronic supplies in the Community by taxable persons who are neither established nor required to be identified for tax purposes within the Community.

(2) The Member State of consumption has primary responsibility for assuring the compliance with their obligations by non-established suppliers. To this end, the information necessary to operate the special scheme for electronically supplied services that is provided for in Article 26c of sixth Council Directive 77/388/EEC of 17 May 1977 on the harmonisation of the laws of the Member States relating to turnover taxes — Common system of value added tax: uniform basis of assessment [5] must be transmitted to those Member States.

(3) It is necessary to provide that the value added tax due in respect of such supplies transferred to accounts designated by the Member States of consumption.

(4) The rules laid down in Directive 77/388/EEC require the non-established taxable person supplying services referred to in the last indent of Article 9(2)e of the Directive to charge VAT to his customer, established or

resident in the Community, unless he is satisfied that his customer is a taxable person. The special scheme provided for in Article 26c of the Directive applies only for services provided to non-taxable persons established or resident in the Community. It is thus clear that the non-established taxable person needs certain information about his customer.

(5) To this end, use could in most cases be made of the facility that is available in Member States in the form of electronic databases which contain a register of persons to whom value added tax identification numbers have been issued in that Member State.

(6) It is accordingly necessary to extend the common system for the exchange of certain information on intra-Community transaction provided for in Article 6 of Regulation (EEC) No 218/92 [6].

(7) The provisions of the Regulation should operate for a temporary period of three years which may be extended for practical reasons and Regulation (EEC) No 218/92 should therefore be temporarily amended accordingly,

HAS ADOPTED THIS REGULATION:

Article 1

Regulation (EEC) No 218/92 is hereby temporarily amended:

1. the second paragraph of Article 1 shall be replaced by the following:

'To that end it lays down procedures for the exchange by electronic means of value added tax information on intra-Community transactions as well as on services supplied electronically in accordance with the special scheme provided for by Article 26c of Directive 77/388/EEC, and also for any subsequent exchange of information and, as far as services covered by that special scheme are concerned, for the transfer of money between Member States' competent authorities.';

[1] OJ C 337 E, 28.11.2000, p. 63.
[2] OJ C 232, 17.8.2001, p. 202, and the Opinion of 25 April 2002 (not yet published in the Official Journal).
[3] OJ C 116, 20.4.2001, p. 59.
[4] See page 41 of this Official Journal.
[5] OJ L 145, 13.6.1977, p. 1, as last amended by Directive 2002/38/EC.

[6] OJ L 24, 1.2.1992, p. 1.

2. in Article 2(1), the ninth indent shall be replaced by the following:

'— "intra-Community supply of services" shall mean any supply of services covered by Article 28b (C), (D), (E) or (F) of Directive 77/388/EEC,';

3. in Article 6, paragraph 4 shall be replaced by the following:

'4.   The competent authority of each Member State shall ensure that persons involved in the intra-Community supply of goods or of services and persons supplying services referred to in the last indent of Article 9(2)e of Directive 77/388/EEC are allowed to obtain confirmation of the validity of the value added tax identification number of any specified person. In accordance with the procedure referred to in Article 10, Member States shall, in particular, provide such confirmation by electronic means.';

4. the following Title shall be added:

'TITLE III A

Provisions concerning the special scheme in Article 26c of Directive 77/388/EEC

Article 9a

The following provisions shall apply concerning the special scheme provided for in Article 26c in Directive 77/388/EEC. The definitions contained in point A of that Article shall also apply for the purpose of this Title.

Article 9b

1.   The information from the non-established taxable person to the Member State of identification when his activities commences set out in the second subparagraph of Article 26c(B)(2) of Directive 77/388/EEC is to be submitted in an electronic manner. The technical details, including a common electronic message, shall be determined in accordance with the procedure provided for in Article 10.

2.   The Member State of identification shall transmit this information by electronic means to the competent authorities of the other Member States within 10 days from the end of the month during which the information was received from the non-established taxable person. In the same manner, the competent authorities of the other Member States shall be informed of the allocated identification number. The technical details, including a common electronic message, by which this information is to be transmitted shall be determined in accordance with the procedure provided for in Article 10.

3.   The Member State of identification shall without delay inform by electronic means the competent authorities of the other Members States if a non-established taxable person is excluded from the identification register.

Article 9c

1.   The return with the details set out in the second subparagraph of Article 26c(B)(5) of Directive 77/388/EEC is to be submitted in an electronic manner. The technical details, including a common electronic message, shall be

determined in accordance with the procedure provided for in Article 10.

2.   The Member State of identification shall transmit this information by electronic means to the competent authority of the Member State concerned at the latest 10 days after the end of the month that the return was received. Member States which have required the tax return to be made in a national currency other than euro shall convert the amounts into euro using the exchange rate valid for the last date of the reporting period. The exchange shall be done following the exchange rates published by the European Central Bank for that day, or, if there is no publication on that day, on the next day of publication. The technical details by which this information is to be transmitted shall be determined in accordance with the procedure provided for in Article 10.

3.   The Member State of identification shall transmit by electronic means to the Member State of consumption the information needed to link each payment with a relevant quarterly tax return.

Article 9d

The provisions in Article 4(1) shall apply also to information collected by the Member State of identification in accordance with Article 26c(B)(2) and (5) of Directive 77/388/EEC.

Article 9e

The Member State of identification shall ensure that the amount the non-established taxable person has paid is transferred to the bank account denominated in euro, which has been designated by the Member State of consumption to which the payment is due. Member States which required the payments in a national currency other than euro shall convert the amounts into euro using the exchange rate valid for the last date of the reporting period. The exchange shall be done following the exchange rates published by the European Central Bank for that day, or, if there is no publication on that day, on the next day of publication. The transfer shall take place at the latest 10 days after the end of the month that the payment was received.

If the non-established taxable person does not pay the total tax due, the Member State of identification shall ensure that the payment is transferred to the Member States of consumption in proportion to the tax due in each Member State. The Member State of identification shall inform by electronic means the competent authorities of the Member States of consumption thereof.

Article 9f

1.   Member States shall notify by electronic means the competent authorities of the other Member States of the relevant bank account numbers for receiving payments according to Article 9e.

2.   Member States shall without delay notify by electronic means the competent authorities of the other Member States and the Commission of changes in the standard tax rate.';

15.5.2002 | EN | Official Journal of the European Communities | L 128/3

5. in Article 13 the present text shall be renumbered as paragraph 2 and a new paragraph 1 shall be inserted as follows:

'1. The Commission and the Member States shall ensure that such existing or new communication and information exchange systems which are necessary to provide for the exchanges of information described in Articles 9b and 9c are operational by the date specified in Article 3(1) of Directive 2002/38/EC. The Commission will be responsible for whatever development of the common communication network/common system interface (CCN/CSI) is necessary to permit the exchange of this information between Member States. Member States will be responsible for whatever development of their systems is necessary to permit this information to be exchanged using the CCN/CSI.'

Article 2

Article 1 shall apply for a period provided for in Article 4 of Directive 2002/38/EC.

No exchange of information under this Regulation shall take place before 1 July 2003.

Article 3

This Regulation shall enter into force on the seventh day following its publication in the *Official Journal of the European Communities.*

This Regulation shall be binding in its entirety and directly applicable in all Member States.

Done at Brussels, 7 May 2002.

For the Council
The President
R. DE RATO Y FIGAREDO

Appendix 10

Directive 97/7/EC of the European Parliament and the Council of the 20th May 1997

THE EUROPEAN PARLIAMENT AND THE COUNCIL OF THE EUROPEAN UNION,
Having regard to the Treaty establishing the European Community, and in particular Article 100a thereof,
Having regard to the proposal from the Commission (1),
Having regard to the opinion of the Economic and Social Committee (2),
Acting in accordance with the procedure laid down in Article 189b of the Treaty (3), in the light of the joint text approved by the Conciliation Committee on 27 November 1996,
(1) Whereas, in connection with the attainment of the aims of the internal market, measures must be taken for the gradual consolidation of that market;
(2) Whereas the free movement of goods and services affects not only the business sector but also private individuals; whereas it means that consumers should be able to have access to the goods and services of another Member State on the same terms as the population of that State;
(3) Whereas, for consumers, cross-border distance selling could be one of the main tangible results of the completion of the internal market, as noted, inter alia, in the communication from the Commission to the Council entitled 'Towards a single market in distribution`; whereas it is essential to the smooth operation of the internal market for consumers to be able to have dealings with a business outside their country, even if it has a subsidiary in the consumer's country of residence;
(4) Whereas the introduction of new technologies is increasing the number of ways for consumers to obtain information about offers anywhere in the Community and to place orders; whereas some Member States have already taken different or diverging measures to protect consumers in respect of distance selling, which has had a detrimental effect on competition between businesses in the internal market; whereas it is therefore necessary to introduce at Community level a minimum set of common rules in this area;
(5) Whereas paragraphs 18 and 19 of the Annex to the Council resolution of 14 April 1975 on a preliminary programme of the European Economic Community for a consumer protection and information policy (4) point to the need to protect the purchasers of goods or services from demands for payment for unsolicited goods and from high-pressure selling methods;
(6) Whereas paragraph 33 of the communication from the Commission to the Council entitled 'A new impetus for consumer protection policy`, which was approved by the Council resolution of 23 June 1986 (5), states that the Commission will submit proposals regarding the use of new information technologies enabling consumers to place orders with suppliers from their homes;
(7) Whereas the Council resolution of 9 November 1989 on future priorities for relaunching consumer protection policy (6) calls upon the Commission to give priority to the areas referred to in the Annex to that resolution; whereas that Annex refers to new technologies involving teleshopping; whereas the Commission has responded to that resolution by adopting a three-year action plan for consumer protection policy in the European Economic Community (1990-1992); whereas that plan provides for the adoption of a Directive;
(8) Whereas the languages used for distance contracts are a matter for the Member States;

(9) Whereas contracts negotiated at a distance involve the use of one or more means of distance communication; whereas the various means of communication are used as part of an organized distance sales or service-provision scheme not involving the simultaneous presence of the supplier and the consumer; whereas the constant development of those means of communication does not allow an exhaustive list to be compiled but does require principles to be defined which are valid even for those which are not as yet in widespread use;

(10) Whereas the same transaction comprising successive operations or a series of separate operations over a period of time may give rise to different legal descriptions depending on the law of the Member States; whereas the provisions of this Directive cannot be applied differently according to the law of the Member States, subject to their recourse to Article 14; whereas, to that end, there is therefore reason to consider that there must at least be compliance with the provisions of this Directive at the time of the first of a series of successive operations or the first of a series of separate operations over a period of time which may be considered as forming a whole, whether that operation or series of operations are the subject of a single contract or successive, separate contracts;

(11) Whereas the use of means of distance communication must not lead to a reduction in the information provided to the consumer; whereas the information that is required to be sent to the consumer should therefore be determined, whatever the means of communication used; whereas the information supplied must also comply with the other relevant Community rules, in particular those in Council Directive 84/450/EEC of 10 September 1984 relating to the approximation of the laws, regulations and administrative provisions of the Member States concerning misleading advertising (7); whereas, if exceptions are made to the obligation to provide information, it is up to the consumer, on a discretionary basis, to request certain basic information such as the identity of the supplier, the main characteristics of the goods or services and their price;

(12) Whereas in the case of communication by telephone it is appropriate that the consumer receive enough information at the beginning of the conversation to decide whether or not to continue;

(13) Whereas information disseminated by certain electronic technologies is often ephemeral in nature insofar as it is not received on a permanent medium; whereas the consumer must therefore receive written notice in good time of the information necessary for proper performance of the contract;

(14) Whereas the consumer is not able actually to see the product or ascertain the nature of the service provided before concluding the contract; whereas provision should be made, unless otherwise specified in this Directive, for a right of withdrawal from the contract; whereas, if this right is to be more than formal, the costs, if any, borne by the consumer when exercising the right of withdrawal must be limited to the direct costs for returning the goods; whereas this right of withdrawal shall be without prejudice to the consumer's rights under national laws, with particular regard to the receipt of damaged products and services or of products and services not corresponding to the description given in the offer of such products or services; whereas it is for the Member States to determine the other conditions and arrangements following exercise of the right of withdrawal;

(15) Whereas it is also necessary to prescribe a time limit for performance of the contract if this is not specified at the time of ordering;

(16) Whereas the promotional technique involving the dispatch of a product or the provision of a service to the consumer in return for payment without a prior request from, or the explicit agreement of, the consumer cannot be permitted, unless a substitute product or service is

involved;

(17) Whereas the principles set out in Articles 8 and 10 of the European Convention for the Protection of Human Rights and Fundamental Freedoms of 4 November 1950 apply; whereas the consumer's right to privacy, particularly as regards freedom from certain particularly intrusive means of communication, should be recognized; whereas specific limits on the use of such means should therefore be stipulated; whereas Member States should take appropriate measures to protect effectively those consumers, who do not wish to be contacted through certain means of communication, against such contacts, without prejudice to the particular safeguards available to the consumer under Community legislation concerning the protection of personal data and privacy;

(18) Whereas it is important for the minimum binding rules contained in this Directive to be supplemented where appropriate by voluntary arrangements among the traders concerned, in line with Commission recommendation 92/295/EEC of 7 April 1992 on codes of practice for the protection of consumers in respect of contracts negotiated at a distance (8);

(19) Whereas in the interest of optimum consumer protection it is important for consumers to be satisfactorily informed of the provisions of this Directive and of codes of practice that may exist in this field;

(20) Whereas non-compliance with this Directive may harm not only consumers but also competitors; whereas provisions may therefore be laid down enabling public bodies or their representatives, or consumer organizations which, under national legislation, have a legitimate interest in consumer protection, or professional organizations which have a legitimate interest in taking action, to monitor the application thereof;

(21) Whereas it is important, with a view to consumer protection, to address the question of cross-border complaints as soon as this is feasible; whereas the Commission published on 14 February 1996 a plan of action on consumer access to justice and the settlement of consumer disputes in the internal market; whereas that plan of action includes specific initiatives to promote out-of-court procedures; whereas objective criteria (Annex II) are suggested to ensure the reliability of those procedures and provision is made for the use of standardized claims forms (Annex III);

(22) Whereas in the use of new technologies the consumer is not in control of the means of communication used; whereas it is therefore necessary to provide that the burden of proof may be on the supplier;

(23) Whereas there is a risk that, in certain cases, the consumer may be deprived of protection under this Directive through the designation of the law of a non-member country as the law applicable to the contract; whereas provisions should therefore be included in this Directive to avert that risk;

(24) Whereas a Member State may ban, in the general interest, the marketing on its territory of certain goods and services through distance contracts; whereas that ban must comply with Community rules; whereas there is already provision for such bans, notably with regard to medicinal products, under Council Directive 89/552/EEC of 3 October 1989 on the coordination of certain provisions laid down by law, regulation or administrative action in Member States concerning the pursuit of television broadcasting activities (9) and Council Directive 92/28/EEC of 31 March 1992 on the advertising of medicinal products for human use (10),

HAVE ADOPTED THIS DIRECTIVE:

Article 1
Object
The object of this Directive is to approximate the laws, regulations and administrative provisions of the Member States concerning distance contracts between consumers and suppliers.

Article 2
Definitions
For the purposes of this Directive:
(1) 'distance contract` means any contract concerning goods or services concluded between a supplier and a consumer under an organized distance sales or service-provision scheme run by the supplier, who, for the purpose of the contract, makes exclusive use of one or more means of distance communication up to and including the moment at which the contract is concluded;
(2) 'consumer` means any natural person who, in contracts covered by this Directive, is acting for purposes which are outside his trade, business or profession;
(3) 'supplier` means any natural or legal person who, in contracts covered by this Directive, is acting in his commercial or professional capacity;
(4) 'means of distance communication` means any means which, without the simultaneous physical presence of the supplier and the consumer, may be used for the conclusion of a contract between those parties. An indicative list of the means covered by this Directive is contained in Annex I;
(5) 'operator of a means of communication` means any public or private natural or legal person whose trade, business or profession involves making one or more means of distance communication available to suppliers.

Article 3
Exemptions
1. This Directive shall not apply to contracts:
- relating to financial services, a non-exhaustive list of which is given in Annex II,
- concluded by means of automatic vending machines or automated commercial premises,
- concluded with telecommunications operators through the use of public payphones,
- concluded for the construction and sale of immovable property or relating to other immovable property rights, except for rental,
- concluded at an auction.
2. Articles 4, 5, 6 and 7 (1) shall not apply:
- to contracts for the supply of foodstuffs, beverages or other goods intended for everyday consumption supplied to the home of the consumer, to his residence or to his workplace by regular roundsmen,
- to contracts for the provision of accommodation, transport, catering or leisure services, where the supplier undertakes, when the contract is concluded, to provide these services on a specific date or within a specific period; exceptionally, in the case of outdoor leisure events, the supplier can reserve the right not to apply Article 7 (2) in specific circumstances.

Article 4
Prior information
1. In good time prior to the conclusion of any distance contract, the consumer shall be provided with the following information:

(a) the identity of the supplier and, in the case of contracts requiring payment in advance, his address;
(b) the main characteristics of the goods or services;
(c) the price of the goods or services including all taxes;
(d) delivery costs, where appropriate;
(e) the arrangements for payment, delivery or performance;
(f) the existence of a right of withdrawal, except in the cases referred to in Article 6 (3);
(g) the cost of using the means of distance communication, where it is calculated other than at the basic rate;
(h) the period for which the offer or the price remains valid;
(i) where appropriate, the minimum duration of the contract in the case of contracts for the supply of products or services to be performed permanently or recurrently.
2. The information referred to in paragraph 1, the commercial purpose of which must be made clear, shall be provided in a clear and comprehensible manner in any way appropriate to the means of distance communication used, with due regard, in particular, to the principles of good faith in commercial transactions, and the principles governing the protection of those who are unable, pursuant to the legislation of the Member States, to give their consent, such as minors.
3. Moreover, in the case of telephone communications, the identity of the supplier and the commercial purpose of the call shall be made explicitly clear at the beginning of any conversation with the consumer.

Article 5
Written confirmation of information
1. The consumer must receive written confirmation or confirmation in another durable medium available and accessible to him of the information referred to in Article 4 (1) (a) to (f), in good time during the performance of the contract, and at the latest at the time of delivery where goods not for delivery to third parties are concerned, unless the information has already been given to the consumer prior to conclusion of the contract in writing or on another durable medium available and accessible to him.
In any event the following must be provided:
- written information on the conditions and procedures for exercising the right of withdrawal, within the meaning of Article 6, including the cases referred to in the first indent of Article 6 (3),
- the geographical address of the place of business of the supplier to which the consumer may address any complaints,
- information on after-sales services and guarantees which exist,
- the conclusion for cancelling the contract, where it is of unspecified duration or a duration exceeding one year.
2. Paragraph 1 shall not apply to services which are performed through the use of a means of distance communication, where they are supplied on only one occasion and are invoiced by the operator of the means of distance communication. Nevertheless, the consumer must in all cases be able to obtain the geographical address of the place of business of the supplier to which he may address any complaints.

Article 6
Right of withdrawal

1. For any distance contract the consumer shall have a period of at least seven working days in which to withdraw from the contract without penalty and without giving any reason. The only charge that may be made to the consumer because of the exercise of his right of withdrawal is the direct cost of returning the goods.

The period for exercise of this right shall begin:

- in the case of goods, from the day of receipt by the consumer where the obligations laid down in Article 5 have been fulfilled,

- in the case of services, from the day of conclusion of the contract or from the day on which the obligations laid down in Article 5 were fulfilled if they are fulfilled after conclusion of the contract, provided that this period does not exceed the three-month period referred to in the following subparagraph.

If the supplier has failed to fulfil the obligations laid down in Article 5, the period shall be three months. The period shall begin:

- in the case of goods, from the day of receipt by the consumer,

- in the case of services, from the day of conclusion of the contract.

If the information referred to in Article 5 is supplied within this three-month period, the seven working day period referred to in the first subparagraph shall begin as from that moment.

2. Where the right of withdrawal has been exercised by the consumer pursuant to this Article, the supplier shall be obliged to reimburse the sums paid by the consumer free of charge. The only charge that may be made to the consumer because of the exercise of his right of withdrawal is the direct cost of returning the goods. Such reimbursement must be carried out as soon as possible and in any case within 30 days.

3. Unless the parties have agreed otherwise, the consumer may not exercise the right of withdrawal provided for in paragraph 1 in respect of contracts:

- for the provision of services if performance has begun, with the consumer's agreement, before the end of the seven working day period referred to in paragraph 1,

- for the supply of goods or services the price of which is dependent on fluctuations in the financial market which cannot be controlled by the supplier,

- for the supply of goods made to the consumer's specifications or clearly personalized or which, by reason of their nature, cannot be returned or are liable to deteriorate or expire rapidly,

- for the supply of audio or video recordings or computer software which were unsealed by the consumer,

- for the supply of newspapers, periodicals and magazines,

- for gaming and lottery services.

4. The Member States shall make provision in their legislation to ensure that:

- if the price of goods or services is fully or partly covered by credit granted by the supplier, or

- if that price is fully or partly covered by credit granted to the consumer by a third party on the basis of an agreement between the third party and the supplier,

the credit agreement shall be cancelled, without any penalty, if the consumer exercises his right to withdraw from the contract in accordance with paragraph 1.

Member States shall determine the detailed rules for cancellation of the credit agreement.

Article 7

Performance

1. Unless the parties have agreed otherwise, the supplier must execute the order within a maximum of 30 days from the day following that on which the consumer forwarded his order to the supplier.

2. Where a supplier fails to perform his side of the contract on the grounds that the goods or services ordered are unavailable, the consumer must be informed of this situation and must be able to obtain a refund of any sums he has paid as soon as possible and in any case within 30 days.

3. Nevertheless, Member States may lay down that the supplier may provide the consumer with goods or services of equivalent quality and price provided that this possibility was provided for prior to the conclusion of the contract or in the contract. The consumer shall be informed of this possibility in a clear and comprehensible manner. The cost of returning the goods following exercise of the right of withdrawal shall, in this case, be borne by the supplier, and the consumer must be informed of this. In such cases the supply of goods or services may not be deemed to constitute inertia selling within the meaning of Article 9.

Article 8
Payment by card
Member States shall ensure that appropriate measures exist to allow a consumer:
- to request cancellation of a payment where fraudulent use has been made of his payment card in connection with distance contracts covered by this Directive,
- in the event of fraudulent use, to be recredited with the sums paid or have them returned.

Article 9
Inertia selling
Member States shall take the measures necessary to:
- prohibit the supply of goods or services to a consumer without their being ordered by the consumer beforehand, where such supply involves a demand for payment,
- exempt the consumer from the provision of any consideration in cases of unsolicited supply, the absence of a response not constituting consent.

Article 10
Restrictions on the use of certain means of distance communication
1. Use by a supplier of the following means requires the prior consent of the consumer:
- automated calling system without human intervention (automatic calling machine),
- facsimile machine (fax).
2. Member States shall ensure that means of distance communication, other than those referred to in paragraph 1, which allow individual communications may be used only where there is no clear objection from the consumer.

Article 11
Judicial or administrative redress
1. Member States shall ensure that adequate and effective means exist to ensure compliance with this Directive in the interests of consumers.
2. The means referred to in paragraph 1 shall include provisions whereby one or more of the following bodies, as determined by national law, may take action under national law before the courts or before the competent administrative bodies to ensure that the national provisions for the implementation of this Directive are applied:

(a) public bodies or their representatives;

(b) consumer organizations having a legitimate interest in protecting consumers;

(c) professional organizations having a legitimate interest in acting.

3. (a) Member States may stipulate that the burden of proof concerning the existence of prior information, written confirmation, compliance with time-limits or consumer consent can be placed on the supplier.

(b) Member States shall take the measures needed to ensure that suppliers and operators of means of communication, where they are able to do so, cease practices which do not comply with measures adopted pursuant to this Directive.

4. Member States may provide for voluntary supervision by self-regulatory bodies of compliance with the provisions of this Directive and recourse to such bodies for the settlement of disputes to be added to the means which Member States must provided to ensure compliance with the provisions of this Directive.

Article 12
Binding nature
1. The consumer may not waive the rights conferred on him by the transposition of this Directive into national law.

2. Member States shall take the measures needed to ensure that the consumer does not lose the protection granted by this Directive by virtue of the choice of the law of a non-member country as the law applicable to the contract if the latter has close connection with the territory of one or more Member States.

Article 13
Community rules
1. The provisions of this Directive shall apply insofar as there are no particular provisions in rules of Community law governing certain types of distance contracts in their entirety.

2. Where specific Community rules contain provisions governing only certain aspects of the supply of goods or provision of services, those provisions, rather than the provisions of this Directive, shall apply to these specific aspects of the distance contracts.

Article 14
Minimal clause
Member States may introduce or maintain, in the area covered by this Directive, more stringent provisions compatible with the Treaty, to ensure a higher level of consumer protection. Such provisions shall, where appropriate, include a ban, in the general interest, on the marketing of certain goods or services, particularly medicinal products, within their territory by means of distance contracts, with due regard for the Treaty.

Article 15
Implementation
1. Member States shall bring into force the laws, regulations and administrative provisions necessary to comply with this Directive no later than three years after it enters into force. They shall forthwith inform the Commission thereof.

2. When Member States adopt the measures referred to in paragraph 1, these shall contain a reference to this Directive or shall be accompanied by such reference on the occasion of their official publication. The procedure for such reference shall be laid down by Member States.

3. Member States shall communicate to the Commission the text of the provisions of national law which they adopt in the field governed by this Directive.

4. No later than four years after the entry into force of this Directive the Commission shall submit a report to the European Parliament and the Council on the implementation of this Directive, accompanied if appropriate by a proposal for the revision thereof.

Article 16
Consumer information
Member States shall take appropriate measures to inform the consumer of the national law transposing this Directive and shall encourage, where appropriate, professional organizations to inform consumers of their codes of practice.

Article 17
Complaints systems
The Commission shall study the feasibility of establishing effective means to deal with consumers' complaints in respect of distance selling. Within two years after the entry into force of this Directive the Commission shall submit a report to the European Parliament and the Council on the results of the studies, accompanied if appropriate by proposals.

Article 18
This Directive shall enter into force on the day of its publication in the *Official Journal of the European Communities*.

Article 19
This Directive is addressed to the Member States.

Done at Brussels, 20 May 1997.
For the European Parliament
The President
J.M. GIL-ROBLES
For the Council
The President
J. VAN AARTSEN

(1) OJ No C 156, 23. 6. 1992, p. 14 and OJ No C 308, 15. 11. 1993, p. 18.
(2) OJ No C 19, 25. 1. 1993, p. 111.
(3) Opinion of the European Parliament of 26 May 1993 (OJ No C 176, 28. 6. 1993, p. 95), Council common position of 29 June 1995 (OJ No C 288, 30. 10. 1995, p. 1) and Decision of the European Parliament of 13 December 1995 (OJ No C 17, 22. 1. 1996, p. 51). Decision of the European Parliament of 16 January 1997 and Council Decision of 20 January 1997.
(4) OJ No C 92, 25. 4. 1975, p. 1.
(5) OJ No C 167, 5. 7. 1986, p. 1.
(6) OJ No C 294, 22. 11. 1989, p. 1.

(7) OJ No L 250, 19. 9. 1984, p. 17.
(8) OJ No L 156, 10. 6. 1992, p. 21.
(9) OJ No L 298, 17. 10. 1989, p. 23.
(10) OJ No L 113, 30. 4. 1992, p. 13.

ANNEX I

Means of communication covered by Article 2 (4)
- *Unaddressed printed matter*
- *Addressed printed matter*
- *Standard letter*
- *Press advertising with order form*
- *Catalogue*
- *Telephone with human intervention*
- *Telephone without human intervention (automatic calling machine, audiotext)*
- *Radio*
- *Videophone (telephone with screen)*
- *Videotex (microcomputer and television screen) with keyboard or touch screen*
- *Electronic mail*
- *Facsimile machine (fax)*
- *Television (teleshopping).*

ANNEX II

Financial services within the meaning of Article 3 (1)
- *Investment services*
- *Insurance and reinsurance operations*
- *Banking services*
- *Operations relating to dealings in futures or options.*
Such services include in particular:
- *investment services referred to in the Annex to Directive 93/22/EEC (1); services of collective investment undertakings,*
- *services covered by the activities subject to mutual recognition referred to in the Annex to Directive 89/646/EEC (2);*
- *operations covered by the insurance and reinsurance activities referred to in:*
- *Article 1 of Directive 73/239/EEC (3),*
- *the Annex to Directive 79/267/EEC (4),*
- *Directive 64/225/EEC (5),*
- *Directives 92/49/EEC (6) and 92/96/EEC (7).*
(1) OJ No L 141, 11. 6. 1993, p. 27.
(2) OJ No L 386, 30. 12. 1989, p. 1. Directive as amended by Directive 92/30/EEC (OJ No L 110, 28. 4. 1992, p. 52).
(3) OJ No L 228, 16. 8. 1973, p. 3. Directive as last amended by Directive 92/49/EEC (OJ No L 228, 11. 8. 1992, p. 1).

*(4) OJ No L 63, 13. 3. 1979, p. 1. Directive as last amended by Directive 90/619/EEC (OJ No L
330, 29. 11. 1990, p. 50).*
(5) OJ No 56, 4. 4. 1964, p. 878/64. Directive as amended by the 1973 Act of Accession.
(6) OJ No L 228, 11. 8. 1992, p. 1.
(7) OJ No L 360, 9. 12. 1992, p. 1.

Statement by the Council and the Parliament re Article 6 (1)
*The Council and the Parliament note that the Commission will examine the possibility and
desirability of harmonizing the method of calculating the cooling-off period under existing
consumer-protection legislation, notably Directive 85/577/EEC of 20 December 1985 on the
protection of consumers in respect of contracts negotiated away from commercial establishments
('door-to-door sales') (1).*
(1) OJ No L 372, 31. 12. 1985, p. 31.

Statement by the Commission re Article 3 (1), first indent
*The Commission recognizes the importance of protecting consumers in respect of distance
contracts concerning financial services and has published a Green Paper entitled 'Financial
services: meeting consumers' expectations'. In the light of reactions to the Green Paper the
Commission will examine ways of incorporating consumer protection into the policy on financial
services and the possible legislative implications and, if need be, will submit appropriate
proposals.*

Appendix 11

DIRECTIVE 2002/65/EC OF THE EUROPEAN PARLIAMENT AND OF THE COUNCIL

of 23 September 2002

concerning the distance marketing of consumer financial services and amending Council Directive 90/619/EEC and Directives 97/7/EC and 98/27/EC

THE EUROPEAN PARLIAMENT AND THE COUNCIL OF THE EUROPEAN UNION,

Having regard to the Treaty establishing the European Community, and in particular Article 47(2), Article 55 and Article 95 thereof,

Having regard to the proposal from the Commission [1],

Having regard to the opinion of the Economic and Social Committee [2],

Acting in accordance with the procedure laid down in Article 251 of the Treaty [3],

Whereas:

(1) It is important, in the context of achieving the aims of the single market, to adopt measures designed to consolidate progressively this market and those measures must contribute to attaining a high level of consumer protection, in accordance with Articles 95 and 153 of the Treaty.

(2) Both for consumers and suppliers of financial services, the distance marketing of financial services will constitute one of the main tangible results of the completion of the internal market.

(3) Within the framework of the internal market, it is in the interest of consumers to have access without discrimination to the widest possible range of financial services available in the Community so that they can choose those that are best suited to their needs. In order to safeguard freedom of choice, which is an essential consumer right, a high degree of consumer protection is required in order to enhance consumer confidence in distance selling.

(4) It is essential to the smooth operation of the internal market for consumers to be able to negotiate and conclude contracts with a supplier established in other Member States, regardless of whether the supplier is also established in the Member State in which the consumer resides.

(5) Because of their intangible nature, financial services are particularly suited to distance selling and the establishment of a legal framework governing the distance marketing of financial services should increase consumer confidence in the use of new techniques for the distance marketing of financial services, such as electronic commerce.

(6) This Directive should be applied in conformity with the Treaty and with secondary law, including Directive 2000/31/EC [4] on electronic commerce, the latter being applicable solely to the transactions which it covers.

(7) This Directive aims to achieve the objectives set forth above without prejudice to Community or national law governing freedom to provide services or, where applicable, host Member State control and/or authorisation or supervision systems in the Member States where this is compatible with Community legislation.

(8) Moreover, this Directive, and in particular its provisions relating to information about any contractual clause on law applicable to the contract and/or on the competent court does not affect the applicability to the distance marketing of consumer financial services of Council Regulation (EC) No 44/2001 of 22 December 2000 on jurisdiction and the recognition and enforcement of judgements in civil and commercial matters [5] or of the 1980 Rome Convention on the law applicable to contractual obligations.

(9) The achievement of the objectives of the Financial Services Action Plan requires a higher level of consumer protection in certain areas. This implies a greater convergence, in particular, in non harmonised collective investment funds, rules of conduct applicable to investment services and consumer credits. Pending the achievement of the above convergence, a high level of consumer protection should be maintained.

(10) Directive 97/7/EC of the European Parliament and of the Council of 20 May 1997 on the protection of consumers in respect of distance contracts [6], lays down the main rules applicable to distance contracts for goods or services concluded between a supplier and a consumer. However, that Directive does not cover financial services.

[1] OJ C 385, 11.12.1998, p. 10 and OJ C 177 E, 27.6.2000, p. 21.
[2] OJ C 169, 16.6.1999, p. 43.
[3] Opinion of the European Parliament of 5 May 1999 (OJ C 279, 1.10.1999, p. 207), Council Common Position of 19 December 2001 (OJ C 58 E, 5.3.2002, p. 32) and Decision of the European Parliament of 14 May 2002 (not yet published in the Official Journal). Council Decision of 26 June 2002 (not yet published in the Official Journal).

[4] OJ L 178, 17.7.2000, p. 1.
[5] OJ L 12, 16.1.2001, p. 1.
[6] OJ L 144, 4.6.1997, p. 19.

(11) In the context of the analysis conducted by the Commission with a view to ascertaining the need for specific measures in the field of financial services, the Commission invited all the interested parties to transmit their comments, notably in connection with the preparation of its Green Paper entitled 'Financial Services — Meeting Consumers' Expectations'. The consultations in this context showed that there is a need to strengthen consumer protection in this area. The Commission therefore decided to present a specific proposal concerning the distance marketing of financial services.

(12) The adoption by the Member States of conflicting or different consumer protection rules governing the distance marketing of consumer financial services could impede the functioning of the internal market and competition between firms in the market. It is therefore necessary to enact common rules at Community level in this area, consistent with no reduction in overall consumer protection in the Member States.

(13) A high level of consumer protection should be guaranteed by this Directive, with a view to ensuring the free movement of financial services. Member States should not be able to adopt provisions other than those laid down in this Directive in the fields it harmonises, unless otherwise specifically indicated in it.

(14) This Directive covers all financial services liable to be provided at a distance. However, certain financial services are governed by specific provisions of Community legislation which continue to apply to those financial services. However, principles governing the distance marketing of such services should be laid down.

(15) Contracts negotiated at a distance involve the use of means of distance communication which are used as part of a distance sales or service-provision scheme not involving the simultaneous presence of the supplier and the consumer. The constant development of those means of communication requires principles to be defined that are valid even for those means which are not yet in widespread use. Therefore, distance contracts are those the offer, negotiation and conclusion of which are carried out at a distance.

(16) A single contract involving successive operations or separate operations of the same nature performed over time may be subject to different legal treatment in the different Member States, but it is important that this Directive be applied in the same way in all the Member States. To that end, it is appropriate that this Directive should be considered to apply to the first of a series of successive operations or separate operations of the same nature performed over time which may be considered as forming a whole, irrespective of whether that operation or series of operations is the subject of a single contract or several successive contracts.

(17) An 'initial service agreement' may be considered to be for example the opening of a bank account, acquiring a credit card, concluding a portfolio management contract, and 'operations' may be considered to be for example the deposit or withdrawal of funds to or from the bank account, payment by credit card, transactions made within the framework of a portfolio management contract. Adding new elements to an initial service agreement, such as a possibility to use an electronic payment instrument together with one's existing bank account, does not constitute an 'operation' but an additional contract to which this Directive applies. The subscription to new units of the same collective investment fund is considered to be one of 'successive operations of the same nature'.

(18) By covering a service-provision scheme organised by the financial services provider, this Directive aims to exclude from its scope services provided on a strictly occasional basis and outside a commercial structure dedicated to the conclusion of distance contracts.

(19) The supplier is the person providing services at a distance. This Directive should however also apply when one of the marketing stages involves an intermediary. Having regard to the nature and degree of that involvement, the pertinent provisions of this Directive should apply to such an intermediary, irrespective of his or her legal status.

(20) Durable mediums include in particular floppy discs, CD-ROMs, DVDs and the hard drive of the consumer's computer on which the electronic mail is stored, but they do not include Internet websites unless they fulfil the criteria contained in the definition of a durable medium.

(21) The use of means of distance communications should not lead to an unwarranted restriction on the information provided to the client. In the interests of transparency this Directive lays down the requirements needed to ensure that an appropriate level of information is provided to the consumer both before and after conclusion of the contract. The consumer should receive, before conclusion of the contract, the prior information needed so as to properly appraise the financial service offered to him and hence make a well-informed choice. The supplier should specify how long his offer applies as it stands.

(22) Information items listed in this Directive cover information of a general nature applicable to all kinds of financial services. Other information requirements concerning a given financial service, such as the coverage of an insurance policy, are not solely specified in this Directive. This kind of information should be provided in accordance, where applicable, with relevant Community legislation or national legislation in conformity with Community law.

(23) With a view to optimum protection of the consumer, it is important that the consumer is adequately informed of the provisions of this Directive and of any codes of conduct existing in this area and that he has a right of withdrawal.

(24) When the right of withdrawal does not apply because the consumer has expressly requested the performance of a contract, the supplier should inform the consumer of this fact.

(25) Consumers should be protected against unsolicited services. Consumers should be exempt from any obligation in the case of unsolicited services, the absence of a reply not being construed as signifying consent on their part. However, this rule should be without prejudice to the tacit renewal of contracts validly concluded between the parties whenever the law of the Member States permits such tacit renewal.

(26) Member States should take appropriate measures to protect effectively consumers who do not wish to be contacted through certain means of communication or at certain times. This Directive should be without prejudice to the particular safeguards available to consumers under Community legislation concerning the protection of personal data and privacy.

(27) With a view to protecting consumers, there is a need for suitable and effective complaint and redress procedures in the Member States with a view to settling potential disputes between suppliers and consumers, by using, where appropriate, existing procedures.

(28) Member States should encourage public or private bodies established with a view to settling disputes out of court to cooperate in resolving cross-border disputes. Such cooperation could in particular entail allowing consumers to submit to extra-judicial bodies in the Member State of their residence complaints concerning suppliers established in other Member States. The establishment of FIN-NET offers increased assistance to consumers when using cross-border services.

(29) This Directive is without prejudice to extension by Member States, in accordance with Community law, of the protection provided by this Directive to non-profit organisations and persons making use of financial services in order to become entrepreneurs.

(30) This Directive should also cover cases where the national legislation includes the concept of a consumer making a binding contractual statement.

(31) The provisions in this Directive on the supplier's choice of language should be without prejudice to provisions of national legislation, adopted in conformity with Community law governing the choice of language.

(32) The Community and the Member States have entered into commitments in the context of the General Agreement on Trade in Services (GATS) concerning the possibility for consumers to purchase banking and investment services abroad. The GATS entitles Member States to adopt measures for prudential reasons, including measures to protect investors, depositors, policy-holders and persons to whom a financial service is owed by the supplier of the financial service. Such measures should not impose restrictions going beyond what is required to ensure the protection of consumers.

(33) In view of the adoption of this Directive, the scope of Directive 97/7/EC and Directive 98/27/EC of the European Parliament and of the Council of 19 May 1998 on injunctions for the protection of consumers' interests (¹) and the scope of the cancellation period in Council Directive 90/619/EEC of 8 November 1990 on the coordination of laws, regulations and administrative provisions relating to direct life assurance, laying down provisions to facilitate the effective exercise of freedom to provide services (²) should be adapted.

(34) Since the objectives of this Directive, namely the establishment of common rules on the distance marketing of consumer financial services cannot be sufficiently achieved by the Member States and can therefore be better achieved at Community level, the Community may adopt measures, in accordance with the principles of subsidiarity as set out in Article 5 of the Treaty. In accordance with the principle of proportionality, as set out in that Article, this Directive does not go beyond what is necessary to achieve that objective,

HAVE ADOPTED THIS DIRECTIVE:

Article 1

Object and scope

1. The object of this Directive is to approximate the laws, regulations and administrative provisions of the Member States concerning the distance marketing of consumer financial services.

2. In the case of contracts for financial services comprising an initial service agreement followed by successive operations or a series of separate operations of the same nature performed over time, the provisions of this Directive shall apply only to the initial agreement.

(¹) OJ L 166, 11.6.1998, p. 51. Directive as last amended by Directive 2000/31/EC (OJ L 178, 17.7.2001, p. 1).
(²) OJ L 330, 29.11.1990, p. 50. Directive as last amended by Directive 92/96/EEC (OJ L 360, 9.12.1992, p. 1).

9.10.2002   EN   Official Journal of the European Communities   L 271/19

In case there is no initial service agreement but the successive operations or the separate operations of the same nature performed over time are performed between the same contractual parties, Articles 3 and 4 apply only when the first operation is performed. Where, however, no operation of the same nature is performed for more than one year, the next operation will be deemed to be the first in a new series of operations and, accordingly, Articles 3 and 4 shall apply.

Article 2

Definitions

For the purposes of this Directive:

(a) 'distance contract' means any contract concerning financial services concluded between a supplier and a consumer under an organised distance sales or service-provision scheme run by the supplier, who, for the purpose of that contract, makes exclusive use of one or more means of distance communication up to and including the time at which the contract is concluded;

(b) 'financial service' means any service of a banking, credit, insurance, personal pension, investment or payment nature;

(c) 'supplier' means any natural or legal person, public or private, who, acting in his commercial or professional capacity, is the contractual provider of services subject to distance contracts;

(d) 'consumer' means any natural person who, in distance contracts covered by this Directive, is acting for purposes which are outside his trade, business or profession;

(e) 'means of distance communication' refers to any means which, without the simultaneous physical presence of the supplier and the consumer, may be used for the distance marketing of a service between those parties;

(f) 'durable medium' means any instrument which enables the consumer to store information addressed personally to him in a way accessible for future reference for a period of time adequate for the purposes of the information and which allows the unchanged reproduction of the information stored;

(g) 'operator or supplier of a means of distance communication' means any public or private, natural or legal person whose trade, business or profession involves making one or more means of distance communication available to suppliers.

Article 3

Information to the consumer prior to the conclusion of the distance contract

1.   In good time before the consumer is bound by any distance contract or offer, he shall be provided with the following information concerning:

(1) the supplier

(a) the identity and the main business of the supplier, the geographical address at which the supplier is established and any other geographical address relevant for the customer's relations with the supplier;

(b) the identity of the representative of the supplier established in the consumer's Member State of residence and the geographical address relevant for the customer's relations with the representative, if such a representative exists;

(c) when the consumer's dealings are with any professional other than the supplier, the identity of this professional, the capacity in which he is acting vis-à-vis the consumer, and the geographical address relevant for the customer's relations with this professional;

(d) where the supplier is registered in a trade or similar public register, the trade register in which the supplier is entered and his registration number or an equivalent means of identification in that register;

(e) where the supplier's activity is subject to an authorisation scheme, the particulars of the relevant supervisory authority;

(2) the financial service

(a) a description of the main characteristics of the financial service;

(b) the total price to be paid by the consumer to the supplier for the financial service, including all related fees, charges and expenses, and all taxes paid via the supplier or, when an exact price cannot be indicated, the basis for the calculation of the price enabling the consumer to verify it;

(c) where relevant notice indicating that the financial service is related to instruments involving special risks related to their specific features or the operations to be executed or whose price depends on fluctuations in the financial markets outside the supplier's control and that historical performances are no indicators for future performances;

(d) notice of the possibility that other taxes and/or costs may exist that are not paid via the supplier or imposed by him;

(e) any limitations of the period for which the information provided is valid;

(f) the arrangements for payment and for performance;

(g) any specific additional cost for the consumer of using the means of distance communication, if such additional cost is charged;

(3) the distance contract

(a) the existence or absence of a right of withdrawal in accordance with Article 6 and, where the right of withdrawal exists, its duration and the conditions for exercising it, including information on the amount which the consumer may be required to pay on the basis of Article 7(1), as well as the consequences of non-exercise of that right;

L 271/20   EN   Official Journal of the European Communities   9.10.2002

(b) the minimum duration of the distance contract in the case of financial services to be performed permanently or recurrently;

(c) information on any rights the parties may have to terminate the contract early or unilaterally by virtue of the terms of the distance contract, including any penalties imposed by the contract in such cases;

(d) practical instructions for exercising the right of withdrawal indicating, *inter alia*, the address to which the notification of a withdrawal should be sent;

(e) the Member State or States whose laws are taken by the supplier as a basis for the establishment of relations with the consumer prior to the conclusion of the distance contract;

(f) any contractual clause on law applicable to the distance contract and/or on competent court;

(g) in which language, or languages, the contractual terms and conditions, and the prior information referred to in this Article, are supplied, and furthermore in which language, or languages, the supplier, with the agreement of the consumer, undertakes to communicate during the duration of this distance contract;

(4) redress

(a) whether or not there is an out-of-court complaint and redress mechanism for the consumer that is party to the distance contract and, if so, the methods for having access to it;

(b) the existence of guarantee funds or other compensation arrangements, not covered by Directive 94/19/EC of the European Parliament and of the Council of 30 May 1994 on deposit guarantee schemes (¹) and Directive 97/9/EC of the European Parliament and of the Council of 3 March 1997 on investor compensation schemes (²).

2.   The information referred to in paragraph 1, the commercial purpose of which must be made clear, shall be provided in a clear and comprehensible manner in any way appropriate to the means of distance communication used, with due regard, in particular, to the principles of good faith in commercial transactions, and the principles governing the protection of those who are unable, pursuant to the legislation of the Member States, to give their consent, such as minors.

3.   In the case of voice telephony communications

(a) the identity of the supplier and the commercial purpose of the call initiated by the supplier shall be made explicitly clear at the beginning of any conversation with the consumer;

(b) subject to the explicit consent of the consumer only the following information needs to be given:

— the identity of the person in contact with the consumer and his link with the supplier,

— a description of the main characteristics of the financial service,

(¹) OJ L 135, 31.5.1994, p. 5.
(²) OJ L 84, 26.3.1997, p. 22.

— the total price to be paid by the consumer to the supplier for the financial service including all taxes paid via the supplier or, when an exact price cannot be indicated, the basis for the calculation of the price enabling the consumer to verify it,

— notice of the possibility that other taxes and/or costs may exist that are not paid via the supplier or imposed by him,

— the existence or absence of a right of withdrawal in accordance with Article 6 and, where the right of withdrawal exists, its duration and the conditions for exercising it, including information on the amount which the consumer may be required to pay on the basis of Article 7(1).

The supplier shall inform the consumer that other information is available on request and of what nature this information is. In any case the supplier shall provide the full information when he fulfils his obligations under Article 5.

4.   Information on contractual obligations, to be communicated to the consumer during the pre-contractual phase, shall be in conformity with the contractual obligations which would result from the law presumed to be applicable to the distance contract if the latter were concluded.

Article 4

Additional information requirements

1.   Where there are provisions in the Community legislation governing financial services which contain prior information requirements additional to those listed in Article 3(1), these requirements shall continue to apply.

2.   Pending further harmonisation, Member States may maintain or introduce more stringent provisions on prior information requirements when the provisions are in conformity with Community law.

3.   Member States shall communicate to the Commission national provisions on prior information requirements under paragraphs 1 and 2 of this Article when these requirements are additional to those listed in Article 3(1). The Commission shall take account of the communicated national provisions when drawing up the report referred to in Article 20(2).

4.   The Commission shall, with a view to creating a high level of transparency by all appropriate means, ensure that information, on the national provisions communicated to it, is made available to consumers and suppliers.

Article 5

Communication of the contractual terms and conditions and of the prior information

1.   The supplier shall communicate to the consumer all the contractual terms and conditions and the information referred to in Article 3(1) and Article 4 on paper or on another durable medium available and accessible to the consumer in good time before the consumer is bound by any distance contract or offer.

2.　The supplier shall fulfil his obligation under paragraph 1 immediately after the conclusion of the contract, if the contract has been concluded at the consumer's request using a means of distance communication which does not enable providing the contractual terms and conditions and the information in conformity with paragraph 1.

3.　At any time during the contractual relationship the consumer is entitled, at his request, to receive the contractual terms and conditions on paper. In addition, the consumer is entitled to change the means of distance communication used, unless this is incompatible with the contract concluded or the nature of the financial service provided.

Article 6

Right of withdrawal

1.　The Member States shall ensure that the consumer shall have a period of 14 calendar days to withdraw from the contract without penalty and without giving any reason. However, this period shall be extended to 30 calendar days in distance contracts relating to life insurance covered by Directive 90/619/EEC and personal pension operations.

The period for withdrawal shall begin:

— either from the day of the conclusion of the distance contract, except in respect of the said life assurance, where the time limit will begin from the time when the consumer is informed that the distance contract has been concluded, or

— from the day on which the consumer receives the contractual terms and conditions and the information in accordance with Article 5(1) or (2), if that is later than the date referred to in the first indent.

Member States, in addition to the right of withdrawal, may provide that the enforceability of contracts relating to investment services is suspended for the same period provided for in this paragraph.

2.　The right of withdrawal shall not apply to:

(a) financial services whose price depends on fluctuations in the financial market outside the suppliers control, which may occur during the withdrawal period, such as services related to:

— foreign exchange,

— money market instruments,

— transferable securities,

— units in collective investment undertakings,

— financial-futures contracts, including equivalent cash-settled instruments,

— forward interest-rate agreements (FRAs),

— interest-rate, currency and equity swaps,

— options to acquire or dispose of any instruments referred to in this point including equivalent cash-settled instruments. This category includes in particular options on currency and on interest rates;

(b) travel and baggage insurance policies or similar short-term insurance policies of less than one month's duration;

(c) contracts whose performance has been fully completed by both parties at the consumer's express request before the consumer exercises his right of withdrawal.

3.　Member States may provide that the right of withdrawal shall not apply to:

(a) any credit intended primarily for the purpose of acquiring or retaining property rights in land or in an existing or projected building, or for the purpose of renovating or improving a building, or

(b) any credit secured either by mortgage on immovable property or by a right related to immovable property, or

(c) declarations by consumers using the services of an official, provided that the official confirms that the consumer is guaranteed the rights under Article 5(1).

This paragraph shall be without prejudice to the right to a reflection time to the benefit of the consumers that are resident in those Member States where it exists, at the time of the adoption of this Directive.

4.　Member States making use of the possibility set out in paragraph 3 shall communicate it to the Commission.

5.　The Commission shall make available the information communicated by Member States to the European Parliament and the Council and shall ensure that it is also available to consumers and suppliers who request it.

6.　If the consumer exercises his right of withdrawal he shall, before the expiry of the relevant deadline, notify this following the practical instructions given to him in accordance with Article 3(1)(3)(d) by means which can be proved in accordance with national law. The deadline shall be deemed to have been observed if the notification, if it is on paper or on another durable medium available and accessible to the recipient, is dispatched before the deadline expires.

7.　This Article does not apply to credit agreements cancelled under the conditions of Article 6(4) of Directive 97/7/EC or Article 7 of Directive 94/47/EC of the European Parliament and of the Council of 26 October 1994 on the protection of purchasers in respect of certain aspects of contracts relating to the purchase of the right to use immovable properties on a timeshare basis (¹).

(¹) OJ L 280, 29.10.1994, p. 83.

L 271/22   EN   Official Journal of the European Communities   9.10.2002

If to a distance contract of a given financial service another distance contract has been attached concerning services provided by the supplier or by a third party on the basis of an agreement between the third party and the supplier, this additional distance contract shall be cancelled, without any penalty, if the consumer exercises his right of withdrawal as provided for in Article 6(1).

8.   The provisions of this Article are without prejudice to the Member States' laws and regulations governing the cancellation or termination or non-enforceability of a distance contract or the right of a consumer to fulfil his contractual obligations before the time fixed in the distance contract. This applies irrespective of the conditions for and the legal effects of the winding-up of the contract.

Article 7

Payment of the service provided before withdrawal

1.   When the consumer exercises his right of withdrawal under Article 6(1) he may only be required to pay, without any undue delay, for the service actually provided by the supplier in accordance with the contract. The performance of the contract may only begin after the consumer has given his approval. The amount payable shall not:

— exceed an amount which is in proportion to the extent of the service already provided in comparison with the full coverage of the contract,

— in any case be such that it could be construed as a penalty.

2.   Member States may provide that the consumer cannot be required to pay any amount when withdrawing from an insurance contract.

3.   The supplier may not require the consumer to pay any amount on the basis of paragraph 1 unless he can prove that the consumer was duly informed about the amount payable, in conformity with Article 3(1)(3)(a). However, in no case may he require such payment if he has commenced the performance of the contract before the expiry of the withdrawal period provided for in Article 6(1) without the consumer's prior request.

4.   The supplier shall, without any undue delay and no later than within 30 calendar days, return to the consumer any sums he has received from him in accordance with the distance contract, except for the amount referred to in paragraph 1. This period shall begin from the day on which the supplier receives the notification of withdrawal.

5.   The consumer shall return to the supplier any sums and/or property he has received from the supplier without any undue delay and no later than within 30 calendar days. This period shall begin from the day on which the consumer dispatches the notification of withdrawal.

Article 8

Payment by card

Member States shall ensure that appropriate measures exist to allow a consumer:

— to request cancellation of a payment where fraudulent use has been made of his payment card in connection with distance contracts,

— in the event of such fraudulent use, to be re-credited with the sum paid or have them returned.

Article 9

Unsolicited services

Without prejudice to Member States provisions on the tacit renewal of distance contracts, when such rules permit tacit renewal, Member States shall take the necessary measures to:

— prohibit the supply of financial services to a consumer without a prior request on his part, when this supply includes a request for immediate or deferred payment,

— exempt the consumer from any obligation in the event of unsolicited supplies, the absence of a reply not constituting consent.

Article 10

Unsolicited communications

1.   The use by a supplier of the following distance communication techniques shall require the consumer's prior consent:

(a) automated calling systems without human intervention (automatic calling machines);

(b) fax machines.

2.   Member States shall ensure that means of distance communication other than those referred to in paragraph 1, when they allow individual communications:

(a) shall not be authorised unless the consent of the consumers concerned has been obtained, or

(b) may only be used if the consumer has not expressed his manifest objection.

3.   The measures referred to in paragraphs 1 and 2 shall not entail costs for consumers.

Article 11

Sanctions

Member States shall provide for appropriate sanctions in the event of the supplier's failure to comply with national provisions adopted pursuant to this Directive.

They may provide for this purpose in particular that the consumer may cancel the contract at any time, free of charge and without penalty.

These sanctions must be effective, proportional and dissuasive.

Article 12

Imperative nature of this Directive's provisions

1. Consumers may not waive the rights conferred on them by this Directive.

2. Member States shall take the measures needed to ensure that the consumer does not lose the protection granted by this Directive by virtue of the choice of the law of a non-member country as the law applicable to the contract, if this contract has a close link with the territory of one or more Member States.

Article 13

Judicial and administrative redress

1. Member States shall ensure that adequate and effective means exist to ensure compliance with this Directive in the interests of consumers.

2. The means referred to in paragraph 1 shall include provisions whereby one or more of the following bodies, as determined by national law, may take action in accordance with national law before the courts or competent administrative bodies to ensure that the national provisions for the implementation of this Directive are applied:

(a) public bodies or their representatives;

(b) consumer organisations having a legitimate interest in protecting consumers;

(c) professional organisations having a legitimate interest in acting.

3. Member States shall take the measures necessary to ensure that operators and suppliers of means of distance communication put an end to practices that have been declared to be contrary to this Directive, on the basis of a judicial decision, an administrative decision or a decision issued by a supervisory authority notified to them, where those operators or suppliers are in a position to do so.

Article 14

Out-of-court redress

1. Member States shall promote the setting up or development of adequate and effective out-of-court complaints and redress procedures for the settlement of consumer disputes concerning financial services provided at distance.

2. Member States shall, in particular, encourage the bodies responsible for out-of-court settlement of disputes to cooperate in the resolution of cross-border disputes concerning financial services provided at distance.

Article 15

Burden of proof

Without prejudice to Article 7(3), Member States may stipulate that the burden of proof in respect of the supplier's obligations to inform the consumer and the consumer's consent to conclusion of the contract and, where appropriate, its performance, can be placed on the supplier.

Any contractual term or condition providing that the burden of proof of the respect by the supplier of all or part of the obligations incumbent on him pursuant to this Directive should lie with the consumer shall be an unfair term within the meaning of Council Directive 93/13/EEC of 5 April 1993 on unfair terms in consumer contracts (¹).

Article 16

Transitional measures

Member States may impose national rules which are in conformity with this Directive on suppliers established in a Member State which has not yet transposed this Directive and whose law has no obligations corresponding to those provided for in this Directive.

Article 17

Directive 90/619/EC

In Article 15(1) of Directive 90/619/EEC the first subparagraph shall be replaced by the following:

'1. Each Member State shall prescribe that a policyholder who concludes an individual life-assurance contract shall have a period of 30 calendar days, from the time when he was informed that the contract had been concluded, within which to cancel the contract.'

Article 18

Directive 97/7/EC

Directive 97/7/EC is hereby amended as follows:

1. the first indent of Article 3(1) shall be replaced by the following:

'— relating to any financial service to which Directive 2002/65/EC of the European Parliament and of the Council of 23 September 2002 concerning the distance marketing of consumer financial services and amending Council Directive 90/619/EEC and Directives 97/7/EC and 98/27/EC (*) applies,

(*) OJ L 271, 9.10.2002, p. 16.';

2. Annex II shall be deleted.

(¹) OJ L 95, 21.4.1993, p. 29.

L 271/24   [EN]   Official Journal of the European Communities   9.10.2002

Article 19

Directive 98/27/EC

The following point shall be added to the Annex of Directive 98/27/EC:

'11. Directive 2002/65/EC of the European Parliament and of the Council of 23 September 2002 concerning the distance marketing of consumer financial services and amending Council Directive 90/619/EEC and Directives 97/7/EC and 98/27/EC (*).

(*) OJ L 271, 9.10.2002, p. 16.'

Article 20

Review

1. Following the implementation of this Directive, the Commission shall examine the functioning of the internal market in financial services in respect of the marketing of those services. It should seek to analyse and detail the difficulties that are, or might be faced by both consumers and suppliers, in particular arising from differences between national provisions regarding information and right of withdrawal.

2. Not later than 9 April 2006 the Commission shall report to the European Parliament and the Council on the problems facing both consumers and suppliers seeking to buy and sell financial services, and shall submit, where appropriate, proposals to amend and/or further harmonise the information and right of withdrawal provisions in Community legislation concerning financial services and/or those covered in Article 3.

Article 21

Transposition

1. Member States shall bring into force the laws, regulations and administrative provisions necessary to comply with this Directive not later than 9 October 2004. They shall forthwith inform the Commission thereof.

When Member States adopt these measures, they shall contain a reference to this Directive or shall be accompanied by such a reference on the occasion of their official publication. The methods of making such reference shall be laid down by Member States.

2. Member States shall communicate to the Commission the text of the main provisions of national law which they adopt in the field governed by this Directive together with a table showing how the provisions of this Directive correspond to the national provisions adopted.

Article 22

Entry into force

This Directive shall enter into force on the day of its publication in the *Official Journal of the European Communities*.

Article 23

Addressees

This Directive is addressed to the Member States.

Done at Brussels, 23 September 2002.

For the European Parliament	*For the Council*
The President	*The President*
P. COX	M. FISCHER BOEL

Appendix 12

Statutory Instrument 2000 No. 2334

The Consumer Protection (Distance Selling) Regulations 2000

© Crown Copyright 2000

STATUTORY INSTRUMENTS

2000 No. 2334

CONSUMER PROTECTION

The Consumer Protection (Distance Selling) Regulations 2000

Made	*31st August 2000*
Laid before Parliament	*1st September 2000*
Coming into force	*31st October 2000*

The Secretary of State, being a Minister designated[1] for the purposes of section 2(2) of the European Communities Act 1972[2] in relation to matters relating to consumer protection, in exercise of the powers conferred on him by section 2(2) of that Act, hereby makes the following Regulations:—

Title, commencement and extent

1.—(1) These Regulations may be cited as the Consumer Protection (Distance Selling) Regulations 2000 and shall come into force on 31st October 2000.

(2) These Regulations extend to Northern Ireland.

Revocation

2. The Mail Order Transactions (Information) Order 1976[3] is hereby revoked.

Interpretation

3.—(1) In these Regulations—

"breach" means contravention by a supplier of a prohibition in, or failure to comply with a requirement of, these Regulations;

"business" includes a trade or profession;

"consumer" means any natural person who, in contracts to which these Regulations apply, is acting for purposes which are outside his business;

---

[1] S.I. 1993/2661.back
[2] 1972 c. 68.back
[3] S.I. 1976/1812.back

"court" in relation to England and Wales and Northern Ireland means a county court or the High Court, and in relation to Scotland means the Sheriff Court or the Court of Session;

"credit" includes a cash loan and any other form of financial accommodation, and for this purpose "cash" includes money in any form;

"Director" means the Director General of Fair Trading;

"distance contract" means any contract concerning goods or services concluded between a supplier and a consumer under an organised distance sales or service provision scheme run by the supplier who, for the purpose of the contract, makes exclusive use of one or more means of distance communication up to and including the moment at which the contract is concluded;

"EEA Agreement" means the Agreement on the European Economic Area signed at Oporto on 2 May 1992 as adjusted by the Protocol signed at Brussels on 17 March 1993[4];

"enactment" includes an enactment comprised in, or in an instrument made under, an Act of the Scottish Parliament;

"enforcement authority" means the Director, every weights and measures authority in Great Britain, and the Department of Enterprise, Trade and Investment in Northern Ireland;

"excepted contract" means a contract such as is mentioned in regulation 5(1);

"means of distance communication" means any means which, without the simultaneous physical presence of the supplier and the consumer, may be used for the conclusion of a contract between those parties; and an indicative list of such means is contained in Schedule 1;

"Member State" means a State which is a contracting party to the EEA Agreement;

"operator of a means of communication" means any public or private person whose business involves making one or more means of distance communication available to suppliers;

"period for performance" has the meaning given by regulation 19(2);

"personal credit agreement" has the meaning given by regulation 14(8);

"related credit agreement" has the meaning given by regulation 15(5);

"supplier" means any person who, in contracts to which these Regulations apply, is acting in his commercial or professional capacity; and

"working days" means all days other than Saturdays, Sundays and public holidays.

(2) In the application of these Regulations to Scotland, for references to an "injunction" or an "interim injunction" there shall be substituted references to an "interdict" or an "interim interdict" respectively.

Contracts to which these Regulations apply

4. These Regulations apply, subject to regulation 6, to distance contracts other than excepted contracts.

---

[4] Directive 97/7/EC was added to Annex XIX to the EEA Agreement by Decision No. 15/98 of the EEA joint Committee which came into force on 1 July 2000 (O.J. No L272, 8.10.98, p.99).back

Excepted contracts

5.—(1) The following are excepted contracts, namely any contract—

(a) for the sale or other disposition of an interest in land except for a rental agreement;

(b) for the construction of a building where the contract also provides for a sale or other disposition of an interest in land on which the building is constructed, except for a rental agreement;

(c) relating to financial services, a non-exhaustive list of which is contained in Schedule 2;

(d) concluded by means of an automated vending machine or automated commercial premises;

(e) concluded with a telecommunications operator through the use of a public pay-phone;

(f) concluded at an auction.

(2) References in paragraph (1) to a rental agreement—

(a) if the land is situated in England and Wales, are references to any agreement which does not have to be made in writing (whether or not in fact made in writing) because of section 2(5)(a) of the Law of Property (Miscellaneous Provisions) Act 1989[5];

(b) if the land is situated in Scotland, are references to any agreement for the creation, transfer, variation or extinction of an interest in land, which does not have to be made in writing (whether or not in fact made in writing) as provided for in section 1(2) and (7) of the Requirements of Writing (Scotland) Act 1995[6]; and

(c) if the land is situated in Northern Ireland, are references to any agreement which is not one to which section II of the Statute of Frauds, (Ireland) 1695[7] applies.

(3) Paragraph (2) shall not be taken to mean that a rental agreement in respect of land situated outside the United Kingdom is not capable of being a distance contract to which these Regulations apply.

Contracts to which only part of these Regulations apply

6.—(1) Regulations 7 to 20 shall not apply to a contract which is a "timeshare agreement" within the meaning of the Timeshare Act 1992[8] and to which that Act applies.

(2) Regulations 7 to 19(1) shall not apply to—

(a) contracts for the supply of food, beverages or other goods intended for everyday consumption supplied to the consumer's residence or to his workplace by regular roundsmen; or

---

[5] 1989 c. 34.back

[6] 1995 c. 7.back

[7] 1695 c. 12(1).back

[8] 1992 c. 35.back

(b) contracts for the provision of accommodation, transport, catering or leisure services, where the supplier undertakes, when the contract is concluded, to provide these services on a specific date or within a specific period.

(3) Regulations 19(2) to (8) and 20 do not apply to a contract for a "package" within the meaning of the Package Travel, Package Holidays and Package Tours Regulations 1992[9] which is sold or offered for sale in the territory of the Member States.

Information required prior to the conclusion of the contract
7.—(1) Subject to paragraph (4), in good time prior to the conclusion of the contract the supplier shall—

(a) provide to the consumer the following information—

(i) the identity of the supplier and, where the contract requires payment in advance, the supplier's address;
(ii) a description of the main characteristics of the goods or services;
(iii) the price of the goods or services including all taxes;
(iv) delivery costs where appropriate;
(v) the arrangements for payment, delivery or performance;
(vi) the existence of a right of cancellation except in the cases referred to in regulation 13;
(vii) the cost of using the means of distance communication where it is calculated other than at the basic rate;
(viii) the period for which the offer or the price remains valid; and
(ix) where appropriate, the minimum duration of the contract, in the case of contracts for the supply of goods or services to be performed permanently or recurrently;

(b) inform the consumer if he proposes, in the event of the goods or services ordered by the consumer being unavailable, to provide substitute goods or services (as the case may be) of equivalent quality and price; and
(c) inform the consumer that the cost of returning any such substitute goods to the supplier in the event of cancellation by the consumer would be met by the supplier.

(2) The supplier shall ensure that the information required by paragraph (1) is provided in a clear and comprehensible manner appropriate to the means of distance communication used, with due regard in particular to the principles of good faith in commercial transactions and the principles governing the protection of those who are unable to give their consent such as minors.

(3) Subject to paragraph (4), the supplier shall ensure that his commercial purpose is made clear when providing the information required by paragraph (1).

(4) In the case of a telephone communication, the identity of the supplier and the commercial purpose of the call shall be made clear at the beginning of the conversation with the consumer.

[9] S.I. 1992/3288.back

Written and additional information

8.—(1) Subject to regulation 9, the supplier shall provide to the consumer in writing, or in another durable medium which is available and accessible to the consumer, the information referred to in paragraph (2), either—

(a) prior to the conclusion of the contract, or

(b) thereafter, in good time and in any event—

(i) during the performance of the contract, in the case of services; and

(ii) at the latest at the time of delivery where goods not for delivery to third parties are concerned.

(2) The information required to be provided by paragraph (1) is—

(a) the information set out in paragraphs (i) to (vi) of Regulation 7(1)(a);

(b) information about the conditions and procedures for exercising the right to cancel under regulation 10, including—

(i) where a term of the contract requires (or the supplier intends that it will require) that the consumer shall return the goods to the supplier in the event of cancellation, notification of that requirement; and

(ii) information as to whether the consumer or the supplier would be responsible under these Regulations for the cost of returning any goods to the supplier, or the cost of his recovering them, if the consumer cancels the contract under regulation 10;

(c) the geographical address of the place of business of the supplier to which the consumer may address any complaints;

(d) information about any after-sales services and guarantees; and

(e) the conditions for exercising any contractual right to cancel the contract, where the contract is of an unspecified duration or a duration exceeding one year.

(3) Subject to regulation 9, prior to the conclusion of a contract for the supply of services, the supplier shall inform the consumer in writing or in another durable medium which is available and accessible to the consumer that, unless the parties agree otherwise, he will not be able to cancel the contract under regulation 10 once the performance of the services has begun with his agreement.

Services performed through the use of a means of distance communication

9.—(1) Regulation 8 shall not apply to a contract for the supply of services which are performed through the use of a means of distance communication, where those services are supplied on only one occasion and are invoiced by the operator of the means of distance communication.

(2) But the supplier shall take all necessary steps to ensure that a consumer who is a party to a contract to which paragraph (1) applies is able to obtain the supplier's geographical address and the place of business to which the consumer may address any complaints.

Right to cancel

10.—(1) Subject to regulation 13, if within the cancellation period set out in regulations 11 and 12, the consumer gives a notice of cancellation to the supplier, or any other person previously notified by the supplier to the consumer as a person to whom notice of cancellation may be given, the notice of cancellation shall operate to cancel the contract.

(2) Except as otherwise provided by these Regulations, the effect of a notice of cancellation is that the contract shall be treated as if it had not been made.

(3) For the purposes of these Regulations, a notice of cancellation is a notice in writing or in another durable medium available and accessible to the supplier (or to the other person to whom it is given) which, however expressed, indicates the intention of the consumer to cancel the contract.

(4) A notice of cancellation given under this regulation by a consumer to a supplier or other person is to be treated as having been properly given if the consumer—

(a) leaves it at the address last known to the consumer and addressed to the supplier or other person by name (in which case it is to be taken to have been given on the day on which it was left);

(b) sends it by post to the address last known to the consumer and addressed to the supplier or other person by name (in which case, it is to be taken to have been given on the day on which it was posted);

(c) sends it by facsimile to the business facsimile number last known to the consumer (in which case it is to be taken to have been given on the day on which it is sent); or

(d) sends it by electronic mail, to the business electronic mail address last known to the consumer (in which case it is to be taken to have been given on the day on which it is sent).

(5) Where a consumer gives a notice in accordance with paragraph (4)(a) or (b) to a supplier who is a body corporate or a partnership, the notice is to be treated as having been properly given if—

(a) in the case of a body corporate, it is left at the address of, or sent to, the secretary or clerk of that body; or

(b) in the case of a partnership, it is left with or sent to a partner or a person having control or management of the partnership business.

Cancellation period in the case of contracts for the supply of goods

11.—(1) For the purposes of regulation 10, the cancellation period in the case of contracts for the supply of goods begins with the day on which the contract is concluded and ends as provided in paragraphs (2) to (5).

(2) Where the supplier complies with regulation 8, the cancellation period ends on the expiry of the period of seven working days beginning with the day after the day on which the consumer receives the goods.

(3) Where a supplier who has not complied with regulation 8 provides to the consumer the information referred to in regulation 8(2), and does so in writing or in another durable medium available and accessible to the consumer, within the period of three months begin-

ning with the day after the day on which the consumer receives the goods, the cancellation period ends on the expiry of the period of seven working days beginning with the day after the day on which the consumer receives the information.

(4) Where neither paragraph (2) nor (3) applies, the cancellation period ends on the expiry of the period of three months and seven working days beginning with the day after the day on which the consumer receives the goods.

(5) In the case of contracts for goods for delivery to third parties, paragraphs (2) to (4) shall apply as if the consumer had received the goods on the day on which they were received by the third party.

Cancellation period in the case of contracts for the supply of services

12.—(1) For the purposes of regulation 10, the cancellation period in the case of contracts for the supply of services begins with the day on which the contract is concluded and ends as provided in paragraphs (2) to (4).

(2) Where the supplier complies with regulation 8 on or before the day on which the contract is concluded, the cancellation period ends on the expiry of the period of seven working days beginning with the day after the day on which the contract is concluded.

(3) Where a supplier who has not complied with regulation 8 on or before the day on which the contract is concluded provides to the consumer the information referred to in regulation 8(2) and (3), and does so in writing or in another durable medium available and accessible to the consumer, within the period of three months beginning with the day after the day on which the contract is concluded, the cancellation period ends on the expiry of the period of seven working days beginning with the day after the day on which the consumer receives the information.

(4) Where neither paragraph (2) nor (3) applies, the cancellation period ends on the expiry of the period of three months and seven working days beginning with the day after the day on which the contract is concluded.

Exceptions to the right to cancel

13.—(1) Unless the parties have agreed otherwise, the consumer will not have the right to cancel the contract by giving notice of cancellation pursuant to regulation 10 in respect of contracts—

(a) for the supply of services if the supplier has complied with regulation 8(3) and performance of the contract has begun with the consumer's agreement before the end of the cancellation period applicable under regulation 12;

(b) for the supply of goods or services the price of which is dependent on fluctuations in the financial market which cannot be controlled by the supplier;

(c) for the supply of goods made to the consumer's specifications or clearly personalised or which by reason of their nature cannot be returned or are liable to deteriorate or expire rapidly;

(d) for the supply of audio or video recordings or computer software if they are unsealed by the consumer;

(e) for the supply of newspapers, periodicals or magazines; or

(f) for gaming, betting or lottery services.

Recovery of sums paid by or on behalf of the consumer on cancellation, and return of security

14.—(1) On the cancellation of a contract under regulation 10, the supplier shall reimburse any sum paid by or on behalf of the consumer under or in relation to the contract to the person by whom it was made free of any charge, less any charge made in accordance with paragraph (5).

(2) The reference in paragraph (1) to any sum paid on behalf of the consumer includes any sum paid by a creditor who is not the same person as the supplier under a personal credit agreement with the consumer.

(3) The supplier shall make the reimbursement referred to in paragraph (1) as soon as possible and in any case within a period not exceeding 30 days beginning with the day on which the notice of cancellation was given.

(4) Where any security has been provided in relation to the contract, the security (so far as it is so provided) shall, on cancellation under regulation 10, be treated as never having had effect and any property lodged with the supplier solely for the purposes of the security as so provided shall be returned by him forthwith.

(5) Subject to paragraphs (6) and (7), the supplier may make a charge, not exceeding the direct costs of recovering any goods supplied under the contract, where a term of the contract provides that the consumer must return any goods supplied if he cancels the contract under regulation 10 but the consumer does not comply with this provision or returns the goods at the expense of the supplier.

(6) Paragraph (5) shall not apply where—

(a) the consumer cancels in circumstances where he has the right to reject the goods under a term of the contract, including a term implied by virtue of any enactment, or

(b) the term requiring the consumer to return any goods supplied if he cancels the contract is an "unfair term" within the meaning of the Unfair Terms in Consumer Contracts Regulations 1999[10].

(7) Paragraph (5) shall not apply to the cost of recovering any goods which were supplied as substitutes for the goods ordered by the consumer.

(8) For the purposes of these Regulations, a personal credit agreement is an agreement between the consumer and any other person ("the creditor") by which the creditor provides the consumer with credit of any amount.

Automatic cancellation of a related credit agreement

15.—(1) Where a notice of cancellation is given under regulation 10 which has the effect of cancelling the contract, the giving of the notice shall also have the effect of cancelling any related credit agreement.

(2) Where a related credit agreement is cancelled by virtue of paragraph (1), the supplier shall, if he is not the same person as the creditor under that agreement, forthwith on receipt of the notice of cancellation inform the creditor that the notice has been given.

(3) Where a related credit agreement is cancelled by virtue of paragraph (1)—

---

[10] S.I. 1999/2083.back

(a) any sum paid by or on behalf of the consumer under, or in relation to, the credit agreement which the supplier is not obliged to reimburse under regulation 14(1) shall be reimbursed, except for any sum which, if it had not already been paid, would have to be paid under subparagraph (b);

(b) the agreement shall continue in force so far as it relates to repayment of the credit and payment of interest, subject to regulation 16; and

(c) subject to subparagraph (b), the agreement shall cease to be enforceable.

(4) Where any security has been provided under a related credit agreement, the security, so far as it is so provided, shall be treated as never having had effect and any property lodged with the creditor solely for the purposes of the security as so provided shall be returned by him forthwith.

(5) For the purposes of this regulation and regulation 16, a "related credit agreement" means an agreement under which fixed sum credit which fully or partly covers the price under a contract cancelled under regulation 10 is granted—

(a) by the supplier, or

(b) by another person, under an arrangement between that person and the supplier.

(6) For the purposes of this regulation and regulation 16—

(a) "creditor" is a person who grants credit under a related credit agreement;

(b) "fixed sum credit" has the same meaning as in section 10 of the Consumer Credit Act 1974[11];

(c) "repayment" in relation to credit means repayment of money received by the consumer, and cognate expressions shall be construed accordingly; and

(d) "interest" means interest on money so received.

Repayment of credit and interest after cancellation of a related credit agreement

16.—(1) This regulation applies following the cancellation of a related credit agreement by virtue of regulation 15(1).

(2) If the consumer repays the whole or a portion of the credit—

(a) before the expiry of one month following the cancellation of the credit agreement, or

(b) in the case of a credit repayable by instalments, before the date on which the first instalment is due,

no interest shall be payable on the amount repaid.

(3) If the whole of a credit repayable by instalments is not repaid on or before the date referred to in paragraph (2)(b), the consumer shall not be liable to repay any of the credit except on receipt of a request in writing, signed by the creditor, stating the amounts of the remaining instalments (recalculated by the creditor as nearly as may be in accordance with the agreement and without extending the repayment period), but excluding any sum other than principal and interest.

[11] 1974 c. 39.back

(4) Where any security has been provided under a related credit agreement the duty imposed on the consumer to repay credit and to pay interest shall not be enforceable before the creditor has discharged any duty imposed on him by regulation 15(4) to return any property lodged with him as security on cancellation.

Restoration of goods by consumer after cancellation

17.—(1) This regulation applies where a contract is cancelled under regulation 10 after the consumer has acquired possession of any goods under the contract other than any goods mentioned in regulation 13(1)(b) to (e).

(2) The consumer shall be treated as having been under a duty throughout the period prior to cancellation—

> (a) to retain possession of the goods, and
> (b) to take reasonable care of them.

(3) On cancellation, the consumer shall be under a duty to restore the goods to the supplier in accordance with this regulation, and in the meanwhile to retain possession of the goods and take reasonable care of them.

(4) The consumer shall not be under any duty to deliver the goods except at his own premises and in pursuance of a request in writing, or in another durable medium available and accessible to the consumer, from the supplier and given to the consumer either before, or at the time when, the goods are collected from those premises.

(5) If the consumer—

> (a) delivers the goods (whether at his own premises or elsewhere) to any person to whom, under regulation 10(1), a notice of cancellation could have been given; or
> (b) sends the goods at his own expense to such a person,

he shall be discharged from any duty to retain possession of the goods or restore them to the supplier.

(6) Where the consumer delivers the goods in accordance with paragraph (5)(a), his obligation to take care of the goods shall cease; and if he sends the goods in accordance with paragraph (5)(b), he shall be under a duty to take reasonable care to see that they are received by the supplier and not damaged in transit, but in other respects his duty to take care of the goods shall cease when he sends them.

(7) Where, at any time during the period of 21 days beginning with the day notice of cancellation was given, the consumer receives such a request as is mentioned in paragraph (4), and unreasonably refuses or unreasonably fails to comply with it, his duty to retain possession and take reasonable care of the goods shall continue until he delivers or sends the goods as mentioned in paragraph (5), but if within that period he does not receive such a request his duty to take reasonable care of the goods shall cease at the end of that period.

(8) Where—

> (a) a term of the contract provides that if the consumer cancels the contract, he must return the goods to the supplier, and
> (b) the consumer is not otherwise entitled to reject the goods under the terms of the contract or by virtue of any enactment,

paragraph (7) shall apply as if for the period of 21 days there were substituted the period of 6 months.

(9) Where any security has been provided in relation to the cancelled contract, the duty to restore goods imposed on the consumer by this regulation shall not be enforceable before the supplier has discharged any duty imposed on him by regulation 14(4) to return any property lodged with him as security on cancellation.

(10) Breach of a duty imposed by this regulation on a consumer is actionable as a breach of statutory duty.

Goods given in part-exchange

18.—(1) This regulation applies on the cancellation of a contract under regulation 10 where the supplier agreed to take goods in part-exchange (the "part-exchange goods") and those goods have been delivered to him.

(2) Unless, before the end of the period of 10 days beginning with the date of cancellation, the part-exchange goods are returned to the consumer in a condition substantially as good as when they were delivered to the supplier, the consumer shall be entitled to recover from the supplier a sum equal to the part-exchange allowance.

(3) In this regulation the part-exchange allowance means the sum agreed as such in the cancelled contract, or if no such sum was agreed, such sum as it would have been reasonable to allow in respect of the part-exchange goods if no notice of cancellation had been served.

(4) Where the consumer recovers from the supplier a sum equal to the part-exchange allowance, the title of the consumer to the part-exchange goods shall vest in the supplier (if it has not already done so) on recovery of that sum.

Performance

19.—(1) Unless the parties agree otherwise, the supplier shall perform the contract within a maximum of 30 days beginning with the day after the day the consumer sent his order to the supplier.

(2) Subject to paragraphs (7) and (8), where the supplier is unable to perform the contract because the goods or services ordered are not available, within the period for performance referred to in paragraph (1) or such other period as the parties agree ("the period for performance"), he shall—

(a) inform the consumer; and
(b) reimburse any sum paid by or on behalf of the consumer under or in relation to the contract to the person by whom it was made.

(3) The reference in paragraph (2)(b) to any sum paid on behalf of the consumer includes any sum paid by a creditor who is not the same person as the supplier under a personal credit agreement with the consumer.

(4) The supplier shall make the reimbursement referred to in paragraph (2)(b) as soon as possible and in any event within a period of 30 days beginning with the day after the day on which the period for performance expired.

(5) A contract which has not been performed within the period for performance shall be treated as if it had not been made, save for any rights or remedies which the consumer has under it as a result of the non-performance.

(6) Where any security has been provided in relation to the contract, the security (so far as it is so provided) shall, where the supplier is unable to perform the contract within the period for performance, be treated as never having had any effect and any property lodged with the supplier solely for the purposes of the security as so provided shall be returned by him forthwith.

(7) Where the supplier is unable to supply the goods or services ordered by the consumer, the supplier may perform the contract for the purposes of these Regulations by providing substitute goods or services (as the case may be) of equivalent quality and price provided that—

(a) this possibility was provided for in the contract;

(b) prior to the conclusion of the contract the supplier gave the consumer the information required by regulation 7(1)(b) and (c) in the manner required by regulation 7(2).

(8) In the case of outdoor leisure events which by their nature cannot be rescheduled, paragraph 2(b) shall not apply where the consumer and the supplier so agree.

Effect of non-performance on related credit agreement

20. Where a supplier is unable to perform the contract within the period for performance—

(a) regulations 15 and 16 shall apply to any related credit agreement as if the consumer had given a valid notice of cancellation under regulation 10 on the expiry of the period for performance; and

(b) the reference in regulation 15(3)(a) to regulation 14(1) shall be read, for the purposes of this regulation, as a reference to regulation 19(2).

Payment by card

21.—(1) Subject to paragraph (4), the consumer shall be entitled to cancel a payment where fraudulent use has been made of his payment card in connection with a contract to which this regulation applies by another person not acting, or to be treated as acting, as his agent.

(2) Subject to paragraph (4), the consumer shall be entitled to be recredited, or to have all sums returned by the card issuer, in the event of fraudulent use of his payment card in connection with a contract to which this regulation applies by another person not acting, or to be treated as acting, as the consumer's agent.

(3) Where paragraphs (1) and (2) apply, in any proceedings if the consumer alleges that any use made of the payment card was not authorised by him it is for the card issuer to prove that the use was so authorised.

(4) Paragraphs (1) and (2) shall not apply to an agreement to which section 83(1) of the Consumer Credit Act 1974 applies.

(5) Section 84 of the Consumer Credit Act 1974 (misuse of credit-tokens) is amended by the insertion after subsection (3) of—

"(3A) Subsections (1) and (2) shall not apply to any use, in connection with a distance contract (other than an excepted contract), of a card which is a credit-token.

(3B) In subsection (3A), "distance contract" and "excepted contract" have the meanings given in the Consumer Protection (Distance Selling) Regulations 2000."

(6) For the purposes of this regulation—

"card issuer" means the owner of the card; and
"payment card" includes credit cards, charge cards, debit cards and store cards.

Amendments to the Unsolicited Goods and Services Act 1971

22.—(1) The Unsolicited Goods and Services Act 1971[12] is amended as follows.

(2) Omit section 1 (rights of recipient of unsolicited goods).

(3) In subsection (1) of section 2 (demands and threats regarding payment), after "them" insert "for the purposes of his trade or business".

(4) The amendments made by this regulation apply only in relation to goods sent after the date on which it comes into force.

Amendments to the Unsolicited Goods and Services (Northern Ireland) Order 1976

23.—(1) The Unsolicited Goods and Services (Northern Ireland) Order 1976[13] is amended as follows.

(2) Omit Article 3 (rights of recipient of unsolicited goods).

(3) In paragraph (1) of Article 4 (demands and threats regarding payment), after "them" insert "for the purposes of his trade or business".

(4) The amendments made by this regulation apply only in relation to goods sent after the date on which it comes into force.

Inertia Selling

24.—(1) Paragraphs (2) and (3) apply if—

(a) unsolicited goods are sent to a person ("the recipient") with a view to his acquiring them;
(b) the recipient has no reasonable cause to believe that they were sent with a view to their being acquired for the purposes of a business; and
(c) the recipient has neither agreed to acquire nor agreed to return them.

(2) The recipient may, as between himself and the sender, use, deal with or dispose of the goods as if they were an unconditional gift to him.

(3) The rights of the sender to the goods are extinguished.

(4) A person who, not having reasonable cause to believe there is a right to payment, in the course of any business makes a demand for payment, or asserts a present or prospective right to payment, for what he knows are—

(a) unsolicited goods sent to another person with a view to his acquiring them for purposes other than those of his business, or
(b) unsolicited services supplied to another person for purposes other than those of his business,

is guilty of an offence and liable, on summary conviction, to a fine not exceeding level 4 on the standard scale.

---

[12] 1971 c. 30.back
[13] S.I. 1976/57 (N.I.1).back

(5) A person who, not having reasonable cause to believe there is a right to payment, in the course of any business and with a view to obtaining payment for what he knows are unsolicited goods sent or services supplied as mentioned in paragraph (4)—

(a) threatens to bring any legal proceedings, or

(b) places or causes to be placed the name of any person on a list of defaulters or debtors or threatens to do so, or

(c) invokes or causes to be invoked any other collection procedure or threatens to do so,

is guilty of an offence and liable, on summary conviction, to a fine not exceeding level 5 on the standard scale.

(6) In this regulation—

"acquire" includes hire;
"send" includes deliver;
"sender", in relation to any goods, includes—

(a) any person on whose behalf or with whose consent the goods are sent;

(b) any other person claiming through or under the sender or any person mentioned in paragraph (a); and

(c) any person who delivers the goods; and

"unsolicited" means, in relation to goods sent or services supplied to any person, that they are sent or supplied without any prior request made by or on behalf of the recipient.

(7) For the purposes of this regulation, an invoice or similar document which—

(a) states the amount of a payment, and

(b) fails to comply with the requirements of regulations made under section 3A of the Unsolicited Goods and Services Act 1971 or, as the case may be, Article 6 of the Unsolicited Goods and Services (Northern Ireland) Order 1976 applicable to it,

is to be regarded as asserting a right to the payment.

(8) Section 3A of the Unsolicited Goods and Services Act 1971 applies for the purposes of this regulation in its application to England, Wales and Scotland as it applies for the purposes of that Act.

(9) Article 6 of the Unsolicited Goods and Services (Northern Ireland) Order 1976 applies for the purposes of this regulation in its application to Northern Ireland as it applies for the purposes of that Order.

(10) This regulation applies only to goods sent and services supplied after the date on which it comes into force.

No contracting-out

25.—(1) A term contained in any contract to which these Regulations apply is void if, and to the extent that, it is inconsistent with a provision for the protection of the consumer contained in these Regulations.

(2) Where a provision of these Regulations specifies a duty or liability of the consumer in certain circumstances, a term contained in a contract to which these Regulations apply, other than a term to which paragraph (3) applies, is inconsistent with that provision if it purports to impose, directly or indirectly, an additional duty or liability on him in those circumstances.

(3) This paragraph applies to a term which requires the consumer to return any goods supplied to him under the contract if he cancels it under regulation 10.

(4) A term to which paragraph (3) applies shall, in the event of cancellation by the consumer under regulation 10, have effect only for the purposes of regulation 14(5) and 17(8).

(5) These Regulations shall apply notwithstanding any contract term which applies or purports to apply the law of a non-Member State if the contract has a close connection with the territory of a Member State.

Consideration of complaints

26.—(1) It shall be the duty of an enforcement authority to consider any complaint made to it about a breach unless—

(a) the complaint appears to the authority to be frivolous or vexatious; or

(b) another enforcement authority has notified the Director that it agrees to consider the complaint.

(2) If an enforcement authority notifies the Director that it agrees to consider a complaint made to another enforcement authority, the first mentioned authority shall be under a duty to consider the complaint.

(3) An enforcement authority which is under a duty to consider a complaint shall give reasons for its decision to apply or not to apply, as the case may be, for an injunction under regulation 27.

(4) In deciding whether or not to apply for an injunction in respect of a breach an enforcement authority may, if it considers it appropriate to do so, have regard to any undertaking given to it or another enforcement authority by or on behalf of any person as to compliance with these Regulations.

Injunctions to secure compliance with these Regulations

27.—(1) The Director or, subject to paragraph (2), any other enforcement authority may apply for an injunction (including an interim injunction) against any person who appears to the Director or that authority to be responsible for a breach.

(2) An enforcement authority other than the Director may apply for an injunction only where—

(a) it has notified the Director of its intention to apply at least fourteen days before the date on which the application is to be made, beginning with the date on which the notification was given; or

(b) the Director consents to the application being made within a shorter period.

(3) The court on an application under this regulation may grant an injunction on such terms as it thinks fit to secure compliance with these Regulations.

Notification of undertakings and orders to the Director

28. An enforcement authority other than the Director shall notify the Director—

(a) of any undertaking given to it by or on behalf of any person who appears to it to be responsible for a breach;

(b) of the outcome of any application made by it under regulation 27 and of the terms of any undertaking given to or order made by the court;

(c) of the outcome of any application made by it to enforce a previous order of the court.

Publication, information and advice

29.—(1) The Director shall arrange for the publication in such form and manner as he considers appropriate of—

(a) details of any undertaking or order notified to him under regulation 28;

(b) details of any undertaking given to him by or on behalf of any person as to compliance with these Regulations;

(c) details of any application made by him under regulation 27, and of the terms of any undertaking given to, or order made by, the court;

(d) details of any application made by the Director to enforce a previous order of the court.

(2) The Director may arrange for the dissemination in such form and manner as he considers appropriate of such information and advice concerning the operation of these Regulations as it may appear to him to be expedient to give to the public and to all persons likely to be affected by these Regulations.

Helen Liddell
Minister of State, Department of Trade and Industry

31st August 2000

SCHEDULE 1

Regulation 3

Indicative list of means of distance communication

1. Unaddressed printed matter.
2. Addressed printed matter.
3. Letter.
4. Press advertising with order form.
5. Catalogue.
6. Telephone with human intervention.
7. Telephone without human intervention (automatic calling machine, audiotext).
8. Radio.
9. Videophone (telephone with screen).

10. Videotext (microcomputer and television screen) with keyboard or touch screen.
11. Electronic mail.
12. Facsimile machine (fax).
13. Television (teleshopping).

SCHEDULE 2

Regulation 5(1)(c)

Non-exhaustive list of financial services

1. Investment services.
2. Insurance and reinsurance operations.
3. Banking services.
4. Services relating to dealings in futures or options.

Such services include in particular:

— investment services referred to in the Annex to Directive 93/22/EEC[14]; services of collective investment undertakings;
— services covered by the activities subject to mutual recognition referred to in the Annex to Directive 89/846/EEC[15];
— operations covered by the insurance and reinsurance activities referred to in:
— Article 1 of Directive 73/239/EEC[16];— the Annex to Directive 79/267/EEC[17];— Directive 64/225/EEC[18];— Directives 92/49/EEC[19] and 92/96/EEC[20].

EXPLANATORY NOTE
(This note is not part of the Regulations)

These Regulations implement Directive 97/7/EC of the European Parliament and the Council of 20 May 1997 (O.J. No. L144, 4.6.97, p.19) on the protection of consumers in relation to distance contracts, with the exception of Article 10.

The Regulations apply to contracts for goods or services to be supplied to a consumer where the contract is made exclusively by means of distance communication, that is any means used without the simultaneous physical presence of the consumer and the supplier

[14] O.J. No. L141, 11.06.1993, p.27.back
[15] O.J. No. L386, 30.12.1989, p.1, to which there are amendments not relevant to these Regulations.back
[16] O.J. No. L228, 16.08.1973, p.3. Relevant amending instruments are Council Directive 84/641/EEC (O.J. No. L339, 27.12.84, p.21); Council Directive 87/343/EEC (O.J. No. L185, 4.7.87, p.72); Council Directive 87/344/EEC (O.J. No. L185, 4.7.87, p.77); Council Directive 90/618/EEC (O.J. No. L330, 29.11.90, p.44); Council Directive 92/49/EC (O.J. No. L228, 11.8.92, p.1.).back
[17] O.J. No. L63, 13.03.1979, p.1, to which there are amendments not relevant to these Regulations.back
[18] O.J. No. L56, 04.04.1964, p.878/64 (O.J./S.E. 1st series 1963–64 p.131), to which there are amendments not relevant to these Regulations.back
[19] O.J. No. L228, 11.08.1992, p.1.back
[20] O.J. No. L360, 09.12.1992, p.1.back

(regulations 3 and 4). Schedule 1 contains an indicative list of means of distance communication.

The Regulations do not apply to those distance contracts excluded by regulation 5(1), such as contracts relating to the supply of financial services.

The Regulations have limited application to contracts for the supply of groceries by regular delivery and contracts for the provision of accommodation, transport, catering or leisure services (regulation 6).

The Regulations require the supplier to provide the consumer with the information referred to in regulation 7 prior to the conclusion of the contract. This includes information on the right to cancel the distance contract, the main characteristics of the goods or services, and delivery costs where appropriate.

Regulation 8 requires the supplier to confirm in writing, or another durable medium which is available and accessible to the consumer, information already given and to give some additional information, including information on the conditions and procedures relating to the exercise of the right to cancel the contract. Regulation 8(3) requires the supplier to inform the consumer prior to conclusion of a contract for services that he will not be able to cancel once performance of the service has begun with his agreement.

Where the Regulations apply, they provide a "cooling off period" to enable the consumer to cancel the contract by giving notice of cancellation to the supplier. The effect of giving notice of cancellation under the Regulations is that the contract is treated as if it had not been made.

Where the supplier supplies the information to the consumer on time, the cooling-off period is 7 working days from the day after the date of the contract, in the case of services, or from the day after the date of delivery of the goods.

Where the supplier fails to comply with the information requirement at all, the cooling-off period is extended by 3 months.

Where the supplier complies with the information requirement later than he should have done but within 3 months the cooling-off begins from the date he provided the information (regulations 10–12).

Certain contracts are excluded from the right to cancel unless the parties agree otherwise, such as a contract for the supply of goods made to the consumer's specifications (regulation 13).

If the consumer cancels, the consumer must be reimbursed within a maximum period of 30 days (regulation 14). Where the consumer cancels the contract, any related credit agreement is automatically cancelled (regulation 15).

Regulation 17 provides that on cancellation of the contract the consumer is under a duty to restore goods to the supplier if he collects them and in the meantime to take reasonable care of them. The Regulations do not require the consumer to return goods but if he is required to under the contract and does not do so, he must pay the cost to the supplier of recovering them.

The Regulations provide that the contract must be performed within 30 days subject to agreement between the parties. However, where the supplier is not able to provide the goods or service ordered, substitutes may be offered if certain conditions are met (regulation 19).

The Regulations provide that where the consumer's payment card is used fraudulently in connection with a distance contract the consumer will be entitled to cancel the payment. If the payment has already been made the consumer will be entitled to a re-credit or to have all sums returned by the card issuer. The Regulations amend the Consumer Credit Act 1974 by removing the potential liability of the debtor under a regulated consumer credit agreement for the first £50 of loss to the creditor from misuse of a credit-token in connection with a distance contract.

The Regulations prohibit the supply of unsolicited goods and services to consumers. Regulation 24 replaces with amendments section 1 of the Unsolicited Goods and Services Act 1971 and Article 3 of the Unsolicited Goods and Services (Northern Ireland) Order 1976. It also creates an offence in similar terms to section 2 of the 1971 Act but extended to the supply of unsolicited services and limited to supply to consumers. The scope of section 2 of the 1971 Act and Article 4 of the 1976 Order (which apply only to goods) is amended to restrict their application to the unsolicited supply of goods to businesses.

The Director General of Fair Trading, Trading Standards Departments in Great Britain and the Department of Enterprise, Trade and Investment in Northern Ireland are enforcement authorities for the purposes of the Regulations. Regulation 26 provides that an enforcement authority must consider complaints about a breach of the requirements of the Regulations. Those bodies are given the power to take proceedings for an injunction against a business to prevent further breaches (regulation 27).

A Regulatory Impact Assessment is available, copies of which have been placed in the libraries of both Houses of Parliament. Copies are also available from the Consumer Affairs Directorate of the Department of Trade and Industry, Room 415, 1 Victoria Street, London SW1H 0ET.

ISBN 0 11 099872 3

Appendix 13

Statutory Instrument 2004 No. 2095

The Financial Services (Distance Marketing) Regulations 2004

© Crown Copyright 2004

STATUTORY INSTRUMENTS

2004 No. 2095

FINANCIAL SERVICES AND MARKETS

The Financial Services (Distance Marketing) Regulations 2004

Made	*4th August 2004*
Laid before Parliament	*5th August 2004*
Coming into force	*31st October 2004*

The Treasury, being a government department designated[1] for the purposes of section 2(2) of the European Communities Act 1972[2] in relation to matters concerning the distance marketing of consumer financial services, in the exercise of the powers conferred on them by that section, hereby make the following Regulations:

Citation, commencement and extent
1. These Regulations may be cited as the Financial Services (Distance Marketing) Regulations 2004 and come into force on 31st October 2004.

Interpretation
2.—(1) In these Regulations—

"the 1974 Act" means the Consumer Credit Act 1974[3];
"the 2000 Act" means the Financial Services and Markets Act 2000[4];
"the Authority" means the Financial Services Authority;

---

[1] S.I. 2004/1283.back
[2] 1972 c. 68; by virtue of the amendment of section 1(2) of the European Communities Act 1972 by section 1 of the European Economic Area Act 1993 (c. 51) regulations may be made under section 2(2) of the European Communities Act to implement obligations of the United Kingdom created or arising by or under the Agreement on the European Economic Area signed at Oporto on 2nd May 1992 (Cm 2073) and the Protocol adjusting the Agreement signed at Brussels on 17th March 1993 (Cm 2183).back
[3] 1974 c. 39.back
[4] 2000 c. 8.back

"appointed representative" has the same meaning as in section 39(2) of the 2000 Act (exemption of appointed representatives);

"authorised person" has the same meaning as in section 31(2) of the 2000 Act (authorised persons);

"breach" means a contravention by a supplier of a prohibition in, or a failure by a supplier to comply with a requirement of, these Regulations;

"business" includes a trade or profession;

"consumer" means any individual who, in contracts to which these Regulations apply, is acting for purposes which are outside any business he may carry on;

"court" in relation to England and Wales and Northern Ireland means a county court or the High Court, and in relation to Scotland means the Sheriff Court or the Court of Session;

"credit" includes a cash loan and any other form of financial accommodation, and for this purpose "cash" includes money in any form;

"designated professional body" has the same meaning as in section 326(2) of the 2000 Act (designation of professional bodies);

"the Directive" means Directive 2002/65/EC of the European Parliament and of the Council of 23 September 2002 concerning the distance marketing of consumer financial services and amending Council Directive 90/619/EEC and Directives 97/7/EC and 98/27/EC[5];

"distance contract" means any contract concerning one or more financial services concluded between a supplier and a consumer under an organised distance sales or service-provision scheme run by the supplier or by an intermediary, who, for the purpose of that contract, makes exclusive use of one or more means of distance communication up to and including the time at which the contract is concluded;

"durable medium" means any instrument which enables a consumer to store information addressed personally to him in a way accessible for future reference for a period of time adequate for the purposes of the information and which allows the unchanged reproduction of the information stored;

"EEA supplier" means a supplier who is a national of an EEA State, or a company or firm (within the meaning of Article 48 of the Treaty establishing the European Community) formed in accordance with the law of an EEA State;

"EEA State" means a State which is a contracting party to the Agreement on the European Economic Area signed at Oporto on 2nd May 1992, as adjusted by the Protocol signed at Brussels on 17th March 1993;

"exempt regulated activity" has the same meaning as in section 325(2) of the 2000 Act;

"financial service" means any service of a banking, credit, insurance, personal pension, investment or payment nature;

"means of distance communication" means any means which, without the simultaneous physical presence of the supplier and the consumer, may be used for the marketing of a service between those parties;

---

[5] O.J. L 271, 9.10.2002, p. 16; the Directive applies to EEA States which are not Member States of the European Community by virtue of Decision No. 47/2003 of the EEA Joint Committee dated 16th May 2003 (O.J. L 193, 31.7.2003, p. 18).back

"the OFT" means the Office of Fair Trading;

"regulated activity" has the same meaning as in section 22 of the 2000 Act (the classes of activity and categories of investment);

"Regulated Activities Order" means the Financial Services and Markets Act 2000 (Regulated Activities) Order 2001[6];

"rule" means a rule—

(a) made by the Authority under the 2000 Act, or

(b) made by a designated professional body, and approved by the Authority, under section 332 of the 2000 Act,

as the context requires;

"supplier" means any person who, acting in his commercial or professional capacity, is the contractual provider of services.

(2) In these Regulations, subject to paragraph (1), any expression used in these Regulations which is also used in the Directive has the same meaning as in the Directive.

Scope of these Regulations

3.—(1) Regulations 7 to 14 apply, subject to regulations 4 and 5, in relation to distance contracts made on or after 31st October 2004.

(2) Regulation 15 applies in relation to financial services supplied on or after 31st October 2004 under an organised distance sales or service-provision scheme run by the supplier or by an intermediary, who, for the purpose of that supply, makes exclusive use of one or more means of distance communication up to and including the time at which the financial services are supplied.

4.—(1) Where an EEA State, other than the United Kingdom, has transposed the Directive or has obligations in its domestic law corresponding to those provided for in the Directive—

(a) regulations 7 to 14 do not apply in relation to any contract made between an EEA supplier contracting from an establishment in that EEA State and a consumer in the United Kingdom, and

(b) regulation 15 does not apply to any supply of financial services by an EEA supplier from an establishment in that EEA State to a consumer in the United Kingdom,

if the provisions by which that State has transposed the Directive, or the obligations in the domestic law of that State corresponding to those provided for in the Directive, as the case may be, apply to that contract or that supply.

(2) Subject to paragraph (5) and regulation 6(3) and (4)—

(a) regulations 7 to 11 do not apply in relation to any contract made by a supplier who is an authorised person, the making or performance of which constitutes or is part of a regulated activity carried on by him;

---

[6] S.I. 2001/544, as amended by S.I. 2001/3544, S.I. 2002/682, S.I. 2002/1310, S.I. 2002/1776, S.I. 2002/1777, S.I. 2003/1475, S.I. 2003/1476, S.I. 2003/2822 and S.I. 2004/1610.back

(b) regulation 15 does not apply to any supply of financial services by a supplier who is an authorised person, where that supply constitutes or is part of a regulated activity carried on by him.

(3) Subject to regulation 6(3) and (4)—

(a) regulations 7 and 8 do not apply in relation to any contract made by a supplier who is an appointed representative, the making or performance of which constitutes or is part of a regulated activity (other than an exempt regulated activity) carried on by him;

(b) regulation 15 does not apply to any supply of financial services by a supplier who is an appointed representative, where that supply constitutes or is part of a regulated activity (other than an exempt regulated activity) carried on by him.

(4) Subject to regulation 6(3) and (4)—

(a) regulations 7 and 8 do not apply in relation to any contract where—

(i) the supplier is bound, or is controlled or managed by one or more persons who are bound, by rules of a designated professional body which are equivalent to those regulations, and

(ii) the making or performance of that contract constitutes or is part of an exempt regulated activity carried on by the supplier;

(b) regulation 15 does not apply to any supply of financial services where—

(i) the supplier is bound, or is controlled or managed by one or more persons who are bound, by rules of a designated professional body which are equivalent to that regulation, and

(ii) that supply constitutes or is part of an exempt regulated activity carried on by the supplier.

(5) Paragraph (2) does not apply in relation to any contract or supply of financial services made by a supplier who is the operator, trustee or depositary of a scheme which is a recognised scheme by virtue of section 264 of the 2000 Act (schemes constituted in other EEA States), where the making or performance of the contract or the supply of the financial services constitutes or is part of a regulated activity for which he has permission in that capacity.

(6) In paragraph (5)—

"the operator", "trustee" and "depositary" each has the same meaning as in section 237(2) of the 2000 Act (other definitions); and

"permission" has the same meaning as in section 266 of that Act (disapplication of rules).

5.—(1) Where a consumer and a supplier enter an initial service agreement and—

(a) successive operations of the same nature, or

(b) a series of separate operations of the same nature,

are subsequently performed between them over time and within the framework of that agreement, then, if any of regulations 7 to 14 apply, they apply only to the initial service agreement.

(2) Where a consumer and a supplier do not enter an initial service agreement and—

    (a) successive operations of the same nature, or

    (b) a series of separate operations of the same nature,

are performed between them over time, then, if regulations 7 and 8 apply, they apply only—

    (i)   when the first operation is performed, and

    (ii) to any operation which is performed more than one year after the previous operation.

(3) For the purposes of this regulation, "initial service agreement" includes, for example, an agreement for the provision of—

    (a) a bank account;

    (b) a credit card; or

    (c) portfolio management services.

(4) For the purposes of this regulation, "operations" includes, for example—

    (a) deposits to or withdrawals from a bank account;

    (b) payments by a credit card;

    (c) transactions carried out within the framework of an initial service agreement for portfolio management services; and

    (d) subscriptions to new units of the same collective investment fund,

but does not include adding new elements to an existing initial service agreement, for example adding the possibility of using an electronic payment instrument together with an existing bank account.

Financial services marketed by an intermediary

6.—(1) This regulation applies where a financial service is marketed by an intermediary.

(2) These Regulations have effect as if—

    (a) each reference to a supplier in the definition of "breach" in regulation 2(1) were a reference to a supplier or an intermediary;

    (b) the reference to the supplier in the definition of "means of distance communication" in regulation 2(1), each reference to the supplier in regulations 7, 8(1) and (2), 10 and 11(3)(b), and the first reference to the supplier in regulation 8(4), were a reference to the intermediary;

    (c) the reference to the supplier in regulation 8(3) were a reference to the supplier or the intermediary;

    (d) for regulation 11(2) there were substituted—

"(2) Paragraph (1) does not apply to a distance contract if the intermediary has not complied with regulation 8(1) (and the supplier has not done what the intermediary was required to do by regulation 8(1)), unless—

    (a) the circumstances fall within regulation 8(1)(b); and

    (b) either—

(i)   the intermediary has complied with regulation 7(1) and (2) or, if applicable, regulation 7(4)(b), and with regulation 7(5), or

(ii)   the supplier has done what the intermediary was required to do by regulation 7(1) and (2) or, if applicable, regulation 7(4)(b), and by regulation 7(5).";

(e)   the reference to a supplier in regulation 22(1) were a reference to an intermediary; and

(f)   each reference to the supplier in paragraphs 2, 4, 5 and 19 of Schedule 1 were a reference to the supplier and the intermediary.

(3) Notwithstanding paragraphs (2) to (4) of regulation 4, regulations 7 and 8 apply in relation to the intermediary unless—

(a)   the intermediary is an authorised person and the marketing of the financial service constitutes or is part of a regulated activity carried on by him;

(b)   the intermediary is an appointed representative and the marketing of the financial service constitutes or is part of a regulated activity (other than an exempt regulated activity) carried on by him; or

(c)   the intermediary is not an authorised person, but—

(i)   he is bound, or is controlled or managed by one or more persons who are bound, by rules of a designated professional body which are equivalent to regulations 7 and 8, and

(ii)   the marketing of the financial service constitutes or is part of an exempt regulated activity carried on by him.

(4) Notwithstanding paragraphs (2) to (4) of regulation 4, regulation 15 applies to the intermediary unless—

(a)   the intermediary is an authorised person and is acting in the course of a regulated activity carried on by him;

(b)   the intermediary is an appointed representative and is acting in the course of a regulated activity (other than an exempt regulated activity) carried on by him; or

(c)   the intermediary is not an authorised person, but—

(i)   he is bound, or is controlled or managed by one or more persons who are bound, by rules of a designated professional body which are equivalent to regulation 15, and

(ii)   he is acting in the course an exempt regulated activity carried on by him.

Information required prior to the conclusion of the contract

7.—(1) Subject to paragraph (4), in good time prior to the consumer being bound by any distance contract, the supplier shall provide to the consumer the information specified in Schedule 1.

(2) The supplier shall provide the information specified in Schedule 1 in a clear and comprehensible manner appropriate to the means of distance communication used, with due

regard in particular to the principles of good faith in commercial transactions and the principles governing the protection of those who are unable to give their consent such as minors.

(3) Subject to paragraph (4), the supplier shall make clear his commercial purpose when providing the information specified in Schedule 1.

(4) In the case of a voice telephone communication—

(a) the supplier shall make clear his identity and the commercial purpose of any call initiated by him at the beginning of any conversation with the consumer; and

(b) if the consumer explicitly consents, only the information specified in Schedule 2 need be given.

(5) The supplier shall ensure that the information he provides to the consumer pursuant to this regulation, regarding the contractual obligations which would arise if the distance contract were concluded, accurately reflects the contractual obligations which would arise under the law presumed to be applicable to that contract.

Written and additional information

8.—(1) The supplier under a distance contract shall communicate to the consumer on paper, or in another durable medium which is available and accessible to the consumer, all the contractual terms and conditions and the information specified in Schedule 1, either—

(a) in good time prior to the consumer being bound by that distance contract; or

(b) immediately after the conclusion of the contract, where the contract has been concluded at the consumer's request using a means of distance communication which does not enable provision in accordance with sub-paragraph (a) of the contractual terms and conditions and the information specified in Schedule 1.

(2) The supplier shall communicate the contractual terms and conditions to the consumer on paper, if the consumer so requests at any time during their contractual relationship.

(3) Paragraph (2) does not apply if the supplier has already communicated the contractual terms and conditions to the consumer on paper during that contractual relationship, and those terms and conditions have not changed since they were so communicated.

(4) The supplier shall change the means of distance communication with the consumer if the consumer so requests at any time during his contractual relationship with the supplier, unless that is incompatible with the distance contract or the nature of the financial service provided to the consumer.

Right to cancel

9.—(1) Subject to regulation 11, if within the cancellation period set out in regulation 10 notice of cancellation is properly given by the consumer to the supplier, the notice of cancellation shall operate to cancel the distance contract.

(2) Cancelling the contract has the effect of terminating the contract at the time at which the notice of cancellation is given.

(3) For the purposes of these Regulations, a notice of cancellation is a notification given—

(a) orally (where the supplier has informed the consumer that notice of cancellation may be given orally),

(b) in writing, or

(c) in another durable medium available and accessible to the supplier,

which, however expressed, indicates the intention of the consumer to cancel the contract by that notification.

(4) Notice of cancellation given under this regulation by a consumer to a supplier is to be treated as having been properly given if the consumer—

(a) gives it orally to the supplier (where the supplier has informed the consumer that notice of cancellation may be given orally);

(b) leaves it at the address of the supplier last known to the consumer and addressed to the supplier by name (in which case it is to be taken to have been given on the day on which it was left);

(c) sends it by post to the address of the supplier last known to the consumer and addressed to the supplier by name (in which case it is to be taken to have been given on the day on which it was posted);

(d) sends it by facsimile to the business facsimile number of the supplier last known to the consumer (in which case it is to be taken to have been given on the day on which it was sent);

(e) sends it by electronic mail to the business electronic mail address of the supplier last known to the consumer (in which case it is to be taken to have been given on the day on which it is sent); or

(f) by other electronic means—

(i) sends it to an internet address or web-site which the supplier has notified the consumer may be used for the purpose, or

(ii) indicates it on such a web-site in accordance with instructions which are on the web-site or which the supplier has provided to the consumer,

(in which case it is to be taken to have been given on the day on which it is sent to that address or web-site or indicated on that web-site).

(5) The references in paragraph (4)(b) and (c) to the address of the supplier shall, in the case of a supplier which is a body corporate, be treated as including a reference to the address of the secretary or clerk of that body.

(6) The references in paragraph (4)(b) and (c) to the address of the supplier shall, in the case of a supplier which is a partnership, be treated as including a reference to the address of a partner or a person having control or management of the partnership business.

(7) In this regulation—

(a) every reference to the supplier includes a reference to any other person previously notified by or on behalf of the supplier to the consumer as a person to whom notice of cancellation may be given;

(b) the references to giving notice of cancellation orally include giving such notice by voice telephone communication, where the supplier has informed the consumer that notice of cancellation may be given in that way; and

(c) "electronic mail" has the same meaning as in regulation 2(1) of the Privacy and Electronic Communications (EC Directive) Regulations 2003 (interpretation)[7].

Cancellation period

10.—(1) For the purposes of regulation 9, the cancellation period begins on the day on which the distance contract is concluded ("conclusion day") and ends as provided for in paragraphs (2) to (5).

(2) Where the supplier complies with regulation 8(1) on or before conclusion day, the cancellation period ends on the expiry of fourteen calendar days beginning with the day after conclusion day.

(3) Where the supplier does not comply with regulation 8(1) on or before conclusion day, but subsequently communicates to the consumer on paper, or in another durable medium which is available and accessible to the consumer, all the contractual terms and conditions and the information required under regulation 8(1), the cancellation period ends on the expiry of fourteen calendar days beginning with the day after the day on which the consumer receives the last of those terms and conditions and that information.

(4) In the case of a distance contract relating to life insurance, for the references to conclusion day in paragraphs (2) and (3) there are substituted references to the day on which the consumer is informed that the distance contract has been concluded.

(5) In the case of a distance contract relating to life insurance or a personal pension, for the references to fourteen calendar days in paragraphs (2) and (3) there are substituted references to thirty calendar days.

Exceptions to the right to cancel

11.—(1) Subject to paragraphs (2) and (3), regulation 9 does not confer on a consumer a right to cancel a distance contract which is—

(a) a contract for a financial service where the price of that service depends on fluctuations in the financial market outside the supplier's control, which may occur during the cancellation period, such as services related to—

    (i)   foreign exchange,

    (ii)   money market instruments,

    (iii) transferable securities,

    (iv) units in collective investment undertakings,

    (v)   financial-futures contracts, including equivalent cash-settled instruments,

    (vi) forward interest-rate agreements,

    (vii) interest-rate, currency and equity swaps,

    (viii) options to acquire or dispose of any instruments referred to in sub-paragraphs (i) to (vii), including cash-settled instruments and options on currency and on interest rates;

(b) a contract whose performance has been fully completed by both parties at the consumer's express request before the consumer gives notice of cancellation;

---

[7] S.I. 2003/2426.back

(c) a contract which—

    (i)   is a connected contract of insurance within the meaning of article 72B(1) of the Regulated Activities Order (activities carried on by a provider of relevant goods or services)[8],

    (ii) covers travel risks within the meaning of article 72B(1)(d)(ii) of that Order, and

    (iii) has a total duration of less than one month;

(d) a contract under which a supplier provides credit to a consumer and the consumer's obligation to repay is secured by a legal mortgage on land;

(e) a credit agreement cancelled under regulation 15(1) of the Consumer Protection (Distance Selling) Regulations 2000 (automatic cancellation of a related credit agreement)[9];

(f) a credit agreement cancelled under section 6A of the Timeshare Act 1992 (automatic cancellation of timeshare credit agreement)[10]; or

(g) a restricted-use credit agreement (within the meaning of the 1974 Act) to finance the purchase of land or an existing building, or an agreement for a bridging loan in connection with the purchase of land or an existing building.

(2) Paragraph (1) does not apply to a distance contract if the supplier has not complied with regulation 8(1), unless—

    (a) the circumstances fall within regulation 8(1)(b); and

    (b) the supplier has complied with regulation 7(1) and (2) or, if applicable, regulation 7(4)(b), and with regulation 7(5).

(3) Where—

    (a) the conditions in sub-paragraphs (a) and (b) of paragraph (2) are satisfied in relation to a distance contract falling within paragraph (1),

    (b) the supplier has not complied with regulation 8(1), and

    (c) the consumer has not, by the end of the sixth day after the day on which the distance contract is concluded, received all the contractual terms and conditions and the information required under regulation 8(1),

the consumer may cancel the contract under regulation 9 during the period beginning on the seventh day after the day on which the distance contract is concluded and ending when he receives the last of the contractual terms and conditions and the information required under regulation 8(1).

Automatic cancellation of an attached distance contract

12.—(1) For the purposes of this regulation, where there is a distance contract for the provision of a financial service by a supplier to a consumer ("the main contract") and there is

---

[8] Article 72B was inserted by article 11 of S.I. 2003/1476, and comes into force on 31st October 2004 for certain purposes and on 14th January 2005 for other purposes: see article 1(3) of S.I. 2003/1476.back

[9] S.I. 2000/2334.back

[10] 1992 c. 35; section 6A was inserted by regulation 11(3) of S.I. 1997/1081.back

a further distance contract ("the secondary contract") for the provision to that consumer of a further financial service by—

(a) the same supplier, or

(b) a third party, the further financial service being provided pursuant to an agreement between the third party and the supplier under the main contract,

then the secondary contract (referred to in these Regulations as an "attached contract") is attached to the main contract if any of the conditions in paragraph (2) are satisfied.

(2) The conditions referred to in paragraph (1) are—

(a) the secondary contract is entered into in compliance with a term of the main contract;

(b) the main contract is, or is to be, financed by the secondary contract;

(c) the main contract is a debtor-creditor-supplier agreement within the meaning of the 1974 Act, and the secondary contract is, or is to be, financed by the main contract;

(d) the secondary contract is entered into by the consumer to induce the supplier to enter into the main contract;

(e) performance of the secondary contract requires performance of the main contract.

(3) Where a main contract is cancelled by a notice of cancellation given under regulation 9—

(a) the cancellation of the main contract also operates to cancel, at the time at which the main contract is cancelled, any attached contract which is not a contract or agreement of a type listed in regulation 11(1); and

(b) the supplier under the main contract shall, if he is not the supplier under the attached contract, forthwith on receipt of the notice of cancellation inform the supplier under the attached contract.

(4) Paragraph (3)(a) does not apply to an attached contract if, at or before the time at which the notice of cancellation in respect of the main contract is given, the consumer has given and not withdrawn a notice to the supplier under the main contract that cancellation of the main contract is not to operate to cancel that attached contract.

(5) Where a main contract made by an authorised person, the making or performance of which constitutes or is part of a regulated activity carried on by him, is cancelled under rules made by the Authority corresponding to regulation 9—

(a) the cancellation of the main contract also operates to cancel, at the time at which the main contract is cancelled, any attached contract which is not a contract or agreement of a type listed in regulation 11(1); and

(b) the supplier under the main contract shall, if he is not the supplier under the attached contract, inform the supplier under the attached contract forthwith on receiving notification of the consumer's intention to cancel the main contract by that notification.

(6) Paragraph (5)(a) does not apply to an attached contract if, at or before the time at which the consumer gives notification of his intention to cancel the main contract by that notification, the consumer has given and not withdrawn a notice to the supplier under the main contract that cancellation of the main contract is not to operate to cancel that attached contract.

Payment for services provided before cancellation

13.—(1) This regulation applies where a cancellation event occurs in relation to a distance contract.

(2) In this regulation, "cancellation event" means the cancellation of a distance contract under regulation 9 or 12.

(3) The supplier shall refund any sum paid by or on behalf of the consumer under or in relation to the contract to the person by whom it was paid, less any charge made in accordance with paragraph (6), as soon as possible and in any event within a period not exceeding 30 calendar days beginning with—

(a) the day on which the cancellation event occurred; or

(b) if the supplier proves that this is later—

(i) in the case of a contract cancelled under regulation 9, the day on which the supplier in fact received the notice of cancellation, or

(ii) in the case of an attached contract under which the supplier is not the supplier under the main contract, the day on which, pursuant to regulation 12(3)(b) or (5)(b), he was in fact informed by the supplier under the main contract of the cancellation of the main contract.

(4) The reference in paragraph (3) to any sum paid on behalf of the consumer includes any sum paid by any other person ("the creditor"), who is not the supplier, under an agreement between the consumer and the creditor by which the creditor provides the consumer with credit of any amount.

(5) Where any security has been provided in relation to the contract, the security (so far as it has been provided) shall, on cancellation under regulation 9 or 12, be treated as never having had effect; and any property lodged solely for the purposes of the security as so provided shall be returned forthwith by the person with whom it is lodged.

(6) Subject to paragraphs (7), (8) and (9), the supplier may make a charge for any service actually provided by the supplier in accordance with the contract.

(7) The charge shall not exceed an amount which is in proportion to the extent of the service provided to the consumer prior to the time at which the cancellation event occurred (including the service of arranging to provide the financial service) in comparison with the full coverage of the contract, and in any event shall not be such that it could be construed as a penalty.

(8) The supplier may not make any charge unless he can prove on the balance of probabilities that the consumer was informed about the amount payable in accordance with—

(a) regulation 7(1) and paragraph 13 of Schedule 1,

(b) regulation 7(4) and paragraph 5 of Schedule 2, or

(c) rules corresponding to those provisions,

as the case may be.

(9) The supplier may not make any charge if, without the consumer's prior request, he commenced performance of the contract prior to the expiry of the relevant cancellation period.

(10) In paragraph (9), the relevant cancellation period is the cancellation period which—

(a) in the case of a main contract, is applicable to that contract, or

(b) in the case of an attached contract, would be applicable to that contract if that contract were a main contract,

under regulation 10, or under rules corresponding to that regulation, as the case may be.

(11) The consumer shall, as soon as possible and in any event within a period not exceeding 30 calendar days beginning with the day on which the cancellation event occurred—

(a) refund any sum paid by or on behalf of the supplier under or in relation to that contract to the person by whom it was paid; and

(b) either restore to the supplier any property of which he has acquired possession under that contract, or deliver or send that property to any person to whom, under regulation 9, a notice of cancellation could have been given in respect of that contract.

(12) Breach of a duty imposed by paragraph (11) on a consumer is actionable as a breach of statutory duty.

Payment by card
14.—(1) Subject to paragraph (2), where—

(a) a payment card has been issued to an individual who, when entering the contract for the provision of that card, was acting for purposes which were outside any business he may carry on ("the card-holder"), and

(b) fraudulent use is made of that card to make a payment under or in connection with a distance contract to which these Regulations apply, by another person who is neither acting, nor to be treated as acting, as the card-holder's agent,

the card-holder may request cancellation of that payment, and is entitled to be recredited with the sum paid, or to have it returned, by the card issuer.

(2) Where paragraph (1) applies and, in any proceedings, the card-holder alleges that any use made of the payment card was not authorised by him, it is for the card issuer to prove that the use was so authorised.

(3) Paragraph (1) does not apply if the contract for the provision of the payment card is an agreement to which section 83(1) of the 1974 Act (liability for misuse of credit facilities) applies.

(4) After subsection (3B) of section 84 of the 1974 Act (misuse of credit-tokens)[11] insert—

" (3C) Subsections (1) and (2) shall not apply to any use, in connection with a distance contract within the meaning of the Financial Services (Distance Marketing) Regulations 2004, of a card which is a credit-token.".

[11] Subsection (3B) was inserted into section 84 by regulation 21(5) of S.I. 2000/2334.back

(5) For the purposes of this regulation—

"card issuer" means the owner of the card;
"payment card" includes a credit card, a charge card, a debit card and a store card.

Unsolicited services

15.—(1) A person ("the recipient") who receives unsolicited financial services for purposes other than those of his business from another person who supplies those services in the course of his business, shall not thereby become subject to any obligation (to make payment, or otherwise).

(2) Where, in the course of any business—

(a) unsolicited financial services are supplied for purposes other than those of the recipient's business, and
(b) a person includes with the supply of those services a demand for payment, or an assertion of a present or prospective right to payment in respect of those services,

that person is guilty of an offence and liable, on summary conviction, to a fine not exceeding level 4 on the standard scale.

(3) A person who, not having reasonable cause to believe that there is a right to payment, in the course of any business and with a view to obtaining payment for what he knows are unsolicited financial services supplied as mentioned in paragraph (2)—

(a) threatens to bring any legal proceedings,
(b) places or causes to be placed the name of any person on a list of defaulters or debtors or threatens to do so, or
(c) invokes or causes to be invoked any other collection procedure or threatens to do so,

is guilty of an offence and liable, on summary conviction, to a fine not exceeding level 5 on the standard scale.

(4) In this regulation, "unsolicited" means, in relation to financial services supplied to any person, that they are supplied without any prior request made by or on behalf of that person.

(5) For the purposes of this regulation, a person who sends to a recipient an invoice or similar document which—

(a) states the amount of a payment, and
(b) does not comply with the requirements, applicable to invoices and similar documents, of regulations made under section 3A of the Unsolicited Goods and Services Act 1971 (contents and form of notes of agreement, invoices and similar documents)[12] or, as the case may be, article 6 of the Unsolicited Goods and Services (Northern Ireland) Order 1976 (contents and form of notes of agreement, invoices and similar documents)[13],

is to be regarded as asserting a right to the payment.

[12] 1971 c. 30; section 3A was inserted by section 1 of the Unsolicited Goods and Services (Amendment) Act 1975 (c. 13).back
[13] S.I. 1976/57 (N.I. 1), amended by S.I. 2000/2334 and S.R. 2004 No. 23.back

(6) Section 3A of the Unsolicited Goods and Services Act 1971 applies for the purposes of this regulation in its application to England, Wales and Scotland as it applies for the purposes of that Act.

(7) Article 6 of the Unsolicited Goods and Services (Northern Ireland) Order 1976 applies for the purposes of this regulation in its application to Northern Ireland as it applies for the purposes of that Order.

(8) This regulation is without prejudice to any right a supplier may have at any time, by contract or otherwise, to renew a distance contract with a consumer without any request made by or on behalf of that consumer prior to the renewal of that contract.

Prevention of contracting-out

16.—(1) A term contained in any contract is void if, and to the extent that, it is inconsistent with the application of a provision of these Regulations to a distance contract or the application of regulation 15 to a supply of unsolicited financial services.

(2) Where a provision of these Regulations specifies a duty or liability of the consumer in certain circumstances, a term contained in a contract is inconsistent with that provision if it purports to impose, directly or indirectly, an additional or greater duty or liability on him in those circumstances.

(3) These Regulations apply notwithstanding any contract term which applies or purports to apply the law of a State which is not an EEA State if the contract or supply has a close connection with the territory of an EEA State.

Enforcement authorities

17.—(1) For the purposes of regulations 18 to 21—

> (a) in relation to any alleged breach concerning a specified contract, the Authority is the enforcement authority;
> (b) in relation to any alleged breach concerning a contract under which the supplier is a local authority, but which is not a specified contract, the OFT is the enforcement authority;
> (c) in relation to any other alleged breach—
>
>> (i) the OFT, and
>> (ii) in Great Britain every local weights and measures authority, and in Northern Ireland the Department of Enterprise, Trade and Investment,
>> is an enforcement authority.

(2) For the purposes of paragraph (1) and regulation 22(6), each of the following is a specified contract—

> (a) a contract the making or performance of which constitutes or is part of a regulated activity carried on by the supplier;
> (b) a contract for the provision of a debit card;
> (c) a contract relating to the issuing of electronic money by a supplier to whom the Authority has given a certificate under article 9C of the Regulated Activities Order (persons certified as small issuers etc.)[14];

---

[14] Article 9C was inserted by article 4 of S.I. 2002/682.back

(d) a contract the effecting or carrying out of which is excluded from article 10(1) or (2) of the Regulated Activities Order (effecting and carrying out contracts of insurance) by article 12 of that order (breakdown insurance), where the supplier is a person who does not otherwise carry on an activity of the kind specified by article 10 of that order;

(e) a contract under which a supplier provides credit to a consumer and the obligation of the consumer to repay is secured by a first legal mortgage on land;

(f) a contract, made before 14th January 2005, for insurance mediation activity other than in respect of a contract of long-term care insurance.

(3) For the purposes of the application of this regulation and regulations 18 to 22 in relation to breaches of, and offences under, regulation 15, "contract"—

(a) wherever it appears in this regulation other than in the expression "contract of long-term care insurance", and

(b) in regulation 22(6),

is to be taken to mean "supply of financial services".

(4) For the purposes of this regulation—

"contract of long-term care insurance" has the same meaning as in the Financial Services and Markets Act 2000 (Regulated Activities) (Amendment) (No. 2) Order 2003[15];

"insurance mediation activity" means any activity which is not a regulated activity at the time the contract is made but will be a regulated activity of the kind specified by article 21, 25(1) or (2), 39A or 53 of the Regulated Activities Order when the amendments to that order made by the Financial Services and Markets Act 2000 (Regulated Activities) (Amendment) (No. 2) Order 2003 come into force[16];

"local authority" means—

(a) in England and Wales, a local authority within the meaning of the Local Government Act 1972[17], the Greater London Authority, the Common Council of the City of London or the Council of the Isles of Scilly,

(b) in Scotland, a council constituted under section 2 of the Local Government etc. (Scotland) Act 1994[18], and

(c) in Northern Ireland, a district council within the meaning of the Local Government Act (Northern Ireland) 1972[19].

---

[15] S.I. 2003/1476, as amended by S.I. 2004/1610.back

[16] Articles 4(1), 5(1), 7 and 9(1) of S.I. 2003/1476 amend articles 21 and 25(1), insert article 39A, and amend article 53 of the Regulated Activities Order with effect from 31st October 2004 for certain purposes and from 14th January 2005 for other purposes: see article 1(3).back

[17] 1972 c. 70; the definition of "local authority" in section 270 has been repealed in part by section 102(2) of and Schedule 17 to the Local Government Act 1985 (c. 51) and amended by section 1(5) of the Local Government (Wales) Act 1994 (c. 19).back

[18] 1994 c. 39.back

[19] 1972 c. 9 (N.I.).back

Consideration of complaints

18.—(1) An enforcement authority shall consider any complaint made to it about a breach unless—

(a) the complaint appears to that authority to be frivolous or vexatious; or

(b) that authority is aware that another enforcement authority has notified the OFT that it agrees to consider the complaint.

(2) If an enforcement authority notifies the OFT that it agrees to consider a complaint made to another enforcement authority, the first mentioned authority shall be under a duty to consider the complaint.

Injunctions to secure compliance with these Regulations

19.—(1) Subject to paragraph (2), an enforcement authority may apply for an injunction (including an interim injunction) against any person who appears to that authority to be responsible for a breach.

(2) An enforcement authority, other than the OFT or the Authority, may apply for an injunction only where—

(a) that authority has notified the OFT, at least fourteen days before the date on which the application is to be made, of its intention to apply; or

(b) the OFT consents to the application being made within a shorter period.

(3) On an application made under this regulation, the court may grant an injunction on such terms as it thinks fit to secure compliance with these Regulations.

(4) An enforcement authority which has a duty under regulation 18 to consider a complaint shall give reasons for its decision to apply or not to apply, as the case may be, for an injunction.

(5) In deciding whether or not to apply for an injunction in respect of a breach, an enforcement authority may, if it considers it appropriate to do so, have regard to any undertaking as to compliance with these Regulations given to it or to another enforcement authority by or on behalf of any person.

(6) In the application of this regulation to Scotland, for references to an "injunction" or an "interim injunction" there are substituted references to an "interdict" or an "interim interdict" respectively.

Notification of undertakings and orders to the OFT

20. An enforcement authority, other than the OFT and the Authority, shall notify the OFT of—

(a) any undertaking given to it by or on behalf of any person who appears to it to be responsible for a breach;

(b) the outcome of any application made by it under regulation 19 and the terms of any undertaking given to, or order made by, the court; and

(c) the outcome of any application made by it to enforce a previous order of the court.

Publication, information and advice

21.—(1) The OFT shall arrange for the publication, in such form and manner as it considers appropriate, of details of any undertaking or order notified to it under regulation 20.

(2) Each of the OFT and the Authority shall arrange for the publication in such form and manner as it considers appropriate of—

(a) details of any undertaking as to compliance with these Regulations given to it by or on behalf of any person;

(b) details of any application made by it under regulation 19[a], and of the terms of any undertaking given to, or order made by, the court; and

(c) details of any application made by it to enforce a previous order of the court.

(3) Each of the OFT and the Authority may arrange for the dissemination, in such form and manner as it considers appropriate, of such information and advice concerning the operation of these Regulations as may appear to it to be expedient to give to the public and to all persons likely to be affected by these Regulations.

Offences

22.—(1) A supplier under a distance contract who fails to comply with regulation 7(3) or (4)(a) or regulation 8(2) or (4) is guilty of an offence and liable, on summary conviction, to a fine not exceeding level 3 on the standard scale.

(2) If an offence under paragraph (1), or under regulation 15(2) or (3), committed by a body corporate is shown—

(a) to have been committed with the consent or connivance of any director, manager, secretary or other similar officer of the body corporate, or any person who was purporting to act in any such capacity, or

(b) to be attributable to any neglect on his part,

he as well as the body corporate is guilty of the offence and liable to be proceeded against and punished accordingly.

(3) If the affairs of a body corporate are managed by its members, paragraph (2) applies in relation to the acts and defaults of a member in connection with his functions of management as if he were a director of the body.

(4) If an offence under paragraph (1), or under regulation 15(2) or (3), committed by a partnership is shown—

(a) to have been committed with the consent or connivance of any partner, or any person who was purporting to act as a partner, or

(b) to be attributable to any neglect on his part,

he as well as the partnership is guilty of an offence and liable to be proceeded against and punished accordingly.

(5) If an offence under paragraph (1), or under regulation 15(2) or (3), committed by an unincorporated association (other than a partnership) is shown—

(a) to have been committed with the consent or connivance of an officer of the association or a member of its governing body, or any person who was purporting to act in any such capacity, or

(b) to be attributable to any neglect on his part,

he as well as the association is guilty of an offence and liable to be proceeded against and punished accordingly.

(6) Except in Scotland—

(a) the Authority may institute proceedings for an offence under these Regulations which relates to a specified contract;

(b) the OFT, and—

(i)   in Great Britain, every local weights and measures authority,

(ii) in Northern Ireland, the Department of Enterprise, Trade and Investment,

may institute proceedings for any other offence under these Regulations.

Functions of the Authority
23. The functions conferred on the Authority by these Regulations shall be treated as if they were conferred by the 2000 Act.

Amendment of the Unfair Terms in Consumer Contracts Regulations 1999
24.—(1) The Unfair Terms in Consumer Contracts Regulations 1999[20] are amended as follows.

(2) After regulation 3(1) (interpretation), insert—

"(1A) The references—

(a) in regulation 4(1) to a seller or a supplier, and

(b) in regulation 8(1) to a seller or supplier,

include references to a distance supplier and to an intermediary.

(1B) In paragraph (1A) and regulation 5(6)—

"distance supplier" means—

(a) a supplier under a distance contract within the meaning of the Financial Services (Distance Marketing) Regulations 2004, or

(b) a supplier of unsolicited financial services within regulation 15 of those Regulations; and

"intermediary" has the same meaning as in those Regulations.".

(3) After regulation 5(5) (unfair terms), insert—

"(6) Any contractual term providing that a consumer bears the burden of proof in respect of showing whether a distance supplier or an intermediary complied with any or all of the obligations placed upon him resulting from the Directive and any rule or enactment implementing it shall always be regarded as unfair.

---

[20] S.I. 1999/2083, amended by S.I. 2001/1186 and S.I. 2003/3182.back

(7) In paragraph (6)—

"the Directive" means Directive 2002/65/EC of the European Parliament and of the Council of 23 September 2002 concerning the distance marketing of consumer financial services and amending Council Directive 90/619/EEC and Directives 97/7/EC and 98/27/EC; and

"rule" means a rule made by the Financial Services Authority under the Financial Services and Markets Act 2000 or by a designated professional body within the meaning of section 326(2) of that Act.".

Amendment of the Consumer Protection (Distance Selling) Regulations 2000

25.—(1) The Consumer Protection (Distance Selling) Regulations 2000[21] are amended as follows.

(2) In regulation 3(1) (interpretation)—

(a) before the definition of "breach" insert—

" "the 2000 Act" means the Financial Services and Markets Act 2000;
"appointed representative" has the same meaning as in section 39(2) of the 2000 Act;
"authorised person" has the same meaning as in section 31(2) of the 2000 Act;";

(b) after the definition of "excepted contract" insert—

" 'financial service' means any service of a banking, credit, insurance, personal pension, investment or payment nature;";

(c) after the definition of "personal credit agreement" insert—

" 'regulated activity' has the same meaning as in section 22 of the 2000 Act;".

(3) In regulation 5(1)(c) (excepted contracts) omit ", a non-exhaustive list of which is contained in Schedule 2".

(4) After regulation 6(3) (contracts to which only part of those Regulations apply) insert—

" (4) Regulations 7 to 14, 17 to 20 and 25 do not apply to any contract which is made, and regulation 24 does not apply to any unsolicited services which are supplied, by an authorised person where the making or performance of that contract or the supply of those services, as the case may be, constitutes or is part of a regulated activity carried on by him.
(5) Regulations 7 to 9, 17 to 20 and 25 do not apply to any contract which is made, and regulation 24 does not apply to any unsolicited services which are supplied, by an appointed representative where the making or performance of that contract or the supply of those services, as the case may be, constitutes or is part of a regulated activity carried on by him.".

(5) Omit Schedule 2 (non-exhaustive list of financial services).

---

[21] S.I. 2000/2334.back

Amendment of the Enterprise Act 2002

26. In Part 1 of Schedule 13 to the Enterprise Act 2002 (listed directives)[22], after paragraph 9 insert—

"9A Directive 2002/65/EC of the European Parliament and of the Council of 23 September 2002 concerning the distance marketing of consumer financial services and amending Council Directive 90/619/EEC and Directives 97/7/EC and 98/27/EC.".

Amendment of the Enterprise Act 2002 (Part 8 Community Infringements Specified UK Laws) Order 2003

27. In the table in the Schedule to the Enterprise Act 2002 (Part 8 Community Infringements Specified UK Laws) Order 2003 (listed directives)[23], after the entry for Directive 2000/31/EC ("Directive on electronic commerce") insert—

Directive 2002/65/EC of the European Parliament and of the Council of 23 September 2002 concerning the distance marketing of consumer financial services and amending Council Directive 90/619/EEC and Directives 97/7/EC and 98/27/EC.	Financial Services (Distance Marketing) Regulations 2004; rules corresponding to any provisions of those Regulations made by the Financial Services Authority or a designated professional body within the meaning of section 326(2) of the Financial Services and Markets Act 2000.".

Amendment of the Enterprise Act 2002 (Part 8 Notice to OFT of Intended Prosecution Specified Enactments, Revocation and Transitional Provision) Order 2003

28. In the table in the Schedule to the Enterprise Act 2002 (Part 8 Notice to OFT of Intended Prosecution Specified Enactments, Revocation and Transitional Provision) Order 2003[24], after the entry for the Fair Trading Act 1973[25] insert—

Financial Services (Distance Marketing) Regulations 2004.	All offences under those Regulations.".

Transitional provisions

29.—(1) In relation to any contract made before 31st May 2005 which is a consumer credit agreement within the meaning of the 1974 Act and a regulated agreement within the meaning of that Act—

    (a) regulations 7, 8, 10 and 11 apply subject to the modifications in paragraphs (2) to (5); and

    (b) references in these Regulations to regulations 7, 8, 10 and 11 or to provisions contained in them shall be construed accordingly.

---

[22] 2002 c. 40.back
[23] S.I. 2003/1374.back
[24] S.I. 2003/1376.back
[25] 1973 c. 41.back

(2) In regulation 7—

    (a) in paragraphs (1) to (3), before "Schedule 1" at each place where it occurs insert "paragraph 13 of"; and

    (b) in paragraph (4)(b), before "Schedule 2" insert "paragraph 5 of".

(3) In regulation 8(1), for "contractual terms and conditions and the information specified in" at each place where it occurs substitute "information specified in paragraph 13 of".

(4) In regulation 10(3), omit—

    (a) "the contractual terms and conditions and"; and

    (b) "those terms and conditions and".

(5) In regulation 11(3), omit "the contractual terms and conditions and" at each place where it occurs.

John Heppell Joan Ryan
Two of the Lords Commissioners of Her Majesty's Treasury

4th August 2004

SCHEDULE 1

Regulations 7(1) and 8(1)

Information required prior to the conclusion of the contract

1. The identity and the main business of the supplier, the geographical address at which the supplier is established and any other geographical address relevant to the consumer's relations with the supplier.

2. Where the supplier has a representative established in the consumer's State of residence, the identity of that representative and the geographical address relevant to the consumer's relations with him.

3. Where the consumer's dealings are with any professional other than the supplier, the identity of that professional, the capacity in which he is acting with respect to the consumer, and the geographical address relevant to the consumer's relations with that professional.

4. Where the supplier is registered in a trade or similar public register, the particulars of the register in which the supplier is entered and his registration number or an equivalent means of identification in that register.

5. Where the supplier's activity is subject to an authorisation scheme, the particulars of the relevant supervisory authority.

6. A description of the main characteristics of the financial service.

7. The total price to be paid by the consumer to the supplier for the financial service, including all related fees, charges and expenses, and all taxes paid via the supplier or, where an exact price cannot be indicated, the basis for the calculation of the price enabling the consumer to verify it.

8. Where relevant, notice indicating that: (i) the financial service is related to instruments involving special risks related to their specific features or the operations to be executed or whose price depends on fluctuations in the financial markets outside the supplier's control; and (ii) historical performances are no indicators for future performances.

9. Notice of the possibility that other taxes or costs may exist that are not paid via the supplier or imposed by him.

10. Any limitations of the period for which the information provided is valid.

11. The arrangements for payment and for performance.

12. Any specific additional cost for the consumer of using the means of distance communication, if such additional cost is charged.

13. Whether or not there is a right of cancellation and, where there is a right of cancellation, its duration and the conditions for exercising it, including information on the amount which the consumer may be required to pay in accordance with regulation 13, as well as the consequences of not exercising that right.

14. The minimum duration of the distance contract in the case of financial services to be performed indefinitely or recurrently.

15. Information on any rights the parties may have to terminate the distance contract early or unilaterally by virtue of the terms of the contract, including any penalties imposed by the contract in such cases.

16. Practical instructions for exercising the right to cancel in accordance with regulation 9 indicating, among other things, the address at which the notice of cancellation should be left or to which it should be sent by post, and any facsimile number or electronic mail address to which it should be sent.

17. The EEA State or States whose laws are taken by the supplier as a basis for the establishment of relations with the consumer prior to the conclusion of the distance contract.

18. Any contractual clause on the law applicable to the distance contract or on the competent court.

19. In which language, or languages: (i) the contractual terms and conditions, and the prior information specified in this Schedule, are supplied; and (ii) the supplier, with the agreement of the consumer, undertakes to communicate during the duration of the distance contract.

20. Whether or not there is an out-of-court complaint and redress mechanism for the consumer and, if so, the methods for having access to it.

21. The existence of guarantee funds or other compensation arrangements, except to the extent that they are required by Directive 94/19/EC of the European Parliament and of the Council of 30 May 1994 on deposit guarantee schemes[26] or Directive 97/9/EC of the European Parliament and of the Council of 3 March 1997 on investor compensation schemes[27].

SCHEDULE 2

Regulation 7(4)(b)

Information required in the case of voice telephone communications

1. The identity of the person in contact with the consumer and his link with the supplier.

2. A description of the main characteristics of the financial service.

[26] O.J. L 135, 31.5.1994, p. 5.back
[27] O.J. L 84, 26.3.1997, p. 22.back

3. The total price to be paid by the consumer to the supplier for the financial service including all taxes paid via the supplier or, if an exact price cannot be indicated, the basis for the calculation of the price enabling the consumer to verify it.

4. Notice of the possibility that other taxes or costs may exist that are not paid via the supplier or imposed by him.

5. Whether or not there is a right to cancel and, where there is such a right, its duration and the conditions for exercising it, including information on the amount which the consumer may be required to pay in accordance with regulation 13, as well as the consequences of not exercising that right.

6. That other information is available on request and the nature of that information.

EXPLANATORY NOTE

(This note is not part of the Regulations)

These Regulations give effect in the United Kingdom to Directive 2002/65/EC of the European Parliament and of the Council of 23 September 2002 concerning the distance marketing of consumer financial services and amending Council Directive 90/619/EEC and Directives 97/7/EC and 98/27/EC (O.J. L 271, 9.10.2002, p.16) ("the Directive") so far as it is not given effect by rules made by the Financial Services Authority under the Financial Services and Markets Act 2000 or made by a professional body designated under that Act.

Regulations 3 to 5 identify the transactions to which the substantive provisions of these Regulations apply. Regulation 3 defines these as "distance contracts", as defined in regulation 2(1) (or, for the purposes of regulation 15, comparable supplies of financial services) made on or after the date on which the Regulations come into force. Regulation 4 then disapplies certain provisions from various categories of contract and supply where equivalent provision is made by other regimes: paragraph (1) excludes contracts and supplies made by suppliers established in another State within the European Economic Area where the law of that State regulates the contract or supply in accordance with the Directive; paragraphs (2) to (4), taken with paragraphs (5) and (6), exclude contracts and supplies in relation to which effect is given to the Directive by rules made or approved by the Financial Services Authority under the Financial Services and Markets Act 2000. Regulation 5 gives effect to Article 1(2) of the Directive in the light of Recital (17) in the Directive's preamble, under which the substantive provisions of the Directive only apply to an "initial service agreement" with a financial services supplier or the first in a series of similar operations, and not to every subsequent transaction carried out under that agreement or in that series.

Regulation 6 sets out how the Regulations apply in cases where financial services are marketed through an intermediary, as contemplated by Recital (19) in the preamble to the Directive. Some provisions of the Regulations apply to the intermediary instead of the supplier; others apply to either or both of them; others again still apply only to the supplier.

Regulations 7 and 8 and the Schedules contain the first set of main provisions, requiring suppliers of financial services, where the Regulations apply, to provide consumers with certain information listed in the Schedules. This information generally has to be provided before the consumer is bound by a distance contract for supply of the financial services in question.

Regulations 9 to 13 contain the next set of main provisions, giving consumers a right to cancel most distance contracts for financial services during a set period after commencement of the contract.

Regulation 9 contains the right to cancel, specifying the means by which the right can be exercised and defining the effect of cancellation as termination of the contract at the time at which the notice of cancellation is given. Regulation 10 defines the period during which the cancellation right can be exercised: generally from the time the consumer is bound by the contract until 14 days after that, or until 14 days after the information required by regulation 8 is provided if later, but until 30 days after the later of those dates in the case of a contract for a personal pension and until 30 days after the day on which the consumer is informed that the distance contract has been concluded in the case of a contract for life insurance. Paragraph (1) of regulation 11 lists certain types of contract to which, as permitted by the Directive, the cancellation right does not apply except in the circumstances dealt with in paragraphs (2) and (3) of that regulation.

Regulation 12 provides that, where a distance contract is cancelled under regulation 9, certain other subsidiary distance contracts connected with that contract—defined in paragraph (1) as "attached contracts"—are automatically cancelled too.

Regulation 13 then provides for the consequences of cancellation of distance contracts, whether by notice under regulation 9 or automatically under regulation 12: the supplier must refund any sums received from the consumer under the contract, less a proportionate charge for any services already supplied, and must release and return to the consumer any security taken under the contract; the consumer must repay to the supplier any money paid to the consumer under the contract, and return any property acquired under it.

Regulation 14 provides that, where a plastic card issued to a consumer is used fraudulently by someone else to make a payment in connection with a distance contract (other than where the Consumer Credit Act 1974 (c. 39) covers the matter), the consumer is entitled to cancel the payment and to have all sums paid recredited or returned by the card issuer.

Regulation 15 prevents consumers from being bound by any obligation in respect of financial services supplied to them but for which they have not asked; and makes it a criminal offence to demand or assert a right to payment with any such supply, or to take or threaten enforcement action with a view to obtaining payment for such a supply, without reason to believe payment is legally due.

Regulation 16 is designed to prevent the Regulations being undermined. It renders void any contractual term which is inconsistent with any provision of these Regulations or purports to impose on a consumer additional or greater duties or liabilities than those provided for in the Regulations; and it overrides any contractual term which aims to apply the law of a non-EEA State so as to prevent a contract or supply closely connected with an EEA State from being governed by the provisions of the Directive.

Regulations 17 to 21 and 26 to 28 contain or provide for enforcement mechanisms in relation to the substantive provisions of the Regulations.

Paragraph (1) of regulation 17 specifies for these purposes that the enforcement authority for certain types of distance contract or supply listed in paragraph (2) is the Financial Services Authority, and that the enforcement authorities for other distance contracts and supplies are the Office of Fair Trading with local weights and measures authorities (in Great Britain) or with the Department of Enterprise, Trade and Investment (in Northern Ireland). Regulation 18 requires any such enforcement authority to consider complaints made to it about breaches of the Regulations unless the complaint is frivolous or vexatious or another enforcement authority has agreed to deal with it. Regulation 19 enables enforcement authorities to apply to the courts for injunctions against persons responsible for breaches of the Regulations, and regulations 20 and 21 provide for notification and publication of details about injunctions granted and undertakings given in relation to such breaches.

Regulations 26 and 27 bring the Directive, these Regulations, and relevant rules corresponding to them, within the scope of Part 8 of the Enterprise Act 2002 (c. 40), which contains special powers for the enforcement of certain consumer legislation; regulation 28 brings offences under these Regulations within the scope of section 230 of that Act, so that local weights and measures authorities must notify the OFT of intended prosecutions under these Regulations.

Regulation 22 provides that breaches of certain provisions of the Regulations are criminal offences, provides for personal criminal liability on the part of certain officers or members of corporate and other bodies where they are responsible for the commission by such bodies of offences under the Regulations, and gives the enforcement authorities power to prosecute offences under the Regulations within their respective spheres of responsibility.

Regulation 23 provides that the functions of the FSA under the Regulations are to be treated as functions under the Financial Services and Markets Act 2000 (c. 8) so as to apply for the purposes of these Regulations various general powers and provisions of that Act.

Regulation 24 amends the Unfair Terms in Consumer Contracts Regulations 1999 (S.I. 1999/2083) so as to deem automatically unfair, for the purposes of those Regulations, any contractual term placing on a consumer the burden of proving whether a supplier or intermediary has complied with obligations deriving from the Directive or any provision implementing it.

Regulation 25 makes amendments to the Consumer Protection (Distance Selling) Regulations 2000 (S.I. 2000/2334) consequential upon the provisions of these Regulations.

Regulation 29 contains transitional provisions in connection with the application of these Regulations to regulated consumer credit agreements.

A full regulatory impact assessment of the effect that this instrument will have on the costs of business is available. Copies of it have been placed in the libraries of both Houses of Parliament, and copies are also available from the Savings and Investment Products Team, HM Treasury, 1 Horse Guards Road, London SW1A 2HQ and at www.hm-treasury.gov.uk.

ISBN 0 11 049681 7

Appendix 14

Statutory Instrument 2000 No. 2699

The Telecommunications (Lawful Business Practice) (Interception of Communications) Regulations 2000

© Crown Copyright 2000

STATUTORY INSTRUMENTS

2000 No. 2699

INVESTIGATORY POWERS

The Telecommunications (Lawful Business Practice)
(Interception of Communications) Regulations 2000

Made	*2nd October 2000*
Laid before Parliament	*3rd October 2000*
Coming into force	*24th October 2000*

The Secretary of State, in exercise of the powers conferred on him by sections 4(2) and 78(5) of the Regulation of Investigatory Powers Act 2000[1] ("the Act"), hereby makes the following Regulations:—

Citation and commencement

1. These Regulations may be cited as the Telecommunications (Lawful Business Practice) (Interception of Communications) Regulations 2000 and shall come into force on 24th October 2000.

Interpretation

2. In these Regulations—

(a) references to a business include references to activities of a government department, of any public authority or of any person or office holder on whom functions are conferred by or under any enactment;

(b) a reference to a communication as relevant to a business is a reference to—

(i) a communication—

(aa) by means of which a transaction is entered into in the course of that business, or

---

[1] 2000 c. 23.back

(bb) which otherwise relates to that business, or

(ii) a communication which otherwise takes place in the course of the carrying on of that business;

(c) "regulatory or self-regulatory practices or procedures" means practices or procedures—

(i) compliance with which is required or recommended by, under or by virtue of—

(aa) any provision of the law of a member state or other state within the European Economic Area, or
(bb) any standard or code of practice published by or on behalf of a body established in a member state or other state within the European Economic Area which includes amongst its objectives the publication of standards or codes of practice for the conduct of business, or

(ii) which are otherwise applied for the purpose of ensuring compliance with anything so required or recommended;

(d) "system controller" means, in relation to a particular telecommunication system, a person with a right to control its operation or use.

Lawful interception of a communication

3.—(1) For the purpose of section 1(5)(a) of the Act, conduct is authorised, subject to paragraphs (2) and (3) below, if it consists of interception of a communication, in the course of its transmission by means of a telecommunication system, which is effected by or with the express or implied consent of the system controller for the purpose of—

(a) monitoring or keeping a record of communications—

(i) in order to—

(aa) establish the existence of facts, or
(bb) ascertain compliance with regulatory or self-regulatory practices or procedures which are—

applicable to the system controller in the carrying on of his business or

applicable to another person in the carrying on of his business where that person is supervised by the system controller in respect of those practices or procedures, or

(cc) ascertain or demonstrate the standards which are achieved or ought to be achieved by persons using the system in the course of their duties, or

(ii) in the interests of national security, or
(iii) for the purpose of preventing or detecting crime, or
(iv) for the purpose of investigating or detecting the unauthorised use of that or any other telecommunication system, or

    (v) where that is undertaken—

        (aa) in order to secure, or
        (bb) as an inherent part of,

the effective operation of the system (including any monitoring or keeping of a record which would be authorised by section 3(3) of the Act if the conditions in paragraphs (a) and (b) thereof were satisfied); or

(b) monitoring communications for the purpose of determining whether they are communications relevant to the system controller's business which fall within regulation 2(b)(i) above; or
(c) monitoring communications made to a confidential voice-telephony counselling or support service which is free of charge (other than the cost, if any, of making a telephone call) and operated in such a way that users may remain anonymous if they so choose.

  (2) Conduct is authorised by paragraph (1) of this regulation only if—

(a) the interception in question is effected solely for the purpose of monitoring or (where appropriate) keeping a record of communications relevant to the system controller's business;
(b) the telecommunication system in question is provided for use wholly or partly in connection with that business;
(c) the system controller has made all reasonable efforts to inform every person who may use the telecommunication system in question that communications transmitted by means thereof may be intercepted; and
(d) in a case falling within—

    (i)   paragraph (1)(a)(ii) above, the person by or on whose behalf the interception is effected is a person specified in section 6(2)(a) to (i) of the Act;
    (ii) paragraph (1)(b) above, the communication is one which is intended to be received (whether or not it has been actually received) by a person using the telecommunication system in question.

  (3) Conduct falling within paragraph (1)(a)(i) above is authorised only to the extent that Article 5 of Directive 97/66/EC of the European Parliament and of the Council of 15 December 1997 concerning the processing of personal data and the protection of privacy in the telecommunications sector[2] so permits.

Patricia Hewitt,
Minister for Small Business and E-Commerce, Department of Trade and Industry

2nd October 2000

[2] O.J. No. L24, 30.1.98, p.1.back

EXPLANATORY NOTE

(This note is not part of the Regulations)

These Regulations authorise certain interceptions of telecommunication communications which would otherwise be prohibited by section 1 of the Regulation of Investigatory Powers Act 2000. To the extent that the interceptions are also prohibited by Article 5.1 of Directive 97/66/EC, the authorisation does not exceed that permitted by Articles 5.2 and 14.1 of the Directive.

The interception has to be by or with the consent of a person carrying on a business (which includes the activities of government departments, public authorities and others exercising statutory functions) for purposes relevant to that person's business and using that business's own telecommunication system.

Interceptions are authorised for—

monitoring or recording communications—

to establish the existence of facts, to ascertain compliance with regulatory or self-regulatory practices or procedures or to ascertain or demonstrate standards which are or ought to be achieved (quality control and training),

in the interests of national security (in which case only certain specified public officials may make the interception),

to prevent or detect crime,

to investigate or detect unauthorised use of telecommunication systems or,

to secure, or as an inherent part of, effective system operation;

monitoring received communications to determine whether they are business or personal communications;

monitoring communications made to anonymous telephone helplines.

Interceptions are authorised only if the controller of the telecommunications system on which they are effected has made all reasonable efforts to inform potential users that interceptions may be made.

The Regulations do not authorise interceptions to which the persons making and receiving the communications have consented: they are not prohibited by the Act.

A regulatory impact assessment is available and can be obtained from Communications and Information Industries Directorate, Department of Trade and Industry, 151 Buckingham Palace Road, London SW1W 9SS. Copies have been placed in the libraries of both Houses of Parliament.

ISBN 0 11 099984 3

Appendix 15

Disability Discrimination Act 1995 (c. 50) 1995 Chapter 50

PART III DISCRIMINATION
IN OTHER AREAS

Goods, facilities and services Discrimination in relation to goods, facilities and services.

19.—(1) It is unlawful for a provider of services to discriminate against a disabled person-

(a) in refusing to provide, or deliberately not providing, to the disabled person any service which he provides, or is prepared to provide, to members of the public;

(b) in failing to comply with any duty imposed on him by section 21 in circumstances in which the effect of that failure is to make it impossible or unreasonably difficult for the disabled person to make use of any such service;

(c) in the standard of service which he provides to the disabled person or the manner in which he provides it to him; or

(d) in the terms on which he provides a service to the disabled person.

(2) For the purposes of this section and sections 20 and 21—

(a) the provision of services includes the provision of any goods or facilities;

(b) a person is "a provider of services" if he is concerned with the provision, in the United Kingdom, of services to the public or to a section of the public; and

(c) it is irrelevant whether a service is provided on payment or without payment.

(3) The following are examples of services to which this section and sections 20 and 21 apply—

(a) access to and use of any place which members of the public are permitted to enter;

(b) access to and use of means of communication;

(c) access to and use of information services;

(d) accommodation in a hotel, boarding house or other similar establishment;

(e) facilities by way of banking or insurance or for grants, loans, credit or finance;

(f) facilities for entertainment, recreation or refreshment;

(g) facilities provided by employment agencies or under section 2 of the Employment and Training Act 1973;

(h) the services of any profession or trade, or any local or other public authority.

(4) In the case of an act which constitutes discrimination by virtue of section 55, this section also applies to discrimination against a person who is not disabled.

(5) Except in such circumstances as may be prescribed, this section and sections 20 and 21 do not apply to—

> (a) education which is funded, or secured, by a relevant body or provided at—
>
> > (i)   an establishment which is funded by such a body or by a Minister of the Crown; or
> > (ii) any other establishment which is a school as defined in section 14(5) of the Further and Higher Education Act 1992 or section 135(1) of the Education (Scotland) Act 1980;
>
> (b) any service so far as it consists of the use of any means of transport; or
> (c) such other services as may be prescribed.

(6) In subsection (5) "relevant body" means—

> (a) a local education authority in England and Wales;
> (b) an education authority in Scotland;
> (c) the Funding Agency for Schools;
> (d) the Schools Funding Council for Wales;
> (e) the Further Education Funding Council for England;
> (f) the Further Education Funding Council for Wales;
> (g) the Higher Education Funding Council for England;
> (h) the Scottish Higher Education Funding Council;
> (i) the Higher Education Funding Council for Wales;
> (j) the Teacher Training Agency;
> (k) a voluntary organisation; or
> (l) a body of a prescribed kind.

Meaning of "discrimination". **20.**—(1) For the purposes of section 19, a provider of services discriminates against a disabled person if—

> (a) for a reason which relates to the disabled person's disability, he treats him less favourably than he treats or would treat others to whom that reason does not or would not apply; and
> (b) he cannot show that the treatment in question is justified.

(2) For the purposes of section 19, a provider of services also discriminates against a disabled person if—

> (a) he fails to comply with a section 21 duty imposed on him in relation to the disabled person; and
> (b) he cannot show that his failure to comply with that duty is justified.

(3) For the purposes of this section, treatment is justified only if—

> (a) in the opinion of the provider of services, one or more of the conditions mentioned in subsection (4) are satisfied; and
> (b) it is reasonable, in all the circumstances of the case, for him to hold that opinion.

(4) The conditions are that—

(a) in any case, the treatment is necessary in order not to endanger the health or safety of any person (which may include that of the disabled person);

(b) in any case, the disabled person is incapable of entering into an enforceable agreement, or of giving an informed consent, and for that reason the treatment is reasonable in that case;

(c) in a case falling within section 19(1)(a), the treatment is necessary because the provider of services would otherwise be unable to provide the service to members of the public;

(d) in a case falling within section 19(1)(c) or (d), the treatment is necessary in order for the provider of services to be able to provide the service to the disabled person or to other members of the public;

(e) in a case falling within section 19(1)(d), the difference in the terms on which the service is provided to the disabled person and those on which it is provided to other members of the public reflects the greater cost to the provider of services in providing the service to the disabled person.

(5) Any increase in the cost of providing a service to a disabled person which results from compliance by a provider of services with a section 21 duty shall be disregarded for the purposes of subsection (4)(e).

(6) Regulations may make provision, for purposes of this section, as to circumstances in which—

(a) it is reasonable for a provider of services to hold the opinion mentioned in subsection (3)(a);

(b) it is not reasonable for a provider of services to hold that opinion.

(7) Regulations may make provision for subsection (4)(b) not to apply in prescribed circumstances where—

(a) a person is acting for a disabled person under a power of attorney;

(b) functions conferred by or under Part VII of the Mental Health Act 1983 are exercisable in relation to a disabled person's property or affairs; or

(c) powers are exercisable in Scotland in relation to a disabled person's property or affairs in consequence of the appointment of a curator bonis, tutor or judicial factor.

(8) Regulations may make provision, for purposes of this section, as to circumstances (other than those mentioned in subsection (4)) in which treatment is to be taken to be justified.

(9) In subsections (3), (4) and (8) "treatment" includes failure to comply with a section 21 duty.

Duty of providers of services to make adjustments. 21.—(1) Where a provider of services has a practice, policy or procedure which makes it impossible or unreasonably difficult for disabled persons to make use of a service which he provides, or is prepared to provide, to other members of the public, it is his duty to take such steps as it is reasonable, in all the circumstances of the case, for him to have to take in order to change that practice, policy or procedure so that it no longer has that effect.

(2) Where a physical feature (for example, one arising from the design or construction of a building or the approach or access to premises) makes it impossible or unreasonably difficult for disabled persons to make use of such a service, it is the duty of the provider of that service to take such steps as it is reasonable, in all the circumstances of the case, for him to have to take in order to—

(a) remove the feature;

(b) alter it so that it no longer has that effect;

(c) provide a reasonable means of avoiding the feature; or

(d) provide a reasonable alternative method of making the service in question available to disabled persons.

(3) Regulations may prescribe—

(a) matters which are to be taken into account in determining whether any provision of a kind mentioned in subsection (2)(c) or (d) is reasonable; and

(b) categories of providers of services to whom subsection (2) does not apply.

(4) Where an auxiliary aid or service (for example, the provision of information on audio tape or of a sign language interpreter) would—

(a) enable disabled persons to make use of a service which a provider of services provides, or is prepared to provide, to members of the public, or

(b) facilitate the use by disabled persons of such a service,

it is the duty of the provider of that service to take such steps as it is reasonable, in all the circumstances of the case, for him to have to take in order to provide that auxiliary aid or service. (5) Regulations may make provision, for the purposes of this section—

(a) as to circumstances in which it is reasonable for a provider of services to have to take steps of a prescribed description;

(b) as to circumstances in which it is not reasonable for a provider of services to have to take steps of a prescribed description;

(c) as to what is to be included within the meaning of "practice, policy or procedure";

(d) as to what is not to be included within the meaning of that expression;

(e) as to things which are to be treated as physical features;

(f) as to things which are not to be treated as such features;

(g) as to things which are to be treated as auxiliary aids or services;

(h) as to things which are not to be treated as auxiliary aids or services.

(6) Nothing in this section requires a provider of services to take any steps which would fundamentally alter the nature of the service in question or the nature of his trade, profession or business.

(7) Nothing in this section requires a provider of services to take any steps which would cause him to incur expenditure exceeding the prescribed maximum.

(8) Regulations under subsection (7) may provide for the prescribed maximum to be calculated by reference to—

(a) aggregate amounts of expenditure incurred in relation to different cases;

(b) prescribed periods;

(c) services of a prescribed description;

(d) premises of a prescribed description; or

(e) such other criteria as may be prescribed.

(9) Regulations may provide, for the purposes of subsection (7), for expenditure incurred by one provider of services to be treated as incurred by another.

(10) This section imposes duties only for the purpose of determining whether a provider of services has discriminated against a disabled person; and accordingly a breach of any such duty is not actionable as such.

Premises Discrimination in relation to premises. 22.—(1) It is unlawful for a person with power to dispose of any premises to discriminate against a disabled person—

(a) in the terms on which he offers to dispose of those premises to the disabled person;

(b) by refusing to dispose of those premises to the disabled person; or

(c) in his treatment of the disabled person in relation to any list of persons in need of premises of that description.

(2) Subsection (1) does not apply to a person who owns an estate or interest in the premises and wholly occupies them unless, for the purpose of disposing of the premises, he—

(a) uses the services of an estate agent, or

(b) publishes an advertisement or causes an advertisement to be published.

(3) It is unlawful for a person managing any premises to discriminate against a disabled person occupying those premises—

(a) in the way he permits the disabled person to make use of any benefits or facilities;

(b) by refusing or deliberately omitting to permit the disabled person to make use of any benefits or facilities; or

(c) by evicting the disabled person, or subjecting him to any other detriment.

(4) It is unlawful for any person whose licence or consent is required for the disposal of any premises comprised in, or (in Scotland) the subject of, a tenancy to discriminate against a disabled person by withholding his licence or consent for the disposal of the premises to the disabled person.

(5) Subsection (4) applies to tenancies created before as well as after the passing of this Act.

(6) In this section—

"advertisement" includes every form of advertisement or notice, whether to the public or not;

"dispose", in relation to premises, includes granting a right to occupy the premises, and, in relation to premises comprised in, or (in Scotland) the subject of, a tenancy, includes—

(a) assigning the tenancy, and

(b) sub-letting or parting with possession of the premises or any part of the premises;

and "disposal" shall be construed accordingly;

"estate agent" means a person who, by way of profession or trade, provides services for the purpose of finding premises for persons seeking to acquire them or assisting in the disposal of premises; and

"tenancy" means a tenancy created—

(a) by a lease or sub-lease,

(b) by an agreement for a lease or sub-lease,

(c) by a tenancy agreement, or

(d) in pursuance of any enactment.

(7) In the case of an act which constitutes discrimination by virtue of section 55, this section also applies to discrimination against a person who is not disabled.

(8) This section applies only in relation to premises in the United Kingdom.

Exemption for small dwellings. 23.—(1) Where the conditions mentioned in subsection (2) are satisfied, subsection (1), (3) or (as the case may be) (4) of section 22 does not apply.

(2) The conditions are that—

(a) the relevant occupier resides, and intends to continue to reside, on the premises;

(b) the relevant occupier shares accommodation on the premises with persons who reside on the premises and are not members of his household;

(c) the shared accommodation is not storage accommodation or a means of access; and

(d) the premises are small premises.

(3) For the purposes of this section, premises are "small premises" if they fall within subsection (4) or (5).

(4) Premises fall within this subsection if—

(a) only the relevant occupier and members of his household reside in the accommodation occupied by him;

(b) the premises comprise, in addition to the accommodation occupied by the relevant occupier, residential accommodation for at least one other household;

(c) the residential accommodation for each other household is let, or available for letting, on a separate tenancy or similar agreement; and

(d) there are not normally more than two such other households.

(5) Premises fall within this subsection if there is not normally residential accommodation on the premises for more than six persons in addition to the relevant occupier and any members of his household.

(6) For the purposes of this section "the relevant occupier" means—

(a) in a case falling within section 22(1), the person with power to dispose of the premises, or a near relative of his;

(b) in a case falling within section 22(4), the person whose licence or consent is required for the disposal of the premises, or a near relative of his.

(7) For the purposes of this section—

"near relative" means a person's spouse, partner, parent, child, grandparent, grandchild, or brother or sister (whether of full or half blood or by affinity); and

"partner" means the other member of a couple consisting of a man and a woman who are not married to each other but are living together as husband and wife.

Meaning of "discrimination" . 24.—(1) For the purposes of section 22, a person ("A") discriminates against a disabled person if—

(a) for a reason which relates to the disabled person's disability, he treats him less favourably than he treats or would treat others to whom that reason does not or would not apply; and

(b) he cannot show that the treatment in question is justified.

(2) For the purposes of this section, treatment is justified only if—

(a) in A's opinion, one or more of the conditions mentioned in subsection (3) are satisfied; and

(b) it is reasonable, in all the circumstances of the case, for him to hold that opinion.

(3) The conditions are that—

(a) in any case, the treatment is necessary in order not to endanger the health or safety of any person (which may include that of the disabled person);

(b) in any case, the disabled person is incapable of entering into an enforceable agreement, or of giving an informed consent, and for that reason the treatment is reasonable in that case;

(c) in a case falling within section 22(3)(a), the treatment is necessary in order for the disabled person or the occupiers of other premises forming part of the building to make use of the benefit or facility;

(d) in a case falling within section 22(3)(b), the treatment is necessary in order for the occupiers of other premises forming part of the building to make use of the benefit or facility.

(4) Regulations may make provision, for purposes of this section, as to circumstances in which—

(a) it is reasonable for a person to hold the opinion mentioned in subsection 2(a);

(b) it is not reasonable for a person to hold that opinion.

(5) Regulations may make provision, for purposes of this section, as to circumstances (other than those mentioned in subsection (3)) in which treatment is to be taken to be justified.

Enforcement, etc. Enforcement, remedies and procedure. **25.**—(1) A claim by any person that another person—

(a) has discriminated against him in a way which is unlawful under this Part; or

(b) is by virtue of section 57 or 58 to be treated as having discriminated against him in such a way,

may be made the subject of civil proceedings in the same way as any other claim in tort or (in Scotland) in reparation for breach of statutory duty. (2) For the avoidance of doubt it is hereby declared that damages in respect of discrimination in a way which is unlawful under this Part may include compensation for injury to feelings whether or not they include compensation under any other head.

(3) Proceedings in England and Wales shall be brought only in a county court.

(4) Proceedings in Scotland shall be brought only in a sheriff court.

(5) The remedies available in such proceedings are those which are available in the High Court or (as the case may be) the Court of Session.

(6) Part II of Schedule 3 makes further provision about the enforcement of this Part and about procedure.

Validity and revision of certain agreements. **26.**—(1) Any term in a contract for the provision of goods, facilities or services or in any other agreement is void so far as it purports to—

(a) require a person to do anything which would contravene any provision of, or made under, this Part,

(b) exclude or limit the operation of any provision of this Part, or

(c) prevent any person from making a claim under this Part.

(2) Paragraphs (b) and (c) of subsection (1) do not apply to an agreement settling a claim to which section 25 applies.

(3) On the application of any person interested in an agreement to which subsection (1) applies, a county court or a sheriff court may make such order as it thinks just for modifying the agreement to take account of the effect of subsection (1).

(4) No such order shall be made unless all persons affected have been—

(a) given notice of the application; and

(b) afforded an opportunity to make representations to the court.

(5) Subsection (4) applies subject to any rules of court providing for that notice to be dispensed with.

(6) An order under subsection (3) may include provision as respects any period before the making of the order.

Alterations to premises occupied under leases. **27.**—(1) This section applies where—

(a) a provider of services ("the occupier") occupies premises under a lease;

(b) but for this section, he would not be entitled to make a particular alteration to the premises; and

(c) the alteration is one which the occupier proposes to make in order to comply with a section 21 duty.

(2) Except to the extent to which it expressly so provides, the lease shall have effect by virtue of this subsection as if it provided—

    (a) for the occupier to be entitled to make the alteration with the written consent of the lessor;

    (b) for the occupier to have to make a written application to the lessor for consent if he wishes to make the alteration;

    (c) if such an application is made, for the lessor not to withhold his consent unreasonably; and

    (d) for the lessor to be entitled to make his consent subject to reasonable conditions.

(3) In this section—

"lease" includes a tenancy, sub-lease or sub-tenancy and an agreement for a lease, tenancy, sub-lease or sub-tenancy; and

"sub-lease" and "sub-tenancy" have such meaning as may be prescribed.

(4) If the terms and conditions of a lease—

    (a) impose conditions which are to apply if the occupier alters the premises, or

    (b) entitle the lessor to impose conditions when consenting to the occupier's altering the premises,

the occupier is to be treated for the purposes of subsection (1) as not being entitled to make the alteration. (5) Part II of Schedule 4 supplements the provisions of this section.

Advice and assistance. 28.—(1) The Secretary of State may make arrangements for the provision of advice and assistance to persons with a view to promoting the settlement of disputes arising under this Part otherwise than by recourse to the courts.

(2) Any person appointed by the Secretary of State in connection with arrangements made under subsection (1) shall have such duties as the Secretary of State may direct.

(3) The Secretary of State may pay to any person so appointed such allowances and compensation for loss of earnings as he considers appropriate.

(4) The Secretary of State may make such payments, by way of grants, in respect of expenditure incurred, or to be incurred, by any person exercising functions in accordance with arrangements made by the Secretary of State under this section as he considers appropriate.

(5) The approval of the Treasury is required for any payment under subsection (3) or (4).

INDEX